Female Index to Genealogical Dictionary
of the First Settlers of New England by James Savage

FEMALE INDEX

to

GENEALOGICAL DICTIONARY
of the
FIRST SETTLERS OF NEW ENGLAND

by
James Savage

Compiled by
Patty Barthell Myers

GENEALOGICAL PUBLISHING COMPANY

Published by Genealogical Publishing Company
3600 Clipper Mill Rd., Suite 260
Baltimore, MD 21211-1953
Library of Congress Catalogue Card Number 2007939017
ISBN 978-0-8063-1785-4
Made in the United States of America

INTRODUCTION

It is universally agreed that James Savage's *Genealogical Dictionary of the First Settlers of New England* is one of the greatest works ever published on New England genealogy. The first edition came out in 1860, and as the four volumes were published in alphabetical sequence by family name, the males were usually found by checking their surname. The females were scattered throughout the four volumes. Some were listed under their fathers' names, some were listed under their husbands' names, and many women had three or more spouses. If the husbands' names were unknown, these ladies could not be found. In 1884 O. P. Dexter prepared a "Genealogical Cross Index" which has appeared in all reprints. It is a surname index only and has all the deficiencies of such an index. This female index, published about 150 years after Savage's *Dictionary* first came out, lists all the females alphabetically by maiden name and all married names, and now they are as easy to locate as are the males.

The reader is advised to check the whole page for a name. The same name may appear two or more times on a single page, but is listed in the index only once per page. Savage spelled the same name differently on different pages. If the spelling is quite different, the name will appear in all versions. If there's a doubt regarding gender, the name is included in the index. When the first name appears on one page and the last name on the next page, the name is listed in the index on both pages. When a name is hyphenated and part appears on one page and the rest on the next page, the name is listed in the index on both pages. Frequently a maiden name is revealed only in the Additions and Corrections section in each volume. All maiden names found in these sections are listed in this index. Some of them are difficult to find, as Savage made corrections to the corrections.

Abbot
—, 1:5
Abiel, 1:4
Abigail, 1:4
Abigail (Lovejoy), 1:4,
　3:122
Ann, 1:4
Catharine, 1:5
Deborah, 1:3-5, 1:55
Dorcas, 1:5
Dorcas (Graves), 1:3,
　2:295
Dorcas (Hibbert), 1:4
Dorothy, 1:2, 1:5
Dorothy (Swain), 1:361,
　4:235
Elizabeth, 1:1-5, 2:74,
　2:361
Elizabeth (—), 1:1
Elizabeth (Ballard), 1:3
Elizabeth (Evarts), 1:4,
　2:128
Elizabeth (French), 1:5
Elizabeth (Geary), 1:5
Elizabeth (Tucker), 1:1
Esther, 1:3
Eunice, 1:3
Frances, 1:4
Hannah, 1:1-6, 1:357,
　2:519
Hannah (—), 1:3, 2:6
Hannah (Chandler), 1:2,
　1:359, 3:360
Hannah (Chubb), 1:3
Hannah (Easty), 1:3
Hannah (Graves), 1:5,
　2:295
Hannah (Gray), 1:5
Hepzibah (Frye), 1:3
Jane, 1:4
Jemima, 1:3
Jemima (—), 1:3
Joanna (—), 1:2
Joyce, 1:5
Joyce (—), 1:5
Joyce (Rice), 3:528
Keziah, 1:4
Lydia, 1:2-3, 1:357
Martha, 1:3, 1:5
Mary, 1:2-5, 1:116
Mary (—), 1:4, 3:545
Mary (Ingalls), 1:2
Mary (Weed), 4:451

Mehitable, 1:2, 1:4
Mercy (—), 1:353
Mercy (Hutchinson), 1:4
Mindwell, 1:4
Priscilla, 1:2-3
Rebecca, 1:4, 4:403
Remember (Fiske), 1:4,
　2:165
Ruth (—), 1:3
Sarah, 1:1-5, 1:358, 2:148,
　4:185
Sarah (—), 1:4-5, 2:519,
　4:78
Sarah (Barker), 1:3, 1:116
Sarah (Farnum), 1:1-2,
　2:143
Sarah (Olmstead), 1:3
Sarah (Steward), 1:5
Susanna, 1:1, 1:4
Tabitha, 1:4
Abby/Abbey/Abbee
Abigail, 1:6
Hannah (—), 1:6
Hepzibah, 1:6
Mary, 1:6
Mary (—), 1:6
Mercy, 1:6
Sarah, 1:6
Sarah (—), 1:6
Sarah (—) Collins
　Warriner, 4:428
Sarah (—) Warriner, 1:6
Tabitha, 1:6
Abdy
Alice (Cox), 1:6, 1:467
Mary, 1:6
Tabitha, 1:6
Tabitha (Reynolds), 1:6,
　3:526
Abel/Abell
— (—) Looman, 3:111
— (Gager), 1:7, 2:221
Abigail, 1:7
Ann, 3:620
Dorothy, 1:7, 4:392
Elizabeth, 1:485
Experience, 1:6, 1:103
Experience (Smith), 1:7,
　4:127
Hannah, 1:7
Joanna, 1:7
Margaret (Post), 1:6
Mary, 1:7

Mary (—) Loomer, 1:7
Abernethy/Ebenatha
Sarah (Doolittle), 1:7, 2:60
Ackerly/Akerly
—, 4:101
Ann (—), 1:7
Hannah (Benton), 3:603
Ackley/Acly
Ann, 1:7
Bethia (—), 1:497
Deborah, 1:497
Desire, 1:497
Elizabeth, 1:497
Elizabeth (—), 1:7
Hannah, 1:7, 3:495
Hannah (—), 1:7
Jerusha, 1:497
Lydia, 1:497
Mary, 1:497, 1:516
Miriam (—), 1:497
Rebecca, 1:497
Sarah, 1:497, 4:150
Acreman/Akerman
Sarah (—) Stickney, 1:7
Sarah (Morse) Stickney,
　4:191
Acres/Ackers
Catharine, 1:7
Deborah, 1:8
Desiretruth, 1:8, 4:291
Desiretruth (Thorne), 1:8,
　4:291
Elizabeth, 1:8, 4:291
Hannah (Silver), 1:7
Joanna, 1:8
Mary, 1:7-8
Adams
— (—) Bradfield, 1:9,
　1:230
— (Clark), 1:398
Abiel, 1:17
Abigail, 1:8-16, 1:497
Abigail (Baxter), 1:13,
　1:141
Abigail (Crafts) Ruggles,
　1:469, 3:586
Abigail (Pinney), 1:12,
　3:439
Abigail (Smith), 4:137
Abigail (Wilmot), 1:8,
　4:581
Alice, 1:17
Alice (Bradford), 1:17,

Adams (continued)
Alice (Bradford)
  (continued)
  1:232, 2:168
Alice (Roper), 1:16
Ann, 1:9-11, 1:497, 4:15
Ann (----), 1:9, 1:11
Ann (Allen), 1:10
Ann (Coolidge), 1:14, 3:60
Ann (Ellen), 1:10, 2:112
Bethia, 1:9, 1:12-14, 4:445
Catharine, 1:15
Cherry, 1:13
Deborah (----), 1:12
Dorcas, 1:13, 4:438
Dorcas (Watson), 4:436
Dorothy, 1:8, 1:10, 1:17,
  1:499
Edith, 1:16
Eleanor, 4:556
Elinor, 1:11
Elinor (----), 1:15
Elinor/Ellen (Newton),
  1:11, 4:603
Elizabeth, 1:8-10, 1:12,
  1:14-17, 1:351, 2:89,
  2:354, 3:404, 4:521,
  4:673, 4:694
Elizabeth (----), 1:9,
  1:12-13, 1:15, 1:17
Elizabeth (Buckland), 1:9,
  4:673
Elizabeth (Dyer), 2:89
Elizabeth (Paine), 1:10,
  3:334
Elizabeth (Portmort), 1:14,
  3:465
Elizabeth (Walley), 4:400
Esther, 1:12, 1:14-16,
  4:161
Esther (Sparhawk), 1:15
Frances (----), 1:9
Frances (Taylor), 4:263
Frances (Vassall), 1:11,
  4:367
Hannah, 1:11-16,
  1:497-498, 4:27, 4:418,
  4:481
Hannah (Bass), 1:13
Hannah (Bent), 1:12
Hannah (Checkley), 1:12,
  1:369
Hannah (Gannett), 2:225

Hannah (Moulton), 1:16
Hannah (Webb), 1:12
Hannah (Wilmot), 1:14,
  4:581
Honor (Hall), 2:591
Jane, 1:8
Jane (James), 1:12
Joanna, 1:15, 2:290
Lucy, 2:353
Lydia, 1:9, 1:13-14
Lydia (----), 1:9
Lydia (Pygan), 3:497
Lydia (Whitney), 1:14,
  4:530
Margaret, 1:11-12, 3:658
Margaret (----), 1:8-9
Margaret (Eames), 1:13,
  2:91
Maria, 1:15
Martha, 1:9, 1:11-12,
  3:426
Martha (Fiske), 1:9, 2:166
Martha (Trescott), 2:408
Mary, 1:8-9, 1:11-17,
  1:497, 2:90, 2:275,
  2:428, 4:446, 4:673,
  4:690
Mary (----), 1:12, 1:14,
  1:16
Mary (----) Bradfield,
  3:596
Mary (Baker), 1:15, 1:99
Mary (Chapin), 1:13,
  1:360
Mary (Coffin), 1:8, 1:419
Mary (Ellis), 1:13, 2:114
Mary (James), 2:536
Mary (Manning), 1:17,
  3:148
Mary (Pettingell), 1:8,
  3:404
Mary (Pinney), 1:9
Mary (Pitty), 1:10, 3:442
Mary (Webb), 1:14
Mehitable, 1:9, 1:13-14,
  2:149
Miriam, 1:9
Patience, 1:12
Patience (Ellis), 1:10,
  2:114
Priscilla, 4:608
Priscilla (Winthrop), 4:608
Rachel, 2:136

Rachel (----), 1:14
Rebecca, 1:10-13, 1:15-16,
  3:369, 4:389, 4:697
Rebecca (----), 1:15
Rebecca (----) Greenhill,
  1:11, 2:308
Rebecca (Andrews), 1:13,
  1:54
Rebecca (Fletcher) Warner,
  1:11, 4:418
Rebecca (Graves), 1:15
Rebecca (Potter), 1:16,
  4:696
Ruth, 1:12-15, 1:196,
  2:161, 2:320
Sarah, 1:8-10, 1:12,
  1:14-16, 1:465, 2:499,
  3:286
Sarah (----), 1:12, 1:14
Sarah (----) Short, 1:15
Sarah (Glover) Short, 4:89
Sarah (Macworth), 1:8
Sarah (Rice), 3:531
Susan (----), 1:15
Susanna, 1:8, 1:11-12,
  1:16
Susanna (----), 1:12
Susanna (Boylston), 1:13
Tamosin (Sheffield), 4:69
Temperance (----), 1:8
Thankful, 1:9
Ursula, 1:10
Addington
Ann, 1:17, 3:83, 3:179,
  3:430
Ann (Leverett), 1:17,
  3:83-84
Elizabeth, 1:17
Elizabeth (----)
  Wainwright), 1:18
Elizabeth (Bowen), 1:17,
  1:222
Elizabeth (Norton)
  Wainwright, 1:498, 3:294,
  4:382
Rebecca, 1:17, 2:11, 3:83
Sarah, 1:17, 3:83, 4:318
Addis
Ann, 1:18, 2:10
Milicent, 1:18, 1:67, 1:153,
  4:141
Adgate
Abigail, 1:18, 4:320

Adgate (continued)
Elizabeth, 1:18, 1:318
Hannah, 1:18, 3:121
Mary (Marvin) Bushnell,
1:18, 1:318, 3:164
Rebecca, 1:18, 2:504
Ruth (Brewster), 1:18
Sarah, 1:18, 2:504
Adjet
Sarah (Howard), 2:471
Adkins
---- (Andrews), 1:19
Abigail, 1:19
Elizabeth, 1:18-19
Elizabeth (Barnes), 1:18
Elizabeth (Whitmore),
1:18-19
Esther, 1:19
Esther (----), 3:596
Hannah, 1:18-19
Jane, 1:19
Jane (Stevens), 1:18
Jemima, 1:18
Mary, 1:19
Mary (Wheeler), 1:19
Naomi, 1:18
Phebe, 1:19
Phebe (Edwards), 1:19
Rachel, 1:18
Rebecca, 1:19
Ruth, 1:18
Sarah, 1:18-19
Adverd/Adford
Elizabeth, 1:19
Mary, 1:19, 2:539
Sarah, 1:19
Thomasine (Manson), 1:19
Agar - see Hagar
Ager
Abigail, 3:17
Ainsworth
Alice (----), 1:19
Elizabeth, 1:19
Hannah, 1:19
Joanna, 1:19
Joanna (Hemenway), 1:19
Akers
Hannah (Silver), 4:98
Priscilla (----), 1:20, 3:34
Rachel, 1:20
Sarah, 1:20
Albee/Alby
Hannah, 1:20, 4:543,

4:659
Lydia, 1:20, 1:498, 3:123
Sarah, 1:498
Albertis
Elizabeth (Way), 4:440
Albeson/Allberson
Elizabeth (Folland), 1:20
Jeconia, 1:20
Alborow/Albro/etc
Dorothy (----) Potter, 1:20,
3:467
Susanna, 1:20, 1:60
Alcock
---- (Hooker), 1:21, 2:459
Ann, 1:21-22, 1:58, 4:562
Constance (Mylam), 1:22,
3:259
Constant, 1:22
Elizabeth, 1:21-22, 1:112,
4:140
Elizabeth (----), 1:21, 2:36
Elizabeth (Mitchell), 1:22,
4:528, 4:673, 4:691
Esther (----), 1:22, 1:357
Hannah, 1:21-22
Joanna, 1:21, 3:596, 3:637
Lydia, 1:21
Margery (----), 1:22, 1:165
Mary, 1:21-22, 3:47, 3:551
Rebecca, 1:22
Sarah, 1:21-22, 4:525
Sarah (----) Butler, 1:22
Sarah (Palsgrave), 1:21,
3:340
Sarah (Stedman) Brackett,
1:22, 1:229, 2:297,
3:413, 4:179
Alden
Abigail (Hallet), 1:24,
2:340
Alice, 1:23
Elizabeth, 1:23-24, 3:375,
4:400
Elizabeth (----), 1:23
Elizabeth (Phillips) Everill,
1:23, 2:131
Elizabeth (Phillips) Everitt,
3:416
Mary, 1:23-24, 2:34
Mary (Simmons), 1:24
Mary (Southworth), 1:23,
4:143
Priscilla, 1:374

Priscilla (Mullins), 1:23,
3:253
Ruth, 1:23, 1:135, 3:596,
4:673
Sarah, 1:23, 1:478, 4:161
Alderman
Jane (----), 1:24
Mary, 1:24
Mary (Case), 1:24, 1:345,
2:422
Sarah, 1:24
Aldis
----, 1:24
Ann, 1:24
Hannah, 1:24
Mary, 1:24-25, 2:163,
3:534
Mary (----), 1:24-25
Mary (Winchester), 1:24
Ruth, 1:24
Sarah, 1:24
Sarah (Eliot), 1:24, 2:111
Sarah (Paine), 1:24, 3:336
Aldrich/Aldridge
Catharine (----), 1:25
Elizabeth (Prentice), 1:25,
3:479
Experience, 1:25
Hannah, 1:25
Hannah (Colburn), 1:25,
1:412
Mary, 1:25, 2:392, 2:576
Mary (----), 1:25, 2:576
Mattithiah, 1:25
Mercy, 1:25
Miriam, 1:25
Patience (Osborne), 1:25
Sarah, 1:25
Sarah (Leach), 1:25, 3:66
Alexander
Abigail, 1:26, 4:450
Beatrice (----), 1:26
Deliverance, 1:26
Dorothy, 1:26, 4:176
Elizabeth, 1:26
Elizabeth (----) Langton,
3:56
Elizabeth (Copley)
Langton, 1:25
Elizabeth (Copley)
Langton Turner, 1:456
Hannah, 1:26, 1:209
Hannah (Allen), 1:26

Alexander (continued)
Martha, 1:26
Mary, 1:26, 1:125, 3:252
Mindwell, 1:26
Ruth, 1:26
Sarah, 1:26
Sarah (Gaylord), 1:26
Susanna (Sage), 1:25
Thankful, 1:26
Alexarson
Ann, 1:96
Mercy, 1:96
Alford
Ann (—), 1:27
Bethia, 1:27
Elizabeth, 1:27, 2:489,
4:54
Judith, 1:26
Margaret (Savage), 1:27
Mary, 1:26-27, 1:321,
3:295, 4:363
Mary (—), 1:27
Mary (Richards), 1:26,
3:532
Mary (Vore/Voar), 4:376
Sarah, 1:26
Alger
—, 1:27, 1:69, 1:80
— (Wilmot), 4:581
Agnes (—), 1:27
Ann (—), 1:28
Deliverance, 1:28
Elizabeth, 1:27-28, 3:341,
4:581
Elizabeth (Packard), 1:28,
3:327
Joanna, 1:27, 3:304
Judith (—), 4:396
Patience (Hayward), 1:28
Allard/Alward
— (—), 1:28
Elizabeth, 1:28, 4:46
Judith, 2:294-295
Allen
—, 1:233
— (—) Atkinson, 1:498
— (Bradley), 1:233
— (Ives), 2:525
— (Kimball), 1:29
— (Martin), 3:163
Abia, 1:30
Abigail, 1:29-35, 1:37-38,
1:345, 1:498, 3:341,
4:563
Abigail (Grannis), 2:290
Abigail (Rogers), 1:37
Ahazadiah, 1:34
Alice (—), 1:37
Amey, 1:32
Amy, 3:630
Ann, 1:10, 1:33-34,
1:37-38, 1:498, 2:597,
3:596
Ann (—), 1:29, 1:31-32,
1:34-35, 1:37, 2:492,
2:506, 2:598
Ann (Bradbury), 1:32
Ann (Brazier), 1:33
Ann (Burr), 1:31, 1:307
Ann (Goodale), 1:37,
2:270-271
Ann (Sadler) Harvard, 1:36,
2:369
Bashua (Haxie), 1:29,
2:385
Bethia, 1:35, 1:37
Bethia (—), 4:673
Catharine, 1:29, 1:31
Catharine (—), 1:30
Christian, 1:29
Constant (—), 1:33
Deborah, 1:34, 1:37, 3:64
Dorcas (—), 4:527
Dorothy, 1:34, 1:38
Elizabeth, 1:29-30,
1:32-34, 1:36, 1:498,
2:140, 2:388, 3:14,
3:541, 4:208, 4:363
Elizabeth (—), 1:32,
1:36-37, 3:596
Elizabeth (Allyn), 1:28,
1:43
Elizabeth (Bacon), 1:32
Elizabeth (Grout), 1:36,
2:319, 3:101
Elizabeth (Houchin)
Endicott, 1:31, 2:123,
2:467-468
Elizabeth (Prichard), 1:33
Elizabeth (Richardson),
1:28
Elizabeth (Sisson), 1:29
Elizabeth (Symonds),
4:247
Esther, 1:32-33
Experience, 1:32, 1:35
Experience (Swift), 1:32
Faith (Ingalls), 1:28, 2:519
Frances, 1:31
Frances (Arnold), 1:66
Frances (Hill), 1:33, 1:81
Frances (Rice), 3:531
Hannah, 1:26, 1:29-31,
1:33-35, 1:37, 1:84,
1:498, 2:8, 2:385, 2:454,
2:534, 3:163
Hannah (—), 1:30-31
Hannah (Dummer), 1:31
Hannah (Leverett), 2:22,
3:83
Hannah (Marshall), 1:498
Hannah (Sabin), 1:34
Hannah (Woodford), 1:35,
4:639
Jane, 1:291, 4:622
Jane (Vining), 4:346
Jane (Vining) Turner,
4:374
Joan, 1:251, 4:214
Joanna (—) Sedgwick,
1:36
Judith, 1:31, 1:38
Judith (—), 1:31
Judith (Beers), 1:155
Leah, 1:31
Lydia, 1:29-30, 1:33, 1:37,
1:166
Lydia (—), 1:29
Lydia (—) Holbrook, 1:34,
2:443
Margaret, 2:485
Margaret (—) Lamb, 1:35,
3:47
Mariana (—), 1:29
Martha, 1:29-31, 1:37,
1:339, 1:498, 4:23
Martha (Way), 1:30
Mary, 1:28-38, 1:398,
1:498, 2:303, 2:311,
3:66, 3:553, 3:610,
3:649, 4:526
Mary (—), 1:28-29, 1:34,
3:231
Mary (—) Andrews, 1:54
Mary (—) Andros, 1:33,
1:57
Mary (—) Pond, 2:404
Mary (Ball) Pond, 1:34,
3:453

Allen (continued)
Mary (Barlow), 1:30
Mary (Bowen), 1:31
Mary (Dexter), 2:45
Mary (Grant), 1:28
Mary (Hannum), 1:33,
2:351
Mary (Harris), 1:37,
2:361-362
Mary (Howland), 1:33
Mary (Nash), 3:262
Mary (Savage) Whitmore,
4:527
Mary (Sherman), 1:29,
4:82
Mary (Towsly), 4:320
Mary (Wright), 4:660
Mehitable, 1:35
Mercy, 1:31-32, 1:36,
3:596
Mercy (Call) Lee, 1:498,
1:511, 3:73
Mercy (Peters), 3:401
Mercy (Rice), 3:529
Mindwell, 1:35
Miriam, 1:31, 1:34
Naomi, 1:30
Patience, 1:34, 3:596
Priscilla, 1:32
Priscilla (Browne), 1:37
Rachel, 1:30, 1:34, 3:596
Rachel (----), 1:31
Rachel (----) Wheeler, 1:29,
4:497
Rachel (Griggs), 1:34,
3:596
Rachel (Houchin), 1:29,
2:468
Rebecca, 1:29-30, 1:32-35,
1:498, 2:274
Rebecca (----), 1:34, 1:37
Rebecca (Cary), 1:344
Rebecca (Skeath), 4:103
Rose, 1:33, 3:596
Rose (Howard), 3:596
Ruth, 1:30, 1:34, 1:37
Ruth (----), 1:498, 3:35
Ruth (Burt), 1:313
Ruth (Leeds), 1:34
Sarah, 1:30-36, 2:239,
3:208, 4:162, 4:484
Sarah (----), 1:30-33
Sarah (Hawkins) Breck,

1:31, 1:241, 2:383
Sarah (Ives), 1:34
Sarah (Kerly), 1:34
Sarah (Partridge), 1:35,
3:365
Sarah (Rust), 1:35
Sarah (Woodford), 1:34,
1:303, 4:639
Silence, 1:34
Susan (Huggins), 2:491
Susanna, 1:30
Susanna (----), 1:30
Susanna (----) Atkinson,
1:499
Thankful, 1:35
Allerton
----, 1:498
Elizabeth, 1:39, 2:134,
4:169
Fear (Brewster), 1:38,
1:246
Joanna (----), 1:38
Mary, 1:38, 1:492, 2:479
Mary (----), 1:38
Mary (Collins), 1:498
Remember, 1:38, 3:181
Sarah, 3:486
Alley
Hannah, 1:39
Joanna (Furnell), 1:39
Martha, 1:39, 3:213
Mary, 1:39, 3:96, 3:646
Rebecca, 1:39
Rebecca (Hood), 1:39,
2:457
Sarah, 1:39, 3:96
Sarah (Silver), 4:98
Susanna (----), 1:39, 3:443,
3:646
Alleyne
Lydia (----), 4:673
Martha, 4:673
Rachel, 4:673
Rachel (Steele), 4:673
Allin
Catharine (----) Hackburne
Dudley, 1:40
Catharine (Dighton)
Hackburne Dudley, 2:78,
2:329
Experience, 4:241
Margaret (----), 1:40

Alline
Mary (Banister), 1:113
Alling
Abigail, 1:41, 3:597
Abigail (Grannis), 3:597
Elizabeth, 1:40-41, 2:464,
3:597
Elizabeth (Cotton), 1:40,
1:463-464, 1:489
Elizabeth (Winston), 1:41,
4:605
Ellen (Bradley), 1:41,
1:233
Esther, 1:41
Hannah, 1:41, 4:690
Joanna, 1:40
Lydia, 1:41
Martha, 1:41
Mary, 1:40-41, 3:246,
3:597
Mary (Nash), 1:41
Rebecca (Pardee), 3:345
Sarah, 1:41, 1:76, 3:382,
3:597
Sarah (Chedsey), 1:41,
1:370
Susanna, 1:41, 3:597
Susanna (Coe), 1:41,
1:418
Allis
Abigail, 1:41, 4:474
Alice (----), 1:42, 2:381
Elizabeth, 1:41
Hannah, 1:41-42, 4:39
Lydia, 1:41
Mary, 1:41-42
Mary (----), 1:42, 1:158,
2:238
Mary (----) Wyatt Graves,
2:295
Mary (Bronson) Wyatt
Graves, 4:662
Mary (Brownson) Wyatt
Graves, 1:42
Mary (Meakins) Clark,
1:41, 1:399, 3:192
Mehitable, 1:42
Rebecca, 1:41-42
Sarah, 1:42
Alliset/Alleset
Deliverance, 1:42
Elizabeth, 1:42
Grace, 1:42

Alliset/Alleset (continued)
Grace (----), 1:42
Allison
Christian (----), 1:42
Mary, 3:155
Ally
Ann (----), 1:498
Jane (----), 1:498
Sarah (Silver), 1:43
Allyn
Abigail, 1:44, 1:186
Abigail (Warham), 1:44,
4:417
Ann, 1:43, 4:519
Ann (Smith), 1:43, 4:115
Deborah, 1:44
Elizabeth, 1:28, 1:43-44
Elizabeth (Gager), 1:43,
2:221
Elizabeth (Otis), 3:117,
3:323
Elizabeth (Sanford), 1:43,
4:16
Elizabeth (Wolcott), 1:498
Esther, 1:44
Hannah, 1:44, 3:576
Hannah (Lamberton)
Welles, 1:43, 3:49, 4:477
Hannah (Walley), 1:44
Jane, 1:44
Margaret, 1:43, 4:142
Martha, 1:43, 1:498
Martha (----) Jepson, 1:44,
2:547
Martha (Wolcott), 1:44,
4:623
Mary, 1:43-44, 3:268,
3:348, 4:522
Mary (Howland), 1:43
Mehitable, 1:44, 1:59
Rebecca, 1:43
Sarah, 1:44, 2:239
Thankful, 1:43
Winifred (----), 1:44
Allyne
Mary, 2:62
Mary (Dotey), 2:62
Almy/Almond
Ann, 1:45, 2:303
Annis, 1:45
Audrey, 1:45
Audrey (----), 1:45
Catharine, 1:45

Deborah, 1:45
Mary, 1:45
Mary (Cole), 1:45, 1:427
Mary (Moore), 3:228
Mary (Unthank), 1:45,
4:360
Susanna, 1:45
Alsop/Alsup
Abigail, 1:45, 3:580
Abigail (Thompson), 1:45
Amy, 1:46
Deborah, 1:46
Elizabeth, 1:45-46, 1:104,
3:597
Elizabeth (Preston), 1:45,
3:483
Hannah, 1:45-46
Hannah (----), 1:46
Jemima, 1:45, 3:597
Lydia, 1:45, 4:332
Mary, 1:45, 3:206, 4:349
Mary (----), 1:45
Sarah, 1:45
Alt/Allt/Ault
Jane, 2:101
Rebecca, 3:598
Remembrance, 1:42, 1:80,
3:504
Remembrance (----), 1:42,
1:80
Alvord
Abigail, 1:46, 3:574
Abigail (Phelps), 1:47,
3:406
Deborah, 1:46
Deborah (Stebbins), 1:46,
1:313, 4:176
Elizabeth, 1:46-47, 1:313,
1:499, 2:70
Elizabeth (----) Bird, 1:47
Experience, 1:46
Hannah, 1:47
Hannah (Brown), 1:47
Jane, 1:47
Joan, 1:46, 2:193
Joan (Newton), 1:46,
3:406
Joanna, 1:47
Joanna (----), 3:26
Joanna (Taylor), 1:47
Mary, 1:46-47, 4:474
Mary (Gull), 1:47
Mary (Vore/Voar), 1:46

Mehitable (Frary) Root,
1:47, 3:572
Mercy (Gull), 2:322
Patience, 1:47
Rebecca, 1:47
Ruth, 1:47
Ruth (Baker), 1:47
Sarah, 1:46-47, 4:428
Thankful, 1:47
Thankful (Miller), 1:47
Amadown
Lydia, 1:47
Sarah, 1:47
Sarah (----), 1:47
Ambeck
Judith, 1:47
Mary (Varleet), 1:47, 4:35,
4:366
Ambler
----, 1:48
Hannah (----), 1:48
Mary, 1:48
Mary (Bates), 1:48, 1:139
Mehitable, 1:48
Sarah, 1:48
Sarah (----), 1:48
Ambrose
---- (----), 1:513, 3:322
---- (Hayes), 2:387
Abigail, 1:48, 3:322
Dorothy, 1:48
Hope (----), 1:48
Margaret, 1:48
Susanna (----), 4:52
Susanna (----) Worcester,
1:48, 4:650-651
Ambry/Ambery
Mary, 1:48
Mary (----), 1:48
Ameredith
Joanna (----), 4:338
Joanna (Treworgye), 1:48,
4:330
Ames
Deliverance, 1:49
Elizabeth, 1:49, 3:411
Elizabeth (Hayward), 1:49
Elizabeth (Wales), 1:49
Hannah, 1:49, 2:386
Hannah (----), 1:49
Joane (----), 1:49
Lydia, 1:49
Rebecca, 1:49

Ames (continued)
Ruth, 1:49, 1:58, 3:303
Sarah, 1:49, 2:394
Sarah (Washburn), 4:429
Sarah (Willis), 1:49, 4:575
Susanna (----), 1:49
Amey/Amee
---- (Johnson), 2:551
Martha, 1:50, 3:597
Martha (Johnson), 1:50
Mary, 1:50
Amory
Mary, 2:119
Mary (----), 1:50
Amos
Ann, 1:50
Mary, 1:50
Amsden
Elizabeth, 1:50
Frances (----), 1:495
Frances (Perriman), 1:50, 3:398
Jane (Rutter), 1:50
Anderson
Amie, 1:228
Ann, 1:51
Catharine, 1:51, 3:412, 4:156
Catharine (----), 1:50
Catharine (Richardson), 1:499
Emma, 1:51, 1:228, 3:135
Hannah (Nichols), 1:499
Hannah (Phillips), 3:414
Jane (----), 1:51
Joanna, 1:51
Mary, 1:51, 2:388, 4:76
Mary (----), 1:51
Mary (----) Hodges, 2:594
Mary (Applin), 1:62
Mary (Hodges), 1:51, 2:24
Andrew
Abigail (----), 3:597
Abigail (Treat), 1:52, 4:327
Elizabeth, 1:52
Elizabeth (White), 1:51
Mary, 1:52
Mary (----), 1:52
Mary (Peck), 3:382
Reana (----) James, 2:535
Andrews
----, 1:19

---- (Curwin/Corwin), 1:488
---- (Jones), 2:569
Abigail, 1:53-56, 1:499, 3:597-598
Abigail (----), 1:56, 1:114
Abigail (Very), 1:55, 4:373
Alice, 1:55, 2:200
Ann (----), 1:56
Ann (Jacob/Jacobs), 2:533
Ann (Tapp) Gibbard, 1:57, 2:244, 4:253
Christian, 1:181
Deborah (Abbot), 1:4, 1:55
Dinah, 1:55
Dorcas, 1:54, 2:11
Elizabeth, 1:53-57, 1:499, 2:261, 2:290, 3:294, 3:597-598, 4:247
Elizabeth (----), 1:55, 1:114
Elizabeth (Nicholson), 1:55, 3:283
Elizabeth (Peck), 1:55, 3:384
Elizabeth (Porter), 1:56, 3:463
Elizabeth (Spencer), 4:149
Elizabeth (Strickland), 1:55, 4:224
Esther, 1:53, 4:149
Grace (----), 3:597
Hannah, 1:52-54, 1:56, 1:470, 1:499, 3:266, 3:375, 3:534, 3:597
Hannah (----), 1:54
Hannah (Jackson), 2:527
Hannah (Kirby), 1:56, 3:30
Hannah (Street), 4:223
Hannah/Susanna, 3:597
Jane, 1:54-55
Jane (----), 1:54-55, 2:151, 3:142
Joan (----), 1:54, 1:77
Joanna, 3:597
Judith (----), 1:54
Love (Knight), 4:687-688
Lucy (----), 1:54
Margaret (----), 1:54, 1:57
Margery, 1:55
Martha, 1:53-54
Mary, 1:52-56, 2:400, 3:443, 3:465, 3:473, 3:539, 3:597, 3:597-600,

4:87
Mary (----), 1:53-54, 1:56
Mary (Chandler), 1:57
Mehitable, 3:539
Patience (Nichols), 1:54
Phebe (Gibbard), 1:55, 2:244
Phebe (Goard), 1:56
Rachel, 1:52, 1:54
Reana, 2:9
Rebecca, 1:13, 1:52-56, 1:164, 1:499, 2:211, 2:470, 3:150
Rebecca (----), 1:56, 4:663
Ruth, 1:53, 1:499, 3:125, 3:404, 3:598
Sarah, 1:52-53, 1:55-56, 1:499, 2:182, 3:597, 4:249, 4:325
Sarah (----), 1:54
Sarah (Holyoke), 2:456
Sarah (Mitton), 1:53, 3:222
Sarah (Porter), 1:52, 3:463
Susanna, 1:55-56, 4:583
Thankful, 1:56
Andros
Mary (----), 1:33, 1:57
Andrus
Elizabeth, 2:246
Angell
Abigail (Dexter), 1:57, 2:44
Alice, 1:57, 4:505
Amphyllis, 1:57, 4:112
Deborah, 1:57
Margery, 1:57
Mary, 1:57, 1:66
Ruth (Field), 1:57, 2:156
Anger
Abigail, 3:17
Angier
Ann (Batt), 1:58, 1:140
Elizabeth, 1:58, 3:433
Elizabeth (----), 1:58
Elizabeth (Shattuck) Goddard, 2:265
Eunice, 1:58
Hannah, 1:58
Hannah (Aspinwall), 1:58, 1:71
Hannah (Oakes), 1:58, 3:303

Angier (continued)
Margaret, 1:58
Mary, 1:58
Ruth, 1:58, 1:371
Ruth (Ames), 1:58
Sarah, 1:58, 4:254
Annable
Ann, 1:59, 1:72
Ann (Alcock), 1:58
Ann (Barker), 1:59
Ann (Clark), 1:58
Deborah, 1:58
Desire, 1:59, 1:115
Elizabeth, 4:534
Hannah, 1:58, 1:215
Jane (----), 1:58
Mehitable (Allyn), 1:44,
1:59
Sarah, 1:58, 2:132
Susanna, 1:58, 2:376
Annesley
Mary (Cook/Cooke), 1:446
Annis
Abigail, 1:59
Ann, 1:59
Dorothy, 1:59
Dorothy (----), 1:59
Hannah, 1:59
Hannah (----), 1:59
Hannah (Osgood), 1:499
Priscilla, 1:59
Sarah, 1:59
Sarah (Chase), 1:59, 1:364
Ansell
Mary, 3:121
Anter
Joan, 2:395
Anthony
Alice, 1:59-60
Alice (Waddell), 1:59,
4:377
Ammi, 1:59
Elizabeth, 1:59-60, 2:301
Frances (----), 1:59
Frances (Waddell), 1:60,
4:377
Mary, 1:59-60
Mary (Wait), 1:60, 4:385
Sarah, 1:60
Sarah (Jones) Bulkley,
2:562
Susanna, 1:59-60, 4:331
Susanna (Alborow), 1:20,

1:60
Antram/Antrim
Hannah, 1:303, 1:499
Martha (Baker), 3:598-599
Mary, 1:60
Applegate
Avis (----), 1:60
Elizabeth (----), 1:60
Appleton
---- (----) Dutch, 1:61
Elizabeth, 1:60-62, 2:79,
2:168
Elizabeth (Rogers), 1:61,
3:562
Elizabeth (Whittingham),
1:62, 3:373
Hannah, 1:61-62, 2:65,
3:333, 3:337
Hannah (Paine), 1:61,
3:337
Joanna, 1:60-61
Judith, 1:61, 3:338, 3:568,
4:623
Margaret, 1:61
Martha, 1:60-62, 2:534
Mary, 1:60-61
Mary (Everard), 1:61
Mary (Oliver), 1:61, 3:309
Priscilla, 1:60-61, 1:334
Priscilla (Baker), 1:60,
3:600
Priscilla (Glover), 1:60,
2:262
Rebecca, 1:60
Rebecca (Ruck), 1:61,
3:584
Sarah, 1:61, 3:414, 3:559
Sarah (----), 1:61
Applin
Abiel, 1:62
Bethshua, 1:62
Bethshua (Bartlett), 1:62,
1:133
Hannah, 1:62, 2:144
Mary, 1:62
Mehitable, 1:62
Apsley
Alice, 2:154
Apthrop
Mary, 1:255
Archer/Archard
Alice, 2:80
Elizabeth (Stow), 1:62,

4:217
Hannah (Osgood), 1:63,
3:320
Rachel, 1:62
Sarah, 2:22
Susanna (----), 1:63, 2:512
Arey
Sarah, 2:356
Armitage/Armatage
---- (Pool/Poole), 3:454
---- (Richardson), 1:63,
3:537
Dorothy (Foy), 3:622
Hannah (----), 3:655
Hannah (Needham), 1:63,
3:655
Jane (----), 1:63
Rebecca, 1:63, 3:182,
3:184, 4:256
Sarah (Webb), 1:63
Arms
Joanna (Hawks), 1:63,
2:381
Armsbee/Armesbey
Abigail, 3:598
Hannah, 3:598
Hannah (----), 3:598
Judith, 1:63
Mary, 1:63, 3:598
Rebecca, 1:63
Sarah, 3:598
Armstrong
Martha, 1:64
Mercy, 1:64
Rachel (----), 1:63
Arnold
---- (Green), 2:305
---- (Tillinghast), 4:303
Abigail, 1:66
Abigail (Frary), 2:201
Ann, 1:64, 1:66
Ann (----), 1:65
Barachiah, 1:64
Barbara, 1:65
Catharine, 1:66
Comfort, 1:64, 1:66
Content, 1:64, 1:66
Damaris, 1:64, 1:66, 1:200
Damaris (Wescott), 1:64,
4:487
Desire, 1:66
Elizabeth, 1:64, 1:66-67,
1:338, 2:305, 2:451,

Arnold (continued)
Elizabeth (continued)
2:462, 3:662
Elizabeth (----), 1:66
Elizabeth (Smith), 4:110
Elizabeth (Wakeman),
4:388
Esther, 1:66
Frances, 1:66
Freelove, 1:64, 1:66, 3:385
Godsgift, 1:64, 1:293,
3:385
Hannah (Wilbore), 4:545
Joanna, 1:67, 3:527
Lucretia, 1:65
Margaret, 1:65
Martha (----), 1:64
Mary, 1:64-66, 1:456,
2:345
Mary (----), 1:65
Mary (Angell), 1:57, 1:66
Mary (Barber) Smith, 1:65
Mary (Barker) Smith,
1:502, 4:112
Mary (Turner), 1:64
Mary (Ward), 1:66, 4:414
Mercy (----) Fosdick, 1:65
Mercy (Picket) Fosdick,
2:185, 3:424
Patience, 1:66
Penelope, 1:64, 1:66,
2:287
Phebe, 1:66
Phebe (----), 1:66
Phebe (Parkhurst), 1:66,
3:358
Priscilla, 1:64
Rebecca (Curtis), 1:65
Ruhamah, 1:65
Sarah, 1:64-66
Sarah (----), 1:66
Sarah (Mumford), 1:64
Sarah (Smith), 1:66, 4:112
Susanna, 1:65-67, 2:143
Susanna (----), 1:65
Susanna (Carpenter), 1:64,
1:338
Arrington - see Harrington
Arsleby
Rebecca (Ayers), 2:130
Arthur
Elizabeth, 4:674
Eunice, 4:674

Keturah, 4:674
Margaret, 4:674
Mary, 4:674
Mary (Folger), 4:674
Persis, 4:674
Priscilla, 4:674
Priscilla (Gardner), 1:67
Rhoda, 4:674
Ash
Mary (Bartlett), 1:67
Milicent (Addis)
Southmayd, 1:18, 1:67,
1:153, 4:142
Ashby
Abigail, 1:67
Abigail (Hutchinson), 1:67,
2:512
Elizabeth, 1:67
Hannah, 1:67
Hannah (----), 1:68
Mary, 1:67
Ashcraft
Hannah, 1:68
Hannah (Osborne), 1:68
Mary, 1:68
Ashfield
Jane (----), 1:68
Mary, 1:68
Ashford
Mary (----) Horton, 2:465
Ashley/Ashly
Abigail, 1:68, 3:88
Ann, 1:69
Dorothy, 1:68
Elizabeth (Batson), 1:139
Hannah, 1:68
Hannah (----) Broome,
1:69, 1:263
Hannah (Glover), 1:68,
2:261
Joanna (----), 1:69
Mary, 1:68-69, 3:572,
4:175
Mary (----), 1:68-69
Mary (Parsons), 1:68,
3:363, 4:578
Mary (Whiting) Sheldon,
4:70
Rebecca, 1:68
Sarah, 1:68-69, 2:522
Sarah (Wadsworth), 1:68,
4:381

Ashton
---- (Alger), 1:27, 1:69
Mary (Edgecomb) Page,
1:69, 2:100, 3:330
Susanna (Foxwell), 1:69,
2:198
Aslett
Elizabeth, 1:69
Hannah, 1:69
Mary, 1:69, 2:214
Mary (Osgood), 1:69,
3:321
Rebecca, 1:69, 2:558
Rebecca (Ayer), 1:69
Ruth, 1:69
Sarah, 1:69
Aspinwall/Aspenall
---- (----) Leavens, 1:70
---- (----) Smith, 1:69
---- (Merrill), 1:70
Abigail (Bowen), 1:70
Alice (Sharp), 1:70
Ann, 1:69
Dorcas, 1:71
Elizabeth, 1:70-71
Elizabeth (Stanley), 1:71,
3:416
Hannah, 1:58, 1:71
Mary, 1:69-71, 2:288
Mary (----), 1:69
Mehitable, 1:70
Remember (Palfrey), 1:70,
3:339
Sarah, 1:70
Sarah (Stevens), 1:70
Astine
---- (Davis), 2:20
Mary, 2:20
Sarah, 2:20
Astwood
Hannah, 4:118
Martha (----), 1:71
Mary, 1:71
Sarah, 1:71
Sarah (----), 1:71
Sarah (----) Baldwin,
1:71-72, 1:105
Atchet
Sarah (Howard), 2:471
Atchinson/Atchison
Elizabeth, 1:72
Mary, 1:72

Athearn
Mary (Butler), 1:72
Zervia, 1:72
Atherton
Ann (Annable), 1:72
Catharine, 1:73, 3:175
Elizabeth (Rigby), 1:73,
3:541
Margaret, 1:73, 4:332
Mary, 1:73, 4:453
Mary (Gulliver), 1:73,
2:322
Patience, 1:73, 2:496
Rest, 1:73, 4:241
Sarah, 1:72
Sarah (Hollister), 1:72,
1:100, 2:449
Thankful, 1:73, 1:182
Atkins
Abigail, 1:74
Abigail (----), 1:74
Abigail (----) Jones, 1:499,
2:599
Ann, 1:74
Ann (----), 1:74
Bethia, 1:74, 2:462
Bethia (Linnell), 1:73
Catharine (Dudley), 1:74
Desire, 1:73
Elizabeth, 1:74
Elizabeth (----), 1:73
Hannah, 1:74
Margaret (----), 1:74
Martha, 1:74
Martha (----), 1:74
Mary, 1:73
Mary (----), 1:74
Mary (Dudley) Wainwright,
2:76
Mercy, 1:74
Atkinson/Adkinson/Atkeson
----, 1:498
Abigail, 1:74-75, 3:176,
4:147
Abigail (----), 1:74-75,
3:175
Abigail (Jones), 1:499
Ann, 3:176
Elizabeth, 1:74-75, 3:62
Elizabeth (Mitchelson),
1:75, 2:41, 3:222
Hannah, 1:74-75, 1:259,
3:176

Helen, 2:418
Jane, 1:372
Margaret (----) Parker,
3:357
Mary, 1:74, 3:176
Mary (Jenkins), 1:74
Mary (Platt), 1:74, 3:445,
4:528
Mary (Wheelwright) Lyde,
1:75, 3:133, 4:503
Rebecca, 1:499, 2:408
Sarah, 1:74, 1:419
Sarah (Mirick), 1:74
Susanna, 1:75, 1:259
Susanna (----), 1:75, 1:499
Atwater
---- (Cotton), 3:366
Abigail, 1:75-76, 2:564,
3:598
Abigail (Heaton), 3:598,
4:701
Abigail (Mansfield), 4:699
Ann/Hannah, 1:76, 2:79
Damaris, 1:75-76, 3:493
Elinor, 1:76
Grace, 1:76
Jane, 1:76
Joanna, 3:598
Lydia, 1:76, 3:598
Lydia (Rockwell), 3:557,
3:598
Mary, 1:75-76, 1:396,
1:443, 4:216
Mary (----), 1:76, 2:414
Mary (Blakeman), 1:76,
1:194
Mary (Cotton), 1:76, 1:464
Mary (Maverick) Smith,
1:76
Mehitable (Wainwright),
1:76, 4:382
Mercy, 1:75, 1:80
Rebecca, 1:76
Rebecca (----), 1:76
Ruth, 1:76
Ruth (Peck), 1:76, 3:381
Sarah (Alling), 1:41, 1:76
Atwell
---- (----), 1:77, 3:162
Elizabeth (Baker), 1:98
Joan (----) Andrews, 1:54,
1:77
Mary, 1:76

Mary (----), 1:76
Atwood
Abigail, 1:77-78, 3:7, 3:19
Abigail (----), 1:78
Abigail (Dunham), 1:78
Ann, 1:77
Ann (----), 1:77
Ann (Betts), 1:78
Ann (Copp), 1:77, 1:457,
4:32
Ann (Snow), 1:77
Apphia (Bangs) Knowles,
1:111, 3:42
Bathsheba (Lattimore),
1:78
Deborah, 1:77
Elizabeth, 1:77-78, 1:465,
2:192
Elizabeth (----), 1:78
Elizabeth (----) Grover,
1:78, 2:321
Esther, 1:78
Esther (----), 1:78
Esther (Walker), 1:77,
4:394
Hannah, 1:78
Joanna, 1:77
Mary, 1:77-78, 1:232,
2:452
Mary (Smith), 1:77
Mehitable (----), 1:456
Mercy, 1:78
Phebe, 1:78
Rachel, 1:78
Rachel (Bachiler), 1:78,
1:89
Rachel (Batchelor), 3:61
Sarah, 1:77-78
Sarah (----), 1:77
Sarah (Masterson), 3:171
Sarah (Tenny), 1:78
Sarah (Terrill), 1:77
Susanna, 1:78
Aubrey
Rachel (Rawson), 1:78,
3:511
Audley
Ann, 1:394
Auger/Agar/Augur
Abigail, 1:79, 3:17
Alice (----), 1:79
Ann, 1:79
Ann (Cromwell), 1:78,

Auger/Agar/Augur
(continued)
Ann (Cromwell)
(continued)
1:476, 3:418
Elizabeth (Packard), 1:79
Esther, 1:79
Hannah (----), 1:79
Mary, 1:79
Mary (Gilbert), 1:79, 2:251
Ruth (Hill), 1:79, 2:415
Augustine
Abigail, 1:80
Elizabeth (Brown), 1:79
Sarah, 1:80
Austin
---- (Alger), 1:27, 1:80
---- (Crumb), 1:481
---- (Davis), 2:20
Abigail, 1:80-81, 1:499,
3:14
Abigail (----), 1:80
Abigail (Batchelder), 1:81,
1:89
Abigail (Batchelor), 3:61
Ann, 1:81, 1:499
Ann (----), 1:81
Catharine (----), 1:80
Constance (----), 1:81
Deborah, 1:419
Dorothy, 1:499
Dorothy (Adams), 1:499
Elizabeth, 1:80-81, 1:499,
2:270, 2:579
Elizabeth (Barnes)
Brockett, 1:257
Elizabeth (Brackett), 1:80
Elizabeth (Jesse), 2:547
Elizabeth (Pitts), 1:81
Elizabeth (Waldo), 1:80
Esther, 1:80, 3:274
Frances (Hill), 1:81, 2:416
Hannah, 1:80
Hannah (Trarice), 1:81
Isabella (----), 1:80
Jemima, 1:80
Lucy (Poor), 3:456
Lydia, 1:80
Mary, 1:80-81, 1:499, 2:20,
2:230, 2:592
Mary (----) Hooker, 1:81
Mary (Littlefield), 3:100
Mehitable, 1:81

Mehitable (Welsteed), 1:81,
1:499
Mercy, 1:80
Mercy (Atwater), 1:75,
1:80
Mercy (Osborn), 2:563
Rachel, 1:81
Rachel (----) Bachilor, 1:89
Rebecca, 1:80, 1:499
Rebecca (Sprague), 1:80
Rose, 1:81, 4:299
Sarah, 1:80-81, 2:20, 3:33
Sarah (----), 1:81
Sarah (Boosey) Standley,
4:165
Sarah (Starbuck) Story,
1:81, 4:172, 4:213,
4:366
Sophia, 1:80
Susanna (Foxwell), 2:198
Thankful (----) Benjamin,
1:80
Averill
Abigail (----), 1:82
Avery
Abigail, 1:83
Abigail (Chesebrough),
1:374
Abigail (Parke), 3:347
Ann (----), 1:499
Ann (Shapley), 1:83
Deborah, 1:83
Deborah (Stallion), 1:82,
4:161
Dorothy, 1:82
Dorothy (Parke), 3:347
Elizabeth, 1:83, 1:296
Elizabeth (Lane), 1:83,
3:52
Elizabeth (White), 1:83
Hannah, 1:82-83, 4:691
Hannah (Minor/Miner),
4:691
Jane (Greenslade), 1:82
Joanna, 1:82
Margaret, 1:82
Margaret (----), 1:83
Mary, 1:82-83, 3:52, 4:307,
4:691
Mary (Lane), 1:83, 3:52
Mehitable (Hinckley)
Worden, 1:83, 2:425,
4:652

Rachel, 1:83, 2:86, 3:52
Rebecca, 1:82
Sarah, 1:83, 3:52, 3:204
Sybil, 1:82
Sybil (Sparhawk), 1:82,
4:541
Awkley
Elizabeth, 1:84
Mary (----), 1:84
Axdell/Axtel/Axtell
Hannah, 4:655
Hannah (----), 1:84
Mary, 1:84, 2:274, 3:186
Mary (----), 1:84
Axley
Frances (----), 1:84
Ayers/Ayer
Abiah, 3:598
Abigail, 3:599
Abigail (----), 1:85
Amy, 3:598
Amy (----), 3:598
Bethia (Millet), 3:213,
3:598
Elizabeth, 3:598-599
Elizabeth (----), 3:598
Elizabeth (Chase), 1:85,
1:364
Elizabeth (Hutchins),
3:599, 3:637
Elizabeth (Palmer), 1:84,
3:340
Elizabeth (Tuttle), 4:352
Hannah, 1:84, 3:321,
3:598-599, 4:450
Hannah (Allen), 1:37, 1:84
Hannah (Pike), 3:599
Love, 3:28, 3:599
Lydia, 3:599
Martha, 2:485, 3:321,
3:599
Mary, 1:84, 2:16, 3:599
Mary (Johnson), 3:599
Mary (Woodham), 3:598,
4:637
Mehitable, 1:85, 3:599
Priscilla (Hovey), 2:470
Rachel, 3:599
Rebecca, 1:69, 1:84, 2:130
Ruth, 3:598-599
Sarah, 1:85, 3:598-599
Sarah (----), 1:85
Sarah (Caldwell), 1:329

Ayers/Ayer (continued)
Sarah (Williams), 1:84, 4:561
Susanna, 4:163
Susanna (Symonds), 3:598, 4:246
Tamosin (Torloar/Thurla), 3:598
Aylett
Lydia (Palsgrave), 3:340
Mary, 1:85
Mary (Hawkins), 1:85, 2:383
Ayrault/Ayrould
Marian (Breton), 1:85
Mary (Robineau), 1:85
Mary Ann (----), 2:275
Babbage/Babbidge
---- (----) Carleton, 3:608
Agnes (----), 1:86
Esther, 3:651
Hannah, 1:86
Hannah (----) Carlton, 1:86
Hannah (Jewett) Carleton, 1:511, 3:608
Mary, 1:86
Ruth, 1:86
Babbit
Mary (Lawton) Babcock, 1:86
Babcock
---- (Crandall), 1:471
Abigail, 1:500
Alice, 2:583
Ann, 1:86
Dorothy (Key), 1:500
Elizabeth, 1:86, 1:500, 3:85
Elizabeth (----), 1:86
Hannah, 1:86, 3:57
Hannah (Coats), 1:500
Jane, 1:86, 3:86
Mary, 1:86, 1:355
Mary (----), 1:86, 2:138
Mary (Lawton), 1:86
Sarah, 1:86, 2:591, 3:86
Babington
Catharine (Haslerigg) Fenwick, 2:154
Babson
Abigail, 3:599
Ann, 3:599
Dorcas (Elwell), 3:599

Elinor, 1:87
Elinor (Hill), 1:87
Elizabeth, 1:87, 3:599
Hannah, 4:168
Hannah (Baker), 3:599
Isabel (----), 1:87
Sarah, 1:87
Bachiler/Bachelor/Bachelder
----, 1:89, 4:11, 4:56
Abigail, 1:81, 1:88-89, 2:32, 3:61
Agnes (----) Gillingham, 1:500
Agnes (Wadlen) Gillingham, 2:586
Bridget (Wines), 4:312
Deborah, 1:89, 4:594
Deborah (Smith), 1:88, 4:120
Elizabeth, 1:87-88, 2:18
Elizabeth (----), 1:88, 3:599
Elizabeth (----) Knill, 1:500, 3:35
Hannah, 1:87-88, 3:599, 3:612, 4:421
Hannah (Warner), 4:418
Jane (----), 1:89
Martha (----), 1:87
Mary, 1:88
Mary (----), 1:88
Mary (Carter) Wyman, 1:88, 1:342, 4:664
Mary (Herrick), 1:88
Mercy, 2:32
Miriam (Moulton), 1:500, 3:249
Rachel, 1:78, 1:89, 3:61
Rachel (----), 1:89
Rebecca (----), 1:88
Ruth, 1:192
Susanna, 1:89, 3:61, 4:447
Theodata, 1:89, 2:507
Backus
Ann (----), 1:89
Elizabeth (Pratt), 1:89, 3:476
Hannah, 1:180
Lydia, 1:89
Mary, 1:89
Ruth, 1:89
Sarah, 1:89
Sarah (Charles), 4:674, 4:677

Sarah (Gardiner), 1:89
Bacon
----, 2:4, 2:215
---- (Aldis), 1:24
Abigail, 1:90-91
Abigail (----), 1:90-91
Alice, 1:500
Ann, 1:90
Ann (Miller), 1:91, 3:211
Beriah, 1:91
Desire, 1:91
Dorothy, 1:90
Dorothy (Bradhurst), 1:90
Elizabeth, 1:32, 1:90-92, 3:536
Elizabeth (----), 1:90
Elizabeth (----) Stanley, 1:89-90, 4:165
Elizabeth (Hancock) Wyman, 4:664
Elizabeth (Howes), 1:90
Elizabeth (Martin), 1:90
Elizabeth (Pierpont), 1:91
Hannah, 1:91-92, 4:333, 4:674, 4:705, 4:712
Hannah (----), 2:19
Hannah (Mayo), 1:91, 3:187
Judith (Wyman), 4:664
Lydia, 1:90-91, 1:500, 3:431, 4:527, 4:627
Lydia (Dewing), 1:91, 2:44
Martha, 1:92
Martha (Foxwell), 1:92, 2:198
Martha (Howland) Damon, 2:4
Mary, 1:90-92, 1:337, 1:500, 2:221, 3:29, 4:527
Mary (----), 1:91
Mary (Howes), 1:91
Mary (Jacob), 1:92
Mary (Noyes), 1:91
Mary (Read), 1:90
Mercy, 1:90-91, 3:323
Patience, 1:91
Rachel, 1:90
Rebecca, 1:90-91, 2:237
Rebecca (----), 1:90
Rebecca (Potter), 1:92
Ruhami, 1:90
Sarah, 1:90-91, 4:244

Bacon (continued)
Sarah (Hinckley), 1:92,
2:425
Sarah (Richardson), 1:91
Susan, 1:90
Susanna, 1:90, 1:500, 2:44
Susanna (Draper), 1:500
Susanna (Spencer), 1:90,
4:148
Badcock
Abigail, 1:92
Dorothy, 1:92, 4:625
Elizabeth, 1:93, 1:500,
4:230
Hannah, 1:92, 1:500,
3:240, 3:614
Hannah (----), 1:92
Hannah (Daniel), 3:599,
3:614
Margaret, 3:77
Mary, 1:500, 3:141
Mary (----), 3:599
Mary (Curtis), 1:487
Sarah, 1:500
Susan, 1:500
Badger
Abigail, 1:93
Elizabeth, 1:93
Elizabeth (----), 1:93, 1:275
Elizabeth (Greenleaf), 1:93,
2:308
Elizabeth
(Hayden/Haydon), 2:386
Hannah, 1:93
Hannah (----), 1:93
Hannah (Swett), 1:93
Lydia, 1:93
Mary, 1:93
Ruth, 1:93
Sarah, 1:93, 4:498
Badlam
Joan (----), 1:93
Mary, 1:93
Mary (----), 1:93
Badman
Lydia, 1:93
Sarah (----), 1:93
Bagg
Hannah, 1:93, 4:96
Hannah (Burt), 1:93,
1:313
Mercy (Thomas), 4:282

Bagley
Abigail, 1:93
Judith, 1:93
Mary, 1:93
Mary (----), 1:93
Mary (Thayer), 1:93
Sarah, 1:93, 3:140
Sarah (Colby), 1:93, 1:424
Sarah (Sargent), 1:93
Bailey - see also Bayley
Abigail, 1:94, 4:268
Abigail (----), 1:94
Abigail (Swan), 4:237
Ann (Bourne), 1:94
Christian, 1:95
Edna (----), 3:289
Edna (Lambert), 1:94
Hannah, 1:94
Lydia, 1:94
Lydia (----), 1:94
Lydia (Redfield), 4:291
Mary, 1:94-95
Mary (----), 1:94
Mary (Carr), 1:338
Rachel, 3:457
Rebecca (----), 1:95
Ruth (----), 1:95
Ruth (Clothier), 1:94
Ruth (Ivory), 1:94, 2:526
Sarah, 1:94-95
Sarah (White), 1:94
Susanna (----), 1:94, 4:272
Bainbridge
Jane, 2:305
Baker
----, 3:554
---- (----) Minter, 3:218
---- (Colyer), 1:98
---- (Lane), 1:98, 3:53
Abiel, 1:96
Alice, 1:99
Alice (----), 1:97
Ann, 1:99
Bathsheba (----), 1:100
Bethia, 1:97
Catharine, 2:551
Catharine (Perkins), 1:97,
3:397
Charity, 1:96
Charity (----), 1:96
Christian, 1:95, 3:547
Christiana (Beal/Beals),
1:146

Christina (Otis), 1:100
Deborah, 1:98, 1:381,
3:600
Deliverance, 1:100
Dorcas, 1:100
Elinor, 1:99
Elinor (Winslow), 1:99,
4:601
Elizabeth, 1:95-100, 2:84,
2:496, 3:117, 3:476,
3:591, 3:600, 4:373,
4:619
Elizabeth (----), 1:95-96,
1:99, 1:500
Elizabeth (Bartlett), 1:98,
1:131
Elizabeth (Chase), 1:95
Elizabeth (Waterhouse),
4:431
Ellen (Winslow), 4:603
Esther, 4:709
Experience, 1:100
Faith (Withington), 1:98,
4:618
Fear (Robinson), 1:99,
3:550
Grace, 1:100
Grace (----), 1:98, 1:501
Grace (Marsh), 1:100,
3:154
Grizzle (Warren) Otis,
3:324
Hannah, 1:95, 1:97-98,
1:500, 3:88, 3:599,
4:616
Hannah (----) Minter,
1:97-98
Hannah (Bauk), 1:97
Hannah (Cooke) Buckland,
1:97, 1:285, 1:449
Hannah (Polley), 1:97
Hannah (Pomeroy), 1:500
Hannah (Tongue), 4:312
Hannah (Willet), 4:556
Hannah (Woodbury), 1:95
Hepzibah, 1:96, 3:450
Isabel (Twining), 1:95
Jane, 3:118
Jane (----), 1:95
Joan (----), 1:100
Joan (Rockwell), 1:96,
2:523, 3:558
Joan (Swift), 1:96, 4:241

14

Baker (continued)
Joanna, 1:100
Judith (----), 1:98
Leah (----), 1:501
Leah (Clark), 1:401
Lydia, 1:97, 1:99
Lydia (Baysey), 1:97,
1:144
Margary, 3:262
Martha, 1:100, 3:598-600,
4:18
Mary, 1:15, 1:95-100,
1:501, 2:193, 3:118,
3:629, 4:231, 4:373
Mary (----), 1:99-100
Mary (Aspinwall), 1:70
Mary (Eddington), 1:100,
2:100
Mary (Gamlin), 1:99,
2:224
Mary (Lewis), 1:99
Mary (Marshall), 1:95,
3:158
Mary (Pemberton), 3:387
Mary (Quincy), 3:501
Mary (Sigourney), 4:95
Mercy, 1:98, 1:100
Mercy (----), 1:100
Patience, 1:98, 1:100
Patience (----) Simmons,
1:99
Pilgrim (Eddy), 1:100,
2:99
Preserved (Trott), 1:97,
4:332
Priscilla, 1:60, 1:99, 3:600
Priscilla (Symonds), 1:99,
4:246
Prudence, 1:100
Rachel, 1:501
Rebecca, 3:600, 4:138
Rebecca (----), 1:96
Rose, 1:388
Ruth, 1:47, 1:97
Ruth (Holton), 1:97, 2:456,
3:135
Sarah, 1:96-100, 1:501,
2:285, 2:511, 2:531,
3:98, 4:510, 4:617
Sarah (Bradford), 1:232
Sarah (Cooke), 1:99, 1:448
Sarah (Hollister) Atherton,
1:72, 1:100, 2:449

Sarah/Mary, 1:501
Silence, 1:97, 3:599
Susanna, 1:96, 1:493
Susanna (Martin), 1:96
Tabitha, 1:95
Temperance (Denslow)
Buckland, 1:285
Thankful, 1:95, 1:97-98,
2:315
Thankful (Foster), 1:97,
2:187, 3:599
Balch
Agnes (----), 1:101
Annis (----), 1:101
Margaret (----), 1:101
Martha, 3:276
Martha (Newmarch),
3:276
Mary, 1:101, 1:501, 2:87
Mary (Conant), 1:101,
1:515, 2:57
Sarah (Gardner), 1:101,
2:230
Balcom
Catharine, 1:101, 2:542
Elizabeth, 1:501
Elizabeth (Haines), 1:101,
2:389
Hannah, 1:501
Sarah, 1:101, 1:501
Sarah (Woodcock), 1:101,
4:637
Baldwicke
Joanna (----), 2:237
Baldwin
---- (----) Mepham, 3:196
---- (Sargent), 4:18
Abigail, 1:102, 1:104-105,
3:516, 3:600
Abigail (----), 1:104, 3:600
Abigail (Baldwin), 1:102
Abigail (Fiske), 1:102,
2:165
Abigail (Lay), 1:105
Ann, 1:105
Ann (----), 1:102
Arabella (Norman), 1:103,
3:288
Deborah, 1:104, 4:705
Dorcas, 1:102
Dorothy, 3:600
Elizabeth, 1:101-105,
1:316, 4:428

Elizabeth (----), 1:103,
1:105, 2:195
Elizabeth (----) Hitchcock
Warriner, 4:428-429
Elizabeth (----) Warriner,
1:103
Elizabeth (Alsop), 1:104
Elizabeth (Botsford), 1:101,
1:217
Elizabeth (Campfield),
1:105, 4:677
Elizabeth
(Huested/Husted), 2:490
Esther, 1:104
Experience (Abell), 1:103
Hannah, 1:102-105, 1:217,
2:166, 2:493
Hannah (----), 1:103
Hannah (Birchard), 1:103
Hannah (Botsford), 1:104,
1:217
Hannah (Bruen), 1:103,
1:281
Hannah (Osborn), 1:103
Hannah (Richardson),
1:102
Isabel (----) Catlin Northam,
1:103, 1:349, 3:289
Jane, 1:103-104
Joanna, 3:600
Joanna (----), 1:102
Joanna (----) Westcoat,
1:104, 4:486, 4:705
Martha, 1:103-105, 3:600
Mary, 1:102-105, 3:446,
4:110
Mary (----), 1:102-103,
1:105, 4:255
Mary (----) Ambry/Ambery,
1:48
Mary (----) Mepham, 1:105
Mary (Beard), 3:602
Mary (Bruen), 1:102,
1:281
Mary (Camp), 1:104
Mary (Richardson), 1:103
Mary (Stream), 1:102,
4:222
Mildred (Prudden), 1:105,
3:492
Phebe, 1:102-103, 3:537
Phebe (Richardson), 1:102,
3:536

Baldwin (continued)
Rachel (----) Dellaclose,
1:501
Rebecca, 1:102-103
Rebecca (----), 1:104
Rebecca (----)
Cheesbrough, 1:103
Rebecca (Palmer)
Chesebrough, 1:373
Ruth, 1:102, 1:105
Ruth (Botsford), 1:217,
4:499
Ruth (Brooks), 4:676
Sarah, 1:102-105, 1:133,
1:284, 1:474, 2:152,
3:541, 4:45, 4:705
Sarah (----), 1:71-72, 1:105
Sarah (Caulkins), 1:105,
1:349-350
Sarah (Coley), 1:432
Sarah (Cooley), 1:103-104
Susanna, 1:102-103
Temperance, 1:104, 1:316
Thankful (Strong), 4:227
Ball
---- (----), 1:501
Abigail, 1:106-107
Abigail (Burt), 1:106,
1:313, 3:254, 4:178
Abigail (Salter), 1:106
Dorothy, 4:380, 4:674
Dorothy (----), 1:105
Elizabeth, 1:107
Elizabeth (Fox), 1:106
Elizabeth (Pierce), 1:106
Esther, 1:106
Hannah, 1:106
Hannah (Nash), 1:106,
3:261, 4:333
Hannah (Rugg), 3:585
Lydia, 1:106
Mabel, 1:106, 4:674
Mary, 1:34, 1:106-107,
3:453, 3:428, 3:453,
4:674
Mary (----), 1:107, 3:600,
4:175
Mary (Brooks), 1:259
Mercy, 1:106, 3:345
Rebecca (Seaverns), 4:47
Ruth, 4:402
Sarah, 1:106, 2:171, 3:600
Sarah (Bullard), 1:106

Sarah (Glover), 1:106,
2:261
Sarah (Thompson), 1:106
Susanna (----) Worthington,
1:106, 4:653
Ballantine/Ballentine
Elizabeth, 1:107
Hannah, 1:107
Hannah (Hollard), 1:107,
2:447
Hannah (Upham), 4:360
Lydia, 1:107
Lydia (Barrett), 1:107
Mary, 1:107
Mary (Winthrop), 1:107,
4:607
Mary (Woodward) Saxton,
1:107
Sarah, 1:107
Susanna, 1:107
Ballard
Abigail, 3:455
Dorothy, 1:108
Eleanor, 2:555
Elizabeth, 1:3, 1:108, 2:68,
4:46
Elizabeth (----), 1:109
Elizabeth (Phelps), 1:108
Esther, 1:108-109, 2:543
Grace (----), 1:109
Hannah (Belcher), 1:108,
1:155
Hannah (Hooper), 1:109
Jane, 1:108
Jemima, 1:108
Lydia, 1:108, 2:252
Lydia (----), 1:108
Lydia (Hale), 1:501
Lydia (Wiswall), 4:616
Mary, 1:108
Priscilla, 1:108
Rachel, 3:200
Rebecca, 1:108-109
Rebecca (----) Horne,
1:108
Rebecca (Hooper), 1:108
Rebecca (Hudson), 1:108
Sarah, 1:108-109, 2:454
Susanna, 1:108
Tabitha, 1:108
Balstone/Baulston
Elizabeth, 1:109, 1:421,
2:588, 2:286, 3:600

Elizabeth (----), 1:109
Judith (----) Winthrop,
1:109
Lydia, 1:109
Lydia (----), 1:109
Mary, 1:109, 4:370
Mary (----), 1:109
Mehitable, 1:109
Meribah, 1:109
Pity, 1:109
Prudence, 1:109
Sarah, 1:109
Sarah (Root), 1:109, 3:573
Bambridge
Justice (----), 1:110
Bancroft
Ann, 2:313
Elizabeth, 1:110-111,
1:272
Elizabeth (----), 1:110,
1:248, 4:21
Elizabeth (Eaton), 1:110
Elizabeth (Metcalf), 1:110,
3:203
Hannah, 1:110
Hannah (Dupper), 1:110
Hannah (Gardner), 1:110
Hannah (Williams), 1:110,
4:561
Jane (----), 1:110
Margaret (Wright), 4:659
Mary, 1:111
Ruhama, 1:111
Ruth, 4:195
Sarah, 1:110-111, 4:31
Sarah (Poole), 1:111
Sarah (Stiles), 1:110, 4:195
Banfield
Elizabeth (Long), 1:501
Bangs
Apphia, 1:111, 3:42
Bethia, 1:111, 2:333
Elizabeth, 1:111
Hannah, 1:111, 2:56
Hannah (Scudder), 1:112,
2:375, 4:43
Hannah (Smalley), 1:111,
4:108
Lydia, 1:111, 2:411
Lydia (Hicks), 1:111,
2:410
Mary, 1:111
Mary (Mayo), 1:111,

Bangs (continued)
Mary (Mayo) (continued)
3:188, 4:233
Mercy, 1:111, 1:501,
3:198
Rebecca, 1:111, 4:145
Ruth (----), 1:112
Ruth (Cole) Young,
1:111-112
Sarah, 1:111, 2:478
Sarah (----), 1:111
Tamosin, 1:111
Banister
Ann, 1:113
Ellen (----), 1:112
Hannah, 1:112
Huldah, 1:112
Jane, 1:112
Jane (Goodenow), 1:112,
2:272
Martha, 1:112
Mary, 1:112-113, 1:501,
3:600, 3:605
Mary (----), 1:501
Ruth, 1:112
Ruth (Eager), 1:112
Sarah, 1:112
Sarah (----), 1:112
Banks
---- (Taintor), 1:112
Abigail (----), 1:112
Elizabeth, 1:190
Elizabeth (Alcock), 1:21,
1:112
Hannah, 1:112
Mary, 1:112
Mary (----), 1:112
Susanna, 1:112
Bant
Elizabeth, 1:113
Mary, 1:113
Mercy (----), 1:113
Barbage
Isabella, 4:617
Barber
---, 2:300
Abiah, 1:113
Abial (Ellis), 1:114
Abiel, 1:114
Abigail, 1:113, 1:508
Abigail (----), 1:113
Abigail (Loomis), 1:113,
3:113

Ann, 1:114
Ann (Chase), 1:114, 1:364
Bathsheba
(Coggin/Cogens), 1:113
Elizabeth, 1:113-114,
1:501, 2:33, 3:238
Elizabeth (----), 1:113
Elizabeth (Clark), 1:113
Elizabeth (Kirk/Reick),
1:114
Esther (Brown), 1:274
Hannah, 1:113, 1:501
Hannah (Drake), 1:113
Hannah (Roper), 1:501
Hannah (Stedman), 1:501
Joan (----), 1:113
Joanna, 1:113, 4:136
Mary, 1:65, 1:113-114,
1:274, 2:256, 3:239
Mary (----), 1:113
Mary (Phelps), 1:114,
3:407
Mary/Mercy, 4:693
Patience, 1:113
Rebecca, 1:501
Ruth, 1:114, 1:501
Ruth (Drake), 1:501
Sarah, 1:113-114, 2:331
Sarah (Mumford), 3:253
Barden
Ann, 1:114
Deborah, 1:114
Deborah (Barker),
1:114-115
Mercy, 1:114
Bardin
Mary (Dodson) Booth,
1:212
Barding/Bearding
Abigail (----) Andrews,
1:56, 1:114
Sarah, 1:114, 4:149
Bardwell
Abigail, 1:114
Esther, 1:114
Mary, 1:114
Mary (Gull), 1:114, 2:322
Sarah, 1:114
Thankful, 1:114
Barefoot
Sarah, 4:540
Barge
Eleanor (----) Bayley,

1:115
Barger
Margaret (----), 1:115
Mary, 1:115
Barker
---, 3:25
--- (Bliss), 1:502
--- (Clark), 1:394
--- (Coddington), 1:502
Abigail, 1:116, 1:508,
2:181
Abigail (Wheeler), 1:115
Alice, 1:116
Alice (---), 1:116
Ann, 1:59, 1:115-116
Ann (Jewett), 1:502, 2:598
Ann (Williams), 1:115,
4:561
Barbara (Dungin), 1:502,
2:580
Christian, 1:502
Deborah, 1:114-116, 4:561
Desire, 1:115
Desire (Annable), 1:59,
1:115
Elizabeth, 1:115, 1:502,
2:94, 4:599
Elizabeth (Easton), 1:502
Elizabeth (Starbuck)
Coffin, 4:172
Esther, 1:116, 2:43, 4:187
Eunice, 1:115, 4:437
Grace, 1:115
Hannah, 1:116, 3:320
Hannah (----), 1:116, 1:200
Hannah (----) Cushing,
1:116
Hannah (Cushing), 1:489
Hannah (Kimball), 1:116
Hannah (Loring) Cushing,
1:489, 3:119
Hannah (Marston), 1:115,
3:160
Jane (----), 1:115-116
Joanna (----), 1:116
Judith, 1:115
Judith (Prence), 1:115,
3:477
Judith (Symonds), 4:247
Lydia, 1:115-116
Margaret, 1:116
Martha, 1:115
Mary, 1:115-116, 1:502,

Barker (continued)
Mary (continued)
4:112, 4:561, 4:655
Mary (----), 1:115-116,
3:560
Mary (Abbot), 1:3, 1:116
Mary (Dix), 1:116
Mary (Lincoln), 1:115,
3:94
Mary (Stevens), 1:116
Rebecca, 1:115-116, 4:139
Ruth, 1:115
Ruth (King), 1:116
Sarah, 1:3, 1:115-116,
1:502, 2:500, 2:592,
3:25
Sarah (----), 1:116
Sarah (Jeffrey), 1:502,
2:540
Sarah (Read), 1:502
Susanna, 1:116
Barley
---- (Stilson), 4:196
Barlow
---- (Stetson), 1:117, 4:184
---- (Stilson), 4:196
Abigail (Lockwood), 1:117,
3:105
Ann (----), 1:117
Beulah (----), 1:116
Deborah, 1:117, 1:502
Elizabeth, 1:116-117,
1:502
Elizabeth (----), 1:117,
1:439, 1:453, 4:424
Elizabeth (Mellins), 1:502
Isabella, 1:117
Jane (----) Bessey,
4:674-675
Martha, 1:117
Mary, 1:30, 1:116-117,
1:502
Mary (----), 1:502
Mary (Pemberton), 1:117,
3:387
Phebe, 1:117
Rose (----), 1:117
Ruth, 1:117, 1:233
Sarah, 1:117, 1:502
Sarah (Huxley), 1:117
Barnaby
Elizabeth, 1:118
Hannah, 1:118

Joanna (----), 1:117
Judith (----) Church, 1:118
Lydia, 1:118
Lydia (Bartlett), 1:117,
1:132, 3:267
Ruth, 1:118
Ruth (Morton), 1:117
Barnard
---- (----), 2:267
---- (Kingman), 3:27
---- (Wentworth), 4:486
Abigail, 1:119, 2:151,
4:674
Abigail (Bull), 1:120
Abigail (Phillips), 1:118,
3:410
Alice (----), 1:119
Ann, 1:119, 2:268
Ann (----), 2:268
Bethia (Folger), 1:119,
2:177
Damaris (Gardner), 1:502
Deborah, 1:130
Deborah (Weed), 4:451
Dorcas (Manning), 4:689
Elinor, 1:120
Elinor (----), 3:99
Elizabeth, 1:118-120,
1:496, 2:53, 4:380
Elizabeth (Negus), 1:120,
3:266
Elizabeth (Paris), 3:345
Elizabeth (Price), 1:120,
3:484
Elizabeth (Roby), 3:549
Elizabeth (Stone), 1:119,
4:206
Esther, 1:120
Esther (----), 1:119
Frances (Foote) Dickinson,
1:118, 2:48, 2:180
Grace, 1:119-120
Hannah, 1:118-120, 2:119,
3:150, 4:184, 4:187,
4:489
Hannah (Marvin), 1:118
Helen (----), 1:120
Jane, 1:119
Joanna (----), 1:120
Judith (Jennison), 1:118,
1:163
Lydia, 1:119
Lydia (Goff), 1:120

Lydia (Howard), 2:471
Martha, 1:120, 4:674,
4:698
Martha (----), 1:119
Mary, 1:118-120, 1:126,
1:152, 2:177, 3:237,
4:674
Mary (----), 1:118
Mary (Barnard), 4:674
Mary (Lugg), 1:119, 3:130
Mary (Morse), 1:119
Mary (Stacy), 1:118
Mary (White) Wells, 4:508
Mercy, 1:120
Mercy (Sherman), 1:120,
4:82
Phebe, 1:119, 1:502
Phebe (----), 1:118
Rebecca, 1:119, 4:573
Rebecca (How), 1:120
Ruth, 1:120, 3:380
Sarah, 1:118-120, 2:326,
4:180, 4:486, 4:674,
4:706
Sarah (----), 1:118-119,
4:591
Sarah (Birchard), 1:118,
1:181, 4:446
Sarah (Clark), 3:600
Sarah (Cutting), 1:119,
1:496
Sarah (Fleming), 1:119,
2:172
Sarah (Peasley), 3:600,
3:659
Sarah (Strong), 1:119,
4:226, 4:476
Sarah (Williamson), 4:573
Thankful, 1:119
Barnes
---- (Hammond), 2:347
Abigail, 1:121-123, 2:361
Abigail (----), 4:674
Abigail (Gibbs), 3:600
Agnes (Bent), 1:122,
1:196, 3:298
Alice, 1:121
Ann, 1:122, 1:254
Ann (----), 1:122
Ann (Canterbury), 1:122,
1:333
Ann (Hyde/Hide), 1:122,
2:515

Barnes (continued)
Deborah, 1:123, 2:21
Deborah (----) Dix, 1:122,
  2:53
Deborah (Orvis), 3:600
Dorothy (Stent/Stint),
  4:182
Elizabeth, 1:18, 1:121-123,
  1:257
Elizabeth (----) Hunt, 1:121,
  2:501
Elizabeth (Heaton), 1:121,
  2:400
Elizabeth (Hedge), 1:121,
  2:400
Elizabeth (Hunt), 1:121,
  2:502
Elizabeth (Stow), 1:121,
  4:218
Esther, 1:121, 3:540,
  3:600
Hannah, 1:121-123, 3:490,
  3:601, 4:674
Hopestill (----), 1:121
Jane (----), 1:121
Joanna/Susanna, 4:674
Lydia, 1:121, 4:92
Martha, 3:601
Mary, 1:121-123, 2:481,
  2:505, 3:157
Mary (----), 1:122, 3:471
Mary (Andrews), 3:597,
  3:600
Mary (Jones), 1:122, 2:564,
  3:601
Mary (Plummer), 1:121
Maybee, 1:122
Mercy, 3:639, 4:674
Mercy (Betts), 4:674
Patience, 3:601
Rachel, 1:123, 3:600, 4:18
Rachel (----), 1:123
Rebecca, 1:123, 3:235,
  3:600
Rebecca (----), 1:121
Ruth, 1:123
Sarah, 3:600, 1:121-123,
  4:36, 4:311, 4:674
Sarah (----), 1:121
Sarah (Ingersoll), 2:520
Susanna, 4:453
Susanna/Joanna, 4:674

Barnett
Elizabeth, 1:502
Hannah, 1:227
Mary, 1:502
Mary (Bishop), 1:502
Barney
Ann (Witt), 1:123, 4:619
Dorcas, 1:124
Hannah, 1:123-124
Hannah (Johnson), 1:123
Mary (Chapman), 1:361
Ruth, 1:124
Sarah, 1:123, 3:626
Barnham
Sarah, 2:141
Barnum/Barnam
Hannah, 1:124
Mary (Hurd), 3:601, 3:637
Sarah (----) Hurd, 3:601
Sarah (Thompson) Hurd,
  3:601, 3:637
Barrell
Abigail, 1:124
Ann, 1:124, 4:51
Ann (----), 1:124
Elizabeth, 1:124
Elizabeth (----), 1:124
Hannah, 1:124
Lydia, 1:124, 4:198
Lydia (Turner) James,
  1:124, 2:536, 4:346
Mary, 1:124
Mary (Colbron), 1:124,
  1:424, 4:343
Barrett
---- (Hawes), 1:125
Catharine (----), 1:125
Deborah (Howe), 2:474
Dorcas (Green), 1:125
Elizabeth, 2:519
Elizabeth (----), 1:125
Elizabeth (Cousins), 1:125
Elizabeth (Dexter)
  Mellen/Melling, 3:194
Frances (Woolderson),
  1:126
Hannah, 1:125, 4:36
Hannah (----), 1:125
Hannah (Fosdick), 1:125,
  2:185
Lydia, 1:107, 1:125-126,
  1:370, 3:454
Lydia (----), 1:126

Margaret (----), 1:126
Martha, 1:126
Mary, 1:125-126, 4:278
Mary (----), 1:125
Mary (Alexander), 1:26,
  1:125
Mary (Barnard), 1:119,
  1:126
Mary (Littlefield), 1:125,
  3:100
Mary (Pond), 1:125
Mary (Sparhawk), 1:126,
  4:144
Rebecca, 1:125, 4:655
Rosamond, 1:125
Sarah, 1:125
Sarah (----), 1:125
Sarah (Champney), 1:126,
  1:356, 3:454
Sarah (Graves), 1:125
Sarah (Learned), 3:68-69
Sarah (Poole), 1:356,
  3:454
Barron
Abigail, 1:126
Dorothy, 1:126
Elizabeth, 1:126-127
Grace, 1:126
Grace (----), 1:126
Hannah, 1:126-127, 1:327,
  1:452
Hannah (----) Hawkins,
  1:126, 2:383
Hannah (Hawkins), 1:126
Lydia (----), 1:126
Lydia (Prescott) Fairbanks,
  2:136
Mary, 1:126, 4:423
Mary (Learned), 1:127,
  3:68
Mary (Sherman), 1:127,
  4:82
Mehitable, 1:126
Rachel (Jennison), 1:127
Ruth (Bonham), 1:210
Sarah, 1:126
Susanna, 1:126, 3:506
Barrows/Barrow
Deborah (----), 1:127
Lydia, 1:127
Lydia (Dunham), 1:127
Mary, 4:486
Ruth (Bonum), 1:127

Barrows/Barrow (continued)
Thankful, 1:127
Barry, 2:176
Abigail (Disbrough) Flood,
2:175
Mary (Chapman), 1:361
Barsham
Amiel (----), 1:127
Annabel, 1:127
Annabel (----), 1:127
Dorothy, 1:127
Elizabeth, 1:127-128,
2:129
Elizabeth (Bond), 1:127,
1:210
Hannah, 1:127-128, 4:157
Mary, 1:127-128, 1:253,
3:350, 4:206
Mehitable (----), 1:127
Rebecca, 1:127-128, 4:597
Sarah, 1:127, 3:149
Susanna, 1:127, 1:333
Barstow
Abigail, 1:128
Ann, 1:129, 1:487
Ann (----), 1:129, 3:132,
3:487
Deborah, 1:128-129, 2:342,
4:62
Grace (Halstead), 1:128,
2:342
Hannah, 1:129
Hannah (----), 1:128
Jerusha, 1:128
Lydia, 1:128
Lydia (----), 1:128, 4:163
Lydia (Hatch), 1:128,
2:376
Marcia (----), 1:128
Margaret, 1:128
Martha, 1:129, 3:487-488,
4:249
Mary, 1:129, 2:523
Mary (----), 1:128
Patience, 1:129
Rebecca, 1:129
Rebecca (Train), 1:129,
4:321
Sarah, 1:129, 1:385, 2:342
Sarah (----), 1:129
Susanna, 1:128-129, 3:505
Susanna (Lincoln), 1:128,
3:94

Susanna (Marrett), 1:128,
3:153
Bartholomew
Abigail, 1:129, 4:579
Catharine (----), 1:129
Catharine (Hutchinson),
2:509
Elizabeth, 1:129-130,
1:353
Elizabeth (----), 1:129
Elizabeth (Scudder), 4:43
Hannah, 1:129, 1:268
Mary, 1:130, 1:503, 2:589,
4:506
Mary (Johnson), 1:130,
2:553
Sarah, 1:502
Bartlett
Abia (Gillet), 1:131, 2:256
Abia/Abial, 1:133, 4:22
Abiah (----), 4:106
Abigail, 1:130-132, 2:119,
4:176, 4:225
Abigail (----), 1:132
Alice, 1:131
Ann, 1:130, 3:535
Ann (----), 3:601
Bethshua, 1:62, 1:133
Captivity (Jennings), 2:545
Cicely (----), 1:130
Concurrence (Crane),
1:130
Deborah, 1:130, 1:132,
1:466, 2:586
Deborah (Barnard), 1:130
Deborah (Weed), 1:130
Dorothy, 1:131
Elizabeth, 1:98, 1:130-133,
1:232, 2:193, 3:478,
4:153
Elizabeth (Titcomb), 1:132
Hannah, 1:130-133, 3:9,
3:22
Hannah (----), 1:131, 1:133
Hannah (Emery), 1:132
Hannah (Peabody), 3:375
Hannah (Pope), 3:459
Hannah (Warren), 2:34
Hepzibah, 1:131, 2:46
Jane, 1:208
Joan (----), 1:131
Joanna, 1:132, 4:307
Lucy, 1:130

Lydia, 1:117, 1:130-133,
3:267
Margaret, 1:134
Martha, 1:130-131, 4:189
Mary, 1:67, 1:130, 1:132,
2:64, 2:190, 3:232,
4:207
Mary (----), 1:130
Mary
(Bridgeman/Bridgman),
1:133, 1:250
Mary (Cruttenden), 1:130,
1:481
Mary (Hoyt), 1:130, 2:481
Mary (Rust), 1:131
Mary (Waite), 1:131
Mary (Walton), 1:132,
4:405
Mary (Warner), 1:130
Mary (Warren), 1:132,
4:427
Mehitable, 1:130-131,
1:133, 4:156
Mercy, 1:132, 2:526
Mercy (Dudley), 2:76
Mercy (Hyde), 1:131
Mindwell, 1:133
Rebecca, 1:130, 1:132,
1:142, 1:232, 2:356
Sarah, 1:130-133, 1:232,
1:503, 2:11, 3:540,
4:524
Sarah (----), 1:131-132
Sarah (Baldwin), 1:103,
1:133
Sarah (Brewster), 1:130,
1:245
Sarah (Knight), 1:131
Sarah (Meigs), 1:130
Sarah/Mary, 4:697
Susanna (----), 1:133
Susanna (Lord), 1:130
Tirzah, 1:133
Tirzah (----), 3:315
Tirzah (Titcomb), 1:133
Bartoll
Alice, 1:133
Mary, 1:133
Parnel (----), 1:133
Susanna, 1:133
Susanna (Woodbury),
1:133

20

Barton
—, 1:133
Elizabeth, 1:134, 1:503, 2:306
Elizabeth (Marston), 1:134
Lydia (Roberts), 1:134
Margaret, 1:134
Margaret (----), 1:134, 4:309
Mary, 2:300
Mary (Butler), 1:134
Mary (Willoughby), 1:134
Naomi, 1:133
Phebe, 1:133-134, 1:417
Ruth, 1:134
Sarah, 1:503
Sarah (----), 1:134
Sarah (Robinson), 3:553
Susanna, 1:133, 1:503
Susanna (Gorton), 1:133, 2:283
Bartram
Elizabeth (----), 1:503
Ellen, 1:134
Esther, 1:134, 3:273
Hannah, 1:134
Rebecca, 1:134
Sarah (----), 1:134
Bascom
Abigail, 1:134, 2:520
Avis (----), 1:134
Hannah, 1:134, 1:263, 2:538
Hepzibah, 1:134, 3:135
Mary, 1:135
Mary (Newell), 1:135, 3:272
Bass
— (Byram), 1:326
Abigail, 1:135
Abigail (Adams), 1:13
Ann (----), 1:135
Deborah, 1:135
Deborah (----), 1:135
Hannah, 1:13, 1:135, 3:335
Lois (Ivory) Bly Rogers, 2:526
Mary, 1:133, 1:135, 1:456
Mary (----), 1:135
Mary (Howard), 1:135, 2:472, 2:561
Mehitable, 1:135

Rebecca (Faxon), 2:149
Ruth, 1:135
Ruth (Alden), 1:23, 1:135
Sarah, 1:135, 3:390, 4:276
Sarah (Wood), 1:135, 4:628
Susanna (----) Blanchard, 1:135
Susanna (Bates) Blanchard, 1:196
Bassaker/Bussaker/Busicot
Abigail, 1:136, 4:205
Mary, 1:136, 4:151
Bassett
— (----) Ives, 1:136, 2:526
— (Burt), 1:503
— (Joyce), 1:136, 2:573
Abia, 3:601, 3:648
Abiah, 1:136
Elizabeth, 1:136-136, 1:302, 1:503, 3:489, 3:614, 4:674
Elizabeth (----), 1:136, 1:503
Hannah, 1:136, 3:352, 3:405, 4:690
Hannah (----), 4:674
Jane, 4:674
Lydia, 4:534, 4:674
Margery (----), 3:601
Martha (Hobart), 1:136, 2:433
Mary, 1:136, 1:503, 3:252, 3:520, 4:674-675
Mary (Burt), 4:675
Mary (Dickerman), 1:136, 2:47
Mercy (Todd), 1:136, 4:309
Miriam, 1:136
Phebe, 3:601
Rachel, 1:136
Rebecca (----), 2:145
Ruth, 4:153, 4:674, 4:680
Sarah, 1:136, 2:116, 3:614, 4:513
Sarah (Hood), 1:136, 2:457
Basseville
Elizabeth, 3:385
Bassom/Bassum
Abigail, 1:136
Hepzibah, 1:136

Bastard
Hannah (----) Wakeman, 1:137
Hannah (Jordan) Wakeman, 4:387
Bastarr
Ann, 3:601
Mary, 1:137
Mary (----), 1:137
Susanna, 1:137
Batchby
Hannah, 2:491
Batchelder - see Bachiler
Bateman
—, 3:137
Abigail, 1:137
Abigail (Richardson), 1:137
Elizabeth, 1:137, 4:658
Elizabeth (Wright), 1:137, 4:658
Hannah, 1:137, 1:445
Hannah (----), 1:137
Martha, 1:137, 2:31
Martha (----), 1:137
Mary, 1:137
Rachel, 1:137
Ruth, 1:137
Sarah, 1:137, 1:324, 2:304
Bates
—, 1:139
Alice (----), 1:138
Ann, 1:138-139
Ann (----), 1:138
Ann (Oldham), 1:138
Ann (Withington), 1:139, 4:618
Bathsheba, 1:139
Elizabeth, 1:139, 3:63
Elizabeth (----), 1:138
Esther (Hilliard), 1:139
Hannah, 1:139, 1:362
Jane (----), 1:138
Lydia, 1:138, 2:174, 4:567
Lydia (Lapham), 1:139, 3:56
Margaret, 1:138-139, 2:248
Mary, 1:48, 1:138-139, 1:516, 2:187, 2:469, 3:563
Mary (----), 1:138
Mary (Chapman), 1:139,

Bates (continued)
Mary (Chapman)
(continued)
1:362
Mary (Cross), 1:516
Mary (Farwell), 2:147
Mary (Leavitt), 3:601
Mary (Lincoln), 1:139,
3:92
Mary (Ross), 4:698
Prudence, 1:138
Rachel, 1:138, 3:91
Rebecca, 1:139
Ruth, 3:601
Ruth (----), 1:138
Ruth (Lyford), 1:138,
3:134
Sarah, 1:139
Sarah (Sprague), 4:153
Silence, 1:139
Susan (----), 1:139
Susanna, 1:138, 1:196,
1:503
Batson
Ann (Winter), 1:139
Elizabeth, 1:139
Elizabeth (Saunders),
1:139
Lydia, 3:601
Margery, 1:139
Mary, 1:139
Mary (----), 1:139
Sarah, 3:601
Batt
Abigail, 1:140
Ann, 1:58, 1:140, 4:449
Ann (----), 1:140
Dorothy, 1:140
Elizabeth, 1:140
Jane, 1:140, 4:255
Lucy (----), 1:140
Lydia (Benjamin), 1:166
Sarah, 1:140
Sarah (Tudman), 3:601
Battelle/Battle/Battles
Abigail, 1:140
Hannah, 1:140
Hannah (Holbrook), 1:140
Martha, 1:140
Mary, 1:140-141, 3:132
Mary (Fisher), 1:140,
2:163
Mary (Onion), 1:140

Sarah, 1:140
Batten
Elizabeth (Cullick), 1:141,
1:482
Ursula (Greenway), 1:141,
2:310
Batter
Elizabeth, 1:141
Martha (Pickman), 1:141,
3:425
Mary, 1:141, 2:117
Mary (Gookin), 1:141,
2:279
Mary (Trask), 4:323
Sarah (----), 1:141
Battey
Margaret (Carr), 1:339
Bauk
Hannah, 1:97
Baxter
Abigail, 1:13, 1:141, 1:503
Abigail (Whitney/Whiterig),
1:503
Ann (----), 1:142
Bethia, 1:141, 2:33
Bridget (----), 1:142
Elizabeth, 1:141, 3:663
Elizabeth (----), 1:141
Elizabeth (----) Mack-
mallen, 1:503, 3:141
Hannah, 1:141, 1:503,
2:88
Hannah (Trumbull), 1:141,
4:336
Hannah (White), 1:141,
4:514
Margaret (Paddy), 1:141
Mary, 1:141-142, 1:293,
1:323, 1:503
Priscilla, 1:141
Rebecca, 1:141, 1:503
Rebecca (Lee)
Saffin/Saffyn, 4:4
Sarah, 1:503
Susanna, 1:141, 2:514,
3:638
Bay/Bayes
Ann (----), 1:142
Ruth, 1:142
Bayard
Ann (Cole), 4:366
Mary (Bowdoin), 1:221

Bayc - see Baysey
Bayley - see also Bailey
Damaris, 1:142, 3:69
Eleanor (----), 1:115
Eleanor (Emery), 1:143
Elinor (----) Jackson, 1:143
Elizabeth, 1:142, 1:504,
3:417
Elizabeth (----), 1:142
Elizabeth (----) Dearing,
1:143, 2:33
Hannah, 1:143
Judith, 1:142-143
Lydia, 1:142-143
Lydia (----), 1:142
Lydia (Redfield), 1:143,
3:521
Lydia (Redfyn), 1:143
Mary, 1:142-143, 2:15
Mary (Carr), 1:142
Mary (Mighill), 1:143
Priscilla, 1:143
Priscilla (----), 1:143
Rachel, 1:143
Rebecca, 1:142-143,
1:267, 1:278
Rebecca (----), 1:142
Rebecca (Bartlett), 1:142
Sarah, 1:142-143, 1:372
Sarah (Emery), 1:142
Baysey
Adrian, 3:115
Elizabeth, 1:144, 3:383
Elizabeth (----), 1:144
Lydia, 1:97, 1:144
Mary, 1:144, 1:307
Beach/Beech
---- (----) Hull, 1:144
---- (Staples), 1:144, 4:169
Abigail, 1:144
Bethia, 3:601
Catharine (----) Hull, 2:492
Elizabeth, 1:504, 3:482
Hannah, 1:144, 1:504
Martha, 1:144, 4:530
Martha (----), 1:144
Mary, 1:144, 1:504
Mary (----), 1:144
Mary (----) Fairchild, 3:601
Mary (Peacock), 3:376,
3:601
Mercy, 1:144
Ruth (Peck), 3:383

Beach/Beech (continued)
Sarah, 1:144, 1:504
Sarah (----), 3:201
Sarah (Platt), 1:144, 3:445
Sarah (Welles), 1:144,
4:475
Beadle
Abigail, 1:144
Dorothy, 1:504
Elizabeth, 1:144-145,
1:504
Elizabeth (Drake), 1:145,
2:69
Hannah, 1:504
Hannah (Lemon), 1:145,
3:78
Mary, 1:144-145, 1:504
Mary (Hicks), 1:144
Susanna, 1:145
Susanna (----), 1:144
Beal/Beals/Beale
Abigail, 1:146
Bridget, 1:155
Catharine (----), 1:145
Christiana, 1:146
Dorothy, 1:146
Elizabeth, 1:145-147, 3:51
Elizabeth (----), 1:146
Elizabeth (Huet), 1:145
Elizabeth (Joy), 2:573
Hannah, 1:146, 2:150
Hannah (Bradstreet),
1:235
Martha, 1:145-146, 1:384,
2:139, 4:203
Martha (Bradstreet), 1:147
Mary, 1:145-146, 2:523,
4:219, 4:532
Mary (----) Jacob, 1:145,
2:534
Mary (----) Stowell, 1:146
Mary (Besbedge/Besbitch),
1:171
Mary (Farrow) Stowell,
2:146
Mary (Gill), 1:146, 2:254
Mary (Hart), 1:147
Mary (Whiting) Hart,
2:368
Mary (Witteridge) Hart,
2:368
Nazareth (----), 1:145
Patience (Lovell), 1:146

Phebe, 1:145
Rebecca, 1:145
Ruth, 1:145
Sarah, 1:145-146, 3:53,
3:155, 4:68, 4:596
Sarah (----), 1:146
Sarah (Lovell), 1:146
Sarah (Ripley), 1:145,
3:543
Susanna, 1:146, 2:560
Susanna (----), 1:146
Beaman/Beamond/Beamon
Abigail, 1:147
Alice (Young), 1:147
Deborah, 1:147, 2:252
Elizabeth, 1:147, 1:361
Elizabeth (----), 1:147
Hannah, 1:504
Hannah (Barnard) Westcar,
1:118, 4:489
Lydia, 1:147, 1:225-226
Lydia (Danforth), 1:147,
2:8
Margaret (Chapman),
1:504
Mary, 1:147, 1:504, 1:515,
4:342
Rebecca, 1:147
Sarah, 1:147
Sarah (----), 1:147
Thankful, 1:147, 1:504
Beament
Sarah, 3:474
Beamsley
Abigail, 1:148
Ann, 1:147-148, 4:643
Ann (----), 1:147
Elizabeth, 1:147-148,
3:330
Grace, 1:147-148, 2:296
Hannah, 1:147-148, 3:394
Martha (----) Bushnell,
1:148, 1:318
Mary, 1:147-148, 2:39,
3:554
Mercy, 1:147-148, 3:401,
4:546
Bean/Beans
Elizabeth, 3:602
Hannah (Very), 4:372
Margaret, 3:602
Mary, 2:575

Beard
----, 3:602
Abigail (Hollinworth),
1:148
Ann, 3:602
Ann (----), 3:602
Esther (----), 1:148
Hannah, 1:148
Hannah (Hawley) Offitt/-
Ufford, 1:148, 3:305
Martha, 3:602, 4:222
Martha (----), 1:148
Mary, 3:602
Mary (----), 1:148
Beardsley/Berslev/etc
Abigail, 1:149
Hannah, 1:149
Mary, 1:148-149, 3:602
Mary (----), 1:148, 3:602
Ruth, 4:698
Sarah, 2:49, 3:602
Bearse/Bearce/Beirce
Abigail, 1:149, 3:279
Esther, 1:149
Hannah, 1:149
Lydia, 1:149
Martha, 1:149
Martha (Taylor), 1:149,
4:263
Mary, 1:149
Priscilla, 1:149, 2:335
Rebecca, 1:149, 2:502
Sarah, 1:149, 2:343
Beauchamp/Becham
----, 3:105
Catharine, 1:149-150
Elizabeth, 1:149, 3:602,
3:625
Elizabeth (----), 1:150
Elizabeth (----) Metcalf,
1:149, 3:203
Isabel (----), 1:150
Margaret, 1:150
Marguerite (----), 1:149
Mary, 1:149-150
Mary (----), 1:149
Mary Ann, 1:150
Susanna, 1:150
Beaudesert
---- (----) Griffin, 2:314
Beaumont/Bement/etc
---- (----) Stent, 1:150,
4:181

Beck
— (Salter), 4:7
Abigail, 1:150
Ann (Frost), 1:150
Deliverance, 1:150
Elizabeth (Hinds), 1:150
Hannah, 1:151
Mary, 1:150
Mary (—), 1:150
Mary (Frost), 1:150
Becket
Hannah, 1:151
Hannah (—), 1:151
Margaret, 1:151
Margaret (—), 1:151
Mary, 1:151, 4:140, 4:443
Sarah, 1:151
Susanna (Mason), 1:151
Beckford/Bickford
— (Cottle), 1:151
Bridget (Furber), 1:151
Christian (—), 1:151
Deborah, 1:151
Elizabeth, 1:151
Elizabeth (Tibbets), 1:151
Hannah, 1:151
Temperance (Furber), 1:151
Beckley
— (Deming), 1:151, 2:35
Abigail, 1:327
Hannah, 1:151, 1:504
Mary, 1:151
Sarah, 1:151, 1:385
Beckwith
—, 1:151, 2:291
— (—), 1:285
Elizabeth, 1:152, 1:181
Elizabeth (—), 1:152
Elizabeth (Griswold)
Rogers Pratt, 1:152, 2:317, 3:474, 3:563
Griswold, 1:152
Mary (Lee), 3:647
Prudence, 1:152, 2:578
Ruth, 1:152
Sarah, 1:151-152
Susanna (—), 1:151
Bedell/Bedle/Beedle
Bethia, 3:415
Elizabeth, 1:152
Elizabeth (—), 2:31
Hannah (—), 1:152

Judith, 1:152
Martha (—), 1:152
Mary, 1:152
Rachel (—) Dean, 2:31
Bedford
Ann (—), 1:152
Bedient
Mary (Barnard), 1:118, 1:152
Bedurtha/Bedortha
Blanch (Lewis), 1:152
Hannah (Marshfield), 3:160
Lydia (—), 1:152
Mary (—) Leonard, 1:152
Mary (Remington)
Leonard, 3:78
Mercy, 1:152
Bedwell
Ann, 2:124
Mary (Hodgkinson), 1:153, 2:440
Beebe/Beeby
Abigail (York), 1:153
Agnes, 1:153, 2:9
Agnes (Keeny), 1:153
Ann, 1:153
Elizabeth (Rogers), 3:560
Hannah, 1:153
Mary, 1:153
Mary (—), 1:153
Mary (Boltwood), 1:153, 1:208
Mary (Keeny), 3:3
Milicent, 1:153
Milicent (Addis)
Southmayd Ash, 1:18, 1:67, 1:153, 4:142
Rebecca, 1:153, 2:454, 3:589
Sarah, 1:153
Sarah (Benedict), 1:153, 1:164
Susanna, 1:153, 2:191
Beecher/Beacher
Abiah, 4:699
Abigail, 4:699
Christian (—) Copper, 1:153, 2:94
Christian (Barker), 1:502
Elizabeth, 4:699
Elizabeth (—), 4:699
Hannah, 4:699

Hannah (—) Potter, 1:153, 3:468
Jemima, 4:699
Joanna, 4:699
Joanna (—), 4:699
Mary, 4:699
Sarah, 4:699
Beeford
Hannah, 1:154
Mary, 1:154
Mary (—), 1:154
Ruth, 1:154
Beeks
Jemima (—) Abbot, 1:3
Beers/Beere
—, 1:155
Abigail, 1:155
Abigail (—), 1:155
Bethia, 1:154, 3:204
Catharine, 1:154
Deborah, 1:154, 2:495
Elizabeth, 1:154-155, 2:10, 2:266
Elizabeth (—), 1:154
Elizabeth (Bullock), 1:155
Elizabeth (Wilcockson), 3:602, 4:547
Esther, 1:154, 3:640
Judith, 1:155
Martha, 1:154, 1:291
Martha (—), 1:154
Martha (Barlow), 1:117
Mary, 1:154-155, 3:164, 3:530, 3:602, 4:122
Mary (—), 1:155
Mary (Fowler), 1:154
Patience, 1:154
Patience (Clifton), 1:154, 1:410
Patience (Scott), 1:154, 4:38
Sarah, 1:155, 4:174
Sarah (Tainter), 1:154, 4:249
Susan (Harrington)
Cutting, 1:496
Susanna (—), 1:412
Susanna (George)
Harrington, 2:360
Susanna (Harrington)
Cutting, 1:154
Beetfield/Bitfield
Elizabeth (—), 1:155

24

Behoney
Bridget (Beal), 1:155
Sarah, 1:155, 3:550
Sarah (----), 1:155
Beighton
Ann, 1:155
Ann (----), 1:155
Belcher
---- (----) Wormwood,
1:156
Abigail, 1:157
Abigail (Thomas), 4:280
Ann, 1:155-156, 3:298,
3:602, 4:212
Catharine (----), 1:156
Deborah, 1:156
Dorothy, 1:157, 2:318
Elizabeth, 1:155-157,
1:206, 3:309, 4:694
Elizabeth (Danforth),
1:155, 2:8
Elizabeth (Ruggles), 3:587
Hannah, 1:108, 1:155
Hannah (Frary), 2:201
Jane, 1:157
Jemima, 1:155, 4:96
Judith, 1:156
Martha, 1:155-156, 3:524
Mary, 1:156, 1:504, 3:592,
3:602, 4:368
Mary (----), 3:284
Mary (Billings), 1:157,
1:178, 3:285
Mary (Lockwood), 1:156
Mary (Simpson), 1:157
Mary (Wigglesworth)
Brackenbury, 4:542
Mary (Wormwood), 1:156
Patience, 3:602
Ranis (Rainsford), 1:157,
3:502
Rebecca, 1:157, 3:211,
3:602, 4:403
Rebecca (----), 1:156
Rebecca (Gill), 2:254
Ruth, 1:157
Ruth (Knight), 1:504
Sarah, 1:156, 2:58
Sarah (----), 1:156
Sarah (Gilbert), 1:156,
2:250
Belconger
Mary, 1:157

Sarah (Kelly), 1:157
Belden/Belding
Abigail, 1:157
Ann, 1:158, 4:279
Elizabeth, 1:157
Elizabeth (Foote), 1:157,
2:180
Esther, 1:157
Hepzibah (Buell) Welles,
1:157
Lydia, 1:158
Lydia (----), 3:602
Margaret, 1:158
Mary, 1:157-158, 2:156,
4:384, 4:655
Mary (----), 1:158
Mary (----) Allis, 1:158
Mary (----) Hastings, 1:158
Mary (----) Wells, 1:158,
4:479
Mary (Burt) Hastings,
1:313, 2:374
Mary (Meakins), 3:191
Mary (Meakins) Clark Allis,
1:42
Sarah, 1:157-158, 1:312
Sarah (----) Wells, 1:158
Sarah (Fellows) Billings,
2:151
Sarah (Hawkes) Mattoon,
1:157, 2:381, 3:178
Sarah (Waite), 4:383
Susanna, 1:158
Thankful, 1:157
Thomasine (----), 1:158
Belknap
Abigail, 1:158
Abigail (Buttolph), 1:158
Deborah (Fitch), 1:158,
2:168
Elizabeth, 1:158
Hannah, 1:158-159, 3:320
Hannah (Meakins), 1:158,
3:192
Jane, 1:159
Jane (Cheney), 1:159,
1:373
Lydia, 1:158
Mary, 1:158-159
Mary (----), 1:504
Patience, 1:159
Ruth, 1:158, 1:504
Ruth (----), 1:158

Ruth (Williams), 4:564
Sarah, 4:102
Sarah (----), 1:159
Sarah (Jones), 2:565
Bell
---- (Endicott), 2:123
Abigail, 1:159
Abigail (Tilton) Filmore,
4:304
Ann (----), 1:160, 3:253
Catharine (----), 1:159
Deborah, 1:160
Deborah (----), 1:160
Dorothy, 1:516, 4:324
Elizabeth, 1:159-160,
1:171, 1:478
Esther, 1:159, 3:157
Hannah, 1:159, 1:505
Hannah (Pray), 3:476
Jane, 1:159
Mary, 1:159-160, 1:459
Mary (Crane), 1:159
Mercy, 1:159
Moremercy, 1:160
Rachel (----), 1:160
Rebecca, 1:159, 4:351
Rebecca (----), 1:159
Rebecca (Ebborne), 1:505,
2:581
Sarah, 1:159-160
Susanna, 1:159
Susanna (Pierson), 1:159,
3:434
Tabitha, 1:160
Bellamy
Bethia, 1:160
Bethia (Ford), 1:160,
2:183
Elizabeth, 1:160
Mary, 1:160
Sarah (Wood), 1:160-161
Bellflower
Abigail (----), 1:161
Deliverance, 1:161
Hannah, 1:161
Bellingham
Elizabeth, 1:162
Elizabeth (----) Savage,
1:162
Grace, 1:161
Hannah, 1:161
Penelope (Pelham), 1:161,
3:282, 3:386

Bellows
Abigail, 1:162, 3:61
Dorcas (----) Willard, 1:162
Dorcas (Cutler) Willard,
  4:553
Esther (----), 1:162
Joanna, 1:162
Judith, 1:162
Mary, 1:162
Mary (Wood), 1:162
Belville
Frances (Hopkins), 1:163
Beman
Phebe (Parke), 3:347
Bemis
Abigail, 1:163
Beriah, 1:163
Elizabeth, 1:163, 2:494
Elizabeth (----), 1:163
Hannah, 1:163
Judith (Jennison) Barnard,
  1:118, 1:163
Lydia, 1:163
Martha, 1:163
Mary, 1:163, 2:328, 4:532
Mary (Barnard), 1:118
Mary (Harrington), 1:163,
  2:360
Rebecca, 1:163, 2:50,
  2:360, 4:511
Sarah, 1:163, 1:176
Sarah (----), 1:163, 2:589
Sarah (Holland) Phillips,
  1:163, 2:447, 3:413
Susanna, 1:163
Bendall
Ann (----), 1:163
Hopedfor, 1:163
Mary, 1:163
Mary (----), 1:163
Mary (Lyell), 1:164, 3:133
Moremercy, 1:163
Reform, 1:163
Restore, 1:163
Benedict
Abigail, 1:164
Betty, 1:164
Elizabeth, 1:164, 4:106
Esther, 1:164
Hannah, 1:164
Joanna, 1:164
Mary, 1:164, 3:312
Mary (Bridgham), 1:164

Mary (Marvin), 1:164,
  3:165
Mary (Messenger), 1:164
Mercy, 1:164
Phebe, 1:164
Phebe (Gregory), 1:164
Rebecca, 1:164, 3:445
Rebecca (Andrews), 1:53,
  1:164
Sarah, 1:153, 1:164
Sarah (Gregory), 1:164,
  2:312
Benfield
Grace (----) Miller, 3:211
Mary, 2:232
Benham
Hannah, 4:699
Hannah (Merriman) Ives,
  4:685
Joanna, 4:675
Margery (---) Alcock, 1:22,
  1:165
Mary, 4:675, 4:699
Mercy (Smith), 1:165,
  4:113
Sarah, 4:699
Sarah (----) Wilson, 3:603
Winifred (King), 1:165,
  3:27
Benjamin
Abigail, 1:165-166, 4:228,
  4:645
Abigail (----), 1:165
Amity (Myrick), 1:165
Ann, 1:165-166
Ann (----), 1:166
Annabel (Eve), 2:129
Elizabeth, 1:165-166
Elizabeth (Barton), 1:134
Elizabeth (Brown), 1:165
Hannah, 1:166
Jemima, 1:166
Jemima (Lambert), 1:166
Jemima (Lumbard), 3:106
Kezia, 1:166
Lydia, 1:165-166
Lydia (---), 1:37
Lydia (Allen), 1:37, 1:166
Martha, 1:165
Mary, 1:165-166
Mary (---), 1:166
Mary (Hale), 1:165
Mehitable (----), 1:166

Mercy, 1:166
Patience, 1:165
Rebecca, 1:165
Sarah, 1:165-166, 2:328
Sarah (----), 1:166
Thankful (----), 1:80, 1:166
Benmore
Elizabeth (----), 1:166
Lydia, 1:166
Martha, 1:166
Rebecca (----) Nock, 1:166
Rebecca (Tibbets) Nock,
  3:286
Bennett
----, 3:333
--- (Goddard), 1:167,
  2:264
Abigail, 3:604
Abigail (----), 1:166
Alice (----), 1:167, 2:511
Audry (----), 1:167
Deborah (Grover), 1:167,
  2:320
Deliverance, 1:516
Dorothy, 1:167
Elizabeth, 1:167, 2:17,
  3:60
Elizabeth (----), 4:593
Elizabeth (----) Smith,
  3:603
Elizabeth (Gillingham),
  1:505
Elizabeth (Parke), 1:168
Elizabeth (Smith), 1:505
Elizabeth (Tarbell), 1:505
Grace, 1:505, 3:603
Hannah, 1:167
Hannah (Wheeler), 1:167,
  4:501
Jane (----), 4:699
Love, 1:167
Lydia, 1:168
Lydia (Perkins), 3:396
Margaret (----), 1:168
Margery (----) Goochfield,
  1:168
Margery (----) Gurgefield,
  1:168
Mary, 1:167, 3:415, 4:699
Mary (----), 1:167, 4:175
Mary (Booth), 3:603
Mary (Broughton), 1:167
Mary (Porter), 1:168,

Bennett (continued)
Mary (Porter) (continued)
3:460
Mary (Simons), 1:166
Rebecca (----), 1:168
Rebecca (Spencer), 1:167,
4:148
Rose, 1:167
Ruth (Bradshaw), 1:505,
1:507
Ruth (Newell), 3:270
Sarah, 1:167, 3:318
Sarah (Champion), 1:167,
1:355
Susanna, 1:168, 1:398
Susanna (Bright), 1:168
Sybil (----), 1:168
Benning
Ann (----), 1:168, 2:41
Mary, 4:485
Bense
Mary, 4:17
Benson
Elizabeth (----), 1:168
Martha, 1:168
Mary, 1:168
Mary (----), 1:168
Sarah, 1:168
Bent
Abigail, 4:321
Abigail (Barnes), 1:122
Agnes, 1:122, 1:169,
1:196, 3:298, 3:528
Agnes (----), 1:122, 1:169,
3:298, 3:448
Ann, 1:169
Elizabeth, 1:169
Elizabeth (----), 1:169
Elizabeth (Bourne), 1:169
Experience, 1:169
Hannah, 1:12, 1:169
Hannah (Stone), 1:169,
4:205
Hopestill, 1:169
Martha, 1:169, 2:476
Martha (----), 1:169
Martha (Rice), 1:169,
3:530
Mary (Paris), 3:345-346
Patience, 1:169
Bentley
Alice, 1:169
Margaret, 1:505

Margaret (----), 1:169
Mary, 1:169, 1:505
Sarah, 1:505
Benton
---- (Peck), 3:383
Abigail (Graves), 4:675
Ann (----), 1:169
Ann (Cole), 1:428, 1:505
Dorothy, 1:169-170
Ellen, 1:170
Hannah, 1:170, 3:603,
4:36
Hannah (Stocking), 4:198
Lydia, 1:170
Martha (Spencer), 4:149
Mary, 1:169-170, 1:176,
1:429, 3:603
Mary (----), 1:170
Rachel
(Goodwin/Goodwyn),
3:625
Rebecca, 1:170
Sarah, 3:603, 4:660
Sarah (Waters), 1:170,
4:433
Tabitha, 3:603
Bernon
Esther (Leroy), 1:170
Mary, 1:170, 4:315
Mary (Harris), 1:170,
2:363
Berry
Abigail, 1:171
Ann (Bully), 1:170
Desire, 1:171
Elizabeth, 1:170-171,
2:563, 3:102
Elizabeth (----) Haskell,
1:170
Elizabeth (Bell), 1:159,
1:171
Elizabeth (Jenness), 2:544
Elizabeth (Travers), 1:170,
4:324
Experience, 1:170
Grace (----), 1:171
Hannah (Hodges), 1:170
Jane, 1:171
Jane (----), 1:171, 2:70
Judah, 1:170
Judah (----), 1:171
Margaret (Rogers), 1:171,
3:562

Mary, 1:170
Mary (Chapman), 1:170
Patience, 1:171
Sarah, 2:69
Sarah (Newmarch), 3:276
Besbedge/Bessbeech/etc
Alice, 1:172, 1:218
Hannah, 1:171
Joanna (Brooks), 1:171
Martha, 1:171, 4:347
Mary, 1:171, 1:277
Sarah (----), 1:171
Bessey/Bessy
Ann, 1:172, 4:675, 4:683,
4:714
Elizabeth, 1:172, 1:211,
4:675
Jane (----), 1:172,
4:674-675
Mary, 1:172, 4:675
Rebecca, 4:675
Best
Susanna, 1:172
Susanna (Duren), 1:172
Betscombe/Betsham
Ann, 3:603
Bett
Grace, 3:235
Bettis
Mary, 2:530
Betts
---- (Bridge), 1:248
Abigail, 1:172-173
Abigail (----), 1:172
Alice (----), 1:173
Ann, 1:78
Ann (----), 1:173, 1:327
Deborah, 1:173
Elizabeth, 1:173, 4:2
Elizabeth (----), 1:172,
2:185
Elizabeth (Bridge), 1:172
Hannah, 1:173, 1:331
Hepzibah, 1:173
Joanna, 1:173, 4:43
Joanna (Riker), 1:173
Judith, 1:173
Judith (Reynolds), 1:173
Margaret, 1:505
Martha, 1:173
Mary, 1:173, 1:505, 3:513
Mary (----), 1:172
Mercy, 1:173, 4:674

Betts (continued)
Mercy (Whitehead), 1:173,
4:2
Sarah, 1:173
Sarah (----), 1:173
Sarah (Marvin), 3:165
Sarah (Nichols) Brinsmead,
1:254
Betty
Mary, 1:174
Sarah (----), 1:174
Sarah (Jeffrey/Jeffries),
2:540
Bevans/Bevens
Abigail, 4:161
Mary (----), 1:174
Bibble
Ann, 1:174, 2:565, 3:301
Sibell/Sybel (----), 1:174,
2:60, 3:301
Bickford
Bridget (Furber), 2:220
Elizabeth (Tibbets), 4:299
Susanna (Furber), 2:220
Temperance (----), 2:220
Bicknell/Bicknall
Agnes, 3:557
Catharine (----), 4:211
Elizabeth, 1:174
Experience, 1:174
Hannah (----), 1:174
Joanna, 1:174
Mary, 1:174
Mary (----), 1:174
Naomi, 1:174
Ruth, 1:174
Sarah, 2:416
Sarah (----), 1:174
Bicknor/Bickner
Hannah (Bell), 1:505
Martha, 1:174
Martha (----), 1:174
Sarah, 1:505, 3:154
Biddle
Elizabeth (Stow), 1:175
Hannah, 1:174
Mary, 1:174, 3:191
Mary (----), 4:546
Rachel (----) Deane, 1:175,
2:31
Sarah, 1:174
Sarah (Harris), 1:175
Sarah (Wells), 1:174

Bidfield/Bedfield/Betfield
Elizabeth, 1:175, 4:190
Elizabeth (----), 1:175
Mary, 1:175
Bidwell
Abigail (Pitkin), 3:440
Elizabeth (Stow), 4:218
Sarah (Harris), 2:360
Sarah (Welles), 4:479
Bigelow
Abial (Pratt), 1:175
Abiel, 1:175
Abigail, 1:175-176, 2:359
Deliverance, 1:176
Elizabeth, 1:175-176
Elizabeth (Child), 1:175
Elizabeth (Flagg), 1:176,
2:171
Hannah, 1:175
Joanna (Erickson), 1:175
Lydia, 1:175
Martha, 1:175-176
Mary, 1:175-176, 2:171,
4:424
Mary (----), 1:176, 4:75
Mary (Benton), 1:176
Mary (Flagg), 1:176, 2:171
Mary (Olcott), 1:176
Mary (Warren), 1:175,
4:424
Mercy, 1:176
Patience, 1:175
Patience (Brown), 1:175
Rebecca, 1:176
Rebecca (Butler), 1:176
Rebecca (Olmsted), 3:312
Rebecca (Shepard), 1:176,
4:75
Sarah, 1:175-176, 3:69
Sarah (Bemis), 1:163,
1:176
Susanna, 1:175
Violet, 1:176
Biggs/Bigg
----, 4:217
Elizabeth, 1:177
Mary, 1:177
Mary (----), 1:176
Mary (Dassett), 1:177,
2:11, 3:217
Rachel, 1:62
Rachel (----), 1:177, 2:187,
4:217

Sarah, 1:177
Bill
Abigail (Willis), 1:177,
4:576
Elizabeth, 1:177
Elizabeth (----), 1:177,
3:409
Elizabeth (Sargent)
Nichols, 1:177, 4:19
Hannah (----), 1:177, 1:285
Lydia (Morrell), 2:320
Margaret, 1:177
Mary, 1:177
Mehitable (----), 1:177
Mercy (Haughton), 1:177,
2:378
Sarah, 1:177
Sarah (Shapley), 1:177
Susanna, 1:177
Billings/Billing
Abigail, 1:178-179
Amie, 1:178
Ann, 1:178, 2:254
Ann (----), 1:178
Beriah, 1:178
Dorothy, 1:179
Elizabeth, 1:178-179,
3:347, 4:288
Elizabeth (Hastings), 1:178
Elizabeth (Pratt), 1:178
Hannah, 1:178, 3:390,
4:384
Hannah (----), 1:178-179
Hannah (Wales), 1:177
Hannah (Wright), 4:659
Hepzibah, 1:178
Jemima, 1:178
Lydia, 1:179
Margaret, 1:178
Margery (----), 1:178
Mary, 1:157, 1:178-179,
3:285, 4:519
Mary (----), 1:178-179
Patience, 1:179
Prudence, 1:179
Sarah, 1:178-179
Sarah (Fellows), 1:179,
2:151
Sarah (Paine), 1:178,
3:335
Seaborn (Tew), 1:178,
4:270
Thankful, 1:178

Billings/Billing (continued)
Zipporah, 1:177-178
Billington
Christian (—) Eaton,
1:179
Christian (Penn) Eaton,
2:95
Hannah (Glass), 2:260
Helen (—), 1:179
Martha, 1:179, 2:97
Mary, 1:179
Mercy, 3:162
Rebecca, 1:179
Bills/Billes
—, 1:179
Ann, 1:179
Ann (Twining), 1:179,
4:353
Elizabeth, 1:179
Joanna, 1:180
Joanna (Twining), 1:179
Mary, 1:179
Mehitable, 1:179
Mercy (Fowler), 2:195
Bingham
Abigail, 1:180
Ann, 1:180
Deborah, 1:180
Hannah (Backus), 1:180
Mary, 1:180
Mary (Rudd), 1:180, 3:585
Mehitable, 1:180
Sarah (Lobdell), 1:180
Bingley
Abigail (Buttolph) Saywell,
1:180, 1:323, 4:33
Elizabeth, 1:180, 1:365
Elizabeth (Preston), 1:180
Binney
Dorcas, 1:180
Elizabeth, 1:180, 2:476
Hannah, 1:180
Hannah (Paine), 1:180
Margaret (—), 1:180
Mercy, 1:180
Mercy (—), 1:180
Phebe, 1:180
Rebecca, 1:180
Rebecca (Vickers), 1:180
Sarah (Crosby), 1:180
Birch
Bathsheba (Sanford),
1:181

Mary, 1:181
Birchard/Birchall/etc
Abigail, 1:181, 1:350
Ann, 1:181
Ann (Caulkins), 1:181
Catharine, 1:181
Christian (Andrews), 1:181
Elizabeth, 1:181
Elizabeth (Beckwith),
1:181
Hannah, 1:103
Jane (—), 1:181
Mary, 1:181
Mary (—), 1:181
Sarah, 1:118, 1:181, 4:446
Sarah (Webb), 1:181
Susan, 1:181
Bird
Abiel, 1:182
Ann, 1:182
Ann (—), 1:182
Bebee, 1:182
Damaris, 1:182
Deiton, 1:182
Elizabeth, 1:182
Elizabeth (—), 1:47
Elizabeth (Williams),
1:182, 4:565
Esther (Woodford), 4:638
Eunice, 1:182
Hannah, 1:182
Lydia, 1:182
Lydia (Steele), 1:182,
4:180
Margaret, 1:460
Mary, 1:182, 4:124
Mary (—), 1:182
Mary (Woodford), 4:638
Mehitable, 1:182
Mercy, 1:182, 2:514
Mindwell, 1:182
Patience, 1:182
Priscilla, 1:182
Rebecca, 1:182
Sarah, 1:182
Sarah (—) Smith, 4:124
Sarah (Woodford), 4:638
Silence, 1:182
Submit, 1:182
Thankful, 1:182
Thankful (Atherton), 1:73,
1:182

Birdley
Elizabeth (—), 1:183
Birdseye/Birdsey/Burdsie
— (Wilcockson), 1:302
Alice (—) Tomlinson,
1:301, 3:603, 4:310
Dinah, 1:302, 1:506, 3:603
Hannah, 1:302, 1:506,
3:603
Joanna, 1:183, 1:302,
4:548
Mary, 1:302, 3:189, 3:603
Phebe (—), 1:506
Phebe (Wilcockson), 3:603,
4:548
Philippa (—), 3:603
Phillis (—), 3:607
Sarah, 3:603
Birdwell
Mary, 2:53
Birge
Abigail, 1:183
Deborah, 1:183
Deborah (Holcomb), 1:183,
2:444
Elizabeth, 1:183
Elizabeth (Gaylord), 1:183,
2:238, 2:466
Esther, 1:183
Hannah, 1:183
Hannah (Watson), 1:183,
4:438
Mary, 1:183
Mary (—), 1:183
Birkbee
Sarah, 4:151
Births
Christian, 2:140
Hannah, 2:540
Bisbee/Bisby
Hannah, 1:262
Joanna (Brooks), 1:263
Mary, 1:277
Phebe, 1:227, 3:163
Sarah (—), 3:92
Sarah (King), 3:26
Biscoe
Mary, 4:98
Bishop
—, 1:185-186, 2:61
— (—) Golt/Gault, 2:587
— (—) King, 3:26
Abigail, 1:184-185,

29

Bishop (continued)
Abigail (continued)
3:603-604, 4:709
Abigail (Bennett), 3:604
Abigail (Willet), 1:185,
4:556
Alice (----) Clark, 1:186
Alice (Martin) Clark, 1:393
Alice (Mattocks), 1:185,
3:87, 3:177
Ann, 3:604, 4:180
Ann (----), 1:185
Ann (Gary), 1:186
Bethia, 1:185
Bridget, 1:184, 3:584
Bridget (Oliver), 1:506,
3:657
Damaris, 4:234
Dinah, 1:184, 3:604
Elizabeth, 1:184-185,
2:253, 3:604
Elizabeth (----), 1:186
Elizabeth (----) Wilbore,
1:184
Elizabeth (Phillips), 1:184
Elizabeth (Tompkins),
1:184
Esther, 1:305
Esther (----), 1:186
Grace, 1:184
Hannah, 1:183-186, 1:506,
3:236, 3:513, 3:603-604
Hannah (----), 1:506
Hannah (----) Talmadge,
3:604
Hannah (Gary), 1:186
Hannah (Yale) Talmadge,
4:709
Joanna, 1:184
Joanna (Boyse) Willet,
3:492
Joanna (Willet) Prudden,
1:185
Joy, 3:604
Leah, 1:186
Margaret (----), 1:186
Mary, 1:183-185, 1:502,
3:604
Mary (----), 3:603, 3:662
Mary (----) Gott/Goult,
1:186, 3:623
Mary (Hall), 2:335
Mary (Williams), 4:560

Mehitable, 1:186
Patience (----), 3:603
Prudence (----), 1:186
Rachel (Sibley), 4:93
Rebecca, 1:184-185,
3:603-604, 4:288
Rebecca (----), 1:185
Rebecca (Kent) Scullard,
1:184, 3:12, 4:43
Ruth, 1:184-185,
3:428-429, 3:603-604,
4:667
Sarah, 1:184-185, 1:287,
1:366, 3:604, 4:44
Sarah (----), 1:184
Sarah (Grannis), 2:290
Sarah (Wells), 4:475
Sarah (Wild), 1:506, 4:549
Susanna, 1:185, 1:198
Susanna (Goldham), 1:185,
2:269
Tabitha, 1:186, 1:337,
2:180
Tabitha (Wilkinson), 1:186
Biss
Jemima (----), 1:186
Martha, 1:186
Bissell
Abigail, 1:187, 2:124,
2:586, 4:20, 4:225,
4:262, 4:341
Abigail (Allyn), 1:186
Abigail (Filley), 1:187,
2:159
Abigail (Holcomb), 1:187,
2:444
Abigail (Moore), 1:187,
3:228
Ann, 1:187
Deborah, 1:187
Deliverance (----) Rockwell
Warner, 4:422
Dorothy, 1:187, 4:438
Dorothy (Fitch), 1:187,
3:619
Elizabeth, 1:187, 4:213
Esther, 1:187
Esther (Strong), 1:187,
4:227
Eunice, 1:187
Hannah, 1:187
Isabel (Mason), 1:187,
3:168

Joyce/Joice, 1:186-187,
3:439
Mary, 1:186-187, 2:69-70,
3:460
Mary (----), 1:186-187,
1:288
Mindwell, 1:187, 2:589
Mindwell (Moore), 1:187,
3:228
Sarah, 1:187
Sarah (White) Loomis,
3:114
Bitner
Sarah (Ingalls), 1:187,
2:596
Bittlestone
Elizabeth, 1:188, 1:256
Elizabeth (----), 1:188
Bixby
Abigail, 1:188
Hannah, 1:188, 1:506
Hannah (Chandler), 1:188,
1:358
Mary, 1:188, 1:506
Mary (----), 1:188
Mehitable, 1:506
Rachel, 1:188
Rachel (----), 1:188
Sarah, 1:188, 1:506
Sarah (Gould), 1:188,
2:285
Sarah (Wyatt) Heard,
1:188, 2:397
Blacey
Abigail (Ingersoll), 2:520
Blachley
Sarah (----) Foot, 1:188,
2:181
Black
Ann, 2:252
Dorothy (----), 1:188
Faith (Bridges), 1:249
Freeborn (----), 1:189
Lydia, 1:189
Mary, 3:80
Persis, 3:621
Ruth, 1:188
Susanna (----), 1:189
Blackburne
Elizabeth (----), 1:189
Blackleach
Abigail (----) Hodson,
3:633

30

Blackleach (continued)
Abigail (Hudson), 3:604,
   3:644, 4:701
Dorcas, 3:151
Dorcas (Bowman), 1:189,
   1:224-225
Elizabeth, 1:189, 1:506
Elizabeth (----), 1:189
Exercise, 1:189, 3:508
Jael, 3:604
Mary, 1:189, 3:306, 4:380,
   4:480
Blackman/Blakeman
----, 1:190
Abigail, 1:195, 2:47, 2:522
Abigail (Curtis), 1:195,
   3:604
Deborah, 1:195
Dorothy, 1:195
Dorothy (----), 4:281
Dorothy (Smith), 1:195,
   2:333, 4:52, 4:115
Elizabeth, 1:190, 1:195
Elizabeth (----), 4:393
Elizabeth (Wheeler), 1:195
Esther (Wheeler), 1:195
Hannah, 1:190, 1:195,
   3:604
Hannah (----), 3:604
Hannah (Hall), 1:195,
   2:333
Hepzibah, 1:190
Jane, 1:190, 1:195, 3:593
Jane (----), 1:194
Jane (Weeks), 1:190,
   4:454
Jemima, 1:190
Joanna, 1:195
Keziah, 1:190
Mary, 1:76, 1:190,
   1:194-195
Mary (Kimberly), 3:604,
   3:644
Mary (Pond), 1:190, 3:453
Miriam, 1:195
Miriam (Wheeler), 1:195,
   3:604, 4:499
Patience (Wilcoxson),
   1:195, 4:547
Rebecca, 1:194-195
Rebecca (Scottow), 1:194,
   4:40
Renew, 1:190

Sarah, 1:190, 1:195, 4:309
Sarah (----), 1:190
Susan, 1:190
Thankful, 1:190
Blackmore
---- (Collamore), 1:432
Elizabeth (----), 1:297
Elizabeth (Banks), 1:190
Mary (----), 1:190
Mary (Hawkins), 1:190,
   2:384
Mary (Trumbull), 1:506
Phebe, 1:190
Blackwell
Alice, 1:191
Desire, 1:191
Jane, 1:191
Lettice, 1:191
Mary, 1:191, 4:168
Sarah, 1:191
Sarah (----), 1:191
Sarah (Warren), 4:426
Blagge
Elizabeth (----), 1:191
Blague
Elizabeth, 1:191
Martha (Kirtland), 1:191
Mary, 1:191
Blaisdell/Blaisdale
----, 2:108
Elizabeth (----), 1:191
Elizabeth (----) Hoyt, 2:481
Mary, 1:191, 4:187, 4:219
Mary (----), 1:191
Sarah, 1:191
Blake
Abigail, 1:192-193
Abigail (Mather), 3:173
Agnes (----), 1:193
Ann, 1:193-194, 3:68
Deborah, 1:192, 3:103
Deborah (----), 1:192
Dorothy, 1:192, 3:103
Dorothy (----), 1:192
Elizabeth, 1:192-193
Elizabeth (----), 1:192
Elizabeth (Clap), 1:192,
   1:389
Elizabeth (Hunt), 1:192
Experience, 1:194
Hannah, 1:192-193
Hannah (----), 1:193, 2:496
Hannah (Macy), 1:192

Hannah (Tolman) Lyon,
   3:649, 4:675
Jane, 1:192
Martha, 1:192
Mary, 1:192-194
Mary (----), 1:193
Mary (----) Shaw, 1:192
Mary (Johnson), 2:553
Mary (Souther) Shaw, 4:65,
   4:141
Mehitable, 1:193-194
Mehitable (----), 1:193
Mercy, 1:193
Patience (Pope), 1:192,
   3:458
Prudence, 1:192, 4:355
Rebecca, 1:192
Ruth, 1:192-193
Ruth (Batchelder), 1:192
Sarah, 1:192-193, 4:252
Sarah (----), 1:193
Sarah (Dearborn), 2:32
Sarah (Hall), 1:193, 2:337
Susan, 1:194
Susanna, 1:192
Zipporah, 1:193
Blakely
Esther, 1:209
Blakesley/Blackley
Abigail, 4:675
Ann, 4:675
Grace, 2:60, 4:675
Grace (Ventris), 4:370,
   4:675
Hannah, 1:189-190, 1:260,
   4:675
Hannah (----), 4:676
Hannah (Potter), 1:189,
   4:675
Mary, 1:189-190, 4:675
Mehitable, 4:675
Miriam, 4:675
Sarah, 1:195, 4:675
Sarah (Kimberly), 4:675
Susanna, 4:675
Tilley, 4:675
Blanchard
----, 1:197
Abiah (Hassell), 1:196,
   2:372
Abigail, 1:196
Agnes (Bent), 1:122,
   1:169

Blanchard (continued)
Agnes (Bent) Barnes,
1:122, 1:196, 3:298
Ann (----), 1:196-197
Ann (Everill), 1:197, 2:131
Ann (Lovejoy), 1:196,
3:122
Ann/Hannah (----), 2:229
Elizabeth, 1:196, 1:506,
2:418, 2:589
Elizabeth (----), 1:195
Esther, 1:196, 2:147
Hannah, 1:195-196, 2:418,
4:76
Hannah (----), 1:196-197
Hannah (Everill), 2:131,
3:147
Hannah (Shepard), 1:196,
4:76
Jane, 1:196
Mary, 1:195-196, 2:149,
3:346
Mary (----), 1:196
Mary (Sweetser), 1:196,
4:239
Mercy, 1:196
Rachel, 1:196
Rose (Holmes), 1:196,
2:451
Ruth, 1:196
Ruth (Adams), 1:196
Sarah, 1:195-196
Sarah (Munroe/Monroe),
3:257
Susanna, 1:196
Susanna (----), 1:135
Susanna (Bates), 1:196,
1:503
Tabitha, 1:196
Tabitha (----), 1:196
Bland
Annabel, 1:197
Isabel, 1:197
Joanna (----), 1:197
Blandford/Blanford
----, 1:197
Dorothy (----) Wright,
1:197, 4:655
Elizabeth (Eames), 1:197
Hannah, 1:197
Mary, 3:328
Mary (----), 1:197, 3:328
Sarah, 1:197, 3:16

Susanna (Long), 1:197,
3:109
Blaney
Ann, 1:507
Catharine, 1:507
Elizabeth, 1:197
Elizabeth (----) Purchase,
1:197, 3:494
Hannah, 1:197
Hannah (King), 1:197,
3:24
Mary, 1:507
Rebecca, 1:507
Sarah, 1:507
Sarah (----) Powell, 1:197,
3:469
Susanna, 1:197
Blanton/Blanding
Bethia (----), 1:198
Mary, 1:197
Phebe, 1:197
Phebe (----), 1:197
Blatchford
Hannah (Willey), 1:198,
4:149, 4:558
Hannah (Willey)
Hungerford, 1:507, 2:498
Joanna, 1:198
Mary, 1:198
Blatchley
Abial, 1:198
Abigail, 1:198
Bashua, 1:198
Hannah, 1:198
Mary, 1:198
Mary (Dodd), 1:198, 2:56
Mehitable, 1:198
Miriam, 1:198, 3:453
Sarah, 1:198
Sarah (----) Foote, 1:198
Susanna, 1:198
Susanna (----), 1:198,
1:257
Susanna (Bishop), 1:185,
1:198
Blaxton
Catharine (----), 1:198
Sarah (----) Stephenson,
1:199, 4:182
Blessing
Joanna, 4:317
Blethin
Jane (Marks), 1:507

Bligh - see also **Bly**
Ruth (Walley) Everton,
2:582
Sarah (----) Everton, 1:507
Sarah (Reynolds), 1:507
Blinman
Mary (Parke), 1:200
Blish/Blush
Alice (Derby), 1:200
Ann, 1:200
Ann (----), 1:200
Ann (Williams) Barker,
1:115
Hannah (----) Barker,
1:200
Hannah (Hull), 1:200
Mary, 1:200
Sarah, 1:200
Thankful, 1:200
Bliss
----, 1:202, 1:502, 2:516,
4:571, 4:571
Ann, 1:202, 1:362, 3:558
Ann (Elderkin), 1:201
Bethia, 1:200-201, 1:336
Catharine (Chapin), 1:201,
1:360, 2:251, 3:160
Damaris (Arnold), 1:64,
1:200
Deliverance, 1:202
Dorothy, 1:200
Elizabeth, 1:200-202,
3:233, 4:112
Elizabeth (----), 1:202
Esther, 1:201, 2:186
Experience, 1:201
Hannah, 1:200-202, 2:332,
4:134, 4:656
Hannah (Cadwell), 4:677
Hannah (Stiles), 1:201,
4:195
Lydia, 1:201
Lydia (Wright), 1:201,
1:438, 3:47, 3:292,
4:659, 4:693
Margaret, 1:201, 2:180
Margaret (----), 1:202
Martha, 1:200-201
Mary, 1:200-202, 1:349,
2:357, 2:444, 3:363,
4:128
Mary (French), 1:201
Mary (Leonard), 1:201,

Bliss (continued)
 Mary (Leonard)
  (continued)
   3:79
 Mary (Wright), 4:654
 Mercy, 1:201
 Miriam, 1:201
 Miriam (Carpenter), 1:201,
  1:338
 Miriam (Harmon), 1:200
 Patience (Burt), 1:200,
  1:313
 Rachel, 1:200, 3:147
 Rebecca, 1:202
 Sarah, 1:201-202, 4:37,
  4:107
 Thankful, 1:201
Blodget
 Abigail, 1:203
 Ann, 1:202
 Hannah, 1:203
 Martha, 1:203
 Mary, 1:203
 Mary (Butterfield), 1:202
 Mary (Rowlandson), 1:203
 Rebecca, 1:203, 1:261
 Rebecca (Tidd), 1:203
 Ruth, 1:203
 Ruth (Iggleden), 1:203,
  2:517
 Sarah, 1:203
 Susanna, 1:203, 4:245,
  4:287
 Susanna (----), 1:203,
  4:285
Blois/Bloys
 Ann, 1:203
 Ann (Cutler), 1:203
 Mary, 1:203
 Mary (----), 1:203
 Michal (Jennison), 1:203,
  2:545, 4:424
 Ruth (Parsons), 1:203
Blomfield/Blumfield
 Mary, 1:203
 Rebecca, 1:204
 Ruth, 1:204
 Sarah, 1:203-204, 4:2
 Susan (----), 1:204
Blood
 Abigail, 1:205
 Abigail (----), 1:204
 Ann, 1:204

Elizabeth, 1:204-205
Elizabeth (----), 1:204
Elizabeth (Longley), 1:204,
 3:110
Elizabeth (Willard), 1:205,
 4:555
Ellen, 1:205
Hannah, 1:204-205
Hannah (----), 1:204
Hannah (Parker), 1:204
Hannah (Purchis), 1:204
Isabel (----), 1:205
Isabel (Farmer), 2:307
Isabel (Farmer) Wyman,
 1:204, 2:141-142, 4:664
Martha, 1:204
Mary, 1:204-205, 2:21
Sarah, 1:204-205, 2:583
Blossom
 Ann (----), 1:205, 3:582
 Elizabeth, 1:205, 2:170
 Mercy, 1:205
 Sarah, 1:205
 Sarah (Bodfish), 1:205,
  1:212
 Sarah (Ewer), 1:205, 2:132
 Thankful, 1:205
Blott
 ----, 1:206, 4:320
 Joanna, 1:206, 3:124
 Lydia, 4:343
 Mary, 1:205, 4:639
 Sarah, 1:206, 2:113
 Susanna (----), 1:205
Blowers
 Ann/Hannah, 1:206
 Elizabeth, 1:206
 Elizabeth (Belcher), 1:155,
  1:206
 Mary, 1:206
 Tabitha, 1:206
 Tabitha (----), 1:206
Blunt
 Abigail, 1:507
 Ann, 1:507
 Ann (----), 1:206
 Ann (Fosdick), 1:507
 Elizabeth (----), 1:206
 Mary, 1:507
Bly - see also Bligh
 ---- (Bishop) King, 1:186
 Hannah, 1:206
 Lois (Ivory), 1:206, 2:526

Mary, 1:206
Rebecca, 1:206, 2:257
Rebecca (Golt/Gott), 1:206
Boade
 Ann (----), 1:207, 4:483
Boardman - see Bordman
Bobbit
 Damaris, 1:207
 Deliverance, 1:207
 Dorcas, 1:207
 Esther, 1:207, 3:372
 Hannah, 1:207
 Ruth, 1:207
 Sarah, 1:207, 3:443
 Sarah (Tarne), 1:207,
  4:257
Bockford
 ---- (Fletcher), 1:207
Boderit
 Jane (----), 1:207
 Susanna, 1:207
Bodfish/Bootfish
 Bridget (----), 1:211,
  2:424-425
 Elizabeth, 1:211-212
 Elizabeth (Bessey), 1:211,
  4:675
 Hannah, 1:211
 Mary, 1:211, 1:474, 4:241
 Meletiah, 1:211
 Rebecca, 1:211
 Sarah, 1:205, 1:211-212
Bodkin
 Abigail, 1:507
 Ann, 1:507
 Elizabeth, 1:207
 Mary, 1:507
 Mary (----), 1:207
Bodman
 Frances (----), 1:207
 Hepzibah (----), 1:207
 Lydia, 1:207
 Mary, 1:207
 Mary (----), 1:207
 Naomi (Church), 1:207
 Rebecca, 1:207
 Sarah, 1:207
 Sarah (----), 1:207
Bodwell
 Bethia, 1:207
 Bethia (Emery), 1:207
Bogle
 Mary, 3:604

Bohonion/Bohannon
Abigail, 1:208
Margaret, 1:208
Mary (----), 1:208
Bollard
Sarah (Jones), 1:208
Bolles
---- (----), 4:202
Mary, 1:208, 2:210, 4:10
Rebecca (Waller), 4:399
Zipporah (----), 1:208, 4:10
Bolt
Sarah (----), 1:208
Susanna, 1:208
Bolton
Abigail, 1:208
Elizabeth, 1:208
Hannah, 1:208
Jane (Bartlett), 1:208
Mary, 1:208
Mary (Dennison), 1:208
Ruth, 1:208
Sarah, 1:208
Sarah (----), 1:208
Boltwood
Elizabeth, 1:209
Hannah (Alexander),
1:209
Lydia, 1:208, 4:421
Martha, 1:208, 4:419
Mary, 1:153, 1:208
Mary (----), 1:208
Rebecca, 1:209
Sarah, 1:208-209, 3:6,
4:419
Sarah (Lewis), 1:209, 3:89
Bond
Abigail, 1:209, 3:571
Bethia, 1:209
Bethia (Fuller), 1:209,
2:216
Deliverance, 1:210
Elizabeth, 1:127,
1:209-210, 1:378, 1:452
Elizabeth (----), 1:209
Elizabeth (----) Eames,
2:90
Elizabeth (----) Nevinson,
1:210, 3:268
Elizabeth (Jackson)
Prentice, 1:209, 2:528,
3:479
Esther, 1:209, 1:364

Esther (----), 4:563
Esther (Blakely), 1:209
Grace (Coolidge), 1:209,
1:451
Hannah, 1:209
Hannah (Coolidge), 1:209,
1:451
Hepzibah (Hastings),
1:210
Margaret, 1:210, 1:451
Mary, 1:209-210, 1:452,
2:319
Pentecost, 3:176
Sarah, 1:209-210, 4:481
Sarah (Briscoe), 1:210,
1:256
Sarah (Rowlandson),
1:209, 3:582
Sarah (Woolson), 1:210,
4:649
Bonett
Priscilla, 1:338
Bonham/Bonum
Hannah, 1:211
Hannah (Fuller),
1:210-211, 2:218
Mary, 1:211
Patience, 1:210, 4:577
Ruth, 1:127, 1:210
Sarah, 1:210-211
Sarah (Morton), 1:210,
3:244
Bonner
Jane, 1:211
Mary, 1:507, 1:211
Mary (----), 1:211, 3:178
Mary (Clark), 1:398, 1:507
Bonney
Dorcas (Sampson), 1:211,
4:10
Mary, 1:211, 3:220
Bonython
----, 1:211
Sarah, 1:211, 2:198
Boosey/Boosy
Alice (----), 1:211, 4:387
Esther (----), 1:211, 1:306
Hannah, 1:211, 3:472
Mary, 1:211, 4:181
Sarah, 1:211, 4:165
Booth
---- (Hawley), 1:212
Abigail, 1:212

Alice, 1:212
Ann, 1:212
Bethia, 1:212
Deborah, 1:212
Deborah (----), 1:212
Dorothy (Hawley), 1:212,
2:385
Elinor, 1:212
Elizabeth, 1:212-213,
3:216, 4:699, 4:704
Elizabeth (----), 1:212
Elizabeth (----) Elmore,
1:213
Elizabeth (Jones), 1:212,
2:564
Elizabeth/Alice (----),
3:604
Ellen, 1:212
Grace, 1:212
Hannah, 1:212, 2:540,
3:604
Hannah (Burroughs),
1:213
Hannah (Wilcockson),
3:604
Joanna, 1:212
Judith, 1:212
Martha, 1:212, 3:44
Mary, 1:212-213, 3:228,
3:389, 3:391, 3:603
Mary (----), 1:212
Mary (Dodson), 1:212,
2:58
Mary (Harmon), 1:213
Mary (Warriner), 1:213
Mary (Welles), 3:604,
4:475
Phebe, 1:213
Rebecca, 1:212
Rebecca (Frost), 1:212-213,
2:210
Rebecca (Symmes), 1:212,
4:244
Sarah, 1:213
Susanna, 1:212
Bootman
Esther (Lambert), 1:213,
3:48
Martha, 1:213
Mary, 1:213
Boradale
Margaret, 4:76

Borden
Amie, 1:213
Amy, 1:213
Ann, 1:213
Dinah, 1:213
Elizabeth, 1:213, 3:538
Elizabeth (Lewis), 1:213,
 3:87
Experience, 1:213
Hannah, 1:213
Hannah (Hough), 1:213,
 2:469
Hope, 1:213
Hope (----), 1:213
Jane (----), 1:213
Joan (----), 1:213
Joanna, 1:213
Mary, 1:213
Mary (----), 1:213
Mary (Harris), 1:213
Mercy, 1:213
Meribah, 1:213
Sarah, 1:213
Sarah (Clayton), 1:213,
 1:406
Bordman/Boardman
Abiah (Kimberly), 3:23
Elizabeth, 1:207, 1:214,
 1:454
Elizabeth (Rider) Cole,
 1:207
Frances, 1:214
Frances (----), 1:214
Hannah, 3:495
Hannah (Hutchinson),
 1:214, 2:512
Hannah (Wright), 4:326
Lucy (----), 1:207
Lydia, 1:214
Martha, 1:214, 2:125
Mary, 1:213-214, 1:372
Mary (Page), 3:330
Rebecca, 1:214, 3:339
Rebecca (----), 1:214, 2:27
Ruth, 3:604
Ruth (Bull), 1:213, 1:294
Sarah, 2:170
Sarah (----), 1:214
Susanna, 1:207
Thankful, 1:207
Borel
Catharine, 1:214
Deborah, 1:214

Isabella, 1:214
Martha (----), 1:214
Boreman
----, 3:30
Abiah (----), 1:214
Abigail, 1:214
Desire, 1:215
Elizabeth (Strong), 1:214
Eunice, 1:214
Hannah, 1:214-215
Hannah (Annable), 1:59,
 1:215
Hannah (Wright), 1:214
Hepzibah, 1:214
Mabel, 1:214
Martha, 1:214
Mary, 1:214-215
Mehitable, 1:215
Mercy, 1:214
Mercy (Hubbard), 1:214
Prudence (Foster), 2:188
Sarah, 1:214-215
Sarah (Steele), 1:214
Borland
Jane, 1:215
Borrodell/Borrowdale
Ann, 2:36
Borth
Hannah, 2:540
Bosseville/Basseville
Elizabeth, 2:356, 3:385
Bostwick
Abigail, 1:215
Abigail (----), 1:215
Ann (Burr), 1:215
Elizabeth, 1:215
Elizabeth (----), 3:604
Ellen (----), 1:215, 4:475
Hannah, 1:215
Jane, 1:215
Martha, 3:604
Mary, 1:215, 2:56, 3:604
Mary (Brimsmead), 1:215,
 1:254
Mary (Hinman), 2:426
Parnel, 1:215
Susanna, 1:215
Boswell
Mary (----), 1:215
Bosworth
Ann (----), 1:216, 1:455
Beatrice (----) Josselyn,
 1:216, 2:570

Bethia, 3:604
Bridget, 1:216, 3:605
Deliverance, 3:604-605
Elizabeth, 1:216, 1:229,
 3:239, 3:604
Elizabeth (Morton), 1:216,
 3:245
Hannah, 1:216, 3:604
Hannah (----), 1:216
Hannah (Howland), 2:480
Hannah (Morton), 1:216,
 3:244
Mary, 1:216, 3:604-605
Mary (----), 1:216
Mehitable, 3:604
Mercy (Bumstead), 1:216,
 1:298
Rebecca, 3:604
Restored, 1:216
Sarah, 1:216
Boteler
Alice (Apsley), 2:154
Both
Mary, 3:228
Botsford
Elizabeth, 1:101, 1:217,
 2:173
Elizabeth (----), 1:217
Elizabeth (Fletcher), 1:217,
 2:173
Esther, 1:217, 4:499-500
Hannah, 1:104, 1:217
Hannah (Baldwin), 1:105,
 1:217
Joanna, 1:217
Mary, 1:217, 4:14
Ruth, 1:217, 4:499
Sarah, 1:217
Boucher
Sarah (Middlecott), 3:205
Boughey
Elizabeth, 1:217, 2:363
Boulter
Elizabeth, 1:217, 3:605
Experience, 1:217
Experience (----), 1:217
Grace, 1:217
Grace (----), 1:217
Hannah, 1:217
Hannah (----), 1:217
Mary, 1:217, 3:480, 3:605
Mary (----), 3:605, 4:12
Rebecca, 1:217

Boulter (continued)
Temperance, 3:605
Boulton
Elizabeth, 1:217
Elizabeth (----), 1:217
Thankful, 1:217
Bound
Ann (----), 1:217
Mary (Haverlad), 1:217
Bounds
Abigail (Prescott), 3:480
Bouren
Elizabeth (Brayton), 1:240
Bourne
Abigail, 1:218
Alice, 1:218
Alice (Besbedge), 1:172, 1:218
Ann, 1:94, 1:218-219, 4:127
Bathsheba, 1:218
Bathshua (Skiff), 1:219, 4:105
Bethia, 1:218
Dorcas, 1:218
Elizabeth, 1:169, 1:218-219, 4:433, 4:475
Elizabeth (----), 1:219
Elizabeth (Rouse), 1:219, 3:579
Hannah, 1:218
Hannah (----), 1:218
Lydia, 1:219, 4:301
Margaret, 1:219, 4:602
Martha, 1:218-219, 1:230, 2:33
Martha (----), 1:219
Mary, 1:218-219
Mary (----), 1:218
Melatiah, 1:219
Patience, 1:219
Patience (Skiff), 1:218, 4:105
Remembrance, 1:219
Ruhama (Hallett), 1:218, 2:340
Ruth (Sargent) Winslow, 1:218, 4:19, 4:602
Sarah, 1:172, 1:218-219
Boutell/Boutwell/Boutelle
Alice (----), 1:219
Elizabeth, 1:219
Elizabeth (----) Bowers,

1:219
Elizabeth (Worthington)
Bowers, 1:223
Grace (----), 2:440
Hannah, 1:219
Hannah (Davis), 1:219
Margaret (----), 1:219
Mary, 1:219
Rebecca, 1:219
Rebecca (Kendall), 1:219, 3:10
Sarah, 1:219-220
Susannah, 1:220
Tabitha, 1:219
Boutineau
Anna, 1:220
Elizabeth, 1:220
Mary, 1:220
Mary (Bowdoin), 1:220, 1:222
Bouton
Abigail, 1:220
Abigail (Marvin), 1:220, 3:164
Bridget, 1:220, 3:4
Mary, 1:220
Mary (Banister), 3:605
Rachel, 1:220
Ruth, 1:220
Ruth (----), 1:220
Bowd
Elizabeth, 1:220
Elizabeth (----), 1:220
Bowden
Elizabeth, 1:220
Hannah, 4:675
Martha (----), 1:220
Mary, 4:429
Mary (Banister), 3:600
Bowditch
Mary (Gardner), 1:220
Mary (Turner), 1:220-221
Sarah (----), 1:220
Temperance (French), 1:220, 2:206
Bowdoin
Elizabeth, 1:221-222
Elizabeth (----), 1:221
Elizabeth (Erving), 1:221
Hannah (Pordage), 1:221, 3:459
Judith, 1:221
Mary, 1:220-222

Mehitable (----) Lillie, 1:221
Phebe (Murdock), 1:222
Sarah, 1:222
Sarah (Bowdoin), 1:222
Sarah (Campbell), 1:221
Bowe
Ann, 1:222
Dorcas (Champney), 1:222
Mary, 1:222
Rebecca, 1:222
Rebecca (Hughes), 1:222
Sarah, 1:222
Sarah (----), 1:222
Sarah (Hubbard), 1:222
Bowen
Abiah, 4:625
Abigail, 1:70, 1:222
Elizabeth, 1:17, 1:222
Elizabeth (----), 1:223
Elizabeth (Johnson), 1:222, 2:553
Esther, 1:222, 3:211
Frances (----), 1:222
Margaret, 1:222, 4:457
Margaret (----), 1:222
Maria, 1:222
Mary, 1:31, 1:222, 4:395
Mary (Titus), 1:222-223
Peniel, 1:222
Penuel, 1:222
Sarah, 4:24
Bowers
---- (Clark), 1:398
Ann, 1:223, 1:507
Barbara, 1:507
Barbara (----), 1:223
Bathsheba, 1:507
Bridget (Thompson), 1:223, 4:283, 4:289
Elizabeth, 1:507
Elizabeth (----), 1:219, 1:507
Elizabeth (Dunster), 1:223, 2:83
Elizabeth (Worthington), 1:223
Hannah (----) Knapp, 1:223
Hannah (Close) Knapp, 3:34
Lydia (French), 1:223
Mary, 1:223, 1:507

Bowers (continued)
Patience, 1:223
Ruth, 1:223, 2:209, 2:430,
    3:622
Ruth (Wooster), 1:223,
    4:649-650
Sarah (Dowd/etc), 2:64
Silence, 1:223
Bowker
Mary (Howe), 1:223,
    2:473
Mary (Potter), 1:223
Bowland
Elizabeth, 1:224
Bowles
Dorothy (----), 1:224
Elizabeth, 1:224, 2:398,
    4:511
Elizabeth (Heath), 1:224,
    2:398
Mary, 1:224, 2:210, 2:231,
    2:398, 2:477
Sarah, 1:224
Sarah (----), 1:224
Sarah (----) Sibley
    Chickering, 1:376
Sarah (Eliot), 1:224, 2:110
Sarah (How) Sibly
    Chickering, 1:224
Bowman
Ann, 1:224
Ann (----), 1:224
Ann (Barnard), 1:119
Dorcas, 1:189, 1:224-225
Joanna, 1:224-225
Martha, 1:224
Martha (Sherman), 1:224,
    4:82
Mary, 1:224, 2:129, 3:605
Phebe (Barnard), 1:502
Rebecca (Smith) Smith,
    1:225, 4:115, 4:132
Bowstreete
Elizabeth, 1:225
Boyden
Christian (Wilcox), 4:547
Elizabeth, 1:225
Frances (----), 1:225
Hannah (----) Morse, 1:225
Hannah (Phillips) Morse,
    3:240
Martha, 1:225, 3:519
Martha (Holden), 1:225,

2:445
Mary, 1:225
Rebecca, 1:225
Sarah, 1:225
Boyen
Frances (Gill), 1:225,
    2:254
Boyer
Johanna (----), 3:255
Marian (Johonnot), 2:560
Boyes/Boyce/Boys
----, 3:514
Elizabeth, 1:225
Esther, 1:225, 4:707
Hannah (Hill), 1:225,
    2:420
Joanna, 3:492
Lydia (----), 3:497
Lydia (Beamond), 1:147,
    1:225-226
Mary, 4:370
Sarah, 1:225
Sarah (Meacham), 1:225,
    3:190
Boykett/Boykim/Boykem
----, 1:226
Bethia, 1:226, 2:37, 4:675
Isabel (----), 1:226
Sarah, 1:226
Boylston
Abigail, 1:226, 1:260,
    2:217
Elizabeth, 1:226, 2:163
Joanna, 1:226
Lucy, 1:226
Mary, 1:226, 2:340, 4:291
Mary (----), 1:226
Mary (Gardner), 1:226,
    2:231
Rebecca, 1:226
Sarah, 1:226, 1:262, 4:135
Sarah (----), 1:226, 2:241
Susanna, 1:13
Boynton/Boyington
Abigail, 1:227
Elinor (----), 2:549
Elizabeth (----), 1:227
Hannah, 4:421
Hannah (Barnet), 1:227
Helen (Pell), 1:227
Mary, 1:227, 2:92
Mary (----), 1:227
Mary (Moore), 1:226

Sarah, 2:578, 4:268
Sarah (Browne), 1:227
Sarah (Southwick), 1:227
Sarah (Swan), 1:227,
    4:237
Brabrook/Braybrook
Abigail (Temple), 1:227
Ann (----), 1:227
Elizabeth, 1:227
Elizabeth (----), 1:227
Joan (----), 3:390
Joanna (----), 1:227
Mehitable, 1:227, 2:67
Sarah (Lewis), 1:227, 3:87
Brackenbury
Alice (----), 1:228
Amie (Anderson), 1:228
Ann, 1:228, 2:191
Ann (----), 1:228
Ann (Chickering), 1:377
Dorcas, 1:507
Dorcas (----), 1:228
Dorcas (Green), 1:507
Elizabeth, 3:368, 3:605
Ellen (----), 1:228
Emma (Anderson), 1:51,
    1:228, 3:135
Hannah, 1:228
Mary, 1:228
Mary (Wigglesworth),
    4:542
Mercy (----), 1:228
Brackett
Alice (----), 1:229
Ann (Grannis), 4:683
Ann (Mitton), 1:228,
    3:222
Eleanor, 2:555
Elinor, 1:228
Elizabeth, 1:80
Elizabeth (Bosworth),
    1:229
Elizabeth (Waldo), 1:229,
    4:389
Hannah, 1:229, 3:29
Hannah (French), 1:229,
    2:208
Jane, 2:390
Kezia, 1:228
Lydia, 1:229
Martha, 1:229, 4:353
Mary, 1:228-229, 4:287
Mary (----) Williams, 1:229,

Brackett (continued)
Mary (----) Williams
(continued)
4:564
Mary (Mitton), 1:229,
3:222
Priscilla (----), 1:229
Rachel, 1:229, 1:477
Ruth (Ellis), 1:229
Sarah, 1:228-229, 1:477
Sarah (----), 1:228
Sarah (----) Foster, 1:229
Sarah (Stedman), 1:22,
1:228, 2:297, 3:413,
4:179
Susanna (Drake), 1:228,
2:69
Bracy/Bracie
Ann, 1:227
Constant, 1:227
Elishaba, 1:227
Elizabeth, 1:227
Phebe, 1:227, 2:48
Phebe (Bisby), 1:227,
3:163
Susanna, 1:227
Bradbury
--- (Perkins), 4:19
Ann, 1:32, 1:230
Elizabeth, 1:230, 1:319
Jane, 1:230, 4:334
Judith, 1:230, 3:225
Mary, 1:230, 4:168
Mary (----), 1:230
Mary (Perkins), 1:230,
3:396
Rebecca (Wheelwright)
Maverick, 1:230, 3:182,
4:503
Sarah, 1:230, 3:234
Sarah (Pike), 1:230, 3:437,
4:199
Bradfield
--- (----), 1:9, 1:230
Martha, 4:516
Mary, 4:675
Mary (----), 3:596
Sarah (----), 4:675
Bradford
--- (----) Wiswall, 1:232
Alice, 1:17, 1:232, 2:168,
3:219
Alice (Carpenter)

Southworth, 1:231,
4:143-144
Alice (Richards), 1:232,
3:534
Ann, 4:544
Ann (Fitch), 2:168
Ann (Smith), 4:127
Bathsheba (Brock), 2:434
Dorothy (May), 1:231
Elizabeth, 1:231
Elizabeth (----), 1:231
Elizabeth (Bartlett), 1:232
Elizabeth (Finney), 1:232
Hannah, 1:232, 3:543
Hannah (Fitch), 1:232
Hannah (Rogers), 1:232
Jael (Hobart), 1:230, 2:435
Julian, 3:8
Margaret (----), 1:231
Martha, 1:231, 3:181
Martha (----), 1:231
Martha (Bourne), 1:219,
1:230
Mary, 1:232
Mary (Atwood) Holmes,
1:232, 2:452
Mary (Chandler), 1:232,
1:357
Mary (Wood) Holmes,
1:232, 2:452
Mary/Mercy, 4:181
Meletiah, 1:232
Mercy, 1:231-232, 4:371
Mercy (Warren), 1:232,
4:425
Rebecca (Bartlett), 1:232
Sarah, 1:232
Sarah (Bartlett), 1:232
Sarah (Merry), 1:230
Bradhurst
Abigail, 1:232
Dorothy, 1:90, 1:232
Hannah, 1:232
Hannah (----), 1:232
Hannah (Gore), 1:232,
2:280
Martha (----), 1:232
Rhoda, 1:232
Brading
Elizabeth, 1:232, 1:258
Hannah (----), 3:551
Hannah (Rock), 1:232,
3:556

Bradish
Hannah, 1:232-233, 4:163
Mary, 1:232-233, 2:246
Mary (----), 1:232
Sarah, 1:232
Vashti (----), 1:233
Bradley/Bradlee
----, 1:233-234
--- (Allen), 1:233
--- (Dorman), 2:61
Abigail, 1:233-234, 3:247
Alice (Prichard), 1:234,
3:486
Ann, 1:234
Ann (----), 1:234
Ann (Thompson), 1:233,
4:286, 4:289
Catharine (----), 1:233
Deliverance, 1:234
Desire, 1:234, 4:699
Elizabeth, 1:233-234, 2:50
Elizabeth (Brewster),
1:234, 1:245, 1:383
Elizabeth (Chedsey), 1:234
Elizabeth (Thompson),
1:233, 4:286, 4:289
Ellen, 1:41, 1:233
Esther, 1:234, 4:699
Esther (----), 1:234
Hannah, 1:233-234, 4:690
Hannah (----), 1:233
Hannah (Munson) Tuttle,
1:234, 4:351
Hannah (Smith), 1:234,
4:113
Lucretia, 1:234, 1:383
Lydia, 4:699
Martha, 1:233-234, 3:257
Martha (Munson), 3:605
Mary, 1:233-234, 3:77,
4:309, 4:699
Mary (----), 1:234
Mary (----) Leete, 1:234,
3:75
Mary (Christophers), 1:234
Mary (Evans), 2:128,
3:605
Mary (Sacket), 3:605
Mary (Williams), 1:233
Miriam, 4:675
Patience, 1:234
Rachel (----) Strong, 1:234
Rachel (Holton) Strong,

Bradley/Bradlee (continued)
Rachel (Holton) Strong
(continued)
4:228
Ruth, 1:233, 4:675
Ruth (Barlow), 1:117,
1:233
Ruth (Dickerman), 2:47,
4:675
Sarah, 1:233-234, 3:605
Silence (Brocket), 1:233,
1:258
Susanna, 1:233
Bradshaw
Abigail, 1:235
Hannah, 1:235
Martha (----) Russell,
1:234, 2:338, 3:595
Mary, 1:235, 3:222
Mary (----), 1:235
Mary (Hall), 2:335
Patience (----), 1:234
Ruth, 1:234-235, 1:505,
1:507
Sarah, 1:234-235
Sarah (Skeath), 4:103
Susanna, 1:235
Bradstreet
----, 4:402
Ann, 1:235-236
Ann (Downing) Gardner,
1:236, 2:66, 2:228
Ann (Dudley), 1:236, 2:78
Ann (Wood) Price, 1:235,
3:484-485
Betty, 1:235
Bridget (----), 1:235
Dorothy, 1:235-236, 1:464,
4:539
Elizabeth, 1:236, 3:422
Hannah, 1:235-236, 2:455,
3:570, 4:539
Lucy, 1:236
Lucy (Woodbridge), 1:236,
2:125, 4:632
Margaret, 1:235
Martha, 1:147, 1:235
Mary, 1:235
Mary (Long), 1:236, 3:108
Mary (Wainwright), 1:235
Mercy, 1:235-236, 3:309,
4:378
Mercy (Tyng), 1:236,

4:358
Rebecca, 1:235
Sarah, 1:235-236, 2:485,
4:341, 4:413
Sarah (----), 1:235
Sarah (Perkins), 1:235,
3:398
Bragdon
Elizabeth (Tucker), 4:339
Bragg
Elizabeth, 1:508
Elizabeth (Mackmallen),
3:141
Elizabeth (McMullen),
1:507
Mary, 1:236, 1:508, 2:129
Sarah, 1:508
Brainard/Brainerd
---- (Hobart), 2:434
Dorothy (Hobart) Mason,
1:237
Hannah, 1:237, 2:236
Hannah (Selden), 4:50
Hannah (Spencer), 1:237,
4:147
Mary, 1:237
Mehitable (Dudley), 3:605
Noadiah, 1:237
Susanna, 1:237
Susanna (----), 1:237
Susanna (Ventris), 4:370,
4:675
Braman
Experience, 1:237
Jane (Babcock), 1:86
Brame/Bram/Bream
Ann, 1:237
Ann (----), 1:237
Elizabeth, 1:237
Elizabeth (----), 1:237
Sarah, 1:237
Bramhall
Grace (----), 1:237
Hannah, 1:237
Martha (----), 1:237
Branch
Catharine (----) Carter
Williams, 1:238, 4:559
Elizabeth, 1:237
Joan (Farnum), 1:238
Lydia (----), 1:237
Mary (Speed), 1:237
Mercy, 1:237, 3:605,

4:152
Brand
Elizabeth, 1:238
Elizabeth (Babcock), 1:86
Martha (Heath), 1:238,
2:398-399
Mary, 1:238
Sarah (----), 1:238
Brandish/Brundish
Rachel (----), 1:281, 4:581
Brandisly
Rachel (----), 1:238
Brandon
Hannah, 1:238
Mary, 1:238
Mary (----), 1:238
Sarah, 1:238
Branker
Abigail (----), 1:238, 3:201,
4:417
Brattle
Bethia, 1:239, 3:363
Catharine, 1:239, 2:133,
4:614
Elizabeth, 1:239, 3:310
Elizabeth (Gerrish) Green,
3:605, 3:626
Elizabeth (Hayman), 1:239,
2:388
Elizabeth (Tyng), 1:238,
4:358
Mary, 1:239, 3:205
Mary (----), 1:238
Brawne
Mary (----), 1:239
Bray
Christian, 1:508
Esther, 1:240, 3:605,
4:168
Hannah, 1:239-240, 3:337,
3:547
Margaret (Lambert), 1:239
Margery, 3:392
Margery (----), 1:239
Mary, 1:239, 3:543, 3:605
Mary (Wilson), 1:239
Priscilla, 1:508
Sarah, 3:605, 4:30
Thomasin (----), 1:239
Brayman
Jane, 2:450
Brayton
Ann, 1:240

Brayton (continued)
Ann (Tolman), 1:240
Elizabeth, 1:240
Martha, 1:240
Mary, 1:240, 2:42
Mary (----), 1:240
Mary (Fish), 1:240, 2:161
Mehitable, 1:240
Preserved, 1:240
Sarah, 1:240
Brazier
Abigail, 1:240
Ann, 1:33
Magdalen (----), 1:508
Rebecca, 1:240
Breadon
Mary, 3:85
Breck
Bethia, 1:241
Elinor, 1:240, 1:471
Elizabeth, 1:240, 1:322, 3:217
Isabel (----), 4:682
Isabel (----) Rigby, 1:240
Margery (----), 1:241
Mary, 1:240-241, 3:372, 4:310
Mary (Hill), 1:241, 2:416-417
Sarah (Hawkins), 1:31, 1:241, 2:383
Susan, 3:329
Susanna, 1:240-241, 2:362
Susanna (----), 1:240
Susanna (Wiswall), 4:615
Breed
Elizabeth, 1:241, 4:95
Elizabeth (Knight), 1:241
Mary, 1:241
Mary (----), 1:241
Mercy (Palmer), 1:241
Sarah, 1:241
Sarah (Hart), 1:241
Sarah (Hathorne), 1:241
Sarah (Newhall), 1:241, 3:273
Breeden
Hannah (Rock/Ruck), 1:241
Mary (----), 3:606
Brelly/Bralley/Burleigh/etc
Mary, 4:561

Breman
Elizabeth (Cadwell), 4:677
Brenton
Abigail, 1:242, 1:315
Ann, 1:242
Elizabeth, 1:242, 3:454
Hannah (----), 1:242
Martha, 1:242, 1:334
Martha (Burton), 1:242, 1:315
Mary, 1:242, 4:15
Mehitable, 1:242, 1:272
Priscilla (----), 1:242
Sarah, 1:242, 2:111
Breton
Marian, 1:85
Brett
Alice, 1:243, 2:393
Ann (----), 1:243
Bethia, 1:243
Elizabeth (Cary), 1:243, 1:344
Hannah, 1:243
Lydia, 1:243
Margaret, 1:243
Margaret (----), 1:243
Mary, 1:243
Mehitable, 1:243
Sarah, 1:243
Sarah (Hayward), 1:243
Bretton
----, 1:243
Ann, 1:243
Elizabeth, 1:243
Jane, 1:243
Mary, 1:243
Rachel, 1:243
Sarah, 1:243
Brewer
----, 4:287
Abigail, 1:243-244
Ann, 1:243
Ann (----), 1:243
Catharine, 1:243
Catharine (Chauncy), 1:243
Elizabeth, 1:244
Elizabeth (----), 1:244
Elizabeth (Graves), 1:244
Elizabeth (Rand), 1:244, 3:504
Elizabeth (Rice), 1:244, 3:529

Eunice, 1:243
Hannah, 1:243-244, 1:358, 2:519
Hannah (Morrill), 1:243, 3:234
Joanna, 1:243-244
Joanna (----), 1:243
Margaret (Weld), 4:473
Martha, 1:244
Mary, 1:244, 3:53, 3:533
Mary (Whitmore), 1:244
Rebecca, 1:243-244
Sarah, 1:243-244, 2:296, 3:183, 4:450
Brewster
----, 2:212, 2:219
--- (---), 3:386
--- (Gager), 2:221
Ann, 1:244
Ann (Dart), 1:244
Elizabeth, 1:234, 1:244-245, 1:383, 2:219
Fear, 1:38, 1:246
Grace, 1:245, 4:491
Hannah, 1:245, 3:606, 4:170
Judith (----), 2:504
Lucretia (----), 1:245
Lucy (----), 1:244
Lydia (Partridge), 1:246, 3:365
Mary, 1:244-245, 4:346
Mary (----), 1:246-247, 3:365
Mary (Knight), 3:39
Patience, 1:246, 3:477
Ruth, 1:18, 1:244-245, 2:415, 3:424
Sarah, 1:130, 1:245, 2:411
Sarah (----), 3:347
Sarah (Collier), 1:245, 1:433
Sarah (Ludlow), 1:245, 3:129
Briars
Elizabeth (Jackson), 3:606
Grace, 3:606
Mary, 3:606
Bricket
Mary, 1:247
Bricknall
Mary, 1:247
Mary (----), 1:247

Bridge
—, 1:248
— (Oldham), 4:693
Abigail, 1:248
Abigail (Russell), 1:248,
3:592
Ann, 1:248, 3:101, 4:480
Ann (Danforth), 1:248, 2:8
Dorcas, 1:248, 1:356
Dorcas (—), 1:248
Elizabeth, 1:172, 1:248,
2:231, 2:359
Elizabeth (—) Bancroft
Saunders, 1:110, 1:248,
4:21
Margaret, 1:248
Martha, 1:248
Mary, 1:247-248, 2:237,
3:37, 3:137, 3:431
Mary (—), 1:247
Persis (—), 1:249, 2:592
Persis (Pierce), 4:675,
4:686, 4:695
Prudence, 1:248, 3:183
Prudence (Robinson),
1:248, 3:555
Rebecca, 1:249
Sarah, 1:248
Bridgeman/Bridgman
Deliverance, 1:250
Elizabeth (—), 1:250
Hannah, 1:250
Joanna (—) Alvord King,
3:26
Joanna (Taylor) Alvord
King, 1:47
Martha, 1:250, 2:49
Martha (—), 1:250
Mary, 1:133, 1:250
Mary (Sheldon), 1:250,
4:69
Patience, 1:250
Sarah, 1:250, 4:302
Bridges
Alice (—), 1:249
Bethia, 1:249, 3:375
Elizabeth, 1:249, 2:102
Elizabeth (—), 1:249,
2:378-379, 3:354
Elizabeth (Norton), 1:249
Faith, 1:249
Hannah, 1:249
Mary, 1:249

Mary (—) Littlehale,
1:249
Mary (—) Post, 1:249
Mary (Lancton) Littlehale,
3:100
Mary (Smith), 1:249
Mehitable, 1:249
Ruth (Greenslip), 1:249
Sarah, 1:249, 3:483
Sarah (—), 4:679
Sarah (How), 1:249, 2:475
Sarah (Marston),
3:160-161
Sarah (Towne), 1:249,
4:317
Bridgham
Abigail, 2:55
Elizabeth (—), 1:249
Mary, 1:164, 2:104
Mercy (Wensley), 1:250,
1:491, 4:483
Briersley/Briers
Elizabeth (—), 1:250
Mary, 1:250
Brigden/Bridgen
Mary, 1:250, 3:22
Mildred (Carthrick), 1:251,
1:343
Sarah, 1:250-251
Thomasine (—), 1:250
Briggs
— (—), 4:423
— (—) Russell, 1:251
Abigail, 4:388
Catharine (—), 1:251
Constant (Lincoln), 3:94
Constant (Mitchell) Fobes,
2:177
Deborah, 1:251
Deborah (Cushing), 1:252,
1:489-490
Deborah (Hawke/Hawkes),
2:381
Elizabeth, 1:252
Elizabeth (—), 1:251
Elizabeth (Garrett), 2:233
Elizabeth (Lincoln), 3:95
Frances, 1:251
Frances (—), 1:252
Frances (Fisher), 1:251,
2:163
Hannah, 1:251-252, 2:362,
3:606, 4:603

Hannah (—), 1:251
Hannah (Bailey), 1:94
Joan (Allen), 1:251, 4:214
Mary, 1:251
Mary (—), 1:251-252
Mary (Garrett), 2:233
Mehitable (Blake), 1:194
Rebecca, 1:252, 2:340
Rebecca (Hoskins), 1:252
Rebecca (Tilden), 1:251
Sarah, 1:252, 4:595
Sarah (Macumber), 1:252,
3:141
Brigham
Elizabeth, 1:252
Elizabeth (Howe), 1:252,
2:474
Hannah, 1:252
Hepzibah, 1:252
Lydia, 1:252
Mary, 1:252-253
Mary (—), 1:252
Mehitable (Spring)
Stimpson, 4:157
Mercy (—), 3:528
Mercy (Hurd), 1:252,
2:502
Persis, 1:252
Sarah, 1:252
Susanna (Shattuck) Morse
Fay, 2:150, 4:62
Bright
Abigail, 1:253, 3:305
Ann, 1:253, 3:587
Ann (Goldstone), 1:253,
2:269
Beriah, 1:253, 2:192
Elizabeth, 1:253, 2:374
Hannah, 1:253
Mary, 1:253, 1:452
Mary (Barsham), 1:128,
1:253, 3:350
Mary (Coolidge), 1:253
Mercy, 1:253
Susanna, 1:168
Brighton
Ann (—), 1:254
Brignall
Martha (Metcalf), 1:254,
3:203, 4:111
Brimblecome
—, 3:606
Barbara (—) Davis, 1:254,

Brimblecome (continued)
  Barbara (----) Davis
    (continued)
    1:351, 2:16
  Mary, 3:606
  Tabitha (----), 3:606
Brimmer
  Susanna (Sigourney), 4:95
Brimsdell/Brimsden
  Ann (Barnes), 1:122,
    1:254
  Bathsheba (Richards),
    1:254
  Desire, 2:87
  Dinah, 2:87
Brimsmead/Brinsmead/etc
  Abigail, 1:254
  Ebbet, 1:254
  Elizabeth, 1:254
  Elizabeth (Hawkins),
    2:382
  Mary, 1:215, 1:254, 3:74
  Mary (----), 1:254
  Ruth, 1:254
  Sarah (Kellogg), 3:4, 3:279
  Sarah (Nichols), 1:254,
    4:499
Brinley
  Ann (Wase), 1:255
  Elizabeth, 1:255
  Grizel, 1:255, 4:99
  Hannah (Carr), 1:255
  Mary, 1:255
  Mary (Apthrop), 1:255
Brintnall
  Dorothy, 1:255
  Esther (----), 1:255
  Hannah (Willard), 1:255,
    4:555
  Jerusha, 1:255
  Mary, 3:336, 4:542
  Mehitable, 1:255
  Parnel, 1:255
  Susanna, 1:255
Briscoe
  Abigail, 1:256
  Abigail (----), 1:316
  Abigail (Compton), 1:256,
    1:439
  Ann, 1:255
  Cicely (----), 1:256
  Dinah, 1:256
  Elizabeth, 1:256, 2:527

Elizabeth (----), 1:256
Elizabeth (Bittlestone),
  1:188, 1:256
Elizabeth (Leavitt) Dudley,
  2:75
Hannah, 1:255-256
Hannah (Stearns), 1:256
Mary, 1:255-256, 1:263
Mary (Camp), 1:256
Rebecca, 1:255-256
Rebecca (----), 1:256
Sarah, 1:210, 1:255-256
Sarah (Long), 1:255, 3:108
Sarah (Wheeler), 1:256,
  4:501
Susanna, 1:256
Bristow/Bristol
  Abigail, 1:257
  Ann, 4:675
  Elizabeth, 3:606, 4:675
  Esther, 3:606, 4:675
  Esther (Sperry), 4:675
  Hannah, 1:257, 3:632
  Lydia, 1:257, 4:125
  Lydia (Brown), 1:257,
    3:606
  Mary, 1:257
  Mehitable, 4:676
  Mercy, 3:606
  Obedience, 4:676
  Rebecca, 1:257, 3:606,
    3:608
  Sarah, 3:606
  Susanna (----) Blatchley,
    1:198, 1:257
Britton
  Jane, 1:427
Britz
  Mary, 1:460
Brock
  Ann, 1:257
  Bathsheba, 2:434
  Elizabeth, 1:257, 3:410
  Elizabeth (----), 1:257
  Grace, 2:434
  Mary, 2:434
  Sarah (Hobart), 2:434
  Sarah (Symmes) Hough,
    1:257, 2:468, 4:244
Brockett
  ---- (Bradley), 1:234
  Abigail, 1:258, 3:657
  Befruitful, 1:257

Elizabeth, 1:258
Elizabeth (Barnes), 1:257
Elizabeth (Doolittle), 2:60
Hannah, 1:257
Mary, 1:257-258,
  3:389-390
Sarah (Bradley), 3:605
Silence, 1:233, 1:257-258
Brocklebank
  Elizabeth, 1:258, 4:309
  Elizabeth (Platts), 1:258
  Hannah, 1:258, 4:192
  Hannah (----), 1:258, 2:59
  Jane (----), 1:258
  Mary, 1:258, 2:59
  Sarah, 1:258, 2:58
Brockway
  Bridget, 1:258
  Deborah, 1:258
  Elizabeth, 1:258
  Hannah, 1:258, 1:355
  Hannah (----), 1:258
  Mary, 1:258
  Sarah, 1:258
Brodbent
  Sarah (----) Osborn, 1:258
Broffe
  Damaris (Threeneedles),
    4:294
  Elizabeth, 4:294
Bromfield
  Abigail, 1:258
  Abigail (Coney), 1:258
  Elizabeth, 1:258, 3:556
  Elizabeth (Brading), 1:232,
    1:258
  Frances, 1:258
  Mary, 1:258-259
  Mary (Danforth), 1:258
  Sarah, 1:258-259
Bromley
  Hannah (Stafford), 1:259,
    4:160
  Thomasine, 1:259
  Thomasine (Packer), 1:259
Bronsden
  Elizabeth, 1:259, 2:311
Bronson - see Brunson
Brook
  Remembrance, 1:269
Brookhouse
  Mary (Batson), 1:139

Brooking/Brucken/Brooken
----, 1:259
Abigail, 1:259
Abigail (----), 1:259
Christian, 1:259
Elinor (----) Knight, 3:36
Elizabeth, 1:259
Elizabeth (----), 1:259
Experience, 4:292
Jane, 1:259
Martha, 1:259, 3:87, 3:524
Mary, 1:259, 3:127
Mary (Walford), 1:259,
   4:392
Mercy, 1:259
Rebecca, 1:259, 3:452
Sarah, 1:259, 1:268
Brookings
Mary, 3:451
Brooks
----, 1:262
Abigail, 1:260-261, 1:508,
   4:177
Abigail (Barker), 1:508
Abigail (Boylston), 1:260
Alice, 1:262
Alice (Spencer), 1:262,
   4:59, 4:147
Ann, 1:260
Ann (----), 1:262
Ann (Meriam), 1:260
Annis (Jaquith), 1:260
Bathsheba, 1:260, 4:394
Bethia, 4:294
Deborah, 1:260, 1:263,
   4:183
Deborah (Garfield), 1:508
Dorothy, 1:261
Dorothy (Wright), 1:261
Elizabeth, 1:260-261,
   1:296, 1:508, 3:606
Elizabeth (----), 1:488
Elizabeth (Curtis), 1:261,
   1:487
Elizabeth (Winslow),
   1:260, 1:262, 1:516,
   4:599
Esther, 1:261, 4:533
Eunice, 1:260, 1:341, 3:9,
   3:250
Eunice (Mousall), 1:260,
   3:250
Grace, 1:261

Grace (----), 1:262
Hannah, 1:260-263, 1:478,
   2:196, 3:426
Hannah (----), 1:262
Hannah (----) Blackley,
   4:676
Hannah (Atkinson), 1:75,
   1:259
Hannah
   (Besbedge/Besbitch),
   1:171
Hannah (Bisby), 1:262
Hannah (Blackley), 1:260
Hannah (Eccles), 1:260,
   2:98
Hannah (Mason), 1:261,
   3:167
Hannah (Potter) Blackley,
   1:190
Joanna, 1:171, 1:260-263,
   3:250, 3:546, 4:183
Lucy (----), 1:262
Lydia, 1:261, 2:71
Martha, 1:260, 1:262
Martha (----), 1:260
Martha (Hotchkiss), 1:262
Mary, 1:259-263, 3:287,
   3:606, 4:501
Mary (Burt), 1:263, 1:313
Mary (Cranston), 1:261
Mary (Griggs), 2:315
Mary (Richardson), 1:261
Mary (Russell), 1:262,
   3:591
Mehitable, 1:262
Mehitable (----) Kingsley,
   1:262
Mercy, 2:415
Miriam, 1:260, 1:263,
   1:486
Miriam (Daniels), 1:260
Priscilla, 1:260
Rachel, 1:260
Rebecca, 1:259-261, 2:592
Rebecca (Blodget), 1:261
Ruth, 1:261, 4:676
Sarah, 1:259-263, 1:283,
   1:508, 3:250, 3:545,
   3:606, 4:262, 4:697
Sarah (----) Carpenter,
   1:260
Sarah (----) Wheeler, 1:263,
   4:501

Sarah (Boylston), 1:262
Sophia, 1:261
Susanna, 1:259, 1:261
Susanna (----), 1:260
Susanna (----) Dunham,
   1:263
Susanna (Atkinson), 1:75,
   1:259
Susanna (Hanmore), 1:261
Tabitha, 1:260, 4:438
Thankful, 1:262
Brooman
Sarah (----) Savage, 1:263
Sarah (Bowen) Savage,
   4:24
Broome
Hannah (----), 1:69, 1:263
Mary (----), 1:69
Broomer
Mary, 2:202, 3:64
Broughton
Abigail, 3:10
Abigail (Reyner), 1:263
Elizabeth, 1:263
Elizabeth (Woodruff),
   1:263, 4:643
Hannah, 1:263
Hannah (Bascom), 1:134,
   1:263, 2:538
Mary, 1:167, 1:263
Mary (Briscoe), 1:256,
   1:263
Patience, 1:263
Sarah, 1:263
Sarah (Rawson), 1:264,
   3:511
Brown/Browne
----, 1:279, 2:118, 3:73,
   4:580, 4:710
---- (----) Ford, 1:274,
   2:182
---- (----) Lovering, 1:265
---- (Ambler), 1:48
---- (Blandford), 1:197
---- (Buckland), 1:270,
   1:285
---- (Eaton), 2:96
---- (Ingersoll), 2:520
Abial (Shaw), 1:277, 4:65
Abiel, 1:271
Abigail, 1:265, 1:267-269,
   1:271-276, 1:508-509,
   2:194, 2:207

Brown/Browne (continued)
Abigail (----), 1:267
Abigail (Barber), 1:508
Abigail (Burrill), 1:272
Abigail (Haynes), 1:267
Abigail (Howe), 3:606,
3:636
Abigail (Macoone/etc),
3:141
Abigail (Trott), 4:711
Abra, 1:273
Alice (Herenden), 1:265
Ann, 1:264, 1:271-272,
1:276, 1:353, 1:509,
4:358, 4:556
Ann (----), 1:272
Ann (----) Lovering, 3:124
Ann (Eaton), 1:266
Ann (Fiske), 1:271, 2:165
Ann (Mason), 3:606,
3:651
Ann (Porter), 1:272, 4:696
Barbara (Eden), 1:275
Bethia, 1:264, 1:276
Bridget (----), 1:276
Catharine (----), 4:17
Charity (----), 1:266
Deborah, 1:271, 1:274,
3:190
Dinah, 1:509
Dorothy, 1:268, 1:508
Dorothy (----), 1:269-270
Dorothy (----) Paris, 1:267
Dorothy (Paris), 3:345
Edith (----), 1:275
Eleanor, 1:273
Eleanor (Watts), 1:273,
4:439
Elethan (Harris), 2:363
Elizabeth, 1:79, 1:165,
1:172, 1:264-275,
1:277-278, 1:321,
1:508-509, 2:289, 3:160,
3:235, 3:350, 3:606,
3:627, 4:23, 4:146,
4:448, 4:676
Elizabeth (----), 1:265-266,
1:268, 1:272-275, 2:531,
3:606
Elizabeth (----) Badger,
1:275
Elizabeth (----) Emerson,
1:271

Elizabeth (----) Foster,
1:265
Elizabeth (Bancroft), 1:111,
1:272
Elizabeth (Bulkley)
Emerson, 1:290, 2:118
Elizabeth (Downs), 1:278
Elizabeth (Greenleaf)
Badger, 1:93, 2:308
Elizabeth (Loomis), 1:509,
3:112
Elizabeth (Marsh), 1:275
Elizabeth (Miner), 1:272
Elizabeth (Munford),
1:278
Elizabeth (Okley), 1:265,
3:304
Elizabeth (Osgood), 1:271,
3:320
Elizabeth (Payson) Foster,
2:188, 3:373
Elizabeth (Polley), 1:272
Elizabeth (Robinson),
3:553
Elizabeth (Ruggles), 1:278,
3:586
Elizabeth (Shepherd),
1:264
Esther, 1:270-271, 1:274,
1:509
Esther (Makepeace), 1:270,
3:144
Eunice, 1:265, 1:509
Faith, 4:418
Faith (----), 1:266
Grace, 1:270, 1:276, 2:37
Grace (----), 1:268
Hallelujah, 3:313
Hannah, 1:47, 1:264-274,
1:277-278, 1:509, 2:128,
2:560, 3:52, 3:353,
3:606, 4:676, 4:697
Hannah (----), 1:267,
1:277-278, 4:704
Hannah (----) Hazen, 1:266
Hannah (----) Williams,
4:559
Hannah (Aslett), 1:69
Hannah (Bartholomew),
1:268
Hannah (Blandford), 1:197
Hannah (Collins), 1:271,
1:277, 1:434

Hannah (Curwin), 1:278,
1:488
Hannah (Earle), 2:135
Hannah (Fellows), 1:273,
2:151
Hannah (Field), 2:156
Hannah (Fitch), 1:273
Hannah (Hobart), 1:271,
2:435
Hannah (House), 1:508
Hannah (Putnam), 1:267
Hannah (Vincent), 1:265,
4:373
Hepzibah, 1:272, 1:274,
1:508
Hildah, 1:508
Hopestill, 1:172
Isabel, 2:466, 2:521
Jane, 1:264
Jane (Skipper), 1:264,
4:106
Jerusha, 1:277
Joanna, 2:361
Joanna (Whitehead), 1:269
Judah, 1:265
Judith, 1:271, 2:24
Judith (----), 1:268
Judith (Perkins), 1:273
Lydia, 1:257, 1:264, 1:266,
1:270, 1:272, 3:46,
3:364, 3:606, 4:644
Lydia (----), 1:264, 1:278
Lydia (Howland), 1:268,
2:480
Mabel, 1:508
Margaret, 1:269, 1:271,
1:509
Margaret (----), 1:269
Margaret (Denison), 2:36
Margaret (Hayward),
1:270
Margaret (Odlin), 1:267
Margaret (Stone), 1:278,
4:205
Martha, 1:267-268, 1:271,
1:273, 1:275-276, 1:278,
1:509, 2:145, 2:543,
2:583, 3:606, 3:619,
4:542
Martha (----), 1:267, 1:274
Martha (----) Chapman,
1:266, 1:361
Martha (----) Oldham,

Brown/Browne (continued)
Martha (----) Oldham
(continued)
1:276
Martha (Eaton) Oldham,
2:98, 3:308
Martha (Harding), 1:276,
2:354
Martha (Hughes), 1:273
Martha (Matthews) Snell,
3:176
Martha (Sherman), 4:83
Martha (Whipple), 1:275
Mary, 1:172, 1:264-278,
1:335, 1:508-509, 2:266,
2:372, 2:482, 3:87,
3:135, 3:188, 3:245,
3:294, 3:354, 3:367,
3:376, 3:527, 3:562,
3:607, 4:425, 4:553,
4:557, 4:613, 4:676
Mary (----), 1:266, 1:270,
1:275-276, 3:531, 4:393,
4:676, 4:694
Mary (----) Hovey, 2:471
Mary (----) Robinson,
1:277, 3:549, 3:607,
4:393
Mary (Barber), 1:274
Mary (Bessbeech), 1:171,
1:277
Mary (Bisby), 1:277
Mary (Buswell), 1:274,
1:319
Mary (Danforth) Phips,
1:277, 2:9
Mary (Dix), 1:264, 2:53
Mary (English), 2:582
Mary (Fellows), 1:273
Mary (Gillett), 1:274,
2:256
Mary (Goodwin), 1:278,
2:587
Mary (Hicks), 1:264
Mary (Holmes), 1:271
Mary (Jaques), 1:275,
2:538
Mary (Johnson), 1:266
Mary (Lothrop/Lathrop),
1:278, 3:120
Mary (Mattocks), 1:276,
3:177
Mary (Murcock), 1:278

Mary (Newhall), 3:274,
3:607
Mary (Shattuck), 1:272,
4:62
Mary (Smith), 4:131
Mary (Tapley), 1:267
Mary (Tilton), 4:304
Mary (Walker), 1:270,
4:394
Mary (Winship), 1:265
Mary (Woodman), 1:271
Mary (Youngs), 1:277
Mehitable, 1:267, 1:272,
1:276
Mehitable (Brenton),
1:242, 1:272
Mercy, 1:269, 1:274-275,
1:278
Mercy (Tuttle), 1:275,
4:352
Mindwell, 1:269, 1:272,
1:509
Mindwell (Loomis), 1:272,
3:113
Patience, 1:172, 1:175,
1:272
Patience (Foster), 1:277
Phebe, 1:270, 1:274, 2:364
Priscilla, 1:37, 1:267,
1:271, 1:277
Prudence, 1:272
Rachel, 1:275-276, 1:508
Rachel (Gardner), 2:228
Rachel (Trott), 4:711
Rebecca, 1:264-265, 1:267,
1:277, 2:488, 3:606
Rebecca (----) Bailey, 1:95
Rebecca (----) Sprague,
1:271
Rebecca (Bayley), 1:267,
1:278
Rebecca (Clark), 3:609
Rebecca (Crawford)
Sprague, 4:156
Rebecca (Usher), 1:264,
4:363
Remembrance (Brook),
1:269
Ruhamah, 1:273
Ruhamah (Wellington),
1:273
Ruth, 1:267, 1:273, 1:509,
3:481, 3:569

Ruth (Huse), 1:272
Sarah, 1:172, 1:227,
1:264-271, 1:273-278,
1:508-509, 2:30, 2:63,
2:299, 2:397, 3:296,
3:358, 3:435, 3:457,
3:606, 4:34, 4:307
Sarah (----), 1:266-267,
1:270, 1:276, 1:278,
2:397
Sarah (Brooking), 1:259,
1:268
Sarah (Brown), 1:264,
1:278
Sarah (Bulkley), 1:266,
1:292
Sarah
(Burrows/Burroughs),
1:310
Sarah (Cutting), 1:268,
1:496
Sarah (Jenks), 2:543
Sarah (Jones), 1:273
Sarah (Kidder), 1:508,
3:18
Sarah (Lamsom), 1:265
Sarah (Sawyer), 1:273
Sarah (Smith), 1:277
Sarah (Walker), 1:270
Susan, 2:540
Susanna, 1:172, 1:274,
1:277, 3:607
Tabitha (Trott) Frost,
4:711
Thankful, 1:172, 1:269
Thomasine (----), 1:277
Unity (----) Buxton, 1:274,
1:325, 3:34
Brownell
Martha, 1:279
Mary, 1:279
Sarah, 1:279
Susanna, 1:279
Susanna (Pierce), 1:279,
3:430
Wait, 1:279
Browning
Deborah, 1:279, 3:396,
3:653
Elizabeth, 1:279, 4:245
Hannah, 1:279
Mary, 1:279, 4:316
Mary (----), 1:279

Browning (continued)
  Rebecca (Wilbor), 1:279,
    4:545
  Sarah, 1:279, 4:563
  Sarah (Freeborn), 1:279
  Zephaniah, 1:279
Brownson - see Brunson
Bruce
  Deliverance, 1:280
  Elizabeth (----), 1:280
  Eunice, 1:280
  Hannah, 1:280
  Martha, 1:280
  Mary, 1:280
  Rebecca, 1:280
  Sarah, 1:280
Bruen
  Esther (----), 1:280
  Hannah, 1:103, 1:281
  Mary, 1:102, 1:281
  Rebecca, 1:281, 3:465
  Sarah (----), 1:281
Brunson/Bronson/Brownson
  ---- (----) Carpenter Orvis,
    1:336
  Abigail, 1:280, 4:591
  Ann, 1:279
  Ann (Griswold), 1:279,
    2:317
  Dorcas, 1:280, 2:462
  Eede/Edith, 1:280
  Elizabeth, 1:279-280
  Elizabeth (----) Carpenter
    Orvis, 1:280, 3:317
  Frances, 1:279
  Hannah, 1:280
  Hannah (Scott), 4:37
  Joanna, 3:650
  Lydia (Warner), 1:280,
    4:420
  Mary, 1:42, 1:279-280,
    2:52, 4:661
  Mary (----) Chatterton,
    4:676
  Mary (Clemence)
    Chatterton, 4:677
  Mary (Root), 3:572
  Mercy, 1:279
  Sarah, 1:279-280, 3:19
  Sarah (Ventris), 4:370,
    4:676
Brush
  Abigail, 1:281

Elizabeth, 1:281
Elizabeth (Clark), 1:281,
  1:404
Elizabeth (Gould), 1:281
Lydia, 1:281
Margery, 1:281
Mary, 1:281, 1:472
Rebecca, 1:281
Bruster
  Mary, 3:39
  Mary (Knight), 1:281, 3:39
  Sarah, 2:411
Bryan
  ---- (----) Fitch, 1:281
  Abigail, 1:282
  Ann, 1:282
  Ann (----), 1:281
  Elizabeth, 1:282
  Elizabeth (----), 4:327
  Elizabeth (Powell)
    Hollingworth, 1:282
  Frances, 1:282
  Hannah, 1:282, 2:358
  Jerusha, 1:282
  Joan (----), 3:233
  Joanna, 1:282
  Martha, 1:282
  Martha (Whiting), 1:282,
    4:518
  Mary, 1:282, 3:145
  Mary (----), 1:282
  Mary (----) Whiting Fitch,
    2:169
  Sarah, 1:282
  Susanna, 1:282
  Susanna (----) Whiting
    Fitch, 4:522
  Sybil, 1:282
  Sybil (Whiting), 1:282,
    4:518
Bryant
  Abigail, 1:283
  Abigail (Bryant), 1:283
  Abigail (Shaw), 1:283,
    4:64
  Agatha, 1:283
  Ann, 1:283
  Deborah, 1:283
  Dorcas (----) Eaton, 2:96
  Elizabeth, 1:283
  Elizabeth (Wetherell),
    1:283, 4:492
  Hannah, 1:283, 4:202

Hannah (----), 1:283
Hannah (Spear), 4:146
Lydia, 1:283, 1:387
Martha, 1:283
Mary, 1:283
Mary (----), 4:183
Mary (Battelle/Battle),
  1:140
Mary (Hiland), 1:283,
  2:516
Mary (Kendall), 1:282-283,
  3:10
Mary (Lewis), 1:283, 3:85
Ruth, 1:283, 4:406
Ruth (----) Frothingham,
  1:283
Ruth (George)
  Frothingham, 2:213
Sarah, 1:283
Sarah (----)
  Magoon/McGown, 3:143
Bryer/Briard
  Abigail, 1:283
  Abigail (Drew), 1:283
  Eleanor (Wright), 1:283
  Elizabeth, 1:283
  Margaret, 1:283
  Mary, 1:283
  Ruth, 1:283
  Sarah, 1:283
Bryers
  Elizabeth, 1:143
Buchanan
  ---- (Clark), 1:400
Buck
  Abigail, 1:283, 3:628
  Abigail (Bull), 1:294
  Ann, 1:284
  Deborah, 1:284, 3:505
  Elizabeth, 1:283-284,
    1:356
  Elizabeth (Churchill),
    1:284, 1:387
  Elizabeth (Holbrook),
    1:284
  Eunice, 1:284
  Frances (----), 1:284
  Frances (Marsh), 3:154
  Hannah, 1:283-284
  Lydia, 3:607, 4:116
  Mabel (Taylor), 4:264
  Margery (Ingersoll) Goffe,
    2:267, 2:520

Buck (continued)
Martha, 1:284, 3:551
Mary, 1:65, 1:284
Mary (Kirby), 1:283, 3:30
Mary (Wilson) Danforth,
4:584
Mehitable, 1:284
Rachel, 1:284, 2:85
Rachel (Andrews), 1:54
Ruth, 1:284, 2:233
Sarah, 1:283-284
Sarah (----), 1:283
Sarah (Brooks), 1:283
Sarah (Faunce) Dotey,
1:284, 2:62
Susanna, 1:284
Susanna (----), 1:284
Buckingham
Ann, 1:285, 4:676
Ann (----), 4:676
Ann (Foster), 1:285, 2:188
Esther, 1:284, 4:676
Esther (Hosmer), 1:284,
2:467
Hannah, 4:455, 4:676
Hannah (Fowler), 1:284,
2:195
Margaret (Griswold),
1:285
Mary, 3:352, 4:676
Mary (----) Hooker, 1:285
Mary (Willet) Hooker,
2:459, 4:557
Ruth, 4:676
Sarah, 4:676
Sarah (Baldwin), 1:105,
1:284
Sarah (Hooker), 1:285,
2:459
Sarah (Lee), 3:647
Temperance, 1:285
Buckland
----, 1:270, 1:285
---- (----) Beckwith, 1:151,
1:285
Abigail, 1:285
Abigail (Vore), 1:285,
4:376
Elizabeth, 1:9, 1:285,
1:509-510, 4:673
Elizabeth (Drake), 1:509
Hannah, 1:285, 2:586,
4:579

Hannah (----) Bill, 1:177,
1:285
Hannah (Cooke), 1:97,
1:285, 1:449
Hannah (Strong), 1:509
Leah, 1:285, 3:119
Lydia, 1:285
Martha, 1:285
Martha (Wakefield), 1:285,
4:386
Mary, 1:285
Rachel (Wheatley), 1:285,
3:118, 4:495
Sarah, 1:285, 3:406
Temperance, 1:285, 3:453
Temperance (Denslow),
1:285, 2:39
Buckley
Joanna (Shute) Nichols,
1:286, 3:281, 4:93
Buckman
Hannah, 1:286
Hannah (----), 1:286
Buckmaster
Abigail, 2:325
Dorcas, 1:457
Mary, 2:4
Sarah, 1:359, 3:62
Buckminster
Dorcas, 1:286
Elizabeth, 1:286
Elizabeth (Clark), 1:286,
1:393
Elizabeth (Spowell), 4:146,
4:153
Hannah, 1:286
Joan (----), 1:286, 2:231
Lydia, 1:397
Martha (Sharp), 1:286
Martha (Vose), 4:376
Mary, 1:286
Mary (----), 1:287
Sarah, 1:286, 3:62
Sarah (Webb), 1:287
Bucknam
---- (Knower), 1:287, 3:40
Elizabeth, 1:287, 4:533
Hannah, 1:287
Hannah (Waite), 1:287,
4:383
Judith, 1:287
Judith (Worth), 1:287
Lydia, 1:287

Martha (Burnet) Haynes,
2:391
Mary, 1:287
Mehitable, 1:287, 4:385
Mercy, 1:287, 4:443
Sarah, 1:287, 4:62
Sarah (----), 1:287
Susanna, 1:287
Bucknell
Sarah, 1:287
Sarah (Bishop), 1:185,
1:287
Buckner
Mary (----), 1:287
Mary (Hunting) Jay, 2:503,
2:539
Buddington
Mary, 4:627
Budley
Elizabeth, 1:288
Elizabeth (----), 1:288
Martha, 1:288
Mary (Conant), 1:288
Rebecca, 1:288
Rebecca (----), 1:288
Rebecca (Stacey), 1:288
Sarah, 1:288
Budlong
Isabel, 1:288
Mary, 1:288
Rebecca, 1:288
Rebecca (Lippit) Howard,
1:288, 3:97
Buell
---- (Fenner), 2:153
Abigail, 1:288-289
Deborah, 1:288
Deborah (Griswold), 1:288,
2:316
Esther, 1:288
Hannah, 1:288-289, 3:342,
3:462
Hepzibah, 1:157,
1:288-289, 4:479
Martha, 1:288
Mary, 1:288-289, 3:215
Mary (----), 1:288
Mary (----) Bissell, 1:186,
1:288
Mehitable, 1:288
Miriam, 1:288
Sarah, 1:288-289

Buffington
Abigail, 1:289
Hannah (Ross), 1:289
Sarah (Southwick), 1:289
Buffum/Buffam
—, 1:289, 4:588
Abigail, 3:632
Damaris (Pope), 1:289, 3:458
Hannah (Pope), 1:289, 3:458
Lydia, 3:632
Margaret, 4:706
Mary, 1:289, 3:264
Thomasin (----), 1:289
Bugby
Abigail, 1:289-290
Abigail (Hall), 1:289
Elizabeth, 1:410
Experience (Pitcher), 1:289, 3:440
Joanna, 1:289
Joanna (----), 1:289
Judith (----), 1:290, 3:355
Mary, 1:289
Mehitable, 1:290
Rebecca, 1:290
Rebecca (----), 1:289
Sarah, 1:289, 1:354
Bulfinch
Ann (----), 1:290
Bulkley
Catharine, 1:290, 4:327
Dorothy, 1:290-292, 4:328
Elinor, 1:292
Elizabeth, 1:290, 2:118
Esther (----), 1:292
Grace, 1:292, 3:19
Grace (Chitwood), 1:291
Hannah, 1:292
Jane, 1:290, 2:174
Jane (Allen), 1:291
Margaret, 1:292
Martha (Beers), 1:154, 1:291
Mary, 1:291, 4:676
Rachel (Talcott), 4:251
Rebecca, 1:291-292, 3:481, 4:504
Rebecca (----), 3:481
Rebecca (Jones) Minot, 2:563, 3:217
Rebecca (Wheeler), 1:291

Sarah, 1:266, 1:290-292
Sarah (----), 1:292
Sarah (Chauncy), 1:290, 1:367
Sarah (Jones), 1:292, 2:562, 4:581-582
Bull
—, 1:294, 1:298
— (—) Easton, 1:293
Abiah, 1:294
Abiah (Perry), 1:294
Abigail, 1:120, 1:292-294
Ann, 1:293
Ann (Clayton) Easton, 1:406, 2:94
Ann (Cole), 1:293
Blyth (—), 1:294
Bridget, 1:96
Deborah, 1:293
Elizabeth, 1:293
Elizabeth (—), 1:293
Elizabeth (—) Underwood, 1:294
Elizabeth (Sage), 4:4
Elizabeth (Underwood), 4:359
Esther, 1:293
Esther (Cowles), 1:294, 1:466
Godsgift (Arnold), 1:293
Hannah, 1:292
Hannah (Chapman), 1:292, 1:362
Hannah (Lewis), 1:294
Margaret, 1:293
Margaret (Damon), 1:293
Martha, 1:293
Mary, 1:293-294, 1:421, 3:253
Mary (Baxter), 1:142, 1:293
Mary (Cheever) Lewis, 4:702
Mary (Pitts), 1:293, 3:442
Mehitable, 1:293
Phebe, 1:293-294, 1:352
Phebe (----), 1:293
Rebecca, 1:294, 1:459
Ruth, 1:213, 1:293-294
Sarah, 1:293-294
Sarah (----), 1:293
Sarah (Manning), 1:293, 3:148

Sarah (Parker), 1:293, 3:351
Sarah (Whiting), 1:293, 4:518
Susanna, 1:292-294
Susanna (----), 1:294
Sybil, 1:293
Bullard
— (Thorpe), 1:294, 4:293
Abigail, 1:295
Ann, 1:294-296, 2:5, 2:561
Ann (----), 1:295, 2:359
Ann (----) Wight, 1:295, 4:543
Beatrice (Hall), 1:295
Elizabeth, 1:294-296, 1:433, 4:46
Elizabeth (----), 1:294
Elizabeth (Avery), 1:296
Elizabeth (Traine) Spring, 4:157
Ellen (----) Dickerman, 2:47
Esther, 1:295
Esther (Morse), 1:295, 3:240
Hannah, 1:294-295, 4:69
Hannah (Jones), 2:566
Hannah (Thorpe), 1:295
Jane (—) Else, 1:510, 2:582
Jemima, 1:296
Joanna, 1:295, 2:396
Judith/Judah, 1:295
Magdalen (----), 1:295
Magdelen, 3:365
Margaret (----), 1:295
Martha, 1:295, 3:203
Martha (Pidge), 1:294
Mary, 1:294-295, 2:146, 2:237, 2:378, 3:38, 3:532
Mary (----) Griswold, 1:295, 2:317
Mary (Marplehead), 1:295
Mary (Richards), 1:295, 3:532
Maudlin, 1:294
Rachel, 1:295
Sarah, 1:106, 1:295
Sarah (----), 1:295
Susanna, 1:295

48

Bullen
Abigail (Sabin), 1:296
Bethia, 1:296
Elizabeth, 1:296
Grace, 1:296
Grace (----), 1:296
Hannah, 1:296
Hannah (Metcalf), 1:296
Judith, 1:296
Judith (Fisher), 1:296
Mary, 1:296, 3:241
Mary (Morse), 1:296,
 3:241
Mary (Pitts), 3:442
Meletiah, 1:296
Miriam, 1:296
Silence, 1:296
Bullier
Elizabeth (Brooks), 1:296
Bullis
Elizabeth, 1:296
Judith (Hart) Ratchell,
 1:296
Judith (Hart) Ratchell
 Reape, 3:508
Judith (Hart) Ratchell
 Rease, 2:367
Rachel, 1:296
Bullivant
Hannah, 1:297
Bullock
Elizabeth, 1:155, 1:510,
 3:607, 3:656
Elizabeth (----), 3:607
Hannah, 1:297
Hannah (----), 1:297
Hopestill, 3:106
Mary, 1:297
Mary (Maverick), 1:510
Mary (Thurber), 1:297
Susan (----), 1:297
Thankful, 1:297
Thankful (Rouse), 1:297
Bully
Ann, 1:170
Ellen (Booth), 1:212
Bumpas/Bumpus
Abigail, 1:298
Elizabeth, 1:298, 3:576
Elizabeth (----) Blackmore,
 1:297
Elizabeth (Banks)
 Blackmore, 1:190

Faith, 1:297
Hannah, 1:297-298
Hannah (----), 1:297
Jane, 1:298
Lydia, 1:297
Mary, 1:297-298, 1:476
Mehitable, 1:298
Penelope, 1:297
Phebe (Lovell), 1:298,
 3:123
Rebecca, 1:297
Sarah, 1:297-298, 2:83
Wybra, 1:297
Wybra (Glass), 2:260
Bumstead
Abigail, 3:607
Hannah, 1:298, 3:305,
 3:607, 4:67
Hannah (----), 3:607
Mary, 1:298, 2:24, 3:607
Mercy, 1:216, 1:298
Sarah, 3:607
Sarah (----), 3:607
Susanna (----), 1:298
Bunce
---- (Bull), 1:294, 1:298
Elizabeth, 1:298, 4:509
Mary, 1:298, 3:192
Sarah, 1:298, 4:381, 4:511,
 4:653
Bundy
Martha, 1:298
Martha (----), 1:298
Mary, 1:298
Patience, 1:298
Ruth (Surney/Turney),
 1:298
Sarah, 1:298
Bunker
Ann, 1:299, 1:431
Elizabeth, 1:299, 1:313,
 3:111, 4:676
Hannah, 1:299, 2:593,
 3:276
Hannah (Miller), 1:299
Jane (----), 4:235
Jane (Godfrey), 1:299
Judith (----), 1:299
Margaret (----) Howe,
 1:299, 2:474
Martha, 1:299, 2:508,
 4:676
Mary, 1:299, 1:419, 4:676

Mary (Gould) Hayward,
 1:510, 2:286
Mary (Macy), 1:299, 3:142
Rebecca (Eaton), 2:95
Bunn/Bunne
Elizabeth, 1:299, 3:18
Elizabeth (Mason), 1:299
Esther, 1:299
Esther (----), 1:299
Bunnill/Bunnell
Ann, 4:700
Ann (Wilmot), 1:300,
 4:580
Elizabeth (----), 4:681,
 4:707
Elizabeth (----) Sperry,
 4:151, 4:700
Judith, 4:700
Lydia, 3:607
Mary, 3:607, 4:695
Rachel, 4:700
Rebecca, 4:700
Rebecca (Mallory), 4:700
Susanna (Whitehead),
 4:700, 4:713
Burbank
Jemima (----), 1:300
Lydia, 1:300
Susanna (Merrill), 1:300
Burbeen
Mary, 1:300
Sarah (Gould), 1:300
Burch
Abigail, 1:300
Elizabeth, 1:300
Elizabeth (----), 1:300
Mary, 1:300
Burchal
Judith, 1:510
Burcham
Frances, 1:300, 4:558
Burchsted
Mary (----) Kirtland, 1:300
Mary (Rand) Kirtland,
 3:32
Burden
Ann (----), 1:301
Deborah (Barker), 4:561
Hannah, 1:301, 1:353
Hannah (Witter), 4:620
Mary (Harris), 2:365
Sarah, 3:187

Burdick
---- (Maxon), 3:652
Deborah, 1:301, 1:471
Jane (----), 1:301
Mary, 1:301
Naomi, 1:301, 3:563
Rachel, 1:301
Ruth, 1:301
Ruth (Hubbard), 1:301,
   2:485
Tacy, 1:301, 3:652
Burditt/Burdett
Elizabeth, 1:301
Elizabeth (----), 1:301
Hannah, 1:301
Hannah (----), 1:301
Hannah (Winter), 1:301,
   4:606
Mary, 1:301
Ruth, 1:301
Sarah, 1:301
Burdsall
Judith, 1:446, 1:510
Burdsie - see Birdseye
Bureau
Ann, 2:139
Burge
Dorothy, 1:302
Elizabeth, 1:302, 3:399
Elizabeth (Bassett), 1:302
Jane (----) Gornell, 1:302,
   2:282
Lydia (----), 1:302
Margaret (----) Cheney,
   1:373
Martha, 1:302
Mary (Nye), 1:302
Mary (Stearns) Larned,
   1:302, 3:68
Mary (Worden), 1:302,
   4:651
Rebecca, 1:302, 4:531
Burgess/Burgiss/Burges
----, 4:263
Eleanor (Munroe/Monroe),
   3:257
Elizabeth (Bassett), 1:136
Joyce (----), 1:302
Lydia (Mead), 1:302,
   3:190
Mercy (Wright), 4:660
Phebe (Peacock), 3:376,
   3:607

Ruth, 4:263
Sarah (Griggs) King, 1:303,
   2:315, 3:27
Sarah (Hall), 1:302
Burk/Burke
Mary (Parmenter), 3:360
Sarah (----), 4:658
Sarah (Woodford) Allen,
   1:34, 1:303
Burkly/Brelly/Burleigh/etc
Mary, 4:561
Burley
Rebecca, 3:30
Burlingham/Burlingame
Martha (Lippit), 1:303,
   3:98
Mary, 1:303
Mary (----), 1:303
Mary (Lippit), 1:303, 3:98
Burlisson
Elizabeth, 1:510
Elizabeth (Buckland),
   1:510
Esther, 1:510
Mary, 1:303, 1:510
Burman
Desire, 1:303
Hannah, 1:303
Hannah (----), 1:303
Mary, 1:303
Mehitable, 1:303
Burnap
Ann, 1:303
Ann (----), 1:304
Hannah (Antram), 1:303,
   1:499
Margaret (Davis), 1:304
Mary, 1:304
Mary (Pearson), 3:378,
   3:607
Sarah, 1:303-304
Sarah (----), 1:304
Burnell
Ann (Moore), 1:510
Sarah, 1:304
Burnett
Margaret (Davis), 2:21
Martha, 2:391
Mary (Pearson), 1:304
Mary (Rice), 1:304
Burnham/Burnam/Burnum
----, 3:227
Abigail, 1:304-305, 4:523

Abigail (Varney), 4:366
Elizabeth, 1:304
Esther, 1:304
Esther (Bishop), 1:305
Frances (----), 1:304
Hannah, 1:304
Hannah (----), 1:383
Hannah (Hobby), 2:437
Joanna, 1:304
Lydia, 1:305
Lydia (Pingree), 1:305
Martha, 1:304
Mary, 1:304-305
Mary (Tuttle), 1:304,
   4:352
Mercy, 1:304
Naomi, 1:305
Naomi (Hull), 1:305,
   2:494
Phebe, 1:305
Rebecca, 1:304
Ruth, 1:304, 1:340
Sarah, 1:304-305
Sarah (Choate), 1:382
Sarah (Humfrey), 1:304,
   2:497
Susanna, 1:304-305
Susanna (----), 1:305
Burph/Burfee
Elizabeth (Perry), 1:305
Burr
Abigail, 1:307-308
Abigail (Glover), 1:305,
   3:624
Ann, 1:31, 1:215,
   1:307-308
Ann (----), 1:305, 1:307
Deborah, 1:307
Elinor (----), 1:305
Elizabeth, 1:306-308
Elizabeth (----), 1:305
Esther, 1:306-308
Esther (----) Boosy, 1:211,
   1:306
Frances (----), 1:307, 2:79
Grace, 3:235
Hannah, 1:305-306, 1:308,
   2:422, 2:434, 3:607
Hannah (Banks), 1:112
Jane, 1:306
Joanna, 1:307
Mary, 1:305-308, 1:399,
   1:479, 3:109

50

Burr (continued)
Mary (Baysey), 1:144,
  1:307
Mary (Lazell), 3:66
Mary (Ward), 1:306, 4:406
Mary (Warren), 1:307,
  4:587
Rebecca, 1:307
Rose, 1:308
Sarah, 1:307-308, 1:368
Sarah (----), 1:308
Sarah (Fitch), 1:307
Sarah (Ward), 1:307,
  4:406-407
Burrage
---- (----), 1:308, 2:345
Bethia, 1:510
Elizabeth, 1:308, 2:31,
  3:457
Elizabeth (----), 1:308
Hannah, 1:308, 2:206
Joanna, 1:510
Joanna (----), 1:308
Mary, 1:308, 1:510
Mary (----), 1:308
Ruth, 1:308, 1:510, 4:509
Sarah, 1:308, 1:510, 2:599
Susanna (Cutler), 1:511
Burrill
Abigail, 1:272
Ann, 1:309
Deborah, 1:308
Deborah (Simpkins), 1:309,
  4:101
Dinah (Nicholson), 3:283
Dorcas (Newberry), 3:269
Elizabeth, 1:308-309,
  2:144
Elizabeth (----), 1:308
Esther, 1:308
Hannah, 1:308
Jane, 3:283
Lois, 1:309
Lois (Ivory), 1:309, 2:526
Lydia, 1:308
Lydia (----), 1:308
Martha (Farrington), 1:309
Mary, 1:308-309
Mary (----), 1:309
Mercy (----), 1:309
Rebecca (----), 1:309
Sarah, 1:308-309, 2:20
Sarah (----), 1:309

Burrington
Abigail, 1:309
Jane (----), 1:309
Burritt
Elizabeth, 1:310
Elizabeth (----), 1:310
Mary, 1:310
Sarah (Nichols), 1:309-310,
  3:280
Burrows/Burroughs
---- (Huet), 1:311
---- (Ruck), 1:311
Abigail, 1:311
Ann (----), 1:311
Elizabeth, 1:310, 4:282
Elizabeth (----) Gross
  Heath, 1:310
Elizabeth (----) Grosse
  Heath, 2:319
Hannah, 1:213, 1:310-311
Hannah (----), 1:310
Hannah (Way), 4:440
Margaret, 1:311
Mary, 1:311, 2:457
Mary (----) Ireland, 1:312,
  2:524
Mary (Culver), 1:311
Mercy (Chester), 1:376
Rebecca, 1:310
Rebecca (----), 1:310
Sarah, 1:310-311
Bursley/Burslem/Burslin
Abigail, 1:312
Elizabeth, 1:312, 2:276
Elizabeth (Howland),
  1:312
Joanna, 1:312, 2:51, 4:676
Joanna (Hull), 1:312,
  2:494
Mary, 1:312, 1:474
Naomi, 2:494
Ruth, 2:494
Temperance, 1:312, 1:475
Burt
----, 1:503
Abigail, 1:106, 1:313,
  3:254, 4:177
Ann (----), 1:313-314
Charity (----), 1:314
Deborah (Stebbins) Alvord,
  1:46, 1:313
Deliverance (----) Hanchet,
  1:314

Deliverance (Langton)
  Hanchet, 2:352
Dorcas, 1:313-314, 4:195
Elizabeth, 1:313-314, 4:96,
  4:659
Elizabeth (Alvord), 1:46,
  1:313
Elizabeth (Bunker), 1:299,
  1:313
Elizabeth (Lobdell), 1:314,
  3:102
Experience, 1:314
Hannah, 1:93, 1:312-313
Hannah (Denslow), 1:313,
  2:39
Mary, 1:263, 1:312-314,
  1:511, 2:374, 4:675
Mary (----), 1:313, 3:573
Mary (Holton), 1:312,
  2:456
Mary (Southwick), 1:314
Mercy, 1:313-314, 4:658
Patience, 1:200, 1:313
Rebecca, 1:314
Rebecca (Sikes), 1:314
Ruth, 1:312-313
Sarah, 1:312-314, 1:511,
  2:60, 2:312, 2:429, 3:36,
  3:463
Sarah (Belden), 1:312
Susan (----), 1:314
Ulalia (----), 1:313
Burton
---- (Clark), 1:316
Abigail (Brenton), 1:242,
  1:315
Ann (Wicks), 4:539
Ann/Hannah (Wicks),
  1:315
Elizabeth, 1:315
Elizabeth (Winslow),
  1:315, 4:603
Frances (----), 1:315
Hannah, 1:315, 3:657
Isabel (Potter), 1:316,
  3:466
Margaret (Otis), 1:315,
  3:323
Martha, 1:242, 1:315
Mercy (Judson), 3:608,
  3:641
Phebe, 1:315
Rose, 1:316

Burton (continued)
Ruth, 1:315
Sarah, 1:315
Susanna, 1:315, 2:283
Burwell
Alice, 1:316
Alice (----), 1:316, 3:382
Ann, 4:700
Benedicta (----), 4:676
Deborah (Merwin), 3:201
Elizabeth, 1:316, 3:382, 4:676
Elizabeth (Baldwin), 1:104, 1:316
Hannah, 4:676
Hannah (----), 4:676
Mary (----) Richards, 3:382
Rebecca (Bunnill), 4:700
Sarah, 1:316
Sarah (Fenn), 1:316, 2:152
Temperance, 1:316
Temperance (Baldwin), 1:104, 1:316
Busbee/Busby
Abigail (----) Briscoe, 1:316
Ann, 1:316, 3:284
Bridget (----), 1:316
Catharine, 1:316
Martha (Cheney) Sadler, 1:316, 1:372, 4:3
Sarah, 1:316, 1:328, 2:319
Bush
Abiah, 1:317
Abigail, 1:317
Ann, 1:316, 3:579
Deborah, 3:141
Elizabeth, 1:316-317
Elizabeth (----), 1:317
Elizabeth (----) Pitman, 1:316
Hannah (----), 1:317
Lydia, 1:317
Mary, 1:317
Mary (----), 1:317
Mary (Hyde), 1:316
Mary (Taylor), 4:264
Mehitable, 1:381
Bushell
Ruth, 1:317, 3:222
Bushnell
----, 2:467
Abigail, 1:317-318, 4:57

Ann, 1:318
Deborah, 1:317
Dorothy, 1:317
Elizabeth, 1:317-318, 2:558
Elizabeth (Adgate), 1:18, 1:318
Hannah, 1:317
Hannah (Beamsley), 1:148, 3:394
Hepzibah, 1:318
Jane, 2:417
Jane (----), 1:317
Jerusha, 1:317
Judith, 1:318, 4:57
Lydia, 1:318, 4:57
Maria, 1:318
Martha, 1:317, 4:124
Martha (----), 1:148, 1:318
Mary, 1:317-318, 2:565, 3:212, 3:550
Mary (----), 1:317
Mary (Leffingwell), 1:317
Mary (Marvin), 1:18, 1:318, 3:164
Patience (Rudd), 1:318, 3:584
Rachel, 1:317
Rebecca, 1:317-318, 3:115
Ruth (Sanford), 1:318, 4:16
Sarah, 1:317, 2:429, 2:522
Sarah (Scranton), 1:317, 4:41
Susanna (----) Wadom/Wadams/etc, 4:379
Bushrod
Abigail, 1:318
Elizabeth, 1:318
Elizabeth (Hannum), 1:318, 2:351
Hannah, 1:318
Busicot - see Bassaker
Buss/Bussey
Ann, 1:319
Ann (----), 1:319
Dorcas, 1:319
Dorcas (----) Jones, 1:319, 2:563
Elizabeth (Bradbury), 1:230, 1:319
Elizabeth (Jones), 1:319,

2:562
Hannah, 4:501-502
Mary (Haven), 1:319
Buswell/Buzzell/Bussell/etc
Hannah (Tyler), 1:319
Margaret (----), 1:319
Mary, 1:274, 1:319
Mary (Eastow), 1:319
Phebe, 1:319, 2:254
Ruth (Stileman), 1:319, 4:192
Sarah, 1:319
Sarah (Keyes), 1:319
Susanna (Perkins), 1:319, 2:220
Butcher
Elizabeth, 1:319, 3:394
Mary (Deane), 1:319
Sarah, 1:319
Sarah (----), 1:319
Butler
Abigail, 1:320
Abigail (Shepard), 4:75
Ann (Holman), 1:320, 2:451
Ann (Phillips), 3:415
Catharine (Haughton), 1:320, 2:378
Dinah, 2:385
Dorothy, 1:321, 3:20
Elizabeth, 1:320-321, 3:608, 4:676
Elizabeth (----), 1:320-321
Elizabeth (Brown), 1:264, 1:321, 4:23
Elizabeth (Morrill), 3:608
Eunice (Coffin), 1:322, 1:419
Grace, 1:320
Grace (----), 1:320
Grace (Newcomb), 3:270
Hannah, 1:321, 1:328, 1:351
Hannah (Savage), 4:24
Jane, 3:327
Jane (----), 1:321
Joan, 1:476
Joyce (----), 1:321
Lydia, 1:321, 3:217, 4:167
Mabel (----), 1:320
Mabel (Olmstead), 3:312, 4:249
Mary, 1:72, 1:134,

Butler (continued)
  Mary (continued)
    1:320-321, 3:608, 3:654,,
    4:429, 4:659
  Mary (----), 1:321, 3:608
  Mary (Alford), 1:27, 1:321,
    3:295, 4:363
  Mary (Goodrich), 1:320,
    2:275
  Patience, 1:321, 2:247
  Phebe, 1:320-321
  Rebecca, 1:176
  Sarah, 1:320, 4:181
  Sarah (----), 1:22, 1:322
  Sarah (Stone), 1:321,
    4:208-209, 4:446
  Susanna, 3:118
  Susanna (Gallop/Gallup),
    2:585
Butley
  Prudence, 2:358
Butman
  Hannah, 3:608
  Mary, 3:608
  Sarah, 3:629
  Sarah (Robinson), 3:608
Butt/Butts
  Barachiah, 1:322
  Deliverance (----), 1:322
  Elizabeth, 1:322
  Elizabeth (Breck), 1:322
  Hannah, 1:322
  Mary, 1:322
Buttels
  Judith (----), 1:322
Butter/Butters
  Lydia, 1:322
  Mary, 4:221
  Rebecca, 1:322
  Rebecca (----), 1:322
Butterfield
  Ann (----), 1:322
  Hannah (----) Whittemore,
    1:322, 4:535
  Jane (----), 3:408
  Mary, 1:202, 1:322, 4:436
Butterworth
  Elizabeth, 1:323, 1:336
  Hannah (Wheaton), 1:323
  Jane, 4:395
  Mary, 1:323, 2:542
Buttolph
  Abigail, 1:158, 1:180,

1:323, 4:33
  Ann (----), 1:323
  Ann/Hannah (Gardner),
    1:323
  Hannah, 1:511
  Hannah (Gardner), 2:227
  Mary, 1:323, 2:276
  Mary (Baxter), 1:142,
    1:323
  Mehitable, 1:323
  Priscilla, 4:555
  Sarah (----), 1:511
  Susanna (----) Sandford,
    1:323, 4:15
Button
  Abigail, 1:324, 2:78, 3:119
  Abigail (Vermaes), 1:324,
    2:509, 4:372
  Eliphal, 1:324
  Elizabeth (Hall), 2:591
  Elizabeth (Wheeler), 4:497
  Grace (----), 1:324
  Hannah, 1:324
  Joan (----), 1:324
  Lettice (----), 1:324
  Mary, 1:324, 3:84
  Mary (----), 1:324
  Mary (Lamphear), 3:50
  Sarah, 1:324, 1:511, 3:28
Buttrick
  Abigail (White), 4:508
  Elizabeth (Hastings), 1:325,
    2:373
  Jane (----) Goodenow,
    1:324
  Mary, 1:324
  Sarah, 1:324
  Sarah (Bateman), 1:324
Buttry/Buttery/Buttress
  Elizabeth, 1:325
  Elizabeth (Knapp), 3:34
  Grace, 1:325, 2:396, 2:525
  Martha (----), 1:325
Buxton
  Abigail, 1:325
  Elizabeth, 1:325, 1:446
  Elizabeth (----), 1:325
  Elizabeth (Holton), 1:325
  Ester (----), 1:325
  Hannah, 1:325
  Lydia, 1:325
  Margaret, 1:329
  Mary, 1:325, 3:608, 3:612

  Mary (Small), 1:325
  Rachel, 1:325
  Sarah, 1:325
  Unity, 1:325
  Unity (----), 1:274, 1:325,
    3:34
Byam
  ---- (Winthrop), 4:611
  Abigail, 1:325
Byfield
  Deborah, 1:325, 3:133
  Deborah (Clark), 1:325,
    1:401
  Sarah (Leverett), 1:325,
    3:83
Byles
  Elizabeth, 3:608
  Elizabeth (Mather)
    Greenough, 1:326, 2:310,
    3:173
  Elizabeth (Patch), 3:368,
    3:608
  Margaret (Corey)
    Cleves/Cleaves, 1:410
  Martha, 3:608
  Mary, 3:608
  Mary (----), 3:608
  Sarah, 1:326, 3:608
  Sarah (----), 1:326
Byley
  Mary, 1:326, 2:77
  Rebecca, 1:326, 2:329
  Rebecca (----), 1:326,
    2:334, 4:246, 4:651
Byram
  ----, 1:326
  ---- (Keith), 1:326
  ---- (Shaw), 1:326
  Abigail, 1:326, 4:524
  Experience, 1:326, 4:575
  Mary, 1:326, 3:67
  Mary (Edson), 2:102
  Mary/Martha (Shaw), 4:63
  Susanna, 2:102
Bywell
  Margaret, 2:154
Cabell
  Ann (----) Betts, 1:173,
    1:327
Cabot
  Mary, 4:54
Cadd
  Mary (----), 1:511

Cadwell
Abigail, 1:328, 4:676-677
Abigail (Beckley), 1:327
Ann, 1:328
Elizabeth, 1:327-328,
4:676-677
Elizabeth (----), 1:327
Elizabeth (Butler), 4:676
Elizabeth (Stebbins)
Wilson, 1:328, 4:175,
4:588
Esther, 3:440
Hannah, 1:328, 4:677
Hannah (Butler), 1:328
Lois, 4:677
Mary, 1:328, 4:676
Mary (Clark), 4:676
Mehitable, 1:328
Rachel, 1:327
Cady/Cade
Abigail, 1:327
Abigail (----), 1:327
Elizabeth, 1:327
Elizabth (----), 1:327
Esther (Chandler), 1:327
Eunice, 1:327
Hannah (Barron), 1:126,
1:327
Jane, 1:327
Joanna, 1:327
Joanna (----), 1:327
Judith, 1:327
Judith (Knapp), 1:327,
3:34
Margaret (----), 1:327
Mary, 1:327
Mary (----), 1:327
Mary (Keyes), 1:327, 3:16
Mercy (Fuller), 1:327
Rachel, 1:327
Sarah, 1:405
Sarah (----), 1:327
Saray (King), 3:24
Caffinch
Elizabeth, 1:328
Mary, 1:328
Mary (Fowler), 1:328
Sarah, 1:328
Cakebread
Hepzibah, 3:608
Hepzibah (Jones), 1:328
Margaret, 3:608
Rebecca, 3:608

Sarah, 1:328, 4:493
Sarah (Busby), 1:316,
1:328, 2:319
Caldwell
Ann, 1:328
Elizabeth, 1:328
Margaret (----), 4:399
Mary, 1:328-329, 2:189
Sarah, 1:328-329
Sarah (Dillingham), 1:328,
2:50
Sarah (Foster), 1:329
Calef/Calfe
Ann, 1:329
Margaret, 1:329
Margaret (Bartlett), 1:134
Margaret (Buxton), 1:329
Martha, 1:329, 2:408
Mary, 1:329
Mary (----), 1:329, 1:383
Call
Bennet (----), 1:330
Elizabeth, 1:330, 1:511,
4:77, 4:305
Elizabeth (Croswell),
1:330
Esther, 1:329-330
Hannah, 1:329-330, 2:596
Hannah (Kettell), 1:329,
3:15
Joanna, 1:330
Joanna (----) Shepardson,
1:330, 4:77
Lydia, 1:511
Lydia (Shepardson), 1:330,
4:77
Margaret, 2:306
Martha (Lowden), 1:330,
3:126
Mary, 1:330, 1:511
Mehitable, 1:329, 3:504
Mercy, 1:330, 1:498,
1:511, 3:73
Temperance (----), 1:330
Temperance (Hurry),
1:511
Callender
Joanna, 1:330
Sarah (----), 1:330
Calley
Catharine (Gilman) Folsom,
2:258

Calloway
Judith (Clock), 1:330
Callum
Margaret (Bentley), 1:505
Calverly
Joan, 4:45
Cammock
Margaret (----), 1:331,
2:570
Camp/Kemp
---- (Beard), 3:602
Abigail, 1:331
Catharine (----) Thompson,
1:331, 4:283
Elizabeth (Smith), 1:331
Hannah, 1:331
Hannah (Betts), 1:331
Mary, 1:104, 1:256, 1:331,
4:688
Mary (Sanford), 1:331,
4:15
Mehitable (Smith), 1:331,
4:120
Sarah, 1:331
Campbell
Agnes, 1:331
Elizabeth, 1:331, 3:622
Mary, 1:331
Mary (----), 1:331
Sarah, 1:221
Susanna, 1:331
Susanna (----), 1:331
Campfield/Canfield
---- (Willoughby), 1:332,
4:579
Abigail, 4:677
Elizabeth, 1:105, 4:677
Elizabeth (Merwin), 3:201
Hannah, 1:332, 4:677
Judith (Mallory), 1:332
Mary, 1:332, 4:677
Mehitable, 4:677
Phebe, 4:123, 4:677
Phebe (----), 1:332, 4:677
Rachel, 1:332
Rebecca, 4:677
Rebecca (----), 4:677
Sarah, 1:332, 4:677
Sarah (Treat), 1:332, 4:326
Canada
Elizabeth, 3:608
Hannah, 3:608
Hannah (Cook), 3:608

Cande/Cambee/Kembee/etc
Abigail, 4:700
Desire, 4:700
Hannah, 4:700
Mary, 4:700
Rebecca, 4:700
Rebecca (Bristol), 3:606,
   3:608
Cane/Canne/Cann
Deborah, 1:328, 3:608
Deborah (Welsh), 1:328
Esther, 1:328
Esther (Reed), 1:332
Margaret (----), 3:608
Margery (----), 1:328
Mary (Parsons), 3:362
Ruth, 1:328
Canney
----, 1:332, 2:436
Esther (Read/Reed), 3:519
Jane, 1:332
Jane (----), 1:332
Mary, 1:332, 4:299
Mary (Clements), 1:332
Sarah (----), 1:332, 4:595
Canning
Ann, 3:404
Cannon
Catharine (Thornton),
   4:293
Canterbury/Cantlebury
Ann, 1:122, 1:333
Beatrice (----), 1:333,
   3:446
Mary, 1:333
Rebecca, 1:333, 4:642
Ruth, 1:333
Capen
---- (Purchis), 1:333
Ann, 1:334
Dorothy, 1:334, 4:361
Elizabeth, 1:333-334,
   4:241
Hannah, 1:333-334, 1:511
Hannah (----), 1:333
Hannah (Lawrence), 1:511
Joanna, 1:333
Mary, 1:333-334, 2:189
Mary (Bass), 1:133, 1:135
Mary (Payson), 1:334,
   3:373
Priscilla, 1:334
Priscilla (Appleton), 1:61,

1:334
Radigan (Clap), 1:333
Ruth, 1:333
Sarah, 1:333-334
Sarah (Trott), 1:333, 4:332
Susanna, 1:333-334
Susanna (Barsham), 1:333
Susanna (Payson), 1:334,
   3:373
Thankful, 1:333
Caper
Mary, 2:259
Capron
Elizabeth, 1:334
Elizabeth (----), 1:334
Sarah, 1:334
Card
Hannah, 3:608
Hannah (----) Coit, 3:608
Martha (Brenton), 1:242
Mary, 1:334, 3:608
Rebecca (----), 4:257
Ruth (Haven/Havens),
   2:379
Carder
----, 2:305
Bethia (----), 1:335
Hannah, 1:335
Martha (Brenton), 1:334
Mary, 1:335, 3:527
Mary (----), 1:335
Mary (Holden), 1:334,
   2:445
Mary (Whipple), 1:334
Sarah, 1:334-335, 2:282
Susanna, 4:432
Carew
---- (Inglefield), 3:627
Carey
Sarah, 2:546
Carkeet/Karkeet/etc
Lydia (----), 3:31
Carleton/Carlton
Abigail (Osgood), 1:335
Hannah (----), 1:86
Hannah (Jewett), 1:511,
   2:598
Hannah (Osgood), 1:335
Prudence (----) Crosby,
   1:335, 1:476
Carlile
Hannah, 1:335
Hannah (----), 1:335

Carman
Abigail, 1:335, 1:417
Florence (----), 1:335
Carnes
Elizabeth, 1:335
Mary (Brown), 1:335
Carpenter
----, 1:337, 4:308
Abiah, 1:337
Abigail, 1:336-338
Abigail (----), 1:337
Agnes, 2:585
Alice, 1:231, 2:585, 4:143
Amy, 1:337
Bethia (Bliss), 1:336
Deliverance (Preston),
   1:337
Dorothy, 1:336
Elizabeth, 1:336
Elizabeth (----), 1:280,
   3:317
Elizabeth (Arnold), 1:338
Elizabeth (Butterworth),
   1:336
Elizabeth (Read), 1:336
Esther, 1:336
Hannah, 1:336-338
Hannah (----), 1:336
Hannah (Burton), 1:315
Hannah (Strong),
   1:335-336
Julian, 3:244
Lydia, 1:338, 4:110, 4:125
Margaret, 1:336-337
Margaret (Hunt), 1:336
Margaret (Sabin), 1:336
Marian, 1:337
Martha, 1:336-337
Mary, 1:336-337
Mary (----), 1:231
Mary (Bacon), 1:337
Mary (Cooper), 1:337
Mary (Hyde), 1:336
Mary (Preston), 1:337
Mary (Tillinghast), 4:303
Miriam, 1:201, 1:338
Miriam (Searle), 1:338
Priscilla, 1:336-338, 4:239,
   4:374
Priscilla (Bonett), 1:338
Rachel (Cooper), 1:337
Rebecca (----), 1:336
Renew (Weeks), 1:335,

Carpenter (continued)
  Renew (Weeks)
  (continued)
    4:454
  Ruth (Follet), 1:337
  Sarah, 1:336-337, 3:400
  Sarah (----), 1:260
  Sarah (Hough), 1:336,
    2:469
  Sarah (Johnson), 1:337
  Sarah (Readaway), 1:337,
    3:522
  Submit, 1:335
  Susanna, 1:64, 1:338
  Tabitha (Bishop), 1:337
Carr
  Ann, 1:338-339, 3:497,
    4:677, 4:697
  Ann (Cotton), 1:464
  Avis, 1:338
  Catharine, 1:339
  Dorothy (----), 1:339
  Elizabeth, 1:338-339,
    4:641
  Elizabeth (----), 1:338-339
  Elizabeth (Pike), 1:339,
    3:437
  Hannah, 1:255, 1:338-339
  Hannah (----), 1:338
  Hepzibah, 1:339
  Jane, 1:339
  Joanna, 1:408
  Margaret, 1:339
  Mary, 1:94, 1:142,
    1:338-339
  Mary (Sears), 1:339
  Mercy, 1:338
  Mercy (----), 1:338
  Patience, 1:338
  Phebe, 1:338
  Rebecca, 1:339
  Rebecca (Nicholson),
    1:339, 3:283
  Sarah, 1:338-339
  Sarah (----), 1:338
  Sarah (Clark), 1:394
  Sarah (Healey), 1:339
  Wait (Easton), 1:339, 2:94
Carrier
  Elizabeth (Sessions), 1:339
  Martha (Allen), 1:339
  Sarah, 1:339, 2:177

Carrington
  Elizabeth, 1:339-340
  Elizabeth (----), 1:339
  Hannah, 1:340
  Joan (----), 1:340
  Mary, 1:340, 4:154
  Mary (Higginson), 3:632
  Sarah, 1:339
  Sarah (Higginson), 3:632
Carroll
  Catharine, 1:340
  Mary, 1:511
  Mary (----), 1:511
Carrow
  Martha (Offitt), 3:305
Carsley - see Kerley
Carter
  ----, 1:359
  ---- (----), 2:566, 3:143
  Abigail, 1:340-342, 3:608,
    3:621, 4:123
  Abigail (Damon), 1:512
  Ann, 1:341-342, 2:192
  Ann (----), 1:341, 2:283
  Ann (Banister), 1:113
  Ann (Fiske), 1:342
  Bethia, 1:340
  Bethia (----), 1:340
  Bethia (Cowdry), 1:512
  Bethia (Pearson), 3:378
  Catharine (----), 1:238,
    1:340, 4:559
  Deborah, 1:342
  Elizabeth, 1:340-342,
    1:516
  Elizabeth (----), 1:340
  Elizabeth (Johnson), 1:512
  Elizabeth (White), 1:342
  Esther, 1:340
  Esther (----), 1:342
  Eunice, 1:341
  Eunice (Brooks), 1:341,
    3:9
  Faith, 1:340
  Hannah, 1:340-341, 1:444
  Hannah (Fiske), 2:165
  Hannah (Gookin), 2:280
  Judith, 1:341-342, 1:444,
    2:158
  Margaret (Whitmore),
    1:342, 4:526
  Martha, 1:342
  Martha (----), 1:340

  Mary, 1:88, 1:340-342,
    1:466, 2:502, 3:504,
    3:608, 3:621, 4:413,
    4:664
  Mary (----), 1:342
  Mary (Dalton), 1:341
  Mary (Field), 1:340, 2:157
  Mary (Tuttle), 1:340,
    4:350
  Phebe, 1:340
  Ruth (Burnham), 1:340
  Sarah, 1:341-342, 2:19
  Sarah (----) Brown, 1:266
  Sarah (Stowers), 1:512
  Susanna, 1:340
  Winifred (----), 1:512
Carteret
  ---- (----) Lawrence, 3:63
Carthrick
  Mildred, 1:251, 1:343
  Sarah (----), 1:343
Cartwright
  Elinor, 1:343
  Elizabeth (Morris), 1:343
  Elizabeth (Trott), 4:677
  Hope, 1:343
  Lydia, 1:343
  Mary, 1:343
  Orange (Rogers), 4:677
  Sarah, 1:343
  Susanna, 1:343
Carver
  Ann, 1:344
  Catharine (----), 1:343
  Elizabeth, 1:343-344
  Elizabeth (Foster), 1:344
  Experience (Blake), 1:194
  Experience (Sumner),
    4:232
  Grace (----), 1:344
  Mary, 1:343
  Mary (----), 1:343
  Mehitable, 1:344
  Mellicent (Ford), 1:343,
    2:71, 2:184
  Mercy, 1:344
  Susanna, 1:344
Carwithen/Carwithey/etc
  Elizabeth, 1:344
  Elizabeth (----), 3:253
  Elizabeth (Farnum), 1:344,
    1:512, 2:142
  Frances (----) Oldham,

56

Carwithen/Carwithey/etc
(continued)
Frances (----) Oldham
(continued)
1:344
Grace (----), 1:344
Cary
Abigail, 1:512
Abigail (Allen), 1:35,
1:345
Eleanor, 1:512
Elinor (----), 1:344
Elizabeth, 1:243,
1:344-345
Elizabeth (----), 1:345
Elizabeth (Godfrey), 1:344,
2:266
Freelove, 1:345
Hannah, 1:344
Hannah (----), 3:608
Hannah (Brett), 1:243
Hannah (Winsor), 1:345
Martha, 1:345
Mary, 1:344-345, 4:524
Mehitable, 1:344, 4:482
Rebecca, 1:344
Sarah, 1:344, 2:364
Case
Abigail, 1:345-346
Amy, 1:346
Amy (Reed), 1:346
Ann (Eno), 1:346
Elizabeth, 1:345-346,
2:315, 3:88, 4:342
Elizabeth (Holcomb),
1:346
Elizabeth (Moore) Loomis,
1:345, 3:113
Elizabeth (Owen) Thrall,
1:346
Elizabeth (Purchase),
1:346, 3:494
Elizabeth (Stafford), 4:160
Eunice, 1:346
Hannah, 1:346
Irene (----), 1:346
Lydia, 1:346
Margaret, 1:346
Mary, 1:24, 1:345-346,
2:422, 3:659, 4:660
Mary (----)
Mecock/Maycock/etc,
3:193

Mary (Humphrey), 1:345
Mary (Olcott), 1:345
Mary (Starkey), 1:512
Mary (Westover), 1:346
Mercy, 1:346
Mindwell, 1:346
Patience (Draper), 1:345
Rachel, 1:346
Sarah, 1:345-346, 3:406
Sarah (Holcomb), 1:346
Sarah (Spencer), 1:345,
4:150
Cash
Ann, 1:347
Elizabeth, 1:347, 4:253
Elizabeth (Lambert), 1:347
Esther, 1:347
Mary, 1:347, 3:190
Ruth, 1:347
Sarah, 1:347
Caskin
Phebe, 1:347
Sarah, 1:347
Casley
---- (----), 3:288
Cass
Abigail, 1:347
Elizabeth (Green) Chase,
1:347
Martha, 1:347, 3:522
Martha (Philbrick), 1:347,
3:408-409
Mary, 1:347
Mary (Hobbs), 1:347
Mary (Sanborn), 1:347
Mercy, 1:347
Patience (Draper), 2:71
Cassell
Mary, 1:405
Castine/Caustine
Isabel (----), 1:347
Lydia, 1:348
Mary (----), 1:348
Castle
Mary, 4:682
Mary (Stowers), 1:348,
4:219-220
Caswell/Casewell/Cassell
Abigail, 1:348
Elizabeth, 1:348, 3:80
Elizabeth (Hall), 1:512
Esther, 1:348
Hannah (Thrasher), 1:348

Mary, 1:348, 4:294
Sarah, 1:348, 2:466
Cate
Rebecca, 4:362
Catlin/Catling
Alice (----), 1:349, 4:280
Elizabeth, 1:349, 1:459
Elizabeth (Norton), 1:512
Hannah, 4:677
Isabel (----), 1:103, 1:349,
3:289
Mary, 1:348-349, 2:208
Mary (Baldwin), 1:103
Mary (Marshall), 1:348,
3:158-159
Caulkins/Calkin/Cawkin
Abigail, 1:350
Abigail (Birchard), 1:350
Ann, 1:181, 1:349
Ann (----), 1:349
Deborah, 1:349, 3:529,
3:569
Elizabeth, 1:349-350
Hannah, 1:350
Hannah (Gifford), 1:350
Lydia, 1:349
Mary, 1:349-350, 3:546
Mary (Bliss), 1:349
Rebecca, 1:349
Ruth, 1:350
Sarah, 1:105, 1:349-350,
2:469
Sarah (Royce), 1:349,
3:570
Sarah (Sluman), 1:349
Cave
Abigail, 3:609
Ann, 3:609
Elizabeth, 2:87
Hannah, 3:609
Mary (Nichols), 3:609,
3:656
Sarah, 3:609
Cawly
Mary (Parmenter), 1:350
Center
Elinor, 1:350
Mary (----), 1:350
Ruth, 1:350
Ruth (----), 1:350, 4:658
Sarah, 1:350
Chadbourne
Lucy (Treworgy), 1:350,

Chadbourne (continued)
Lucy (Treworgy)
  (continued)
  4:330, 4:579
Mary, 1:350
Mary (----), 1:350
Patience, 4:149
Chadwell
Abigail (----) Jones, 1:512,
  2:566
Ann, 1:351
Barbara (----) Davis
  Brimblecom, 1:351, 2:17
Catharine (----) Presbury,
  1:351
Elizabeth, 1:350
Elizabeth (----), 1:350,
  2:548
Elizabeth (Hawes), 1:512
Lois, 1:350
Margaret, 1:351
Margaret (----), 1:351
Mary, 1:350
Ruth, 2:367, 3:265
Sarah, 1:350
Sarah (Ivory), 1:350, 1:475,
  2:526
Susanna, 2:280
Chadwick
Abigail, 1:351
Elizabeth, 1:351, 1:502,
  2:416, 4:649
Elizabeth (----), 1:351,
  2:197
Hannah, 1:351
Hannah (Butler), 1:351
Jemima, 1:351
Joan (----), 1:351
Lydia, 1:351
Martha, 1:351
Mary, 1:351
Mary (Stocker), 1:351
Sarah, 1:351, 2:321
Sarah (----), 1:351
Sarah (Whitney), 4:532
Sarah (Wolcot), 1:351
Chaffee/Chaffy/Chaffin
Dorothy, 1:351
Elizabeth (Adams), 1:14,
  1:351
Experience, 1:352
Experience (----), 1:352
Mary, 1:351

Rachel, 1:352
Sarah (----), 1:352
Chalice/Challis/Chellis
Elizabeth, 1:352, 4:19
Hannah, 1:352
Lydia, 1:352
Mary, 1:352, 4:19
Mary (Sargent), 1:352,
  4:19
Chalker
Catharine, 1:352
Catharine (----), 2:417
Catharine (Post), 1:352,
  3:465
Hannah, 1:352
Hannah (Sanford), 1:352,
  4:16
Jane, 1:352
Mary, 1:352, 1:460-461
Mehitable, 1:352
Phebe, 1:352
Phebe (Bull), 1:294, 1:352
Ruth, 1:352
Sarah, 1:352
Sarah (Ingham), 1:352
Chalkley/Chaulkey
Elizabeth (----), 1:352
Chamberlain/Chamberlin
Abigail (----), 1:354
Ann, 1:353-354
Ann (Brown), 1:353
Catharine (----), 1:353
Deborah, 1:353
Deborah (----), 1:353
Deborah (Templar), 1:512,
  4:266
Elizabeth, 1:353-354,
  4:515
Elizabeth (Bartholomew),
  1:353
Elizabeth (Hammond),
  1:354
Experience (----), 1:353
Hannah, 1:353, 1:512
Hannah (----), 1:353
Hannah (Burden), 1:353
Jane, 1:353-354
Jane (----), 1:353
Joanna, 1:354
Joanna (----), 1:353
Mary, 1:352-354, 2:295
Mary (----), 1:354
Mary (Child), 1:353

Mary (Graves), 1:354
Mary (Parker), 1:354
Mary (Randall), 3:506
Mary (Turner), 1:352
Mehitable, 1:354
Mercy (----) Abbot, 1:353
Mercy (Dickinson), 1:354,
  2:48
Rebecca, 1:354, 4:62
Rebecca (----), 1:354
Sarah, 1:352-354, 2:19,
  4:68
Sarah (Bugby), 1:289,
  1:354
Sarah (Faxon) Weld, 4:458
Sarah (Proctor), 1:354
Susanna, 1:353, 4:340
Ursula, 1:353
Chambers
Margaret (Vaughan),
  4:369
Champernoon
Mary (----) Cutts, 1:355,
  1:495
Champion
Deborah (----, 1:355
Hannah (Brockway),
  1:258, 1:355
Mary, 1:355
Sarah, 1:167, 1:355
Susanna (DeWolf), 1:355
Champlin
Ann, 1:355
Elizabeth (----) Davoll,
  1:355, 2:579
Mary, 1:355
Mary (Babcock), 1:86,
  1:355
Sarah (Brown), 1:267
Champney
---- (----), 1:126
Abigail, 1:356
Deborah, 1:356
Dorcas, 1:222, 1:356
Dorcas (Bridge), 1:248,
  1:356
Esther, 1:356, 1:444
Hepzibah, 1:356
Hepzibah (Corlet) Minot,
  1:356, 1:458, 3:217
Jane (----), 1:356
Joan (----), 1:356, 3:227
Lydia, 1:356, 2:373

58

Champney (continued)
Margaret (----), 1:356
Mary, 1:356, 2:205, 3:538
Ruth (Michelson) Green,
2:303, 3:609
Sarah, 1:126, 1:356, 1:394,
3:454, 3:591
Sarah (----), 1:356
Sarah (Hubbard), 1:356,
2:484
Chandler
---- (Carter), 1:359
---- (Lord), 1:359, 3:116
Abiel, 1:357
Abigail, 1:357-358
Ann, 1:356
Ann/Hannah/Annis (----),
2:6, 3:360
Annis, 1:358
Annis (----), 1:359
Bridget, 1:357, 1:359
Bridget (Henchman)
Richardson, 1:359, 3:536
Deborah, 1:357
Dorcas, 1:358
Dorothy, 1:358
Elinor, 1:359
Elinor (Phelps), 1:359
Elizabeth, 1:357-359,
3:169
Elizabeth (Buck), 1:356
Elizabeth (Douglas), 1:357,
2:63
Esther, 1:327, 1:359
Esther (----) Alcock, 1:357
Eunice, 1:358
Hannah, 1:2, 1:188,
1:357-359, 2:71, 3:360
Hannah (----), 1:359
Hannah (Abbot), 1:2,
1:357
Hannah (Brewer), 1:358
Hannah (Clary), 1:358
Hannah (Huntington),
1:359
Hepzibah, 1:358
Jemima, 1:358
Lydia, 1:357-358, 2:412
Lydia (Abbot), 1:3, 1:357
Martha, 1:356
Mary, 1:57, 1:232,
1:356-359, 2:6, 3:126,
4:86

Mary (----), 1:359
Mary (Dane), 1:359, 2:6
Mary (Hall), 1:358
Mary (Lord), 1:359
Mary (Peters), 1:358,
3:401
Mary (Raymond), 1:357
Mary (Simonds), 1:358
Mary (Stevens), 1:359
Mehitable, 1:357-358,
1:422
Mehitable (Russell), 1:357
Mercy (Perkins), 1:358
Patience (----) Griggs,
1:358
Phebe, 1:357-359
Rhoda, 1:358-359
Ruth, 1:356
Sarah, 1:356-359, 1:409,
1:423, 3:360, 3:407,
4:130
Sarah (----) Davis, 1:358
Sarah (Abbot), 1:5, 1:358
Sarah (Buckmaster), 1:359
Sarah (Burrill) Davis,
1:309, 2:21
Susanna, 1:358
Susanna (Perrin), 1:358
Chanterel/Cantrel/Chantrel
Emma, 1:513
Mary, 1:513, 3:159
Mary (----), 1:513
Chapin
Abilene (Coley), 1:432
Abilene (Cooley), 1:360
Bethia, 4:677
Bethia (Cooley), 1:360,
1:453
Catharine, 1:201, 1:360,
2:251, 3:160
Cicely (----), 1:360
Dorothy (Root), 1:360
Hannah, 1:359-360, 2:428,
4:677
Hannah (Sheldon), 1:360,
4:69
Lydia, 1:359-360
Lydia (Crump), 1:360
Mary, 1:13, 1:360, 4:655
Mary (----), 1:360
Mary (Read/Reed), 3:518
Sarah, 1:360, 4:282, 4:677
Sarah (----), 1:359

Sarah (Wright), 4:654
Susanna, 3:558
Union, 4:677
Chapleman
Rebecca, 3:609
Rebecca (Needham), 3:609,
3:655
Chaplin/Chaplain
Ann, 2:263
Elizabeth (----), 1:360
Elizabeth (West), 1:361
Mary (----), 1:513
Sarah (Hinds), 1:360
Chapman
Abiel, 1:363
Abigail, 1:361, 1:363
Ann, 1:361-362
Ann (Bliss), 1:202, 1:362
Betty, 1:513
Dorcas, 1:362
Dorothy, 4:640
Dorothy (Swain) Abbot,
1:361, 4:235
Elizabeth, 1:361, 1:363,
2:576
Elizabeth (----), 1:362,
1:478
Elizabeth
(Beamond/Beamon),
1:147, 1:361
Elizabeth (Fox), 1:361
Elizabeth (Hawley), 1:361,
2:384
Esther (Selden), 4:50
Florence (----), 1:362
Hannah, 1:292, 1:361-362,
1:513
Hannah (----) Stearns,
4:174
Hannah (Bates), 1:362
Hannah (Grant), 1:513
Joan (----), 1:362
Lydia, 1:361-362, 2:50
Lydia (Gilbert) Richardson,
2:250
Lydia (Willis), 1:362
Lydia (Wills), 1:362
Margaret, 1:361, 1:504
Martha (----), 1:266, 1:361
Mary, 1:139, 1:170,
1:361-362, 1:513, 4:331
Mary (----), 1:362
Mary (----) Sheather, 1:362,

Chapman (continued)
Mary (----) Sheather
(continued)
4:67
Mary (Collins), 1:361
Mary (Symonds), 1:361,
4:246
Mehitable, 1:361-363
Mercy, 1:363
Rachel (Ingersoll), 2:520
Rebecca, 1:361, 1:363
Rebecca (Leonard), 1:361
Rebecca (Smith), 1:361
Sarah, 1:361-363, 1:513,
3:287, 3:474
Sarah (Griswold), 1:362,
2:590
Sarah (Mirick), 1:513
Susan, 1:362
Chappel/Chappell
Christian, 1:364
Christian (----), 1:363,
4:161
Elizabeth, 1:363
Esther, 1:363
Margery (----), 1:363
Mary, 1:363-364, 2:9
Rachel, 1:363
Sarah, 1:363
Chard
Elizabeth (Pratt), 1:364
Grace (----), 1:364
Joanna, 1:364
Mary, 1:364
Mary (----), 1:364
Patience, 1:364
Charles
----, 4:677, 4:698
Hannah, 4:677
Hannah (----), 4:677
Mary, 4:300, 4:677, 4:710
Sarah, 1:364, 4:674, 4:677
Sarah (----), 1:364, 3:609
Charlett
Catharine (----), 1:364,
2:378
Elizabeth, 1:364
Mary, 1:364
Chase
Abigail, 1:364
Abigail (Shearman), 4:704
Ann, 1:114, 1:364-365
Ann (----), 3:258

Ann (Follansbee), 1:365
Ann (Wheeler), 1:364,
4:497
Dorothy, 1:365
Elizabeth, 1:85, 1:95,
1:364-365
Elizabeth (Baker), 1:95
Elizabeth (Bingley), 1:180,
1:365
Elizabeth (Green), 1:347
Elizabeth (Mooers), 1:365
Elizabeth (Philbrick),
1:365, 2:232, 3:409,
3:548
Esther, 1:364
Esther (Bond), 1:209,
1:364
Hannah, 1:364-365
Hannah (Carpenter), 1:338
Jemima, 1:364
Judith, 1:365
Lydia, 1:365
Lydia (----), 1:365
Martha, 1:364
Martha (Kimball), 1:364
Mary, 1:364-365, 4:187
Mary (----), 1:365
Mary (Knowles), 3:42
Mary (Perkins), 1:365,
3:395
Mehitable, 1:365
Phebe, 1:365
Priscilla, 1:364-365, 3:199
Rachel, 1:365
Rachel (Partridge), 1:365,
3:367
Rebecca, 1:364-365
Rebecca (Follansbee),
1:365, 2:178
Ruth, 1:364-365
Sarah, 1:59, 1:364-365
Sarah (Jacobs), 1:365
Chatfield
Abigail, 1:366
Alister, 1:366
Ann (Higginson), 1:366,
2:413
Esther, 1:366
Esther (Hall), 1:366
Isabel (Nettleton), 1:366
Mary, 1:366
Mercy, 1:366
Naomi, 1:366

Sarah (Bishop), 1:366
Chatterton
Hannah, 4:677
Mary, 4:677
Mary (----), 4:676
Mary (Clark), 4:677-678
Mary (Clemence), 4:677
Mercy, 4:677
Sarah, 4:677
Susanna, 4:677
Chatwell
Hannah, 3:609
Mary, 3:609
Prisca, 3:609
Sarah (----) March, 3:609
Chauncy
Abiah, 1:513
Abigail, 1:369
Abigail (Strong), 1:369,
3:452, 4:227
Ann, 1:369
Catharine, 1:243, 1:369
Catharine (Eyre), 1:367
Elizabeth, 1:368
Elizabeth (----), 1:513
Hannah, 1:368
Mary, 1:368, 3:112, 4:400
Mary (Nichols), 1:368,
3:280
Sarah, 1:290, 1:367, 1:369
Sarah (Burr), 1:307, 1:368
Sarah (Hodshon), 1:368,
2:440
Sarah (Walley), 1:368,
4:400
Sarah (Wolcott), 1:368
Thomasine (----), 1:368
Cheater
Alice (----), 1:369, 2:323
Hannah, 1:369
Lydia, 1:369
Checkley
Ann, 1:369-370
Ann (Eyre), 1:369,
2:133-134
Elizabeth, 1:369-370,
3:109
Elizabeth (----), 1:370
Elizabeth (Rolfe), 1:370
Hannah, 1:12, 1:369
Hannah (Wheelwright),
1:369, 2:512, 4:503
Lydia, 1:369

60

Checkley (continued)
Lydia (Scottow) Gibbs,
1:369, 2:246, 4:40
Mary, 1:369-370
Mary (Scottow), 1:369,
4:40
Rebecca, 1:369-370
Rebecca (Miller), 1:369
Sarah, 1:369
Chedsey/Chidsey
Abigail, 1:370
Ann (Thompson), 1:370
Dinah, 1:370
Elizabeth, 1:234, 1:370
Elizabeth (----), 1:370
Hannah, 1:370
Hannah (Dickerman),
1:370, 4:680
Mary, 1:370
Priscilla (Thompson),
1:370, 4:286
Rachel, 1:370
Sarah, 1:41, 1:370
Sarah (----), 1:370
Sarah (Hull), 4:678
Cheeny
Mary, 2:442
Cheever
Abigail, 1:371, 3:609
Abigail (Leffingwell),
3:609
Elizabeth, 1:370-371,
2:270, 3:342, 3:609
Elizabeth (Warren), 1:372
Ellen (Lothrop), 1:371,
2:289
Esther, 1:371
Esther (----), 1:371
Hannah, 1:371
Lydia, 1:370-371
Lydia (Barrett), 1:370
Lydia (Haley), 1:513,
2:591, 4:700
Mary, 1:370-371, 3:85,
3:89, 4:702
Mary (Bordman), 1:372
Ruth (Angier), 1:58, 1:371
Sarah, 1:370-371
Susanna, 1:371
Chenery
Sarah (----) Boylston,
1:226

Chenevard
Margaret (Beauchamp),
1:150
Cheney
Abiel, 1:373
Abigail, 1:373
Dorothy (Hawley), 2:384
Elinor, 1:372, 4:61
Elinor (Woodhouse), 4:639
Elizabeth, 1:372
Ellen, 2:551, 4:678
Hannah, 1:372-373
Hannah (Noyes), 1:372,
3:298
Hannah (Woods), 1:373
Hulda/Huldah, 1:372,
4:651
Jane, 1:159, 1:373
Jane (Atkinson), 1:372
Jemima, 1:372, 3:403
Judith, 1:372
Margaret, 1:372-373,
2:374, 4:678
Margaret (----), 1:373
Martha, 1:316, 1:372, 4:3
Martha (----), 1:372
Mary, 1:372, 4:650
Mary (Plummer), 1:372,
3:446
Mehitable, 1:373
Melicent, 1:373
Rebecca, 1:373
Rebecca (Newell), 1:373,
3:271
Sarah, 1:372, 3:446
Sarah (----), 1:372
Sarah (Bayley), 1:372
Cheny
Lydia, 3:11
Mary, 3:19
Cherrall
Ursula (----), 1:373
Chesebrough/Cheesbrook/etc
Abigail, 1:373-374
Abigail (----), 1:373
Ann, 1:373-374
Ann (Stevenson), 1:374
Bridget, 1:373
Elizabeth, 1:373
Hannah, 1:373-374
Hannah (Denison), 1:373
Margaret, 1:373
Martha, 1:374

Mary, 1:373-374
Mary (----), 1:374
Mary (McDowell), 1:374
Mary (Minor), 1:373
Priscilla, 1:374
Priscilla (Alden), 1:374
Prudence, 1:374
Rebecca (----), 1:103
Rebecca (Palmer), 1:373,
3:342
Sarah, 1:373-374, 2:223
Sarah (Stanton), 1:373
Chesholme/Chisholm/etc
Isabel (----), 1:374
Chesley
Elizabeth, 1:375
Elizabeth (----), 1:375
Elizabeth (Leighton)
Cromwell, 1:375, 3:44
Elizabeth (Thomas), 1:375
Esther, 1:375
Hannah, 1:375
Joanna (----), 1:375
Mary, 1:375, 2:337
Sarah, 1:375
Sarah (----), 1:375
Susanna, 1:375
Thomasin (Wentworth),
2:387
Chester
---- (Stebbins), 4:175
Dorcas, 1:375, 4:521
Dorothy (Hooker), 1:375
Elizabeth (Pitman), 1:513
Eunice, 1:375, 4:155,
4:189
Hannah, 1:376
Hannah (----), 1:376
Hannah (Talcott), 4:251
Jemima (Treat), 4:325
Mary, 1:375, 4:622
Mary (----), 1:376, 1:438,
3:594
Mary (Treat), 4:327
Mary (Wade) Sharpe,
1:375
Mercy, 1:375-376
Prudence, 1:375, 3:594,
4:326
Sarah, 1:375, 4:623
Sarah (Welles), 1:375,
4:478
Susanna, 1:376

Chichester
---- (Porter), 1:376, 3:462
Elizabeth, 1:376
Martha, 1:376
Mary, 1:376, 3:609, 3:651
Mary (----), 1:376
Sarah, 1:376
Susanna, 1:376
Chick
---- (Spencer), 4:149
Chickering
Abigail, 1:377
Ann, 1:376-377, 3:336
Ann (----), 1:376
Ann (Fiske), 1:376
Bethia, 1:376, 3:276
Catharine, 1:376-377,
  1:513
Deborah (Wright), 1:377
Elizabeth, 1:376-377
Elizabeth (----), 2:297
Elizabeth (Hagborne),
  1:376-377
Esther, 1:376, 4:111
Lydia, 1:377
Lydia (Fisher), 1:377,
  2:162
Mary, 1:376-377, 3:202
Mary (Judson), 1:377
Mary (Thorpe), 1:377
Mercy, 1:376, 4:72
Prudence, 1:377
Sarah (----) Sibley, 1:376
Sarah (How) Sibly, 1:224
Susanna (----), 1:377
Susanna (Symmes), 1:513
Chidester
Mabel (Tuller), 4:342
Child/Childs
Abigail, 1:378
Ann, 1:378
Catharine (----), 3:45
Eleanor, 3:489
Elizabeth, 1:175,
  1:377-379
Elizabeth (----), 1:210
Elizabeth (----) Palmer,
  1:377
Elizabeth (Bond) Palmer,
  1:378
Elizabeth (Crocker), 1:379
Elizabeth (Morris), 1:378,
  3:235

Experience, 1:378, 2:171
Grace, 1:377
Grace (Morris), 1:377,
  3:235
Hannah, 1:378-379
Hannah (French), 2:208
Hannah (Train), 1:378,
  4:321
Lydia, 1:378
Margaret, 1:377-378,
  3:484
Martha, 1:377
Martha (----), 1:378
Mary, 1:353, 1:377-378
Mary (----), 1:377-378
Mary (Linnell), 1:378,
  3:97
Mary (Truant), 1:378
Mary (Warren), 1:378,
  2:167, 4:423
Mehitable, 1:377-378
Mehitable (Dimick), 1:378
Mercy, 1:379
Prudence, 1:378
Rebecca, 1:378
Ruth, 2:522
Ruth (----) Maddock, 1:378
Ruth (Church) Maddocks,
  3:142
Sarah, 1:378, 2:531
Sarah (----), 2:342
Sarah (Norcross), 1:378,
  3:287
Sarah (Platts), 1:378
Thankful, 1:379
Chillingworth
Elizabeth, 1:379
Jane (----), 1:379
Joan/Jane (----), 2:2
Mary, 1:379, 2:189
Mehitable, 1:379, 2:90
Sarah, 1:379, 4:156
Chilson/Chilstone
Sarah, 1:379
Sarah (Jenks), 1:379,
  2:543
Chilton
Mary, 1:379, 4:195, 4:601
Chin
Rebecca (Merritt), 3:200
Chipman
Bethia, 1:380
Deborah, 1:380

Desire, 1:380
Elizabeth, 1:380, 2:573
Hannah, 1:380, 2:487
Hannah (Fessenden),
  2:583
Hope, 1:380, 2:487
Hope (Howland), 1:380,
  2:480
Lydia, 1:380, 4:17
Mary, 1:380, 4:706
Mercy, 1:380
Rebecca, 1:380
Ruth, 1:380, 1:474
Ruth (Sargent) Winslow
  Bourne, 4:19
Sarah, 1:380
Sarah (Cobb), 1:380,
  1:413
Chittenden
Abigail, 1:381
Alethia, 1:381
Deborah, 1:381-382
Deborah (Baker), 1:98,
  1:381
Elizabeth, 1:381-382,
  4:660
Elizabeth (Stevens), 4:189
Hannah, 1:381-382
Hannah (Fletcher), 1:381,
  2:173
Joan (Sheaffe), 1:382
Joanna, 1:381-382
Joanna (----), 1:481
Joanna (Jordan), 1:381
Lydia, 1:381
Mary, 1:381-382, 3:75
Mary (Vinal), 1:381, 4:373
Mehitable, 1:381
Mehitable (Buck), 1:284
Mehitable (Bush), 1:381
Rebecca, 1:381
Rebecca (----), 1:381
Ruth, 1:381
Sarah, 1:381, 1:432
Sarah (----), 1:381
Susanna, 1:381
Chitwood
Grace, 1:291
Choate
Abigail, 1:383
Ann, 1:383
Ann (----), 1:382
Dorothy, 1:382

Choate (continued)
Elizabeth (Giddings),
1:382
Elizabeth (Graves), 1:382
Hannah (----) Burnham,
1:383
Margaret, 1:382
Mary, 1:382-383
Mary (----) Calef, 1:383
Mary (Varney), 1:383
Mary (Williams), 1:383
Mercy (Varney), 4:366
Prudence (Marshall),
1:382
Rachel, 1:383
Rebecca (----), 1:383
Sarah, 1:382-383
Sarah (Perkins), 1:382
Christophers/Christopher
----, 1:383
Ann (----), 1:384
Catharine, 4:678
Deborah, 1:384
Elizabeth, 4:678
Elizabeth (Brewster)
Bradley, 1:234, 1:383
Elizabeth (Mulford), 1:383
Elizabeth (Saltonstall),
4:678
Grace, 4:678
Grace (Turner), 1:383
Joanna, 1:383, 3:184,
4:678
Lucretia, 4:678
Lucretia (Bradley), 1:234,
1:383
Lydia, 1:384, 4:678
Margaret, 1:383, 1:460,
4:678
Mary, 1:234, 1:383, 4:678
Mary (----), 1:383
Ruth, 4:678
Sarah (----), 4:678
Chubb
Hannah, 1:3
Hannah (Faulkner), 1:384,
2:148
Chubbuck
---- (----) Garnet, 1:384,
2:233
Alice, 1:384
Alice (----), 1:384
Martha, 1:384

Martha (Beal), 1:146,
1:384, 4:203
Mary, 1:384, 3:95
Mary (----) Gardner, 2:228
Rebecca, 1:384, 2:593
Sarah, 1:384, 2:168
Church
Abigail, 1:385-386, 4:275
Abigail (Cadwell),
4:676-677
Abigail (Severance), 1:385
Abigail (Strong), 4:228
Alice, 1:385, 3:609
Alice (Southworth), 1:384,
4:143
Ann, 1:385
Ann (----), 1:386
Deborah, 1:385-386, 2:525
Deliverance, 1:385
Elizabeth, 1:384-385,
1:513, 2:432
Elizabeth (----), 3:114
Elizabeth (Warren), 1:386,
4:427
Hannah, 1:386
Hepzibah, 1:385, 4:149
Joanna (Sprague), 1:385,
4:156
Judith (----), 1:118
Lydia, 1:385, 2:374
Mary, 1:385-386, 2:294,
3:593, 4:133, 4:678
Mary (----), 1:385
Mary (Churchill),
1:386-387
Mary (Tucker), 1:385,
2:558, 4:338
Naomi, 1:207
Priscilla, 1:386, 2:525
Rebecca, 1:385-386, 4:50,
4:426
Rebecca (Shattuck), 1:386,
4:62
Ruth, 1:385, 3:142
Sarah, 1:385, 4:687
Sarah (----), 1:385
Sarah (Barstow), 1:129,
1:385
Sarah (Beckley), 1:151,
1:385
Churchill/Churchall/etc
Abigail, 1:386
Ann, 1:387

Desire (Holmes), 2:452
Elizabeth, 1:284, 1:387
Elizabeth (Foote), 1:387,
2:180
Hannah, 1:386-387
Hannah (Pontus), 1:386,
3:454, 3:540
Joanna, 1:386
Lydia, 1:387
Lydia (Bryant), 1:387
Margaret, 1:387
Mary, 1:386-387, 2:34
Mary (----), 1:386-387
Mary (----) Dotey, 1:386
Prudence, 1:386, 2:274
Rebecca, 1:387
Rebecca (Delano), 1:387
Sarah, 1:387
Sarah (Hicks), 1:387
Churchman
Ann, 1:387, 3:561
Hannah, 1:513
Churchwood
Hannah, 1:387, 3:570
Chute
---- (Epes), 1:387
Ann, 1:387
Elizabeth, 1:387, 4:192
Hannah, 1:388
Martha, 1:387
Mary, 1:387
Mary (Wood), 1:387
Rose (Baker), 1:388
Ruth, 1:388
Claghorn
Abia, 1:388
Abigail (Lombard), 1:388
Bethia (Lothrop), 1:388
Elizabeth, 1:388
Jane, 1:388
Jane (----), 1:388
Mary, 1:388, 2:19
Sarah, 1:388
Thankful, 1:388
Clap
---- (----), 2:61
Abigail, 1:389, 1:391
Abigail (----) Sharp, 1:390,
4:60
Abigail (Pond), 1:389
Ann, 3:609
Bethia, 1:391
Charity, 1:389

Clap (continued)
Deborah, 1:390-391
Deborah (----) Smith,
1:388
Elizabeth, 1:192,
1:389-391, 2:336, 2:452,
3:26, 4:230-231
Elizabeth (----), 1:388
Elizabeth (----) Goodspeed,
1:389
Elizabeth (Bursley)
Goodspeed, 1:312, 2:276
Elizabeth (Dickerman),
1:388
Elizabeth (Smith), 1:389
Esther, 1:389, 4:228
Experience, 1:388,
1:390-391
Experience (Houghton),
1:389, 2:469
Hannah, 1:390-391, 3:208,
4:225
Hannah (Gill), 1:391,
2:254
Hannah (Leeds), 1:390,
3:74
Jane, 1:389, 1:391, 4:453
Joan (----), 1:389, 2:113
Joanna (Ford), 1:390,
2:183
Judith, 1:388-389, 3:373
Mary, 1:389-391, 3:440,
3:609
Mary (----), 1:390
Mary (Fisher), 1:391,
2:163
Mehitable, 1:389
Prudence, 1:389, 1:391,
3:384
Prudence (Clap), 1:389
Radigan/Redigon, 1:333
Ruth, 1:389
Sarah, 1:388-390, 3:174,
3:609
Sarah (Clap), 1:390
Sarah (Leavitt), 1:390,
3:70
Sarah (Newberry), 1:390,
3:269
Sarah (Pond), 1:388, 3:453
Submit, 1:390
Supply, 1:389-390
Susanna, 1:389

Susanna (----), 1:389
Susanna (Swift), 1:389,
4:241
Thankful (King), 3:25
Thanks, 1:390
Unite, 1:389-391
Wait, 1:390, 4:101
Waitstill, 1:390
Clapham
Isabella (Barlow), 1:117
Clark/Clarke
----, 1:115, 1:316, 1:394,
1:398, 1:400, 1:402,
3:242, 3:616
---- (Harges), 1:395
---- (Hart) Williams, 4:560
---- (Holbrook), 2:443
---- (Howard), 2:472
---- (Pratt), 3:473
---- (Tibbets), 1:393
---- (Wilbor/Wilbore),
4:545
Abigail, 1:393-395,
1:397-399, 1:405, 3:434,
3:443, 3:609-610, 4:19,
4:251, 4:678
Abigail (----), 1:397
Abigail (Lothrop), 1:394,
3:120
Abigail (Maverick), 1:399,
3:180
Abigail (Pierson), 3:434
Agnes, 3:390
Agnes (----), 1:393, 3:609
Agnes (Tybott), 4:299
Alice (----), 1:186, 1:398,
1:400
Alice (Hallett) Nichols,
1:400, 2:340, 3:281
Alice (Martin), 1:393
Ann, 1:58, 1:394, 1:397,
1:402, 2:540, 2:597,
3:639
Ann (----), 1:401, 1:405
Ann (----) Wakefield, 4:386
Ann (Audley), 1:394
Ann (Lutterell), 1:393
Bethia, 1:399
Bethia (----), 1:400
Bethia (Hubbard), 1:398,
2:485
Catharine, 1:399, 1:403,
2:285, 3:610

Catharine (----), 1:404
Charity, 1:402
Content, 1:403, 1:514
Content (----), 1:403
Deborah, 1:325, 1:397,
1:401-402, 2:561, 3:610
Deborah (Gould/Gold),
2:286
Deborah (Peacock), 3:376,
3:610
Deliverance, 1:403, 1:458,
1:514
Dorothy, 1:392, 1:402
Dorothy (Lettis/Lettice)
Gray, 3:81
Elinor (----), 1:394
Elinor (Dearnford), 1:405
Elizabeth, 1:113, 1:281,
1:286, 1:392-394,
1:396-397, 1:399-402,
1:404, 1:448, 2:70,
2:202, 2:485, 2:510,
3:172, 3:398, 3:476,
3:518, 3:626, 3:632,
4:41, 4:357, 4:641
Elizabeth (----), 1:393,
1:395, 1:399, 1:401
Elizabeth (----) Crow,
1:400
Elizabeth (Bishop), 1:185
Elizabeth (Clark), 1:397
Elizabeth (Cook), 1:398
Elizabeth (Edwards), 1:400
Elizabeth (Greenleaf),
1:393
Elizabeth (Hutchinson),
1:397
Elizabeth (Mitton), 1:400,
3:222
Elizabeth (Norman), 1:397
Elizabeth (Sisson), 4:103
Elizabeth (Somerby),
1:399, 2:329, 4:140
Elizabeth (Stebbins), 1:396,
4:177
Elizabeth (Toppan), 1:399
Elizabeth (Whiting), 1:402
Elizabeth (Williams),
1:396
Elizabeth (Woodbridge),
1:397
Else (----), 1:402
Esther, 1:395, 1:397-398,

Clark/Clarke (continued)
Esther (continued)
3:127, 3:280
Experience, 1:397, 1:404,
3:260
Experience (Hinsdale),
2:427
Faith, 1:403, 2:62
Faith (----), 1:403
Frances, 1:394, 1:403,
2:445, 3:514
Frances (----), 2:43, 3:405,
4:227, 4:368
Frances (Latham), 3:58
Freeborn (Williams) Hart,
1:403, 2:368, 4:569
Hannah, 1:392, 1:394,
1:396-400, 1:403-405,
2:210, 2:240, 2:499,
3:292, 3:444, 3:559,
3:609, 4:642, 4:678
Hannah (----), 1:514
Hannah (Davis), 1:399
Hannah (Fordham), 1:400,
2:184
Hannah (Griswold), 1:405,
2:317
Hannah (Heath), 1:394,
2:399
Hannah (Jones) Falconer,
2:568
Hannah (Odlyn), 1:394
Hannah (Pratt), 1:392,
3:471
Hannah (Scott), 1:403
Hannah (Strong), 1:405,
4:227
Hannah (Tuttle), 4:678,
4:711
Hope, 1:394, 1:513
Hope (----), 1:513
Hope (Power), 1:394
Jane, 1:437
Jane (----), 1:393
Jane (Fletcher), 3:610
Jane (Pepperell), 3:392
Jemima, 1:395, 1:397,
2:72
Joan, 1:402
Joan/Jane, 4:209
Joanna, 1:400, 1:405
Joanna (----), 1:403
Judith, 1:393, 1:399, 3:652

Leah, 1:401
Lucy, 1:402
Lydia, 1:398, 1:404, 2:284
Lydia (Buckminster),
1:397
Lydia (Titcomb), 1:398
Margaret, 3:584, 3:610
Margaret (----), 1:398
Margery (----), 1:404
Martha, 1:186, 1:393-394,
1:396-397, 1:402, 1:404
Martha (Clark), 1:396
Martha (Curtis), 1:402,
1:487
Martha (Farr), 1:405,
2:144
Martha (Nash), 1:405,
3:262
Martha (Pease), 1:403
Martha (Pitkin) Wolcott,
1:392, 3:441, 4:623
Martha (Saltonstall), 1:395
Martha (Whittingham),
1:396
Mary, 1:392-397,
1:399-400, 1:402-405,
1:472, 1:507, 2:43,
2:238, 2:257, 2:284,
2:357, 2:483, 3:103,
3:218, 3:239, 3:340,
3:357, 3:363, 3:609-610,
3:635, 4:22, 4:182,
4:226-227, 4:270,
4:676-678
Mary (----), 1:396, 1:398,
1:401-405
Mary (----) Fletcher, 1:396
Mary (----) Ward Fletcher,
2:173
Mary (Allen), 1:398
Mary (Atwater), 1:76,
1:396, 1:443
Mary (Bonner), 1:507
Mary (Bullen), 1:296
Mary (Burr) Crow, 1:305,
1:399, 1:479
Mary (Clark), 3:609
Mary (Crow), 1:397, 1:479
Mary (Easton), 1:403, 2:94
Mary (Magoon), 1:398,
3:143
Mary (Meakins), 1:41,
1:399, 3:192

Mary (Newberry), 1:392,
3:269
Mary (Poor), 1:397
Mary (Sheffield), 4:69
Mary (Sherman), 4:84
Mary (Strong), 1:396-397,
4:227
Mary (Tully), 4:343
Mary (Twelves) Tyng,
4:353
Mary (Voaker), 3:610
Mary (Walker), 4:678
Mary/Mercy, 1:392
Mehitable, 1:391,
1:401-402
Mehitable (----), 1:391
Mehitable (Thrall), 1:400
Mercy, 1:392, 1:394,
1:399, 1:402, 3:610
Mercy (----), 2:273
Miriam, 1:400
Phebe, 3:610
Prudence, 3:610
Rachel, 1:394-395,
1:401-402
Rachel (----), 1:405
Rachel (Nichols), 1:400
Rebecca, 1:392-393,
1:396-398, 1:404, 3:595,
3:609-610, 4:431, 4:643
Rebecca (----), 1:392,
1:405
Rebecca (Cooper), 1:396,
1:455
Rebecca (Glover) Smith,
2:261
Rebecca (Lincoln),
3:92-93
Rebecca (Miller), 1:402,
3:209
Rebecca (Parker), 1:396
Rebecca (Thurston), 1:404,
4:296
Redigan, 4:620
Ruhama, 1:399-400
Ruth, 3:609-610
Ruth (Judd), 3:610
Ruth (Spencer), 1:399,
4:147
Sarah, 1:392-400, 1:402,
1:404, 1:459, 2:258,
2:305, 2:428, 2:504,
3:60, 3:165, 3:315,

Clark/Clarke (continued)
  Sarah (continued)
    3:363, 3:439, 3:526,,
    3:600, 3:610, 4:96,,
    4:450, 4:477, 4:678
  Sarah (----), 1:392, 1:397,
    1:402, 1:404
  Sarah (----) Cooper, 1:404
  Sarah (----) Stiles, 1:400,
    4:194
  Sarah (Barnham), 2:141
  Sarah (Burnham/Burnam),
    1:305
  Sarah (Champney), 1:394
  Sarah (Crisp) Harris
    Leverett, 1:397, 1:437,
    1:473, 2:366
  Sarah (Lynde), 1:402,
    4:239
  Sarah (Peck), 3:383
  Sarah (Prior) Gould, 1:403,
    3:489
  Sarah (Shrimpton), 1:397,
    4:91
  Sarah (Smith), 1:396,
    4:113, 4:678
  Sarah (Stow), 1:393
  Sarah (Wolcot), 1:405
  Susan, 4:678
  Susanna, 1:391, 1:394,
    1:398-400, 1:402-403,
    2:241, 3:119
  Susanna (----) Story, 1:397
  Susanna (Bennett), 1:168,
    1:398
  Susanna (Ring), 1:400,
    3:542
  Thankful, 1:397
Clary
  Ann (Dickinson), 1:405,
    2:48
  Hannah, 1:358
  Mary, 1:405
  Mary (Cassell), 1:405
  Sarah, 1:405, 3:400
  Sarah (Cady), 1:405
Clason/Classon
  Abigail (Bushrod), 1:318
  Priscilla (Abbot), 1:2
Clay
  Catharine (----), 1:406
  Elizabeth, 1:406
  Hannah, 1:406

Mary, 1:406
Mary (Allen), 3:610
Mary (Law), 1:406
Sarah, 1:406
Clayton
  Ann, 1:406, 2:94
  Sarah, 1:213, 1:406
Cleaveland
  Abiel, 1:406
  Abigail, 1:407
  Ann, 1:407
  Ann (Winn), 1:406, 4:596
  Deliverance, 1:406
  Dorcas, 1:406
  Dorcas (Wilson), 1:406
  Elizabeth (----), 1:406
  Hannah, 1:406-407, 2:404
  Isabel, 1:406
  Jane (Keyes), 1:407, 3:16
  Joanna, 1:406-407
  Lydia, 1:406
  Margaret (----) Fish, 1:407
  Mary, 1:406-407
  Mary (----), 1:406
  Miriam, 1:406-407, 1:514
  Persis, 1:407
  Persis (Hildreth), 1:407
  Prudence (----), 1:406
  Rachel, 1:406
  Ruth (Norton), 1:407
  Sarah, 1:406
Clegstone
  ---- (Wakeman), 4:388
Clement/Clemens/Clemence
  ---- (Fawne), 1:408, 2:149
  Abigail, 1:408, 3:438
  Ann, 1:408
  Ann (Taylor), 1:408
  Deborah (----), 1:408
  Elizabeth, 1:407-408,
    1:514, 4:232
  Elizabeth (----), 1:407-408
  Elizabeth (Richardson),
    1:408
  Grace, 4:324
  Hannah, 1:408
  Hannah (Gove), 1:407
  Hannah (Ingles/Inglish),
    2:522
  Hannah (Inglis), 1:408
  Hannah (Ings), 1:408
  Joanna, 1:407
  Joanna (----) Leighton,

1:407, 3:44
Joanna (Carr), 1:408
Joanna (Riland), 1:408
Judith, 4:529
Lydia (----), 1:407
Margaret (----), 3:131
Margaret (Dummer),
  1:407
Martha, 3:469
Martha (----), 1:408
Martha (Deane), 1:175,
  1:407
Mary, 1:332, 1:408, 3:36,
  3:320, 4:677
Mary (Rock), 1:408
Rebecca, 1:408, 1:434
Sarah, 1:408, 3:234
Sarah (----), 1:408
Sarah (Osgood), 1:408,
  3:320
Clesson
  Mary, 1:408
  Mary (Phelps), 1:408,
    3:406
Cleverly
  Elizabeth, 2:466, 4:684
  Sarah (----), 1:409
Cleves/Cleaves
  Bethia, 1:409
  Deborah, 1:409
  Elinor, 1:409
  Elizabeth, 1:409, 3:222
  Hannah, 1:409
  Joan (----), 1:409
  Lydia, 1:409
  Margaret, 1:409
  Margaret (Corey), 1:409
  Martha, 1:409
  Martha (Corey), 1:409,
    1:460
  Mercy (Eaton), 1:409
  Rebecca, 1:409
  Rebecca (Conant), 1:409
  Rebecca (Corning), 1:409
  Rebecca (Whittredge),
    1:410, 4:533
  Sarah, 1:409
  Sarah (Chandler), 1:359,
    1:409, 3:360
  Sarah (Stone), 1:409
Clifford
  Ann (----), 1:410
  Bridget (----) Huggins,

66

Clifford (continued)
Bridget (----) Huggins
(continued)
1:410, 2:491
Hannah, 1:410, 3:145
Mehitable, 1:410
Sarah (Godfrey), 1:410,
2:266
Clift
Lydia (Willis), 1:410,
4:577
Clifton
Mary (----), 1:410
Patience, 1:154, 1:410
Clinton
Arbella, 2:552
Susan, 2:496
Clisby/Cleesby/Clesby
Abigail (Frothingham),
1:410
Elizabeth (----), 1:410
Hannah, 1:410
Mary, 1:410
Sarah (----), 1:410
Cloade
Elizabeth, 1:410
Elizabeth (Bugby), 1:410
Mary, 1:410
Clock
Judith, 1:330
Clopton
Bridget, 4:10
Thomasine, 4:610
Close
Hannah, 3:33
Sarah (Hardy/Hardie),
2:355
Clothier
Ruth, 1:94
Clough
Elizabeth, 1:411
Elizabeth (----), 1:411,
3:610
Elizabeth (Brown), 1:278
Jane (----), 1:411
Martha, 1:410-411
Martha (----), 1:410-411
Martha (Goodwin), 2:587
Mary, 1:410-411, 3:60
Mary (----), 1:411
Mary (Adams), 1:15
Mercy (Page), 1:411
Priscilla, 1:411

Ruth (Conner), 1:443
Sarah, 1:411, 3:199
Susanna, 1:411
Susanna (----), 1:411
Tabitha, 1:411
Thankful (----), 1:410
Cloutman
Elizabeth (----), 1:411
Elizabeth (Story), 3:610
Mary, 1:411
Cloyes/Cloyce
---- (Mills), 1:412
Abigail, 1:411
Abigail (----), 1:411
Hannah, 1:412, 2:108,
3:610
Hannah (----), 1:412
Jane (----) Spurwell, 1:411
Martha, 1:411
Mary, 1:411-412, 3:610
Mary (Long), 1:412, 3:109
Sarah, 1:411
Sarah (----), 1:412
Sarah (----) Bridges, 4:679
Sarah (Mills), 1:514
Sarah (Towne), 3:300
Sarah (Towne) Bridges,
1:249, 4:317
Susan (Harrington) Beers,
1:496
Susanna (----) Beers, 1:412
Susanna (George)
Harrington Beers, 2:360
Susanna (Harrington)
Cutting Beers, 1:154
Susanna (Lewis), 1:412,
3:86
Clugstone
---- (Wakeman), 1:412
Clutterbuck
Elizabeth (----), 1:412
Coalborne
Hannah, 1:412
Priscilla (----), 1:412
Rebecca, 1:412
Sarah, 1:412
Coates/Coats
Abigail, 1:412, 3:527
Elizabeth, 3:527
Hannah, 1:500
Jane, 3:527
Mary, 1:412
Mary (Witherdin), 1:412

Cobb
---- (----), 3:414
Abigail, 1:412
Bethia, 1:412
Elizabeth, 1:412-414
Elizabeth (Taylor),
1:413-414, 4:263
Eunice, 1:413
Experience, 1:413-414
Hannah, 1:413, 2:506,
3:85
Hope (Huckins), 1:413
Jane (Woodward), 1:413
Lois, 1:413
Lois (Hallett), 1:413
Lydia, 1:413-414
Martha, 1:413
Martha (Nelson), 1:413
Mary, 1:413, 2:81, 2:506,
4:572
Mary (Haskins), 1:413,
2:466
Mehitable, 1:413-414
Mercy, 1:412-413
Patience, 1:413, 2:506,
3:356
Patience (Hurst), 1:413,
2:506
Sarah, 1:380, 1:413-414,
2:424
Sarah (Hacket), 2:590
Sarah (Hinckley), 1:413,
2:425
Sarah (Lewis), 1:413, 3:85,
4:145
Thankful, 1:413
Cobbett
Elizabeth, 1:414
Elizabeth (----), 1:414
Margaret, 1:414
Mary (----), 1:414
Ruth, 1:414
Cobble
Elizabeth, 1:415
Judith, 1:415
Judith (----), 1:415
Mary, 1:415
Sarah, 1:415
Cobham
Marah, 1:415
Martha, 1:415
Mary, 1:415
Mary (----), 1:415

Cobham (continued)
Sarah, 1:415
Cobleich
Mary (----), 1:415
Coburn
Hannah, 4:178
Cock
Mary, 3:654
Susanna (Upshall), 4:361,
4:679
Cockerum
Christian (----), 1:415
Cockshott
Elizabeth (----), 1:415
Coddington
----, 1:502
Ann, 1:415-416
Ann (----), 1:416
Catharine, 1:415
Emma (----), 1:415, 2:546
Hannah (----), 1:415
Hannah (Gardner), 1:415,
2:585
Mary, 1:416
Mary (----), 1:416
Mary (Howard), 1:416
Mary (Moseley), 1:416
Priscilla (----), 1:416
Sarah, 1:415
Susanna (Hutchinson),
1:415, 2:509
Codman
---- (Bonython), 1:211
Elizabeth, 1:514
Elizabeth (----), 1:417
Elizabeth (Randall), 1:514,
3:506
Hepzibah, 1:417, 4:706
Parnell (Foster), 1:417
Susanna, 1:417
Codner
Elizabeth, 1:417
Martha, 1:417
Mary, 1:417, 1:514
Phebe (Barton), 1:134,
1:417
Priscilla (----), 1:417
Rachel, 1:417
Rachel (Neighbors), 1:417,
3:267
Coe
----, 1:418, 2:521
Abigail, 1:418

Abigail (Carman), 1:417
Ann (----), 1:418
Catharine, 1:418
Elizabeth, 1:417-418
Elizabeth (Wakley), 1:418
Hannah, 1:417-418, 2:426,
3:610
Hannah (----), 1:418, 2:115
Jane, 1:418
Lydia, 1:417
Margaret, 1:418
Margaret (Van Zandt),
1:418
Martha, 1:418
Martha (Ramsey), 1:417
Mary, 1:418
Mary (Hawley), 1:418,
2:384
Sarah, 1:417-418, 4:682,
3:610, 3:638, 4:683
Sarah (Peabody), 1:417
Susanna, 1:41, 1:418
Coffin
Abigail, 1:419, 1:514,
2:24, 2:229
Abigail (Starbuck), 1:419,
4:172
Ann, 3:613
Ann (Gardner), 2:228
Apphia, 1:419
Apphia (Dole), 1:419, 2:59
Damaris (Gayer), 2:238
Deborah, 1:420, 3:38
Deborah (Austin), 1:419
Dinah, 1:419
Dionis (Stevens), 1:419
Dorcas, 4:706
Elinor, 1:418
Elizabeth, 1:418-420,
2:308
Elizabeth (Starbuck),
1:419, 4:172
Eunice, 1:322, 1:419
Florence, 1:418
Florence (Hooke), 1:418
Hannah, 1:419
Hope (Gardner), 2:229
Jane, 1:419
Joanna, 1:418
Joanna (----), 1:419
Joanna (Gilman), 2:258
Judith, 1:418-420, 4:12
Judith (Greenleaf)

Somerby, 1:420, 2:308,
4:140
Love, 1:419
Love (Gardner), 4:679,
4:682
Lydia, 1:418-420, 3:99,
3:436
Mary, 1:8, 1:418-420,
2:228, 3:99, 4:172,
4:696
Mary (Bunker), 1:419,
4:676
Mary (Gardner), 2:228
Mary (Severance), 1:418,
4:52
Priscilla, 1:419
Ruth (Gardner), 1:418,
2:228
Sarah, 1:418-419
Sarah (Atkinson), 1:419
Sarah (Dole), 1:419
Coffley
Agnes, 3:38
Coggan/Cogan/Coggin
Abigail, 1:420, 1:514,
2:206
Abigail (----), 1:420, 3:417
Ann, 1:420
Ann (----), 1:420
Bathsheba, 1:113
Elizabeth, 1:420, 3:556,
4:664
Lydia, 1:420
Martha (----) Coytemore
Winthrop, 1:420
Martha (Nowell)
Coytemore Winthrop,
4:611
Martha (Rainsborough)
Coytemore Winthrop,
1:468
Mary, 1:420, 3:554, 4:637
Mary (----), 1:420-421
Mary (Long), 1:421, 1:514
Ruth, 4:264
Sarah, 1:421, 1:468, 4:290
Coggeshall/Coxsall
Ann, 1:421, 2:94, 2:580
Ann (----) Wakefield, 4:700
Bedaiah, 1:421
Comfort (Freeborne),
2:202
Constant, 1:421

Coggeshall/Coxsall
(continued)
Content, 1:421
Elizabeth, 1:421
Elizabeth (Balstone), 1:110,
 1:421, 2:588
Elizabeth (Timberlake),
 1:421, 4:305
Freegift, 1:421
Humilis, 1:422
Joan (West), 1:422
Mary, 1:421-422, 3:253
Mary (----), 1:421
Mary (Bull), 1:293, 1:421
Mercy (Freeborne), 2:202
Patience, 1:421
Patience (Throgmorton),
 1:421, 4:294
Rachel, 3:313
Rebecca, 1:421
Rebecca (Russell), 1:422
Sarah (----), 3:610
Wait, 1:421, 2:284
Cogswell
----, 1:422, 4:389
Abigail, 1:422
Elizabeth, 4:379, 4:481
Elizabeth (----), 1:422
Elizabeth (Wainwright),
 1:422, 4:382
Hannah, 1:422
Hannah (Brown), 4:676
Martha (----), 4:508
Martha (Emerson), 1:422
Mary, 1:422
Sarah, 1:422, 3:299, 4:352
Susanna, 1:422, 4:508
Susanna (Haven/Havens),
 2:379
Susanna (Hearn), 1:422
Wastall, 1:422
Coit/Coyte
Abigail, 1:422, 2:129,
 3:618, 3:653
Elizabeth, 1:423
Hannah (----), 3:608
Martha, 1:422, 3:247,
 4:512
Martha (Harris), 1:423,
 2:365
Mary, 1:422, 4:187
Mary (----), 1:422, 2:112,
 2:169

Mary (Stevens), 1:422,
 3:611
Mehitable (Chandler),
 1:357, 1:422
Sarah (Chandler), 1:357,
 1:423
Coke
Ann, 4:567
Coker
---- (Hathorne/Hawthorne),
 3:664, 4:701
Catharine (----), 1:423
Hannah, 1:423, 3:131
Judith, 1:423
Martha (Perley), 1:423
Mary, 1:423
Mary (----) Woodbridge,
 1:423
Mary (Jones) Woodbridge,
 4:633
Mercy, 1:423
Sarah, 1:423, 4:117
Sarah (Hathorne), 1:423
Colbron/Colborne/Colburn
Bethia, 1:423
Bethia (Bullen), 1:296
Deborah, 1:423, 4:543
Elizabeth, 1:424
Experience, 1:423
Experience (Leland), 1:423,
 3:77
Hannah, 1:25, 1:412,
 1:423
Mary, 1:124, 1:424, 2:162,
 4:343
Mary (Holbrook), 2:443
Priscilla, 3:240
Rhoda (Bradhurst), 1:232
Sarah, 1:424, 3:367, 3:432
Sarah (----), 3:611
Sarah (Golt/Gault), 2:587
Colby
Dorothy, 1:424, 2:482,
 4:19
Elizabeth, 1:424, 4:19
Elizabeth (Sargent), 1:424,
 4:19
Frances, 1:424
Frances (Hoyt), 1:424,
 2:481
Martha (----), 1:424
Mary, 1:424, 4:19
Rebecca, 1:424, 4:562

Sarah, 1:93, 1:424
Susanna, 1:424
Susanna (----), 1:424,
 4:533
Colcord
Abigail, 1:424
Deborah, 1:424
Elizabeth, 1:425
Hannah, 1:424, 2:32
Mary, 1:424, 2:158
Mary (----), 1:425
Mehitable, 1:424, 4:188
Sarah, 1:424, 2:436
Shuah, 1:424
Coldam/Coldham/Coldom
Elizabeth, 1:425, 3:294
Joanna (----), 3:611
Judith, 1:425
Martha, 4:531
Mary (----), 1:425
Mary (Pierce), 3:428
Coldfax
Mary (Day), 2:578
Cole/Coale/Coales
----, 1:429
Abigail, 1:426-427, 1:430,
 4:97-98
Abigail (Stanley), 1:430
Ann, 1:293, 1:425-430,
 1:505, 4:318, 4:366
Ann (----), 1:429-430,
 3:611
Ann (----) Edwards, 1:427,
 2:104
Ann (----) Keayne, 1:429,
 3:2
Arrold (----), 1:429
Bethia (----) Silsbee, 1:425
Deliverance, 4:319
Dorothy, 1:428, 1:430
Elizabeth, 1:426-427,
 1:429-430, 1:491, 4:318,
 4:452
Elizabeth (----), 1:426
Elizabeth (----) Cook,
 1:427, 1:446
Elizabeth (Knight), 4:688
Elizabeth (Lettice)
 Shurtleff Cook, 3:81, 4:92
Elizabeth (Rider), 1:207,
 1:428, 3:540
Elizabeth (Weeden), 1:429,
 4:452

Cole/Coale/Coales
(continued)
Elizabeth (Woodford),
4:638
Esther, 1:426
Esther (----), 2:105
Eunice (----), 1:430
Frances (----), 1:426
Hannah, 1:426-428, 1:430,
1:514
Hannah (Snow), 1:430
Hepzibah, 1:425, 1:428,
2:55
Jane, 1:429-430
Jane (Britton), 1:427
Jeannett, 1:425
Joan (----), 1:427
Joanna, 1:426
Joanna (----), 1:427
Lydia, 1:428, 4:585
Lydia (----), 1:425, 2:105
Lydia (Davis), 1:429
Margaret, 2:63
Margaret (----) Green,
1:429, 3:583
Martha, 1:427, 1:430
Martha (----), 1:430
Martha (Jackson), 1:429
Mary, 1:45, 1:425-430,
1:514, 2:461, 2:527,
2:585, 2:587, 3:120
Mary (----), 1:426-427,
1:429-430, 2:370
Mary (----) Morton, 1:427
Mary (Benton), 1:429
Mary (Foxwell), 1:426,
2:198
Mary (Gallop), 1:428,
2:223
Mary (Knight), 1:514
Mary (Paine) Rogers,
3:337
Mary (Rogers), 1:427
Mary (Tilson), 1:427,
4:304
Mehitable (----), 1:428
Mercy (Fuller), 2:219
Rachel, 1:428, 4:112
Rachel (----), 1:428
Rebecca, 1:426-427
Rebecca (Collier), 1:427,
1:433
Rebecca (Gray), 1:426

Ruth, 1:111, 1:425-428,
4:353, 4:670
Ruth (----), 1:425-426
Ruth (Snow), 1:428
Sarah, 1:426-430, 1:514
Sarah (----), 1:426
Sarah (Aslett), 1:69
Sarah (Davis), 1:514,
2:578
Sarah (Rusco), 1:426,
3:589
Sarah (Train), 1:427,
4:321
Staines, 1:429
Susanna, 1:426, 1:430,
2:512
Susanna (Cunliffe), 1:429,
1:484, 4:445
Susanna (Hutchinson),
1:428, 2:513
Susanna (Upshur), 1:428
Coleman - see also Colman
----, 1:431, 2:20
Abigail, 1:430
Ann, 1:431, 2:578
Ann (Bunker), 1:299,
1:431
Bethia, 1:431
Deborah, 1:431, 2:323
Dorcas, 4:304
Frances (----) Welles, 1:431
Hannah, 1:431, 3:262
Hannah (Porter), 4:679
Joanna, 1:431
Joanna (Folger), 1:430,
2:177
Judah, 1:431
Lydia, 1:431, 3:537
Margery (----) Osgood
Rowell, 3:581
Margery (Fowler) Osgood
Rowell, 1:431, 3:657
Mary (----) Ely Stebbins,
4:178
Mary (----) Johnson, 1:431,
2:550
Mary (Crow), 1:431, 1:479
Mary (Day) Ely Stebbins,
1:431, 2:27, 2:117
Phebe, 1:430
Sarah, 1:431, 2:463, 4:326
Susanna, 1:431
Susanna (----), 1:431

Coles
Maher (Gorton), 2:283
Mary, 4:169
Colet
Elizabeth, 2:226
Coley
Abilene, 1:431
Ann, 1:431
Ann (Prudden), 1:431,
3:491
Elizabeth, 1:431
Hannah, 1:431, 2:233
Martha (Stream), 1:432
Mary, 1:431, 4:222
Sarah, 1:431
Colfax/Colefox
Bridget (----) Roe, 1:432
Elizabeth, 1:514
Hannah, 1:514
Mary, 1:514
Mary (Day), 1:514
Collamore/Cullimore/etc
----, 1:432
Abigail, 1:432
Abigail (Davis), 1:432
Elizabeth, 1:432, 3:576
Margaret (----), 1:432
Margery (Page), 1:432
Martha, 1:432
Mary, 1:432
Mary (----), 1:432
Sarah, 1:432
Sarah (Chittenden), 1:381,
1:432
Collar/Coller
Ann (Cutler), 1:493
Elizabeth (----), 1:432
Hannah, 1:432, 1:496
Hannah (Cutler), 1:432
Priscilla, 1:432
Susanna, 1:432
Sybilla, 1:432
Collicott
Bethia, 1:432, 2:279
Elizabeth, 1:432, 2:337
Experience, 1:432
Joanna (----), 1:432
Thomasin (----), 1:432
Collier/Collyer/Colyer
----, 1:98
Abigail, 1:433
Ann, 1:433
Elizabeth, 1:433, 4:143

Collier/Collyer/Colyer
(continued)
Elizabeth (Bullard), 1:295,
1:433
Elizabeth (Jones), 1:433
Elizabeth (Sanford), 1:433,
4:15
Jane (----), 1:98, 1:433
Jane (Jones), 2:565
Mary, 1:433, 2:204, 3:406,
3:477
Rebecca, 1:427, 1:433
Sarah, 1:245, 1:433
Susanna, 1:433
Colliham
Ann, 3:168
Collins
----, 3:570
---- (Alger), 1:27
---- (Hutchinson), 1:436,
2:513
Abigail, 1:434-436, 1:515,
2:145, 2:346, 3:611,
4:318, 4:556
Abigail (----), 3:611
Abigail (House), 1:436
Alce/Alice, 1:435
Amy/Ammi (----) Ward,
4:414
Ann, 1:433-436, 2:535,
3:270, 3:611
Ann (----), 1:434, 1:436,
4:118
Ann (Leete) Trowbridge,
1:434, 3:75, 4:333
Dorcas, 1:435
Dorcas (Swain) Taintor,
1:435
Dorothy, 1:435
Duty (Knowles), 1:435
Elizabeth, 1:433-435,
3:523, 4:310
Elizabeth (----), 1:435
Elizabeth (----) Putnam,
1:433
Esther, 1:435
Hannah, 1:271, 1:277,
1:434-435, 1:515, 2:521,
3:611
Hannah (----), 1:515
Hannah (Lamson), 1:434
Hannah (Ward) Pitman,
4:410

Jane, 1:435
Jane (----), 1:434
Joan, 1:435, 4:34
Joan (----), 1:435
Lois, 1:435
Lydia, 1:435
Margery, 1:434
Martha, 1:434, 1:436,
3:226, 3:629
Martha (----), 1:434
Martha (Eaton), 1:433,
2:96
Mary, 1:361, 1:433,
1:435-436, 1:498, 2:116,
2:344, 2:557, 3:611,
3:614, 3:643
Mary (----) Kingsnoth,
1:435
Mary (Dixwell), 2:55
Mary (Stevens) Kingsnoth,
3:30, 4:186
Mary (Tolman), 4:310
Mary (Whiting), 1:436,
4:522
Mehitable, 1:434, 4:679
Mehitable (Giles), 1:435,
1:515, 2:253
Patience, 1:434
Phebe, 1:434
Priscilla, 1:433
Priscilla (Kirtland), 1:433
Rebecca, 1:434
Rebecca (----) Hunt, 1:436
Rebecca (Clement), 1:434
Sarah, 1:434-436, 2:579,
4:679
Sarah (----), 1:434, 4:428
Sarah (Morrill), 4:679
Sarah (Tibbals), 1:434,
4:298
Sarah (White), 1:436
Sarah (Wright), 1:434
Sibyl/Sybil, 1:434, 1:436,
4:518
Susanna, 1:433, 1:435-436,
2:344, 2:362, 4:397
Susanna (----), 1:435
Thankful, 1:436
Collishaw
Ann (----) Morrice, 1:437
Colman - see also Coleman
----, 4:344
Abigail, 1:437

Bridget (----) Rowe, 3:580,
3:611
Elizabeth, 1:437
Elizabeth (----), 1:437
Frances (----) Welles, 4:479
Jane, 1:437
Jane (Clark), 1:437
Lydia (Scottow) Gibbs
Checkley, 1:369, 2:246,
4:40
Margaret (Lumbard),
1:437, 3:106
Martha, 1:437
Mary, 1:437
Mary (Pepperell) Frost,
1:437, 2:211, 3:392
Mary (Prescott), 3:480
Sarah (----), 1:437
Sarah (Crisp) Harris
Leverett Clark, 1:397,
1:437, 1:473, 2:366
Colpit
Sarah (Pierce), 3:432
Colson
Ann, 1:437
Elizabeth, 1:437
Lydia, 1:437
Mary (----), 1:437
Susanna (----), 1:437
Colt
Esther, 3:114
Ruth (Loomis), 3:114
Sarah, 1:437
Coltman
Mary, 1:438
Colton
Abigail (Parsons), 3:363
Deborah, 1:438
Deborah (Gardner), 1:438
Esther, 1:438
Esther (Mansfield), 1:438
Esther (Marshfield), 3:160
Hepzibah, 1:438, 4:476
Joanna (Wolcott), 4:623
Lydia (Wright) Bliss
Norton Lamb, 1:438,
4:659
Mary, 1:438
Mary (----), 4:175
Mary (Drake), 1:438
Mercy, 1:438
Rebecca, 1:438
Sarah, 1:438, 3:3

Colton (continued)
Sarah (Griswold), 1:438,
2:317
Colver/Culver
Ann (----), 1:438
Combs/Coombs/Coomes/etc
Bathsheba (Raymond),
3:513
Bathshua (Raymond),
1:453
Elizabeth, 1:439, 1:491
Elizabeth (----) Barlow,
1:117, 1:439, 1:453,
4:424
Hannah, 1:453
Joan (----), 1:515
Mary, 1:439, 3:261, 3:638,
4:424
Mary (----), 1:453
Mary (Nash), 3:261
Sarah (----), 1:439
Sarah (Cuthbertson), 1:453,
1:492
Come
Martha (Munroe), 3:257
Comee/Comy/Comey
Elizabeth, 3:9
Mary, 1:439, 3:17
Comer
---- (Gilbert), 1:439, 2:586
Elinor (----), 1:439
Mary, 1:439
Sarah, 1:439
Sarah (----), 1:439
Compton
Abigail, 1:256, 1:439
Susanna (----), 1:439
Comstock
----, 4:120
---- (Elderkin), 1:439,
2:107
Abigail, 1:439, 2:505,
3:377
Abigail (----), 1:440
Bethia, 1:439, 4:175
Christian, 1:439
Elizabeth, 1:439, 4:33,
4:87
Elizabeth (----), 1:440
Elizabeth (Wheeler), 1:439
Hannah, 1:439
Hannah (Platt), 1:439,
3:445

Mary, 1:439-440
Mercy, 1:439
Pelatiah (----), 1:439
Sarah, 1:440
Sarah (Hanford), 1:440,
2:350
Conant
Christian (Mower), 3:611,
3:654
Elizabeth, 1:440-441,
3:148, 3:631
Elizabeth (Walton), 4:405
Martha, 1:440
Mary, 1:101, 1:288, 1:441,
1:515-515, 2:57, 4:370,
4:524
Rebecca, 1:409, 1:441
Sarah, 1:440-441
Sarah (----), 1:440-441
Seeth (----), 1:515
Concklin
Elizabeth, 1:441
Mary (Gardiner), 1:441,
2:226
Condy/Coundy/Candy
Ann, 3:612, 4:703
Ann (----), 3:612, 4:248
Elizabeth, 4:248
Elizabeth (----), 1:441,
4:281
Esther, 3:611
Mary (Parker), 1:441,
3:355
Rebecca (----), 3:611
Sarah (Drowne), 2:74
Susanna (----), 1:441
Cone
Abigail, 1:442
Ann, 1:442
Beriah, 1:442
Deborah, 1:442
Dorothy, 1:442
Elenor, 1:442
Elizabeth, 1:441-442
Elizabeth (----), 1:441
Elizabeth (Cunningham),
1:442
Elizabeth1, 1:441
Esther, 1:442
Hannah, 1:442
Helena, 1:442
Jemima, 1:442
Lucy, 1:442

Lydia, 1:442
Mary, 1:442
Mary (Gates), 1:442
Mary (Hungerford), 1:442
Mehitable, 1:442
Mehitable (Spencer), 1:442,
4:147
Phebe, 1:442
Rebecca, 1:442
Ruth, 1:442
Sarah, 1:442
Sarah (Hungerford), 1:442
Susanna, 1:442
Coney
Abigail, 1:258
Ann, 2:198
Elizabeth, 1:442
Elizabeth (Nash), 1:442,
3:262
Experience, 1:442
Margaret (Christophers),
1:383
Mary, 1:442
Mary (Atwater) Clark, 1:76,
1:396, 1:443
Mehitable, 2:197
Patience, 1:442
Rebecca, 1:442
Sarah, 1:442
Sarah (----), 1:443
Congdon
Frances (Stafford), 4:160
Conklin
Mary, 4:707
Conner
Ann (Gove), 1:443, 2:288
Dorothy, 1:443
Elizabeth, 1:443
Elizabeth (----), 1:443
Mary, 1:443
Mary (Gilman), 2:258
Rebecca, 1:443
Ruth, 1:443
Sarah, 1:443
Sarah (----), 1:443
Ursula, 1:443
Connoway
Ann (----), 1:443
Ann (Wilson), 1:515
Constable
Ann (----), 1:443, 3:108
Convers/Converse
Abigail, 1:444, 3:15

Convers/Converse
(continued)
Ann, 1:444
Ann (Long), 1:444, 3:109
Deborah, 1:444, 3:429
Dorothy, 1:444
Elizabeth, 1:443-445
Esther, 1:444
Esther (Champney), 1:356,
  1:444
Hannah, 1:443-445, 1:515,
  3:430
Hannah (----), 1:444
Hannah (Bateman), 1:445
Hannah (Carter), 1:444
Joan (Corbin) Sprague,
  4:155
Joanna (----) Sprague,
  1:444
Judith (Carter), 1:342,
  1:444, 2:158
Kezia, 1:444
Lydia, 1:444
Mary, 1:443-444, 2:20,
  4:288
Patience, 1:444
Rebecca, 1:444
Ruth, 1:444-445, 2:7,
  4:243
Ruth (Marshall), 1:444
Sarah, 1:443-444
Sarah (----), 1:443-445
Sarah (Stone), 1:444
Cook/Cooke
----, 3:612, 4:248
---- (Ford), 1:445, 2:183
---- (Howell), 2:478
Abigail, 1:448-449, 1:515,
  3:451, 3:612
Abigail (Griggs), 1:450,
  2:315
Alice, 1:448, 1:450, 4:189,
  4:519
Alice (----), 1:446
Ann, 1:448, 4:138
Bethia, 1:448, 2:354
Bridget, 1:445
Damaris (Hopkins), 1:446,
  2:462
Deborah, 1:448
Deborah (Hopkins), 1:448
Deliverance, 1:450
Elizabeth, 1:398,

1:445-450, 1:515, 2:62,
  2:367, 2:589, 3:364,
  3:612, 4:116, 4:546,
  4:681
Elizabeth (----), 1:427,
  1:448-449, 2:361
Elizabeth (----) Shurtleff,
  1:446
Elizabeth (Buxton), 1:325,
  1:446
Elizabeth (Clark), 1:392,
  1:448, 2:70
Elizabeth (King) Deane,
  1:448
Elizabeth (Lettice)
  Shurtleff, 3:81, 4:92
Elizabeth (Leverett), 1:445,
  3:83
Elizabeth (Nash), 1:445,
  3:261
Elizabeth (Ring) Dean,
  2:30
Esther, 1:446-447, 1:449
Esther (----), 1:446
Frances (----) Wheeler,
  1:449, 2:306, 4:497
Grace, 1:448
Hannah, 1:97, 1:285,
  1:446-449, 3:608, 3:612
Hannah (Dean), 2:29
Hannah (Harris), 1:447,
  2:360
Hannah (Lindon), 1:450
Hope, 1:450
Hope (Parker), 1:450,
  3:350
Jane, 1:446-447, 3:219
Jane (Middlecott), 1:445,
  3:205
Jane (Sewall), 4:56
Jemima, 1:515
Joan (Denslow), 1:445,
  2:39
Joanna, 1:445, 3:463,
  4:623
Judith, 1:446, 1:450, 3:492
Judith (Burchal), 1:510
Judith (Burdsall), 1:446
Lydia, 1:447-448, 1:515,
  3:612
Lydia (Miller), 1:447,
  3:209
Lydia (Vore), 1:448, 4:376

Lydia (White), 4:512
Mabel, 1:450
Margaret, 1:447
Martha, 1:446, 1:450,
  1:491
Martha (----), 1:450
Martha (Allyn), 1:43
Martha (Stedman), 1:448,
  4:179
Mary, 1:446-450, 1:487,
  1:515, 2:306, 2:558,
  3:249, 3:612-613, 4:250,
  4:679
Mary (----), 1:446-447,
  1:450, 3:523
Mary (Buxton), 3:608,
  3:612
Mary (Downs), 1:448
Mary (Elwell), 1:447
Mary (Hale), 3:612
Mary (Haven/Havens),
  2:379
Mary (Haynes/Haines),
  2:389
Mary (Lamson), 1:449,
  3:49
Mary (Parmenter), 1:445
Mehitable, 1:450, 2:478
Mercy, 1:447
Miriam, 1:445, 1:449-450,
  3:74
Patience, 3:624
Phebe (----), 1:448
Rachel, 1:446, 3:17, 3:612,
  4:375
Rachel (----), 3:612
Rachel (Spencer), 4:149
Rebecca, 1:447
Rebecca (Flagg), 1:450
Rebecca (Foote) Smith,
  1:445, 2:180, 4:128
Ruth, 1:446, 1:448
Ruth (----), 1:447-448
Ruth (Barton), 1:134
Sarah, 1:99, 1:445,
  1:447-450, 1:515, 2:338,
  2:376, 2:471, 4:32
Sarah (----), 1:448-450
Sarah (Coleman), 1:431
Sarah (Fiske), 1:448
Sarah (Mason), 1:450
Sarah (Nash), 1:449
Sarah (Place), 3:443

Cook/Cooke (continued)
Sarah (Very), 3:612, 4:372
Sarah (Warren), 1:447,
  4:427
Sarah (Westwood), 1:445,
  4:491
Susanna, 1:446, 4:102
Susanna (----), 4:157
Susanna (----) Goodwin,
  1:446
Tamar (Tyler), 1:450,
  4:355
Cookery
Hannah (Long), 1:451,
  3:109
Mary (Beaman), 1:504,
  1:515
Cooledge/Coolidge
Abigail, 1:451-452
Ann, 1:14, 1:451-452,
  3:60
Deborah, 1:451
Elizabeth, 1:451-453,
  1:468
Elizabeth (Bond), 1:452
Elizabeth (Rouse), 1:452
Esther (Mason), 1:452
Experience (Thornton)
  Wakefield, 4:293
Grace, 1:209, 1:451
Hannah, 1:209, 1:451-452
Hannah (Barron), 1:126,
  1:452
Hannah (Livermore),
  1:451, 3:101
Hepzibah, 1:451-452,
  4:206
Huldah, 1:451
Lydia, 1:452
Lydia (Jones), 1:452
Margaret (Bond), 1:451
Martha, 1:451-452
Martha (Rice), 1:451
Mary, 1:253, 1:451-452,
  3:223, 4:481
Mary (----), 1:451
Mary (----) Mattocks,
  1:451
Mary (Bond), 1:210, 1:452
Mary (Bright), 1:253,
  1:452
Mary (Smith), 1:453
Mary (Wellington)

Maddocks, 3:142, 4:481
Melicent, 1:451
Mercy, 1:452
Mindwell, 1:451
Priscilla (Rogers), 1:452,
  3:561
Rebecca, 1:451-452, 4:541
Rebecca (----), 1:452
Rebecca (Frost), 1:452
Sarah, 1:451-453, 2:155,
  2:167, 2:374
Sarah (Eddy), 1:453
Susanna, 1:452
Susanna (----), 1:452
Tabitha, 1:453
Thankful, 1:452
Cooley
Abilene, 1:360
Bethia, 1:360, 1:453
Elizabeth (Wolcott), 1:453,
  4:623
Hannah, 3:362
Hannah (Tibbals), 1:453,
  4:298
Martha (Stream/Streame),
  4:222
Mary, 1:453, 4:270
Rebecca (----), 1:453,
  4:421
Rebecca (Williams), 4:561
Sarah, 1:103, 1:453
Sarah (----), 1:453
Cooper
----, 1:453, 2:151
---- (----) Smith, 1:455,
  4:126
Abigail, 1:454
Ann, 1:454, 3:243, 3:439
Ann (----) Bosworth, 1:216,
  1:455
Ann (Sparhawk), 1:454,
  4:144
Deborah, 3:476
Deliverance (Marston),
  3:612, 3:651
Desire (Lamberton), 1:455,
  3:49
Elizabeth, 1:454, 3:612
Elizabeth (----), 1:453,
  1:455
Elizabeth (Bordman),
  1:454
Hannah, 1:454, 3:466,

4:679
Hannah (Hastings), 1:454
Humility, 4:302
Jane, 4:605
Jane (----) Hall, 4:679
Jane (Wallen/Woolen) Hall,
  3:627
Judith, 1:455, 4:560
Judith (Sewall), 4:55
Lydia, 1:454, 2:164, 2:199,
  2:288, 3:244, 4:204
Lydia (----), 1:454, 4:204
Martha, 1:454
Mary, 1:337, 1:454, 3:197,
  3:615, 4:679
Mary (Rogers), 3:560
Mary (Thompson), 1:454
Mary (Tucker), 1:454
Mehitable (Minot), 1:455,
  3:217, 4:18, 4:201
Mercy, 1:453
Priscilla (----) Wright,
  1:454
Rachel, 1:337
Rebecca, 1:396, 1:453-455,
  3:625, 4:679
Sarah, 1:454-455, 2:27,
  2:401, 3:231, 3:369,
  4:679
Sarah (----), 1:404
Sarah (----) Southwick,
  3:612
Sarah (Morse), 1:455,
  3:240
Waitawhile (Makepeace),
  1:454, 3:144
Copeland
Abigail, 1:456
Bethia, 1:455
Elizabeth, 1:456
Hannah, 1:456
Lydia, 1:455-456
Lydia (Townsend), 1:455
Mary, 1:456
Mary (Arnold), 1:456
Mary (Bass) Webb, 1:456
Mary (Holbrook), 2:443
Mehitable (----) Atwood,
  1:456
Mercy, 1:455
Mercy (----), 1:456
Ruth, 1:455
Ruth (----), 1:455

Copeland (continued)
Sarah, 1:456
Copley
Elizabeth, 1:25, 1:456
Elizabeth (----), 1:456,
3:406
Mary, 2:75
Copp
Ann, 1:77, 1:457, 4:32
Joanna, 1:457
Judith (----), 1:457
Lydia, 1:457
Margaret (----), 1:456
Naomi, 1:457
Obedience (Topliff), 1:456,
4:313
Rebecca, 1:457
Ruth, 1:457
Sarah, 1:456
Copper
Christian (----), 1:153, 2:94
Corbee/Corby
---- (Langton), 3:56
Hannah, 1:457
Mary, 1:457
Mary (Crippin), 1:457,
1:515
Corbet/Corbett
Dorcas (Buckmaster),
1:457
Dorcas (Buckminster),
1:286, 1:457
Mehitable (Holbrook),
2:443
Sarah (Haynes/Haines),
2:390
Corbin/Corbyn
Dorcas, 1:457
Dorcas (Buckminster),
1:286
Joan, 4:155
Joanna, 1:457
Lydia (Martin), 1:457,
3:162
Margaret, 1:457
Mary (Morse), 3:237
Corlet
Barbara (Cutter), 1:458,
1:496
Hepzibah, 1:356, 1:458,
3:217
Joanna, 3:589
Rebecca, 1:458

Corliss
----, 1:457, 3:43
Huldah, 1:458, 3:29
Joane (----), 1:457
Mary, 1:457, 3:266
Cornell
Deliverance (Clarke),
1:458
Sarah (Earle), 2:134
Corney/Curney
Abigail, 1:458
Abigail (Skilling), 1:458
Cornhill/Corning
Hannah (Bachiler), 3:599,
3:612
Rebecca, 1:409
Sarah, 1:458
Cornish
Damaris, 4:342
Elizabeth (Wolcott), 1:458,
4:620
Martha (----), 1:459
Mary (Stone), 1:459
Remember, 1:459
Cornwell
Elizabeth, 1:459
Esther, 1:459, 4:217,
4:547
Experience, 1:459
Hannah, 1:459, 2:60
Joan (----), 1:459
Martha, 1:459, 2:485
Martha (Peck), 1:459,
3:383
Mary, 1:459
Mary (----), 1:459
Mary (Bell), 1:459
Mary (White), 1:459
Rebecca, 1:459
Rebecca (Bull), 1:459
Sarah, 1:459, 2:483
Sarah (Clark), 1:459
Thankful, 1:459
Corrington
Mary (----), 1:459
Corse
Elizabeth, 1:459
Elizabeth (Catlin), 1:349,
1:459
Cory/Coree/Corey
----, 3:248
Deliverance, 1:460, 3:612
Elizabeth, 1:460

Margaret, 1:409, 1:460
Margaret (----), 1:460
Margaret (Christophers),
1:460
Martha, 1:409, 1:460
Martha (----), 1:460
Mary, 3:612, 3:658
Mary (Britz), 1:460
Mary (Earle), 2:134
Cosin/Cozens/Cousins/etc
Ann (Hunt) Edwards,
1:460
Bethia, 1:461
Elizabeth, 1:125
Elizabeth (----), 1:460
Hannah, 1:461
Margaret (Bird), 1:460
Mary, 1:460
Mary (Boylston), 4:291
Mary (Chalker), 1:352,
1:460-461
Mary (Eames), 1:460
Rebecca, 3:612
Rebecca (----), 3:612
Sarah, 1:460-461
Susanna, 2:178
Cosseboom
Patience (Jones), 2:564
Coster
Esther
(Auger/Agar/etc), 1:79
Costin/Costing
Phebe, 1:461
Sarah, 1:461
Cotta/Cotty/Cottey
Bathshua, 1:461
Joan (----), 1:461
Mary, 1:461
Mary (Moore), 1:461
Sarah (Wharton), 1:461,
4:494
Cotter
Elinor (----), 1:461
Cotterill/Cottrell
Charity (Hall), 2:591
Dorothy, 1:461
Elizabeth, 1:461
Martha, 3:201
Mary, 1:461, 3:57
Cottle
----, 1:151
Ann, 1:461, 4:308
Dorothy, 1:461

Cottle (continued)
Elizabeth, 1:461
Judith, 1:461
Judith (----), 1:461
Lydia, 1:461
Mary, 1:461
Mary (Woodbridge), 1:461
Sarah, 1:461
Susanna, 1:461
Cotton
----, 3:366
Abiah, 1:464
Ann, 1:464
Ann (----), 1:464
Ann (Lake), 1:463, 3:45,
3:173
Bridget (Hoar), 2:432
Dorothy, 1:463-464, 2:280,
4:125
Dorothy (Bradstreet),
1:236, 1:464
Elizabeth, 1:40, 1:462-464,
1:489, 2:105, 4:66
Elizabeth (Horrocks),
1:462
Elizabeth (Saltonstall)
Denison, 1:463, 2:37
Hannah, 1:464
Joanna (Rossiter), 1:462,
3:577
Lydia, 1:464
Maria, 1:462-463, 3:173
Mary, 1:76, 1:462-464,
3:173-175, 4:342
Mary (----), 1:465
Mary (Moore), 3:228
Mercy, 1:464
Prudence (Wade) Crosby,
1:464, 1:477, 4:378
Rebecca, 1:464
Ruth (Taylor), 4:259
Sarah, 1:462-464, 3:220,
3:430
Sarah (----), 3:174
Sarah (----) Day Story,
4:244
Sarah (----) Story, 1:462
Sarah (Hubbard), 1:463,
2:485
Couch
Abigail, 1:465
Hannah, 1:465
Martha, 1:465

Mary, 1:465
Rebecca, 1:465
Sarah, 1:465
Susanna, 1:465
Counts
Elizabeth, 1:465
Sarah, 1:465, 3:60
Sarah (Adams), 1:15,
1:465
Courser
Deliverance, 1:465
Joanna, 1:465
Cousins - see Cosin
Covell
Elizabeth (Atwood), 1:465
Sarah, 1:465
Covey
Rachel, 3:50
Sarah
(Landfear/etc), 3:50
Cowdall
Mary (----) Davis, 1:465,
2:22
Cowdry
Bethia, 1:466, 1:512
Elizabeth, 1:465
Elizabeth (----), 1:465
Mary (----), 1:465
Cowell
Alice, 1:466
Alice (Palmer), 1:466
Elizabeth, 1:466
Margaret (----), 1:466
Mary, 4:680
Mary (Carter) Hunter,
1:341, 1:466, 2:502
Sarah, 1:466
Sarah (Hobart), 1:466,
2:434
Cowen
Deborah (Litchfield),
1:466
Elizabeth, 1:466
Hannah, 1:466
Mary, 1:466
Rebecca, 1:466, 2:380
Rebecca (----) Man, 1:466
Sarah, 1:466
Cowes
Mary, 3:660
Cowland
Alice (----) Shotten, 1:466,
4:89

Mary, 1:466
Sarah (----), 1:466
Cowles
----, 1:466
Abigail, 3:464, 4:679
Abigail (Stanley), 4:165
Abigail (Woodford), 4:638
Deborah (Bartlett), 1:132,
1:466
Elizabeth, 3:134, 4:679
Esther, 1:294, 1:466,
4:679
Hannah, 4:163, 4:679
Hannah (----), 1:466
Hannah (Pitkin), 3:441
Mary, 4:679
Rachel (Porter), 3:660
Sarah, 2:277, 4:679
Cox/Cock/Coxe
----, 1:467, 2:544
Alice, 1:6, 1:467
Alice (----), 1:467
Ann, 1:467
Elizabeth, 1:467
Leah, 1:467, 3:395
Margaret (----), 1:466-467
Martha (----), 1:467
Mary, 1:467, 1:515, 2:266
Mary (----), 1:467
Mary (Ingersoll), 1:467
Mary (Mason), 1:515,
3:166
Prudence (Marston), 3:161
Sarah, 3:614
Sarah (----), 1:467
Susanna, 1:467, 3:117
Susanna (Upshall), 1:467
Coy
Elizabeth (Roberts), 1:467
Martha (----), 1:467
Mary, 1:467, 3:45
Coytemore
Catharine (----) Gray,
2:297, 3:295
Catharine (Myles) Gray,
1:467, 4:358
Elizabeth, 1:467-468,
4:358
Martha (----), 1:420
Martha (Nowell), 4:611
Martha (Rainsborough),
1:467
Sarah, 1:467

Cozens - see Cosin
Crabb
  Hannah (Emmons), 1:468,
    2:120
Crabtree
  Alice (----), 1:468, 2:408
  Deliverance, 1:468
  Mary, 1:468
  Mary (----), 1:468
Crackbone
  Elizabeth (Cooledge),
    1:453, 1:468
  Hannah, 1:468
  Judith, 1:468
  Mary, 1:468
  Sarah, 1:468
Craford/Crafford
  Elizabeth, 1:469
  Elizabeth (----), 3:612
  Judith (----), 1:469
  Mary, 1:469
  Mary (----), 1:469
  Susanna (----), 1:469
Crafts/Craft
  Abigail, 1:469-470, 2:275,
    2:441, 3:586
  Alice (----), 1:469
  Dorcas (----), 1:469
  Elizabeth, 1:470
  Elizabeth (Seaver), 1:470
  Hannah, 1:469-470, 2:557,
    4:586
  Lydia, 1:469
  Mary, 1:469-470, 2:315
  Mary (Hudson), 1:469
  Mehitable, 1:469
  Rebecca, 1:469, 4:660
  Rebecca (Gardner), 1:469
  Rebecca (Wheelock),
    1:469, 4:502
  Sarah, 1:469
  Ursula (----) Hosier, 4:223
  Ursula (----) Robinson,
    1:469
  Ursula (----) Robinson
    Hosier Streeter, 3:555
Cragg
  Catharine (----), 2:137
Craggan/Craggin
  Abigail, 1:470, 3:37
  Ann, 1:470
  Elizabeth, 1:470
  Leah, 1:470

  Mercy, 1:470
  Rachel, 1:470
  Sarah, 1:470
  Sarah (Dawes), 1:470
Cram
  Argentine (Cromwell),
    1:470, 1:476
  Esther (----), 1:470
  Hannah, 2:158
  Lydia, 1:470
  Mary, 1:470
  Sarah, 4:2
Crampton
  Abigail, 1:470
  Elizabeth, 1:470, 3:72
  Frances (----), 1:470
  Hannah, 1:470, 4:41
  Hannah (Andrews), 1:53,
    1:470
  Mary (Parmelee), 1:470
  Sarah, 1:470, 2:129
  Sarah (----) Munger, 1:470
  Sarah (Hull) Munger,
    4:692
  Sarah (Rockwell), 1:470,
    3:557
Cramwell
  Rebecca, 1:471
  Rebecca (----), 1:471
Crandall
  ----, 1:471
  ---- (Landfear/Lamphear),
    3:50
  Ann, 1:471
  Deborah (Burdick), 1:301,
    1:471
  Elizabeth, 1:471
  Elizabeth (----), 1:471
  Elizabeth (Gorton), 1:471,
    2:283
  Experience, 1:471
  Hannah, 1:471
  Mary, 1:471
  Mary (----), 1:471
  Patience, 1:471
  Priscilla (----), 1:471
  Sarah, 1:471
  Susanna, 1:471
Crane
  ---- (Kingsley/Kinsley),
    1:471, 3:30
  Abigail, 3:612
  Concurrence, 1:130

  Concurrence (Meigs),
    3:193
  Deborah (Griswold), 1:472,
    2:590
  Deliverance, 1:471
  Elinor (Breck), 1:471
  Elizabeth, 1:471, 3:612
  Esther, 1:472
  Hannah, 1:471-472, 2:504,
    3:612
  Hannah (Leonard), 1:472
  Margaret, 3:564
  Martha (Credan), 4:269
  Mary, 1:159, 1:471-472,
    2:590, 3:504
  Mary (----), 1:472
  Mercy, 1:471, 2:429
  Sarah, 1:472
  Sarah (Kilbourn/Kilborne),
    1:472, 3:19
Craniver
  Elizabeth, 1:472
  Elizabeth (Woolland),
    1:472
Cranston
  Mary, 1:261
  Mary (Brush), 1:281,
    1:472
  Mary (Clark), 1:394, 1:472
  Mary (Hart), 1:472, 2:368
  Mary (Williams), 4:560
Crary
  Ann, 1:472
  Christobel, 1:472
  Christobel (Gallup), 1:472,
    2:223
  Margaret, 1:472
Crason
  Esther, 3:634
Crawford
  Rebecca, 4:156
Crawley
  Phebe, 1:472
Creatty
  Mary (----), 3:616
Credan
  Hannah, 4:269
  Martha, 4:269
Crehore
  Mary (Spurr), 1:472, 4:158
Crippin
  Catharine, 1:515, 3:582
  Elizabeth, 1:516

Crippin (continued)
Experience, 1:515
Frances, 1:515
Hannah, 1:516
Lydia, 1:515-516
Mary, 1:457, 1:515
Mary (Ackley), 1:516
Mehitable, 1:515
Mercy, 1:515
Susanna, 1:515
Thankful, 1:515
Thankful (Fuller), 1:515
Crisp/Crispe
Bridget (----), 1:473
Elizabeth, 1:473, 3:61
Hannah (Hudson)
Richards, 1:473, 2:489,
3:532
Joanna (----), 1:473
Joanna (----) Longley,
1:473, 3:110
Mary, 1:473
Mehitable, 1:473
Sarah, 1:397, 1:437, 1:473,
2:366
Sarah (Wheelwright),
1:473, 3:544, 4:503
Critchley
Alice, 1:473
Alice (----) Dinely, 1:473,
2:51
Elizabeth, 1:473
Jane, 1:473
Jane (----), 1:473
Mary, 1:473
Crittenden
Lydia (Thompson), 4:283
Croad/Croade
Deborah (Thomas),
1:473-474, 4:282
Elizabeth, 1:473, 3:485
Elizabeth (Price), 1:473,
3:485, 3:584
Frances (Hersey), 1:474,
2:406
Hannah, 1:473-474
Judith, 1:474, 3:264
Mary (----), 3:613
Sarah, 1:474, 2:275
Croakham/Crocum/etc
Hannah, 1:474
Joan (----) Waller, 1:474,
4:399

Rebecca (Josselyn), 1:474,
2:364, 2:570, 4:185
Crocker
Abigail, 1:475
Alice, 1:475
Alice (----), 1:475
Ann (Beebe), 1:153
Bathshua, 1:475
Bethia, 1:474
Elizabeth, 1:379,
1:474-475
Elizabeth (Bodfish), 1:212
Experience, 1:475
Hannah, 1:474-475, 3:121
Hannah (Taylor), 1:474,
4:263
Joan (----), 1:474
Joanna, 1:475
Martha, 1:475
Mary, 1:474-475
Mary (Bodfish), 1:474
Mary (Bursley), 1:312,
1:474
Mary (Walley), 1:474,
4:401
Meletiah, 1:475
Meletiah (Hinckley), 1:475,
2:425
Mercy, 1:475
Rachel (----), 1:475
Rachel (Chappell), 1:363
Rebecca, 1:474
Remember, 1:475
Ruth, 1:474
Ruth (Chipman), 1:474
Sarah, 1:474
Sarah (Baldwin), 1:474
Temperance, 1:475
Temperance (Bursley),
1:312, 1:475
Thankful, 1:474
Croe
Abigail, 4:699
Croft
Abigail, 1:475
Abigail (Dickinson), 1:475,
1:480, 2:48
Ann (----) Ivory, 1:475,
2:526
Elizabeth, 1:475
Mary, 1:475
Crompton
Jane (----), 3:613

Cromwell
----, 2:41, 2:567
Alice (Wiseman), 1:476
Ann, 1:78, 1:476, 3:418
Ann (----), 1:476, 2:573,
3:39
Argentine, 1:470, 1:476
Catharine, 2:568
Dorothy, 1:476
Dorothy (----), 1:476
Dorothy (----) Kingston,
1:516
Elizabeth, 1:476, 3:484
Elizabeth (Leighton),
1:375, 1:476, 3:44
Elizabeth (Thomas), 1:476
Hannah (----), 1:476
Hannah (Barney), 1:124
Jane, 1:476, 3:423
Joan (Butler), 1:476
Margaret (----), 1:476
Margaret (----) Becket,
1:151
Mary (----) Lemon, 1:476,
3:78
Rebecca, 1:476
Rebecca (----), 1:476
Sarah, 1:476, 2:182, 4:485
Crook/Crooke
Elizabeth, 3:626
Rebecca, 2:229
Ruth, 3:519
Crooker
Elizabeth, 3:125
Mary (Bumpas), 1:476
Mary (Gaunt), 1:476
Sarah, 3:141
Crosby
Ann, 1:477
Ann (----), 1:477, 4:289
Deliverance (Corey),
3:612-613
Dorothy, 3:437
Elizabeth, 1:477
Ellen (Veazie) Paine,
3:336
Hannah, 1:476-477, 2:554
Hannah (----), 1:477
Jane, 3:422
Mary, 1:477
Mary (Nickerson), 1:477
Mercy, 1:477
Patience (Freeman), 1:477

78

Crosby (continued)
Prudence (----), 1:335,
1:476
Prudence (Wade), 1:464,
1:477, 4:378
Rachel, 1:477, 3:18
Rachel (Brackett), 1:229,
1:477
Rebecca, 1:477
Sarah, 1:180, 1:477
Sarah (Brackett), 1:229,
1:477
Sarah (French), 2:208
Cross
---- (Bates), 1:139
---- (Jones), 2:569
Ann, 1:477
Ann (----), 1:477
Elizabeth, 3:613
Elizabeth (----), 1:478
Elizabeth (----) Chapman,
1:478
Elizabeth (Fox) Chapman,
1:361
Frances (----), 1:478
Hannah, 1:478, 1:516,
2:347
Jane (Pudeater), 3:613
Martha, 1:478, 2:83, 4:263
Martha (Treadwell), 1:478
Mary, 1:477, 1:516, 2:405,
2:419, 3:389, 3:424
Mary (----), 1:477-478,
4:22
Mary (Grant), 1:516
Mary (Phillips) Munjoy
Lawrence, 1:478, 3:63,
3:255
Sarah, 2:419
Susanna, 1:478
Crossman
Elizabeth, 1:478
Elizabeth (Bell), 1:478
Hannah (Brooks), 1:478
Joanna (Thayer), 1:478,
4:277
Mary, 1:478, 2:285
Mary (Sawyer), 1:478
Mercy, 1:478
Sarah, 4:645
Sarah (----), 1:478
Sarah (Alden), 1:478
Susanna, 1:478

Crossthwayte/Croswait
Judith (----), 1:478
Crosswell/Croswell
Elizabeth, 1:330
Hepzibah, 2:592
Naomi, 2:5
Priscilla, 2:589
Priscilla (Upham), 1:479,
4:360
Croutch/Crouch
Elizabeth, 1:479
Hannah, 1:479
Mary, 1:479
Mary/Mercy, 2:277
Mercy, 2:587
Sarah (----), 1:479
Crow
Ann, 1:479
Deborah, 1:480
Deborah (----), 1:480
Deliverance (Bennett),
1:516
Elishua (----), 1:479
Elizabeth, 1:479-480,
4:427
Elizabeth (----), 1:400
Elizabeth (Goodwin),
1:479, 2:278
Esther, 1:479, 2:344
Hannah, 1:479-480, 1:516,
2:49
Hannah (Lewis), 3:89,
3:154
Hannah (Winslow), 1:480,
4:229, 4:602
Lydia, 1:480
Margaret, 1:479
Martha, 1:479, 1:516
Martha (Moses), 1:516
Mary, 1:397, 1:431,
1:479-480, 3:225
Mary (Burr), 1:305, 1:399,
1:479
Mehitable, 1:479-480,
3:366
Mehitable (Miller), 1:479,
3:209
Ruth, 1:479, 2:239, 2:332
Sarah, 1:479, 4:23, 4:508
Sarah (Fuller), 2:218
Sarah (Lewis), 1:480
Susanna, 1:480

Crowell
Agnes (----), 1:480
Lydia, 1:480, 2:276
Mary (Lothrop), 3:121
Crowfoot
Abigail (Dickinson) Croft,
1:475, 1:480, 2:48
Mary, 1:480
Mary (Hillier), 1:516
Mary (Warner), 1:480
Sarah, 1:480
Crown
Agnes, 1:480
Alice (Rogers), 1:480
Elizabeth, 1:480
Rebecca, 1:480
Crumb/Cromb
---, 1:481
Alice (----) Haughton,
1:481
Elizabeth, 1:481
Hannah (----), 1:481
Jemima, 1:481
Mercy, 1:481
Rachel, 1:481
Crump
Lydia, 1:360
Cruttenden
Abigail, 1:481
Abigail (Hull), 1:481
Ann, 1:481
Bathsheba, 1:481
Bathsheba (Johnson),
1:481
Deborah, 1:481
Elizabeth, 1:481
Esther, 1:481
Hannah, 1:481
Jane, 1:481
Joan (Sheaffe) Chittenden,
1:382
Joanna (----) Chittenden,
1:481
Lydia, 1:481
Lydia (----), 3:194
Lydia (Thompson), 1:481,
4:289
Mary, 1:130, 1:481
Mary (----), 1:481
Mary (Hoyt), 1:481
Mehitable, 1:481
Mercy, 1:481
Naomi, 1:481

Cruttenden (continued)
Rachel, 1:481
Sarah, 1:481
Susanna, 1:481
Susanna (Grigson), 1:481,
2:316
Susanna (Kirby), 1:481,
3:30
Cudworth
—— (Stoughton), 3:613
Abigail, 1:482
Bethia, 1:482
Elizabeth, 1:482
Hannah, 1:482
Joanna, 1:482
Mary, 1:481-482, 4:508
Mary (——), 1:482
Rachel, 1:482
Sarah, 1:482
Sarah (Jackson), 1:482
Cullick
Elizabeth, 1:141, 1:482
Elizabeth (Fenwick), 1:482,
2:117, 2:153
Hannah, 1:482, 2:262
Mary, 1:482
Culver
Abigail, 1:483
Ann, 4:679
Ann (——), 1:482
Elizabeth, 4:679
Elizabeth (Ford), 1:483,
2:183
Hannah, 1:482
Mary, 1:311
Mary (——), 1:483
Sarah, 1:483
Sarah (——), 1:482
Cumby/Cumbee
Esther, 1:483
Sarah (——), 1:483
Cumming
——, 2:198
Cummings/Cummens/etc
Ann, 1:483-484, 3:379
Elizabeth, 1:483, 2:548
Elizabeth (——), 1:483
Lydia, 1:483
Mary, 1:483
Mary (——), 1:483
Priscilla, 1:483
Priscilla (Warner), 1:483
Sarah, 1:483, 2:207

Sarah (——), 1:483
Sarah (Howlett), 1:483,
2:480
Cunliff/Cunliffe/Cunlith
Susanna, 1:429, 1:484,
3:451, 4:445
Susanna (——), 1:484
Cunnill
Elizabeth, 3:201
Cunningham
Elizabeth, 1:442
Curney/Corney
Abigail, 1:484
Abigail (Skilling), 1:458,
1:484, 4:105
Mary, 3:613
Mary (Cook), 3:613
Rebecca (Smith), 3:613
Currier
Ann (——), 1:484
Hannah, 1:484, 2:181
Martha, 1:484
Mary, 2:482
Mary (Hardy), 1:484,
2:355
Sarah, 1:484
**Curtice/Curtise/Curtize - see
Curtis**
Curtis
——, 4:680
—— (——) Kimberly, 3:604
Abiel, 1:486
Abigail, 1:195, 1:486-488,
3:548, 3:604, 3:613
Abigail (Grout), 2:319
Abigail (Thompson), 1:486,
3:613, 3:637, 4:85,
4:285, 4:287, 4:710
Alice (——), 1:488
Ann, 1:486-488, 3:622
Ann (Barstow), 1:487
Ann (Hallet), 1:486, 2:340
Deborah, 1:484, 1:486-487
Elizabeth, 1:261,
1:485-488, 2:287, 3:271,
4:200
Elizabeth (——), 1:485-487,
4:474
Elizabeth (Abell), 1:485
Esther (Judson), 2:576
Eunice, 1:486
Experience (Palmer),
1:486

Hannah, 1:485-488, 2:240,
3:262
Hannah (——), 1:195
Hannah (——) Kimberly,
3:644
Hannah (Gore), 1:485
Hannah (Polley), 1:485,
3:450
Hannah (Smith), 1:485
Jane (——), 1:485
Joan (——), 1:488
Lydia, 1:484
Lydia (——), 1:487
Margaret (——), 1:486
Martha, 1:402, 1:486-487
Mary, 1:484, 1:486-488,
2:530, 3:613
Mary (Cook), 1:487
Mary (Guy), 1:485, 2:325
Mary (Merriman), 4:690
Mary (Sylvester), 1:484
Mehitable, 1:485, 1:487
Mercy, 1:486
Mercy (——), 1:486
Miriam, 1:487
Miriam (Brooks), 1:263,
1:486
Obedience (Holland),
1:486, 2:224, 2:447
Priscilla (Gould/Gold),
2:285
Rebecca, 1:65, 1:485-486
Rebecca (——), 1:484-486
Rebecca (Wheeler), 1:486,
4:500
Ruth, 1:484, 1:487
Sarah, 1:484, 1:486-488,
3:613
Sarah (——), 1:486-487
Sarah (——) Goodrich,
1:487
Sarah (——) Strange, 1:486
Sarah (Alexander), 1:26
Sarah (Foote/Foot), 2:181
Sarah (Foxwell), 1:486,
2:198
Sarah (Locke), 1:486
Sarah (Marvin) Goodrich,
2:275
Susanna, 1:484-485
Thankful, 1:486
Curwin/Corwin
——, 1:488

Curwin/Corwin (continued)
Abigail, 1:488, 2:377, 3:590
Ann, 1:488
Elizabeth, 1:488
Elizabeth (----), 3:24
Elizabeth (----) Brooks, 1:488
Elizabeth (Herbert) White, 1:488
Elizabeth (Sheaffe) Gibbs, 1:488, 2:247, 4:66
Elizabeth (Winslow) Brooks, 1:262, 1:516, 4:599
Hannah, 1:278, 1:488, 4:274
Lucy, 1:488
Margaret (Winthrop), 1:488, 4:613
Penelope, 1:488, 4:622
Sarah, 1:488
Susanna, 1:488, 3:133
Cushing
---- (Jacob) Thaxter, 4:275
Ann (Coffin), 3:613
Deborah, 1:252, 1:489-491, 3:119, 4:256
Deborah (Jacob), 1:491
Deborah (Loring), 1:490, 3:119
Deborah (Thaxter), 1:491, 4:275
Elizabeth, 1:491
Elizabeth (----) Wilkie, 1:489
Elizabeth (Cotton) Alling, 1:41, 1:463-464, 1:489
Elizabeth (Jacob) Thaxter, 1:489
Elizabeth (Thaxter), 1:489, 4:275
Hannah, 1:489, 1:491
Hannah (----), 1:116
Hannah (Hawke), 1:491, 2:381
Hannah (Loring), 1:489, 3:119
Jael, 1:491
Jael (Jacob), 1:491, 2:533
Judith (Parmenter), 1:489
Lydia (Gilman), 1:489, 2:257

Margaret, 1:491
Mary, 1:490
Mary (Pickels), 1:490
Mary (Thaxter), 1:491, 4:275
Mercy (Pickels), 1:490
Mercy (Wensley) Bridgham, 1:250, 1:491, 4:483
Nazareth, 1:490
Nazareth (Pitcher), 1:490
Sarah, 1:490, 2:80, 2:532
Sarah (----) Holmes, 1:490
Sarah (Hawks), 1:490, 2:381
Sarah (House), 2:470
Sarah (Jacob), 1:490, 2:534
Cushman
Abigail (Fuller), 1:492, 2:218
Elizabeth, 1:491
Elizabeth (Cole), 1:491
Elizabeth (Combes), 1:491
Esther, 4:423
Esther (----), 4:423
Fear, 1:491-492
Lydia, 1:491-492, 3:628
Martha, 1:491
Martha (Cooke), 1:446, 1:491
Mary, 1:491-492
Mary (Allerton), 1:38, 1:492, 2:479
Mary (Singleton), 1:492
Mehitable, 1:491
Rebecca, 1:491
Rebecca (Rickard), 1:491
Ruth (Howland), 1:492, 2:480
Sarah, 1:491-492, 2:381, 2:439
Cuthbertson
----, 1:492, 3:475
Sarah, 1:453, 1:492
Sarah (----) Priest, 1:492
Sarah (Allerton) Priest, 3:486
Cutler
Abigail, 1:494, 4:680
Abigail (----), 1:494
Ann, 1:203, 1:493-494
Ann (----), 1:493, 4:680

Ann (Woodmansey), 1:493, 4:642
Dorcas, 4:553
Dorothy (----), 1:494
Dorothy (Bell), 1:516, 4:324
Elizabeth, 1:493-494, 4:680
Elizabeth (----), 1:494
Elizabeth (Carter), 1:516
Elizabeth (Felch), 1:494
Elizabeth (Fitch), 1:494
Elizabeth (Hilton), 1:494, 2:594
Hannah, 1:432, 1:493-494, 2:589, 3:496, 4:552-553, 4:680
Jemima, 1:493
Joanna, 1:493
Joanna (Dodd) Richards, 4:680, 4:697
Lydia (Moore) Wright, 1:493
Margaret, 1:494, 1:516
Martha (----), 1:494
Martha (Wiswall), 1:516
Mary, 1:493-494, 1:516, 2:139, 4:126, 4:680
Mary (----), 1:493
Mary (----) King, 1:493, 3:26
Mary (Brown) Lewis, 1:264, 3:87
Mary (Cowell), 4:680
Mary (Gile/Gyles/etc), 2:253
Mary (Stearns), 1:494, 4:174
Mary (Very), 1:494, 4:372
Mehitable (Nowell) Hilton, 1:493, 2:423, 3:295
Olive (Thompson), 1:493
Phebe, 1:493
Phebe (Page), 1:493, 3:330
Rebecca, 1:493-494, 1:516, 2:126, 4:527
Rebecca (----), 1:494
Ruth, 1:494, 4:680
Ruth (----), 4:680
Sarah, 1:493-494, 1:516, 2:246, 3:409, 4:680
Susanna, 1:493, 1:511
Susanna (Baker), 1:493

Cutt/Cutts
Bridget, 1:495, 2:10, 2:289
Dorcas (Hammond), 1:495, 2:345
Elizabeth, 1:494-495, 2:109
Hannah, 1:494, 4:390
Hannah (Star), 1:494
Joanna (Wills), 1:495, 4:579
Margaret, 1:495, 4:368
Mary, 1:494-495, 3:388
Mary (----), 1:355, 1:495
Sarah, 1:495
Ursula (----), 1:495
Cutter
Barbara, 1:458, 1:496
Bethia, 1:495
Bethia (Wood), 1:495
Deborah (Stone), 4:206
Deborah (Wiswall), 4:616
Elizabeth, 1:495-496, 2:336
Elizabeth (----), 1:495-496
Frances (----) Amsden, 1:495
Frances (Perriman) Amsden, 1:50
Hannah, 1:495-496, 2:339, 3:155
Hepzibah, 1:496
Isabel, 1:495
Joanna (Dodd) Richards, 3:534
Lydia, 1:495, 2:336
Lydia (Hall), 1:495, 2:339
Lydia (Moore) Wright, 4:659
Mary, 1:495-496, 4:16
Mary (Fillebrown), 1:495, 2:159
Rebecca, 1:496, 2:159
Rebecca (Rolfe), 1:496
Ruhamah, 1:496
Sarah, 1:496, 3:102, 3:347
Cutting
Elizabeth, 1:496
Hannah (Collar), 1:432, 1:496
Lydia, 1:496-497, 4:157, 4:427
Mary, 1:496, 3:226, 3:297
Mary (----), 1:496, 3:210

Mercy, 3:226
Sarah, 1:119, 1:268, 1:496
Sarah (----), 1:496
Susanna, 1:496, 3:270
Susanna (Harrington), 1:154, 1:496
Dade/Davy/Dady
Abigail, 2:1
Dorothy (----), 2:1
Hannah, 2:1
Hannah (Miller), 2:1, 2:101, 3:129, 3:210-211
Martha (----), 2:1
Dafforne/Daffern
Mary, 2:1
Mary (----), 2:1
Dagan
Elizabeth, 2:2
Daggett/Doggett
Abigail, 2:2
Bathsheba, 2:2
Bathsheba (----) Pratt, 2:2
Bathsheba (Holmes), 2:2, 2:451
Elizabeth, 2:2
Jane (----) Chillingworth, 1:379
Joan/Jane (----) Chillingworth, 2:2
Lydia, 2:2
Mary, 2:2
Mary (Rogers), 2:2
Mehitable (Truant), 2:2, 4:334
Persis, 2:2
Persis (Sprague), 2:2, 4:156
Rebecca, 2:2
Sarah, 2:2
Daille
Esther (Latonice), 2:2
Martha (----), 2:2
Psyche (----), 2:2
Dakin/Dakyngs/Daking
Huldah (Cheney) Worcester, 4:651
Sarah, 2:2
Sarah (----), 2:2
Sarah (Woodis), 4:639
Susan (----), 2:2
Susan (----) Stratton, 2:2
Dale
Abigail, 2:3

Ann, 2:577
Elizabeth, 2:577
Elizabeth (----), 2:577
Joanna, 2:3
Joanna (Farrar), 2:3
Lydia, 2:577
Martha, 2:3
Mary, 2:577
Rebecca, 2:3
Daley
Ann, 2:577
Mary, 2:577
Dalisson/Dalison
Margaret (----) Story, 2:3
Mary (----), 2:3
Dalton/Dolton
Abigail (Gove), 2:3, 2:288, 4:11
Dorothy (----), 2:3, 2:31-32
Hannah (----), 2:3
Mary, 1:341
Mehitable (----), 4:244
Mehitable (Palmer), 2:3, 3:340
Ruth (----), 1:341, 2:3
Dame/Damme/Dam
---- (Hall), 2:591
Abigail, 2:3, 4:171
Alice, 2:4
Elizabeth, 2:3
Elizabeth (----), 2:3
Elizabeth (Furber), 2:4, 2:220
Jane (Rowe), 2:3, 3:580
Judith, 2:3, 4:299
Leah, 2:4, 2:388
Martha, 2:4
Martha (Pomfret), 2:4, 3:452
Mary, 2:3, 4:307
Sarah, 2:4
Susanna, 2:3
Damerill
Sarah (----), 2:4, 2:383
Damon/Daman/etc
---- (Bacon), 2:4
Abiah, 2:4
Abigail, 1:512
Catharine (Merritt), 2:4
Deborah, 2:4, 2:443, 4:647
Elizabeth, 2:4
Hannah, 2:4, 2:259
Margaret, 1:293, 2:4

Damon/Daman/etc
(continued)
Martha (Howland), 2:4
Martha (Woodworth), 2:4,
4:648
Mary, 2:4
Silence, 2:4
Susan (----), 2:4
Susanna, 2:4
Dana
Abiah, 2:5
Ann (Bullard), 2:5
Deliverance, 2:5
Elizabeth, 2:5, 4:643
Elizabeth (Haskett), 3:630
Hannah, 2:5
Lydia (Trowbridge), 2:5,
4:334
Mary, 2:217
Mary (Buckmaster), 2:4
Mary (Goble), 2:5
Naomi (Crosswell), 2:5
Patience (----), 2:5
Sarah, 2:5
Dane
Abigail, 2:6, 2:148
Ann/Annis (----) Chandler,
3:360
Ann/Hannah/Annis (----)
Chandler, 1:359, 2:6
Deliverance (----), 2:5-6
Deliverance (Hazeltine),
2:6, 2:395
Elizabeth, 2:6, 2:190,
2:474-475, 2:557
Elizabeth (----), 2:6-7
Elizabeth (Ingalls), 2:519,
2:577
Francis (----), 2:6
Hannah, 2:6-7, 2:273,
3:321
Hannah (----) Abbot, 2:6
Hannah (Chandler) Abbot,
1:2, 1:359
Hannah (Poor), 2:6, 3:456
Martha, 2:7
Martha (----), 2:7
Mary, 1:359, 2:6-7, 3:386
Mary (Thomas), 2:6
Mary (Thompson), 2:7
Phebe, 2:6, 3:553
Rebecca, 2:6
Ruth, 2:7

Ruth (Converse), 2:7
Sarah, 2:6-7, 2:396, 4:419
Danforth
Ann, 1:248, 2:7-8, 4:520
Bethia, 2:8-9
Elizabeth, 1:155, 2:7-9,
2:197, 2:394, 4:293
Elizabeth (----), 4:216
Elizabeth (Minot), 2:7,
3:217
Elizabeth (Poulter), 2:7,
3:469
Elizabeth (Symmes), 2:7
Hannah, 2:8
Hannah (Allen), 2:8
Lydia, 1:147, 2:8
Martha, 2:8
Mary, 1:258, 1:277, 2:7-9,
3:420
Mary (Wilson), 2:8, 4:584
Mary (Withington), 2:8,
4:618
Mehitable, 2:7
Rachel, 2:8
Rebecca, 2:7
Rebecca (Parker), 2:7
Sarah, 2:8, 4:519
Sarah (Thurlo), 2:9
Daniel/Daniels
----, 2:10
Agnes (Beebe), 1:153, 2:9
Alice, 2:10, 2:302, 3:29
Ann (Gregson), 2:316
Anna, 2:10
Anna/Hannah (Gregson),
2:9
Bridget (Cutt/Cutts), 1:495,
2:10, 2:289
Catharine (Greenway),
2:310
Catharine (Grinoway),
2:10
Christian, 2:9
Elizabeth, 2:9-10, 2:140,
4:605
Elizabeth (----), 2:9
Elizabeth (Chamberlain),
1:354
Hannah, 2:9, 3:599, 3:614
Joanna, 2:9-10, 4:700
Lydia (Adams), 1:9
Mary, 2:9, 2:577, 3:487
Mary (Chappell), 1:363,

2:9
Mary (Grant), 2:9
Mary (Prince), 2:577,
3:487
Mary/Mercy (Grant),
2:291
Maudlin, 4:223
Miriam, 1:260
Rachel, 2:9
Reana (Andrews), 2:9
Reanna (----), 2:211
Rebecca, 2:10
Sarah, 2:9
Susanna, 2:577
Susanna (----) Hyde, 4:702
Susanna (Baxter) Hyde,
3:638
Susanna (Hyde), 2:577
Dants/Danks
Elizabeth, 2:10
Elizabeth (----) Webb, 2:10
Elizabeth (Swift) Webb,
4:445
Mehitable, 2:10
Mercy, 2:10
Darby - see also Derby
Alice, 3:440
Elizabeth, 3:107
Jane (James), 2:535
Ruth (Whitmarsh), 4:526
Dare
Sarah, 3:364
Darley
Mary, 4:241
Susanna (Hooke), 2:10
Darling
Catharine (----), 2:10
Elizabeth, 2:543
Elizabeth (Beers), 1:154,
2:10
Hannah (Lewis), 3:86
Joanna (----), 2:10
Margaret, 2:577
Mary, 2:577, 4:65
Darrow/Darrah
---- (----) Sharswood, 4:61
Jane, 2:10
Mary, 2:10
Mary (----), 2:10
Milicent (Beebe), 1:153
Dart
Abiah, 2:578
Ann, 1:244, 2:10, 2:578

Dart (continued)
Ann (Addis), 1:18, 2:10
Bethia, 2:10, 2:578
Bethia (----), 2:10
Dinah, 2:10
Elizabeth, 2:10, 2:577
Elizabeth (Douglas), 2:10
Elizabeth (Strickland),
2:578, 4:224
Hannah, 2:578
Lucy, 2:578
Lydia, 2:578
Margaret, 2:578
Maria, 2:578
Mary, 2:10, 2:578
Mary (----), 2:578
Mary (----) Wadley, 3:641
Mary (Roe/Stow), 3:617
Prudence, 2:578
Prudence (Beckwith),
2:578
Ruth, 2:578
Sarah, 2:10
Darvall/Darvill/Darvell
Dorothy, 2:11
Elizabeth, 2:11, 3:298
Esther (----), 2:11
Mary, 2:11, 3:297
Dassett
Ann (Flint/Flynt), 2:11,
2:174
Hannah (Flynt), 2:11
Martha (----), 2:11
Mary, 1:177, 2:11, 3:217
Sarah, 2:11
Davenport
Abigail, 2:11, 2:13, 3:432
Abigail (Pierson), 2:13,
3:434
Ann (Snelling), 2:12
Bridget (Watkins), 2:13
Deotate, 2:13
Dorcas (Andrews), 1:54,
2:11
Elizabeth, 2:13-14, 2:108
Elizabeth (----), 2:13-14
Elizabeth (Thacher), 2:13,
2:21, 4:273
Elizabeth (Wainwright),
4:382
Esther, 2:11, 2:436
Eunice, 2:11
Experience, 2:14

Hannah, 2:13
Hannah (----), 2:13
Hepzibah, 2:11
Martha (Gold) Sellick, 2:13,
4:51
Mary, 2:11, 2:13-14, 3:183
Mary (----), 2:14
Mehitable, 2:13-14
Naomi (----), 2:13
Patience (----), 2:11
Rachel (Holmes), 2:12
Rebecca, 2:11
Rebecca (Addington), 1:17,
2:11, 3:83
Sarah, 2:11, 2:13-14
Sarah (Bartlett), 2:11
Tabitha, 2:11
Thankful, 2:11
Truecross, 2:14, 3:217
Waitstill, 2:11
Waitstill (----), 2:11
Zeruiah, 2:11
Davie
Elizabeth, 2:15
Elizabeth (Richards), 2:15,
3:532
Mary, 2:15
Mary (----), 2:15
Sarah, 2:15
Sarah (----) Richards, 2:14
Sarah (Gibbons) Richards,
3:532, 4:357
Davies - see Davis
Davis
----, 2:17, 2:20
---- (----), 3:41
---- (----) Guernsey, 4:700
---- (Bills), 1:179
---- (Coleman), 1:431, 2:20
---- (Eaton), 2:17, 2:96
---- (Kingman), 3:27
Abigail, 1:432, 2:17-18,
2:22, 4:233
Alice (Thorp), 2:23
Ann, 2:19, 2:23
Ann (----), 2:21
Ann (Tayler), 2:19
Ann (Taylor), 4:263
Barbara (----), 1:254, 1:351,
2:16
Bathsheba, 2:17
Bridget, 3:26
Bridget (----), 2:21

Bridget (Kinsman), 2:22
Christian (----), 2:22
Cicely (----), 2:17
Constance, 2:578
Deborah, 2:21, 2:23
Deborah (----), 2:21
Deborah (Barnes), 1:123,
2:21
Dorothy (Mixer), 3:223
Elizabeth, 2:16-19,
2:21-24, 2:339,
3:188-189, 4:680
Elizabeth (----), 2:15-16,
2:23, 2:578
Elizabeth (----) Isaacs, 2:20,
2:525
Elizabeth (Bachelor), 2:18
Elizabeth (Bennet), 2:17
Elizabeth (Hidden), 2:16
Elizabeth (Randall), 2:18
Elizabeth (Saywell), 2:19,
4:33
Elizabeth (Scott), 4:37
Elizabeth (Smead), 2:21
Elizabeth (Thacher)
Davenport, 2:13, 2:21,
4:273
Elizabeth (Woodhouse),
4:639
Ellen, 2:17, 2:21
Experience (Lynnell), 2:17,
3:97
Grace, 2:19
Grace (Brock), 2:434
Hannah, 1:219, 1:399,
2:16-19, 2:21-23, 2:315,
2:561, 3:16
Hannah (----), 3:485
Hannah (----) Bacon, 2:19
Hannah (Gridley), 2:16,
2:313
Hannah (Leverett) Allen,
2:22, 3:83
Hannah (Lynnell), 2:16,
2:18, 3:97
Huldah, 2:23
Huldah (Symmes), 2:23,
4:244
Jane, 2:18
Jane (Andrews), 1:54
Jane (Peaslee), 2:18, 3:380
Jemima, 2:18
Joanna, 2:23

Davis (continued)
Joanna (----), 2:17
Joanna (Hull) Bursley,
1:312
Josebeth, 2:17
Joshabeth, 4:594
Judith, 2:16, 2:18, 2:24,
2:253
Judith (----), 2:23
Judith (Brown), 2:24
Lydia, 1:429
Lydia (----), 3:204, 4:587
Lydia (----) Waller, 4:399
Margaret, 1:304, 2:21,
2:23
Margaret (----), 2:24
Margaret (Pynchon), 2:23,
3:498
Margery (Willard), 2:16
Martha (Wakeman),
2:22-23
Mary, 2:16-24, 2:249,
2:276, 2:398-399, 2:526,
3:86, 3:88, 4:680
Mary (----), 1:465, 2:17-19,
2:21-22, 2:24, 2:578
Mary (Ayers), 2:16
Mary (Bayley), 1:143, 2:15
Mary (Blood), 2:21
Mary (Chamberlain),
1:353
Mary (Claghorn), 1:388,
2:19
Mary (Collins), 3:614
Mary (Collins) Elwell,
3:611
Mary (Convers), 2:20
Mary (Devotion), 2:19
Mary (Edmunds), 2:578,
2:581
Mary (Eires), 2:16
Mary (Hamblen), 2:19
Mary (Johnson), 2:16
Mary (Kelly), 2:24
Mary (Leek), 3:75
Mary (Mead), 2:21
Mary (Meddowes), 2:21
Mary (Parker), 2:23, 3:355
Mary (Spring), 2:18
Mehitable, 2:19
Mehitable (----), 2:17
Mercy, 2:17
Patience, 2:17, 2:578

Phebe, 2:18
Rachel, 2:19-20, 2:23,
2:265
Rebecca, 2:21, 2:23
Remember Mercy, 2:16
Return (Gridley), 2:19,
2:313
Ruhamah (Dow), 2:20
Ruth, 2:16, 2:19, 2:23,
2:338, 3:97
Ruth (Goodspeed), 2:19,
2:277
Sarah, 1:514, 2:17-23,
2:578, 3:234, 3:330,
3:595, 4:117, 4:189,
4:593, 4:670
Sarah (----), 1:358, 2:15,
2:17-18, 2:20, 2:23,
3:343
Sarah (Archer), 2:22
Sarah (Boynton), 2:578
Sarah (Burrill), 1:309, 2:20
Sarah (Carter), 2:19
Sarah (Chamberlain), 2:19
Sarah (Kirtland), 2:19,
3:32
Sarah (Morrill), 2:22,
3:234
Sarah (Richards), 2:15,
3:532
Sarah (Thayer), 2:21,
2:393, 4:277
Susanna, 2:16-18
Susanna (----), 2:23
Thankful, 2:16
Trine, 2:22
Davison
Abigail, 2:24
Abigail (----), 2:24
Abigail (Coffin), 1:514,
2:24
Joanna, 2:24
Joanna (----), 3:12
Joanna (Hodges), 2:24
Margaret (----), 2:25
Mary, 2:24
Sarah, 2:24, 3:135
Davoll
Elizabeth (----), 1:355
Dawes
Elizabeth, 2:24
Hannah, 3:614
Mary, 2:24-25

Mary (----), 2:25
Mary (Bumstead), 1:298,
2:24
Mehitable (Gardner),
2:228
Priscilla, 3:561
Rebecca, 2:24
Sarah, 1:470
Susan, 2:25
Susanna, 2:24
Susanna (Mills), 3:214,
3:614
Dawson
----, 1:392
Elizabeth, 2:25
Hannah, 2:25
Hannah (----) Russell, 2:25,
3:592
Margaret (----), 2:25
Martha (Howland), 2:478
Sarah (Tuttle), 2:25
Dawstin
Hannah, 2:25
Sarah, 2:25
Day
----, 2:26
Abiel, 2:26
Abigail, 2:26-27, 2:578
Abigail (Leach), 2:26
Abigail (Pond), 2:26, 3:452
Ann, 2:578
Ann (Coleman), 2:578
Betty, 1:462, 4:244
Bridget, 3:640
Editha (----), 2:456, 3:185
Editha (Stebbins), 2:26-27
Elizabeth, 2:25-26, 2:28,
4:244
Elizabeth (Andrews), 1:55
Elizabeth (Gouge), 3:615
Hannah, 2:27, 2:540
Mary, 1:431, 1:514,
2:26-27, 2:117, 2:578,
3:103, 3:333
Mary (----), 2:26, 2:578,
3:653
Mary (Laughton), 2:27
Mary (Rowe), 3:614
Phebe (----), 2:28
Phebe (Wildes), 3:615
Rachel (Rowe), 3:615
Rebecca (----) Bordman,
1:214, 2:27

Day (continued)
Ruth (Rowe), 3:615
Sarah, 2:26-27, 2:165, 2:323, 3:6
Sarah (----), 4:244
Sarah (Cooper), 2:27
Sarah (Fuller), 2:26
Sarah (Maynard), 2:26
Susan, 2:26
Susan (Fairbanks), 2:26, 2:136
Susanna, 2:25, 3:615
Susanna (----), 2:25
Thankful, 4:260
Daynes/Deans/Daines
Joanna, 2:28
Sarah, 2:28
Sarah (Peake), 2:28, 3:377
Deacon
Alice (----), 2:28
Elizabeth (----), 2:578
Elizabeth (----) Pickering, 2:28, 3:423
Deale
Pity (----), 2:28
Dean/Deane
Abiah, 2:29
Abigail, 2:29, 2:31
Alice, 2:29, 2:31
Alice (----), 2:29
Ann (Farr), 2:30
Bethia, 2:29
Bethia (Edson), 2:29, 2:102
Catharine, 2:31, 3:80
Catharine (Stephens), 2:31
Damaris, 2:28
Deborah, 2:29-31
Desire, 2:30
Eleanor (Strong), 2:31, 4:226
Elizabeth, 2:28-31, 2:102, 4:353
Elizabeth (----), 2:29-30
Elizabeth (----) Beedle, 2:31
Elizabeth (Burrage), 1:308, 2:31, 3:457
Elizabeth (Flint), 2:30
Elizabeth (Fuller), 2:30
Elizabeth (King), 1:448
Elizabeth (Ring), 2:30, 3:542

Eunice (----), 2:30
Hannah, 2:28-31, 3:615
Hannah (Leonard), 2:29, 3:79
Jane, 2:31, 2:578
Jane (----), 2:578
Jane (Scammon), 2:31, 4:34
Judith, 2:31
Lydia, 2:28, 2:31
Margaret, 2:29
Martha, 1:175, 1:407, 2:31
Martha (Bateman), 2:31
Mary, 1:319, 2:28-31, 3:386
Mary (----), 2:30-31
Mary (Farmer), 2:30, 2:141
May/Mary (Smith), 4:117
Mehitable, 2:28-29, 4:544
Mehitable (Wood), 2:31
Mercy, 2:31
Mildred (----), 2:30
Miriam, 2:30, 4:594, 4:680
Molly, 2:30
Naomi, 2:28
Rachel (----), 1:175, 2:31
Rebecca, 2:30
Ruth (Convers/Converse), 1:444
Sarah, 2:28-31, 2:472
Sarah (----), 2:29
Sarah (Blanchard), 1:195
Sarah (Brown), 1:277, 2:30
Sarah (Edson), 2:29, 2:102
Sarah (Peake), 3:377
Sarah (Williams), 2:28
Susanna, 2:29-30, 3:564, 4:139
Dear/Deare
Elizabeth (Griffin), 2:31, 2:313
Dearborn
Abigail, 2:31-32
Abigail (Bachelder), 2:32
Abigail (Sanborn), 2:31
Ann, 2:32
Deborah, 2:32
Dorothy (----) Dalton, 2:3, 2:31-32
Elizabeth, 2:32
Elizabeth (Marion), 2:32

Esther, 2:32, 4:89
Esther (----), 2:32
Hannah, 2:32
Hannah (Colcord), 1:424, 2:32
Hannah (Dow), 2:32
Huldah, 2:33
Huldah (Smith), 2:33
Lydia, 2:32
Mary, 2:31-33
Mary (----), 2:32
Mary (Roby), 2:32
Mary (Ward), 2:32, 4:413
Mehitable, 2:31-32
Mercy, 2:32
Mercy (Bachelder), 2:32
Ruth, 2:32
Sarah, 2:31-32, 3:299
Sarah (----), 2:32
Sarah (Gove), 2:32, 2:288
Theodate, 2:33
Dearing/Deering/Dering
Abigail, 2:41
Ann, 2:41
Ann (----) Benning, 1:168, 2:41
Bethia, 2:33
Bethia (Baxter), 1:141, 2:33
Elizabeth, 2:41, 4:482
Elizabeth (----), 1:143, 2:33
Elizabeth (Mitchelson) Atkinson, 1:75, 2:41, 3:222
Elizabeth (Packer), 2:41
Hannah, 2:33
Hannah (----), 2:33
Hannah (Davis), 2:18
Martha, 2:41
Mary, 2:33, 2:41, 4:146-148
Mary (Newcomb), 2:33, 3:270
Mary (Ray), 2:33, 3:512
Rachel, 2:33, 4:146
Sarah, 2:33, 2:41
Dearnford
Elinor, 1:405
Death
Abigail, 2:33
Elizabeth (Barber), 2:33
Hepzibah, 2:33
Lydia, 2:33

Death (continued)
Mary, 2:33
Mary (Peabody), 2:33, 3:375
Ruth, 2:33
Waitstill, 2:33
Waitstill (----), 2:33
Decrow
Martha (Bourne), 2:33
Delano
Bethia, 2:34
Elizabeth (Dewsbury), 2:34
Elizabeth (Standish), 2:34
Esther, 2:34
Hannah (Dotey), 2:62
Hannah (Warren) Bartlett, 2:34
Jane, 2:34
Mary, 2:34, 2:81
Mary (Alden), 1:23, 2:34
Mary (Churchill), 2:34
Mary (Pontus) Glass, 2:34, 2:260, 3:454
Mary (Warren) Bartlett, 1:132
Mercy, 2:34
Mercy (Warren), 2:34, 4:426
Rebecca, 1:387, 2:34
Sarah, 2:34
Susanna, 2:34
Delene
Ruth (Redman), 3:522
Delis
Eunice (Dodson), 2:58
Dell/Dill
Abigail (----), 2:34, 2:351
Elizabeth (----), 2:34
Elizabeth (Bright), 1:253
Dellaclose
Rachel (----), 1:501
Deming/Demon/Dement
----, 1:151, 2:35
Ann, 2:35
Ann (Wickham), 4:538
Elizabeth, 2:35, 2:180
Elizabeth (Gilbert), 2:35
Honour, 2:35
Honour (Treat), 2:35, 4:326
Mary, 2:35, 2:505
Mary (----), 2:35

Mary (Mygate/Mygatt/etc), 2:35, 3:259
Mary (Sheaffe), 2:35
Mehitable, 2:35
Prudence, 2:35
Rachel, 2:35, 3:233
Rebecca (Treat), 4:326
Sarah, 2:35, 3:226
Sarah (----), 2:35
Sarah (Kirby), 2:35
Dengayne/Dingham
Elizabeth (----) Alcock, 2:36
Denison
---- (Boykett/Boykim), 1:226
Abigail, 2:37
Ann, 2:36-37, 3:340
Ann (Borrodell/Borrodale), 2:36
Bethia (Boykem), 2:37, 4:675
Borrodell, 2:36, 4:167
Bridget (Thomson), 2:36
Deborah, 2:36
Desire, 2:37
Dorothy (Weld), 2:38, 4:473, 4:570
Elizabeth, 2:36-37, 3:513, 3:562
Elizabeth (Giddings) Haskell, 3:630
Elizabeth (Saltonstall), 1:463, 2:37
Elizabeth (Weld), 2:36, 4:458
Esther, 2:37
Grace (Brown), 2:37
Hannah, 1:373, 2:36-37, 4:32
Lydia, 2:37
Margaret, 2:36, 3:651
Margaret (----), 2:37
Martha, 2:37
Martha (Symonds), 2:37, 4:246
Mary, 1:208, 2:36-37, 3:345
Mary (Gorham), 2:36, 2:281
Mary (Parker), 2:37
Mary (Symonds), 3:164
Mary (Wetherell) Harris,

2:364, 4:491
Mehitable, 2:37
Mercy, 2:37
Mercy (Gorham), 2:36
Patience (Dudley), 2:36, 2:78
Phebe, 2:37
Phebe (Lay), 2:37, 3:65
Sarah, 2:36-38, 3:397, 3:615, 4:167
Sarah (Stanton) Prentice, 2:37-38, 3:480, 4:167
Sybil, 2:37
Thankful, 2:37
Denman
---- (Sleeper) Perkins, 2:38
Elizabeth, 2:38
Hannah, 2:38
Mary, 2:38, 3:182
Sarah, 2:38
Denning
Ann (----), 2:38
Dennis
----, 2:39
Agnes, 3:615
Elizabeth (----) Raymond, 2:38
Elizabeth (Smith) Raymond, 3:513
Judith, 2:39, 3:99
Judith (----), 2:39
Martha, 2:38
Mary, 2:38-39, 3:609, 3:615
Mary (----), 2:38
Mary (Beamsley) Robinson, 1:148, 2:39, 3:554
Ruth (----) White, 4:515
Sarah, 2:38-39, 2:284
Sarah (----), 2:38, 3:315
Sarah (Howland), 2:39
Denny
---- (Wakeman), 4:388
Denslow
Abigail, 2:39
Deborah, 2:39, 2:466
Elizabeth, 2:39, 2:579, 3:27
Elizabeth (----), 2:39
Hannah, 1:313, 2:39, 2:579
Joan, 1:445, 2:39

Denslow (continued)
Mary, 2:39, 3:582
Mary (Eggleston), 2:39
Mary (Roe), 3:559
Ruth, 2:39
Sarah, 2:579
Susanna, 2:39, 2:438,
2:578
Temperance, 1:285, 2:39
Denton
Abigail, 2:39, 4:175
Hannah, 2:39
Hannah (Leonard), 2:39,
3:79
Ruth (Tileston), 2:40,
2:191, 4:302
Sarah, 2:39
Derby - see also Darby
Alice, 1:200
Ann, 2:579, 3:530
Ann (----), 2:40
Elizabeth, 2:40, 2:579,
3:107
Elizabeth (----), 2:40, 2:579
Experience, 2:40
Jane (Plympton), 3:448
Lucretia, 2:40
Lucretia (Hilman/Kilham),
2:40
Margaret, 2:40, 2:579
Martha, 2:40, 2:579
Martha (Haskett), 2:40
Mary, 2:40
Ruth (----), 2:40, 2:442
Sarah, 3:106
Susanna (Hooke), 2:40
Desbrough/Desborough
---- (Cromwell), 2:41
Mary, 3:488
Rose (----) Penoyer, 2:41
Sarah, 2:41
Devell/Devel/Davoll/Devill
Elizabeth (----), 2:579
Mary, 2:42, 4:252
Mary (Brayton), 2:42
Devenish/Davenish
Bethia, 2:42
Mary, 2:42
Mary (----), 2:42
Susanna (Dwinell/Dunnell),
2:87
Devereaux
Ann (----), 2:42

Susanna, 2:42, 3:356
Devotion
----, 2:43
Abigail, 2:43
Deborah, 2:42
Elizabeth, 2:42, 4:458
Elizabeth (Stafford), 4:160
Hannah, 2:42-43, 3:587
Hannah (----), 2:43
Hannah (Pond), 3:452
Martha, 2:42, 3:587
Mary, 2:19, 2:579
Mary (----), 2:42
Naomi (Taylor), 4:259
Sarah, 2:42
Dew/Due
Esther (Barker), 1:116,
2:43
Patience, 2:43
Dewer
Ann (----), 2:43
Dewey
Abigail, 2:43
Abigail (Drake), 2:43, 2:70
Ann, 2:43, 4:645
Constance (Hawes), 2:43,
2:380
Elizabeth, 2:43, 3:286
Elizabeth (Wright), 4:654
Experience, 2:43
Experience (----), 2:43
Frances (----) Clark, 2:43,
3:405, 4:227
Hannah, 2:43, 3:269,
3:285
Hepzibah (Lyman), 2:43,
3:134
Margaret, 2:43
Mary, 2:43
Rhoda, 4:260
Sarah, 2:43
Sarah (----), 2:43
Sarah (Orton), 3:317
Sarah (Warner), 4:421
Dewing/Dewen
Ann, 2:44
Hannah, 4:542
Lydia, 1:91, 2:44
Rachel, 2:44
Susanna (Bacon), 1:90,
2:44
DeWolf
Hannah (----), 2:44

Mary, 3:73
Phebe, 2:44
Sarah, 2:44
Sarah (Lay), 2:44
Susanna, 1:355
Dewsbury
Elizabeth, 2:34
Dexter
Abigail, 1:57, 2:44-45
Abigail (----), 2:44
Alice, 2:45, 3:258
Ann, 2:45, 2:579
Ann (Sanders), 2:45
Bridget (----), 2:45
Content, 2:45
Elizabeth, 2:44-45, 3:194,
3:615
Elizabeth (----), 2:45
Frances, 4:637
Hannah (Sigourney), 4:95
Isabel, 2:44
Marian, 2:45
Mary, 2:45
Mehitable (Hallet), 2:44
Mercy, 2:45
Phebe, 2:45
Ruth (Wilkinson), 4:552
Sarah, 2:45, 2:579, 3:439
Sarah (----), 2:44
Sarah (Vincent), 2:45
Dibble/Deeble/Deble
---- (----), 2:46
Abigail, 2:46
Elizabeth, 2:46
Elizabeth (----) Hawks
Hinsdale, 2:381, 2:427
Elizabeth (----) Hinsdale,
2:46
Elizabeth (Hull), 2:46
Hepzibah, 2:46, 2:247
Hepzibah (Bartlett), 2:46
Joanna, 2:46
Lydia, 2:46, 3:443
Lydia (Tift/Teffe), 2:46
Martha, 2:46
Mary, 2:46, 2:124
Mary (----), 2:422
Mary (Tucker), 2:46
Mary (Wakefield), 2:46,
4:386
Mindwell, 2:46
Miriam, 2:46, 2:256
Patience, 2:46

Dibble/Deeble/Deble
(continued)
Sarah, 2:46
Sarah (Loomis), 3:114
Sarah (Waterbury), 2:47,
4:430, 4:449
Thankful, 2:46
Dibbs
Hepzibah (Merrill), 2:47
Dickarson
Elizabeth (Howland) Hicks,
2:47, 2:410
Dickens/Dickins
Joan (----) Tyler, 2:47
Mary (Cadwell), 4:676
Dickerman
Abigail, 2:47
Ann, 2:47
Elizabeth, 1:388
Elizabeth (----), 2:47
Ellen (----), 2:47
Hannah, 1:370, 2:47,
4:680
Lydia, 2:47
Mary, 1:136, 2:47
Mary (Cooper), 3:615,
4:679
Rebecca, 2:47, 2:179
Ruth, 2:47, 4:675
Sarah, 2:47
Dickinson
---- (Reeve/Reeves), 3:523
Abigail, 1:475, 1:480,
2:47-49
Abigail (Blackman), 2:47,
2:522
Abigail (Blakeman), 1:195
Alice (----) Roper, 2:48
Alice (Roper), 3:575
Ann, 1:405, 2:48-49
Ann (----), 2:48
Ann (Crow), 1:479
Dorcas (----), 2:47, 3:155
Elizabeth, 2:47-49, 3:616,
3:657
Elizabeth (----) Wright,
2:48
Elizabeth (Burt) Wright,
4:659
Elizabeth (Howland) Hicks,
2:480
Esther, 2:49, 4:127
Esther (Gilbert), 2:250

Frances (Foote), 1:118,
2:48, 2:180
Hannah, 2:48-49, 2:256,
2:545
Hannah (----), 2:48
Hannah (Crow), 1:479,
2:49
Hannah (Gough), 2:48
Joanna, 2:47
Lydia (----), 2:49
Martha (Bridgman), 1:250,
2:49
Mary, 2:48-49, 3:289,
3:580, 4:127
Mary (----), 2:47, 2:49
Mary (Cole), 1:430
Mary (Cowles), 4:679
Mary (Payne), 2:49, 3:336
Mehitable, 2:48-49, 2:523
Mehitable (----), 2:49
Mercy, 1:354, 2:48
Nodiah, 2:49
Phebe (Bracy), 1:227, 2:48
Rebecca, 2:48-49, 4:125
Rebecca (----), 2:47
Rebecca (Barrett) Wright,
4:655
Sarah, 2:48-49, 2:597, 3:5,
3:53
Sarah (----), 2:48
Sarah (Beardsley), 2:49,
3:602
Susanna (Smith), 4:125
Sybel, 2:49
Dicksey - see also Dixey
Elizabeth, 2:138
Dickson
Abigail, 2:49
Hannah, 2:50, 2:199
Jane (----), 2:49
Lydia, 2:49
Margery (Winship), 2:49
Mary, 2:49
Rachel, 3:265
Dighton
Catharine, 2:78, 2:328-329
Frances, 4:565
Dike/Dyke/Dikes
Elizabeth, 3:616, 4:300
Experience (----)
Chamberlain, 1:353
Hannah, 3:616
Margery, 3:616

Margery (----), 3:616
Mary, 2:50, 3:616
Rebecca, 2:171, 3:616,
4:248
Rebecca (Doliver), 2:50
Sarah, 2:50
Dillingham
Abigail, 2:50
Deborah, 4:594
Elizabeth (Feake), 2:50,
2:150
Hannah, 2:50
Lydia, 2:50
Lydia (Chapman), 2:50
Oziah, 4:595
Rebecca, 2:50
Sarah, 1:328, 2:50
Sarah (----), 2:50
Thankful, 2:50
Dimmock/Dimuck/Dimick
Ann (----), 4:681
Elizabeth, 4:46
Elizabeth (----), 2:51
Hannah, 2:51
Joanna, 2:51
Joanna (Bursley), 2:51,
4:676
Mary, 2:51
Mehitable, 1:378, 2:51
Mehitable (----), 2:51
Sarah, 2:51
Thankful, 2:51
Dimon/Diamond/etc
Abigail, 2:50
Abigail (----), 2:50
Elizabeth, 2:51
Elizabeth (Bradley), 1:234,
2:50
Esther, 2:50
Grace, 2:50-51
Joan (----), 2:51
Margaret, 2:51
Mary (----), 2:50
Rebecca (Bemis) Minter,
1:163, 2:50
Ruth, 2:51
Dinan
Mary, 4:619
Dinely
Abigail, 2:51
Alice (----), 1:473, 2:51
Hannah (Porter), 2:51,
3:460

Dingham/Dengham
Elizabeth (----) Alcock,
  1:21
Dingley
Elizabeth (----), 2:52
Elizabeth (Newton), 3:277
Hannah, 2:52, 3:3
Mary, 2:52, 4:162
Sarah, 2:52, 2:184
Sarah (----), 2:52, 2:584
Dinsdale
Martha, 2:52
Martha (----), 2:52
Mary, 2:52
Sarah, 2:52
Disbrow/Disbrough/etc
----, 2:52
Abigail, 2:52, 2:175
Elizabeth, 2:554, 3:523,
  3:571
Elizabeth (----) Strickland,
  2:52
Mary, 2:52, 4:148
Mary (Brunson), 2:52
Mercy (----), 2:52
Phebe, 2:52, 3:7
Sarah (Knapp), 2:52, 3:34
Diser/Dicer
Elizabeth, 2:579
Elizabeth (Austin), 2:579
Honor, 2:579
Dival
Mary, 3:59
Diven
Mary, 2:53, 4:619
Dix
Abigail, 2:53-54, 3:348,
  4:321
Deborah, 2:53
Deborah (----), 1:122, 2:53
Elizabeth, 2:53-54
Elizabeth (Barnard), 1:119,
  2:53
Esther (----), 2:54
Hannah, 2:54
Jane, 2:53
Jane (Wilkinson), 2:53
Joane (----), 2:54
Margery, 2:579
Margery (----), 2:579
Martha (Lawrence), 3:61
Mary, 1:116, 1:264, 2:53,
  2:579

Mary (Birdwell), 2:53
Mercy, 2:54
Priscilla, 2:54
Rebecca, 2:53, 2:171
Rebecca (----), 2:53
Sarah (----), 2:53
Susanna (----), 2:53
Tabitha (----), 2:53
Dixey/Dixy
Abigail, 2:54
Ann, 2:54, 3:616, 3:636
Elizabeth, 2:54, 3:616,
  3:654
Margaret, 2:54
Mary, 2:54, 4:634
Sarah (Collins), 2:579
Dixon
----, 3:206
Joan (----), 2:54
Susanna, 2:54
Dixwell
Abigail (Bridgham), 2:55
Bathsheba (How), 2:55
Bethia (Howe), 3:636
Bethia/Bathsheba (How),
  3:616
Elizabeth, 2:55
Joanna (----) Ling, 2:55,
  3:97
Mary, 2:55
Mary (Prout), 2:55, 3:490
Doane
Abigail, 2:56
Abigail (----), 2:56
Ann, 2:56, 4:669
Apphia, 2:55
Constance, 4:63-64
Constant, 2:55
Hannah (Bangs), 1:111,
  2:56
Hepzibah (Cole), 2:55
Lydia, 2:56, 2:410
Mercy (Knowles), 2:55,
  3:42
Patience, 2:55
Rebecca, 2:56, 3:332
Ruhama, 2:55
Dobson/Dobyson
Mary (Bostwick), 2:56
Sarah (Masters), 3:170
Dodd
Elizabeth, 2:20, 2:56,
  3:583

Hannah, 2:56
Joanna, 3:534, 4:680,
  4:697
Mary, 1:198, 2:20, 2:56
Mary (----), 2:56
Mary (Stevens), 2:56
Mehitable, 2:20, 3:616
Patience, 2:56
Sarah (Stevens), 2:56,
  4:188-189
Dodge
---- (Haskell), 3:616
Abigail, 2:57
Amy, 2:57
Ann, 2:57
Charity, 2:57
Deborah, 2:57, 3:455
Deliverance, 2:56
Edith, 2:56
Edith (----), 2:57
Elinor, 2:56
Elizabeth, 3:616
Hannah, 2:56-57, 3:463,
  3:616, 4:636
Jane, 4:160
Joanna (Hale) Larkin,
  3:616
Martha, 2:56-57
Mary, 2:56-57, 2:406
Mary (----) Creatty, 3:616
Mary (Conant), 1:441
Mary (Conant) Balch,
  1:101, 1:515, 2:57
Mary (Eaton), 2:57
Mary (Haskell), 2:56,
  2:372
Mary (Parker), 2:57
Prudence, 2:57
Rebecca, 3:616
Ruth, 2:56
Sarah, 2:56-57, 3:616,
  4:636
Sarah (----), 2:56
Sarah (Eaton), 2:57
Sarah (Proctor), 2:56,
  3:489
Dodson
Abigail (Gannett), 2:58,
  2:225
Bethia, 2:58
Deborah, 2:58
Eunice, 2:58
Hannah, 2:58

Dodson (continued)
Mary, 1:212, 2:58
Mary (Williams), 2:57,
  4:561
Patience, 2:58, 3:429
Sarah, 2:57-58, 4:184
Doe
Elizabeth, 2:58
Martha (----), 2:58
Dolbeare
Elizabeth, 2:579
Sarah, 2:579
Dolberry/Dolbery
Elizabeth, 2:58, 4:281
Elizabeth (----), 2:58
Dole
---- (Saunders), 4:21
Ann, 2:58
Apphia, 1:419, 2:58-59
Elizabeth, 2:58-59, 3:447
Frances (Sherburne), 2:58
Hannah, 2:58-59
Hannah (----) Brocklebank,
  1:258, 2:59
Hannah (Rolfe), 2:58,
  3:571
Love, 2:58
Mary, 2:58-59
Mary (Brocklebank), 1:258,
  2:59
Mary (Gerrish), 2:58,
  2:244
Mary (Jewett), 2:58
Patience, 2:59
Patience (----) Walker, 2:59
Patience (Jewett) Walker,
  4:397
Sarah, 1:419, 2:58-59,
  2:308
Sarah (Belcher), 2:58
Sarah (Brocklebank),
  1:258, 2:58
Sarah (Greenleaf), 2:59
Doleman
Elizabeth, 2:158
Dolens
Mary, 3:200
Dolhaff/Dolhert
Catharine, 2:59
Mary, 2:59
Prudence, 2:59
Doliber/Doliver/etc
Ann (Higginson), 2:59,

2:414
Mary, 2:59
Mary (----), 2:59
Mary (Elwell), 3:616
Mary (Ward), 3:181
Rebecca, 2:50
Sarah, 2:59
Donnell/Dennell/Dunnell
---- (Reading), 2:59
Alice, 3:294
Elizabeth, 2:270
Doolittle
Abigail, 2:60
Abigail (----), 2:60
Abigail (Moss), 4:681,
  4:692
Elizabeth, 2:60, 4:681
Elizabeth (Thorpe), 2:60,
  4:293
Grace (Blakesley), 2:60
Hannah (Cornwell), 2:60
Mary, 2:60, 4:681
Mary (Peck), 2:60
Mercy (Holt), 2:60, 2:455
Ruth (Lothrop), 2:60
Sarah, 1:7, 2:60
Sarah (Brown), 1:276
Sarah (Hall), 2:60
Sibell/Sybel (----) Bibble
  Nutt, 1:174, 2:60, 3:301
Susanna, 2:60
Dorchester
---- (----) Harmon, 2:60,
  2:357
Esther, 2:60
Martha (----) Kitcherell,
  2:60, 3:33
Mary, 2:60
Mary (Harmon), 2:61,
  2:357
Sarah, 2:60, 4:176-177
Sarah (----), 2:60
Sarah (Burt), 1:314, 2:60,
  2:429
Sarah (Parsons), 2:61,
  3:361
Dorland/Durland
---- (Bishop), 1:185, 2:61
Mary, 2:61
Dorlow
---- (Gridley), 2:313
Dorman
----, 2:61

Elizabeth (----) Bunnell,
  4:681, 4:707
Elizabeth (----) Sperry
Bunnill, 4:700
Hannah, 2:61
Hannah (Hull), 2:61, 3:637
Mary, 2:61
Mary (Wilmot), 4:681
Ruth (Johnson), 4:686
Dorr
---- (----) Clap, 2:61
Ann, 2:61
Clemence, 2:61
Elizabeth (Dickerman)
  Clap, 1:388
Elizabeth (Hawley), 2:61,
  2:385
Dorset
Comfort, 2:61
Doryfall/Dorifield
Ann, 2:61
Dotey/Doty/Dote/Doten
Deborah, 2:62
Desire, 2:62, 2:452, 4:85,
  4:161
Elizabeth, 2:62, 3:579
Elizabeth (Cook) Wilcox,
  4:546, 4:681
Elizabeth (Cooke), 1:446,
  2:62
Faith, 2:62
Faith (----), 3:412
Faith (Clark), 1:403, 2:62
Hannah, 2:62
Martha, 2:62
Mary, 2:62
Mary (----), 1:386, 2:62
Mercy, 2:62
Patience, 2:62
Sarah, 2:62, 4:424
Sarah (----), 2:62
Sarah (Faunce), 1:284,
  2:62, 2:148
Doughty
----, 2:62
Elizabeth, 2:62
Lydia, 2:62
Lydia (Turner), 2:62,
  4:345
Martha, 2:62
Mary, 2:62
Sarah, 2:62
Susanna, 2:62

Douglass
---- (----) Nason, 2:63
Abiah, 2:63
Abiah (Hough), 2:63,
  2:469
Ann, 2:63, 2:240, 2:407,
  4:431
Ann (Mable), 2:63
Elizabeth, 1:357, 2:10,
  2:63
Hannah, 2:63
Mary, 2:63
Mary (Hempstead), 2:63,
  2:402
Phebe, 2:63
Rebecca, 2:63
Sarah, 2:63, 3:3
Dove
Bethia, 2:63
Deborah, 2:63
Dorcas, 2:63, 2:579
Elizabeth, 2:63
Hannah, 2:63
Ruth, 2:579
Sarah, 2:579
Dover
Mary, 4:695
Dow
---- (----) Nudd, 3:299
Abigail (----), 2:64
Hannah, 2:32, 2:63-64,
  2:312, 2:363
Hannah (Page), 2:63,
  3:331
Joan (----), 2:63
Margaret (----) Nudd, 2:63
Margaret (Cole), 2:63
Martha, 2:64
Mary, 2:63-64
Mary
  (Chalice/Challis/Chellis),
  1:352
Mary (Graves), 2:64, 2:294
Mary (Mussey), 2:63,
  3:258
Mehitable (Green), 3:331
Phebe (----), 2:64
Ruhamah, 2:20
Sarah (----), 2:64
Sarah (Brown), 2:63
Sarah (Wall), 2:64, 4:398
Susanna (----), 2:64

Dowd
Elizabeth, 2:64
Elizabeth (----), 2:64
Hannah (----), 2:64
Mary, 2:64
Mary (Bartlett), 2:64
Mehitable, 2:64
Rebecca, 2:64, 2:128
Ruth (Johnson), 2:64
Sarah, 2:64
Dowden
Mercy (Paddy), 2:64,
  3:329
Dowell
Elizabeth, 3:373
Elizabeth (Wing), 4:594
Dowling
Mary, 3:200
Dowman
Joanna, 3:476
Downam/Deerman
Dorothy, 2:64
Dorothy (----), 2:64
Elizabeth, 2:64
Elizabeth (----), 2:64
Hannah, 2:580
Mercy, 2:64
Sarah, 2:580
Downe/Downs/Downes
---- (Umberfield), 4:358
Abigail (----) Hall, 2:65
Abigail (Roberts) Hall,
  2:591
Catharine (----), 2:65
Deliverance, 2:65
Dorothy, 3:616
Dorothy (----), 2:65
Elizabeth, 1:278, 2:65
Hannah, 2:65
Hannah (Appleton), 1:61,
  2:65, 3:333
Martha (----), 2:65
Mary, 1:448, 2:65
Mary (Umphrevile), 2:65
Rebecca, 2:65
Ruth, 2:65
Sarah (Hall), 2:591
Susanna (Eliot), 2:65
Susanna (Eliot) Hobart,
  2:109
Downer
Hannah, 2:65
Hannah (----), 2:65

Mary, 2:65, 4:46
Mary (Knight), 2:65
Sarah, 2:65
Sarah (Eaton), 2:65, 2:96
Susanna (Huntington),
  2:65
Downing
----, 2:66
Abigail, 3:225
Ann, 1:236, 2:66-67,
  2:228
Catharine, 2:67
Catharine (Salisbury), 2:66
Dorcas, 2:66
Elizabeth, 2:67
Frances (Howard), 2:66
Hannah, 2:67, 2:188
Joanna, 2:67
Joanna (----), 2:67, 2:580,
  2:595
Lucy, 2:66, 3:293
Lucy (Winthrop), 2:65
Margaret, 2:67
Margaret (Sullivan), 2:67
Mary, 2:66-67, 4:199
Mary (----), 2:67
Mary (----) Meakins, 2:67
Mary (Bunce) Meakins,
  1:298, 3:192
Mehitable (Brabrook),
  1:227, 2:67
Priscilla, 2:67
Rebecca (----), 2:67
Sarah, 2:67
Sarah (Hunter), 2:65,
  2:502
Susan, 2:66
Downton
Elizabeth, 2:67
Mary, 2:67, 3:620, 3:641
Mary (----), 2:67
Mary (Lovell), 3:123
Rebecca (----), 3:641
Dowse
Alice, 2:68
Ann, 2:69
Catharine, 2:68
Catharine (----), 2:68
Catharine (Herbert), 2:68,
  2:592
Deborah, 2:68
Dorothy, 2:69
Dorothy (Edmunds), 2:69

Dowse (continued)
  Elizabeth, 2:68-69, 2:580,
    3:57, 3:207, 4:155
  Elizabeth (Ballard), 2:68
  Faith (Jewett), 2:69, 2:549
  Hannah, 2:68-69
  Hannah (Ludkin), 2:69,
    3:129
  Joanna, 2:69
  Lydia, 2:68
  Margery, 2:68
  Margery (Rand), 2:68,
    3:504
  Martha, 2:68-69
  Martha (----), 2:68
  Mary, 2:68-69, 2:580,
    4:155
  Mary (Edmunds), 2:68
  Mary (George), 2:68,
    2:242
  Mary (Hewin), 2:68
  Naomi, 2:68
  Relief, 2:68
  Relief (----), 2:191
  Relief (Holland), 2:68,
    2:447, 3:67
  Sarah, 2:68-69
  Sarah (Berry), 2:69
  Susanna, 2:69
Doxy
  Catharine (----), 2:69, 3:51
Doyle
  Joanna (Farrar), 2:69,
    2:145
Drake
  ----, 1:113
  Abigail, 2:43, 2:70-71
  Amy, 2:71
  Ann, 2:580
  Ann (----), 2:71
  Edee, 2:580
  Elishama (----), 2:70
  Elizabeth, 1:145, 1:509,
    2:69-70, 2:107, 2:239,
    2:344
  Elizabeth (Alvord), 1:46,
    2:70
  Elizabeth (Clark) Cooke,
    1:392, 1:448, 2:70
  Esther, 2:70, 2:318
  Frances, 2:580
  Hannah, 1:113, 2:69-70,
    2:414, 2:580

  Hannah (Mills), 2:580
  Hannah (Moore), 2:70,
    3:228
  Hepzibah, 2:70
  Jane, 2:69-70
  Jane (----), 2:69, 2:71
  Jane (----) Berry, 1:171,
    2:70
  Jane (Holbrook), 2:443
  Joan (----), 2:71
  Lydia, 2:70, 3:113
  Mary, 1:438, 2:69-71,
    2:238, 3:158-159
  Mary (Bissell), 1:187,
    2:69-70
  Mary (Wolcott), 2:70,
    4:621
  Mellicent (Ford) Carver,
    1:344, 2:71
  Mindwell, 2:70
  Prudence, 2:70
  Rachel, 2:70
  Ruth, 1:501, 2:70
  Ruth (----), 2:71
  Sarah, 2:69-71, 2:580,
    4:623
  Sarah (----), 2:69-71
  Sarah (Knowles), 2:70
  Sarah (Porter), 2:69
  Susanna, 1:228, 2:69-70
Drakeley
  Ann, 2:71
  Beatrice, 2:71
  Comfort, 2:71
  Eunice, 2:71
  Eunice (Hickok), 2:71
  Lydia, 2:71
  Lydia (Brooks), 2:71
  Mary, 2:71
  Mary (Warner), 2:71
  Mercy, 2:71
Draper
  Abigail, 2:71
  Abigail (Whiting), 2:71
  Elizabeth, 2:71
  Elizabeth (----), 2:71
  Elizabeth (Aspinwall)
    Stevens, 1:70
  Eunice, 2:71
  Hannah, 2:71
  Hannah (Chandler), 1:357,
    2:71
  Lydia, 2:72, 3:60

  Mary, 3:105
  Mary (----), 2:71, 3:625
  Mary (Thacher), 3:616,
    4:272
  Patience, 1:345, 2:71
  Sarah, 2:327
  Susanna, 1:500
Dresser
  Elizabeth, 2:72
  Lydia, 2:72
  Martha, 2:72
  Martha (Thorla), 2:72
  Mary, 2:72
  Mary (----), 2:72
  Mary (Leaver), 2:72
  Sarah, 2:72
Drew
  Abigail, 1:283, 2:72
  Elizabeth, 1:395, 2:72,
    3:616
  Elizabeth (----), 2:73, 2:178
  Hannah (----), 2:72
  Jemima (Clark), 1:395,
    2:72
  Mary (Druce), 2:72, 2:75
Drinker
  Elizabeth, 2:73
  Elizabeth (----), 2:73
  Hannah (----), 2:73
  Mary, 2:73
  Mary (Emmons), 2:73
  Sarah, 2:73
Driscoll
  Florence, 2:73
Driver
  Elizabeth, 2:580
  Elizabeth (----), 2:73
  Mary (----), 2:74
  Ruth, 2:74, 3:467
  Sarah, 2:73
  Sarah (Salmon), 2:73
Drowne/Drown
  ---- (Clark), 3:616
  ---- (Tillinghast), 4:303
  Bathsheba, 2:74
  Catharine (Clark), 3:610
  Elizabeth, 2:74
  Elizabeth (Abbot), 2:74
  Esther, 2:74
  Mary, 2:74
  Sarah, 2:74
  Susanna, 2:74

Druce/Druse
Deliverance, 2:75
Elizabeth (----), 2:75
Hannah, 2:74
Jane (----), 3:616
Mary, 2:72, 2:74-75
Mary (----), 2:74
Mehitable, 2:75
Drummond
Lydia (----) Hallet, 2:75,
2:340
Drury
Elizabeth, 2:75
Lydia, 2:75
Lydia (----), 2:75
Mary, 2:75
Mary (----), 2:75
Mary (----) Fletcher, 2:75,
2:173
Rachel, 2:75
Rachel (Rice), 2:75, 3:529
Dubbin
Elizabeth, 4:24
Dudley
Abigail, 2:77-78, 3:12
Ann, 1:236, 2:76-78,
2:422
Ann (Robinson), 2:76
Catharine, 1:74, 2:76
Catharine (----) Hackburne,
1:40
Catharine (Dighton)
Hackburne, 2:78, 2:329
Deborah, 2:78, 4:284,
4:378
Dorothy, 2:77, 3:70
Dorothy (----), 2:78
Elizabeth, 2:75, 2:77-78,
2:336
Elizabeth (----), 2:77
Elizabeth (Gilman), 2:75,
2:258
Elizabeth (Hill), 2:420
Elizabeth (Leavitt), 2:75
Hannah (----), 2:77
Hannah (Poulter), 2:75,
3:469
Jane (Lutman), 2:78
Joanna, 2:77
Lucia, 2:454
Lucretia, 2:454
Lucy (Wainwright), 2:76,
4:382

Margaret, 2:77
Martha (French), 2:75
Mary, 2:75-78, 2:355,
3:169
Mary (----), 2:78
Mary (Byley), 2:77
Mary (Copley), 2:75
Mary (Hill), 2:420
Mary (Leverett), 2:77, 3:83,
4:319
Mary (Roe/Stow), 2:78,
3:617
Mary (Thing), 2:77
Mary (Winthrop), 2:77,
4:611
Mehitable, 3:605
Mercy, 2:75-76, 2:78,
4:632
Mercy (Gilman), 2:77
Naomi, 2:75
Patience, 2:36, 2:78
Rebecca, 2:76-77, 3:133,
4:56
Rebecca (Tyng), 2:76,
4:357
Ruth, 2:78, 4:537
Sarah, 2:75, 2:77-78,
2:367, 3:1-2, 3:327
Sarah (Gilman), 2:77,
2:258
Sarah (Wheeler), 2:75
Dudson
Abigail, 2:78, 3:21
Abigail (----), 2:510
Abigail (Button), 1:324,
2:78, 3:119
Martha, 2:78
Martha (----), 2:78
Dugall/Dougall
Elizabeth, 2:79
Hannah (----), 2:79
Mary, 2:79
Dumaresque
---- (Bretton), 1:243
Dumbleton
Lydia (Leonard), 2:79,
3:79
Rebecca, 3:80
Sarah, 2:79, 3:80
Dummer
---- (Rishworth), 2:80
Alice (Archer), 2:80
Ann, 2:79

Ann/Hannah (Atwater),
1:76, 2:79
Catharine (Dudley), 2:76
Dorothy, 2:80
Elizabeth, 2:79, 2:330
Elizabeth (Appleton), 1:61,
2:79
Frances (----) Burr, 1:307,
2:79
Hannah, 1:31, 2:79
Jane, 2:80, 3:447, 3:448,
4:53
Joan (----), 2:80
Joanna, 2:80
Lydia (Alcock), 1:21
Margaret, 1:407
Mary (----), 2:79
Mehitable, 2:80
Dunbar
Mary, 2:361
Sarah, 2:226
Sarah (Cushing), 2:80
Sarah (Thaxter), 4:275
Duncan/Dunkin
Abigail (Sherman), 4:83
Deliverance, 2:81
Deliverance (----), 2:81
Elizabeth, 2:80
Elizabeth (----), 2:80
Hannah, 4:38
Margaret, 2:81
Margery, 2:80
Martha, 2:80
Mary, 3:617, 4:19
Mary (Epes), 1:387, 4:246
Mary (Epes) Symonds,
2:80
Priscilla, 2:80
Ruth, 2:80
Sarah, 2:81, 3:138
Dunen/Dunnin
Eunice, 2:80
Ruth, 2:80
Dungan/Dungin
Barbara, 1:502, 2:580
Frances (----), 2:580
Dunham
---, 2:81, 4:629
Abigail, 1:78
Abigail (----), 2:81
Desire, 2:81
Elizabeth, 2:80
Elizabeth (Tilson), 2:80,

Dunham (continued)
Elizabeth (Tilson)
(continued)
4:304
Esther (Wormall), 2:81,
4:486
Hannah, 2:80, 3:540
Lydia, 1:127
Martha (Beal) Falloway,
1:145, 2:139
Martha (Knott), 2:81
Mary, 2:343
Mary (----) Falloway, 2:81
Mary (Cobb), 1:413, 2:81,
2:506
Mary (Delano), 2:81
Mary (Porter), 4:681
Mary (Smith), 2:81
Mary (Tilson), 2:81, 4:304
Mercy, 2:81
Mercy (Morton), 2:81,
3:244
Patience, 2:81
Persis, 2:81, 3:471, 4:65
Sarah, 2:81
Susanna, 2:342
Susanna (----), 1:263
Duning
---- (Goodenow), 2:272
Dunk/Dunck
Elizabeth (Stedman), 2:81
Mary (Price) Petersfield
North, 2:81, 3:289
Dunkler
Mary (French), 2:208
Dunn
Elizabeth (Haskett), 2:580
Dunning
Sarah (Joy), 2:82, 2:573
Dunster
Abigail (Eliot), 2:82
Deborah (Wade), 2:82
Dorothy, 2:82
Elizabeth, 1:223, 2:82-83,
4:555
Elizabeth (----), 3:617
Elizabeth (----) Glover,
2:262, 3:617
Faith, 2:82-83, 3:330
Mary, 2:82, 3:153, 4:555
Rose, 2:82, 2:417
Ruth (----), 3:153

Duntlen/Duntlin
Hannah, 3:76
Ruth, 4:582
Dunton
---- (Felch), 2:83, 2:151
Elizabeth, 2:83
Hannah, 2:83
Mary, 2:83
Sarah, 2:83
Dupper
Hannah, 1:110
Durand
Eliz (Powell) Hollingworth
Bryan, 1:282
Duren
---- (Hayward), 2:83
Susanna, 1:172
Durges
Rebecca (Tilton) Lamb,
4:304
Durgin/Durgy/Dirgey
Martha, 2:83
Martha (Cross), 1:478,
2:83
Durham
Mary (Delano), 2:34
Sarah (Bumpas), 1:297,
2:83
Durine
Mary (----), 2:83
Durkee
Martha (Cross), 1:478
Durren/Durin/etc
Elizabth (Guttridge), 2:83
Jane, 2:582
Mary, 4:399
Dustin/Duston
---- (----), 1:457, 3:266
Hannah (Emerson), 2:83
Martha, 2:84
Dutch
Abigail, 2:84
Abigail (Gidding), 2:84
Alice, 3:617
Elizabeth, 2:84, 3:542
Elizabeth (Baker), 2:84
Elizabeth (Roper), 2:84
Esther, 2:84, 2:116
Grace, 3:617
Grace (----), 2:84
Hannah, 2:84
Hannah (Lovell), 3:123
Hannah (Lowell), 2:84

Jane, 2:84
Mary, 2:84, 2:116, 3:617
Mary (Roper), 2:84, 3:575
Susanna, 2:84
Dutchfield/Ditchfield
Ann (----), 2:84
Joan, 2:84
Dutton
Elizabeth, 2:84
Mary, 2:84, 2:344
Ruth (Hooper), 2:85
Sarah, 2:84
Susan (----), 2:84
Susanna, 2:84
Dwelley
Deborah, 2:85
Elizabeth, 2:85
Elizabeth (Simmons), 2:85
Eunice (Glass), 2:85
Lydia, 2:85
Margaret, 2:85
Mary, 2:85
Rachel, 2:85
Rachel (Buck), 2:85
Ruth, 2:85
Susanna, 2:85
Thankful, 2:85
Dwight
Abia, 2:86
Ann, 2:85-86
Ann (Flint), 2:86
Ann (Flynt) Dassett, 2:11
Bethia (Morse), 2:87
Dorcas (Watson), 2:86,
4:437
Dorothy, 2:85-86
Elizabeth (----), 2:87
Elizabeth (----) Thaxter
Ripley, 2:85, 3:543, 4:275
Esther (Fisher), 2:87,
2:162
Eunice, 2:86
Hannah, 2:85, 4:519
Hannah (----), 2:85
Lydia, 2:85
Lydia (Hawley), 2:85,
2:384
Martha (----) Dassett, 2:11
Mary, 2:85-86, 3:410
Mary (----) Edmunds, 2:86
Mary (Partridge), 2:86,
3:366
Mehitable, 2:86

Dwight (continued)
Mehitable (Partridge), 2:86,
3:366
Rachel, 2:86
Rachel (Avery), 2:86
Ruth, 2:86
Sarah, 2:85-86, 3:526
Sarah (Powell), 2:86,
3:469
Sarah (Sibley), 2:86
Dwinell/Duennell/Dunnell
Abigail, 2:87
Desire (Brimsdell), 2:87
Dinah (Brimsdell), 2:87
Elizabeth, 2:87
Elizabeth (Cave), 2:87
Elizabeth (Fiske), 2:87
Hannah, 2:87
Hannah (----), 2:87
Joanna, 2:87
Keziah, 2:87
Magdalen, 2:87
Mary, 2:87
Mary (----), 2:87
Mary (Balch), 2:87
Mary (Read), 2:87
Maudlin, 2:87
Mercy, 2:87
Prudence (----), 2:87
Ruth, 2:87
Sarah, 2:87
Susanna, 2:87
Tryphena, 2:87
Tryphosa, 2:87
Dyer
----, 2:89
Abigail, 2:89
Agnes (Reed), 2:89
Ann (Hutchinson), 2:509,
4:372
Elizabeth, 2:88, 4:329
Elizabeth (----), 2:88-89
Hannah, 2:88
Hannah (----), 2:88, 3:240
Hannah (Avery), 1:83
Hannah (Baxter), 1:141,
2:88
Hannah (Frary), 2:88
Isabel, 2:89
Joanna (Gilman) Coffin,
2:258
Judah, 2:89
Lydia, 2:89

Mary, 2:88-89, 3:453,
4:514
Mary (----), 2:88-89
Mary (Taylor), 2:89
Mehitable, 2:88
Sarah, 2:89, 3:586
Eager
Hannah, 3:617, 4:708
Lydia (----) Cole, 1:425
Rebecca (Hyde), 3:617,
3:638
Eames/Emmes
---- (Johnson), 2:551
Abigail, 2:90
Ann, 2:90
Ann (----), 2:90
Dorothy, 2:90
Elizabeth, 1:197, 2:90,
3:622, 4:549
Elizabeth (----), 2:90
Hannah, 2:90, 2:187
Hannah (Johnson), 2:90,
2:557, 4:414
Hannah (Truant), 2:90,
4:334
Lydia, 2:90-91
Lydia (Wheeler), 2:90
Margaret, 1:13, 2:90-91
Margaret (----), 2:91
Margery, 2:89-90, 2:533
Martha, 2:90
Martha (Johnson), 2:90
Mary, 1:460, 2:90-91
Mary (----) Paddleford,
2:91
Mary (Adams), 1:11, 2:90
Mary (Blandford)
Paddleford, 3:328
Mary (Peabody) Death,
2:33
Mehitable (Chillingworth),
1:379, 2:90
Mercy (Sawyer), 2:90
Milicent, 4:156
Patience (Twitchell), 2:90
Priscilla, 2:90
Rebecca, 2:90
Rebecca (----), 2:90
Sarah, 2:91
Earle
---- (Sprague), 2:91
Dorcas (----), 2:134
Hannah, 2:135

Joan (----), 2:91
Martha, 2:134, 4:630
Mary, 2:91, 2:134, 2:171,
2:485
Mary (----), 2:135
Mary (Lawrence), 2:91,
3:61
Mary (Webb), 2:91, 4:445
Prudence (----), 2:135
Sarah, 2:134
Early
Abigail, 2:92
Abigail (Foote), 2:92,
2:181
East
Abigail (Phillips), 3:411
Abigail (Phillips)
Woodbury, 2:92, 4:403,
4:635
Elizabeth, 2:92
Mary, 2:92
Mary (----), 2:92
Mary (----) Plum, 2:92
Mary (Baldwin) Plum,
3:446
Rebecca, 2:92
Sarah, 2:92
Eastman
---- (Corliss), 1:457
Ann (Pitts) Joy, 2:92,
2:572
Deborah (----), 3:29
Elizabeth, 2:92-93
Elizabeth (Haddon), 2:92
Elizabeth (Screven), 2:93,
4:41
Elizabeth (Severance),
2:93
Hannah, 2:92
Hannah (Healey), 2:92,
2:397
Jane, 2:93
Jemima, 2:92
Lydia, 2:93
Lydia (Markham), 2:93,
3:153
Mary, 2:92-93
Mary (----) Morse, 2:93
Mary (Barnard) Morse,
3:237
Mary (Boynton), 1:227,
2:92
Mary (Morss), 2:93

Eastman (continued)
   Mary (Tilton), 2:92, 2:322,
     4:305
   Ruth, 2:93
   Sarah, 2:92-93, 2:207,
     4:76
   Sarah (----) Brown Carter,
     1:266
Easton
   ---- (----), 1:293
   Abigail, 2:94
   Alice (----), 2:93
   Ann, 2:94
   Ann (Clayton), 1:406, 2:94
   Ann (Coggeshall), 1:421,
     2:94, 2:580
   Christian (----) Copper
     Beecher, 1:153-154, 2:94
   Christian (Barker) Beecher,
     1:502
   Elizabeth, 1:502, 2:94
   Elizabeth (Barker), 1:502,
     2:94
   Freelove, 2:94
   Mary, 1:403, 2:93-94
   Mehitable, 2:94
   Mehitable (Gault/Gaut),
     2:93, 2:236
   Patience, 2:94, 3:144,
     4:689, 4:698
   Sarah, 2:94
   Sarah (Spencer), 4:149
   Wait/Waite, 1:339, 2:94
Eastow/Estow
   Mary, 1:319, 2:94, 2:127,
     3:161
   Sarah, 2:94, 2:127, 2:436,
     4:240
Eastwick/Estick/Estwick
   Elizabeth, 2:95, 3:425,
     3:618
   Esther, 2:95, 3:618
   Esther (----), 2:580, 3:618
   Hannah, 2:95, 3:618
   Sarah, 2:95, 3:618
   Sarah (----), 2:95
Easty/Esty
   Hannah, 1:3
   Mary (Town), 2:94
   Mary (Towne), 4:317
Eaton
   ----, 2:17, 2:96, 2:98
   ---- (----) Yale, 4:667

   ---- (Ingall/Ingalls), 2:519
   Abby, 3:227
   Abigail, 2:95, 3:169
   Abigail (----), 2:95, 2:98
   Alice (----), 2:96
   Ann, 1:266, 2:95-96
   Ann (Morton) Yale, 2:97
   Audrey, 2:345
   Christian (----), 1:179
   Christian (Penn), 2:95,
     3:389
   Dorcas, 2:96
   Dorcas (----), 2:96
   Elizabeth, 1:110, 2:96,
     2:319
   Elizabeth (----), 2:96
   Elizabeth (Fuller), 2:219
   Esther, 2:96
   Eunice/Unice (Singletary),
     2:98, 4:102
   Grace, 2:96
   Grace (----), 2:96, 4:98
   Hannah, 2:97-98, 2:567,
     3:368
   Hannah (Hubbard), 2:98
   Jane, 2:95
   Judith, 2:96
   Mabel (----) Haynes, 2:97,
     3:617
   Mabel (Harlakenden)
     Haynes, 3:631
   Martha, 1:433, 2:95-96,
     2:98, 3:308
   Martha (----), 2:96, 2:98
   Martha (Billington), 1:179,
     2:97
   Mary, 2:57, 2:95-98, 2:250,
     2:420, 3:35, 3:168
   Mary (----), 2:95-96
   Mary (French), 2:96
   Mary (True), 2:95
   Mehitable, 2:95
   Mercy, 1:409
   Phebe, 2:96
   Priscilla, 2:95
   Rachel, 2:95, 3:503
   Rebecca, 2:95
   Rebecca (----), 2:95
   Rebecca (Kendall), 2:96,
     3:9
   Ruth, 2:96
   Sarah, 2:57, 2:65, 2:96
   Sarah (----), 2:95

   Sarah (Hoskins), 2:95
Ebenatha - see Abernethy
Eborne/Ebborne/Eburne
   ---- (Gilbert), 2:98, 2:586
   Catharine (Smith), 2:580,
     4:117
   Hannah, 2:581
   Mary, 2:98
   Rebecca, 1:505, 2:98,
     2:581
   Sarah, 2:98, 3:617
   Sarah (Haines), 3:617
   Susanna, 2:581
   Susanna (Trask), 2:581,
     4:323
Eccles/Ecles/Eckles/Eckels
   Hannah, 1:260, 2:98
   Martha, 2:98
   Mary, 2:98
   Mary (----), 2:98
Eddy
   Abigail, 2:99
   Abigail (Devotion), 2:43
   Alice, 2:99
   Alice (Paddock), 2:99,
     3:328
   Amie (----), 2:98
   Deliverance, 2:99
   Deliverance (Owen), 2:99,
     3:326
   Elinor, 2:99
   Elizabeth, 2:99, 3:106,
     4:507
   Elizabeth (----), 2:98-99
   Elizabeth (Woodward),
     4:644
   Hannah, 2:99
   Hasadiah, 2:99
   Hepzibah (----), 2:99
   Jane, 3:641
   Joanna, 2:99
   Joanna (----), 2:99
   Mary, 2:99
   Mercy, 2:99
   Patience, 2:99
   Pilgrim, 1:100, 2:98-99
   Ruth, 2:99, 4:206
   Sarah, 1:453, 2:99, 3:152
   Sarah (Meade), 2:99,
     3:190
   Sarah (Woodward), 4:644
   Susanna, 2:99
   Susanna (Paddock), 2:99,

Eddy (continued)
    Susanna (Paddock)
       (continued)
       3:328
Eden
    Alice, 3:248
    Barbara, 1:275
Edenden/Eddington
    Hannah, 3:263
    Mary, 1:100, 2:100
    Mehitable, 2:99-100
    Rebecca, 2:100, 3:116
    Sarah, 2:100, 3:505
Edes/Eads/Eades
    Catharine (----), 2:100
    Elizabeth, 2:100
    Elizabeth (----), 2:100
    Grace (Lawrence), 2:100,
       3:61
    Joanna (Willet), 3:617
    Martha, 3:617
    Martha (Frothingham),
       3:617
    Martha (Mudge), 3:617
    Mary, 2:100, 3:617
    Mary (Tufts), 2:100, 4:342
    Sarah, 2:100, 3:617
    Susanna (Welch), 3:617
Edgarton
    Ann/Hannah, 2:100
    Elizabeth, 2:100
    Lydia, 2:100
    Mary, 2:100
    Mary (Sylvester), 2:100
    Sarah, 2:100
Edgecomb
    Joanna, 2:100
    Margaret, 2:100
    Mary, 1:69, 2:100, 3:330
    Rachel (Gibbins), 2:100,
       2:245
    Sarah, 2:100
    Sarah (Stallion), 2:100,
       4:161
Edgerly
    ---- (Ault), 1:42, 1:80
    Jane (----) Whidden, 4:505
    Jane (Ault) Wheedon,
       2:101
    Rebecca (Ault), 3:598
    Rebecca
       (Hallowell/Holloway),
       2:101

Edlin/Edling
    Elizabeth (----), 2:101
Edmaster
    Hannah, 2:581
    Hannah (----), 2:581
    Mary, 2:581
    Prudence, 2:101, 2:581
Edmunds/Edmonds/Edmands
    Abigail, 2:102
    Alice, 4:408
    Alice (----), 2:101-102
    Ann (----) Martin, 2:102
    Dorothy, 2:69, 2:101
    Dorothy (----), 2:102
    Elizabeth, 2:101-102,
       3:234
    Elizabeth (----), 2:102,
       3:163, 3:234
    Elizabeth (Bridges), 2:102
    Elizabeth (Meriam), 2:102
    Hannah (Miller) Dade, 2:1,
       2:101, 3:129, 3:211
    Mary, 2:68, 2:101-102,
       2:508, 2:578, 2:581,
       3:466
    Mary (----), 2:86, 2:102
    Mary (Hearndale), 2:405
    Mary (Herendean), 2:101
    Mary (Sprague), 2:101,
       4:155
    Mary (Willard), 2:581,
       4:555
    Mary (Wiswall), 4:616
    Ruth, 2:102, 2:581
    Sarah, 2:101
    Sarah (Hudson), 2:101
    Susanna (----), 2:101
Edsall/Edsell
    Elizabeth (Farman), 2:102
    Sarah, 3:377
Edson
    Bethia, 2:29, 2:102
    Elizabeth, 2:102, 3:414
    Elizabeth (Dean), 2:29,
       2:102
    Experience, 2:442
    Experience (----), 2:102
    Mary, 2:102
    Mary (----), 2:102
    Sarah, 2:29, 2:102
    Sarah (Hoskins), 2:102,
       2:466
    Susanna, 2:102, 3:4

Susanna (----), 2:102
Susanna (Byram), 2:102
Edwards
    ---- (----), 2:581
    ---- (Myles), 2:103
    Abigail, 2:103-104, 2:581,
       4:215
    Agnes (----) Spencer, 2:104,
       4:150
    Ann, 2:103-104, 2:581
    Ann (----), 1:427, 2:104
    Ann (Hunt), 1:460
    Catharine (Thornton)
       Cannon, 4:293
    Christian, 2:104
    Christian (----), 2:104
    Dorothy (----) Finch, 2:103,
       2:159, 4:315
    Dorothy (Moulton), 3:249
    Elizabeth, 1:400,
       2:103-104, 2:274, 2:581,
       3:454
    Elizabeth (----), 2:103
    Elizabeth (Tuttle), 2:103,
       4:352
    Esther, 2:103, 2:581
    Esther (Stoddard), 2:104
    Eunice, 2:581
    Frances, 2:103
    Hannah, 2:103, 2:581
    Hannah (----), 4:175
    Hannah (Noble) Goodman,
       3:286
    Jerusha, 2:581
    Joan (----), 2:103
    Joanna (----), 3:513
    Lucy, 2:103, 2:581
    Lydia, 2:103
    Mabel, 2:103-104
    Margaret, 2:103
    Margaret (----), 2:103
    Martha, 2:581
    Mary, 2:103, 2:130, 2:156,
       2:581, 3:454
    Mary (Bridgham), 2:104
    Mary (Poole), 2:103, 3:454
    Mary (Sams), 2:103
    Mary (Solart), 4:706
    Mary (Strong), 4:228
    Mary (Talcott), 2:103,
       4:251
    Mercy (Newland), 3:274
    Phebe, 1:19

Edwards (continued)
Ruth, 2:103-104, 2:330
Sarah, 2:103-104, 3:454
Sarah (----), 2:103
Sarah (----) Searl, 2:103
Sarah (Baldwin) Searle,
4:45
Sarah (Boykim), 1:226
Sybel (Newman), 3:274
Thankful (Sheldon), 2:103,
4:69
Eells/Ells/Eels/Eales
Ann, 2:105
Ann (Lenthall), 2:105
Elizabeth, 2:105
Hannah, 2:105
Hannah (North), 2:104
Martha (Pitkin), 3:440
Mary, 2:105
Sarah, 2:104
Sarah (----) Peck, 2:105
Egard
Esther, 4:211
Eger/Eager
Elizabeth, 2:105
Esther (----) Cole, 2:105
Hannah, 2:581
Hannah (Kerley), 2:105
Lydia (----), 2:105
Lydia (----) Cole, 1:425,
2:105
Margaret, 2:105
Martha, 2:105
Mercy, 2:105
Rebecca (Hyde), 2:581
Ruth, 1:112, 2:105
Ruth (----), 2:105
Sarah, 2:105
Eggington
Elizabeth, 1:462, 2:105
Elizabeth (Cotton), 1:462,
2:105
**Eggleden/Eggleton - see
Iggleden**
Eggleston

(Disbrow/Disborow/etc),
2:52
Abigail, 2:106, 3:318
Deborah, 2:106
Dorothy, 2:106
Esther, 2:106
Esther (----), 2:106, 2:124,

4:562
Hannah, 2:106, 4:268
Hannah (Osborne)
Shattuck, 2:106, 3:318,
4:58
Mary, 2:39, 2:106, 4:22
Mercy, 2:106
Rebecca, 2:106
Sarah, 2:106, 3:403, 3:488
Sarah (----), 2:106
Susanna, 2:106
Eglin
Mary, 2:106, 4:566
Phebe, 2:106
Phebe (Williams), 2:106,
4:566
Egron
Elizabeth, 2:106
Elcock
Martha (Munson), 4:681
Mary, 2:107
Sarah, 2:107
Elder
Lydia, 2:107
Lydia (Homes), 2:107
Remember, 2:107
Elderkin
----, 1:439, 2:107
Abigail, 2:107
Abigail (Fowler), 2:107
Ann, 1:201, 2:107
Bathshua, 2:107
Elizabeth (Drake) Gaylord,
2:107, 2:239
Eldred
---- (----), 2:107
---- (Lumpkin), 2:107
Ann, 2:107
Bethia, 2:107
Elizabeth, 2:107
Elizabeth (----), 2:107
Elizabeth (Nickerson),
3:284
Margaret (Houlden), 2:107,
2:445
Mary, 2:107
Sarah, 2:107
Eldridge/Eldredge
---- (Lumpkin), 3:130
Desire, 2:108
Elizabeth, 2:108, 2:398
Elizabeth (----), 2:108
Elizabeth (Nickerson),

2:108
Martha, 2:108
Martha (Knowles), 3:41
Mary, 2:108, 4:122
Elgarr
Abigail (Filley), 2:108
Eliot/Elliot/Elliott
----, 2:111, 4:122
---- (Blaisdell), 2:108
---- (Hadden), 2:108
Abiel, 2:111
Abigail, 2:82, 2:109, 4:662
Ann, 2:109-111
Ann (Mountfort/Mumford),
2:109
Asaph, 2:109
Bashua, 2:111
Deborah, 2:109
Deborah (----) York, 2:109,
4:669
Elizabeth, 2:108,
2:110-111, 4:368, 4:619
Elizabeth (----), 2:111
Elizabeth (Cutts), 1:495,
2:109
Elizabeth (Davenport),
2:14, 2:108
Elizabeth (French), 2:208
Elizabeth (Gookin), 2:110,
2:279, 3:500
Elizabeth (Stoughton),
4:213-214
Elizabeth (Stoughton)
Mackman, 3:141, 4:215
Hannah, 2:109, 2:201,
2:261, 4:577
Hannah (----), 2:108, 2:111
Hannah (Cloyes), 2:108,
3:610
Hannah (Gould), 2:581,
2:588
Jane, 2:111, 2:210, 3:392
Jemima, 2:111
Lydia, 4:543
Margaret (----), 2:110
Margery (----), 2:109
Martha, 2:110
Mary, 2:108-109, 2:111,
2:432, 2:456, 3:167,
3:372
Mary (----) Wilcock, 2:109,
4:546
Mary (Saunders), 2:108,

Eliot/Elliot/Elliott
(continued)
Mary (Saunders)
(continued)
4:21
Mary (Shattuck), 2:108
Mary (Wolcott), 4:622
Mary (Wyllis), 2:111,
4:577
Mehitable, 2:109, 2:111
Rachel, 2:109, 3:468,
4:527
Rebecca, 2:111
Ruth, 2:108
Ruth (Symonds), 2:108
Sarah, 1:24, 1:224,
2:109-111
Sarah (----), 2:108
Sarah (Brenton), 1:242,
2:111
Sarah (Willet), 2:110,
4:557
Susanna, 2:65, 2:109,
2:434
Elithorp/Elithorpe/Elithrop
---- (----), 2:112
Abigail, 2:112
Abigail (----), 2:566
Margaret, 4:629
Mary, 2:112, 3:446
Elkins/Elking
Esther (Waldron), 2:112,
3:71, 4:390
Esther (Waldron) Lee,
2:570
Lydia, 3:617
Magdalen, 3:617
Margaret, 3:617
Mary, 2:112, 3:617
Sarah, 3:617
Sarah (----), 3:617
Ellen
Ann, 1:10, 2:112
Mary (Ball) Pond, 3:453
Ellery
Abigail, 2:112
Abigail (Norwood), 3:618,
3:656
Abigail (Wilkins), 3:617,
4:551
Ann (Remington), 2:113
Ann (Sargent), 3:618
Elinor, 3:618

Hannah (Vincent), 2:112
Hannah (Vinson), 4:375
Jemima, 3:618
Lucy, 3:618
Mary, 2:112, 3:618
Mary (----) Coit, 2:112
Sarah (Warner), 3:618
Susanna, 2:112
Ellet/Ellit
Alice, 3:163
Ann, 2:113
Margaret (----), 2:113
Martha, 2:113
Sarah, 2:113
Sarah (----), 2:113
Ellingwood
Abigail, 3:618
Elizabeth, 2:113, 2:581
Ellen (Lynn), 2:581
Martha (----), 3:618
Mary, 2:113
Sarah, 2:113
Ellis
---- (Genery), 2:242
Abial, 1:114
Abiel, 2:114
Ann, 2:113
Bennet, 2:113
Elizabeth (Freeman), 2:113,
2:203
Elizabeth (Genery), 2:114
Esther (Nichols), 3:279
Experience, 2:114
Hannah, 2:113, 2:298,
3:558
Joan (----) Clap, 1:389,
2:113
Joanna, 2:114
Joanna (Willis), 4:576
Juda, 2:114
Juda/Judith, 4:681
Mary, 1:13, 2:114, 2:161
Mary (Lane), 3:52
Mary (Wight), 2:114,
4:543
Patience, 1:10, 2:114
Rebecca, 2:163
Remember, 2:114
Ruth, 1:229, 2:114, 2:242
Sarah, 2:113
Sarah (----), 3:618
Sarah (Blott), 1:206, 2:113
Susan (Chapman), 1:362

Susan (Lumber), 2:113
Ellison
Experience, 2:114
Hannah, 2:114
Lydia (Morton), 2:114,
3:244
Mary, 2:114
Sarah, 2:114
Temperance, 2:114
Thomasine, 2:114
Thomasine (----), 2:114
Ellmes
Catharine (Whitcomb),
2:114, 4:507
Hannah, 2:114
Joanna, 2:114
Mary, 2:114
Sarah, 2:114, 2:375
Waitstill, 2:114
Ellsworth
Abigail, 2:115
Elizabeth, 2:114-115,
3:113
Elizabeth (Holcomb),
2:114, 2:444
Esther (White), 2:115
Martha, 2:114-115
Martha (Gaylord), 2:115,
2:238
Mary, 2:114-115, 3:111
Mary (----) Smith, 2:114,
4:116
Mary (Trumbull), 2:115
Sarah (Grant), 2:115
Sarah (Jewett), 2:581,
2:598
Elmer/Ellmer
Elizabeth, 2:115
Mary, 2:115
Sarah, 2:115
Elmore
Elizabeth (----), 1:213
Else/Elzie/Elsey
Hannah, 4:575
Hannah (----) Coe, 1:418,
2:115
Jane (----), 1:510, 2:582
Elson/Elsen/Elsing
---- (----), 2:115, 3:252
Abigail, 2:115
Dinah, 3:638, 3:641
Elizabeth (----), 2:582
Joanna (----), 3:641

Elson/Elsen/Elsing
(continued)
Margaret (----) Hilliard,
2:421, 4:660
Mary, 3:641
Mary (----), 3:641
Sarah, 3:641
Sarah (----), 2:115
Sarah (Hayman), 2:582
Thomasin, 2:582, 2:592
Elthan
Hannah, 2:115
Elton
Ann, 2:116
Jane (----), 2:116
Mary, 2:116
Elwell
Abigail, 2:116
Abigail (Vincent), 2:116
Alice (Leach), 2:116
Bethia, 2:116
Dorcas, 2:116, 3:599
Elizabeth, 2:116
Esther, 2:116
Esther (Dutch), 2:84,
2:116
Hannah, 2:116
Jane, 2:582
Jane (----), 2:116
Jane (Durin), 2:582
Joan, 2:116
Mary, 1:447, 2:116, 3:616
Mary (----) Rowe, 3:618
Mary (Collins), 1:435,
2:116
Mary (Dutch), 2:116,
3:617
Mehitable (----), 2:116
Mehitable (Millet), 3:618
Sarah, 2:116
Sarah (Bassett), 2:116
Sarah (Whedon), 4:496
Ely
Ann, 2:117
Elizabeth, 2:117
Elizabeth (----), 2:117
Elizabeth (Fenwick)
Cullick, 1:482, 2:117
Martha (----), 2:116
Mary (----), 4:178
Mary (Day), 1:431, 2:27,
2:117
Mary (Marvin), 3:165

Ruth, 2:116
Emands
Dorothy, 2:593
Emerson
---- (Brown), 2:118
Ann, 2:118
Barbara (Lothrop), 2:117,
3:120
Dorothy, 2:117
Elizabeth, 2:117
Elizabeth (----), 1:271,
2:118
Elizabeth (Bulkley), 1:290,
2:118
Elizabeth (Leach), 3:66
Hannah, 2:83, 2:118
Judith (----), 2:118
Martha, 1:422, 2:117
Martha (Woodward),
2:118
Mary, 2:117-118, 3:176,
3:415, 4:622
Mary (Batter), 2:117
Mary (Moody), 2:118
Phillis (Perkins), 2:118
Ruth, 2:117, 3:275
Ruth (Symonds), 2:117,
4:246
Sarah, 2:118
Sarah (----), 2:117-118
Sarah (Stowers) Carter,
1:512
Emery/Emory
Abigail, 2:119
Abigail (Bartlett), 2:119
Ann, 2:119, 3:315
Bethia, 1:207, 2:119
Ebenezer, 2:119, 2:430
Eleanor, 1:143
Elizabeth, 2:119, 3:7,
3:286
Hannah, 1:132, 2:119
Judith, 2:119
Lydia, 2:119
Martha (Shepard), 4:71
Mary, 2:119, 4:31
Mary (----), 3:618
Mary (----) Webster, 2:119,
4:448
Mary (Sawyer), 2:119,
4:31
Mary (Woodman) 2:119
Ruth, 2:119

Ruth (Jaques), 2:119
Sarah, 1:142, 2:119
Emmons
Alice (----), 3:618
Elizabeth, 2:120, 2:402
Hannah, 1:468, 2:119-120
Martha (----), 2:120
Mary, 2:73, 2:119
Mary (----), 2:73, 2:119
Mary (Amory), 2:119
Mary (Scott), 2:119, 4:38
Endicott
---, 2:123
Ann (Gower), 2:122
Elizabeth, 2:123, 2:582
Elizabeth (----), 2:123
Elizabeth (Gibson), 2:123
Elizabeth (Houchin), 1:31,
2:123, 2:467
Elizabeth (Kimball), 2:123
Elizabeth (Winthrop)
Newman, 2:123, 3:274,
4:613
Hannah, 2:123
Hannah (Felton), 2:152
Joanna (----), 2:123
Lydia, 2:123
Mary, 2:123, 2:406
Mary (----), 2:123
Mehitable, 2:123
Sarah, 2:123
England
Ellen, 2:123, 4:486
English/Engles
Abigail, 2:123
Elizabeth, 2:123
Hannah, 2:124
Jane (----), 2:123
Joanna (Farnum), 2:123,
2:143
Mary, 2:123-124, 2:582
Mary (----), 2:124, 2:582
Mary (Hollingworth),
2:124, 2:595
Mary (Waters), 2:123,
4:435
Sarah (----), 2:124
Sarah (----) Ingersoll, 2:522,
2:582
Susanna, 2:582
Engs
Mary, 2:124
Mary (----), 2:124, 3:72

Eno/Eanno/Enno/Ennoe
---- (----) Holcomb, 2:124
Abigail, 2:124
Abigail (Bissell), 2:124
Ann, 1:346, 2:124, 2:582
Ann (Bedwell), 2:124
Esther (----) Eggleston, 2:106, 2:124
Martha, 2:582
Mary, 2:124, 2:582
Mary (Dibble), 2:46, 2:124
Sarah, 2:124, 2:443, 2:582
Susanna, 2:124
Ensign
Elizabeth, 2:125, 4:378
Elizabeth (Wilder), 2:125
Hannah, 2:125, 3:325, 4:76, 4:361
Hannah (Shepard), 4:75
Lydia, 2:125
Mary, 2:124-125, 4:132
Mehitable (Gunn), 2:124, 2:324, 4:69
Sarah, 2:124-125, 3:557
Epes/Eppes
----, 1:387
Elizabeth, 2:125
Elizabeth (Symonds), 2:125, 4:246
Hannah (----) Wainwright, 2:125, 4:382
Lucy (Woodbridge) Bradstreet, 1:236, 2:125, 4:632
Margaret, 2:125
Martha, 2:125
Martha (----), 1:387, 2:125, 4:246
Martha (Bordman), 1:214, 2:125
Martha (Reed), 4:246
Mary, 1:387, 2:80, 2:125, 4:246-247
Ruth, 2:125
Erickson
Joanna, 1:175
Errington
Ann (----), 2:126
Hannah, 2:126
Mary, 2:126
Rebecca, 2:126, 2:248, 4:437
Rebecca (Cutler), 1:494,

2:126
Sarah, 2:126
Erving
Elizabeth, 1:221
Estabrook/Easterbrook
Abigail (Willard), 2:126, 4:328
Ann, 2:126
Elizabeth, 2:126
Hannah, 2:126
Hannah (Leavitt) Loring, 2:126, 3:118
Mary, 2:126
Mary (Mason), 2:126, 3:167
Melicent, 2:126
Melicent (Woodhouse), 2:126, 4:639
Prudence (----), 3:256
Sarah (----), 2:126
Estes
---- (Jenkins), 2:126
Alice (----), 2:127
Mary (Robinson), 2:126
Philadelphia (Jenkins), 2:542
Sarah, 2:127
Eustis
Sarah (----), 2:127
Sarah (Cutler), 1:516
Sarah (Scolley), 4:36
Evance
Mary, 2:127
Susanna (----), 2:378
Susanna/Hannah (----), 4:681
Evans
Abigail, 2:128
Amy (----), 2:127
Ann, 2:128
Ann (----), 2:128
Barbara, 3:441
Deborah (----), 2:127
Dorcas (----), 2:127
Elinor, 2:127-128
Elizabeth, 2:127
Elizabeth (----), 2:128
Esther (----), 2:127
Hannah, 2:128, 2:410
Hannah (Brown), 2:128
Jane, 4:304
Joanna, 2:128, 2:401
Martha, 2:127

Mary, 2:128, 2:584, 3:605
Mary (----), 2:127-128
Mary (Hawks) Hinsdale, 2:127, 2:381, 2:427
Patience, 2:128
Patience (Meade), 2:127, 3:190
Rachel, 2:127
Rebecca, 2:128
Rebecca (----), 2:128
Sarah, 2:128
Thomasin, 2:128
Evarts
Dorothy, 2:128
Elizabeth, 1:4, 2:128-129
Elizabeth (----) Parmelee, 2:128, 3:359
Hannah, 2:128-129
Lydia, 2:128
Lydia (Guttridge), 2:128
Mary, 2:128-129
Mary (----), 2:128
Mary (French), 2:128, 2:208
Mary (Hayden), 2:129, 2:387
Mehitable, 2:129
Patience, 2:129
Rebecca (Dowd), 2:64, 2:128
Sarah, 2:128-129
Sarah (Crampton), 1:470, 2:129
Silence, 2:129
Eve
Annabel, 2:129
Elizabeth (Barsham), 1:128, 2:129
Eveleth
Abigail (Coit), 1:422, 2:129, 3:618, 3:653
Bridget (----) Parkman, 2:129, 3:359
Elizabeth, 2:129
Hannah, 2:129
Mary, 2:129, 3:653
Mary (----), 2:129
Mary (Bowman), 2:129
Mary (Bragg), 1:236, 2:129
Susanna, 3:618, 4:186
Susanna (----), 2:129

Eveley
    Margaret, 2:223
Everard
    Mary, 1:61
    Sarah, 3:559
Evered
    Mary (----), 2:130
    Sarah (Fillebrown), 2:130
Everenden
    Ruth (Redman), 3:522
Everest
    Joanna (----), 2:130
    Lydia, 2:130
Everett
    Abigail, 2:130-131, 3:493
    Abigail (----), 2:130
    Bethia, 2:130
    Elizabeth, 2:130
    Elizabeth (Pepper), 2:130,
        3:392
    Hannah, 2:130
    Judith, 2:131
    Mary, 2:131
    Mary (----), 2:131
    Mary (Edwards), 2:130
    Mary (Pepper), 2:131,
        3:392
    Mary (Winch), 2:131
    Rachel, 2:130
    Rachel (----), 2:130
    Ruth, 2:131
    Sarah, 2:131, 2:162
    Tabitha, 2:130
Everill
    Ann, 1:197, 2:131
    Elizabeth, 2:131
    Elizabeth (----), 2:131
    Elizabeth (Phillips), 1:23,
        2:131
    Hannah, 2:131, 3:147
Everitt
    Elizabeth (Phillips), 3:416
Everton
    Catharine, 2:132
    Catharine (----), 2:132
    Elizabeth, 2:132
    Joanna, 2:132
    Joanna (----), 2:132
    Joanna (Lynd), 3:411
    Ruth, 2:132
    Ruth (Walley), 2:132,
        2:582
    Sarah, 2:132

Sarah (----), 1:507, 2:132
Everts
    Mary, 3:254
Ewell
    Abia, 2:132
    Deborah, 2:132
    Eunice, 2:132
    Hannah, 2:132
    Mary, 2:132
    Mary (Goodale), 2:132,
        2:271
    Sarah, 2:132, 3:290
    Sarah (Annable), 1:59,
        2:132
Ewer
    Elizabeth, 2:132-133
    Elizabeth (Lovell), 2:133,
        3:123
    Hannah (----), 2:132
    Mary, 2:542
    Mehitable, 2:133
    Sarah, 1:205, 2:132-133
    Sarah (Larned), 2:132,
        3:122
    Thankful, 2:133
Exell/Exile
    Abigail, 2:133
    Hannah (----) Reeves,
        2:133
    Hannah (Rowe) Reeves,
        3:523
    Mary, 2:133, 3:560
Eyre/Eire/Eyers
    ---- (Paine), 3:338
    Ann, 1:369, 2:133-134,
        3:338
    Ann (----), 3:618
    Ann (Still), 1:367
    Bethia, 2:133
    Bethia (Millet), 3:213
    Catharine, 1:367, 2:133,
        2:597, 3:639
    Catharine (Brattle), 1:239,
        2:133, 4:614
    Christian, 2:133, 3:338
    Dorothy, 2:133, 3:338
    Dorothy (----), 2:133
    Elizabeth, 3:618
    Elizabeth (Allerton) Starr,
        1:39, 2:134, 4:169
    Hannah (Knowles), 3:42
    Lydia, 3:618
    Lydia (Starr), 2:134

Maria, 2:133
Martha (Hubbard)
    Whittingham, 2:133,
        2:486, 4:536
Mary, 2:16, 2:133-134,
        3:338, 3:652
Rebecca, 2:133, 3:338
Sarah, 2:133, 3:431
Fabens/Fabin/Fabins
    ---- (Gilman), 2:135, 2:257
    Elizabeth, 2:135
Fairbanks
    Abigail, 2:136
    Anne (----), 2:137
    Comfort, 2:136
    Constance, 2:137, 3:177
    Deborah, 2:136
    Deborah (Shepard), 2:136,
        4:71
    Dorothy, 2:136
    Elizabeth (----), 2:137
    Grace, 2:136
    Grace (----), 2:136
    Hannah, 2:136-137
    Hannah (----), 2:136
    Lydia, 2:135, 3:528
    Lydia (Prescott), 2:136,
        3:481
    Margaret, 2:135-136
    Martha, 2:135-136
    Martha (----), 2:135
    Mary, 2:135-137, 3:204,
        4:111
    Mary (----), 2:135
    Mary (Howard), 2:137
    Mary (Penfield), 3:388
    Mary (Smith), 3:203
    Mary (Wilder), 4:549
    Mercy, 2:135
    Rachel, 2:136
    Rachel (Adams), 2:136
    Sarah, 2:136
    Sarah (----), 2:136
    Susan, 2:26, 2:136
    Susan (----), 2:136
    Susanna, 2:136
    Susanna (----), 2:136
Fairchild
    ---- (Seabrook), 2:137, 4:43
    Catharine (----), 2:576
    Catharine (----) Cragg,
        2:137
    Dinah, 2:137

Fairchild (continued)
Emma, 2:137, 3:482
Mary (----), 3:601
Ruth, 2:409
Sarah, 3:619
Fairfield
Elizabeth, 2:137, 3:619, 4:141
Elizabeth (----), 2:137, 3:339
Mary, 2:137, 3:352
Ruth (----) Marshall, 2:137, 3:157
Sarah, 2:137
Sarah (----), 2:137, 3:619, 3:643
Triphena, 3:619
Fairman
Sarah, 3:588
Fairweather/Fayerweather
Elizabeth (Dicksey), 2:138
Jerusha (Grosse), 2:319
Mary, 2:138, 2:273
Mary (----), 2:138, 2:273
Penelope, 2:138
Penelope (Turner), 4:347
Sarah (Turner), 2:138, 4:348
Falconer
Hannah (Jones), 2:568
Fales/Vales
Abigail (Hawes), 2:138
Falloway/Fallowell
Ann, 3:459
Catharine (----), 2:138
Martha (Beal), 1:145, 2:139
Mary (----), 2:81
Sarah (Wood), 2:138, 4:627
Fane
Elizabeth (----), 2:139
Faneuil
Ann (Bureau), 2:139
Mary, 2:139, 3:414
Mary (Cutler), 2:139
Fannin
Jane, 3:214
Fanning
Elizabeth, 2:140
Elizabeth (Allen), 2:140
Elizabeth (Boulter), 1:217
Elizabeth (Daniel), 2:9,

2:140
Mary, 2:140, 2:490, 3:68
Sarah, 2:140
Fargo
Sarah (----), 2:140
Farley
Beatrice (----), 2:140
Christian (----), 2:141
Christian (Births), 2:140
Jane, 2:141
Lydia (----), 2:140
Mary (----) Woodbury, 2:141
Mehitable, 2:141
Sarah (Barnham) Clark, 2:141
Sarah (Burnham) Clark, 1:305
Farman
Alice (----), 2:141
Elizabeth, 2:102
Mary, 2:141
Farmer
Abigail, 2:142
Abigail (----), 2:142
Abigail (Johnson), 2:142
Ann (Morley), 3:233
Barbara, 2:141-142
Betty, 2:142
Dorothy, 2:142
Elizabeth, 2:141-142
Elizabeth (Hunt), 2:142
Isabel, 1:204, 2:141, 2:307, 4:664
Isabella, 2:141-142
Isabella (----), 2:141
Isabella (Barbage), 4:617
Lydia (Richardson), 2:142
Mary, 2:30, 2:141-142
Mary (----), 2:141
Mary (Richardson), 2:141
Rachel (Shed), 2:142
Rebecca, 2:142
Sarah, 2:141-142, 3:449
Susanna, 2:142
Farnham/Farnam/Farnum
Ann, 2:143
Elizabeth, 1:344, 1:512, 2:142, 3:401
Elizabeth (----), 2:142
Elizabeth (Holt), 2:143, 2:455
Elizabeth (Sibborns), 2:143

Hannah, 2:142-143
Hannah (Holt), 2:143
Hannah (Hutchinson), 2:143
Hannah (Wilcoxson), 2:143
Joan, 1:238
Joanna, 2:123, 2:142-143
Martha (Coe), 1:418
Mary, 2:143, 3:122, 3:456
Mary (Tyler), 2:143
Mehitable, 2:556
Priscilla (Holt), 2:142
Rachel, 2:142, 3:163
Rebecca (Kent), 2:143, 3:13
Sarah, 1:1-2, 2:143
Susanna (Arnold), 1:67, 2:143
Tabitha, 2:214
Farnsworth
Elizabeth, 2:143, 3:149
Elizabeth (----), 2:143
Esther, 2:143
Hannah, 2:143, 3:384
Mary, 2:143-144, 3:543, 4:273
Mary (----), 2:143
Mary (----) Long, 2:143, 3:108
Mary (Moses), 2:144, 3:246
Mary (Stoughton), 2:144, 4:215
Rebecca, 2:143
Ruth, 2:143, 3:493
Farr
---- (Stowers/Stower), 4:219
Ann, 2:30
Elizabeth, 2:144, 2:508
Elizabeth (----), 2:144
Elizabeth (Burrill), 2:144
Hannah (Applin), 1:62, 2:144
Hannah (Walden), 2:144
Hannah (Whitney), 4:531
Martha, 1:405, 2:144
Mary, 2:144, 3:259
Sarah, 2:144
Farrabas
Deborah (Rediat), 4:190
Dorothy (Rediat), 2:144,

Farrabas (continued)
Dorothy (Rediat)
(continued)
3:521
Elizabeth, 2:144
Rebecca, 2:144
Rebecca (Perriman), 2:144,
3:399
Farrand
Elizabeth, 2:144, 4:136
Hannah, 2:144, 4:292
Farrar
Abigail (Collins), 2:145
Ann (----), 4:46
Christina, 4:524
Elizabeth, 2:145
Elizabeth (----), 2:145
Hannah, 2:145, 4:665
Hannah (----), 2:145
Hannah (Hayward), 2:391
Joanna, 2:3, 2:69, 2:145
Mary, 2:145
Mary (How), 2:144
Mehitable, 2:145
Mercy, 2:145
Sarah, 2:145, 3:121
Susanna, 2:145
Susanna (Rediat), 3:521
Farrington
Abigail, 2:146, 2:430
Abigail (----), 2:145
Elizabeth, 2:145-146
Elizabeth (----), 2:145,
2:295
Hannah, 2:146
Judith, 2:146
Lydia (Hudson), 2:146
Martha, 1:309, 2:146
Martha (Browne), 2:145
Mary, 2:146
Mary (Bullard), 1:295,
2:146
Sarah, 2:145-146
Farris
Mary, 3:394
Farrow
Abigail, 2:146
Ann (Whitmore), 2:146
Christian, 2:147
Esther, 2:146
Frances (----), 2:146
Hannah, 2:146-147, 2:178,
2:571

Joanna (May) Gardner
Whiton, 2:147, 2:227,
4:533
Martha, 2:146
Mary, 2:146, 4:219
Mary (Garnett), 2:147,
2:233
Mary (Hilliard), 2:146,
2:421
Patience, 2:147
Priscilla, 2:146
Remember, 2:146, 4:407
Sarah, 2:146
Farwell
Elizabeth, 2:147
Esther (Blanchard), 2:147
Hannah (----), 2:147
Hannah (Learned), 2:147,
3:68
Mary, 2:147
Mary (Munroe/Monroe),
3:257
Olive, 2:147, 4:145
Olive (----), 2:147
Sarah, 2:147, 2:563
Sarah (----), 2:147, 4:90
Sarah (Wheeler), 2:147
Susanna, 2:147
Faulkner
Abigail (Dane), 2:6, 2:148
Dorothy (Robinson), 2:147
Elizabeth, 2:148
Elizabeth (----), 2:147
Hannah, 1:384, 2:148
Martha, 2:147
Mary, 2:147, 3:150
Mary (----), 2:147
Sarah, 2:148
Sarah (Abbot), 1:3, 2:148
Faunce
Elizabeth, 2:148
Hannah, 2:148
Jane, 2:148
Jane (Nelson), 2:148,
3:268
Joanna, 2:148
Judith (Rickard), 2:148
Martha, 2:148
Mary, 2:148, 2:357
Mehitable, 2:148
Mercy, 2:148, 2:453
Patience, 2:148, 2:452,
3:643

Patience (Morton), 2:148,
3:244
Priscilla, 2:148, 4:425
Sarah, 1:284, 2:62, 2:148
Favor/Feaver
Ann, 2:148
Mary (Osgood), 2:148
Fawer/Fower
Dinah (----), 2:148
Grace (----), 2:554
Grace (Negoose), 2:148
Grace (Negus/Negos),
3:267
Mary (----), 2:542
Mary (Preston), 2:149,
3:482
Fawne
----, 1:408, 2:149
Elizabeth (----), 2:149
Faxon
Abigail, 2:149
Deborah, 2:149, 4:28
Deborah (Thayer), 2:149
Elizabeth, 2:149
Elizabeth (----), 2:149,
2:432
Hannah, 2:149
Joanna, 2:149, 2:162,
4:391
Lydia, 2:149
Mary, 2:149
Mary (Blanchard), 1:196,
2:149
Mehitable, 2:149
Mehitable (Adams), 1:9,
2:149
Rebecca, 2:149
Sarah, 2:149, 4:458
Sarah (----) Savil, 2:149
Sarah (Gamitt) Savil, 4:28
Fay
Deliverance, 2:150
Mary (----), 2:149
Ruth, 2:150
Susanna (Shattuck) Morse,
2:149, 3:240, 4:62
Feake
Elizabeth, 2:50, 2:150
Elizabeth (Fones)
Winthrop, 2:150, 4:608
Fearing
Elizabeth, 2:150
Elizabeth (Wilder), 2:150,

Fearing (continued)
  Elizabeth (Wilder)
    (continued)
    4:549
  Hannah, 2:150
  Hannah (Beal), 1:146,
    2:150
  Margaret, 2:150
  Margaret (----), 2:150,
    4:566
  Margaret (Hawks), 2:381
  Mary, 2:150, 2:406
  Rachel, 2:150
  Sarah, 2:150, 3:91
  Susanna, 2:150
Felch
  ----, 2:83, 2:151, 2:393
  Elizabeth, 1:494, 2:150
  Elizabeth (----), 2:151
  Hannah, 2:150
  Hannah (Sargent), 3:619,
    4:19
  Margaret (----), 2:151
  Mary, 2:150
Fellows
  Abigail, 2:151
  Abigail (Barnard), 2:151
  Ann, 2:151
  Ann (----), 2:151
  Elizabeth, 2:151
  Hannah, 1:273, 2:151
  Mary, 1:273, 2:151
  Rachel (Varney), 4:366
  Sarah, 1:179, 2:151
  Ursula (----), 2:151
Felmingham/Fillingham
  ---- (Cooper), 1:453, 2:151
  Mary, 4:710
Felt
  ---- Andrews, 2:151
  ---- Mackworth, 2:151
  Elizabeth, 2:151, 3:58,
    4:257
  Elizabeth (----), 2:151
  Elizabeth (Wilkinson),
    2:151, 4:551
  Mary, 2:151, 3:280
Felton
  Ann (Horn), 2:464
  Elizabeth, 2:152, 3:619
  Ellen (----), 2:151
  Exercise, 3:653
  Hannah, 2:152, 3:619

  Judith, 2:596, 3:638
  Mary, 2:152, 3:619
  Mary (----), 2:151, 3:619
  Mary (Tompkins), 3:619,
    4:311, 4:700
  Remember, 2:152, 4:703
  Ruth, 2:152
  Susanna, 2:152
Fenn
  Deborah, 2:152
  Deborah (----), 2:152
  Esther (----), 3:619
  Hannah, 2:152
  Martha, 2:152, 3:278
  Mary, 2:152
  Mary (----) Hawkins, 2:152,
    2:383, 4:90
  Mehitable, 2:152
  Mehitable (----), 2:152
  Mehitable (Gunn), 2:323,
    3:619
  Sarah, 1:316, 2:152, 4:435
  Sarah (Baldwin), 1:105,
    2:152
  Susanna, 2:152
  Susanna (Ward), 2:152
Fenner
  ----, 2:153
  Howlong (Harris), 2:153,
    2:365
  Mehitable (Waterman),
    4:432
  Phebe, 2:153
  Sarah (----), 2:153
Fenton
  Dorothy, 4:682
  Dorothy (----), 2:153
  Frances, 2:153
Fenwick
  Alice (Apsley) Boteler,
    2:154
  Catharine (Haslerigg),
    2:154
  Dorothy, 2:153-154
  Elizabeth, 1:482, 2:117,
    2:153-154
  Mary, 2:153
Ferguson
  Mary (----), 2:154
  Mary (Maverick), 2:154,
    3:181
Ferman
  Dorothy, 3:619

  Elizabeth, 3:619
  Elizabeth (----), 3:619
Fernald
  Joanna (----), 2:154
  Mary, 3:365
  Sarah, 3:133
Fernes
  Elizabeth, 3:619, 4:151
Ferneside/Ferniside/etc
  Elizabeth, 2:154
  Elizabeth (----), 3:234
  Elizabeth (Starr), 2:154,
    4:169
  Hannah, 2:154, 2:494
  Lydia, 2:154
  Mary, 2:154, 2:492
  Ruth, 2:154
Ferris
  Elizabeth, 2:583
  Hannah, 2:155
  Mary, 2:155
  Ruth, 3:383
  Ruth (Knapp), 2:155, 3:34
  Sarah, 2:155
  Sarah (Blood), 2:583
  Susanna (----), 2:582
  Susanna (----) Lockwood,
    3:105
Ferry
  Elizabeth, 2:155
  Mary, 2:155
  Sarah, 2:155, 4:421
  Sarah (Harmon), 2:155,
    2:357
Fessenden
  Abigail (Locke), 2:583
  Abigail (Patten), 2:583
  Alice (Babcock), 2:583
  Ann (Fillebrown), 2:583
  Hannah, 2:155, 2:583,
    4:54
  Jane, 2:155, 2:583
  Jane (----), 2:155
  Margaret, 2:583
  Margaret (----), 2:155
  Martha (Brown), 2:583
  Martha (Wyeth), 2:583
  Mary, 2:583
  Mindwell (Oldham), 2:583
  Rebecca (Smith), 2:583
  Sarah (Coolidge), 2:155
Feveryear
  Elizabeth, 2:155

Feveryear (continued)
Mary, 2:155
Mary (Grafton) Hardy,
2:155, 2:355
Priscilla, 2:155
Tabitha (Pickman), 2:155,
3:425
Field
Abigail, 2:156
Abilene, 2:156
Bethia, 2:156
Deborah, 2:156
Elizabeth, 2:156-157,
2:565
Gillian (----) Mansfield,
2:155, 3:149
Hannah, 2:156
Joanna, 2:156
Joanna (Wyatt), 2:156,
4:662
Lydia, 2:156
Martha, 2:156
Mary, 1:340, 2:156-157,
2:374, 3:619, 4:641
Mary (----), 2:157, 3:307
Mary (Belding), 2:156
Mary (Bennett), 1:167
Mary (Bishop) Johnson
Hodgkin, 1:185
Mary (Edwards), 2:103,
2:156
Mary (Leach), 3:67, 3:619
Mary (Stanley), 2:156,
3:416
Phebe (Titus) Scudder,
4:43
Ruth, 1:57, 2:156
Sarah, 2:156-157
Sarah (----), 2:157
Sarah (Gilbert), 2:157
Sarah (Webb), 2:157,
4:445
Thankful, 2:156
Fielder
Mary (Griggs), 2:157,
2:315
Sarah, 2:157, 2:315
Fiennes
----, 2:158
Fifield
Deborah, 2:158, 2:530
Elizabeth, 3:43
Hannah (Cram), 2:158

Judith (Carter) Convers,
1:342, 2:158
Lydia, 3:144
Maria (Mather) Green,
3:173
Mary, 2:158, 2:390
Mary (----), 2:158
Mary (Colcord), 1:424,
2:158
Mary (Perkins), 2:158
Mehitable, 2:158
Filer/Fyler
Abigail, 2:158
Bethesda (Pool), 2:158,
3:456
Elizabeth, 2:159
Elizabeth (Doleman),
2:158
Experience, 2:159
Experience (Strong), 2:158,
4:227
Jane, 2:158
Judith, 2:158
Fillebrown
Ann, 2:583
Anna, 2:159
Anna (----), 2:159
Mary, 1:495, 2:159
Rebecca (Cutter), 1:496,
2:159
Sarah, 2:130
Filley
Abigail, 1:187, 2:108,
2:159
Abigail (Dibble), 2:46
Ann, 2:159
Ann (Gillet), 2:159, 2:256
Deborah, 2:159
Elizabeth, 2:159, 4:591
Margaret, 2:159
Mary, 2:159, 2:583, 4:105
Filmore
Abigail (Tilton), 4:304
Finch
Dorothy (----), 2:103,
2:159, 4:315
Elizabeth (----) Thompson,
2:159, 4:285
Elizabeth (Austin), 1:80
Judith (----) Graves Potter,
3:468
Judith (----) Potter, 2:160
Judith (Alward) Graves

Potter, 2:295
Martha (----), 2:160
Mary (Hoadley), 2:430
Finney - see also Phinney
Christian (----), 2:160
Elizabeth, 1:232
Phebe (----), 2:160
Firmin/Ferman/Firman
Sarah (----), 2:160
Susan (Ward), 2:160,
4:411
Fisen
Ann, 3:564
Fish
---- (Starke/Start), 4:172
Abigail, 2:161
Abigail (Mumford), 2:161,
3:253
Alce, 2:161
Alice, 2:161
Comfort, 2:161
Deborah, 2:161
Elizabeth (----), 2:161
Grizigon (Strange), 2:161
Grizzel, 2:161
Hope, 2:161
Lydia (Miller), 2:161,
3:209
Margaret (----), 1:407
Mary, 1:240, 2:161
Mary (----), 2:161
Mary (Hall), 2:161, 2:339
Mehitable, 2:161
Ruth, 2:161
Sarah, 2:161
Fisher
---- (Wiswall), 4:616
Abigail, 2:162-164, 2:455,
4:682
Abigail (Marrett), 2:162,
3:153, 3:241
Ann, 2:162, 2:398
Ann (----), 2:163
Ann (Whitney), 2:162,
4:530
Bethia, 3:391
Constance, 2:163
Dorothy, 2:162
Elizabeth, 2:161-163,
2:583, 3:448, 3:619,
4:682
Elizabeth (----), 4:682
Elizabeth (Boylston),

Fisher (continued)
  Elizabeth (Boylston)
    (continued)
    1:226, 2:163
  Esther, 2:87, 2:162
  Esther (Hunting), 2:164,
    2:503
  Experience, 2:162
  Frances, 1:251, 2:163
  Hannah, 2:162-164, 4:682
  Hannah (----), 4:682
  Hannah (Hill), 2:162,
    2:416
  Hannah (Leonard), 2:163
  Isabel (----) Breck, 4:682
  Isabel (----) Rigby Breck,
    1:240
  Joanna (Faxon), 2:162
  Judith, 1:296
  Leah, 2:162, 2:265
  Leah (Heaton), 2:162,
    2:400
  Lydia, 1:377, 2:162, 3:153,
    3:237, 4:682
  Lydia (----) Oliver, 2:163,
    3:311
  Lydia (Holten/Houlton),
    2:164
  Lydia (Walker), 4:394
  Margaret, 2:163
  Mary, 1:140, 1:391,
    2:161-163, 4:324, 4:682
  Mary (----), 2:163-164
  Mary (Aldis), 1:25, 2:163
  Mary (Colburn), 2:162
  Mary (Ellis), 2:114, 2:161
  Mary (Fuller), 2:163
  Mary (Treadway), 2:163,
    2:383, 4:324
  Mehitable, 2:162
  Mehitable (Veazie), 2:164,
    4:369
  Melatiah, 4:682
  Meletiah, 3:202
  Meletiah (----), 2:164
  Meletiah (Bullen), 1:296
  Meletiah (Snow), 4:682
  Mercy, 2:162
  Milcha (Snow), 2:164
  Rebecca, 4:682
  Rebecca (Ellis), 2:163
  Rebecca (Partridge), 4:682
  Rebecca (Woodward),

2:164, 4:643-644, 4:646
  Ruth, 2:161, 2:163, 3:466
  Ruth (Adams), 2:161
  Sarah, 2:131, 2:162, 2:332
  Sarah (Everett), 2:131,
    2:162
Fiske
  ----, 2:164
  Abigail, 1:102, 2:164-167,
    3:224
  Abigail (Park), 2:166,
    3:348
  Ann, 1:271, 1:342, 1:376,
    2:164-165, 2:167
  Ann (----), 2:165
  Ann (Gipps), 2:165
  Ann (Shepard) Quincy,
    2:166, 3:500
  Ann (Warren), 2:167
  Bathsheba (Morse), 2:164
  Bridget (----), 3:662
  Bridget (Musket), 2:167
  Elizabeth, 2:87, 2:164-167
  Elizabeth (----), 2:166
  Elizabeth (----) Henchman,
    2:165, 2:402
  Elizabeth (Haman), 2:166
  Elizabeth (Reed), 2:165,
    3:515
  Hannah, 2:164-167, 2:583
  Hannah (Baldwin),
    1:102-103, 2:166
  Hannah (Coolidge) Smith,
    1:452
  Hannah (Richards), 2:166
  Hannah (Smith), 2:167
  Hepzibah, 2:166
  Lydia, 2:164, 2:167, 4:204,
    4:425, 4:663
  Lydia (Cooper), 1:454,
    2:164, 4:204
  Lydia (Fletcher), 2:166
  Margaret, 2:166
  Martha, 1:9, 2:166-167,
    2:169, 3:346, 4:284,
    4:359
  Mary, 2:166-167, 3:168
  Mary (Warren) Child,
    1:378, 2:167, 4:423
  Rebecca (Perkins), 2:167,
    3:398
  Remember, 1:4, 2:165
  Remember (----), 2:165,

2:273
  Sarah, 1:448, 2:164-167,
    2:221
  Sarah (Cooledge), 1:451,
    2:167
  Sarah (Day), 2:27, 2:165
  Sarah (Smith), 2:164
  Sarah (Symmes), 2:166,
    4:243
  Sarah (Wyeth), 2:165,
    4:663
  Seaborn (Wilson), 2:164,
    4:589
  Susanna, 2:166-167
  Susanna (----), 2:166
Fitch
  ---- (----), 1:281
  ---- (Fiske), 2:164
  Abigail, 2:168, 2:584,
    3:619-620, 3:651
  Abigail (----), 2:168
  Abigail (Goodrich), 2:170,
    2:275
  Abigail (Whitfield), 4:517
  Alice (Bradford) Adams,
    1:17, 1:232, 2:168
  Ann, 2:168, 3:620
  Ann (Abel), 3:620
  Ann (Whiting), 3:620
  Bridget, 3:620
  Deborah, 1:158, 2:168
  Dorothy, 1:187, 2:168,
    3:619
  Elizabeth, 1:494,
    2:168-169, 3:620, 4:259
  Elizabeth (----) Wyborne,
    4:662
  Elizabeth (Appleton),
    2:168
  Elizabeth (Mason), 3:619
  Elizabeth (Waterman),
    3:620, 4:433
  Esther (----), 2:168
  Hannah, 1:232, 1:273,
    2:168-169, 3:223, 3:620
  Hannah (----), 2:169
  Hannah (Sweetser), 4:239
  Lucy, 2:584
  Margaret, 2:168
  Margaret (Clark), 3:610
  Martha, 2:169
  Martha (----), 3:620
  Martha (----) Messinger,

Fitch (continued)
Martha (----) Messinger
(continued)
3:202
Martha (Brown), 3:619
Martha (Fiske), 2:169
Mary, 2:168-169, 3:619
Mary (----), 2:170
Mary (----) Coit, 2:169
Mary (----) Whiting, 2:169
Mary (Het), 2:168
Mary (Stevens) Coit, 3:611
Mary (Stone), 2:169, 4:208
Mehitable, 3:620
Mindwell (Tisdale), 3:620
Miriam, 2:584, 3:620
Priscilla, 2:584, 3:620
Priscilla (Mason), 2:168,
3:168
Rachel, 3:620
Rebecca, 2:169, 3:517,
3:620
Rebecca (Lindall), 2:169,
3:95
Ruth, 3:620
Ruth (----), 3:620
Sarah, 1:282, 1:307,
2:169-170, 3:169, 3:620,
4:214, 4:427
Sarah (----), 3:620
Sarah (Boardman), 2:170
Sarah (Bryan), 1:282
Sarah (Chubbuck), 1:384,
2:168
Sarah (Lane), 2:169, 3:52
Sarah (Mason), 3:620
Sibbil, 2:170
Susanna (----) Whiting,
4:522
Fitts
Grace (----), 2:170
Margaret (Choate), 1:382
Sarah (----), 2:170
Sarah (Ordway), 2:170
Sarah (Thompson), 2:170,
4:288
Fitz
---- (Davis), 2:17
Fitzgerald
Elizabeth (Brooks) Bullier,
1:296
Fitzrandle/Fittsrandolfe/etc
Elizabeth (Blossom), 1:205,

2:170
Hannah, 2:170, 4:261
Hope, 2:170
Mary, 2:170, 2:425
Mary (Holley), 2:170
Fitzroy
----, 4:365
Flack
Ann (----), 3:620
Deborah, 2:170
Hannah, 2:170, 3:620
Jane (----), 2:170
Mary (----), 2:170
Flagg
Abigail, 2:171
Deliverance, 2:171
Dinah, 2:171
Elizabeth, 1:176, 2:171
Experience, 2:171
Experience (Child), 2:171
Hannah, 2:171
Hannah (Leffingwell),
2:171
Hepzibah, 2:172
Jemima, 2:172
Mary, 1:176, 2:171
Mary (----), 2:171
Mary (Bigelow), 2:171
Mary (Earle), 2:171
Mary (Gale), 2:171, 2:222
Mary (Lawrence) Earle,
2:91, 3:61
Mercy, 2:171
Priscilla, 2:171
Prudence, 2:171
Rebecca, 1:450, 2:171-172
Rebecca (Dikes), 2:171
Rebecca (Dix), 2:53, 2:171
Sarah, 2:171
Sarah (Ball), 2:171
Flamsworth
Martha, 3:229
Flanders
Abigail, 2:172
Elizabeth, 2:172
Elizabeth (Sargent), 2:172
Jane, 2:172
Jane (----), 2:172
Mary, 2:172
Naomi, 2:172
Sarah, 2:172
Flatman
Elizabeth, 2:172

Fleming
Ann (----), 2:172
Elizabeth, 2:172
Joanna (----), 2:172
Mary, 2:172
Sarah, 1:119, 2:172
Fletcher
----, 1:207
Abigail, 2:173
Elizabeth, 1:217, 2:173
Elizabeth (Allen), 1:29
Elizabeth (Wheeler), 2:173
Hannah, 1:381, 2:173
Hope, 4:218
Jane, 3:610
Lydia, 2:166, 2:174
Lydia (Bates), 2:174
Margaret (Hailstone),
2:173, 2:329
Mary, 2:173
Mary (----), 1:396, 2:75,
2:172-173
Mary (Evans), 2:584
Mary (Pendleton), 2:173,
3:388
Mary (Ward), 2:173
Rebecca, 1:11, 2:173,
4:418
Sarah, 2:173, 4:164
Sarah (----) Dingley, 2:584
Sarah (Hill), 2:173
Flinders
Hannah, 3:641
Jane, 3:641
Jane (----), 2:584
Jane (Eddy), 3:641
Flint - see also Flynt
Abigail, 2:584, 3:620
Alice, 2:175, 3:423
Ann, 2:86, 2:174, 3:620
Ann (----), 3:620
Dorothy, 2:174, 4:75
Elizabeth, 2:30, 3:620,
3:646
Elizabeth (Hart), 3:620
Elizabeth (Johnson), 3:620
Elizabeth (Putnam), 2:174,
3:496
Esther (Willet), 2:174,
4:557
Hannah, 3:620-621, 4:410
Hannah (Moulton), 3:620
Jane (Bulkley), 1:290,

Flint (continued)
  Jane (Bulkley) (continued)
    2:174
  Joanna, 2:174, 3:275
  Lydia, 3:620
  Margaret, 2:174
  Margaret (Hoar), 2:431
  Margery (Hoar), 2:174
  Mary, 2:174, 2:584, 3:620
  Mary (Downton), 3:620,
    3:641
  Mary (Oakes), 2:174,
    3:657
  Ruth, 2:174, 3:620
  Sarah, 3:620, 3:663
Flood/Floyd
  Abigail, 2:175
  Abigail (Disbrough), 2:52,
    2:175
  Dorothy, 2:176
  Elinor, 2:176
  Elinor (----), 2:176
  Elizabeth, 4:412
  Elizabeth (----), 2:176,
    2:543
  Esther, 2:175
  Hannah, 2:176
  Hannah (----), 2:175
  Joanna, 2:176
  Lydia, 2:175-176
  Lydia (----), 2:176, 2:313
  Mary, 2:175-176
  Mary (----), 2:175
  Rachel, 2:175-176
  Rachel (----), 2:176
  Ruth, 2:176
  Sarah, 2:175-176
  Sarah (----), 2:175-176
Flower/Flowers
  Ann, 2:176
  Elizabeth, 2:176
  Hannah, 2:219
  Lydia, 2:176
  Lydia (Smith), 3:621,
    4:125
  Mary, 2:176
Flucker
  Judith (Bodoin), 1:221
Fluster
  Jane, 2:592
Flynt - see also Flint
  Ann, 2:11
  Dorothy, 3:501

  Hannah, 2:11
Fobes
  Bethia, 2:176, 3:4
  Constant (Mitchell), 2:176
  Elizabeth, 2:176-177, 3:4
  Elizabeth (Howard), 2:176,
    2:472
  Elizabeth (Southworth),
    2:177, 4:143
  Hannah, 2:176, 3:4
  Mary, 2:176
  Sarah, 2:176
  Sarah (Gager), 2:176
Fogg
  Mary (Page), 3:331
  Sarah (Carrier), 2:177
  Sarah (Currier), 1:484
  Susanna, 3:621
  Susanna (----), 2:177,
    3:621
Folger
  Abiah, 2:177, 2:200
  Bathshua, 2:177, 3:458
  Bethia, 1:119, 2:177
  Dorcas, 2:177, 3:474
  Experience, 2:177
  Joanna, 1:430, 2:177
  Mary, 2:177, 4:674
  Mary (Barnard), 2:177
  Mary (Morrill), 2:177
  Meribah (Gibbs), 2:177
  Patience, 2:177, 2:228,
    2:356
  Sarah, 2:177
  Sarah (Gardner), 2:177,
    2:229
Folland
  Elizabeth, 1:20, 2:562
Follansbee
  Abigail (----), 2:178
  Ann, 1:365
  Hannah, 2:178
  Mary, 2:178
  Rebecca, 1:365, 2:178
  Sarah (----), 2:178
Follet/Follett
  ---- (----), 3:263
  Elizabeth (----) Drew, 2:73,
    2:178
  Hannah, 3:621
  Hannah (----), 2:178
  Mary, 3:621, 3:631
  Persis (Black), 3:621

  Rebecca, 3:621
  Ruth, 1:337, 3:621
  Sarah, 2:178
  Susanna, 3:621, 4:93
Folsom
  Abigail (Perkins), 2:178,
    3:394
  Catharine (Gilman), 2:258
  Elizabeth, 2:178
  Hannah (Farrow), 2:146,
    2:178
  Mary, 2:178, 3:150
  Mary (Gilman), 2:178
  Mary (Roby), 2:178
  Mercy, 2:178
  Susanna, 2:178, 2:257
  Susanna (Cousins), 2:178
Fones
  Ann, 2:179
  Ann (----), 2:179
  Elizabeth, 2:150, 4:608
  Elizabeth (----), 2:179
  Lydia (----), 2:179
  Lydia (Smith), 4:110
  Margaret, 2:179
  Margaret (----), 2:179
  Martha, 4:611
  Mary, 2:179, 2:301
  Meribah (----), 2:179
Foote/Foot
  Abigail, 2:92, 2:179, 2:181
  Abigail (Barker), 2:181
  Abigail (Ingalls), 2:179
  Abigail (Jeggles), 2:179,
    3:639
  Abigail (Johnson), 2:179,
    2:554
  Bathsheba (----), 2:179,
    2:181
  Dorcas, 2:180
  Elizabeth, 1:157, 1:387,
    2:179-181
  Elizabeth (----), 4:478
  Elizabeth (Deming), 2:180
  Elizabeth (Nash), 2:181
  Elizabeth (Smith), 2:180,
    2:322, 4:132
  Eunice, 2:180
  Frances, 1:118, 2:48,
    2:180
  Hannah, 2:179
  Hannah (----) Howd, 2:181
  Hannah (Currier), 1:484,

Foote/Foot (continued)
Hannah (Currier)
(continued)
2:181
Lydia, 2:181
Margaret, 2:180
Margaret (----), 2:389
Margaret (Bliss), 1:201,
2:180
Margaret (Stallion), 2:181,
4:161
Martha, 2:181
Martha (Ward), 2:181,
4:410
Mary, 2:179-181, 2:274,
3:576, 4:200
Mary (----), 2:179
Mary (Merrick), 2:181
Mehitable, 2:179
Patience, 2:179
Rebecca, 1:445, 2:180-181,
4:128
Rebecca (Dickerman),
2:47, 2:179
Sarah, 2:180-181, 2:575,
3:307
Sarah (----), 1:188, 1:198,
2:181
Sarah (Rose), 2:180
Susanna (----) Frisbie,
2:180
Tabitha (Bishop), 1:186,
2:180
Thankful, 2:181
Footman
Catharine (----), 2:182
Sarah (Cromwell), 2:182
Forbas
Kate (Robinson), 2:182
Forbes
---- (Gager), 2:221
Dorothy, 2:182
Mary, 2:182
Sarah, 2:182
Sarah (Andrews) Treat,
1:53, 2:182, 4:325
Sarah (Treat), 2:182, 4:325
Forbush
Hannah (----), 2:182
Force
Elizabeth (----), 2:182
Ford/Foorde
----, 1:445, 2:183

---- (----), 1:274
---- (Kent), 2:182
Abigail, 2:183, 4:226-227
Abigail (Snow), 2:183,
4:138
Ann, 2:182-183, 3:269
Ann (----), 2:184
Ann (----) Scott, 2:183,
4:39
Ann (Phippen), 3:418
Barbara, 2:183
Bethia, 1:160, 2:183
Bethia (Hatch), 2:183
Elinor (----), 2:182
Elizabeth, 1:483,
2:182-183
Elizabeth (----), 2:183
Elizabeth (Hopkins), 4:682
Elizabeth (Knowles),
2:183, 3:41
Hannah, 2:183, 3:621
Hannah (----), 2:182
Hepzibah, 2:183, 3:134,
3:154
Joanna, 1:390, 2:183
Joanna (----), 2:183
Lydia, 2:183
Lydia (Griffin), 2:182
Margaret, 2:184
Martha, 2:182, 3:268
Mary, 2:183-184, 4:523
Mary (----), 2:182, 2:584
Mary (Brooks), 1:261
Mehitable (Phippen),
2:183, 3:418
Mellicent, 1:343, 2:71,
2:184
Mercy, 2:184, 4:282
Milicent, 2:184
Patience, 2:183
Prudence, 2:182, 3:92
Ruth, 2:182-183
Sarah, 2:182-183, 2:571
Sarah (Dingley), 2:52,
2:184
Silence, 2:182
Susanna, 2:183
Fordham
----, 2:184
Elizabeth (----), 2:184
Hannah, 1:400, 2:184
Mary, 2:477
Mary (Maltby), 2:184,

3:145
Forman/Furman
Abigail, 2:184
Mary (Wilbore), 2:184,
4:545
Forster
Susanna (Parker), 3:355
Fort
Hannah (----) Hutchinson,
2:185
Forth
Mary, 4:610
Forward
Ann (----), 2:185
Fosdick
Ann, 1:507, 2:185
Ann (Shapleigh), 2:185
Elizabeth (----) Betts, 1:172,
2:185
Hannah, 1:125, 2:185
Martha, 2:185, 2:445
Mary, 2:185
Mercy, 2:185
Mercy (----), 1:65
Mercy (Picket), 2:185,
3:424
Ruhami, 2:185
Ruth, 2:185
Sarah (----), 2:185
Foskett
Abigail, 2:185
Elizabeth, 2:185
Elizabeth (----), 2:185
Elizabeth (Leach), 2:584
Hannah (----), 2:584
Mary, 2:185
Miriam (Cleaveland),
1:514
Foss
Sarah (----) Heard, 2:397
Sarah (Goffe), 2:185
Fossaker/Fossecar/etc
Elizabeth (----) Johnson,
2:185, 2:556
Foster
Abigail, 2:188
Abigail (----), 2:186,
2:189-190
Abigail (Foster), 2:188
Abigail (Hawkins) Moore
Kellond, 2:383, 3:6, 3:230
Abigail (Lord), 3:116
Ann, 1:285, 2:188,

Foster (continued)
Ann (continued)
2:190-191, 2:584, 3:409,,
3:621
Ann (----) Wilson, 3:621,
4:588
Ann (Brackenbury), 1:228,
2:191
Ann (Lane), 2:189, 3:52
Catharine, 2:186
Catharine (----), 2:186
Comfort, 2:187
Deborah, 2:191
Elizabeth, 1:344, 2:186,
2:188-191, 2:211, 2:490,
2:584, 3:557, 3:621,
4:370, 4:629
Elizabeth (----), 1:265,
3:430
Elizabeth (----) Whittemore,
2:188, 2:584
Elizabeth (Dane), 2:6,
2:190
Elizabeth (Harris), 2:187,
2:365
Elizabeth (Mumford),
3:253
Elizabeth (Payson), 2:188,
3:373
Elizabeth (Pierce)
Whittemore, 4:535
Ellen, 2:189
Esther, 2:186, 2:190
Esther (----), 2:190
Esther (Bliss), 2:186
Esther (Foster), 2:186
Esther (Kempe), 3:8
Experience, 2:206
Frances (----), 2:186
Hannah, 2:187-190, 3:621,
4:204
Hannah (----), 3:621
Hannah (Downing), 2:188
Hannah (Eames), 2:90,
2:187
Hannah (Very), 2:186,
3:621, 4:372-373
Hepzibah, 2:186
Hopestill, 4:217
Jemima, 2:187
Judith, 2:188-189
Judith (----), 2:189-190
Lettice, 4:311

Lettice (Hanford), 2:186,
2:350
Margaret, 3:621
Margery, 3:621
Margery (----), 3:621
Martha, 2:188, 4:629
Martha (----), 3:621
Martha (Hall), 2:188
Martha (Kinsman), 2:188
Mary, 2:186-191, 2:485,
2:584, 3:20, 3:122,
3:374, 3:621, 3:640, 4:5
Mary (----), 2:186, 3:621
Mary (Bartlett), 1:132,
2:190, 3:232
Mary (Bates), 1:138, 2:187
Mary (Caldwell), 2:189
Mary (Capen), 1:333,
2:189
Mary (Chillingworth),
1:379, 2:189
Mary (Dresser), 2:72
Mary (Jackson), 2:188,
2:532
Mary (Russ), 2:186, 3:589
Mary (Sherwin), 3:621,
4:86
Mary (Stuard), 3:621
Mehitable, 2:186, 2:188
Mehitable (Wyllis) Russell,
2:188, 3:589, 4:577,
4:633
Mercy, 2:188, 3:621
Naomi, 2:190-191
Parnell, 1:417, 2:190
Parnell (Winslow), 2:190
Patience, 1:277
Patience (----), 2:187
Prudence, 2:188, 2:191
Rebecca, 2:186, 2:190-191
Relief (----) Dowse, 2:191
Relief (Holland) Dowse,
2:68, 3:67
Rose, 2:187
Ruth, 2:188-189, 2:191,
3:621
Ruth (Tileston) Denton,
2:40, 2:191, 4:302
Sarah, 1:329, 2:188-190,
2:510, 3:207, 3:621
Sarah (----), 1:229,
2:189-190, 4:516
Sarah (Martin), 2:189-190

Sarah (Parker), 2:190,
3:356
Sarah (Payson), 2:187,
3:373, 4:615
Sarah (Stuard), 3:621
Susanna, 2:190
Susanna (----), 2:191
Susanna (Parker), 2:190
Thankful, 1:97, 2:187,
2:189, 3:599
Fountain
Susanna (Beebe), 1:153,
2:191-192
Fowkes
Jane (----), 2:192, 2:465
Fowle
Abigail, 2:192, 4:137,
4:665
Abigail (----), 2:192
Abigail (Carter), 3:608,
3:621
Ann, 2:192, 3:621
Ann (Carter), 1:341, 2:192
Beriah (Bright), 1:253,
2:192
Elizabeth, 2:192, 3:627
Elizabeth (Atwood), 1:78,
2:192
Grissel (----), 2:193
Hannah, 2:192-193, 3:587,
4:665
Margaret (----), 2:192
Mary, 2:192
Mary (----), 2:192-193
Mary (Carter), 3:608,
3:621
Mercy, 2:192
Sarah, 2:192
Fowler
---- (Tapp), 2:195, 4:253
Abigail, 2:107, 2:193-195,
4:95
Abigail (Brown), 1:274,
2:194
Ann, 2:194
Ann (Johnson), 2:194,
2:558
Deborah, 2:195, 3:48
Elizabeth, 2:193-194
Elizabeth (----) Baldwin,
2:195
Elizabeth (Alsop) Baldwin,
1:104

Fowler (continued)
Elizabeth (Bartlett), 1:131,
2:193
Elizabeth (Herrick), 2:194
Elizabeth (Reynolds),
2:194
Esther, 2:194
Hannah, 1:284, 2:193-195,
3:543, 4:32
Hannah (----), 2:195
Hannah (----) Norton,
2:194
Hannah (Scott), 2:194,
4:37
Hannah (Worthen), 2:195
Isabel, 2:194
Joan (Alvord), 1:46, 2:193
Margery, 3:657
Margery/Margaret, 1:431,
2:194, 3:320
Martha, 2:194
Martha (----), 2:194
Mary, 1:154, 1:328,
2:193-195, 2:278, 2:464,
3:24
Mary (----), 2:194
Mary (----) Norton, 2:194,
3:291
Mary (Baker), 2:193
Mary (Hubbard), 2:193,
2:483
Mehitable, 2:193-194
Mercy, 2:193, 2:195
Mercy (Miller), 2:193,
3:212
Mindwell, 2:193-194
Rose (Burton), 1:316
Ruth, 2:193
Sarah, 2:194-195, 4:120
Sarah (----), 3:621
Sarah (Welch), 4:676
Susanna, 2:195
Fownell
Mary (----), 2:195, 2:596
Sarah, 2:195, 3:22
Fox
---- (Frost), 2:211
Abigail, 2:196
Abigail (----), 2:196
Bathshua (Rogers) Smith,
2:196, 3:560, 4:131
Beriah (Smith), 2:196,
4:130

Elizabeth, 1:106, 1:361,
2:196, 3:622
Elizabeth (----), 3:622
Elizabeth (----) Chadwick,
1:351, 2:196-197
Ellen (----) Green, 2:196,
2:304
Esther (----), 2:196
Hannah, 2:196, 3:114
Hannah (Brooks), 1:262,
2:196
Hannah (Burrows), 1:311
Hannah (Isbell) Stedman,
2:196, 4:179
Joanna (----), 2:196
Judith, 2:196
Judith (Rayner), 2:196,
3:514, 4:357
Lydia (Jaquith), 2:195
Mary, 2:196
Mary (----), 2:196, 3:72
Mary (Lester), 2:196
Mary (Stone) Hunt, 2:195,
4:205
Mary (Wheeler), 2:195,
4:497
Rebecca (----), 2:196
Rebecca (----) Wyeth,
4:682
Sarah, 2:196
Sarah (Larrabee), 2:196,
3:646
Susanna, 2:448
Foxall
Ruth, 2:197
Foxcraft/Foxcroft
Ann (Coney), 2:198
Catharine, 2:197
Elizabeth, 2:197
Elizabeth (Danforth), 2:9,
2:197
Martha, 2:197
Mehitable, 2:197
Mehitable (Coney), 2:197
Phebe, 2:197
Foxwell
---- (Cumming), 2:198
Ann (Shelley), 2:198
Deborah (----), 2:198
Ester, 2:198
Lucretia, 2:198, 3:552
Martha, 1:92, 2:198
Mary, 1:426, 2:198, 3:291

Ruth, 2:198
Sarah, 1:486, 2:198
Sarah (Bonython), 1:211,
2:198
Susanna, 1:69, 2:198
Foy/Foye
Dorothy, 3:622
Dorothy (----), 2:198
Elizabeth, 2:198, 2:497,
3:622
Elizabeth (Campbell),
3:622
Elizabeth (Emmes), 3:622
Hannah, 2:198, 3:622
Mary, 3:622
Rochard (----), 2:198
Sarah (Belcher), 1:156
Sarah (Lynde), 3:622
Fraile
Deborah, 2:199
Elizabeth, 2:199, 4:66
Elizabeth (----), 2:199
Eunice, 2:199, 3:368
Hannah, 2:199
Ruth, 2:199
Frame
Mary (----), 2:199
Francis
Alce/Alice (----), 2:199
Ann, 2:199
Elizabeth, 2:199
Hannah, 2:199
Hannah (Dickson), 2:199
Hannah (Hall), 2:199
Joan (----), 2:199
Lydia, 2:199
Lydia (Cooper), 2:199
Mary, 2:199
Rebecca, 2:199
Rose (----), 2:199
Sarah, 2:199
Susanna, 2:199, 3:656
Franklin
Abiah (Folger), 2:177,
2:200
Alice (Andrews), 1:55,
2:200
Ann, 2:200
Ann (----), 2:200
Catharine (----), 2:199
Deborah (Reed), 2:200
Elizabeth, 1:55, 2:200,
3:183

Franklin (continued)
  Hannah, 2:200
  Jane, 2:200
  Jane (----), 2:201
  Joanna, 2:199
  Joanna (----), 2:200
  Lydia, 2:200
  Martha, 3:417
  Mary, 2:199-200
  Phebe (----), 2:199-200,
    3:96
  Sarah, 2:199-200
Franks
  Deborah, 2:201
  Grace (----), 2:201
  Sarah, 2:201
  Sarah (Weld), 2:201, 4:458
Frary
  ----, 2:201
  Abigail, 2:201
  Bethia, 2:201
  Elizabeth (----) Harding,
    2:584
  Hannah, 2:88, 2:201
  Hannah (Eliot), 2:201
  Hannah
    (Eliot/Elliot/Elliott), 2:109
  Mary, 2:201, 3:572
  Mary (----), 2:201
  Mary (Graves), 2:201
  Mary/Mercy, 3:572
  Mehitable, 1:47, 2:201,
    3:572
  Prudence, 2:201
  Prudence (----), 2:201
  Susanna, 2:201
Fraye
  Ann (Upton), 4:362
Frazer
  Abigail, 2:202
  Hannah, 2:202
  Martha (Stuart), 2:202
Freake
  Elizabeth, 2:202
  Elizabeth (Clark),
    1:401-402, 2:202, 2:510
  Jane, 2:202
  Mary, 2:202
  Mehitable, 2:202
Freeborne/Freebourne/etc
  ----, 4:406
  Ann, 2:202
  Comfort, 2:202

  Martha, 2:202
  Mary, 2:202, 4:442
  Mary (----), 2:202
  Mary (Broomer) Lawton,
    2:202, 3:64
  Mercy, 2:202
  Patience, 2:202
  Sarah, 1:279, 2:202, 4:406
  Sarah (----), 2:202
  Susanna, 2:202
Freelove
  Elizabeth (Wilbore), 2:202,
    4:545
Freeman
  ---- (----) Perry, 3:399
  Alice, 2:203, 3:329
  Ann (Stearns), 4:173
  Apphia, 2:204, 3:391,
    4:145
  Cecilia, 2:203
  Deborah, 2:203
  Dorothy, 2:204
  Dorothy (Haynes), 2:204,
    2:389
  Elizabeth, 2:113,
    2:203-204, 2:236
  Elizabeth (----), 2:203-204
  Hannah, 2:204-205, 3:187,
    4:354
  Hannah (----), 2:204, 3:462
  Lydia (----), 2:205
  Margaret, 2:203
  Margaret (Ingraham),
    2:203, 2:523
  Margaret (Young), 2:203
  Martha, 3:660
  Mary, 2:203-205, 3:399
  Mary (----), 2:204, 3:477
  Mary (Collier), 1:433,
    2:204
  Mercy, 2:204, 3:42
  Mercy (----) Watson, 4:437
  Mercy (Prence), 2:204,
    3:477
  Mercy (Southworth),
    2:204, 4:143
  Patience, 1:477, 3:335
  Rachel, 2:203
  Rebecca, 2:203-205
  Rebecca (Prence), 2:203,
    3:477
  Rebecca (Sparrow),
    2:204-205

  Sarah, 2:203-204, 3:641
  Sarah (----), 2:203
  Sarah (Mayo), 4:233
  Sarah (Merrick), 2:204
  Sarah (Smith), 4:117
Freeze/Frieze
  Elizabeth (----), 2:205
Freke
  Mary, 4:388
French
  ----, 2:205
  ---- (Kingsley), 2:206, 3:29
  Abigail, 2:206-208
  Abigail (Beal/Beals), 1:146
  Abigail (Brown), 1:267,
    2:207
  Abigail (Coggan), 1:420,
    2:206
  Alice, 2:207, 2:480
  Alice (----), 2:207
  Ann, 2:205-206, 3:108,
    3:622
  Ann (----), 2:205
  Ann (Bowers), 1:223
  Ann (Marsh), 2:207, 3:154
  Deborah, 2:206
  Dorcas, 3:377
  Elinor (Thompson) Veazey,
    2:206, 4:289, 4:369
  Elizabeth, 1:5, 1:146,
    2:205-208, 2:525, 2:585,
    3:622, 4:502
  Elizabeth (----), 2:208
  Esther, 2:207
  Esther (----), 2:207
  Experience (Foster), 2:206
  Experience (Thayer),
    2:206
  Grace, 2:206
  Grace (----), 2:205-206
  Hannah, 1:146, 1:229,
    2:205-208, 3:3, 3:33,
    3:409, 4:484, 4:497,
    4:511
  Hannah (----) Edwards
    Stebbins, 4:175
  Hannah (Burrage), 1:308,
    2:206
  Hannah (Jacob/Jacobs)
    Loring, 3:119
  Hannah (Whitman), 2:207,
    4:523
  Jane, 3:622

French (continued)
  Jemima, 2:585
  Jemima (Cheney), 1:372,
    3:403
  Joan (----), 2:205
  Joanna, 2:207
  Joanna (----), 2:207
  Lydia, 1:223, 3:622
  Lydia (----), 3:622
  Margery, 2:585
  Martha, 2:75
  Martha (----), 2:207-208
  Mary, 1:146, 1:201, 2:96,
    2:128, 2:205-208, 2:515,
    2:585, 3:25, 3:154,
    3:379, 4:177
  Mary (----), 2:207
  Mary (Catlin), 2:208
  Mary (Champney), 1:356,
    2:205
  Mary (Lothrop) Stearns,
    2:208, 3:122, 3:223,
    4:174
  Mary (Marsh), 2:205
  Mary (Noyes), 2:206,
    3:297
  Mary (Palmer), 2:206
  Mary (Tisdale), 2:207
  Mary (Winsley), 2:205
  Phebe, 2:285
  Rachel, 2:208
  Rachel (Twelves), 2:209,
    4:353
  Rebecca, 2:205, 2:585
  Rebecca (----), 2:205
  Sarah, 2:205-208, 3:377,
    4:317, 4:335
  Sarah (Cummings), 1:483,
    2:207
  Sarah (Eastman), 2:93,
    2:207, 4:76
  Susanna, 2:207, 3:622
  Susanna (----), 2:206
  Temperance, 1:220,
    2:205-206
Frese
  Elizabeth, 3:542
Friend
  Ann (Curtis), 3:622
  Bethia, 2:209
  Elizabeth, 3:384
  Mary, 3:622
  Mary (Curtis), 3:613

  Mary (Moulton), 3:248
Friese
  Elizabeth (----), 2:209
Frink, 3:479
  Deborah, 2:209, 3:48
  Grace (----), 2:209
  Hannah (Prentice), 3:478
  Mary (----), 2:209
Frisbie
  Abigail, 2:209, 2:430,
    3:622
  Hannah, 3:622
  Hannah (Ross), 4:698
  Lydia, 3:622
  Rebecca, 3:622
  Ruth (Bowers), 1:223,
    2:209, 2:430, 3:622
  Silence, 3:622
  Susanna (----), 2:180
Frissell/Frizell
  Abigail, 3:335
  Elizabeth, 2:210
  Hannah, 2:209-210
  Hannah (Clark), 1:404,
    2:210
  Martha, 2:210
  Martha (----), 2:210
  Mary, 2:210
  Mary (----), 2:210
  Sarah, 2:209
  Sarah (----), 2:209
Frost
  ----, 2:211
  Abigail, 2:210-212, 3:622
  Ann, 1:150
  Catharine, 2:212, 2:345,
    3:44
  Dorothy, 2:211
  Elizabeth, 2:210, 2:212,
    2:298, 3:622
  Elizabeth (----), 2:210
  Elizabeth (Barlow), 1:117
  Elizabeth (Foster), 2:211
  Elizabeth (Miller), 2:212,
    3:209
  Elizabeth (Wakefield),
    2:211-212, 4:386
  Esther, 2:211
  Faith, 2:212
  Hannah, 2:211-212, 3:622
  Hannah (Johnson), 2:212
  Hannah (Marshcroft/etc),
    3:159

  Hannah (Miller), 2:212,
    3:209
  Hepzibah (----), 2:211
  Jane, 2:210-211
  Jane (Eliot) Pepperell,
    2:210-211, 3:392
  Lydia, 2:210, 2:212, 2:298
  Margery, 2:211
  Martha (----) Rankin,
    3:507
  Mary, 1:150, 2:210-212,
    3:622
  Mary (----), 2:211, 3:622
  Mary (Bowles), 1:224,
    2:210
  Mary (Cole), 2:585
  Mary (Gibbs) Goodridge,
    2:212, 2:247
  Mary (Pepperell), 1:437,
    2:211, 3:392
  Mary (Rowland), 3:581
  Mehitable, 2:210
  Mercy (Paine), 3:622,
    4:694
  Miriam, 2:211
  Rachel, 2:211
  Reana (----) Daniels, 2:211
  Reana (Andrews) Daniels,
    2:9
  Rebecca, 1:212, 1:452,
    2:210-211, 2:533, 3:622
  Rebecca (Andrews), 1:56,
    2:211
  Rebecca (Hamlet), 2:211,
    2:344
  Sarah, 2:210-212, 3:622,
    4:133
  Sarah (----), 2:211
  Sarah (Singletary), 2:212
  Sarah (Wainwright),
    2:210, 4:382
  Susanna, 2:212, 4:534
  Susanna (Dixon), 2:54
  Tabitha (Trott), 4:711
  Thomasine (----), 2:211
Frothingham
  Abiel, 2:213
  Abigail, 1:410, 2:213
  Ann, 2:213
  Ann (----), 2:213
  Bethia, 2:213
  Elizabeth, 2:213
  Esther, 3:394

Frothingham (continued)
Hannah, 2:212-213, 3:15
Hannah (Rand), 3:505
Martha, 2:213, 3:617
Mary, 2:212-213, 4:515
Mary (Hett), 2:212, 2:407, 3:16
Mary (Lowden), 2:213
Rebecca, 2:213
Ruth, 2:213
Ruth (----), 1:283
Ruth (George), 2:213, 2:242
Sarah, 2:213
Frow/Fro
Abigail, 2:213
Priscilla (----) Hunter, 2:213, 2:502
Frye
Ann, 2:213-214
Ann (----), 2:214
Bethia, 2:213, 3:516
Deborah, 2:214
Dorothy, 2:214
Elizabeth, 2:214, 4:195
Elizabeth (----), 2:214
Esther, 2:213
Eunice (Potter), 2:214, 3:466
Hannah, 2:214
Hannah (----), 2:214
Hepzibah, 1:3, 2:213
Lydia, 2:214
Lydia (Osgood), 2:214, 3:321
Mary, 2:213-214, 4:221
Mary (Aslett), 1:69, 2:214
Mary (Parker), 2:213
Mehitable, 2:213
Naomi, 2:213, 4:668
Phebe, 2:214, 3:402
Ruth, 2:213, 4:313
Sarah, 2:214
Susan, 2:214
Tabitha (Farnum), 2:214
Fryer/Frier
---- (Scarlet), 4:35
Catharine (----), 2:214
Christian (----), 2:214
Dorothy (Woodbridge), 2:214
Elizabeth, 2:214
Elizabeth (----), 3:622

Margaret, 4:686
Sarah, 2:214
Fugill
Mercy, 2:215
Pledge, 2:215
Fulham/Fullam
Hannah, 2:215
Mary, 2:215
Mary (Woolson) Jones, 2:215
Sarah, 2:215, 4:334
Sarah (Livermore), 2:215
Fuller
---- (Bacon), 2:215
---- (Brewster), 2:212
---- (Tead), 4:265
Abiel, 2:216
Abigail, 1:492, 2:215, 2:217-219
Abigail (Boylston), 2:217
Abigail (Titus), 2:216
Agnes (Carpenter), 2:585
Ann, 2:217, 2:219, 3:67, 4:125-126
Ann (----), 2:215, 2:217
Ann (Fuller), 2:217, 2:219
Bethia, 1:209, 2:216, 3:622
Bridget (----), 2:218
Bridget (Lee), 2:585
Deborah, 2:219, 3:536
Desire, 2:219
Dorothy, 2:215
Elizabeth, 2:30, 2:215-217, 2:219, 2:514, 3:28, 3:204, 3:582, 3:622, 4:72, 4:362, 4:502
Elizabeth (----), 2:215-216, 2:219
Elizabeth (----) Bowen, 1:223
Elizabeth (Brewster), 2:219
Elizabeth (Lothrop), 3:121
Elizabeth (Tidd), 2:219
Elizabeth (Ward), 2:217, 4:409
Elizabeth (Wilmot), 2:217
Elsie (Glascock), 2:585
Experience, 2:217, 2:219
Frances (----), 2:217, 2:219
Hannah, 1:210, 1:211, 2:215-219

Hannah (----), 2:216
Hannah (Flower), 2:219
Hannah (Marsh), 4:682
Jane (Lothrop), 2:218, 3:120
Judith, 2:216
Judith (Grey), 2:216
Lydia, 2:216-217
Lydia (Jackson), 2:217, 2:528
Margaret (----), 2:218
Margaret (Hicks), 2:217
Mary, 2:163, 2:215, 2:217-219, 2:536-537, 2:564, 4:564
Mary (----), 2:215, 2:217, 2:219
Mary (Champion), 1:355
Mary (Dana), 2:217
Mary (Ide), 2:219, 2:517
Mehitable, 2:217
Mehitable (----), 2:216
Mehitable (Rowley), 3:582
Mercy, 1:327, 2:217-219
Mindwell (Trowbridge), 2:217, 4:332
Patience, 2:217
Rachel (----), 2:215
Rebecca (Putnam), 3:496, 3:622, 4:704
Reliance, 2:216
Ruth, 2:215, 2:217, 2:219, 4:501
Ruth (----), 3:622
Sarah, 2:26, 2:215, 2:217-219, 2:470
Sarah (----), 2:217-218
Sarah (Gates), 2:235
Sarah (Mirick), 3:219
Sarah (Nutt) Wyman, 2:219, 3:301, 4:664
Sarah (Wyman), 2:219
Susanna, 4:213
Susanna (Perkins) Buswell, 1:319
Susanna (Perkins) Buzzell, 2:220
Thankful, 1:515, 2:216
Thankful (----), 2:215
Fullford
Elizabeth, 2:599
Elizabeth (Pierce), 2:599

Furber
Bridget, 1:151, 2:220
Elizabeth, 2:4, 2:220
Susanna, 2:220
Temperance, 1:151
Furbush
Dorothy (Pray), 3:476
Furnell
Elinor (----), 2:220, 3:48
Elizabeth, 2:220
Ellen (----), 2:220
Joanna, 1:39, 2:220
Mary, 2:220
Mary (----), 2:220
Sarah, 2:220
Susanna, 2:220
Gaffell/Gassell
Mary, 4:234
Gage
Ann (----), 2:220
Elizabeth, 2:221
Elizabeth (Northend)
Hobson, 2:221, 2:438,
3:290
Faith (Stickney), 2:220,
4:192
Mary, 3:482
Mary (Weeks) Green,
2:306
Prudence (Leaver), 2:220,
3:69, 4:192
Sarah (----), 2:220
Sarah (----) Keyes, 2:220,
3:16
Gager
----, 1:7
Bethia, 2:221
Elizabeth, 1:43, 2:221
Elizabeth (----), 2:221
Hannah, 2:221
Lydia, 2:221
Mary, 2:221
Mehitable (Taylor), 4:259
Rebecca (Lay) Raymond,
3:512
Sarah, 2:176, 2:221
Gaille
Elizabeth, 3:550
Gaines/Gaynes
Ann (Wright), 2:221
Jane (----), 2:585
Mary, 4:263

Gale
Abia, 2:222
Abigail, 2:221-222
Charity, 2:221
Elizabeth, 2:221-222,
3:574
Elizabeth (Spring), 2:222,
3:194, 4:157
Hannah, 2:222
Lydia, 2:221
Martha (Lemon), 2:221,
3:647
Mary, 2:171, 2:221-222,
3:622
Mary (Bacon), 2:221
Mary (Castle), 4:682
Mercy, 2:221
Rebecca (Swett), 2:222
Sarah, 2:221-222, 2:232
Sarah (Fiske), 2:166, 2:221
Gall
Mary (Ward), 2:222
Gallop/Gallup
Ann (----), 2:222
Christobel, 1:472, 2:223
Christobel (----), 2:222
Elizabeth, 2:223, 4:186
Elizabeth (Wheeler), 2:223,
4:500
Esther, 2:222-223, 2:439
Esther (Prentice), 2:222,
3:478
Hannah, 2:222-223, 2:249
Hannah (Lake), 2:223,
3:45
Joan, 2:222, 2:572
Lucy, 2:222
Margaret, 2:222-223
Margaret (Eveley), 2:223
Mary, 1:428, 2:222-223
Mary (Phillips), 2:223
Mehitable, 2:585
Sarah, 2:223
Sarah (Chesebrough),
1:374, 2:223
Susanna, 2:585
Temperance, 2:223
Gally/Galley
Elizabeth, 2:223, 2:253,
4:322
Florence (----), 2:223
Galpin
Ann (Knight), 4:688

Elizabeth, 2:223
Elizabeth (Smith), 2:223
Esther, 2:224
Esther (Thompson), 2:224,
4:285
Martha, 2:223
Rachel, 2:223
Rebecca, 2:223
Rebecca (----), 2:223
Sarah, 2:223
Thankful, 2:223
Galusha
Rachel, 2:224
Gamitt/Jarmill
Sarah, 4:27-28
Gamlin/Gamblin/etc
Elizabeth, 2:224, 2:241
Elizabeth (----) Mayo,
2:224
Hannah, 2:224
Mary, 1:99, 2:224
Obedience, 2:224
Obedience (Holland)
Curtis, 1:486, 2:224, 2:447
Gammon
Catharine, 2:567
Mary (Parrott), 2:224
Gannett
---- (----) Sharpe, 2:224
Abigail, 2:58, 2:225
Deborah, 2:224
Elizabeth, 2:225
Hannah, 2:224-225
Sarah (----), 2:225
Ganson
Elizabeth, 3:623
Elizabeth (----), 3:623
Gardiner
Abigail, 3:556
Elizabeth, 2:225-226,
2:476
Elizabeth (Allyn) Allen,
1:28, 1:43
Mary, 1:441, 2:226
Mary (----) Lungman,
2:225
Mary (Williamson), 2:226
Sarah, 1:89
Sarah (Chandler) Coit,
1:423
Gardner
----, 2:227
---- (Downing), 2:66

Gardner (continued)
Abigail, 2:229-231, 2:585, 4:614
Abigail (Coffin), 2:229
Ann, 2:228-229
Ann (Downing), 1:236, 2:66, 2:228
Ann/Hannah, 1:323
Ann/Hannah (----) Blanchard, 1:196, 2:229
Bethia, 2:228, 2:231, 2:585, 3:623
Bethia (Macy), 2:228, 3:142
Christian, 2:228
Damaris, 1:502, 2:228-229
Damaris (----), 3:623
Damaris (----) Shattuck, 4:62, 4:700
Deborah, 1:438, 2:228-230, 3:142
Elinor, 2:590
Elizabeth, 2:227-228, 2:230-231, 2:523, 2:585
Elizabeth (----), 2:227
Elizabeth (----) Grafton, 3:623
Elizabeth (----) Stone, 2:227
Elizabeth (Allen) Stone, 4:208
Elizabeth (Goodwin), 2:277
Elizabeth (Horn), 2:464
Elizabeth (Lane), 2:585
Elizabeth (Vincent/Vinson), 2:227
Elizabeth (Ward), 2:227
Esther, 2:229-230, 2:551
Eunice (Starbuck), 2:227, 4:172
Hannah, 1:110, 1:415, 2:226-229, 2:231, 2:241, 2:414, 2:585, 3:623
Hannah (----), 2:227, 2:230
Hannah (Nelson), 2:585
Hope, 2:228-229
Joanna, 2:231, 4:167, 4:421
Joanna (May), 2:147, 2:227, 4:533
Judith, 2:229
Judith (Tower), 2:231

Love, 2:229, 4:679, 4:682
Lucy, 2:231, 3:224, 4:346-347
Lucy (Smith), 2:231
Lydia, 2:230, 2:384
Margaret, 2:227, 2:229-230, 3:358
Margaret (----), 2:230
Margaret (Fryer), 4:686
Mary, 1:220, 1:226, 2:227-228, 2:230-231, 2:403, 4:392, 4:682, 4:685, 4:711
Mary (----), 2:228-229
Mary (Austin), 1:499, 2:230
Mary (Bowles), 1:224, 2:231
Mary (Coffin) Pinkham, 2:228
Mary (Porter), 2:231, 3:461
Mary (Starbuck), 2:227, 4:172
Mary (Stowell), 2:228, 4:219
Mary (Weld), 2:229, 4:457
Mary (White), 2:230
Mehitable, 2:227-229
Miriam, 2:229-230, 4:652
Patience, 2:230
Patience (Folger) Harker, 2:177, 2:228, 2:356
Priscilla, 1:67, 2:228
Priscilla (Grafton), 2:228, 2:289
Rachel, 2:228
Rachel (Gardner) Brown, 2:228
Rebecca, 1:469, 2:227, 2:229, 4:527
Rebecca (Crooke), 2:229
Remember, 2:228
Ruth, 1:415, 1:418, 2:227-230, 2:546, 3:630
Sarah, 1:101, 2:177, 2:226-231, 2:280, 3:483
Sarah (----), 2:226, 2:230, 4:587
Sarah (Dunbar), 2:226
Sarah (Mason), 2:226, 3:167
Sarah (Shattuck), 2:229

Seeth, 2:230, 2:289
Susanna, 2:227, 2:229
Susanna (Shelley), 2:230
Garfield
Abigail, 2:231-232, 2:260, 3:358
Ann, 2:231-232
Deborah, 1:508, 2:232
Elizabeth, 2:231-232
Elizabeth (Bridge), 2:231, 2:359
Grace, 2:232
Jerusha, 2:232
Joan (----) Buckminster, 1:286, 2:231
Lydia, 2:232
Mary, 2:231-232
Mary (Benfield), 2:232
Mehitable, 2:231
Mehitable (Hawkins), 2:231, 2:383
Mercy, 2:232
Rachel, 2:232
Rebecca, 2:231-232, 3:223
Rebecca (----), 2:231
Ruth, 2:232
Sarah, 2:232, 3:176
Sarah (Gale), 2:222, 2:232
Susanna (----), 2:232
Garford
Ann (----), 2:232
Garland
Dorcas, 2:232
Dorcas (----), 2:232
Elizabeth (Philbrick), 3:408
Elizabeth (Philbrick) Chase, 1:365, 2:232, 3:409, 3:548
Joan (----), 2:232
Lydia, 2:232
Mary, 2:232
Rebecca, 2:232
Rebecca (Sears), 2:232
Garnett/Garnet
---- (----), 1:384, 2:233
Deborah, 2:585
Joanna, 2:233
Judith, 2:233, 4:71
Mary, 2:147, 2:233
Mary (----), 2:146
Sarah (Warren), 2:233

Garnsey
  Hannah (Coley), 1:432,
    2:233
  Rose (----) Waterbury,
    2:233, 4:430
  Sarah, 2:233
Garretson
  Alice (Willey), 2:234
Garrett/Garrad/Garrard
  Ann, 2:234
  Deborah, 2:234
  Deborah (----), 2:233
  Elizabeth, 2:233, 4:301
  Hannah, 2:233
  Jael, 2:233
  Lydia, 3:623
  Lydia (Tilden), 2:233,
    4:301
  Mary, 2:233-234, 2:586
  Mary (----), 2:234
  Persis (Pierce), 2:234
  Priscilla, 2:233
  Ruth, 2:233
  Ruth (Buck), 1:284, 2:233
  Sarah, 2:234
Garrison
  Joan (Pullen), 2:234
Garven
  Elizabeth, 3:623
Gary
  Ann, 1:186
  Hannah, 1:186
Gascoyne/Gaskin/Gaskell
  Abigail (----), 2:234
  Elizabeth, 2:234
  Elizabeth (----), 2:234
  Elizabeth (Sherman),
    2:234, 4:82
  Hannah, 2:234, 3:623
  Mary, 2:234
  Provided, 3:623
  Provided (Southwick),
    3:623
  Sarah, 2:234, 3:623, 3:640
  Sarah (----), 2:234
Gassell/Gaffell
  Mary, 4:234
Gatchell/Getchell
  Dorcas, 2:235
  Dorcas (----), 2:235
  Eleanor, 2:235
  Elizabeth (Jones), 2:235
  Hannah, 2:235

  Mary, 2:235
  Mary (----) Wodell, 2:235
  Priscilla, 2:235
  Sarah (Brayton), 1:240
  Susanna, 2:235, 3:293
Gates
  Abigail, 2:235-236, 4:144
  Ann, 2:236
  Ann (----), 2:236, 4:646
  Deborah, 2:236
  Elizabeth, 2:235-236, 3:65
  Elizabeth (----), 2:235
  Elizabeth (Freeman), 2:236
  Esther, 2:235-236
  Esther (----), 2:235
  Hannah, 2:235-236
  Hannah (Brainard), 1:237,
    2:236
  Hannah (Oldham), 3:308
  Judah, 2:235
  Margaret, 2:235
  Margaret (----), 2:235
  Margaret (Geer), 2:239
  Mary, 1:442, 2:235-236,
    2:586, 3:186
  Patience, 2:235
  Rachel, 2:235
  Rebecca, 2:235-236
  Rebecca (----), 2:235
  Ruth, 2:235
  Sarah, 2:235-236
  Sarah (Olmstead), 2:235,
    3:312
  Sarah (Woodward), 2:236,
    4:643-644
  Susanna, 2:235
Gatline/Gattliffe
  Mary, 2:236
  Mary (Richardson), 2:236,
    3:535
  Prudent, 2:236
  Prudent (----), 2:236
Gault/Gaut/Golt - see also
  Gott
  ---- (----), 2:587
  Deborah, 2:270
  Mehitable, 2:93, 2:236
  Rebecca, 2:587
  Sarah, 2:270, 2:587
Gaunt
  Mary, 1:476
Gavett
  Catharine, 3:437

Gawdren
  Mary (Cole), 2:527
Gay
  ---, 2:237
  Abiel, 2:237
  Abigail, 2:237
  Abigail (----), 2:237
  Elizabeth, 2:237, 3:162
  Hannah, 2:237
  Hannah (----), 2:237
  Joanna, 2:237
  Joanna (----) Baldwicke,
    2:237
  Judith, 2:237
  Lydia, 2:237, 3:623
  Lydia (----), 2:236
  Lydia (Lusher), 2:237
  Mary, 2:237
  Mary (Bridge), 1:248,
    2:237
  Mary (Bullard), 2:237,
    3:532
  Rebecca, 2:237
  Rebecca (Bacon), 1:90,
    2:237
  Sarah, 2:237
Gayer
  Damaris, 2:237-238
  Dorcas, 2:237-238, 4:172
  Dorcas (Starbuck), 2:237,
    4:171
Gaylord/Gaylor/etc
  Abigail, 2:238, 2:586,
    2:590
  Abigail (Bissell), 1:187,
    2:586
  Ann, 2:238-239, 3:405
  Ann (Porter), 2:239
  Elizabeth, 1:183, 2:238,
    2:466, 2:586
  Elizabeth (Drake), 2:107,
    2:239
  Elizabeth (Hull), 2:238
  Esther, 2:586
  Hannah, 2:239, 2:586
  Joanna, 2:238, 3:461
  Margaret (Southmayd),
    4:142
  Martha, 2:115, 2:238,
    2:586
  Martha (Thompson), 2:586
  Mary, 2:238, 2:317, 3:113
  Mary (----) Allis, 2:238

Gaylord/Gaylor/etc
(continued)
Mary (----) Wyatt Graves
   Allis, 2:295
Mary (Bronson) Wyatt
   Graves Allis, 4:662
Mary (Brownson) Wyatt
   Graves Allis, 1:42
Mary (Clark), 1:392, 2:238
Mary (Drake), 2:238
Mary (Stebbins), 2:238,
   4:175
Rachel, 2:586
Ruth, 2:586
Ruth (Crow), 1:479, 2:239,
   2:332
Sarah, 1:26, 2:238, 3:407
Sarah (Rockwell), 2:238,
   3:558
Sarah (Standley), 2:238,
   4:164
Gears/Geer/Geers
Ann, 2:239
Deborah, 2:239
Deborah (----), 2:240
Dorothy, 2:239
Elizabeth, 2:239-240
Esther, 2:239
Esther (----), 2:239
Experience (----), 2:239
Hannah, 2:239
Jerusha, 2:239
Keziah, 2:239
Lucy, 2:239
Margaret, 2:239
Martha, 2:239-240
Martha (----), 2:239
Martha (Tyler), 2:240
Mary, 2:239-240
Mary (----), 2:239
Sarah, 2:239, 4:559
Sarah (Abby/Abbey), 1:6
Sarah (Allen), 2:239
Sarah (Allyn), 1:44, 2:239
Sarah (Howard), 2:239
Thankful, 2:239
Zerviah, 2:239
Geary
Ann (Douglas), 2:63,
   2:240
Deborah, 2:240
Elizabeth, 1:5, 2:240
Elizabeth (----), 2:240

Elizabeth (Parker), 2:240
Frances (----), 2:240
Hannah, 2:240
Hannah (Curtis), 1:487,
   2:240
Mary, 2:240
Rebecca, 2:240
Sarah, 2:240, 2:455
Gedney/Gidney
----, 3:496
Ann, 2:240
Bethia, 2:240
Catharine (----), 2:241
Deborah, 2:240
Elizabeth, 2:240
Elizabeth (Turner), 2:240,
   4:346
Hannah, 2:240-241
Hannah (Clark), 2:240
Hannah (Gardner), 2:241
Lydia, 2:240-241
Margaret, 2:241
Martha, 2:240-241
Mary, 2:240, 3:467
Mary (----), 2:241
Mary (Patteshall), 2:240
Priscilla, 2:240
Ruth, 2:240-241
Sarah, 2:241, 3:623
Sarah (----), 2:241
Susanna, 2:241
Susanna (----), 3:359
Susanna (Clark), 2:241
Gee
Elizabeth (Thacher), 3:623,
   4:272
Elizabeth (Thornton),
   2:241, 4:292
Grace (----), 2:241
Genery/Chenerie
----, 2:242
---- (----) Ellis, 2:242
Elizabeth, 2:114, 2:586
Elizabeth (Gamlyn), 2:241
Mary, 2:242
Sarah (----) Boylston,
   2:241
Thomasin (Hewes), 2:242
George
Abigail (----), 2:586
Ann (----) Goldstone, 2:242,
   2:269
Elizabeth, 2:242-243,

2:260, 2:353, 3:523
Elizabeth (----), 2:242,
   2:404
Hannah, 2:242-243, 3:208
Lydia (Lee), 2:242, 3:172
Martha, 2:242
Mary, 2:68, 2:242-243
Mary (----), 2:242
Mary (Lowden), 2:586
Mary (Pelham), 3:386
Mary (Pell), 2:242-243,
   3:386
Ruth, 2:213, 2:242
Sarah (----), 2:242
Susan, 2:242
Susanna, 2:242, 2:359
Geraerd/Geraerdi/etc
Deliverance (----), 2:243
Mary, 2:243
Meribah (Sweet), 2:243,
   4:238
Renewed (Sweet), 4:238
Gerard
---- (Beckwith), 1:151
Germaine
Mary, 4:94
Gerrish
Abigail, 2:244
Ann, 2:243-244
Ann (----), 2:244, 2:346
Ann (Paine), 3:623
Ann (Parker) Manning,
   2:244
Ann (Waldron), 2:243,
   4:390
Bridget (Vaughan), 4:369
Elizabeth, 2:243-244,
   2:304, 2:309, 3:605,
   3:626
Elizabeth (Higginson),
   2:243
Elizabeth (Turner), 3:624
Elizabeth (Waldron), 2:243,
   4:390
Hannah (Ruck), 2:243,
   3:584
Jane (Sewall), 2:243, 4:53
Joanna, 2:243
Joanna (----) Oliver, 2:244
Joanna (Goodale) Oliver,
   3:309
Judith, 2:244
Mary, 2:58, 2:243-244

Gerrish (continued)
Mary (Sewall), 4:55
Sarah, 2:243
Gibbard/Gibbert
Abigail, 2:244, 3:625,
4:683
Ann (Tapp), 1:57, 2:244,
4:253
Esther, 2:244
Hannah, 2:244
Mary, 2:244
Phebe, 1:55, 2:244
Rebecca, 2:244, 4:667
Sarah, 2:244
Sarah (----), 4:694
Sarah (Coe), 4:683
Gibbes
Sarah, 3:302
Gibbons/Gibbins
Ann, 2:245, 3:205
Charity, 2:245
Dorcas (/Seely), 2:245
Dorcas (Seely), 4:50
Elizabeth, 2:245
Esther, 2:245
Jerusha, 2:245
Judith (Lewis), 2:245
Margaret (----), 2:245
Rachel, 2:100, 2:245
Rebecca, 2:245, 4:77
Sarah, 2:245, 3:532, 4:357
Ursula (----), 2:245
Gibbs
Abigail, 2:246, 3:600,
4:241
Alice (Warren), 2:247,
4:426
Ann (Gleason), 2:246
Bethia, 2:247
Catharine, 2:247
Catharine (----), 2:246
Cutbury, 4:332
Elizabeth, 2:246-247
Elizabeth (Andrus), 2:246
Elizabeth (Moore), 2:247
Elizabeth (Sheaffe), 1:488,
2:247, 4:66, 4:444
Esther, 3:20
Experience, 2:247
Hannah, 2:247, 4:590
Hannah (Punderson),
2:246, 3:493
Hepzibah, 2:247

Hepzibah (Dibble), 2:46,
2:247
Joanna, 2:247, 3:113
Joyce (----) Osborn, 2:246
Lydia, 2:246
Lydia (Scottow), 1:369,
2:245, 4:40
Margaret, 2:246-247
Mary, 2:212, 2:246-247
Mary (Bradish), 1:233,
2:246
Mary (Middlecott), 3:205
Mary (Moore), 2:247
Mary (Shrimpton), 2:247,
4:55
Mehitable, 2:246
Mercy, 2:246
Mercy (Greenough), 2:246,
2:310
Meribah, 2:177
Miriam, 2:247
Patience, 2:247
Patience (Butler), 2:247
Sarah, 2:246-247
Sarah (Cutler), 2:246
Gibson
Elizabeth, 2:123
Elizabeth (Remington)
Stedman, 2:248, 4:179
Hannah (Phippen), 2:248,
3:418
Hannah (Underwood),
2:248, 4:359
Joanna (----) Prentiss,
2:248, 3:478
Margaret (Bates), 1:138,
2:248
Martha, 2:248, 3:271
Mary, 2:248, 3:586
Mehitable (Welsteed)
Austin, 1:499
Rebecca, 2:248, 4:173
Rebecca (----), 2:248
Rebecca (Errington), 2:248
Sarah (Pemberton), 2:248,
3:387
Silence, 2:248
Thankful, 2:248
Giddings/Gittings/Gidding
Abigail, 2:84
Elizabeth, 1:382, 3:630
Elizabeth (----), 2:249
Hannah (Martin), 2:249

Jane (Tuttle), 2:249, 4:350
Mary, 2:249
Mary (Goodhue), 2:249,
2:273
Sarah, 3:628
Sarah (----), 2:405
Sarah (Alcock), 1:21
Gifford
Grace, 2:385
Hannah, 1:350, 2:249
Hannah (Gallop), 2:223,
2:249
Hannah (Gove), 2:249
Margaret, 2:249
Margaret (Temple), 2:249
Mary, 2:249
Mary (Caulkins), 1:350
Mary (Davis), 2:249
Ruth, 2:249
Gilbert
----, 1:439, 2:98, 2:249,
2:586, 2:592
Abigail, 2:249
Abigail (Heaton) Atwater,
4:701
Abilene (Marshfield),
3:160
Amie (Lord), 3:116
Amy, 2:250-251
Amy (Lord), 2:250
Ann, 2:252, 3:624
Ann (Black), 2:252
Ann (Blake), 1:194
Catharine (Chapin) Bliss,
1:201, 1:360, 2:251,
3:160
Deborah
(Beamond/Beamon),
1:147
Deborah (Beamont), 2:252
Dorothy, 2:250
Dorothy (Stow), 2:250,
4:218
Elizabeth, 2:35, 2:249-252,
3:624, 4:291
Elizabeth (----), 2:249,
2:251-252, 3:515
Elizabeth (----) Olmstead,
2:251, 3:312, 4:49
Elizabeth (Belcher), 1:156
Elizabeth (Kilham), 2:250
Elizabeth (Smith), 2:251,
4:125

Gilbert (continued)
Esther, 2:249-250
Hannah, 2:251-252, 3:354, 3:624, 3:641, 4:683
Hannah (----), 3:624
Harriet, 4:686
Jane, 2:251, 4:570
Jane (----), 3:624
Jane (Rossiter), 2:251, 3:578
Lydia, 2:250-252
Lydia (Ballard), 2:252
Martha, 2:250
Mary, 1:79, 2:249-252, 2:455, 3:342, 3:578, 3:624
Mary (Eaton), 2:250
Mary (Griswold), 2:250
Mary (Harris) Ward, 2:250, 2:365, 4:409
Mary (Rogers), 2:251, 3:568
Mary (Trowbridge), 2:252
Mary (Ward), 2:251
Mary (Welles), 1:431, 2:250
Mary (Whight), 2:250
Mary (White), 2:250, 4:510
Mehitable, 2:252
Rachel, 2:250, 3:159
Rebecca, 2:251, 3:624
Rebecca (----), 2:252
Sarah, 1:156, 2:157, 2:250-252, 3:624, 3:636, 4:309, 4:382, 4:685
Sarah (----), 3:624
Sarah (Gregson), 2:250, 2:316, 4:517
Winifred (----), 2:249

Gile/Guile/Gyles/Giles
Abigail, 2:253
Bridget, 2:253
Bridget (----) Very, 2:253, 4:372
Elizabeth, 2:253
Elizabeth (Bishop), 1:184, 2:253
Elizabeth (Gally) Trask, 2:223, 2:253, 4:322
Hannah, 2:253, 2:325, 4:372
Judith (Davis), 2:253

Margaret, 2:326
Mary, 2:253, 2:326
Mary (----), 2:253
Mehitable, 1:435, 1:515, 2:253
Remember, 2:253, 3:245
Ruth, 2:253
Sarah, 2:253
Sarah (More), 2:253
Susanna, 2:253
Gilford
Mary (----), 2:253-254
Priscilla, 2:254
Susanna, 2:253-254
Susanna (Pullen), 2:254
Gill
Abigail, 2:255
Agnes (----), 2:254
Ann (Billings), 2:254
Deborah, 2:254, 3:53
Elizabeth, 2:254-255, 4:202
Elizabeth (Ware), 2:254, 4:417
Frances, 1:225, 2:254
Hannah, 1:391, 2:254-255
Hannah (Meacham), 2:255, 3:190
Hannah (Otis), 2:254, 3:323
Isabel, 4:346
Judith, 2:254
Martha (----), 2:254
Mary, 1:146, 2:254, 3:323
Phebe, 2:254
Phebe (Buswell), 1:319, 2:254
Rachel, 2:254, 4:219
Rebecca, 2:254
Ruth (Lincoln), 2:254, 3:94
Sarah, 2:254, 3:55
Sarah (Worth), 2:254
Susanna, 2:255
Susanna (Wilson), 2:254, 4:586
Gillam
Ann, 2:255
Ann (----), 2:255
Dyonisia, 2:255
Elizabeth, 2:255, 2:325
Faith, 2:255
Hannah, 2:255, 3:414

Hannah (----), 4:364
Hannah (Savage), 2:255, 4:27, 4:99
Martha, 2:255, 3:624
Mary, 2:255
Phebe (Phillips), 2:252, 3:416
Gillett/Jellett
Abia, 1:131, 2:256
Abigail, 2:255-256, 2:586
Ann, 2:159, 2:256, 2:586
Azanah, 2:586
Deborah, 2:586
Deborah (Bartlett), 2:586
Dinah, 2:586
Dorothy, 2:586
Elizabeth, 2:256, 2:541, 2:586
Elizabeth (----), 4:416
Elizabeth (----) Perry, 2:255
Elizabeth (Hawks), 2:256, 2:381
Esther, 2:255, 3:112
Esther (Gull), 2:322
Hannah, 2:255-256, 2:586
Hannah (Buckland), 2:586
Hannah (Dickinson), 2:48, 2:256, 2:545
Joanna, 2:255-256, 4:227
Joanna (Taintor), 2:256, 4:249
Mary, 1:274, 2:255-256, 2:595
Mary (Barber), 1:114, 2:256
Mary (Barker), 3:291
Mary (Kelsey), 2:256
Mary/Mercy, 2:586
Mary/Mercy (Barber), 4:693
Mercy (Barker), 3:291
Mindwell, 2:586
Miriam, 2:256
Miriam (Deeble), 2:46, 2:256
Priscilla, 2:255
Priscilla (Kelsey), 2:586
Rebecca, 2:256
Rebecca (Owen), 2:586
Sarah, 2:255-256
Zabed, 2:586

Gillingham
Agnes (----), 1:500
Agnes (Wadlen), 2:586
Deborah, 2:257
Elizabeth, 1:505
Hannah, 2:257
Martha, 2:257
Mary, 2:257
Rebecca, 2:257
Rebecca (Bly), 1:206,
2:257
Gillow
Mary, 3:624
Sarah, 2:257
Sarah (Keyzer), 2:257
Gilman
----, 2:135, 2:257, 2:264
---- (Goddard), 2:264
Abigail, 2:258, 4:279
Abigail (Mandrake), 3:624
Abigail (Maverick), 2:257,
3:179
Alice, 2:258
Ann, 2:258
Ann (----), 2:258
Catharine, 2:257-258
Deborah, 2:258
Elizabeth, 2:75, 2:257-258,
3:43
Elizabeth (----), 2:258
Elizabeth (Adkins), 1:19
Elizabeth (Hersey), 2:258
Elizabeth (Treworgy),
2:257, 4:330
Elizabeth (Trueworthy),
2:257
Hannah, 2:257-258
Joanna, 2:258
Judith, 2:258
Lydia, 1:489, 2:257-258
Maria, 2:258
Maria (Hersey), 2:258
Martha, 2:258
Mary, 2:178, 2:257-258,
4:279
Mary (Clark), 2:257
Mary (Wiggin), 2:257
Mercy, 2:77
Sarah, 2:77, 2:257-258
Sarah (Clark), 2:258
Susanna (Folsom), 2:257
Gilson
Ann, 2:259

Elizabeth (----), 2:259
Frances (----), 2:259
Hepzibah (----), 2:259
Mary, 2:259, 3:649
Mary (Caper), 2:259
Sarah, 2:258-259
Sarah (----), 2:258
Susanna, 2:258
Gipps
Ann, 2:165
Girdler
Ann, 2:259
Hannah, 2:259
Mary, 2:259
Gisborne
Mary (Wicks), 2:259,
4:539
Glading
Elizabeth, 2:259
Elizabeth (Rogers), 2:259
Hannah, 2:259
Mary, 2:259
Susanna, 2:259
Glanfield
Abigail, 2:259
Lydia, 2:259
Lydia (Ward), 2:259,
4:410
Sarah, 2:259
Glascock
Elsie, 2:585
Glass
Amy, 2:260, 4:574
Elizabeth, 2:260
Elizabeth (----), 2:260
Emma, 2:260
Eunice, 2:85
Hannah, 2:259-260
Mary, 2:260
Mary (----), 2:260
Mary (Pontus), 2:34, 2:259,
3:454
Wybra, 2:260
Glazier
Elizabeth, 2:260
Elizabeth (George), 2:242,
2:260
Ruth, 2:260
Gleason
Abiah (----), 2:260
Abigail, 2:260
Abigail (Garfield), 2:260
Ann, 2:246, 2:260

Elizabeth, 3:506
Esther, 2:260
Hannah (----), 2:260
Joyce, 2:260, 3:271
Martha, 2:260
Martha (----), 2:260
Mary, 2:260
Mary (Ross), 2:260
Patience, 2:260
Sarah, 2:260
Sarah (----), 2:260
Susanna, 2:260
Susanna (----), 2:260
Glide
Mary (----), 3:624
Glover
Abigail, 1:305, 2:261-262,
3:624
Abigail (----), 2:261
Abigail (Henderson), 2:262
Ann, 2:262-263, 3:511
Ann (----), 2:261
Elinor (----), 3:641
Elizabeth, 2:262, 3:624,
4:606
Elizabeth (----), 2:82,
2:261-262
Elizabeth (Andrews),
2:261
Esther (----) Saunders,
2:261
Hannah, 1:68, 2:261-262,
3:624, 4:223
Hannah (----), 2:262
Hannah (Cullick), 1:482,
2:262
Hannah (Eliot), 2:110,
2:261
Hannah (Hinckley), 2:262,
2:425
Hannah (Parsons), 3:363
Joanna (Daniel), 2:10,
4:700
Mary, 2:261-263
Mary (----), 2:261
Mary (Guppy), 2:262
Mary (Smith), 2:262,
2:425, 4:118, 4:121
Mehitable, 3:624
Mercy, 2:261, 3:624,
3:650
Priscilla, 1:60, 2:262
Rachel, 4:288

Glover (continued)
Rebecca, 2:261, 4:135
Rebecca (----), 2:261
Ruth (Adams), 1:15
Ruth (Stephens), 2:263
Ruth (Stevens), 4:189
Sarah, 1:106, 2:261-262,
  2:299, 4:88, 4:607
Sarah (----), 2:587
Goad/Goard
---- (Haynes/Haines), 2:391
Ann, 2:263
Ann (Chaplin), 2:263
Hannah, 2:263
Lydia, 2:263
Mary, 2:263
Phebe, 1:56, 2:263
Phebe (Howes), 2:263
Sarah, 2:263
Goble
Abigail, 2:264
Alice (Mousall), 2:264
Elsey, 2:264
Hannah, 2:264
Hannah (----), 2:264, 3:574
Mary, 2:5, 2:264
Mary (Mousall), 3:251
Ruth, 2:264
Ruth (----), 2:264
Sarah, 2:264
Goddard
----, 1:167, 2:264
Abigail, 2:265
Deborah, 2:265
Deborah (Treadway),
  2:265, 4:325
Elizabeth, 2:264-265
Elizabeth (----), 2:265
Elizabeth (Shattuck), 2:265
Hannah, 2:264
Hannah (Jamison) Stone,
  2:264
Jane, 2:265
Leah (Fisher), 2:265
Lucy (Seaver), 2:264
Martha, 2:264
Martha (Palfrey), 3:339
Mary, 2:264-265
Mary (Woodward), 2:264
Mehitable, 2:265
Mehitable (Spring), 2:265
Rachel, 2:265
Rachel (Davis), 2:265

Sarah, 2:264-265
Susanna, 2:264
Susanna (Stone), 2:264,
  4:209
Tryphena, 2:264
Welthea (----), 2:264
Godfrey
----, 4:450
---- (----) Webster, 4:448
---- (Turner), 2:266
Deborah, 2:266
Elizabeth, 1:344, 2:266
Elizabeth (----), 2:266
Hannah, 2:266
Hannah (Hacket), 2:587,
  2:590
Hannah (Kimball), 2:266
Hannah (Meriam), 2:266
Jane, 1:299, 4:644
Joanna, 2:266
Margaret, 2:266, 3:536
Margaret (----) Webster,
  2:266
Margery (----) Webster,
  4:450
Martha (Joyce), 2:573
Mary, 2:266, 3:315
Mary (Brown), 1:276,
  2:266
Mary (Cox), 2:266
Mary (Richmond), 2:266,
  3:539
Ruth, 2:266
Sarah, 1:410, 2:266
Goding/Godding
Elizabeth, 2:266-267
Elizabeth (Beers), 2:266
Godman
Elizabeth (----), 2:267
Godsoe
Elizabeth (----), 2:267
Goffe/Goff
----, 4:494
---- (----), 4:621
Abiah, 2:267, 4:617, 4:621
Amy (----), 2:267
Ann, 2:267-268
Ann (Barnard), 2:268
Deborah, 2:267-268
Elizabeth, 2:268
Eunice, 2:267
Frances, 2:268
Frances (Whalley), 2:268

Hannah, 2:267-268, 3:229,
  4:617
Hannah (Barnard),
  1:118-119
Hannah (Sumner), 2:268,
  4:232
Joyce (----), 2:267
Lydia, 1:120, 2:267-268,
  4:153, 4:617
Mabel, 2:267
Margaret (----), 4:617
Margaret (Wilkinson),
  2:267, 4:552
Margery (Ingersoll), 2:267,
  2:520
Mary, 2:267-268, 4:333
Mary (Briscoe), 1:256
Rebecca, 2:268
Sarah, 2:185, 2:268
Sarah (----), 2:267
Susan, 2:267
Susanna, 2:268
Goldham
Frances (Munger), 2:269
Susanna, 1:185, 2:269
Golding
Abigail, 2:269
Elizabeth, 2:269
Frances, 2:269
Jane, 2:269
Jane (----), 2:269
Martha, 2:269
Mary, 2:269
Mercy, 2:269
Sarah, 2:269
Sarah (----), 2:269
Goldman
Mary (Crow), 3:225
Goldsmith
Mary, 3:368
Mary (Huntington), 2:269,
  2:504
Susanna (----) Sheather,
  2:269
Goldstone
Ann, 1:253, 2:269
Ann (----), 2:242, 2:269
Mary, 2:269-270, 2:408
Goldthwait
Elizabeth, 2:270, 3:25
Elizabeth (----), 2:587
Elizabeth (Cheever), 2:270,
  3:609

Goldthwait (continued)
Hannah, 2:270
Mehitable, 2:270
Goldwyer
Martha, 2:270, 3:437
Golt - see Gault
Gooch
----, 2:270
Lydia (----), 2:270
Ruth (----), 2:270
Goochfield
Margery (----), 1:168
Goodale
Abigail, 3:625
Ann, 1:37, 2:270
Catharine (----), 2:271
Dorothy (----), 2:270
Elizabeth, 3:126, 4:316
Elizabeth (----), 2:271
Elizabeth (Beacham),
3:625
Elizabeth (Beauchamp),
3:602
Esther, 3:624
Hannah, 2:271, 3:643-644
Hannah (Haven), 2:270,
2:379
Joanna, 2:271, 3:309
Martha, 2:270
Mary, 2:132, 2:270-271,
3:625
Mary (----), 2:271
Mary (Cole), 1:426, 2:587
Patience (Cook), 3:624
Sarah (----) Rix, 2:270,
3:545
Susanna, 2:271, 4:253
Goodall
Mary, 3:171
Gooddin
Elizabeth (Beers), 1:154
Mary (Beers), 1:154
Goode/Good
Abigail (----), 2:271
Deborah, 2:271
Sarah, 2:270-271
Goodenhouse
Bethia (----), 2:271
Goodenow/Goodenough/etc
----, 2:272
Abigail, 2:272
Ann (----), 2:271
Dorothy, 2:271

Dorothy (Mann), 2:271
Elizabeth, 2:272
Hannah, 2:271-272, 3:388,
4:117
Jane, 1:112, 2:271-272,
4:543
Jane (----), 1:324,
2:271-272
Joanna (----), 2:272
Lydia, 2:271-272
Mary, 2:271-272
Mary (----), 2:272
Mary (----) Axtell, 1:84
Mercy, 2:271-272, 3:371
Rebecca, 2:271
Rebecca (----), 2:271
Sarah, 2:271-272, 3:14,
4:397, 4:645
Susanna, 2:272
Ursula, 2:272
Goodfellow
Mary (Grant), 2:272, 2:292
Goodhue
Bethia, 2:273
Bethia (----) Lothrop
Grafton, 2:273
Bethia (Rea) Lothrop
Grafton, 2:289, 3:122,
3:512
Elizabeth, 2:273
Hannah, 2:273
Hannah (Dane), 2:6, 2:273
Jane (----), 2:273
Margery, 2:273
Margery (Watson), 2:273
Mary, 2:249, 2:273, 3:290
Mary (----) Fayerweather
Webb, 2:273
Mercy (----) Clark, 2:273
Rachel (----) Todd, 2:273
Remember (----) Fiske,
2:165, 2:273
Sarah, 2:273
Sarah (Whipple), 2:272,
4:505
Susanna, 2:273
Gooding
Bridget (----) Salisbury, 4:5
Seaborn/Sibborn, 3:419
Goodman
Elizabeth, 2:274, 4:419
Hannah, 2:274
Hannah (Noble), 3:286

Mary, 2:274
Mary (Axtell), 2:274
Mary (Terry), 2:274, 4:269
Goodrich
Abigail, 2:170, 2:274-275,
3:625
Abigail (Crafts), 2:275
Ann, 2:274-275
Elizabeth, 2:274-275,
3:575, 3:625, 4:41,
4:477
Elizabeth (Edwards),
2:104, 2:274
Eunice, 2:275
Grace (Riley), 2:275,
3:542
Hannah, 2:274, 3:186
Hannah (Wright), 2:274
Jerusha (Treat) Wells,
2:274, 4:325, 4:480
Joanna, 3:625
Lucenia, 2:275
Lucy, 2:275
Mary, 1:320, 2:274-275,
3:519, 3:625
Mary (----), 2:274, 3:625
Mary (Adams), 1:15
Mary (Foote) Stoddard,
2:180, 2:274, 4:200
Mary Ann (----) Ayrault,
2:275
Milicent, 2:274
Prudence, 2:274
Prudence (Churchill),
2:274
Rebecca, 2:274-275, 4:655
Rebecca (Allen), 1:498,
2:274
Sarah, 2:274-275, 2:449,
3:19
Sarah (----), 1:487
Sarah (Marvin), 2:275,
3:164
Sarah (Treat), 2:274, 4:327
Goodridge
Abigail, 2:276
Deborah (----), 2:275
Elizabeth, 2:275-276
Hannah, 2:275-276
Margaret, 2:276
Margaret (----), 2:276,
2:493
Martha, 2:276

Goodridge (continued)
Martha (Moores), 2:276
Mary, 2:275-276, 4:294,
4:640
Mary (----), 2:276
Mary (Adams), 2:275
Mary (Buttolph) Thaxter,
2:276
Mary (Gibbs), 2:212,
2:247
Mary (Jordan), 2:275
Mary Ann, 2:276
Prudence (----), 2:275
Rebecca (Halsey), 2:276
Sarah (Croad), 2:275
Susanna, 2:276
Goodsell
Abigail, 2:276
Deborah, 2:276
Lydia, 2:276
Mary, 2:276
Sarah, 2:276
Sarah (Hemmingway),
2:276
Goodspeed
Alice, 2:276
Alice (Layton), 2:276
Bathsheba, 2:276
Elizabeth, 2:277
Elizabeth (----), 1:389
Elizabeth (Bursley), 1:312,
2:276
Experience, 2:276
Experience (Holley), 2:276
Lydia, 2:276
Lydia (Crowell), 1:480,
2:276
Mary, 2:276-277, 2:425
Mary (----), 2:424
Mary (Davis), 2:18, 2:276
Mehitable, 2:276
Mercy, 2:276, 2:564
Patience, 2:276
Reliance, 2:276
Rose, 2:276
Ruth, 2:19, 2:276-277
Goodwin/Goodwyn/etc
---- (Cowles), 1:466
Alice, 2:277
Deborah, 2:277
Deborah (Walker), 2:587
Eleanor, 2:278
Elizabeth, 1:479,

2:277-278, 3:625
Elizabeth (----), 2:277
Elizabeth (Pratt), 2:277,
3:471
Elizabeth (Shepard), 4:75
Hannah, 2:277-278, 3:441
Hannah (Jones), 2:278
Hannah (Major), 2:278
Joanna (----), 2:277
Joanna (----) Johnson,
2:587
Joanna (Long) Johnson,
2:599
Margaret (Trowbridge),
4:334
Martha, 2:277, 2:587
Martha (Lathrop), 2:277,
3:120
Martha (Williamson),
4:573
Mary, 1:278, 2:277-278,
2:587, 3:625
Mary (----), 2:277
Mary (Fowler), 2:278
Mary/Mercy (Crouch),
2:277
Mehitable, 2:277
Mehitable (Gould), 2:286,
2:587
Mehitable (Porter), 2:277,
3:463
Mercy (Crouch), 2:587
Mercy (Roby), 3:549
Rachel, 2:278, 3:625
Rebecca, 2:278
Ruth, 2:277
Sarah, 2:277-278
Sarah (Cowles), 2:277
Seaborn/Sibborn, 3:419
Susanna, 2:278
Susanna (----), 1:446,
2:278
Susanna (----) Wheeler,
2:277
Violet, 2:278
Goodyear
---- (----) Lamberton, 2:278,
3:49
Abigail, 3:625
Abigail (Gibbard), 3:625,
4:683
Elizabeth, 2:278
Esther, 2:278, 3:625,

4:127
Hannah, 2:278, 4:388
Lydia, 2:278, 3:45
Mary, 2:278, 3:45
Obedience, 4:700
Gookin
Bethia, 2:279
Bethia (Collicott), 1:432,
2:279
Dorothy (Cotton), 2:280
Elizabeth, 2:110, 2:279,
3:500
Elizabeth (Quincy), 2:279,
3:501
Hannah, 2:279-280
Hannah (Savage), 2:279,
4:24
Hannah (Stearns) Briscoe,
1:256
Hannah (Tyng) Savage,
2:279, 4:357
Mary, 1:141, 2:279
Mary (----), 2:279
Goole
Rose (----), 2:280
Goose
Elizabeth (Foster), 2:584
Mary, 2:280, 4:647
Mary (----), 2:280
Mary (Robinson), 3:625
Rebecca, 2:280
Sarah (----), 2:280
Sarah (Trerice), 2:587
Susanna (Chadwell), 2:280
Susanna (Jones), 2:566,
2:587
Gore
Abigail, 2:280-281
Elizabeth (Weld), 2:281,
4:457
Hannah, 1:232, 1:485,
2:280
Mary, 2:280, 3:259
Rhoda (----), 2:280, 3:524
Sarah, 2:280
Sarah (Gardner), 2:229,
2:280
Gorham/Gorum/Goram
Abigail, 2:282
Desire, 2:281-282, 2:380
Desire (Howland), 2:281,
2:479-480
Dorcas (Coffin)

Gorham/Gorum/Goram
(continued)
Dorcas (Coffin)
Soley/Solly (continued)
Soley/Solly, 4:706
Elizabeth, 2:281
Experience, 2:281, 3:122
Hannah, 2:281-282, 4:689
Hannah (Huckins), 2:281,
2:487
Lydia, 2:281-282, 4:271
Mary, 2:36, 2:281-282
Mary (Joyce), 2:573
Mary (Otis), 2:282, 3:323
Mehitable, 2:281
Mercy, 2:36, 2:281-282
Priscilla (Hussey), 2:282
Rachel (Trott), 4:711
Ruth, 2:282
Temperance, 2:281-282
Thankful, 2:282
Theodate, 2:282
Gorlick
—— (Blanchard), 1:197
Gornell
Jane (——), 1:302, 2:282
Gornock
Margaret (——), 2:282
Gorton
——, 2:305
Alice, 2:282
Ann, 2:283, 4:421
Elizabeth, 1:471,
2:282-283
Hannah, 2:282
Maher, 2:283
Maplet, 2:282
Margaret (Wheaton),
2:282
Mary, 2:282-283, 2:305,
3:159, 4:14
Mary (——), 2:282
Mary (Sumner), 2:282
Sarah, 2:282-283, 3:140
Sarah (Carder), 1:335,
2:282
Susanna, 1:133, 2:283
Susanna (Burton), 1:315,
2:283
Gosier/Gazeau
Elizabeth, 2:283
Elizabeth (——), 2:283

Goss
Elizabeth, 2:284
Hannah, 2:284
Hannah (Hopkins), 2:284
Mary, 2:284
Sarah (——), 2:284, 3:282
Gott/Goult - see also Gault
Deborah, 2:284
Elizabeth (Morris), 2:284
Lydia (Clark), 2:284
Mary, 2:284
Mary (——), 1:186, 3:623
Rebecca, 1:206
Sarah (Dennis), 2:284
Gouge
Elizabeth, 3:615
Gough
Hannah, 2:48
Gould/Gold
——, 2:286
—— (Slawson), 2:285,
4:106
—— (Sumner), 4:232
Abigail, 2:285-287, 3:138
Ann, 2:287, 2:304
Catharine (Clarke), 2:285
Content, 2:284, 2:588
Deborah, 2:286-287
Dorcas, 2:284
Dorcas (——), 2:588
Elizabeth, 1:281,
2:285-287, 2:588
Elizabeth (——), 2:284,
2:286, 3:625
Elizabeth (Balstone), 2:286
Elizabeth (Balstone)
Coggeshall, 1:110, 1:421,
2:588
Elizabeth (Curtis), 2:287
Elizabeth (Mott), 2:588
Frances (Robinson), 2:287
Grace (——), 2:285
Hannah, 2:284-286, 2:435,
2:581, 2:588
Hannah (——), 2:284-287
Hannah (Talcott), 2:286,
4:251
Jane, 2:285
Jane (Harris) Smith, 2:286,
2:364
Joanna, 2:285, 2:588
Joanna (——), 2:285, 2:588
Judith (——), 2:286

Lydia, 2:285
Margaret, 2:286
Margaret (Stone), 2:286
Martha, 2:13, 2:286-287,
3:276, 4:51
Martha (——) Harvey,
2:286, 2:369
Mary, 1:510, 2:284-287,
2:540, 2:588, 3:521,
4:105-106
Mary (——), 2:285-286
Mary (Clark), 2:284
Mary (Crossman), 1:478,
2:285
Mehitable, 2:286, 2:587
Mercy, 2:287
Mercy (Sumner), 2:287
Patience, 2:286
Phebe, 2:285, 2:287, 3:397
Phebe (French), 2:285
Priscilla, 2:284-285, 2:287,
2:588, 4:548
Priscilla (Grover), 2:588
Priscilla (Perkins), 2:285
Rebecca, 3:625
Rebecca (——), 2:284
Rebecca (Cooper), 3:625
Rose (——), 2:284-285
Ruth, 2:285
Sarah, 1:188, 1:300,
2:285-287
Sarah (——), 2:285
Sarah (Baker), 2:285
Sarah (Prior), 1:403, 2:588,
3:489
Susanna, 2:287
Wait, 2:284, 2:588
Wait (Coggeshall), 1:421,
2:284
Goulder
Catharine (——), 2:287
Goulding
Penelope (Arnold), 1:64,
2:287
Gove
Abigail, 2:3, 2:288, 4:11
Ann, 1:443, 2:288
Elizabeth (——) Walden,
2:288
Hannah, 1:407, 2:249,
2:287-288
Hannah (——), 2:288
Judith, 2:287

Gove (continued)
  Judith (Sanborn), 2:287
  Keziah, 2:288
  Lydia, 2:287-288
  Lydia (Cooper), 2:288
  Mary, 2:287-288, 4:12
  Mary (Aspinwall), 2:288
  Mary (Woodhead), 2:288
  Peniel, 2:288
  Rachel, 2:287
  Sarah, 2:32, 2:287-288
  Sarah (----), 2:288
Gower
  Ann, 2:122
Gowing/Gowen
  Elizabeth, 2:288
  Elizabeth (----), 2:289
  Joanna, 2:288
  Joanna (----), 2:288
  Lois, 2:288
Goyt
  Mary, 2:289
  Mary (----), 2:289
Gozzard
  Elizabeth, 2:289
  Elizabeth (----), 2:289
Graffort
  Bridget (Cutt) Daniel,
    1:495, 2:10, 2:289
Grafton
  ----, 4:21
  Abigail, 2:289
  Bethia (----) Lothrop,
    2:273
  Bethia (Rea) Lothrop,
    2:289, 3:122, 3:512
  Elizabeth, 2:289, 2:532
  Elizabeth (----), 3:623
  Elizabeth (Brown), 2:289
  Elizabeth (Maverick),
    2:289, 3:180
  Hannah (Hobart), 2:289,
    2:594
  Margaret, 2:289
  Martha, 2:289
  Mary, 2:155, 2:289, 2:292,
    2:355
  Mary (----), 2:289
  Mary (Belknap), 1:158
  Priscilla, 2:228, 2:289,
    2:532
  Remember, 2:289
  Seeth, 2:289

  Seeth (Gardner), 2:230,
    2:289
Gragg/Griggs
  Mary, 4:218
Graham
  Abigail (Humphrey), 2:289,
    2:497
  Elizabeth, 3:647
  Sarah, 3:164
  Sarah (Mygate) Webster,
    2:588, 3:259
  Susanna, 3:165
Grame
  Mary, 2:290
Granger
  Deliverance, 2:290
  Dorothy, 2:290, 3:307
  Elizabeth, 2:290, 4:96
  Esther, 2:290
  Esther (Hanchet), 2:290
  Eunice, 2:290
  Grace (----), 2:290
  Hannah, 2:290, 4:265
  Joanna (Adams), 1:15,
    2:290
  Lydia (Younglove), 2:290,
    4:671
  Martha (Poor), 2:290,
    2:329, 3:456
  Mary, 2:290
  Mary (----), 2:329
  Mindwell (Taylor), 2:290
  Rebecca, 2:290, 4:622
Grannis
  Abigail, 2:290, 3:597
  Ann, 2:290, 4:683
  Elizabeth (Andrews), 1:56,
    2:290
  Hannah, 2:290, 2:417
  Hannah (Russell), 2:290
  Hannah (Wakefield), 2:290,
    4:386
  Mabel, 2:290, 4:686,
    4:701
  Sarah, 2:290
Grant
  ---- (Beckwith), 1:151,
    2:291
  Abigail, 2:291-292, 3:576
  Ann (Nevinson), 3:268
  Bathsheba, 2:292
  Elizabeth, 2:292, 4:422
  Experience, 2:291

  Frances, 3:16
  Hannah, 1:513, 2:292-293
  Hannah (Palmer), 2:292
  Jane, 4:424
  Jane (----), 2:292
  Joanna, 2:292
  Margaret (----), 2:291
  Mary, 1:28, 1:516, 2:9,
    2:272, 2:291-292, 4:111
  Mary (----), 2:291-292
  Mary (----) Draper, 3:625
  Mary (Foster), 2:188
  Mary (Grafton), 2:292
  Mary (Hull), 2:292
  Mary (Porter), 2:292
  Mary (Thacher) Draper,
    4:272
  Mehitable, 2:292
  Mercy, 2:291-292
  Priscilla, 2:292, 2:497,
    2:588
  Priscilla (----), 2:291-292
  Sarah, 2:115, 2:291-293,
    4:47, 4:100
  Sarah (----), 2:291-292
  Sarah (Adams), 1:8
  Sarah (Ward/Weare),
    2:291
  Sarah (Ware), 4:417
  Susanna (----) Rockwell,
    2:292
  Susanna (Chapin)
    Rockwell, 3:558
  Susanna (Groves), 2:321
Graves
  ---- (----) Dibble, 2:46
  Abigail, 2:295-296, 4:675,
    4:683
  Amy, 2:295, 3:537
  Amy (----), 2:295
  Amy/Ann, 3:662
  Ann, 3:527
  Ann (----), 2:294
  Bethia, 2:295
  Catharine, 2:295, 2:297
  Catharine (Gray),
    1:467-468, 2:297
  Deliverance, 2:295-296
  Dorcas, 1:3, 2:295
  Elizabeth, 1:244, 1:382,
    2:294-297, 2:372
  Elizabeth (----) Chickering,
    2:297

Graves (continued)
Elizabeth (----) Farrington, 2:145, 2:295
Elizabeth (Cruttenden), 1:481
Elizabeth (Foote/Foot), 2:181
Elizabeth (Hagborne) Chickering, 1:377
Elizabeth (Maynard), 2:295, 3:186
Elizabeth (Russell), 2:295, 2:404, 3:594
Elizabeth (Stillwell), 2:295, 4:196
Elizabeth (Ventris), 2:294
Esther, 2:295
Grace (Beamsley), 1:148, 2:296
Hannah, 1:5, 2:294-296, 3:187, 3:468, 4:137, 4:683
Joanna (----), 2:296
Judith (----), 3:468
Judith (Allard), 2:294
Judith (Alward), 2:294
Martha, 2:295-296
Martha (----), 2:295
Martha (Mitton), 2:295, 3:222
Mary, 1:354, 2:64, 2:201, 2:294-296, 2:371, 3:527, 3:534, 4:370, 4:383, 4:710
Mary (----) Wyatt, 2:295
Mary (Bronson) Wyatt, 4:662
Mary (Brownson) Wyatt, 1:42
Mary (Chamberlain), 1:354, 2:295
Mary (Church), 1:386, 2:294
Mary (Hoar), 2:295
Mary (James) King, 3:23
Mary (Ross), 2:295
Maud, 2:295
Mehitable, 2:294, 3:245, 4:653
Mercy, 2:294
Rebecca, 1:15, 2:294, 2:296-297
Ruth, 2:295-296, 3:32

Sarah, 1:125, 2:294-296, 3:44, 4:175, 4:683
Sarah (----), 2:297
Sarah (Brewer), 2:296
Sarah (Stedman) Brackett Alcock, 1:22, 1:229, 2:297, 3:413, 4:179
Sarah (Wyatt), 2:294, 4:662
Susanna, 2:297, 4:244
Gray/Grey
Abigail, 3:626
Abigail (Lord), 2:299, 3:648
Ann, 2:298, 4:601
Bethia, 2:298
Catharine, 1:467, 2:297, 2:299
Catharine (----), 2:297, 3:295
Catharine (Myles), 1:467, 4:358
Christian, 3:625
Deborah (Williams), 3:625
Desire, 2:298, 4:143
Dorothy (Abbot), 1:5
Dorothy (Lettice), 2:298, 3:81
Elizabeth, 2:298-299, 3:486
Elizabeth (----), 2:298, 3:625, 3:650
Elizabeth (Frost), 2:212
Elizabeth (Frost) Watson, 2:298
Hannah, 1:5, 2:298-299
Hannah (Ellis), 2:298
Hannah (Holt), 2:299
Hannah (Hyde), 3:625, 3:638
Hannah (Lumpkin), 2:298, 3:130
Jemima, 2:299
Joanna (Smith), 4:114
Judith, 2:216
Lucy (Palmes), 2:299, 3:343
Lydia, 2:298, 3:117
Lydia (Frost), 2:212, 2:298
Mary, 2:212, 2:298, 2:588, 3:625-626, 3:645, 4:697
Mary (Winslow), 2:298, 4:601

Mehitable, 2:298
Meletiah, 2:298
Meletiah (Lewis), 2:298
Mercy, 2:298
Parnell, 1:467, 3:295
Priscilla, 2:298
Rebecca, 1:426, 2:299
Rebecca (Hill), 2:298
Sarah, 2:298-299, 3:99
Sarah (Glover), 2:299
Susanna, 2:298-299
Susanna (----), 2:299
Susanna (Harrison), 2:298
Susanna (Langdon), 3:626
Sybil (Whiting) Bryan, 1:282
Thankful, 2:298
Grazillier
Mary (----), 2:299
Greaves
Elizabeth (Hagborne) Chickering, 1:377
Greeley/Greely/Grele
Abigail, 2:299
Hannah, 2:299
Hannah (Ilsley), 2:299
Judith, 2:299
Mary, 2:299, 4:482
Mary (----), 2:299
Rachel, 2:299
Ruth, 2:299
Sarah, 2:299
Sarah (Brown), 1:267, 2:299
Green/Greene
----, 2:303, 2:305, 4:148, 4:313
---- (----), 2:307
---- (Barber), 2:300
---- (Barton), 1:133
---- (Blott) Tozer, 1:206
---- (Carder), 2:305
---- (Gorton), 2:305
---- (Johnson), 2:302
---- (Sayles), 2:301, 2:305
---- (Slocum), 2:300, 2:305
Abigail, 2:301, 3:626, 4:190
Alice (Daniels), 2:302
Amy, 2:301, 2:305
Ann, 2:303-304, 2:306-307
Ann (----), 2:301

Green/Greene (continued)
Ann (----) Grosse, 4:67
Ann (Almy), 1:45, 2:303
Ann (Gould), 2:287, 2:304
Ann (Green), 2:303, 2:306
Ann (Turner), 2:304,
  4:346
Audrey, 2:305
Barbara, 2:305
Bethia, 2:303, 2:411
Catharine, 2:301, 2:303,
  2:444
Deborah, 2:305
Deliverance, 2:301
Deliverance (Potter), 2:301,
  3:467
Dorcas, 1:125, 1:507,
  2:300-301, 2:305-306
Eleanor, 2:305
Elizabeth, 1:347,
  2:301-307, 2:335, 3:109,
  3:440, 3:516, 3:525,
  3:626
Elizabeth (----), 2:300-301,
  2:306
Elizabeth (----) Kingsbury,
  3:28
Elizabeth (----) Long,
  2:589, 3:109
Elizabeth (Anthony), 1:59,
  2:301
Elizabeth (Arnold), 2:305
Elizabeth (Barton), 2:306
Elizabeth (Farmer), 2:141
Elizabeth (Gerrish), 2:304,
  3:605, 3:626
Elizabeth (Nichols), 2:305
Elizabeth (Sill), 2:306,
  4:97
Elizabeth (Warren), 4:426
Elizabeth (Webb), 2:306
Elizabeth (Wheeler), 1:449,
  2:307, 4:497
Elizabeth (Whitman),
  2:304, 4:523
Ellen (----), 2:196, 2:304
Esther, 2:300-301, 3:226
Esther (Condy/Candy),
  3:611
Esther (Hasey), 2:300
Esther (Swett), 4:240
Frances (----) Wheeler
  Cook, 1:449, 2:306

Frances (Stone), 2:300,
  4:209
Hannah, 2:304, 2:306-307,
  2:402, 3:43, 3:536,
  4:375, 4:683
Hannah (----), 2:307
Hannah (Bateman), 1:137
Hannah (Butler), 1:321
Hannah (Kendall), 3:9
Isabel, 2:305
Isabel (Farmer) Blood,
  2:307
Jane, 2:307, 4:177
Jane (Bainbridge), 2:305
Jane (Pygan), 2:304, 3:497
Joanna, 2:300
Joanna (----), 2:304
Joanna (----) Shatswell,
  2:302, 4:61
Lydia, 2:300, 2:305, 2:376
Margaret, 2:302
Margaret (----), 1:429,
  3:583
Margaret (Call), 2:306
Maria, 2:300
Maria (----), 2:300
Maria (Mather), 2:589,
  3:173
Martha, 2:306
Martha (----) Page, 2:300
Mary, 2:301-307, 2:315,
  3:110, 3:525, 3:612,
  3:626, 4:238
Mary (----), 2:304, 2:307
Mary (Allen), 2:303
Mary (Bartholomew)
  Whipple, 1:503, 2:589
Mary (Barton), 2:300
Mary (Cook), 1:449, 2:306
Mary (Cowland), 1:466
Mary (Estabrook), 2:126
Mary (Fones), 2:179,
  2:301
Mary (Gorton), 2:283,
  2:305, 4:14
Mary (Houchin), 2:304,
  2:468
Mary (Jeffrey), 2:304,
  2:540
Mary (Jenkins), 2:303
Mary (Jones), 2:562
Mary (Robinson), 2:589
Mary (Warren), 3:626

Mary (Weeks), 2:306
Mehitable, 2:307, 3:331
Mercy, 2:301
Perseverance (----), 2:301
Phebe, 1:430, 2:300-301,
  2:396-397, 3:583
Philippa (----), 2:302
Rachel, 2:300
Rebecca, 2:300-301,
  2:305-306
Rebecca (----), 2:300,
  2:305
Rebecca (Hills), 2:306
Rebecca (Jones), 2:301,
  2:566
Ruth, 2:303-304, 2:411
Ruth (Michelson), 2:303,
  3:222, 3:609
Sarah, 2:300-301,
  2:303-305, 2:307, 3:55,
  3:525, 3:626
Sarah (----), 1:466
Sarah (Bateman), 1:137,
  2:304
Sarah (Clark), 1:398,
  2:305
Sarah (Wheeler), 1:449,
  2:303, 4:497
Susan (Holden), 2:445
Susanna, 2:301, 2:303,
  4:148
Susanna (----), 2:304,
  2:306, 4:67
Susanna (Houlden), 2:300
Welthean, 2:305-306
Greenfield
Ann, 2:460
Barbara, 2:307
Barbara (----), 2:307
Mary, 2:307
Susan (----) Wise, 2:307
Susanna (----) Wise, 4:614
Greenhill
Rebecca, 2:308, 4:74
Rebecca (----), 1:11, 2:308
Greenland
----, 2:589
Elizabeth, 2:589
Lydia, 2:308
Lydia (----), 2:308
Greenleaf
Abigail, 2:308
Abigail (Somerby), 2:308

Greenleaf (continued)
  Bethia, 2:308
  Catharine (----), 2:308
  Elizabeth, 1:93, 1:393,
    2:308-309, 3:299
  Elizabeth (Coffin), 2:308
  Elizabeth (Gerrish), 2:244,
    2:309
  Elizabeth (Hills), 2:308
  Esther (----) Swett, 2:309
  Esther (Weare) Swett,
    4:240
  Hannah (Veazie), 2:308,
    4:369
  Jane, 2:308
  Judith, 1:420, 2:308-309,
    4:140
  Margaret (Piper), 2:309
  Martha, 2:308
  Mary, 2:308-309, 3:554,
    4:476
  Mary (----), 2:308
  Rachel, 2:308
  Rebecca, 2:308
  Ruth, 2:308
  Sarah, 1:146, 2:59,
    2:308-309, 4:255
  Sarah (Beal), 1:146
  Sarah (Dole), 2:308
  Sarah (Kent), 2:308
Greenough
  Abigail, 2:309
  Abigail (Hammond), 2:309,
    2:346, 4:507
  Ann, 2:310
  Consider, 2:310
  Dorothy, 2:310
  Elizabeth, 2:309-310,
    3:329, 3:549
  Elizabeth (----), 3:329
  Elizabeth (Grosse), 2:309,
    2:319
  Elizabeth (Mather), 1:326,
    2:310, 3:173
  Elizabeth (Rainsford),
    2:310, 3:502
  Elizabeth (Upshall), 2:309,
    4:362
  Jerusha, 2:309
  Mary, 2:309-310, 3:329,
    3:374
  Mercy, 2:246, 2:310
  Rebecca (Haggett), 2:309

  Ruth (Swift), 2:310, 4:241
  Sarah, 2:309-310
  Sarah (Shove), 2:310
Greenslade
  Jane, 1:82
Greenslip
  Ruth, 1:249
Greenway/Grinaway/etc
  ----, 3:213
  Ann, 2:310, 3:430
  Catharine, 2:10, 2:310
  Mary, 2:310
  Mary (----), 2:310
  Ursula, 1:141, 2:310
Greenwich
  Sarah, 3:659
Greenwood
  Abigail, 2:311
  Abigail (----), 2:311
  Abigail (Woodward),
    4:645
  Alice (Lyon), 2:311
  Ann, 2:311
  Ann (Lynde), 2:311, 3:413
  Elizabeth, 2:311
  Elizabeth (Bronsden),
    1:259, 2:311
  Elizabeth (Wiswall), 2:311
  Esther, 2:311
  Hannah, 2:311
  Hannah (Trowbridge),
    2:311, 4:332
  Hannah (Ward), 2:311,
    4:409
  Martha, 2:311
  Mary, 2:311
  Mary (----), 2:311
  Mary (Allen), 1:35, 2:311
  Priscilla, 2:311
  Ruth, 2:311
  Sarah, 2:311
  Susanna, 2:311
  Thankful (Wilson), 2:311
Greet
  ---- (Hart), 2:312, 2:367
Gregory
  Abigail, 2:312
  Elizabeth, 2:312
  Elizabeth (Moulthrop),
    3:248, 3:626
  Elizabeth (Pardee/Pardie),
    2:312, 3:345
  Hannah, 2:312

  Hannah (----), 2:312
  Hannah (Dow), 2:312
  Hannah (Haite), 2:312
  Lydia, 2:312
  Martha, 2:312
  Mary, 2:312
  Percie, 2:312
  Phebe, 1:164
  Sarah, 1:164, 2:312
  Sarah (Burt), 1:313, 2:312
Grice/Grise
  ----, 2:312, 3:326
  Margery (----), 2:312
Gridley
  ----, 2:313
  ---- (----), 3:54, 3:646
  Elizabeth, 2:313
  Elizabeth (----), 2:313
  Elizabeth (Clark), 1:396,
    3:626
  Esther, 2:313
  Esther (Thompson), 3:626,
    4:288
  Grace (----), 2:313
  Hannah, 2:16, 2:313,
    4:275
  Lydia (----) Flood, 2:313
  Lydia (----) Floyd, 2:176,
    2:313
  Mary, 2:313, 3:574, 3:626
  Mary (----), 4:380
  Mary (Humphrey), 3:626
  Mary (Seymour), 2:313,
    4:58
  Return, 2:19, 2:313
  Sarah, 2:313
Griffin/Griffing
  Abigail, 2:313-314
  Ann (----), 2:314
  Ann (Bancroft), 2:313
  Deborah (Norton) Hill,
    2:314, 2:593, 3:290
  Dorothy (Skidmore), 3:626,
    4:105
  Elinor (----), 2:589
  Elizabeth, 2:31, 2:313-314,
    4:493, 4:683
  Elizabeth (----), 2:313, 4:86,
    4:683
  Elizabeth (----) Upson,
    2:313
  Elizabeth (Ring), 2:314
  Esther, 2:314

Griffin/Griffing (continued)
Hannah, 2:313-314, 3:452,
  3:626
Hannah (Cutler), 1:494,
  2:589
Joan (----), 2:589
Judith, 2:314
Lydia, 2:182, 2:313, 4:713
Maria, 2:314
Mary, 2:313-314, 3:626,
  3:647, 4:588
Mary (----), 2:314
Mary (----) Harrod, 2:314
Mindwell, 2:313
Phebe, 4:683
Priscilla, 2:314
Priscilla (----), 2:314
Priscilla (Crosswell), 2:589
Rebecca, 2:314
Remember, 2:314
Ruth, 2:313, 4:438
Sarah, 2:313-314, 3:626,
  4:163
Sarah (----), 2:314
Sarah (Devotion), 2:42
Susanna, 2:314
Susanna (Price), 2:314
Griggs
---- (Hannaford), 2:315
Abigail, 1:450, 2:315
Alice (----), 2:315
Ann, 2:315, 2:561, 3:59
Eleanor (Haskell), 3:630
Elizabeth, 2:315, 3:626
Elizabeth (Case), 2:315
Grissel/Grizel (----) Jewell,
  2:315, 2:548
Hannah, 2:315, 3:626
Hannah (----), 3:509
Hannah (Davis), 2:315
Joanna, 2:315
Mary, 2:157, 2:315, 4:218
Mary (----), 2:315
Mary (Crafts), 2:315
Mary (Green), 2:307,
  2:315
Mary (Patten), 2:315
Patience (----), 1:358
Rachel, 1:34, 3:596, 3:626
Rachel (----), 3:626
Sarah, 1:303, 2:315, 3:18,
  3:27, 3:626
Thankful (Baker), 1:98,

2:315
Grigson/Gregson
Abigail, 2:316
Ann, 2:316
Anna/Hannah, 2:9
Jane (----), 2:315
Mary, 2:316
Phebe, 2:316, 4:518
Sarah, 2:250, 2:316, 4:517
Susanna, 1:481, 2:316
Grihme/Grihmes
Abigail (Humphrey), 2:316
Elizabeth, 2:316
Rebecca, 2:316
Sarah, 2:316
Sarah (Webster), 2:316
Susanna, 2:316
Grimes
Ann (----), 2:316
Elizabeth (Blanchard),
  1:506, 2:589
Frances (----), 2:316
Mary, 2:316
Sarah, 3:164
Susanna, 2:316, 3:165,
  4:368
Grimstone/Grimsted
Margaret (----), 2:316
Grinnel
Mary (Waddell), 4:377
Grissell
Hannah, 3:11
Griswold
Abigail, 2:317-318, 2:590
Abigail (Gaylord), 2:590
Abigail (Williams), 2:590,
  4:561
Ann, 1:279, 1:279,
  2:316-317, 2:589
Ann (Wolcott), 2:317,
  4:621
Azubah, 2:589
Bathsheba, 2:590
Bathsheba (----), 2:590
Deborah, 1:288, 1:472,
  2:316-317, 2:589-590
Dorothy, 2:590
Elizabeth, 1:152, 2:317,
  2:589, 3:474, 3:563
Elizabeth (----), 4:482
Elizabeth (Cooke), 1:448,
  2:589
Esther, 2:318, 2:589-590

Esther (Drake), 2:70,
  2:318
Hannah, 1:405, 2:316-317,
  2:589-590
Hannah (----), 2:590
Hannah (Lee), 3:647
Lucy, 2:590
Lydia, 2:317, 2:590
Margaret, 1:285, 2:317,
  2:590
Margaret (----), 2:598
Martha, 2:590
Mary, 2:250, 2:316-318,
  2:589-590, 3:407
Mary (----), 1:295, 2:316,
  2:590
Mary (----) Lee, 2:317
Mary (DeWolf) Lee, 3:73
Mary (Gaylord), 2:317
Mary (Holcomb), 2:317
Mary (Howard), 2:471
Mindwell (Bissell), 2:589
Patience, 2:317
Phebe, 2:317
Phebe (Hyde), 2:317
Rachel, 2:590
Sarah, 1:362, 1:438,
  2:316-318, 2:590, 3:407,
  3:439
Sarah (----) Bemis, 1:163,
  2:589
Susanna (Huntington),
  2:318, 2:503
Zerviah, 2:589
Groat
Susanna (Hagar), 2:328
Groom
Miriam (Wheeler)
  Blakeman, 3:604
Gross/Grosse
---- (----), 2:318, 4:117
Abigail, 2:319, 4:87
Alice, 2:319
Ann, 2:318
Ann (----), 2:318-319, 4:67
Catharine (----), 2:318
Dorothy (Belcher), 2:318
Elinor (----), 2:318
Elizabeth, 2:309,
  2:318-319, 4:252
Elizabeth (----), 1:310,
  2:318-319
Hannah, 2:318-319

Gross/Grosse (continued)
Huldah, 2:319
Jerusha, 2:319
Lydia, 2:318, 2:361
Martha, 2:318
Mary, 2:318-319
Mary (----), 2:318
Mary (Bond), 2:319
Mary (Trott), 2:318
Ruth, 2:318
Sarah, 2:318
Susanna, 2:318
Grosvenor
Esther (----), 2:319
Susanna, 2:319
Groth
Elizabeth, 2:319
Elizabeth (Eaton), 2:96,
2:319
Grout
Abigail, 2:319-320
Elizabeth, 1:36, 2:319-320,
3:101
Mary, 2:319, 3:34
Mary (----), 2:319
Mehitable, 2:320
Rebecca, 2:320
Rebecca (Toll), 2:319-320
Sarah, 2:319-320
Sarah (----), 2:320
Sarah (Busby) Cakebread,
1:316, 1:328, 2:319
Susanna, 2:319-320
Susanna (Hagar), 2:320
Grove
Ann, 3:97-98
Elizabeth (----), 2:320
Mary, 2:225, 2:320, 2:428
Ruth (Foster), 2:188
Tryphena (Lisle) Lloyd,
2:432
Grover
Deborah, 1:167, 2:320
Elizabeth, 2:320-321
Elizabeth (----), 1:78,
2:320-321
Grace, 2:321
Hannah, 2:320, 3:626
Hannah (----), 2:320
Hannah (Hills), 2:320
Lydia, 2:320
Margaret (----), 2:320
Margaret (Winthrop),

4:608
Mary, 2:320, 4:625
Naomi, 2:320
Priscilla, 2:588
Ruth (Adams), 2:320
Ruth (Haskell), 3:630
Sarah, 2:321, 3:626
Sarah (----), 2:320
Sarah (Barlow), 1:502
Sarah (Barney), 3:626
Sarah (Chadwick), 1:351,
2:321
Groves
Ann (----), 2:321
Elizabeth, 2:321, 3:462
Hannah, 3:462
Martha (Mitton), 2:321
Susanna, 2:321
Grow
Hannah, 2:321
Hannah (Lord), 2:321
Mary, 2:321
Ruth, 2:321
Ruth (----), 2:321
Growth
Elizabeth (----), 2:508
Grubb
Abiah, 2:321
Ann (----), 2:321
Elizabeth, 2:321
Gruman
Sarah (Try), 2:321, 4:337
Grundy
Elizabeth, 2:322
Rebecca, 2:322
Guernsey
---- (----), 4:700
Mary (Tilton) Eastman,
2:92, 2:322, 4:305
Guild
Elizabeth, 2:322
Elizabeth (Crook), 3:626
Joanna, 2:322
Mary (Woodcock), 3:627
Sarah, 2:322
Sarah (----), 2:322
Gull
Ann, 2:322, 3:573
Elizabeth (Smith) Foote,
2:180, 2:322, 4:132
Esther, 2:322
Mary, 1:47, 1:114, 2:322
Mercy, 2:322

Gulliford/Gullifer/Gulliver
---- (Kingsley), 3:30
Elinor (Kingsley), 2:322
Elizabeth, 2:322, 2:340
Hannah, 2:322
Lydia, 2:322, 3:79
Mary, 1:73, 2:322
Susanna, 2:548
Gully
Mary, 2:323
Mercy (----), 2:323
Gunn
Ann, 2:323
Christian, 3:627
Christian (----), 3:627
Deborah, 2:323-324, 4:293,
4:323
Deborah (Coleman), 1:431,
2:323
Elizabeth, 2:323, 3:627
Elizabeth (Wyatt), 2:323,
4:662
Hannah (----), 3:627
Mary, 2:323
Mary (Smith), 2:323,
4:120
Mary (Williams), 2:323,
4:561
Mehitable, 2:124,
2:323-324, 3:619, 4:69
Sarah, 3:627
Sarah (----), 3:627
Sarah (Day), 2:27, 2:323,
3:6
Gunnison/Gullison
Deborah, 2:324
Elizabeth, 2:324
Elizabeth (----), 2:324
Margery (Pepperell)
Whittemore, 3:392
Sarah, 2:324
Sarah (----) Lynn, 3:137
Guppie/Guppy/Guppey
Abigail, 2:324
Abigail (----), 2:324
Abigail (Kitchen), 3:627
Abigail (Kitchin), 3:644
Elizabeth, 2:324
Elizabeth (----), 2:324
Ellen (----), 2:324
Mary, 2:262
Rachel, 3:419

Gurdon
Meriel, 4:8
Gurgefield
Margery (----), 1:168
Gurley
Abigail, 2:324
Esther, 2:324
Esther (Ingersoll), 2:324, 2:521, 2:560
Eunice, 2:324
Experience, 2:324
Experience (Rust), 2:324
Lois, 2:324
Margaret, 2:324
Mary, 2:324
Gurney
Elizabeth, 2:325
Elizabeth (----), 2:325
Mary, 2:325
Rebecca (Taylor), 2:325, 4:261
Gustin
Elizabeth (Brown), 1:271, 3:627
Gutch
Deborah, 2:325
Elizabeth, 2:325
Lydia, 2:325
Magdalen, 2:325
Patience, 2:325
Sarah, 2:325
Gutterson
Abigail, 2:325
Abigail (Buckmaster), 2:325
Elizabeth (----), 3:627
Mary, 2:325
Sarah, 2:325
Susanna, 3:483
Guttridge
Elizabeth, 2:83
Lydia, 2:128
Mary, 4:146
Mary (----), 1:41
Guy
----, 2:325
Jane (----), 2:325
Mary, 1:485, 2:325, 4:249
Gwin/Gwinn
Elizabeth (Gillam), 2:255, 2:325
Mary (----), 2:590, 3:132

Habberfield
Mary (----), 2:326
Hack
Mary (----), 2:326
Hackburne
Catharine (----), 1:40
Catharine (Dighton), 2:78
Hannah, 2:503
Hacker
Bethia, 2:326
Bethia (Meacham), 2:326, 3:190
Sarah, 2:326
Hackett
Elinor (Gardner), 2:590
Hannah, 2:326, 2:587, 2:590
Judah, 2:326
Mary, 2:326
Mary (Crane), 1:471, 2:590
Rebecca, 2:326
Rebecca (----), 2:326
Sarah, 2:326, 2:590
Sarah (Barnard), 1:120, 2:326
Hacklinton/Hackleton
Joanna (Wakeman), 2:327, 4:388
Hadborne
Ann, 2:327
Ann (----), 2:327
Rebecca, 2:327
Hadden/Haddon
----, 2:108
Catharine (----), 2:327
Elizabeth, 2:92, 2:327
Margaret (----), 2:327
Sarah, 2:327
Haddock
Hannah, 4:487
Hadlock
Deborah, 3:627, 4:266
Hannah, 2:327, 4:487
Margery, 2:327
Mary, 2:327, 3:627
Mary (----), 2:327
Rebecca, 2:327
Rebecca (Hutchinson), 2:327, 2:596
Remember (Jones), 2:327, 3:640
Sarah, 2:327, 2:512

Sarah (Draper), 2:327
Sarah (Pasco), 2:327
Sarah (Pasque), 2:327
Haffell/Haffield
Martha, 2:328
Martha (----), 2:328
Mary, 2:328
Rachel, 2:328
Ruth, 2:328
Sarah, 2:328
Hagar/Agar
Abigail, 2:328, 4:528
Hannah, 2:328
Mary, 2:328
Mary (Bemis), 2:328
Mehitable, 2:328, 3:287
Mercy, 2:328
Rebecca, 2:328, 2:396
Ruhamah, 2:328, 4:384
Sarah, 2:328, 4:531
Sarah (Benjamin), 1:166, 2:328
Sarah (Mixer), 2:328, 3:223
Susanna, 2:320, 2:328
Hagborne/Hackborne
Catharine (Dighton), 2:328
Elizabeth, 1:376-377, 2:328, 4:267, 4:315
Elizabeth (----), 2:328
Hannah, 2:328-329
Sarah, 2:328
Haggert
Hannah, 4:455
Haggett
Abigail, 2:329, 4:151
Deliverance, 2:329
Hannah, 2:329
Joanna (Johnson), 2:329
Martha (Poor) Granger, 2:290, 2:329
Mary, 2:329
Mary (Middlecott) Gibbs, 3:205
Rebecca, 2:309
Hailstone
Margaret, 2:173, 2:329
Haimes
Catharine, 2:329
Mary (----), 2:329
Haines - see Haynes
Haite
Elizabeth, 4:52

Haite (continued)
Hannah, 2:312
Hakes
Ann, 2:590
Elizabeth, 2:590
Joanna, 2:590
Mary, 2:590
Sarah, 2:590
Halbridge/Halbich/etc
Mercy, 2:329
Hale
Abigail, 2:331, 3:456,
3:576
Ann (----), 2:329, 2:332
Dorothy, 2:330
Edna, 2:331
Elizabeth, 2:331, 3:422
Elizabeth (Dummer),
2:330
Elizabeth (Somerby) Clark,
1:399, 2:329, 4:140
Eunice, 2:331
Hannah, 2:331, 3:376,
4:146
Hannah (Nott), 3:294
Hannah (Tillinghast),
4:303
Jane (Lord), 2:331
Joan (----), 2:534
Joanna, 2:329, 2:331, 3:57,
3:616
Joanna (----), 2:330
Judith, 2:330
Lydia, 1:501, 2:330-331
Lydia (----), 2:330
Martha, 2:331
Mary, 1:165, 2:330-331,
3:263, 3:612, 4:582
Mary (Hutchinson), 2:331,
2:596
Mary (Nash), 2:331, 3:263
Mary (Watson), 2:330,
4:438
Mary (Welles), 2:331,
4:477
Mary (Williams), 4:560
Naomi, 2:331
Naomi (Kilborne), 2:331,
3:19
Priscilla, 2:331
Priscilla (Markham), 2:331,
3:153
Rebecca, 2:329-330

Rebecca (Byley), 1:326,
2:329
Rebecca (Lowell), 2:330
Ruth, 2:330-331
Ruth (Edwards), 2:104,
2:330
Sarah, 2:331, 4:704
Sarah (Barber), 2:331
Sarah (Ilsley), 2:330, 2:518
Sarah (Jaques), 2:538
Sarah (Northend), 2:331
Sarah (Noyes), 2:329,
3:296
Sarah (Somerby), 2:330
Sarah (Symonds), 2:330
Thomasin (----), 2:331
Vine, 2:331
Haley
---- (West), 2:332, 4:488
Ann, 2:332, 4:488
Hannah (Bliss), 2:332,
4:134
Lydia, 1:513, 2:332, 2:591,
4:488, 4:700
Ruth (Crow) Gaylord,
1:479, 2:239, 2:332
Hall
----, 2:591
---- (----) Byley, 2:329
---- (Wilcox), 4:547
Abigail, 1:289, 2:335,
2:338-339, 4:409
Abigail (----), 2:65, 2:339
Abigail (Roberts), 2:335,
3:546-547
Alice, 2:339
Alice (Tripp), 2:339, 4:331
Amie, 2:591
Ann, 2:337
Ann (----) Newell, 2:592
Ann (Ratchell), 2:332,
3:508
Ann (Thornton), 2:336,
4:292
Ann (Wilcox), 2:591,
4:546
Barshua, 2:591
Beatrice, 1:295
Bethia, 2:333
Bethia (----), 2:333
Bethia (Bangs), 1:111,
2:333
Charity, 2:333, 2:591

Constant (----), 2:333
Deliverance, 2:339, 4:330
Dependence, 2:337
Dorcas, 2:592
Dorothy (----) Blakeman,
4:281
Dorothy (Smith) Blakeman,
1:195, 2:333, 4:52,
4:115
Elizabeth, 1:512,
2:333-338, 2:591, 3:57,
3:627, 4:627
Elizabeth (----), 2:333,
2:338
Elizabeth (Clap), 2:336
Elizabeth (Collicott), 1:432,
2:337
Elizabeth (Cornwell),
1:459
Elizabeth (Cutter), 1:496,
2:336
Elizabeth (Davis), 2:339
Elizabeth (Dudley), 2:77,
2:336
Elizabeth (Folland), 2:562
Elizabeth (Fowle) Walker,
3:627
Elizabeth (Green), 2:304,
2:335
Elizabeth (Holbrook),
2:337
Elizabeth (Johnson), 2:338,
2:558
Elizabeth (Laighton),
2:591, 3:44
Elizabeth (Larned), 2:334
Elizabeth (Pollard),
2:333-334
Elizabeth (Rand), 2:336
Elizabeth (Smith), 2:335,
2:591, 4:113
Elizabeth (Withington),
2:336
Esther, 1:366, 2:332-333,
2:335, 2:338, 2:569
Esther (----), 2:332, 2:339
Esther (Chesley), 1:375
Experience, 2:337, 2:422
Frances (Parker), 2:332,
3:350
Grace, 2:332, 2:337-338,
2:591, 4:508
Grace (----), 2:339

Hall (continued)
Grace (Willis), 2:338
Hannah, 1:195, 2:199,
2:333, 2:336, 2:338-339,
2:591-592
Hannah (----), 2:336
Hannah (Bramhall), 1:237
Hannah (Cutter), 2:339
Hannah (Miller), 2:336,
3:209
Hannah (Penniman), 2:335
Hannah (Sheather), 2:338,
4:67
Hannah (Walker), 2:338,
4:394
Honor, 2:591
Huldah, 2:337
Jane, 2:337, 2:591
Jane (----), 4:679
Jane (Wallen/Woolen),
2:334, 3:627
Jane (Willis), 2:336, 4:577
Jemima, 2:335
Jemima (Sill), 2:335, 4:97
Joan (----), 2:338
Joanna, 3:371
Joice (----) Staines, 4:160
Lydia, 1:495, 2:333, 2:336,
2:338-339
Lydia (----), 2:333
Lydia (Cutter), 2:336
Lydia (Jackson) Leavitt ,
2:527, 3:70
Margaret (----), 2:332
Margery, 2:336
Martha, 2:188, 2:333,
2:335, 2:337, 2:592,
3:468, 4:559
Martha (----), 2:333, 2:591
Martha (----) Russell
Bradshaw, 1:234, 2:338,
3:595
Martha (Hill), 2:338
Mary, 1:358, 2:161,
2:332-333, 2:335-339,
2:591-592, 3:161, 3:190,
4:112
Mary (----), 1:495, 2:333,
2:336-339
Mary (----) Hall, 2:332
Mary (----) Hubbard, 2:335,
2:486
Mary (----) Morton, 2:591

Mary (Chesley), 1:375,
2:337
Mary (Hilton), 2:336,
2:423
Mary (Parker), 2:335,
3:350
Mary (Rutherford), 2:332,
3:490, 3:579, 3:627
Mary (Spencer), 4:18
Mehitable, 2:337
Mehitable (Matthews),
2:332
Mercy, 2:333, 2:336
Mercy (----), 2:591
Phebe, 2:333
Phebe (----), 2:338
Priscilla, 2:335-336
Priscilla (Bearse), 2:335
Rachel (Macoone/etc),
3:141
Rebecca, 2:332-333, 2:339
Rebecca (----) Byley, 1:326,
2:334, 4:246, 4:651
Rebecca (Jones), 2:562
Rebina (----), 2:335
Ruth, 2:338-339, 3:513
Ruth (Davis), 2:16, 2:338
Sarah, 1:193, 1:302, 2:60,
2:332-339, 2:559,
2:591-592, 4:528
Sarah (----), 2:332, 2:591
Sarah (Babcock), 1:86,
2:591
Sarah (Barker), 2:592
Sarah (Cook), 1:450,
2:338
Sarah (Fisher), 2:332
Sarah (Meriam), 2:339
Sarah (Rand), 2:333
Sarah (Rockwell), 3:557
Silence, 2:335
Susan, 4:547
Susanna, 2:332-333,
2:335-337, 2:339
Susanna (Sheffield), 4:69
Tabitha, 2:333, 2:336
Hallam
Alice (----), 2:339, 3:101
Elizabeth, 2:340
Elizabeth (Gulliver)
Meades, 2:340
Mary, 2:340
Prudence, 2:339

Prudence (Richardson),
2:339, 3:535
Sarah (Pygan), 2:339,
3:497
Hallet/Hallett/Hollet
Abigail, 1:24, 2:340
Abigail (Dexter), 2:45
Alice, 1:400, 2:340, 3:281
Ann, 1:486, 2:340
Ann (----), 2:340
Ann (Bessey), 4:675,
4:683, 4:714
Dorcas, 2:340
Hannah, 2:376
Lois, 1:413
Lydia (----), 2:75, 2:340
Mehitable, 2:44, 2:340
Ruhama, 1:218, 2:340
Sarah, 3:410
Hallowell/Holloway/etc
Ann, 2:340
Ann (----), 2:341
Ann (Blake) Leager, 3:68
Decline (----), 2:341
Elizabeth (----), 2:341
Esther, 2:341
Mary, 2:340-341
Mary (----), 2:341
Mary (Boylston), 2:340
Mary (Stocker), 2:340
Rebecca, 2:101
Rebecca (Briggs), 2:340
Sarah, 2:340-341
Halsall/Hansell/Halsey
Elizabeth, 2:341, 2:478
Elizabeth (----), 2:341
Hannah, 2:341
Hannah (Grosse), 2:319
Joan/Joan (Ruck), 2:341
Joan/Joane (Ruck), 3:584
Mary, 2:477
Mehitable, 2:341
Rebecca, 2:276
Sarah, 2:341
Sarah (----), 2:341
Halstead/Halsteed
Edna (----), 2:342
Grace, 1:128, 2:342
Isabel (----), 2:341
Susanna, 1:128, 2:342
Ham
Abigail, 2:342
Ann, 2:342

Ham (continued)
Elizabeth, 2:342
Joanna, 2:342
Mary, 2:342
Mary (Heard), 2:342,
2:397
Patience, 2:342
Thomasine, 2:342
Thomasine (Messerve),
2:342
Haman
Elizabeth, 2:166
Hamblen
Abigail, 2:343
Abigail (----), 2:342
Ann (----), 2:342
Bethia, 2:342
Elizabeth, 2:343
Esther, 2:343
Experience, 2:342-343,
2:542
Hannah, 2:343
Hope, 2:343
Jemima, 2:342
Martha, 2:343
Mary, 2:19, 2:342-343,
3:630
Mary (Dunham), 2:343
Mehitable, 2:342
Mehitable (Jenkins), 2:342,
2:542
Meletiah, 2:343
Mercy, 2:342
Mercy (----), 2:342
Patience, 2:342
Priscilla, 2:343
Reliance, 2:342
Sarah, 2:343
Sarah (Bearse), 2:343
Susanna, 2:342
Susanna (Dunham), 2:342
Thankful, 2:343
Hamby
Catharine, 2:509
Hamilton/Hambleton
Elizabeth, 2:343
Mary (Richardson), 2:343
Sarah, 2:343
Hamlet
Abigail, 2:344
Hannah (Parker), 2:344
Mary (----), 2:344
Mary (Dutton), 2:344

Rebecca, 2:211, 2:344
Sarah, 2:344
Sarah (----) Hubbard, 2:344,
2:484
Hamlin
Elizabeth, 2:344, 4:43
Elizabeth (Drake), 2:344
Elizabeth (Partridge),
3:366
Esther, 2:344, 4:142
Esther (Crow), 1:479,
2:344
Mable, 2:344
Mary, 2:344, 3:593
Mary (Collins), 1:436,
2:344
Mehitable, 2:344, 2:459
Sarah, 2:592
Sarah (----), 2:592
Sarah (Bierse/Bearse),
1:149
Sibil, 2:344
Susanna, 2:344
Susanna (Collins), 1:436,
2:344
Hammant
Elizabeth, 2:344
Sarah, 2:592
Sarah (----), 2:592
Hammatt
---- (----) Burrage, 1:308,
2:345
Hammond/Hammons
----, 2:347
---- (----), 3:580
---- (Sampson), 4:10
Abigail, 2:309, 2:345-346,
2:373, 4:507
Abigail (----), 2:345
Abigail (Collins) Willet,
2:346, 4:556
Agnes (Penny), 3:627
Ann, 2:347
Ann (----) Gerrish, 2:244,
2:346
Audrey (Eaton), 2:345
Catharine (Frost) Leighton,
2:212, 2:345, 3:44
Dorcas, 1:495, 2:345
Elizabeth, 1:354,
2:345-348, 2:470, 3:168,
3:338, 4:335, 4:644
Elizabeth (----), 2:346

Elizabeth (Noyes), 2:347,
3:298
Elizabeth (Payne), 2:347,
3:330
Elizabeth (Stedman), 2:347,
4:178
Esther, 2:346, 3:479
Hannah, 2:345-347, 3:338,
3:469
Hannah (Cross), 2:347
Hepzibah, 2:345
Jane, 2:346
Jane (----), 4:579
Margaret (----) Willoughby,
2:346, 4:579
Maria, 2:346
Martha, 2:346
Mary, 2:345-346
Mary (----), 2:346
Mary (Arnold), 2:345
Mary (Somes), 2:345,
4:140
Mary (Vincent), 3:627
Philippa (----), 2:354
Prudence (----), 2:345
Rose (Trippe), 2:347
Rosimund, 2:346
Ruth (Stanwood), 3:627
Sarah, 2:345-347, 4:179,
4:453, 4:559
Sarah (Nichols), 2:345
Sarah (Pickard), 2:347
Susanna (Cross), 1:478
Hanbury
Hannah, 2:348
Hannah (----), 2:551
Hannah (Souther), 2:348
Hancock
Abigail, 2:349
Ann, 2:349
Elizabeth, 2:348-349,
2:592, 4:628, 4:663
Hannah, 2:348
Joan (----), 2:348
Judith (Winthrop), 4:613
Lydia, 2:348
Mary, 2:348-349
Mary (Prentice), 2:349,
3:478
Ruth (----), 2:348
Sarah, 2:348-349
Sarah (----), 2:348
Silence, 2:348

Hancox
Mehitable, 2:349
Rachel, 2:349
Rachel (Leonard), 2:349,
3:79
Hand
Alice, 4:87
Hannah (Seward), 2:349,
4:57
Jane (Wright), 2:349,
4:654
Hands
Abra (----), 2:349
Ann, 3:628
Hannah
(Hanniford/Hannifall),
2:350-351
Mary, 2:349
Mary (----), 2:349
Mehitable, 2:349
Phebe, 3:628
Sarah, 3:628
Sarah (Ward), 3:628,
4:414
Silence, 4:546
Hanford/Handford
---- (Hatherly), 2:186
Catharine, 2:350
Eglin, 4:44
Eglin (Hatherly),
2:349-350, 4:44
Elizabeth, 2:350
Hannah, 2:350, 3:444
Hannah (Newbury), 2:350,
3:269
Lettice, 2:186, 2:350
Margaret, 2:350, 3:550
Mary, 2:350
Mary (----) Ince, 2:350
Mary (Miles) Ince, 2:518,
3:207
Sarah, 1:440, 2:350
Susanna, 3:307
Hanmer/Hanmore
Bethia, 2:350, 4:196
Elizabeth, 2:350, 2:410
Hannah, 2:350
Rebecca, 2:350, 2:410
Susanna, 1:261
Hannadown
Lydia, 2:350
Sarah (----), 2:350

Hannah
Martha (Clark), 1:393
Mary, 2:350
Mary (Wilson), 2:350,
4:588
Hanniford/Hannifall/etc
----, 2:315
Abigail, 3:628
Abigail (----) Dell, 2:34,
2:351
Hannah, 2:350-351
Hannah (----), 2:350
Sarah, 2:351
Hannison
Miriam, 4:702
Hannum
Abigail, 2:351
Elizabeth, 1:318, 2:351
Elizabeth (Wright)
Stebbins, 4:178
Esther, 2:351
Esther (Langton), 2:351,
3:56
Experience, 2:351
Hannah, 2:351
Honor (----), 2:351
Joanna, 2:351
Mary, 1:33, 2:351
Mindwell, 2:351
Ruth, 2:351
Sarah, 2:351
Sarah (Weller), 2:351,
4:474
Hansett/Hanchet/etc
Bathsheba, 2:351
Deliverance, 2:352, 4:474
Deliverance (----), 1:314
Deliverance (Langton),
2:352, 3:56
Elizabeth, 2:351-352
Elizabeth (Loomis), 2:352,
3:114
Elizabeth (Perry), 2:351
Esther, 2:290, 2:351
Esther (Pritchet), 2:351
Hannah, 2:351-352, 3:114
Huldah, 2:351
Mary, 2:351
Mary (Parker), 2:351,
3:352
Mehitable, 2:351
Sarah, 2:352

Hanson
Abigail, 2:352
Elizabeth, 2:352
Mary, 2:352, 3:90, 3:628
Mary (----), 2:352
Mary (----) Robinson,
3:628
Mary (Mumford), 3:253
Mercy, 2:352
Hapgood
Elizabeth, 2:353, 4:683
Elizabeth (Treadway),
2:352, 4:324
Elizabeth (Ward), 2:352
Hepzibah, 2:353
Huldah, 2:353, 4:683
Judith, 4:683
Judith (----), 2:353
Mary, 2:352-353, 4:530
Sarah, 2:352-353, 4:530
Harberfield
Mary (----), 2:326
Harbert/Herbert
Catharine, 2:592
Elizabeth (George), 2:353
Hannah, 2:353
Jael (Thayer), 2:353
Lucy (Adams), 2:353
Mary, 2:353
Mary (----), 2:353
Harbottle
Dorothy, 3:47
Harbour
Christian (Nethercoot),
2:353
Elizabeth (----) George,
2:242
Jane (----), 2:353
Harcutt/Harker/Harkett
Dorothy, 2:353
Elizabeth, 2:353, 4:671
Elizabeth (Potter), 2:353,
3:467
Isabel, 2:353, 4:539
Mary, 2:353, 3:14
Mercy, 2:353
Meribah, 2:353, 4:318
Sarah, 2:353
Hard
Elizabeth (Barlow), 1:502
Hardier
----, 2:353
Elizabeth, 2:353

Hardier (continued)
Elizabeth (----), 2:353
Lydia, 4:21
Margaret (Tomlinson),
  4:310
Mary, 2:353
Harding/Harden
---- (----) Tybbot, 3:628
---- (Dyer), 2:89
Abiah, 2:354
Bethia (Cook), 1:448,
  2:354
Elizabeth, 2:354
Elizabeth (----), 2:354,
  2:584
Elizabeth (Adams), 2:354
Esther (Willis), 2:354
Hannah, 2:354
Hannah (Wood), 2:354,
  4:628
Hester (Willis), 4:574
Jane, 3:628
Martha, 1:276, 2:354
Martha (----), 2:354
Mary, 2:354, 2:592
Maziah, 2:354
Philippa (----) Hammond,
  2:354
Susanna (----) Haviland,
  2:354, 2:379
Hardman
Mary, 2:355
Sarah (----), 2:355
Hardy/Hardie
----, 2:355
Ann (Huested), 2:355
Ann (Huested/Husted),
  2:490
Elizabeth, 2:355, 2:371,
  3:424
Elizabeth (----), 2:355
Hannah, 2:355
Lydia (----), 2:355
Martha (----), 2:355
Mary, 1:484, 2:355
Mary (----), 2:355, 3:456
Mary (Dudley), 2:77,
  2:355
Mary (Grafton), 2:155,
  2:289, 2:355
Mercy (Tenny), 2:355
Rebecca (Hobby), 2:437
Ruth, 2:355

Ruth (Marsh), 2:355
Ruth (Tenny), 2:355
Sarah, 2:355
Seeth, 2:355
Susanna, 2:355
Hare
Joanna (----), 2:356
Mary (----), 2:356
Susanna, 2:356
Harger/Hardger/Hardyear
Abigail, 2:356
Ann, 2:356
Hannah (----), 3:628
Margaret, 3:628
Margaret (Tomlinson),
  2:356
Mary, 2:356
Sarah, 2:356
Harges
----, 1:395
Harker
Dorothy (----) Mills, 2:356,
  3:214
Elizabeth, 2:356
Elizabeth (----), 2:356
Mary, 2:356
Mary (----), 2:356
Mercy, 2:356
Patience (Folger), 2:177,
  2:228, 2:356
Sarah, 2:356
Harlakenden
Dorothy, 4:709
Elizabeth, 2:356
Elizabeth
  (Bosseville/Basseville),
  2:356, 3:385
Mabel, 2:356, 2:389,
  3:631
Margaret, 2:356
Harley
Abigail (Saltonstall), 4:8
Harlock
---- (Mayhew), 2:356
Sarah (Arey), 2:356
Sarah (Stuart), 2:356
Harlow
Abigail, 3:628
Abigail (Buck), 3:628
Bathsua, 2:357
Elizabeth, 3:628
Hannah, 2:357, 3:628
Hannah (----), 3:628

Joanna, 2:357
Judith, 2:357
Lydia, 3:628
Lydia (Cushman), 1:492,
  3:628
Mary, 2:357, 3:628
Mary (Faunce), 2:148,
  2:357
Mary (Shelly), 2:357,
  3:243, 3:628, 4:71
Mehitable, 2:357
Priscilla, 3:628
Priscilla (----), 3:628
Rebecca, 2:357, 3:628
Rebecca (Bartlett), 1:132,
  2:356
Repentance, 2:357
Harman/Harmon/Herman
---- (----), 2:60
---- (Sampson), 2:357
Elizabeth, 2:357
Hannah, 2:592
Mary, 1:213, 2:61, 2:357
Mary (Bliss), 1:202, 2:357
Miriam, 1:200
Sarah, 2:155, 2:357
Harndale/Horndel/Harndel
Mary, 2:357, 4:166
Rebecca, 2:357, 3:246
Harnett
---- (Porter), 2:358, 3:462
Eunice, 2:358
Priscilla (----), 2:358
Harper
Deborah (----), 2:358
Dorcas, 2:358, 4:637
Experience, 2:358
Hannah, 2:358
Mary, 2:358
Mercy, 2:358
Prudence (Butley), 2:358
Harraden/Harrendine/etc
Ann, 2:358
Deborah (Norwood), 3:628
Elizabeth, 3:488
Hannah, 4:18
Hannah (York), 3:628
Mary, 3:147, 3:549
Sarah, 2:358
Sarah (----), 2:358
Sarah (Giddings), 3:628
Sarah (Haskell), 3:628,
  3:630

Harriman
—, 2:358
Abigail (—), 2:358
Ann, 2:358
Elizabeth, 2:358, 3:206,
3:628
Elizabeth (—), 2:358
Hannah, 2:391
Hannah (Bryan), 1:282,
2:358
Margaret (—), 2:359
Margaret (Wood), 2:358
Mary, 4:683
Sarah (—), 2:358
Harrington
—, 4:493
Abigail, 2:359-360
Abigail (Bigelow), 2:359
Ann, 2:359-360
Ann (—) Bullard, 2:359
Elizabeth, 2:359-360,
2:592, 4:374
Elizabeth (—), 2:359
Elizabeth (Bridge) Garfield,
2:231, 2:359
Elizabeth (Warren), 4:424
Grace, 2:360
Grace (Livermore), 2:360
Hannah, 2:359
Hannah (Winter), 2:359
Joanna, 2:359
Joanna (Mixer), 2:359,
3:223, 4:412
Lydia, 2:359
Lydia (Fiske) Warren,
4:425
Mary, 1:163, 2:359-360,
2:592, 4:264
Mary (Brown) Warren,
4:425
Mary (Ockington), 2:359,
3:304
Mary (Winter), 4:606
Mindwell, 2:359
Patience, 2:359
Prudence, 2:360
Rebecca, 2:360
Rebecca (Bemis) White,
1:163, 2:360, 4:511
Ruth, 2:359
Sarah, 2:359-360
Sarah (Whitney), 2:359,
4:530

Susan, 1:496
Susanna, 1:154, 1:496,
2:359-360
Susanna (George), 2:242,
2:359
Thankful, 2:359
Harris
—, 3:548
Abigail, 2:361-362
Abigail (—), 2:361
Abigail (Barnes), 2:361
Abigail (Morey), 2:364,
3:232
Agnes (Way), 2:363
Alice (—), 2:362
Amity, 2:363
Amy (—), 2:362
Ann, 2:360-361, 3:180,
4:184
Bridget, 2:362
Bridget (—), 2:361
Deborah, 2:361
Desire, 2:361
Edith (—), 2:365
Elethan, 2:363
Elizabeth, 2:187,
2:360-365, 2:499, 3:512,
4:30, 4:499, 4:530
Elizabeth (—), 2:360,
2:363, 2:365, 4:184
Elizabeth (—) Cook,
2:361
Elizabeth (Abbot), 1:5,
2:361
Elizabeth (Blackleach),
1:189
Elizabeth (Boughey),
1:217, 2:363
Elizabeth (Hazen), 2:362,
2:395
Elizabeth (Lane), 2:362
Elizabeth (Manwaring),
2:363, 3:150
Elizabeth (Wells), 2:362
Elnathan (Tew), 4:270
Esther (—), 2:362
Hannah, 1:447, 2:360-362,
2:365, 2:433, 3:628-629,
4:526
Hannah (—), 2:362-363,
2:365
Hannah (Briggs), 1:252,
2:362

Hannah (Dove), 2:63
Hannah (Dow), 2:363
Hepzibah, 2:364
Hepzibah (—), 2:364
Hepzibah (Crosswell),
2:592
Hope, 2:360
Howlong, 2:153, 2:365
Huldah, 2:362
Jane, 2:361-362, 2:364,
2:286
Joanna, 2:361
Joanna (—), 2:361-362
Joanna (Brown), 2:361
Lydia, 2:361
Lydia (—) Smith, 2:365
Lydia (Grosse), 2:318,
2:361
Lydia (Post) Moore, 3:465
Lydia (Wright) Smith,
4:124
Margaret, 2:361, 2:364,
4:163, 4:230
Margaret (—), 2:363
Martha, 1:423, 2:360-361,
2:364-365
Martha (—), 2:360
Martha (Collins), 3:629
Martha (Lake), 2:364, 3:45
Mary, 1:37, 1:170, 1:213,
2:250, 2:360-365, 2:553,
3:628-629, 4:409
Mary (—), 2:360, 2:362,
2:365
Mary (Dunbar), 2:361
Mary (Sanger), 2:362, 4:16
Mary (Shepard), 2:364
Mary (Tew), 2:360, 4:270
Mary (Weld), 2:360, 4:458
Mary (Wetherell), 2:364,
4:491
Mary (Winslow), 4:601
Mehitable, 2:361, 2:364
Mercy, 2:361, 2:363,
2:365
Mercy (Latham), 2:361
Mindwell (Lyman), 2:362
Naomi, 2:362
Naomi (—), 2:362
Naomi (Stevens), 2:592
Parnel, 2:366
Patience, 2:361, 2:365,
3:152

Harris (continued)
Phebe (Brown), 2:364
Phebe (Pearson), 2:364,
3:378
Priscilla, 2:361, 2:363
Prudence, 2:360, 3:629
Rachel, 2:362, 4:170
Rebecca, 2:364
Rebecca (Josselyn)
Croakham, 1:474, 2:364,
2:570, 4:185
Rebecca (Kettle), 2:362
Sarah, 1:175, 2:360-363
Sarah (----), 2:361-362,
2:364
Sarah (----) Miller, 2:364
Sarah (Cary) Matthews,
2:364
Sarah (Crisp), 1:437, 1:473,
2:366
Sarah (Nettleton) Miller,
3:211
Sarah (Vinting/Vinton),
2:361
Sibil, 3:629
Silence, 2:364
Susan (----), 2:365
Susanna, 2:361, 2:592
Susanna (----), 2:365
Susanna (Breck), 1:240,
2:362
Susanna (Collins), 2:362
Thomasin, 2:361
Thomasin (----), 2:361
Thomasin (Elson), 2:582,
2:592
Toleration, 2:360
Harrison
---- (----) Thompson, 2:366,
4:285
Abigail, 2:366, 3:629
Ann, 2:366, 3:152
Bethia, 4:700
Catharine (----), 2:366
Dorothy (Symonds), 2:366,
4:246
Elinor (----), 2:366
Elizabeth, 2:366, 3:629
Elizabeth (Denison), 2:37
Elizabeth (Stent/Stint),
2:366, 4:181
Ellen, 4:285
Grace (----), 2:366

Jemima, 3:629
Lydia, 3:629
Margaret (Stent), 3:629
Martha (Montague), 2:366,
3:225
Mary, 2:366, 3:434
Persis (----), 2:366
Persis (----) Bridge, 2:592
Persis (Pierce) Bridge,
4:675, 4:686, 4:695
Rebecca, 2:366
Sarah, 2:366
Sarah (Hubbard), 2:483
Susanna, 2:298
Harrod
Alice, 3:629
Elizabeth (Cooke), 1:447,
2:367
Hannah, 2:367, 4:501
Mary (----), 2:314
Rachel (----), 2:367
Susanna (----), 2:367
Hart
----, 2:312, 2:367, 4:560
---- (Needham), 3:655
Abigail, 2:367, 3:655
Abigail (Lambard), 2:368
Alice, 2:367, 3:427
Ann, 2:367-368
Deborah, 3:233
Dorothy (Jones), 2:367
Elizabeth, 2:367-368,
3:620, 4:590
Elizabeth (Ingalls), 2:368
Freeborn (Williams), 1:403,
1:472, 2:368, 4:569
Jane (Rossiter), 3:578
Judith, 1:296, 2:367, 3:508
Lucy, 2:367
Lydia, 3:629
Lydia (Neal), 3:629, 3:655
Margaret (----) Smith,
2:368, 4:110
Martha, 2:367, 3:263
Mary, 1:147, 1:472,
2:367-368, 3:71, 3:629,
3:655
Mary (----), 2:367-368,
3:629
Mary (Moore), 3:654
Mary (Needham), 3:629
Mary (Stone), 4:203
Mary (Whiting/Whitridge),

2:368
Rebecca, 2:367, 3:655
Ruth, 3:629
Ruth (Chadwell), 2:367
Ruth (Howkins), 4:700
Sarah, 1:241, 2:367-368,
3:264, 3:464, 4:36,
4:179
Hartley
Martha, 2:368
Mary (----), 2:368
Hartshorn
Sarah (----), 2:368
Sarah (----) Lamson, 2:592,
3:50
Susan, 2:368
Susan (----), 2:368
Hartwell
Abigail, 2:369
Abigail (Stearns), 4:174
Elizabeth, 2:369
Hannah, 2:369
Jane, 2:369
Jessie (----), 2:369
Martha, 2:369
Mary, 2:369
Priscilla (Wright), 2:369
Rebecca, 2:369
Ruth, 2:369
Ruth (Wheeler), 2:369
Sarah, 2:369, 3:349
Sarah (Wilder), 4:550
Susan (----), 2:369
Harty
Margaret, 4:526
Harvard
Ann (Sadler), 1:36, 2:369
Harvey
---- (Gilbert), 2:249, 2:592
---- (Staples), 2:370
Abigail, 2:370
Ann, 4:496
Ann (----), 2:370
Elizabeth, 2:370, 2:515
Elizabeth (Cleves) Mitton,
1:409, 3:222
Elizabeth (Wall), 2:370,
4:398
Elizabeth (Willis), 4:575
Experience, 2:370
Hannah, 2:369, 3:642,
4:683, 4:686
Hannah (Gilbert), 3:641,

Harvey (continued)
  Hannah (Gilbert)
    (continued)
    4:683
  Harriet (Gilbert), 4:686
  Jehoadan (Horn), 2:464
  Joan (----), 2:370
  Joanna (----), 2:370
  Margaret (----), 2:370
  Martha, 2:370
  Martha (----), 2:286,
    2:369-370, 4:270
  Mary, 2:370, 3:642, 4:683,
    4:686
  Mary (----), 2:370
  Mary (----) Cole, 1:429,
    2:370
  Mary (Staples), 4:169
  Patience (York), 3:629
  Rose, 3:629
  Sarah, 2:370, 3:629, 3:642,
    4:18, 4:683, 4:686
  Sarah (----), 3:629
  Sarah (Barnes) Rowell,
    1:123
  Sarah (Butman), 3:629
Harwood/Harward
  Ann, 2:371
  Deliverance, 2:370
  Elizabeth, 2:370-371,
    2:592
  Elizabeth (----), 2:370-371,
    2:592
  Hannah, 2:371
  Hannah (----), 2:371
  Jane (----), 2:370
  Joanna, 2:370
  Joanna (----), 2:371
  Rachel, 2:371
  Rachel (Smith) Woodward,
    2:371, 4:119, 4:646
Hasey
  Esther, 2:300
  Judith (----), 2:371
  Sarah, 4:154
  Sarah (----), 2:371
  Susanna, 2:371
Haskell/Hascall
  ----, 3:616
  Abigail, 2:372, 3:364
  Bethia (Parsons), 3:158
  Edith, 3:629
  Eleanor, 2:371-372, 3:630

  Elizabeth, 2:371
  Elizabeth (----), 1:170,
    3:630
  Elizabeth (Giddings),
    3:630
  Elizabeth (Hardy), 2:355,
    2:371
  Hannah, 2:371, 3:630
  Hannah (Woodbury),
    4:636
  Jane, 3:630
  Lydia, 2:372, 3:361
  Mary, 2:56, 2:371-372,
    3:629
  Mary (Baker), 3:629
  Mary (Brown), 2:372,
    3:607
  Mary (Graves), 2:371
  Mary (Riggs), 2:371,
    3:542
  Mary (Tybbot), 2:372,
    4:299
  Miriam (Hill), 2:372
  Ruth, 2:372, 3:629-630
  Sarah, 2:372, 3:628, 3:630,
    4:636
Haskett
  ----, 3:425
  Elizabeth, 2:580, 3:630
  Elizabeth/Ellen (----),
    3:630
  Ellen (----), 2:372
  Hannah, 2:372
  Martha, 2:40
  Mary, 2:372
  Sarah, 2:372
Haskins - see Hoskins
Haslerigg
  Catharine, 2:154
Hassell
  Abiah, 1:196, 2:372
  Ann, 2:372
  Ann (----), 2:372
  Elizabeth, 2:372, 4:658
  Esther, 2:372, 3:400
  Joan (----), 2:372
Hastings
  Abigail, 2:373-374, 4:425
  Abigail (Hammond), 2:345,
    2:373
  Ann (----) Mean, 2:373,
    3:192
  Ann (Hawkes), 2:374,

    2:381
  Elizabeth, 1:178, 1:325,
    2:373-374
  Elizabeth (Bright), 1:253,
    2:374
  Elizabeth (Clark), 1:403
  Elizabeth (Graves), 2:294,
    2:372
  Elizabeth (Nevinson),
    2:374, 3:268
  Hannah, 1:454, 2:372-374
  Hannah (----), 2:374
  Hannah (Moore), 2:373,
    3:227
  Hepzibah, 1:210,
    2:373-374
  Lydia, 2:373-374
  Lydia (Champney), 1:356,
    2:373
  Lydia (Church), 2:374
  Margaret, 2:374
  Margaret (Cheney), 1:372,
    2:374
  Martha, 2:373-374
  Martha (Shepherd), 2:373
  Mary, 2:374
  Mary (----), 1:158
  Mary (----) Parsons, 2:373
  Mary (Burt), 1:313, 2:374
  Mary (Field), 2:374
  Mary (Mean), 2:374,
    3:192
  Mary (Nevinson), 2:373,
    3:268
  Mehitable, 2:374
  Ruth (Rice), 2:373, 3:530
  Sarah, 2:373-374
  Sarah (----), 2:373
  Sarah (Coolidge), 1:452,
    2:374
  Sarah (Mean), 2:374,
    3:192
  Sarah (Sharp), 4:570
  Silence, 2:374
  Submit, 2:373
  Susan (----), 2:374
  Susanna, 2:373
  Thankful, 2:374
Hatch
  Abigail, 2:375, 3:630
  Abigail (----), 2:376
  Abigail/Elizabeth (Walker),
    3:630

Hatch (continued)
Alice, 2:375, 3:424, 3:576
Amy, 3:630
Amy (Allen), 3:630
Ann, 2:376, 4:313
Bethia, 2:183, 2:375,
  3:630
Elizabeth (Holbrook),
  2:375, 2:443
Elizabeth (Walker), 3:630
Grace (----), 2:375
Hannah, 2:375-376, 3:630,
  4:364
Hannah (Scudder) Bangs,
  1:112, 2:375
Jane, 2:375-376, 3:123,
  4:82
Jane (----), 2:375, 3:26
Joanna, 3:630
Keturah, 2:375
Lydia, 1:128, 2:375-376,
  3:630, 4:260
Margaret, 2:375
Mary, 2:375-376, 3:630
Mary (Hamblen), 3:630
Mary (Hewes), 2:375,
  2:407
Meletiah, 3:630
Phebe, 2:376
Ruth, 3:630
Sarah, 2:375, 3:630
Sarah (Ellmes), 2:114,
  2:375
Sarah (Rowley), 3:582,
  3:630
Susanna (Annable), 1:59,
  2:376
Hatfield
Sarah (Gilbert), 2:252
Hathaway/Hadaway
Hannah, 2:376
Hannah (Hallet), 2:376
Hepzibah (Starbuck),
  4:172
Rebecca, 4:249
Rebecca (Wilbore), 2:593
Sarah, 2:376
Sarah (Cook), 1:447,
  2:376
Hatherly
----, 2:186
Abigail, 2:376
Abigail (----), 2:376

Eglin, 2:350, 4:44
Lydia (----) Tilden, 2:377
Lydia (Greene), 2:376
Hathorne/Hawthorne
----, 3:664, 3:644, 4:701
Abigail, 3:514, 3:630,
  3:644, 4:701
Abigail (Curwin), 1:488,
  2:377, 3:590
Ann, 2:377, 3:462
Ann (----), 3:644, 4:701
Elizabeth, 2:377, 3:460,
  3:630
Esther (Witt), 2:377, 4:619
Mary, 2:377
Phebe, 2:377
Priscilla, 2:377, 4:88
Ruth, 2:227
Ruth (Gardner), 2:227,
  3:630
Sarah, 1:241, 1:423, 2:377,
  2:593
Sarah (----), 3:631, 3:644,
  4:701
Hathwit - see Huthwit
Hatsell
Susanna (----) Evance,
  2:127, 2:378
Susanna/Hannah (----)
  Evance, 4:681
Haughton
Abigail, 2:378, 3:67
Alice (----), 1:481, 2:378
Catharine, 1:320, 2:378
Catharine (----) Charlett,
  1:364, 2:378
Hannah, 2:378
Mercy, 1:177, 2:378
Sarah, 2:378
Sarah (Phippen), 2:378,
  3:418, 4:110
Haven/Havens
Dennis/Dionis (----), 2:379
Dinah, 2:379
Elinor (Thurston), 2:378,
  4:296
Elizabeth, 2:379
Elizabeth (----), 2:379
Elizabeth (----) Bridges,
  2:378-379
Experience, 2:379
Hannah, 2:270, 2:378-379
Hannah (Hitchings), 2:378

Jane, 2:378, 4:90
Margaret, 2:379
Martha, 2:379
Mary, 1:319, 2:378-379,
  4:256
Mary (Ballard), 1:108
Mary (Bullard), 2:378
Mary (Hearing/Herring),
  2:379
Mercy, 2:379
Moriah, 2:379
Rebecca, 2:379
Ruth, 2:379
Sarah, 2:378-379, 3:274,
  4:355, 4:530
Sarah (----), 2:379
Susanna, 2:378-379
Susanna (----), 2:379
Susanna (Newhall), 3:274,
  3:631
Haverlad
Mary, 1:217
Haviland
Susanna, 2:379
Susanna (----), 2:354,
  2:379
Hawes
----, 1:125
---- (----) Edwards, 2:581
Abigail, 2:138, 2:379
Abigail (----), 2:379
Alice, 2:380
Ann, 2:380
Ann (----), 2:380
Bethia, 2:380
Constance, 2:43, 2:380
Deborah, 3:452
Deliverance, 2:380
Desire, 2:380
Desire (Gorham), 2:281,
  2:380
Elizabeth, 1:512, 4:543,
  4:696
Mary, 2:380
Mary (----), 2:380
Mary (Humphrey), 2:380,
  2:497
Rebecca (Cowen), 1:466,
  2:380
Ruth, 2:379
Ruth (Haynes), 2:379,
  2:388
Sarah, 2:380

Hawes (continued)
 Susanna, 2:380
 Susanna (----), 2:380
Hawke/Hawkes/Hawks
 ---- (----) Edwards, 2:593
 Alice (----) Allis, 1:42,
  2:381
 Ann, 2:374, 2:381
 Ann (----), 2:380
 Bethia, 2:381
 Deborah, 2:380-381
 Elizabeth, 2:256,
  2:380-381, 3:93
 Elizabeth (----), 2:427
 Elizabeth (Pratt), 2:380,
  3:475
 Hannah, 1:103, 1:491,
  2:381, 4:38
 Hannah (Beebe), 1:153
 Joanna, 1:63, 2:381
 Judith (Smead), 2:380
 Margaret, 2:380-381
 Margaret (----), 2:381-382
 Martha (Baldwin), 1:103
 Mary, 2:127, 2:381, 2:427,
  3:117, 3:371
 Rebecca, 2:381
 Rebecca (Maverick), 2:381,
  3:181
 Sarah, 1:157, 1:490,
  2:380-381, 2:551, 3:178,
  4:415
 Sarah (Cushman), 1:492,
  2:381
 Sarah (Hooper), 2:380
 Sarah (Jacob), 2:380
 Susanna, 2:380-381
Hawkehurst/Hauxhurst
 ---- (Reddock), 2:382,
  3:521
Hawkesworth/Hauxworth
 Mary, 2:382, 3:331
 Mary (----), 2:382, 4:578
Hawkins
 Abigail, 2:383, 3:6, 3:230,
  3:631
 Abigail (Holbrook), 3:631,
  3:634
 Agnes, 3:631
 Agnes (Stilson), 4:196
 Ann, 2:382
 Ann (Welles) Thompson,
  2:382, 4:288, 4:478

 Damaris, 2:382, 4:294
 Dorothy (----), 2:384
 Elizabeth, 2:382-383,
  3:533, 4:607
 Elizabeth (----), 2:382
 Esther, 1:66, 2:382
 Esther (----), 2:382
 Frances (----), 2:382
 Grace (----), 2:383
 Hannah, 1:126, 2:382-383,
  2:471, 2:510, 4:58
 Hannah (----), 1:126, 2:383
 Hope, 2:383
 Jane (----), 2:383
 Lois, 3:631
 Lydia (Gardner), 2:384
 Martha, 2:382, 3:663
 Mary, 1:85, 1:190,
  2:382-384, 2:426, 2:574,
  3:631
 Mary (----), 2:152,
  2:382-383, 4:90
 Mary (Mills), 3:214, 3:631
 Mary (Sherman), 2:383,
  4:82
 Mary (Treadway) Fisher,
  2:383, 4:324
 Mehitable, 2:231, 2:383
 Rebecca, 2:383
 Rebecca (----), 2:383,
  4:176
 Ruhamah (Johnson),
  2:383
 Sarah, 1:31, 1:241,
  2:382-383
 Sarah (----) Damerill, 2:4,
  2:383
 Susan, 2:382
Hawley
 ----, 1:212
 ---- (Gould/Gold), 2:286
 Abia, 2:384, 4:624
 Amy (----), 2:385
 Catharine (----), 2:384
 Dorothy, 1:212, 2:384-385
 Dorothy (----) Lamb, 2:385
 Dorothy (Harbottle) Lamb,
  3:48
 Elizabeth, 1:361, 2:61,
  2:384-385
 Emma (----), 2:385
 Esther (----), 3:279
 Esther (----) Ward, 2:384,

  4:414
 Hannah, 1:148, 2:384,
  3:281, 3:305
 Lydia, 2:85, 2:384
 Lydia (Marshall), 2:384,
  3:157
 Mary, 1:418, 2:384
 Mary (Thompson), 4:288
 Rebecca (Stoddard), 2:384
 Sarah (Welles), 2:384,
  4:477
Haxie/Hauksie/Hoxie
 ---- (Hull), 2:385
 Ann, 2:385
 Ann (Richmond), 2:385
 Bashua, 1:29, 2:385
 Content, 2:385
 Deborah, 2:385
 Desire, 2:385
 Dinah (Butler), 2:385
 Dorothy (----) Wing, 2:385
 Elizabeth, 2:385
 Elizabeth (Wing), 2:385
 Grace, 2:385
 Grace (Gifford), 2:385
 Hannah, 2:385
 Hannah (Allen), 2:385
 Kezia, 2:385
 Maria, 2:385
 Martha, 2:385
 Mary, 2:385
 Mary (Presbury), 2:385
 Sarah, 2:385
 Sarah (----), 2:385
 Sherebiah, 2:385
Hay
 Bridget (----), 2:386
 Sarah, 2:386
Hayden/Haydon
 ---- (----), 2:386
 Abigail, 2:386, 4:275
 Amy, 2:386
 Ann (----), 2:386
 Concurrance, 2:387
 Elizabeth, 2:386, 3:476
 Elizabeth (----), 2:386
 Elizabeth (Goodenow),
  2:272
 Elizabeth (Ladd), 2:386
 Experience, 2:387
 Hannah, 2:386-387, 4:277
 Hannah (Ames), 1:49,
  2:386

Hayden/Haydon (continued)
Hannah (Mayne), 2:386
Hannah (Neal), 2:387,
3:264
Hannah (Thayer), 2:387
Hannah (Wilcockson),
2:386, 4:548
Lydia, 2:386, 4:375
Margaret, 2:386
Margaret (----) Wilcockson,
2:387
Mary, 2:129, 2:386-387
Mercy, 2:386, 3:16
Rachel, 2:387
Ruhamah, 2:386
Ruth, 2:386
Sarah, 2:386-387
Sarah (Parmelee),
2:386-387
Susanna, 2:387
Susanna (----), 2:386
Hayes
----, 2:387
---- (Tuttle), 4:351
Abigail, 2:387-388
Abigail (----), 2:387
Abra, 2:387
Ann, 2:388
Elizabeth, 2:387-388, 3:23
Elizabeth (----), 2:388
Elizabeth (Langton), 3:646
Hannah, 2:387-388
Hannah (Sanborn), 2:388
Jane (----) Heard, 2:387
Leah (Dame), 2:388
Mary, 2:388, 3:23
Mary (----) Wingate, 2:387
Mary (Horne), 2:387,
2:464
Mary (Kimberly), 2:388,
3:23
Mary (Tuttle), 2:387
Mehitable, 2:388
Patience, 2:388
Sarah, 2:387-388
Sarah (Wingate), 2:388
Thomasin (Wentworth)
Chesley, 2:387
Hayman/Heyman
Elizabeth, 1:239, 2:388
Elizabeth (Allen), 1:498,
2:388
Grace, 2:388

Grace (----), 2:388
Hannah, 2:388
Hannah (----), 2:388
Mary, 2:388, 3:118, 3:413
Mary (Anderson) Lynde
Shepard, 1:51, 2:388, 4:76
Sarah, 2:388, 2:582
Haynes/Haines
----, 2:390-391, 4:10
---- (Starke/Start), 4:172
Abigail, 1:267, 2:390
Ann, 2:439
Ann (Clark), 1:402
Ann (Estabrook), 2:126
Deliverance, 3:557
Dorothy, 2:204, 2:389
Dorothy (Noyes), 2:389,
3:298
Elinor, 2:390
Elizabeth, 1:101,
2:389-391, 4:453
Elizabeth (----), 2:389,
2:391
Elizabeth (Noyes), 2:390,
3:298
Elizabeth (Rice), 2:390,
3:531
Ellen, 2:391
Esther, 2:390
Hannah, 2:388, 2:391,
3:573
Hannah (----), 3:56
Hannah (Harriman), 2:391
Isabella, 3:363
Jane (Brackett), 2:390
Lydia, 2:391
Mabel, 2:389-390, 3:590
Mabel (----), 2:97, 3:617
Mabel (Harlakenden),
2:356, 2:389, 3:631
Margaret, 2:390
Margaret (----) Foote,
2:389
Margaret (Stallion) Foot,
2:181
Margery (----) White,
2:391
Martha (Burnet), 2:391
Mary, 2:388-391, 2:476,
3:299
Mary (----), 2:388, 2:390
Mary (Fifield), 2:158,
2:390

Mary (Glover), 2:263
Mary (Moulton), 2:389,
3:249
Mehitable, 2:391
Rachel, 2:389
Rachel (Davis), 2:20
Ruth, 2:379, 2:388-390,
4:203, 4:577
Sarah, 2:388-391, 3:29,
3:432, 3:617
Sarah (Ingersoll), 2:391,
2:521, 2:593, 2:595
Sarah (Lord), 2:390, 3:115
Sarah (Moulton), 2:389,
3:249
Sarah (Noyes), 2:389
Sarah (Rea), 2:391
Sufferance, 3:299, 4:324
Suffrance, 2:391
Susanna, 4:645
Tabitha (Stone), 2:388
Hayward
----, 2:83
---- (Atkinson), 1:498
---- (Dawson), 1:392
---- (Felch), 2:393
---- (Ruggles), 3:587
Abiel, 2:393
Abigail, 2:393-394, 3:103,
3:302, 4:361
Abigail (Newbury), 2:391
Alice (Brett), 1:243, 2:393
Ann, 2:392
Ann (White), 2:392
Deborah, 2:394
Dorothy, 2:393
Elizabeth, 1:49, 2:393-394
Elizabeth (----), 2:393,
4:617
Elizabeth (----) Oakes,
2:393
Elizabeth (----) Oakes
Sweetser, 4:239
Elizabeth (----) Oakes
Sweetster, 2:394, 3:302
Elizabeth (----) Warren
Sendall, 2:392, 4:51,
4:425, 4:587
Elizabeth (Danforth),
2:394
Elizabeth (Treadway)
Hapgood, 2:352, 4:324
Elizabeth (Treadwell),

Hayward (continued)
Elizabeth (Treadwell)
(continued)
2:393
Esther, 2:393
Hannah, 2:391-393, 2:416,
4:275
Hannah (----), 4:278
Hannah (Hosmer), 2:393,
2:467
Hannah (Mitchell), 2:393,
3:220
Hannah (Willis), 2:393,
4:575
Hulda, 4:276
Isabel (----), 2:393
Judith, 2:392
Judith (----), 4:247
Judith (Phippen), 2:392,
3:419
Lydia, 2:393
Lydia (Kilborne), 2:393,
3:20
Margaret, 1:270
Margery, 2:394
Margery (----), 2:394
Martha, 2:393-394, 2:471
Mary, 2:391-394, 3:219,
4:553
Mary (----), 1:392, 2:391
Mary (----) Aldridge
Judson, 1:25, 2:392, 2:576
Mary (Gould), 1:510
Mercy, 2:392
Patience, 1:28, 2:393
Persis, 3:9
Rebecca, 2:392-393
Rebecca (Atkinson), 1:499
Sarah, 1:243, 2:391-392,
3:587, 4:275
Sarah (----), 2:394, 2:593,
3:537
Sarah (Ames), 1:49, 2:394
Sarah (Mitchell), 2:392,
3:220
Sarah (Thayer), 2:392
Sarah (Thayer) Davis, 2:21,
2:393
Silence (----), 2:392
Susanna, 2:392-393
Susanna (----), 2:394
Susanna (Wilkinson),
2:593

Tabitha, 2:393
Haywood
Margaret (----), 2:394
Sarah (Symonds), 4:247
Hazard
Abigail (Gardiner), 3:556
Elizabeth, 2:395, 3:44
Hannah, 2:395, 4:547
Martha, 2:395, 3:466
Martha (----), 2:395
Mary, 3:552
Hazeltine/Hazelton
Ann, 2:395
Ann (----), 2:395
Deliverance, 2:6, 2:395
Elizabeth, 2:395
Elizabeth (Jewett), 2:395,
2:549
Elizabeth (Langhorne),
2:395
Joan (Anter), 2:395
Mary, 2:395, 3:21
Hazelwood
Mary, 2:396
Sarah (----), 2:396
Hazen
Edna, 2:395, 3:397
Elizabeth, 2:362, 2:395
Hannah (----), 1:266
Priscilla, 3:378
Headley
Mehitable (Applin), 1:62
Heald
Ann, 2:396
Ann (Vinton), 2:396
Dorcas, 2:396
Dorothy, 2:396
Dorothy (----), 2:396
Hannah, 2:396
Sarah, 3:79
Sarah (Dane), 2:396
Healey/Haley
Abigail, 2:396
Elizabeth, 2:396
Grace, 2:396, 2:596
Grace (Buttress), 1:325,
2:396
Grace (Buttry), 2:525
Grace (Ives), 2:396
Hannah, 2:92, 2:396-397
Hannah (Smith), 2:396
Joanna (Bullard), 2:396
Lydia, 2:396

Martha, 2:396
Mary, 2:396-397, 4:627
Phebe (Greene), 2:396-397
Rebecca, 2:396
Rebecca (Hagar), 2:328,
2:396
Ruth, 2:396
Sarah, 1:339, 2:396, 3:151
Sarah (----) Brown, 2:397
Sarah (Brown), 2:397
Heard
Abigail, 2:397-398, 2:562
Abigail (----), 2:398
Catharine, 2:397
Dorcas, 2:397
Elizabeth, 2:397-398,
3:301
Elizabeth (Hull), 2:397,
2:492
Elizabeth (Roberts), 2:397,
3:547
Elizabeth (Warner), 2:397
Experience, 2:397
Experience (Otis), 2:397,
3:325
Grace, 2:397
Hannah, 2:397, 3:263
Jane (----), 2:387
Jane (Cole) Litchfield,
1:429
Keziah, 2:398
Mary, 2:342, 2:397-398
Ruth (----), 2:397
Sarah (----), 2:397
Sarah (Wyatt), 1:188,
2:397
Shuah (----), 2:397, 3:324
Hearing/Herring
Mary, 2:379
Hearn
Susanna, 1:422
Hearndale
Abigail, 2:405
Deliverance (----), 2:405
Esther, 2:405
Kezia, 2:405
Martha, 2:405
Mary, 2:405
Meribah, 2:405
Hearsey
---- (Richards), 3:532
Heath
Abigail, 2:398-399

Heath (continued)
Ann, 2:398
Ann (----), 4:671-672
Ann (Fisher), 2:398
Dorothy, 2:399
Elizabeth, 1:224,
2:398-399, 4:67
Elizabeth (----), 2:398,
2:561
Elizabeth (----) Gross,
1:310, 2:319
Elizabeth (Eldridge), 2:398
Esther, 2:399
Hannah, 1:394, 2:399,
2:561
Hannah (Weld), 2:399,
4:457
Lydia, 2:399
Margaret, 2:399
Martha, 1:238, 2:398-399
Martha (----), 2:399, 3:331
Mary, 2:398-399
Mary (----), 2:398-399
Mary (Davis), 2:18,
2:398-399
Mehitable, 2:399
Sarah (Partridge), 2:398,
3:366
Susanna, 2:399
Susanna (King), 2:399
Heaton
Abigail, 2:400, 3:598,
3:631, 4:701
Ann, 3:631
Elizabeth, 1:121,
2:399-400
Elizabeth (----), 2:399,
3:186, 3:386, 4:580
Experience, 2:399
Experience (Mede), 2:399,
3:190
Leah, 2:162, 2:399-400
Mary (----), 2:400
Sarah, 2:400
Sarah (Streete), 2:399,
4:223
Hedge
Blanch (----) Hull, 2:400
Elizabeth, 1:121, 2:400
Mary, 2:400, 4:229
Sarah, 2:400, 3:652
Thankful (Lathrop), 2:400

Hedger
Elizabeth (Burton), 1:315
Hedges
Ann (Nickerson), 2:400
Grace, 2:400
Mary (Andrews), 2:400,
3:443
Hedley
Elizabeth, 2:400
Mary, 2:400
Mary (----), 2:400
Sarah, 2:400
Helme
Margaret (----), 2:401
Helson
Joan (Warwick), 2:401,
4:429
Helyer
Experience (Hall), 2:337
Hemmenway/Hemingway
Abigail, 2:401
Elizabeth, 2:401
Elizabeth (Hewes), 2:401
Hannah, 2:401
Joanna, 1:19, 2:401
Joanna (Evans), 2:128,
2:401
Mary, 2:401
Mary (----), 2:401
Mary (Trescott), 2:401,
4:329
Ruth, 2:401
Sarah, 2:276, 2:401
Sarah (Cooper), 1:454,
2:401
Thankful, 2:401, 3:350
Hempstead
Elizabeth, 2:401
Elizabeth (----), 2:401
Elizabeth (Larrabee), 3:631,
3:646
Hannah, 2:401-402
Lucy, 2:401
Mary, 2:63, 2:401-402
Patience, 2:401
Phebe, 2:401
Henbury
Elizabeth, 2:402
Hannah, 2:402
Lydia (Hill), 2:402
Martha, 4:74
Martha (----), 2:402, 4:75
Mary, 2:402

Susanna, 2:402
Henchman/Hinchman
Abigail, 2:402
Abigail (----), 2:402
Bridget, 1:359, 2:403,
3:536
Deborah, 2:402
Elizabeth, 2:402, 4:368
Elizabeth (----), 2:165,
2:402
Elizabeth (Emmons),
2:120, 2:402
Hannah, 2:402, 2:416
Hannah (Green), 2:402
Jane, 2:402
Margaret, 2:402
Mary, 2:402-403
Mary (Philbird), 2:403
Mary (Poole), 2:402, 3:456
Sarah, 2:402
Sarah (----), 2:402
Susanna, 2:402
Henderson
Abigail, 2:262
Hendrick
Abigail (Morse), 2:403
Dorothy, 2:403
Dorothy (Pike), 2:403,
3:435
Hannah, 2:403
Mary (----) Stockbridge,
2:403, 4:197
Sarah, 2:403, 2:519
Hendrickson
Hannah (----), 4:97
Hendy/Handy/Hendee
Elizabeth, 3:631
Elizabeth (Conant), 3:631
Hannah, 3:631
Mary, 3:631
Sarah, 3:631
Sarah (Smith), 3:631
Henfield
Elizabeth, 3:631
Elizabeth (Preston), 3:631
Hannah, 3:631
Mary, 2:403
Mary (Gardner), 2:230,
2:403
Henley/Hanley
Sarah (Thompson), 2:403
Henrickson
Mary, 2:403

Henryson
Elizabeth, 2:404
Martha (----), 2:404
Mary, 2:404
Miriam, 2:404
Sarah, 2:404
Henshaw/Hinshaw/Hinshew
Catharine, 2:404
Elizabeth, 2:404
Elizabeth (Sumner), 2:404,
  4:232
Mary (----) Pond Allen,
  2:404
Mary (Ball) Pond Allen,
  1:34, 3:453
Mary (Webster), 2:404
Thankful, 2:404
Hensher/Heinsher
Elizabeth, 2:404
Hannah, 2:404
Hannah (Cleaveland),
  1:407, 2:404
Hepburn/Hepbourne/etc
Abigail, 2:404
Hannah, 3:129
Hannah (----), 2:404
Rebecca, 2:404
Sally, 2:404
Sarah, 2:404
Herbert
Catharine, 2:68
Elinor (----) Miller, 2:404,
  3:210
Elizabeth, 1:488, 2:593
Elizabeth (----) George,
  2:404
Elizabeth (Russell) Graves,
  2:295, 2:404, 3:594
Mary, 2:404
Mary (----), 2:404
Mary (Follett), 3:631
Herenden/Henrendean
---- (----), 3:476
Alice, 1:265
Mary, 2:101
Sarah, 2:524
Herrick
---- (----), 4:405
Abigail, 2:406
Abigail (Wheeler), 2:406
Ann, 2:405
Edith, 2:406
Edith (Laskin), 2:405

Elizabeth, 2:194,
  2:405-406, 4:209
Hannah, 2:406
Lydia, 2:405
Lydia (----), 2:405
Martha, 2:405-406
Martha (----), 2:405
Martha (Tappan), 4:255
Mary, 1:88, 2:405-406
Mary (----) March, 2:406
Mary (Cross), 2:405
Mary (Dodge), 2:57, 2:406
Mary (Endicot), 2:406
Mary (Folsom) March,
  3:151
Mary (Redington), 2:406
Ruth, 2:406
Sarah, 2:405-406
Sarah (----) Giddings,
  2:405
Sarah (Leach), 2:406, 3:67
Tryphena, 2:406
Tryphosa, 2:406
Herring
Mary (Pierce), 2:406,
  3:430
Hersey
---- (Gilman), 2:257
Alice (Bradford) Mitchell,
  3:219
Deborah, 3:93
Elizabeth, 2:258, 2:406
Elizabeth (----), 2:406
Frances, 1:474, 2:406
Judith, 2:406-407, 4:583
Maria, 2:258
Mary (Fearing), 2:150,
  2:406
Mary (Hawke/Hawkes),
  2:381
Rebecca (Chubbuck),
  1:384, 2:593
Sarah (Hawke/Hawkes),
  2:381
Hervey
---- (Clark), 1:400
Het/Hett
Ann, 2:407
Ann (Douglas), 2:63,
  2:407
Ann (Needham), 2:407
Dorothy, 2:407
Dorothy (----), 2:407, 3:15

Dorothy (Emands), 2:593
Elizabeth, 2:407
Hannah, 2:593, 2:596
Mary, 2:168, 2:212, 2:407,
  2:593, 3:16
Mary (----), 2:593
Mehitable, 2:407, 4:345
Mercy, 2:407
Hewes - see also Hughes
Alice (----) Crabtree, 1:468,
  2:408
Bethia (Sweetman), 2:407,
  4:239
Elizabeth, 2:401, 2:407
Elizabeth (----), 2:407
Hannah, 2:408
Martha (Calef), 1:329,
  2:408
Mary, 2:375, 2:407-408
Mary (----), 2:407
Mary (Allen), 1:37
Mary (Goldstone), 2:270,
  2:408
Rachel, 2:407
Rebecca, 2:407
Remember, 3:396
Ruth (Sawtell), 2:407, 4:30
Sarah, 2:407
Thomasin, 2:242
Hewett - see Huet
Hewins/Huen/Hewens
Hannah, 2:408
Martha, 2:408
Martha (Trescott), 2:408,
  4:329
Mary, 2:68, 2:408, 4:329
Mary (----), 4:683
Mercy, 2:408, 4:329
Heylet
Lydia (Palsgrave), 3:340
Heywood
Rebecca, 2:408
Rebecca (Atkinson), 2:408
Sarah (Symonds), 2:408
Hibbell
Elizabeth (Meigs),
  3:193-194
Hibbert/Hibbard/Hebard
Abigail, 2:408
Dorcas, 1:4
Elizabeth, 2:408
Joan (----), 2:408
Joanna, 2:408

Hibbert/Hibbard/Hebard
(continued)
Mary, 2:408, 4:137
Sarah, 2:408
Hibbins/Hibbens
Ann (----), 2:409
Ann (----) Moore, 3:229
Mary (Pennell), 2:409
Hibbs
Abigail, 2:409
Elizabeth, 2:409
Elizabeth (----), 2:409
Hichborn
Catharine, 2:409
Catharine (----), 2:409
Hickens
Ann, 2:411, 2:577
Hickocks/Hickox/Hicock
Elizabeth, 2:409, 3:631
Eunice, 2:71, 2:409
Hannah, 2:409
Hannah (Skeel), 2:409,
4:103
Lois, 2:409
Mary, 2:409, 3:631
Mercy, 2:410
Ruth, 2:409
Ruth (Fairchild), 2:409
Sarah, 2:409
Susan, 2:409
Hicks
Bethia (Green), 2:303,
2:411
Dorcas, 2:410
Dorcas (----), 2:410
Dorcas (Veren), 3:632,
4:371
Elizabeth, 2:410-411,
3:266
Elizabeth (Davis), 2:18
Elizabeth (Hanmore),
2:350, 2:410
Elizabeth (Howland), 2:47,
2:410, 2:480
Elizabeth (Sills/Scill/Skill),
2:410, 4:96
Hannah, 2:411
Hannah (Evans), 2:128,
2:410
Joanna, 4:670
Lydia, 1:111, 2:410
Lydia (Doane), 2:56, 2:410
Margaret, 2:217, 2:410

Margaret (----), 2:410
Martha (Derby), 2:40
Mary, 1:144, 1:264, 2:410
Mary (----), 2:410
Mary (----) Washburn,
2:410
Mary (Butler) Washburn,
1:321
Phebe, 2:410, 4:437
Rebecca, 2:410
Rebecca (Hanmore), 2:350,
2:410
Rebecca (Palfrey), 3:339
Ruth (Greene), 2:411
Sarah, 1:387
Sarah (----) Mather, 2:410
Sarah (Davis), 2:18
Hickson
Elizabeth, 4:684
Sarah (Brewster/Bruster),
2:411
Sarah (White) Hinsdale,
2:411, 2:427
Sarah (White) Taylor
Hinsdale, 4:264, 4:510
Hidden
Elizabeth, 2:16
Higason
Margaret, 3:654
Higby
Rebecca (----), 2:411
Higginbottom
Elizabeth (Munson), 2:411,
3:257
Eunice (----), 2:411
Rebecca, 2:411
Higgins
Beriah, 2:412
Elizabeth, 2:412
Elizabeth (Rogers),
2:411-412, 3:564
Jemima, 3:252
Judah, 2:412
Lydia, 2:411-412
Lydia (Bangs), 1:111,
2:411
Lydia (Chandler), 2:412
Mary, 2:412
Mary (----) Yates, 4:668
Mary (Yates), 2:412
Rebecca, 2:412
Sarah, 2:412
Susanna (----), 2:411

Susanna (Westoe), 2:412
Zeruiah, 2:412
Higginson
Ann, 1:366, 2:59,
2:413-414
Ann (----), 2:413
Elizabeth, 2:243, 2:414
Elizabeth (Richards),
2:414
Hannah (Gardner), 2:414
Margaret, 2:414, 3:654
Margaret (Sewall), 4:56
Mary, 2:412, 2:414, 3:632
Mary (----) Atwater, 2:414
Mary (Blackman) Atwater,
1:76
Sarah, 2:414, 3:632, 4:494
Sarah (Savage), 2:414,
4:25, 4:27
Sarah (Warner), 2:414,
4:420
Sarah (Whitefield), 2:413
Sarah (Whitfield), 4:517
Higley
Catharine, 2:414
Hannah, 2:414, 4:336
Hannah (Drake), 2:414
Hiland - see Hyland
Hildreth/Hildrick
Abigail, 2:415, 3:354
Abigail (Wilson), 2:415
Elizabeth, 2:414-415
Elizabeth (----), 2:414-415
Jane, 3:490
Joanna, 2:414
Margaret (Ward), 2:414
Mary, 2:414
Persis, 1:407, 2:414-415
Sarah, 2:414-415, 4:204
Sarah (----), 2:415
Hill/Hills
----, 2:417, 4:383
---- (----), 3:124
Abiah, 2:419
Abigail, 2:416, 2:418-419,
2:421, 2:593, 3:77,
3:632
Abigail (Buffam), 3:632
Abigail (Wakeman), 4:387
Abigail (Wheeler), 2:419
Abigail (Wooden), 3:632,
4:638
Adeline (----) Johnson,

Hill/Hills (continued)
Adeline (----) Johnson
  (continued)
  2:419, 3:632, 4:41,, 4:686
Ann, 2:416, 4:582
Ann (----), 2:415
Ann (----) Lunt, 2:418,
  3:131
Catharine (----) Chalker,
  2:417
Catharine (Post) Chalker,
  1:352
Charity, 2:416
Deborah, 2:418
Deborah (----), 3:389
Deborah (Norton), 2:314,
  2:421, 2:593, 3:290
Dorothy, 2:417-418
Dorothy (----), 2:417
Elinor, 1:87
Elinor (----) Munt, 2:420,
  3:257
Elizabeth, 2:308,
  2:416-421, 3:632
Elizabeth (----), 2:416-417,
  2:420
Elizabeth (Chadwick),
  1:351, 2:416
Elizabeth (Clark), 3:632
Elizabeth (Jones), 2:562
Elizabeth (Strong), 2:417,
  4:226
Elizabeth (Williams),
  2:419
Ellen (----), 2:418
Esther, 2:421
Esther (----) Hawley
  Nichols, 3:279
Frances, 1:33, 1:81, 2:416
Frances (----), 2:416-417,
  2:420
Hannah, 1:225, 2:162,
  2:320, 2:416, 2:418-421,
  3:20, 3:107, 3:389,
  3:632, 4:210, 4:375
Hannah (----), 2:320,
  2:415-416, 2:418, 2:593,
  3:389, 3:632
Hannah (----) Mellows,
  2:418, 3:195
Hannah (Bunker), 2:593
Hannah (Grannis), 2:290,
  2:417

Hannah (Hayward), 2:416
Hannah (Henchman),
  2:416
Hannah (Howard), 2:416,
  2:472
Hannah (Smith), 2:418
Hannah (Stowers), 2:415,
  4:220
Helen (Atkinson), 2:418
Jane, 2:415
Jane (Bushnell), 2:417
Joanna, 2:421
Lydia, 2:402, 2:418, 3:632
Lydia (Buffam), 3:632
Margaret (----), 2:416
Margaret (----) Toothacker,
  4:312
Margaret (Toothaker),
  2:418
Margery, 3:232
Martha, 2:338, 2:418-419
Martha (----), 2:419
Martha (Toothaker), 2:418
Mary, 1:241, 2:415-421,
  3:99, 3:632, 4:32
Mary (----), 2:417, 2:420,
  3:632
Mary (Cross), 2:419
Mary (Eaton), 2:97, 2:420,
  3:35
Mary (Frost), 2:210
Mary (Hoyt), 2:418
Mary (Sharswood), 4:61
Mary (Warner) Steele,
  2:420, 4:181, 4:418
Mary (White), 4:512
Mehitable, 2:418
Mercy, 2:416, 2:419
Mercy (Brooks), 2:415
Miriam, 2:372, 3:632,
  3:644
Miriam (----), 3:632, 3:644
Miriam (Gardner), 2:230
Phebe (Leonard), 3:80
Phillis, 2:421
Phillis (Lyman), 2:420,
  3:134
Prudence, 4:85
Rachel (Mason), 2:415,
  3:168
Rebecca, 2:298, 2:306,
  2:418
Rose (Dunster), 2:82-83,

  2:417
Ruth, 1:79, 2:415
Ruth (Brewster) Picket,
  1:245, 2:415, 3:424
Sarah, 2:173, 2:415-417,
  2:419-421, 3:112, 3:389,
  3:632
Sarah (----), 2:415-416,
  2:419, 4:141
Sarah (Bicknall), 2:416
Sarah (Cross), 2:419
Sarah (Long), 2:415, 3:109
Sarah (Paige), 3:332
Sarah (Stone), 2:416,
  4:205
Susan, 3:632
Susanna, 2:420, 3:19,
  3:632, 3:644
Tabitha, 2:416
Thankful, 2:417, 2:419
Thankful (----), 2:417
Thankful (Stow), 4:218
Thomasine, 2:416
Wait, 2:418
Hilliard
---- (Merry), 2:421, 3:200
Abigail, 2:421
Ann, 2:421
Apphia, 2:421
Apphia (----), 2:421
Elizabeth, 2:421, 3:632,
  3:659
Esther, 1:139, 2:421
Esther (----), 2:421
Margaret (----), 2:421,
  4:660
Martha (----), 2:421
Mary, 2:146, 2:421, 2:594,
  4:488
Mary (----), 2:594
Mary (King), 3:24
Mary (Oliver), 2:421
Sarah, 2:421
Sarah (----), 2:421
Hillier/Hiller/Hillyer
Abigail, 2:422
Ann, 2:594
Deborah, 2:422, 4:17
Elizabeth, 2:422, 2:594
Experience (Hall), 2:422
Hannah, 2:422
Hannah (Burr), 1:305,
  2:422

Hillier/Hiller/Hillyer
(continued)
Mary, 1:516, 2:422
Mary (----) Dibble, 2:422
Mary (Case) Alderman,
   1:24, 1:345, 2:422
Mary (Wakefield) Dibble,
   2:46, 4:386
Rose (----), 2:422, 2:487
Sarah, 2:422
Hilman
Lucretia, 2:40
Hilton
----, 2:422, 3:340
Ann, 2:422-423
Ann (Dudley), 2:77, 2:422
Ann (Hilton), 2:423
Catharine (Shapleigh)
   Treworthy, 2:422, 4:330
Elizabeth, 1:494, 2:423,
   2:594
Elizabeth (----), 2:423
Elizabeth (Lord), 2:594
Frances (----) White, 2:423
Hannah, 4:641
Jane, 2:422-423, 3:178
Mary, 2:336, 2:422-424,
   3:159, 3:248, 4:46
Mehitable (Nowell), 1:493,
   2:423, 3:295
Sarah, 2:423, 4:600
Sobriety, 2:422-423
Sobriety (Hilton), 2:423
Hinckley
Abiah, 2:424
Abigail, 2:425
Admire, 2:425
Bathshua, 2:425
Bethia, 2:424
Bethia (Lothrop), 2:424,
   3:122
Bridget (----) Bodfish,
   1:211, 2:424-425
Elizabeth, 2:424-425,
   3:350
Experience, 2:425, 4:505
Hannah, 2:262, 2:424-425
Mary, 2:424-425, 3:488
Mary (----) Goodspeed,
   2:424
Mary (Fitzrandle), 2:170,
   2:425
Mary (Goodspeed), 2:277,

2:425
Mary (Richards), 2:425,
   3:534
Mary (Smith) Glover,
   2:262, 2:425, 4:118,
   4:121
Mary (Stone), 2:424
Mehitable, 1:83, 2:425,
   4:651
Meletiah, 1:475, 2:425
Mercy, 2:424-425
Rachel, 2:424
Reliance, 2:425-426, 4:207
Sarah, 1:92, 1:413,
   2:424-425
Sarah (----), 2:424, 2:487
Sarah (Cobb), 1:413,
   2:424
Sarah (Pope), 2:425
Susanna, 2:424-425, 4:119
Thankful, 2:424-425,
   3:184
Thankful (Trott), 2:424,
   4:332
Hinckson/Hinksman
---- (Walford), 2:426,
   4:392
Elizabeth, 4:368
Elizabeth (Parsons), 2:426,
   3:362
Mary, 2:426
Mary (----), 2:426
Rebecca, 2:594
Hinds
Abigail (Ward), 3:181
Elizabeth, 1:150
Sarah, 1:360
Hine
Alice, 3:632
Elizabeth, 3:632
Hannah (Bristoll), 3:632
Hinman
Annis, 2:426
Elizabeth, 2:426
Elizabeth (Lamb/Lumm),
   2:426
Eunice, 2:426
Hannah, 2:426
Hannah (----), 3:632
Hannah (Coe), 2:426
Hannah (Stiles), 2:426,
   4:194
Mary, 2:426

Mary (Hawkins), 2:426
Mercy, 2:426
Patience, 2:426
Rachel, 2:426
Sarah, 2:426
Sarah (----), 2:426
Wait, 2:426
Hinsdale/Hensdale/Hindsell
Abigail (----), 2:427
Ann, 2:427, 3:5
Ann (----), 2:427
Elizabeth, 2:427, 3:544,
   4:684
Elizabeth (----), 2:46, 2:427
Elizabeth (----) Hawks,
   2:381, 2:427
Experience, 2:427
Martha (Smith), 4:125
Mary, 2:427, 4:70, 4:701
Mary (Hawks), 2:127,
   2:381, 2:427
Mary (Plimpton), 3:632
Mehitable, 2:427
Mehitable (----), 3:573
Mehitable (Johnson),
   2:427
Mehitable (Plympton),
   3:448
Sarah, 2:427, 2:538, 4:684
Sarah (White), 2:411
Sarah (White) Taylor,
   2:427, 4:264, 4:510
Hipdich
Mary (Adams), 1:14, 2:428
Hirst
Elizabeth, 2:428
Elizabeth (Sewell), 2:428,
   4:55
Hannah, 2:428
Jane, 2:428
Mary, 2:428, 3:393
Mary (Grove), 2:320,
   2:428
Hiskett
Sarah (Clark), 1:402,
   2:428
Hitchcock
Abiah, 2:429
Abigail, 2:428, 3:632
Abigail (Merriman), 3:632,
   3:653
Ann, 2:429
Elizabeth, 2:429, 3:633,

Hitchcock (continued)
  Elizabeth (continued)
    3:636
  Elizabeth (----), 3:633,
    4:428
  Elizabeth (Moss), 2:429,
    3:246
  Frances, 4:686
  Hannah, 2:428, 4:111
  Hannah (Chapin), 1:360,
    2:428
  Jerusha, 2:429
  Lucretia (----), 2:429
  Lydia, 2:429
  Lydia (----), 4:428
  Margaret, 2:429
  Mary, 2:428-429, 3:593,
    3:632, 4:699
  Rebecca, 2:429
  Sarah, 2:428, 3:551
  Sarah (Burt) Dorchester,
    1:314, 2:60, 2:429
  Sarah (Mirick), 2:428
Hitchen/Hitchings/Hitchins
  ---- (Hardy/Hardie), 2:355
  Elizabeth, 2:429
  Hannah, 2:378
  Martha, 2:429
  Rebecca, 2:429
  Ruth, 2:429
  Sarah, 2:429
Hoadly/Hoadley/Hodley
  Abigail, 2:430
  Abigail (Farrington), 2:430
  Abigail (Frisbie), 2:209,
    2:430
  Athia, 2:429
  Dinah, 2:430
  Elizabeth, 2:430
  Elizabeth (----), 2:429-430
  Hannah, 2:430
  Jemima, 2:430
  Lydia, 2:430
  Mary, 2:430
  Mary (----), 2:430
  Mercy (Crane), 1:471,
    2:429
  Rachel, 2:429
  Ruth (Bowers) Frisbie,
    1:223, 2:209, 2:430,
    3:622
  Sarah (Bushnell), 2:429
  Thomasine, 2:429

Hoag
  Ebenezer (Emery), 2:430
  Hannah, 2:430
  Judith, 2:430
Hoar
  Abigail, 2:432
  Alice (----), 2:431
  Ann, 3:644
  Bridget, 2:431-432
  Bridget (Lisle), 2:431,
    4:363
  Dorcas, 2:432
  Elizabeth, 2:430, 3:481
  Hannah, 2:432, 3:633
  Hannah (Wright), 2:432,
    3:542
  Joanna, 2:431, 3:238,
    3:500
  Joanna (----), 2:431
  Lydia, 2:430, 2:594
  Margaret, 2:431
  Margery, 2:174, 2:431
  Mary, 2:295, 2:430
  Mary (----) Fox Lee, 3:72
  Mary (Lee), 2:430
  Mary (Stratton), 2:430,
    4:221
  Mercy, 2:430
  Rebecca (----), 3:633
  Sarah, 2:430, 2:594, 4:214
  Sarah (Wilbore), 2:432
Hobart
  ----, 2:434
  ---- (----) Lyford, 2:433
  ---- (Whiting), 2:434
  Abigail, 2:434-435
  Abigail (Burnham)
    Whitman, 4:523
  Ann (----) Lyford, 3:133
  Bathsheba, 2:435, 3:70,
    4:347
  Bethia, 2:435
  Deborah, 2:433-434, 3:92
  Dorothy, 1:237, 2:433,
    4:684
  Elizabeth, 2:432-433,
    2:435, 3:543, 4:339,
    4:574
  Elizabeth (----), 2:433
  Elizabeth (----) Faxon,
    2:149, 2:432
  Elizabeth (Church), 1:513,
    2:432

  Elizabeth (Warren), 2:433
  Elizabeth (Whiting), 4:520,
    4:684
  Ellen (Ibrook), 2:434,
    2:516
  Hannah, 1:271, 1:308,
    2:289, 2:432-436, 2:594,
    3:520
  Hannah (Beal), 1:146
  Hannah (Burr), 1:308,
    2:434
  Hannah (Gold), 2:435,
    2:588
  Hannah (Harris), 2:433
  Jael, 1:230, 2:433-435
  Jane (----), 2:435
  Joanna, 2:433
  Joanna (Quincy), 2:433,
    3:501
  Judith, 2:433
  Lydia, 2:433, 2:435, 3:95
  Martha, 1:136, 2:433
  Mary, 2:432-433
  Mary (----), 2:435
  Mary (----) Stowell, 2:435
  Mary (Allen) Rainsford,
    1:32
  Mary (Eliot), 2:109, 2:432
  Mary (Sunderland)
    Rainsford, 3:503
  Mehitable, 3:52
  Patience (----) Jones, 2:433
  Rebecca, 2:433-435, 3:166
  Rebecca (Ibrook), 2:435,
    2:516
  Rebecca (Sumner),
    4:231-232
  Ruth, 2:433
  Sarah, 1:466, 2:433-434,
    3:147
  Sarah (----), 2:433
  Sarah (Jackson), 2:435,
    2:528
  Sarah (Joyce), 2:433
  Sarah (Wetherill),
    2:433-434, 4:492
  Susanna (Eliot), 2:109,
    2:434
Hobbs
  ---- (Canney), 1:332, 2:436
  Abigail, 2:437, 3:633
  Bethia, 2:437
  Deborah, 2:437

Hobbs (continued)
Deliverance (----), 3:633
Dorcas, 2:436
Esther, 2:436
Esther (Davenport), 2:436
Hannah, 2:436
Jane, 2:436
Joanna, 2:437
Joanna (----), 2:437
Mary, 1:347, 2:436-437,
3:12, 3:22, 3:658
Mary (----), 2:436
Sarah, 2:436-437
Sarah (Colcord), 1:424,
2:436
Sarah (Eastow), 2:94,
2:436, 4:240
Sarah (Estow), 2:127
Sarah (Swett), 2:436,
4:240
Susanna, 2:436
Tabitha, 2:436
Tabitha (----), 2:436
Hobby
Ann, 2:438
Ann (----), 2:438
Elizabeth, 2:437-438
Hannah, 2:437
Hannah (----), 2:437
Judith, 2:438
Martha, 2:437
Mary, 2:437
Mercy, 2:438
Rachel, 2:437
Rebecca, 2:437
Hobson
Ann (Reyner), 2:438,
3:513
Dorcas (Pearson), 2:438
Elizabeth (Northend),
2:221, 2:438, 3:289
Elizabeth (Shipman), 4:87
Mary (----), 2:438, 3:267
Hoddy
Mary (----), 3:1
Mary (Roddam), 2:438
Hodgdon
Ann (Wingate), 4:595
Hodge
Abigail, 2:438
Elizabeth, 2:438
Mary, 2:438
Susanna, 2:438

Susanna (Denslow), 2:438,
2:578
Hodges
Abigail, 2:439
Ann (----), 2:439
Bethia, 3:633
Catharine, 2:439
Charity, 2:439
Dorcas, 2:439
Elizabeth, 2:439, 3:633
Elizabeth (Macy), 2:439,
3:142
Esther, 2:439
Esther (Gallop), 2:223,
2:439
Exercise (Razor), 2:439
Hannah, 1:170, 2:439,
3:633
Joanna, 2:24
Lydia (----) Brown, 1:264
Mary, 1:51, 2:24, 2:439,
3:633, 4:263
Mary (----), 2:440, 2:594
Mary (Andrews), 1:53,
3:443
Mary (Hudson), 2:439
Mary (Pickman), 3:425,
3:633
Sarah, 2:439, 3:230, 3:419,
3:633
Sarah (Phippen), 2:439,
3:419
Tabitha, 3:633
Hodgkin/Hodgkins
Abigail, 2:439, 3:633
Abigail (Hovey), 2:470
Ann, 3:633
Ann (Haynes), 2:439
Elizabeth, 2:439, 3:343,
3:633, 4:575
Elizabeth (Cleverly), 4:684
Experience, 3:633
Grace, 4:257
Grace (Dutch), 3:617
Hannah, 3:633
Hannah (----), 3:633
Martha, 3:633
Mary, 2:439, 3:633
Mary (----), 3:633, 3:639
Mary (Bishop) Johnson,
1:185
Mary (Stockbridge), 3:633
Mercy, 3:633

Patience, 3:633
Sarah, 2:439
Sarah (Cushman), 2:439
Sarah (Talmadge), 2:439
Hodgkinson
Mary, 1:153, 2:440
Hodgman
Catharine (More), 3:633
Elizabeth (----), 2:440
Grace (----) Boutell, 2:440
Mary (----) Morrill, 2:440,
3:234
Hodsden
Esther, 2:440, 4:493
Hodson/Hodgson/Hodshon
Abiah, 2:440
Abigail, 2:440
Abigail (----), 3:633
Abigail (Turner), 2:440
Alice, 2:440
Ann, 2:440, 3:633
Elizabeth (Trowbridge),
2:440, 4:333
Jane (----), 2:440
Mary, 2:440, 3:633
Rachel (Shotten/Shotton),
2:440, 4:89
Sarah, 1:368, 2:440
Hogg
Joan (----), 2:441
Mary, 2:441
Holbrook
----, 2:443
---- (Kingman), 3:27
Abigail, 2:441-443, 3:631,
3:634
Abigail (Craft), 2:441
Abigail (Pierce), 2:442
Agnes (----), 3:633
Alice (----), 2:442
Ann, 2:443
Deborah (Damon), 2:443
Elizabeth, 1:284, 2:337,
2:375, 2:441-443, 3:188,
3:262, 4:153
Elizabeth (----), 2:442-443
Elizabeth (----) Stream,
2:441
Elizabeth (Seaver), 2:441
Elizabeth (Stream), 3:323
Eunice, 2:441-442, 3:127
Experience, 2:441, 2:443
Experience (----), 2:441

Holbrook (continued)
Experience (Leland), 2:443, 3:77
Hannah, 1:140, 2:442-443, 3:427, 3:634
Hannah (Merwin), 3:201
Hannah (Shepard), 2:594
Hopestill, 3:518
Jane, 2:442-443
Jane (----), 2:443
Joanna, 2:443
Joanna (----), 2:443
Lois, 2:441
Lydia (----), 1:34, 2:442
Margaret, 2:441, 3:557
Margaret (----), 2:443
Margery (----), 2:441
Mary, 2:442-443, 3:634, 4:496
Mary (----), 2:442, 3:633
Mary (----) Loring, 2:442
Mary (Cheeny), 2:442
Mary (White), 2:443
Mehitable, 2:441-443
Milicent, 2:443
Miriam, 2:594, 2:598
Miriam (----), 2:441
Patience, 3:77, 3:634
Persis, 2:442-443
Sarah, 2:441, 2:443
Sarah (----), 2:441-442
Sarah (Turner), 2:441, 4:346
Susanna, 2:443, 4:555
Holcomb
---- (----), 2:124
Abigail, 1:187, 2:444
Ann, 2:444
Deborah, 1:183, 2:444
Elizabeth, 1:346, 2:114, 2:444
Hannah, 2:444
Mary, 2:317, 2:444, 2:594
Mary (Bliss), 2:444
Mindwell, 2:444
Ruth, 2:444
Ruth (Sherwood), 2:444
Sarah, 1:346, 2:444, 3:326
Sarah (Eno), 2:124, 2:443
Holden/Houlden
Abigail, 2:444, 2:446
Abigail (----), 2:444
Ann, 2:444, 2:446

Ann (----), 2:446
Barbara, 2:445, 4:538
Bethia (Waterman), 2:445
Catharine, 2:444
Catharine (Green), 2:303, 2:444
Elizabeth, 2:444-446, 3:516, 3:529
Elizabeth (----), 2:444
Frances, 2:444-445, 2:452
Frances (Clark), 1:394, 2:445
Grace, 2:444-445
Grace (Jennison), 2:444
Judith, 2:444
Lydia, 2:446
Margaret, 2:107, 2:445
Martha, 1:225, 2:442, 2:444-445
Martha (Fosdick), 2:185, 2:445
Mary, 1:334, 2:445-446, 4:571
Mary (----), 2:445
Mary (Rutter), 2:444
Mercy, 2:446
Sarah, 2:444-446, 4:160, 4:236
Sarah (Pierce), 2:444
Susan, 2:445
Susanna, 2:300, 2:445-446
Susanna (----), 2:445
Susanna (Shattuck), 2:446
Waite, 2:445
Holder
Ann, 2:446
Content, 2:446
Elizabeth, 2:446
Hope, 2:446
Hope (----), 2:446
Mary, 2:446
Mary (Scott), 2:446, 4:38
Patience, 2:446
Holdridge/Holdred
Abigail, 2:446
Elizabeth, 2:446
Elizabeth (----), 2:446
Isabella (----), 2:446
Lydia (Quimby), 3:500, 3:634
Mary, 2:446, 3:7
Mehitable, 2:446
Mercy, 2:446

Rebecca, 2:446, 3:151
Sarah, 2:446
Holdsworth
Sarah (Rawlins), 2:446, 2:594
Holgate
Magdalen (Dwinell/Dunnell), 2:87
Holgrave/Halgrave
Elizabeth, 2:446
Elizabeth (----), 2:446
Love, 2:446
Lydia (----), 2:446
Martha, 2:446, 3:348
Holland/Hollon
---- (----), 3:23
Abigail, 2:447
Ann (----), 2:447
Ann (Quiddington), 3:499
Bridget, 2:447
Deborah, 2:447
Elizabeth, 2:447
Elizabeth (----), 3:61
Elizabeth (Park), 2:447
Elizabeth (Parke), 3:348
Elizabeth (Shattuck) Goddard Angier, 2:265
Hannah, 2:447
Joanna, 2:447
Judith (----), 2:447
Mary, 2:447
Mary (----), 2:447
Obedience, 1:486, 2:224, 2:447
Relief, 2:68, 2:447, 3:67
Ruth, 2:447
Sarah, 1:163, 2:447, 3:413
Sarah (Hosier), 2:447
Hollard
Catharine (----), 2:447, 4:360
Elizabeth, 2:447
Hannah, 1:107, 2:447, 2:595
Hepzibah, 2:447
Joanna, 2:447
Sarah, 2:447
Holley/Holly
Bethia, 4:451
Elizabeth (----), 2:448
Experience, 2:276
Joanna (----) Downing, 2:580, 2:595

Holley/Holly (continued)
Mary, 2:170
Sarah (Shute), 4:93
Holliday
Abigail, 2:448
Catharine (Hunter), 2:448,
2:502
Mary, 2:448
Sarah, 2:448
Hollidge
Ann (----), 2:448
Holliman/Hollyman/etc
Mary (----) Sweet, 2:448,
4:238
Priscilla, 2:448, 4:420
Renewed, 2:243
Susanna (Fox), 2:448
Susanna (Oxston), 2:448
Hollingworth/etc
----, 2:595, 4:170
Abigail, 1:148, 2:448,
3:634
Abigail (----), 3:634
Elinor (----), 2:448, 3:634
Elinor (Story), 2:595
Elizabeth, 2:448
Elizabeth (Powell), 1:282,
2:448, 3:469
Mary, 2:124, 2:448, 2:595
Susan, 2:448
Susan (----), 2:448
Susanna, 3:634, 4:707
Hollis
----, 3:56
Abigail, 4:523
Elizabeth, 2:449, 3:634
Elizabeth (----), 2:449
Mary, 3:634
Mary (----), 2:449
Mercy, 2:449
Hollister
Abiah, 2:450
Abigail, 2:449-450
Abigail (Treat), 2:449,
4:326
Ann, 2:449
Elizabeth, 2:449, 4:477
Elizabeth (----) Reynolds,
2:449
Elizabeth (----) Williams,
4:559
Elizabeth (Lattimore),
2:449, 3:59

Eunice, 2:449
Jerusha, 2:449
Joanna (Treat), 2:449,
4:326
Mary, 2:449-450, 4:476
Sarah, 1:72, 1:100,
2:449-450
Sarah (Goodrich), 2:275,
2:449
Holloway/Holway
Grace, 3:517
Grace (----), 3:412
Hannah, 2:450
Jane (Brayman), 2:450
Mary, 2:450
Mary (----), 2:450
Rebecca, 2:101
Rose, 3:274
Holman
---- (Brimblecombe), 3:606
Abigail, 2:450-451
Abigail (----), 2:450
Abigail (Rigby), 2:451,
3:541
Ann, 1:320, 2:451
Ann (----), 2:450
Ann (Quincy), 3:500
Deborah, 2:450
Elizabeth, 2:451
Hannah, 2:451, 4:147
Hannah (Turner), 2:451
Margaret, 2:450
Mary, 2:450-451, 3:169
Mary (----), 2:451
Mary/Mercy (----), 2:450
Mehitable, 2:450
Patience, 2:451
Sarah, 2:450-451, 3:356
Sarah (Pitts), 2:450
Seeth, 2:451, 3:577
Susanna (----), 2:450
Winifred (----), 2:451
Holmes/Homes
---- (Walford), 2:452
Abigail, 2:453
Abigail (----), 2:452
Abigail (----) Chesebrough,
1:374
Abigail (Nichols), 2:451
Ann, 4:13
Ann (Rouse), 3:579
Ann (Rowe), 2:452
Bathsheba, 2:2, 2:451

Bethia, 2:453
Catharine (----), 2:453
Charity, 2:453
Consider, 2:454
Deborah, 2:451
Desire, 2:452
Desire (Dotey) Sherman,
2:62, 2:452, 4:85, 4:161
Dorcas, 2:453
Elizabeth, 2:451-454,
3:455, 3:634
Elizabeth (----), 2:454
Elizabeth (Arnold), 1:66,
2:451
Elizabeth (Clap), 1:390,
2:452
Esther, 2:453
Esther (Morse), 2:453,
3:237
Fear (Sturges), 2:453
Frances (Holden), 2:445,
2:452
Hannah, 2:452-453, 4:273
Hannah (Newell), 2:452,
3:271
Hannah (Sampson), 2:453,
4:10
Hannah (Thatcher), 2:452,
4:273
Jane, 3:634
Jane (----), 2:451, 2:453
Lucia/Lucretia (Dudley),
2:454
Lydia, 2:107
Margaret, 2:451
Margaret (Fones), 2:179
Martha, 2:453, 4:303
Mary, 1:271, 2:453-454,
4:302
Mary (Atwood), 1:232,
2:452
Mary (Hobby), 2:437
Mary (Wood), 1:77, 1:232,
2:452, 4:627
Mehitable, 2:452-453
Mercy (Faunce), 2:148,
2:453
Obedience, 2:453
Patience, 2:452-453
Patience (Faunce), 2:148,
2:452
Patience (Topliff), 2:453,
4:313

Holmes/Homes (continued)
Phebe (Blackmore), 1:190
Rachel, 2:12
Rachel (Waterbury), 4:430
Rebecca, 2:454
Rose, 1:196, 2:451
Sarah, 2:452-454, 3:634
Sarah (----), 1:490, 2:452
Sarah (----) Hone, 3:634
Sarah (Wiswall), 4:617
Temperance, 2:453
Thankful, 2:453
Holt
----, 3:174
---- (----) Preston, 2:455,
3:483
Abigail, 3:634
Elizabeth, 2:143,
2:454-455, 3:634
Elizabeth (French), 3:622
Elizabeth (Thomas), 2:454,
4:280
Hannah, 2:143, 2:299
Hannah (Allen), 2:454
Hannah (Bradstreet) Rolfe,
1:235, 2:455, 3:570
Lydia, 3:634
Mary, 2:558, 3:634
Mary (Russell), 2:455
Mercy, 2:60, 2:455
Priscilla, 2:142, 2:455
Rebecca (Beebe), 1:153,
2:454
Rhoda (Chandler), 1:359
Sarah, 3:634
Sarah (----), 2:455, 3:384,
3:634
Sarah (Ballard), 1:109,
2:454
Sarah (Geary), 2:455
Susanna, 3:634
Tabitha, 3:634
Tabitha (Thomas), 3:634
Holton/Holten/Houlton
----, 2:456
Abigail, 2:455
Abigail (Fisher), 2:162,
2:455
Ann (----), 2:455, 4:395
Elizabeth, 1:325, 2:595
Lydia, 2:164
Mary, 1:312, 2:455-456,
3:495

Mary (----), 3:634
Mary (Gilbert) Rossiter,
2:250, 2:455, 3:578
Rachel, 2:455-456, 4:228
Ruth, 1:97, 2:455-456,
3:135, 3:599
Ruth (----), 4:684
Sarah, 2:455-456, 2:595,
3:24, 3:495
Sarah (----), 3:634
Sarah (Ingersoll) Haines,
2:521, 2:593, 2:595
Sarah (Marshfield), 2:456,
3:160
Holyoke
---- (Stebbins), 4:175
Ann, 2:456, 3:497
Editha (----) Day Maynard,
2:456
Editha (Stebbins) Day
Maynard, 2:27
Elizabeth, 2:456, 3:16
Hannah, 2:456, 4:251
Mary, 2:456, 4:350
Mary (Eliot), 2:109, 2:456
Mary (Pynchon), 2:456,
3:498
Prudence (Stockton),
2:456
Sarah, 2:456
Susanna, 2:456, 3:162
Holyroad
Love, 4:707
Homan
Esther (Crason), 3:634
Homer
Margery/Mary (Stevens),
2:457
Mary, 2:457
Mary (----), 2:457
Mary (Burrows), 2:457
Homwood aka Holman
Elizabeth, 2:457
Winifred (----), 2:457
Hone
Sarah (----), 3:634
Hood
Ann, 2:457
Barbara, 2:457
Elizabeth, 3:273
Elizabeth (----), 2:457
Hannah, 2:457
Huldah, 2:457

Joanna (Dwinell/Dunnell),
2:87
Lydia, 2:457
Mary, 2:457
Rebecca, 1:39, 2:457
Sarah, 1:136, 2:457
Sarah (----), 2:457
Hooke
---- (Whalley), 2:458
Eleanor (----) Norton,
2:458
Elizabeth, 2:458
Elizabeth (----), 2:458
Ellen, 2:458
Florence, 1:418
Martha, 2:458
Mary, 2:458
Mary (Maverick) Palsgrave,
2:457, 3:181, 3:339
Susanna, 2:10, 2:40
Hooker, 3:635
----, 1:21, 2:459, 3:416
Abigail, 2:458
Abigail (Standley), 2:458,
4:164
Dorothy, 1:375
Esther, 3:634
Hannah (Weld), 4:458
Joanna, 2:459, 4:76
Mable (Hamlin), 2:344
Mary, 2:459, 3:277, 3:321,
3:432
Mary (----), 1:81, 1:285,
2:458
Mary (Leete), 2:458, 3:75
Mary (Smith) Lord, 2:460,
3:115
Mary (Standley), 2:458,
4:165
Mary (Willet), 2:458,
4:557
Mehitable (Hamlin), 2:344,
2:459
Sarah, 1:285, 2:459
Sarah (Standley), 2:458
Susanna, 2:460
Susanna (----), 2:459
Susanna (Fenn), 2:152
Hooper
Ann (Greenfield), 2:460
Elizabeth, 2:460
Elizabeth (----), 2:460
Hannah, 1:109, 2:460

Hooper (continued)
Margaret, 3:493
Martha, 3:493
Mary, 2:460
Mary (Litchfield), 2:460
Mary (Norman), 2:460
Mary (White), 2:460
Rebecca, 1:108, 2:460
Remember (----), 2:460
Ruth, 2:85, 2:460, 4:388
Sarah, 2:380
Hopcot
Sarah, 3:142
Hopewell
Sarah, 2:595
Hopkins
----, 4:287, 4:493
Abigail, 2:461, 3:198
Abigail (Whipple), 2:463,
4:506
Ann (Yale), 2:461, 4:666
Bethai (Atkins), 2:462
Bethia, 2:461, 4:180,
4:198-199
Catharine (Wheldon),
2:461, 4:504
Constance, 2:462, 4:138
Damaris, 1:446, 2:462
Deborah, 1:448, 2:461-462,
3:542
Dorcas, 2:462
Dorcas (Bronson), 1:280,
2:462
Elizabeth, 2:461-462,
4:682
Elizabeth (----), 2:462
Elizabeth (Arnold), 1:67,
2:462
Frances, 1:163
Hannah, 2:284, 2:462-463
Hannah (----), 2:463
Hannah (Mumford), 3:253
Hannah (Strong), 4:227
Hannah (Turner), 2:462,
4:347-348
Jane (----), 2:461, 4:411
Judah, 2:462
Lydia, 2:461
Mary, 2:461-463, 3:89,
4:48-49, 4:132
Mary (----), 2:462, 3:89,
4:516
Mary (Butler), 1:321

Mary (Cole), 1:426, 2:461
Mary (Judd), 2:575
Mary (Merrick), 2:462,
3:198
Mary (Smith), 2:462
Phebe, 2:462
Ruth, 2:461-462
Ruth (Long), 2:595
Ruth (Wilkinson), 2:463,
4:552
Susanna (Andrews), 1:55
Thankful, 2:461
Wait, 2:462
Hopkinson
---- (Swan), 2:463, 4:237
Elinor, 4:639
Elizabeth (Dresser), 2:72
Elizabeth (Pearson), 3:378,
3:635
Sarah (Coleman), 2:463
Sarah (Wallingford), 2:463
Sarah (Wheeler) Spofford,
4:151
Hoppin
Deliverance, 2:463
Hannah, 2:463
Hannah (Makepeace),
2:463, 3:144
Mabel (----) Shippie, 2:595
Mabel (Mitchell) Shippey,
4:88
Opportunity, 2:463, 3:131
Opportunity (----), 3:144
Sarah, 2:463
Susanna (Jacklin), 2:595
Hopson - see also Hobson
Abigail, 2:463
Dorothy (Leete), 2:464
Dorothy (Lord), 2:464
Elizabeth, 2:463-464
Elizabeth (Alling), 1:41,
2:464
Elizabeth (Shipman),
2:463
Mary (Fowler), 2:464
Sarah, 2:464
Sarah (----), 2:463
Horn/Horne
Ann, 2:464
Ann (----), 2:464
Elizabeth, 2:464
Elizabeth (----), 2:464,
4:389

Jehoadan, 2:464
Margaret, 2:464
Mary, 2:387, 2:464, 3:635
Mary (Clark), 3:635
Naomi (----), 3:635
Rebecca (----), 1:108
Rebecca (----) Stevens,
3:635
Recompense, 2:464
Hornden/Horndall
Mary, 2:464
Horrocks
Elizabeth, 1:462
Horsey
Elizabeth (Saltonstall), 4:9
Horsley
Martha (Parker), 2:465,
3:352
Hortman
Catharine (----), 2:465
Horton
Mary, 2:465
Mary (----), 2:465
Hosford
Deborah (Brown), 1:274
Esther, 2:465
Jane (----) Fowkes, 2:192,
2:465
Mary, 2:465
Philippa (Thrall), 2:465,
4:293
Phillis (Thrall), 4:323
Sarah, 2:465, 4:264
Susanna, 3:307
Hosier
Sarah, 2:447
Ursula (----) Streeter, 2:466,
3:555, 4:223
Hoskins/Haskins
Ann, 2:466, 2:595
Ann (----), 3:635
Constant, 2:595
Deborah, 2:595
Deborah (Denslow), 2:39,
2:466
Elizabeth, 2:466, 2:595,
4:304
Elizabeth (Cleverly), 2:466
Elizabeth (Gaylord) Birge,
1:183, 2:238, 2:466
Grace, 2:466
Grace (----), 2:372
Hannah, 2:595

Hoskins/Haskins (continued)
Hannah (Hall), 2:592
Isabel, 2:466
Isabel (Brown), 2:466
Jane, 2:466, 2:595
Jane (Fluster), 2:592
Mabel, 2:595
Mary, 1:413, 2:466
Mary (Austin), 2:592
Mary (Gillett), 2:595
Patience (Soule), 4:141
Rebecca, 1:252, 2:466, 3:7
Rebecca (Brooks), 2:592
Ruth (----) Peck, 3:382,
   3:635
Sarah, 2:95, 2:102, 2:466,
   2:595
Sarah (Casewell), 1:348,
   2:466
Hosmer
---- (Bushnell), 2:467
Abigail, 2:467, 4:630
Abigail (Wood), 2:467,
   4:628, 4:630
Alice (----), 2:466
Ann, 2:466
Ann (----), 2:466
Catharine (----) Wilton,
   2:467, 4:590
Clemence, 2:467, 2:500
Deborah, 2:467
Dorothy, 2:467
Ellen (----), 2:467
Esther, 1:284, 2:467,
   3:440
Hannah, 2:393, 2:466-467,
   4:554
Mary, 2:466-467, 4:135
Mary (----), 2:466
Sarah (White), 2:467
Hotchkiss
Abigail, 2:467, 3:635
Ann, 3:635
Desire, 3:635
Dorcas, 3:635
Elizabeth, 3:635, 4:690
Elizabeth (Peck), 3:635,
   3:659
Esther, 3:635
Esther (----), 3:635
Esther (Sperry), 3:635,
   4:150
Hannah, 3:635

Hannah (----), 3:635
Jemima, 3:635
Lydia, 3:635
Martha, 1:262, 3:635
Mary, 2:439, 2:467, 3:635
Mary (Pardee), 2:467,
   3:345
Priscilla, 3:635
Rebecca, 3:635
Sarah, 2:439, 2:467, 3:635
Sarah (Talmage), 2:439,
   2:467, 4:252
Sarah (Wilmot), 3:635,
   4:581
Houchin/Houtchin/etc
Alce, 2:468
Elizabeth, 1:31, 2:123,
   2:467-468
Esther, 2:468, 4:504
Esther (----), 2:467
Mary, 2:304, 2:467-468
Mehitable, 2:467
Rachel, 1:29, 2:468
Rachel (----), 2:468
Sarah, 2:467
Hough/Haugh
Abiah, 2:63, 2:469
Abigail, 2:469
Ann, 2:468-469
Ann (Lothrop), 2:469,
   3:121
Ann (Rainsford), 2:468,
   3:502
Deborah, 2:469
Elizabeth, 2:468
Elizabeth (----), 2:468
Hannah, 1:213, 2:469
Mary, 2:468
Mary (Bates), 1:139, 2:469
Mercy (Winthrop), 4:608
Priscilla, 4:608
Rebecca, 2:468
Sarah, 1:336, 2:468-469,
   4:23
Sarah (Caulkins), 1:349,
   2:469
Sarah (Post), 2:468
Sarah (Symmes), 1:257,
   2:468, 4:244
Susanna, 2:469
Susanna (----), 2:468
Susanna (Wrotham), 2:468,
   4:661

Houghton
Abigail, 2:469
Abigail (Barron), 1:126
Beatrice, 2:469
Beatrice (----), 2:469
Experience, 1:389, 2:469
Isabel, 2:469
Jane (----), 2:469
Mary, 2:469
Mary (----), 2:469
Mercy, 2:469
Sarah, 2:469
House
Abigail, 1:436
America, 3:635
Elizabeth, 2:469, 4:233
Elizabeth (Hammond),
   2:347, 2:470
Elizabeth (Peck), 3:383
Hannah, 1:508
Mary (----), 3:635
Rebecca, 2:470
Rebecca (Nichols), 2:470,
   3:282
Sarah, 2:469-470
Sarah (Biddle), 1:174
Housing
Sarah (----), 2:470
Sarah (Cloyes), 1:411
Hovey
Abigail, 2:470-471
Deborah (Barlow), 1:502
Dorcas, 2:470-471
Dorcas (Ivory), 2:470
Elizabeth, 2:470
Esther, 2:471, 4:263
Esther (Treadwell), 2:470,
   4:325
Hannah, 2:470-471
Hannah (Pratt), 2:470,
   3:475
Joanna, 2:471
Mary, 2:470
Mary (----), 2:471
Mary (Dwinell/Dunnell),
   2:87
Mary (Marrett), 2:470,
   3:153, 3:355
Mercy, 2:470
Mercy (----) Clark
   Goodhue, 2:273
Miriam, 2:471
Priscilla, 2:470

Hovey (continued)
Rachel, 2:471
Rebecca (Andrews), 1:55,
2:470
Rebecca (Dane), 2:6
Sarah, 2:470-471
Sarah (Cook), 2:471
Sarah (Fuller), 2:470
Susanna, 2:470
Howard
----, 2:472
Abiel, 2:472
Abigail, 2:472-473
Abigail (----)
Diman/Dymond/Diamond,
2:50
Abigail (Newberry), 3:269
Amy, 2:472
Ann, 2:473
Ann (----), 2:575
Ann (Brenton), 1:242
Ann (Dixey), 3:616, 3:636
Bethia, 2:471-472, 3:202
Deborah, 2:473
Deborah (----), 4:533
Deborah (Pitts), 2:471,
3:442
Elizabeth, 2:176,
2:471-473
Elizabeth (----), 2:472
Elizabeth (----) Sweetser,
2:472
Elizabeth (Lee), 2:472,
3:73
Elizabeth (Washburn),
2:471, 4:429
Frances, 2:66
Hannah, 2:416, 2:471-473,
3:217, 3:636, 4:18
Hannah (Hawkins), 2:383,
2:471
Isabel (----), 2:473
Jane, 2:471
Kezia, 2:472
Lydia, 2:471
Lydia (Kilborne), 3:20,
3:306
Martha, 2:471-473
Martha (----), 2:471, 2:473
Martha (Hayward), 2:394,
2:471
Mary, 1:135, 1:416, 2:137,
2:471-473, 2:561, 3:636,

4:456
Mary (----), 2:472
Mary (----) Welcome,
4:456
Mary (Gould), 1:510
Mary (Keith), 2:471, 3:4
Mary (Wellman), 2:473,
3:231, 4:481
Mercy, 2:471, 2:473
Rebecca, 4:148
Rebecca (Lippit), 1:288,
2:472, 3:97
Rose, 3:596
Ruth (Jones), 2:473, 3:640
Sarah, 2:239, 2:471-473,
3:327, 3:636, 4:202
Sarah (----), 2:473
Sarah (Dean), 2:472
Sarah (Latham), 2:472
Sarah (Parker), 2:472
Sarah (Stone), 2:471
Sarah (Willard), 2:472,
4:555
Silence, 2:471
Susanna, 2:471-472
Susanna (Keith), 3:4
Susanna (Wilkinson),
2:472
Temperance, 2:472
Howd
Elizabeth (----), 2:473
Elizabeth (Hitchcock),
3:633, 3:636
Hannah (----), 2:181
Howe/How
---- (----), 2:474
---- (Curtis), 4:680
Abigail, 2:473-475, 3:606,
3:636
Abigail (Mixer), 3:223
Ann, 2:474, 4:205
Ann (----), 3:636
Bathsheba, 2:55, 2:475,
3:616
Bathsheba (How), 2:475
Bethia, 2:475, 3:636
Bethia/Bathsheba, 3:616
Bethia/Bathshua, 4:684
Deborah, 2:473-475
Deborah (Howe), 2:475
Dorothy, 2:476
Elizabeth, 1:252,
2:473-476, 3:14, 3:349,

3:491, 3:521, 3:636,
4:684
Elizabeth (----), 2:474,
2:476, 3:261, 3:655
Elizabeth (Binney), 2:476
Elizabeth (Bunn), 1:299
Elizabeth (Dane), 2:6,
2:474-475
Elizabeth (Jackson), 2:475,
2:532
Elizabeth (Kerley), 2:474
Elizabeth (Morse), 2:571
Elizabeth (Woolson),
4:649
Esther, 2:473, 3:167,
3:636, 4:332
Esther (----), 4:685
Frances (Marshall), 3:158
Frances (Marshall) Willey,
2:476
Frances (Woods), 2:475
Hannah, 2:473-476, 2:595
Hannah (Howe), 2:474
Hannah (Ward), 2:473
Lydia, 2:476, 2:595
Margaret (----), 1:299,
2:474
Martha, 2:474, 2:476,
4:397
Martha (Bent), 1:169,
2:476
Mary, 1:223, 2:144,
2:473-476, 2:595, 3:636,
4:359
Mary (----), 2:474-476
Mary (Bellamy), 1:160
Mary (Haynes), 2:476
Mary (Sumner), 2:476,
4:232
Prudence, 2:476
Rebecca, 1:120, 2:473-474
Ruth, 2:476, 2:595
Sarah, 1:224, 1:249,
2:473-475, 3:39, 4:221,
4:295, 4:351, 4:413
Sarah (----), 2:476
Sarah (Foote/Foot) Curtis,
2:181
Sarah (Gilbert), 3:636
Sarah (Leavitt) Clap, 1:390,
3:70
Sarah (Peabody), 3:375
Sarah (Prence), 3:477

Howe/How (continued)
  Sufferance, 2:474, 4:324
  Susanna (----), 2:475
  Tabitha, 2:476
  Thankful, 2:475
  Zeruiah, 2:474
Howell
  ----, 2:478
  ---- (Fordham), 2:184
  ---- (Wakeman), 4:388
  Abiah, 2:477
  Abigail, 2:477
  Abigail (White), 2:476, 4:510
  Ann (James), 2:476
  Catharine (Lee), 3:73, 3:172, 4:56
  Deborah, 2:477
  Dorothy, 2:478
  Elinor, 2:477
  Elizabeth, 2:226, 2:476-477
  Elizabeth (Gardiner), 2:226, 2:476
  Elizabeth (Halsey), 2:341, 2:478
  Eunice, 2:477-478
  Hannah, 2:477-478
  Hannah (----), 2:478
  Hannah (Rayner), 2:476, 3:515
  Jerusha, 2:477
  Martha, 2:477
  Martha (White), 2:477, 4:510
  Mary, 2:477
  Mary (----) Taylor, 2:477
  Mary (Bowles), 2:477
  Mary (Bryan) Maltby, 1:282
  Mary (Fordham), 2:477
  Mary (Halsey), 2:477
  Mehitable, 2:477
  Penelope, 2:477
  Phebe, 2:477
  Prudence, 2:477
  Sarah, 2:477
  Sarah (Judson), 2:477, 2:576
  Sarah (Sayre), 2:477
  Susanna, 2:477-478
  Sybil, 2:477
  Thomasine, 2:477

Howen
  Elizabeth (----), 2:478
Howes
  Dorcas (Joyce), 2:573
  Elizabeth, 1:90, 2:478, 3:198
  Elizabeth (Mayo), 2:478, 3:187
  Elizabeth (Paddock), 2:478
  Hannah, 2:478
  Lydia (Joyce), 2:573
  Mary, 1:91, 2:478
  Mary (----), 2:478
  Mary (Matthews), 2:478
  Phebe, 2:263
  Rebecca, 2:478
  Sarah, 2:478
  Sarah (Bangs), 1:111, 2:478
  Sarah (Prince), 2:478
  Thankful, 3:210
Howkins
  Ruth, 4:700
Howland
  Abigail, 2:479-480
  Abigail (----), 2:480
  Ann, 2:480
  Bethia, 2:479
  Bethia (Thacher), 2:479, 4:271
  Deborah, 2:478, 4:121
  Desire, 2:281, 2:479
  Elizabeth, 1:312, 2:47, 2:410, 2:478-480, 3:125
  .Elizabeth (Prence), 3:477
  Elizabeth (Prince), 2:479
  Elizabeth (Southworth), 2:480, 4:143
  Elizabeth (Tilley), 1:343, 2:479, 4:303
  Elizabeth (Vaughan), 2:479
  Experience, 2:479-480
  Hannah, 2:480
  Hope, 1:380, 2:480
  Judah, 2:479
  Lydia, 1:268, 2:480, 2:542
  Margaret (----) Read, 2:478
  Martha, 2:4, 2:478
  Mary, 1:33, 1:43, 2:478-480, 4:573
  Mary (----), 2:479
  Mary (Lee), 2:480, 3:72

  Mercy, 2:480
  Patience (Stafford), 4:160
  Ruth, 1:492, 2:480
  Sarah, 2:39, 2:479-480
Howlett
  Alice (French), 2:480
  Rebecca (----), 2:480
  Sarah, 1:483, 2:480
  Susanna (----), 2:480
  Susanna (Hudson), 3:394, 3:636-637
Howse
  Elizabeth, 3:338
Hoyt
  Abigail, 2:480-482
  Abigail (----), 3:570
  Abigail (----) Pomeroy, 2:480
  Abigail (Cook) Pomeroy, 1:449, 3:451
  Ann, 2:482
  Deborah, 2:481
  Deliverance, 2:482
  Dorothy, 2:481-482, 3:122
  Dorothy (Colby), 2:482
  Dorothy (Worthen), 2:481
  Elizabeth, 2:481-482
  Elizabeth (----), 2:481
  Frances, 1:424, 2:481
  Frances (----), 2:481
  Grace, 2:481
  Hannah, 2:482, 3:636
  Hannah (Weed), 4:451
  Hope/Hopestill, 2:482
  Judith, 2:481
  Lydia, 2:481
  Margaret, 2:481
  Martha, 2:482
  Martha (Stevens), 2:482
  Mary, 1:130, 1:481, 2:418, 2:480-482
  Mary (----), 2:480, 3:636
  Mary (Barnes), 1:123, 2:481
  Mary (Bell), 1:159
  Mary (Brown), 2:482
  Mary (Currier), 2:482
  Mary (Lindall), 2:481, 3:95
  Mary (Wells), 2:480
  Mehitable, 2:481
  Mercy, 3:636
  Miriam, 2:482
  Naomi, 2:481, 3:649,

Hoyt (continued)
Naomi (continued)
4:684
Rachel, 2:481
Sarah, 2:480-481
Sarah (Pond), 2:481, 3:453
Sarah (Wells), 2:480
Sarah (Wilson), 2:480
Susanna, 2:482
Susanna (Joyce), 2:481
Hubbard
— (Miriam), 2:484
Abigail, 2:483, 2:485-486,
4:150
Agnes (Spencer)
Humphrey, 2:497, 4:149
Alice (----), 2:482
Ann, 2:483-484
Ann (Leverett), 2:484,
3:83
Ann (Warner), 2:484
Bethia, 1:398, 2:485
Comfort, 2:485
Elizabeth, 1:185,
2:483-485, 3:292, 4:528,
4:684, 4:688
Elizabeth (----), 2:482,
2:486
Elizabeth (Clark), 1:396,
2:485, 3:172
Elizabeth (Jordan), 2:483
Elizabeth (Watts), 2:483,
4:439
Esther, 2:483, 2:485
Esther (Rice), 2:483, 3:531
Hannah, 2:98, 2:482-485,
3:196
Hannah (Ives), 2:484,
2:525
Hannah (Rice), 3:531
Jane, 2:484
Jane (----), 2:484
Jane (Latham), 2:484, 3:58,
4:563
Jemima, 2:485
Judith (----), 2:486
Kezia, 2:485
Lydia, 2:484
Margaret, 2:483-484,
2:486-487, 3:498, 3:560,
4:39
Margaret (Allen), 2:485
Margaret (Rogers), 2:486,

3:564
Martha, 2:133, 2:485-486,
4:536
Martha (Allen), 1:37
Martha (Ayer), 2:485
Martha (Cornwell), 2:485
Mary, 2:193, 2:483-486,
3:55, 3:507, 3:590, 4:32
Mary (----), 2:335, 2:483,
2:486
Mary (----) Pearce, 2:487
Mary (Brown), 4:676
Mary (Clark), 2:483
Mary (Earle), 2:485
Mary (Foster), 2:485
Mehitable, 2:483
Mehitable (Russell), 3:589
Mercy, 1:214, 2:484
Naomi, 2:485
Rachel, 2:482-485, 3:56
Rebecca, 2:483
Rebecca (----), 2:484
Ruth, 1:301, 2:485
Sarah, 1:222, 1:356, 1:463,
2:482-486
Sarah (----), 2:344, 2:484
Sarah (Aldis), 1:24
Sarah (Bradstreet), 1:236,
2:485, 4:413
Sarah (Cornwell), 1:459,
2:483
Sarah (Kirby), 2:485, 3:30
Sarah (Winship), 2:484
Thankful, 2:485
Tracy (----), 3:636
Hucking
---- (----) Tilley, 4:302
Huckins/Huckens
Elizabeth, 2:487
Experience, 2:487
Hannah, 2:281, 2:487
Hannah (Chipman), 1:380,
2:487
Hope, 1:413, 2:487
Hope (Chipman), 1:380,
2:487
Lydia, 2:487
Mary, 2:487, 4:211
Mary (Wells), 2:487
Rose (----) Hillier, 2:422,
2:487
Sarah, 2:487
Sarah (----) Hinckley,

2:487
Sarah (Pope) Hinckley,
2:425
Huddlestone
Catharine (----), 2:487
Hudson
—, 2:488
Abigail, 2:488-489, 3:604,
3:644, 4:701
Abigail (----), 2:488
Abigail (Shore), 2:489,
4:88
Abigail (Turner), 4:347
Ann, 2:488
Ann (----), 2:488-489
Ann (Rogers), 2:488,
3:561
Bethia, 2:488
Deborah, 2:488
Elizabeth, 2:488-489,
4:438
Elizabeth (----), 2:488
Elizabeth (Alford), 1:27,
2:489
Hannah, 1:473, 2:488-489,
3:83, 3:532, 4:346
Joanna, 2:488
Joanna (----), 2:488
Lydia, 2:146, 2:488
Mary, 1:469, 2:439, 2:488
Mary (----), 2:488-489
Mary (----) Fownell, 2:195,
2:596
Mary (Maynard), 2:488,
3:186
Mary (Orcutt), 3:315
Rebecca, 1:108
Rebecca (Brown), 1:277,
2:488
Rebecca (Rugg), 3:585
Rhoda, 2:488
Sarah, 2:101, 2:488
Sarah (----), 2:489
Sarah (Wickham), 4:538
Susan (----), 2:489
Susanna, 2:488, 3:394,
3:636
Huested/Husted
Angel, 2:490
Ann, 2:355, 2:490
Elizabeth, 2:490
Elizabeth (----), 2:490
Mary (Lockwood), 2:490,

Huested/Husted (continued)
Mary (Lockwood)
(continued)
3:105
Rebecca (----), 2:490
Huet/Huitt/Hewett
----, 1:311
---- (----), 3:512
Bridget, 2:490
Content, 2:490
Elizabeth, 1:145, 2:490
Elizabeth (Foster), 2:490
Hannah, 2:490
Hannah (----), 4:183
Hannah (Palmer), 2:491,
3:342
Isabel (----), 2:490
Jael, 2:490
Lydia, 2:490, 4:124
Lydia (Uttley), 2:491,
4:364
Martha (Winter), 2:490,
4:605
Mary, 2:490, 4:228
Mary (----) Cutler, 1:493
Mary (Fanning), 2:140,
2:490
Mercy, 2:490
Ruth, 2:490
Sarah, 2:490
Susanna, 2:490, 3:51
Huggins
Bridget, 2:491, 4:449
Bridget (----), 1:410, 2:491
Experience (Jones), 2:491
Hannah, 2:491, 4:648
Hannah (Batchby), 2:491
Margaret, 2:491
Sarah, 2:491
Sarah (----), 2:491
Susan, 2:491
Hughes - see also Hewes
Elizabeth, 2:491
Elizabeth (----), 2:491
Elizabeth (Grafton), 2:289
Martha, 1:273
Mary (----), 2:491, 4:210
Mary (Dowd), 2:64
Rachel, 3:637
Rebecca, 1:222
Hulbert/Hulburd
---- (----) Allen, 1:35
Ann, 2:491

Ann (----) Allen, 2:491-492
Hepzibah, 2:491
Ruth
(Salmon/Sammon/etc),
4:6
Sarah, 2:491
Hull
----, 2:385
---- (----), 1:144
---- (Hyland), 2:516
Abigail, 1:481
Agnes (----), 2:494
Blanch (----), 2:400
Catharine (----), 2:492
Deborah (Beers), 1:154,
2:495
Dodavah, 2:494
Elinor (Newman), 2:492
Elizabeth, 2:46, 2:238,
2:397, 2:492-494, 3:637
Elizabeth (----) Storer,
2:495, 4:210
Elizabeth (Bemis), 2:494
Elizabeth (Burr), 1:306
Elizabeth (Greene), 2:301
Elizabeth (Loomis), 3:112
Hannah, 1:200, 2:61,
2:492-495, 3:637, 4:55
Hannah (Baldwin), 1:103,
2:493
Hannah (Ferniside), 2:154,
2:494
Hannah (Prindle), 2:494
Hannah (Townsend),
2:495, 4:320, 4:440-441
Joanna, 1:312, 2:494
Judith (----) Quincy Paine,
2:495, 3:334, 3:500
Judith (Quincy), 2:493,
3:500
Margaret (----) Goodridge,
2:276, 2:493
Martha, 2:492, 2:494,
3:637
Mary, 2:292, 2:492-495,
3:439, 3:637, 3:639
Mary (Fernside), 2:492
Mary (Merwin), 3:201
Mary (Nichols), 2:494,
3:279
Mary (Sanford), 4:14
Mary (Spencer), 2:493,
3:421, 4:148

Mehitable (Smead), 2:493,
3:285
Mercy (Jacobs), 3:637,
3:639
Naomi, 1:305, 2:494
Rebecca, 2:492, 2:494
Sarah, 2:492, 2:494-495,
3:254, 3:637, 4:97,
4:678, 4:692
Sarah (----) Phippen, 2:492,
3:418
Sarah (Jones), 2:492
Sarah (Sanford), 4:14
Hulton
Dorothy, 2:495
Martha (----), 2:495
Hum
Priscilla (Kitchen), 3:644
Humfrey
----, 3:325
Ann, 2:496, 3:344
Dorcas, 2:496
Lydia, 2:496
Sarah, 1:304, 2:496
Susan (Clinton), 2:496
Hummerston
Abigail, 4:684
Elizabeth, 4:685
Elizabeth (Sanford), 4:685
Esther (----) Howe, 4:685
Hannah, 4:685
Hannah (Johnson),
4:685-686
Joan (----), 4:688-689
Joan (Walker), 2:496,
4:684
Lydia, 4:684
Mary, 4:684-685
Sarah, 4:684
Sarah (Tuttle), 4:684,
4:711
Silence, 4:685
Humphrey/Humphries/etc
---- (Lane), 2:497
Abigail, 2:289, 2:316,
2:497
Agnes (Spencer), 2:497,
4:149
Ann, 2:103, 3:259
Elizabeth, 2:497
Elizabeth (----), 2:497
Elizabeth (Baker), 2:496
Frances (----), 2:497

Humphrey/Humphries/etc
(continued)
Hannah, 2:497
Hannah (----) Blake, 2:496
Hannah (Lane), 3:52
Jane (----) Weeks, 2:497
Martha, 2:497
Martha (----), 2:497
Mary, 1:345, 2:380, 2:497,
3:626
Mary (----), 2:497
Mary (Tuller), 4:342
Patience (Atherton), 1:73,
2:496
Priscilla (Grant), 2:292,
2:497
Ruth, 2:497
Sarah, 2:497
Susanna, 2:497, 4:513
Hungerford
---- (----), 4:149
Hannah, 2:498
Hannah (Willey), 1:507,
2:498
Mary, 1:442
Sarah, 1:442, 2:498
Hunking/Hunkins
---- (Lee), 3:71
Agnes, 2:498
Agnes (----), 2:498
Ann (----), 2:498
Mary, 2:498
Sarah, 2:498
Hunlock/Hunloke
Elizabeth, 2:498, 4:587
Joanna, 2:498
Joanna (Sendall), 2:498,
4:51
Margaret, 2:498
Margaret (----), 2:498
Martha, 2:498
Mary, 2:498
Sarah, 2:498
Hunn
Ann (----), 2:499, 3:417
Sarah, 2:499
Sarah (----), 2:499
Hunnewell
Elizabeth (Harris), 2:360,
2:499
Sarah (Adams), 1:14,
2:499

Hunt
Abigail, 2:499
Ann, 1:460, 2:501-502,
3:415
Ann (----), 2:499
Ann (Richards), 3:534
Ann/Ellen, 4:53
Clemence, 2:500
Clemence (----), 4:120
Clemence (Hosmer), 2:467,
2:500
Dorothy (----), 3:398
Ebbet/Ebbot (----), 2:500
Elizabeth, 1:121, 1:172,
1:192, 2:142, 2:500-502,
2:504, 4:556
Elizabeth (----), 1:121,
2:501-502
Elizabeth (Jessop), 2:597
Esther, 2:499
Hannah, 1:172, 2:499-500,
2:502, 4:508, 4:655
Hannah (Clark), 2:499
Jane (----), 4:358
Joanna, 2:501
Joanna (----), 2:501
Joanna (Alcock), 3:637
Judith (----), 2:501
Margaret, 1:336, 2:501,
3:176
Margaret (----), 2:501
Margaret (Keith), 3:4
Martha, 2:500-501
Martha (Neighbors), 2:500,
3:267
Martha (Williams), 2:501
Mary, 2:500-502, 2:520,
3:76, 3:268, 4:69, 4:449
Mary (----), 2:501-502
Mary (Bradford), 1:232
Mary (Glass), 2:260
Mary (Paine), 2:500, 3:336
Mary (Stone), 2:195, 2:500,
4:205
Mary (Webster), 4:449
Mehitable (----), 2:500
Mercy (----) Brigham Rice,
3:528
Mercy (Hurd) Brigham
Rice, 1:252, 2:502
Naomi, 2:499, 3:64
Priscilla, 2:501
Rebecca (----), 1:436

Rebecca (Paine), 2:501,
3:335, 3:384
Ruth (Quincy), 2:500,
3:501
Sarah, 2:499-501
Sarah (----), 2:502
Sarah (Barker), 2:500,
3:25
Sarah (Betts), 1:173
Tabitha, 2:501
Hunter
Abilene, 2:502
Alice, 4:675, 4:685
Catharine, 2:448, 2:502
Christina, 2:502
Cicely (----), 2:502
Elizabeth, 2:502
Hannah, 2:502
Mary, 2:502
Mary (----), 2:502
Mary (Carter), 1:341,
1:466, 2:502
Priscilla, 2:502, 3:13
Priscilla (----), 2:213, 2:502
Rebecca, 4:675, 4:685
Rebecca (Bearce), 1:149,
2:502
Rebecca (Bessey), 4:675
Sarah, 2:65, 2:502
Hunting
----, 2:503
Ann, 2:503, 3:410
Catharine, 2:503, 2:596
Elizabeth, 2:503
Elizabeth (Paine), 3:336
Elizabeth (Payne), 2:503
Esther, 2:164, 2:503
Esther (Seaborn), 2:503
Hannah, 2:503
Hannah (----), 2:503
Hannah (Hackburne),
2:329, 2:503
Margaret, 2:503, 4:416
Mary, 2:503, 2:539
Mercy, 2:503
Rebecca, 2:503
Rebecca (Woodward),
4:645
Susanna, 3:532
Huntington
---- (Gager), 2:221
Ann, 2:503
Elizabeth, 2:504

Huntington (continued)
Elizabeth (Hunt), 2:504
Hannah, 1:359, 2:504
Hannah (Crane), 1:471,
2:504
Joan (----), 2:504
Judith, 2:504
Judith (----) Brewster,
2:504
Lydia, 2:503
Margaret (----), 2:503,
4:214
Mary, 2:269, 2:504
Mary (----), 2:504
Mary (Clark), 1:395
Rebecca (Adgate), 1:18,
2:504
Ruth, 2:503-504, 4:162
Ruth (Rockwell), 2:503,
3:558
Sarah, 2:504
Sarah (Adgate), 1:18,
2:504
Sarah (Clark), 2:504
Susanna, 2:65, 2:318,
2:503
Huntley
Abigail (----) Comstock,
1:440
Abigail (Comstock), 2:505
Alice, 2:505
Elizabeth, 2:505, 3:87
Jane (----), 2:504
Mary, 2:505
Mary (----), 2:505
Mary (Barnes), 2:505
Sarah, 2:505
Hurd
Abigail, 2:505, 3:190
Ann, 2:505
Ann (----) Judson, 2:505,
2:576
Ann (Willson), 2:505
Elizabeth, 2:505
Elizabeth (----), 2:505
Esther, 2:505
Hannah, 2:505
Hannah (----), 2:505
Joanna (Alcock), 3:596
Martha, 2:505
Mary, 2:505, 3:601, 3:637
Mary (----), 2:505
Mehitable, 2:505

Mercy, 1:252, 2:502
Ruth, 2:505
Sarah, 2:505
Sarah (----), 2:505, 3:601
Sarah (Kimberly), 3:637,
3:644
Sarah (Thompson), 2:505,
3:637, 4:285, 4:287
Hurlbut/Hulbert
Ann (----) Allen, 2:506
Jemima, 2:506
Jerusha, 2:506
Margaret, 2:506
Mary, 2:506
Mary (----), 2:506
Mary (Deming), 2:35,
2:505
Mehitable, 2:506
Mercy, 3:637
Phebe, 2:506
Rebecca, 2:506
Ruth (Salmon), 4:6
Sarah, 2:506
Sarah (----), 2:506
Hurry
Abigail, 2:506
Hannah, 2:506
Hannah (----), 2:506
Hannah (Call), 2:596
Hannah (Hett), 2:593,
2:596
Rachel, 2:506
Rebecca, 2:506
Sarah, 2:506
Temperance, 1:511, 2:506
Hurst
Abigail (Thompson) Curtis,
3:637
Alice (----), 2:506
Catharine (----), 2:506
Catharine (Thurston),
2:507
Elizabeth, 2:507
Hannah, 2:506-507
Mary, 2:506
Patience, 1:413, 2:506
Sarah, 2:507, 4:588
Huse
Abigail (Thompson) Curtis,
3:613, 4:85, 4:710
Amy, 2:507
Ann, 2:507
Ann (Russell), 2:507

Ebenezer, 2:507
Elinor (----), 2:507
Hannah, 2:507
Hannah (----), 2:507
Judith (----), 2:507
Mary, 2:507
Mary (----) Sears, 2:507
Ruth, 1:272, 2:507
Sarah, 2:507
Hussey/Huzzey
Abigail, 2:508
Ann (----) Mingay, 2:507,
3:215
Huldah, 2:507
Martha (Bunker), 2:508,
4:676
Mary, 2:507-508, 4:240,
4:320
Mary (----), 2:507
Priscilla, 2:282
Puella, 2:508
Rebecca (Perkins), 2:507
Theodata, 2:507
Theodata (Bachiler), 1:89,
2:507
Theodate, 2:508
Hutchins/Hutchings
Abiah, 2:508
Abigail (Whitney), 4:531
Ann, 2:508
Barbarie, 2:508
Elizabeth, 2:508, 3:599,
3:637
Elizabeth (----) Growth,
2:508
Elizabeth (Eaton) Groth,
2:319
Elizabeth (Farr), 2:144,
2:508
Elizabeth (Wilder), 4:549
Frances (----), 2:508
Hannah (Johnson), 2:508
Jane (----), 2:508
Love, 2:508, 4:78
Mary, 4:447
Mary (Edmunds), 2:102,
2:508
Mary (Stevenson), 2:508,
4:182
Sarah, 2:508
Hutchinson
----, 1:436, 2:510, 2:513,
4:482

Hutchinson (continued)
Abigail, 1:67, 2:510-512, 2:596
Abigail (Vermaes) Button, 1:324, 2:509, 4:372
Alice (----), 2:512
Alice (----) Bennett, 1:167, 2:511
Ann, 2:509, 3:396, 4:372
Ann (Marbury), 2:513
Bethia, 2:511-512
Bridget, 2:513
Catharine, 2:509-510
Catharine (Hamby), 2:509
Elizabeth, 1:397, 2:509-512, 2:596, 4:600
Elizabeth (----), 2:511
Elizabeth (----) Bridges Parker, 3:354
Elizabeth (----) Parker, 2:512
Elizabeth (Clark) Freak, 1:402, 2:202, 2:510
Faith, 2:512-513, 4:26
Hannah, 1:214, 2:143, 2:509-512, 4:395
Hannah (----), 2:185
Hannah (Hawkins), 2:383, 2:510
Lydia, 2:511, 2:596
Lydia (Small), 2:511
Margaret, 2:511
Margaret (----), 2:511
Martha (Stearns), 4:173
Mary, 2:331, 2:508, 2:510, 2:513, 2:596, 4:502
Mary (----), 2:513
Mary (Cushman), 1:492
Mehitable, 2:510-511
Mercy, 1:4
Rebecca, 2:327, 2:596
Ruth, 2:511
Sarah, 2:510, 2:596
Sarah (----), 2:508, 2:512
Sarah (----) Standish, 2:596
Sarah (Baker), 2:511
Sarah (Foster), 2:510
Sarah (Leighton), 2:510
Sarah (Putnam), 2:511, 3:496
Sarah (Shrimpton), 2:510
Susan, 2:512
Susanna, 1:415, 1:428,
2:509, 2:513
Susanna (----), 2:508, 2:513, 4:502
Susanna (----) Archer, 1:63, 2:512
Thankful, 2:511
Zuriel, 2:513
Huthwit/Hathwit
Ann, 2:513, 3:429
Elizabeth, 2:513
Judith (----), 2:513
Martha, 2:513
Mary, 2:513
Hutson
Barbarie, 2:508
Huxley/Huxly
Elizabeth, 2:514
Hannah, 2:514
Mary, 2:514
Sarah, 1:117, 2:514
Sarah (Spencer), 2:514, 4:149
Hyatt
Mary (Sension), 2:514
Rebecca, 2:514
Hyde/Hides
Abigail, 2:515
Ann, 1:122, 2:515
Ann (----), 2:514, 4:456
Bethia, 2:514-515
Bethia (Hyde), 2:514
Christian, 2:514-515
Dorothy, 2:515
Dorothy (Kidder), 2:515, 3:18
Elizabeth, 2:514-516, 3:322
Elizabeth (Caulkins), 1:350
Elizabeth (Fuller), 2:216, 2:514
Elizabeth (Harvey), 2:370, 2:515
Elizabeth (Hyde), 2:516
Elizabeth (Olcott), 2:516, 3:307
Esther, 2:515-516, 3:465
Eunice, 2:515
Hannah, 2:514-515, 3:625, 3:638
Hannah (----), 2:514
Hannah (Hyde), 2:514
Hannah (Jackson) Kenrick,
2:515, 2:530, 3:11
Hannah (Stedman), 2:516, 4:178
Jane (----) Plympton, 3:638
Jane (Dummer) Plympton, 3:448
Jane (Lee), 2:516, 3:73
Lydia, 2:515
Martha, 2:514
Mary, 1:316, 1:336, 2:514-515, 4:436
Mary (French), 2:515
Mary (Rediat), 2:515
Mary (Williams), 2:515
Mercy, 1:131
Mercy (Bird), 2:514
Mindwell, 2:514
Patience, 2:531
Phebe, 2:317, 2:516
Rebecca, 2:515, 2:581, 3:617, 3:638
Relief, 2:515
Ruth, 2:515
Sarah, 2:514-516, 3:323, 4:649
Sarah (Dana), 2:5
Sarah (Hyde), 2:514
Sarah (Prentice), 3:479
Susanna, 2:577
Susanna (----), 4:702
Susanna (Baxter), 1:141, 2:514, 3:638
Temperance (----), 2:516
Hyland/Hiland/Highland
----, 2:516
Deborah, 2:516, 3:638, 4:300
Elizabeth, 2:516, 3:638
Elizabeth (Stockbridge), 2:516, 4:197-198
Hannah, 3:638
Hannah (----), 3:638
Hannah (Cruttenden), 1:481
Mary, 1:283, 2:516, 3:638
Ruth, 2:516
Sarah, 2:516, 4:348
Ibrook
Ellen, 2:434, 2:516
Margaret, 2:516, 4:316
Rebecca, 2:435, 2:516
Ide
---- (Bliss), 2:516

Ide (continued)
  Martha, 2:516-517, 4:396
  Mary, 2:219, 2:516-517
  Mary (Ormsbee), 2:517
Iggleden/Eggleden/Eggleton
  Ann (Prince), 2:517
  Elizabeth, 2:517, 3:191
  Elizabeth (----), 2:517,
    3:369
  Peaceable (----), 2:106,
    4:97
  Ruth, 1:203, 2:517
  Sarah, 2:517, 3:301
Ilsley
  Abigail, 2:517
  Abigail (Plummer), 2:517
  Barbara, 2:517
  Barbara (----), 2:518
  Elizabeth, 2:517
  Hannah, 2:299, 2:517
  Hannah (Poor), 2:517
  Judith, 2:517
  Lydia, 2:517
  Mary, 2:517-518, 3:231
  Ruth, 2:517
  Sarah, 2:330, 2:517-518
  Sarah (----), 2:517
  Sarah (Little), 2:517
Ince
  Mary (----), 2:350
  Mary (Miles), 2:518, 3:207
Indicutt/Indicott
  Ann, 2:518
  Elizabeth, 2:518
  Elizabeth (----), 2:518
  Mary (----), 2:518
  Sarah, 2:518
Ines/Innes/Innis/Iyans/Irons
  Ann, 2:518
  Ann (----), 2:518
  Catharine, 2:518, 4:689
  Elizabeth, 2:518
  Rebecca, 2:518, 4:280
Ingall/Ingalls
  ----, 2:519
  Abigail, 2:179, 2:519
  Ann (----), 2:519
  Deborah, 2:519
  Dinah, 3:638
  Dinah (Elson), 3:638,
    3:641
  Elizabeth, 2:368, 2:519
  Elizabeth (Barrett), 2:519

Faith, 1:28, 2:519
Hannah, 2:519, 4:159
Hannah (Abbot), 1:3,
  2:519
Hannah (Brewer), 2:519
Mary, 1:2, 2:519, 3:638,
  4:187
Mary (----) Tripp, 2:519
Mary (Osgood), 2:519,
  3:320
Rebecca (Leighton), 2:519
Ruth (Eaton), 2:96
Sarah, 1:187, 2:519, 2:596
Sarah (----), 2:519
Sarah (----) Abbot, 2:519
Sarah (Farnum) Abbot, 1:3
Sarah (Hendrick), 2:403,
  2:519
Sarah (Russell), 2:519
Ingersoll
  ----, 2:520
  ---- (Coe), 1:418, 2:521
  Abiah, 2:520
  Abigail, 2:520, 3:545,
    4:579
  Abigail (Bascom), 1:134,
    2:520
  Abigail (Blackman)
    Dickinson, 2:47, 2:522
  Alice, 2:521, 4:622
  Ann (----), 2:521, 3:36
  Bathsheba, 2:521, 3:36
  Bethia, 2:520
  Catharine, 2:520
  Catharine (----), 2:520
  Deborah, 2:520, 3:57
  Deborah (----), 2:520
  Dorcas, 2:521
  Dorothy, 2:520, 3:116,
    3:405
  Dorothy (Lord), 2:520,
    3:116
  Elizabeth, 2:519-520,
    3:638
  Elizabeth (----), 2:519
  Esther, 2:324, 2:520,
    2:560
  Hannah, 2:520, 2:596, 3:7,
    3:116, 3:638
  Hannah (Collins), 1:515,
    2:521
  Isabel, 2:521
  Isabel (Brown), 2:521

Joanna, 2:521, 3:403
Judith (----), 2:521
Judith (Felton), 2:596,
  3:638
Lydia, 2:520
Margaret, 2:522, 3:116
Margery, 2:267, 2:520
Mary, 1:467, 2:519-521,
  3:638
Mary (Coombs), 3:638
Mary (Hunt), 2:520
Mary (Preston), 3:638
Miriam, 2:522
Rachel, 2:520
Rebecca, 2:521
Ruth, 2:520, 3:575, 3:638
Ruth (Childs), 2:522
Sarah, 2:391, 2:520-522,
  2:593, 2:595, 3:575,
  3:638
Sarah (----), 2:521
Sarah (Ashley), 2:522
Sarah (Coe), 3:638
Susanna, 2:522
Ingham
  Abigail, 2:522
  Hannah, 2:522
  Mary, 2:522
  Mary (----), 2:522
  Rebecca, 2:522
  Rebecca (Williams), 2:522
  Sarah, 1:352, 2:522
  Sarah (Bushnell), 2:522
Ingleby
  Elizabeth, 3:294
Inglefield
  ----, 3:627
Ingles/Inglish
  Hannah, 2:522
  Mary, 2:522
  Mary (----), 2:523
Inglesby/Ingoldsby
  Ruth (----), 2:523
  Sarah, 4:46
Inglis
  Hannah, 1:408
Ingram/Ingraham
  Deliverance, 2:523
  Elizabeth, 2:523
  Elizabeth (----), 2:523
  Elizabeth (Gardner), 2:523
  Experience, 2:523
  Hannah, 2:523

Ingram/Ingraham
(continued)
Joan (Rockwell) Baker,
1:96, 2:523
Lydia (----), 2:523
Margaret, 2:203, 2:523
Mary, 2:523
Mary (Barstow), 1:129,
2:523
Mehitable, 2:523
Mehitable (Dickinson),
2:48, 2:523
Rebecca, 2:523
Rebecca (Seale/Searle),
2:523
Sarah (Shaler) Lord, 4:685
Ings
Hannah, 1:408
Mary (Beal), 2:523
Inman
Barbara (----), 2:523
Joanna, 2:524, 3:232
Sarah (Herenden), 2:524
Ireland
----, 2:589
---- (Greenland), 2:589
Abiel, 2:524
Grace (----), 2:524
Grace (Healy), 2:596
Margaret, 2:597
Martha, 2:524
Mary (----), 1:312, 2:524
Ireson
Elizabeth (----), 2:524
Hannah, 2:524
Mary (Leach), 2:524
Rebecca (May), 2:524
Ruth, 2:524, 3:638
Irish
Content, 2:524
Deborah (Church), 1:386,
2:525
Dorothy (Witherell), 2:524,
4:492
Elizabeth, 2:524
Elizabeth (----), 2:524
Joanna, 2:524
Mary, 2:524
Priscilla, 2:524
Priscilla (Church), 1:386,
2:525
Sarah, 2:524

Isaac/Isaacs
Elizabeth (----), 2:20, 2:525
Rebecca, 2:525
Isbell
Ann (----), 3:282
Elizabeth, 2:525
Elizabeth (French), 2:525
Hannah, 2:196, 2:525,
4:179
Issam
Hannah, 2:525
Jane, 2:525
Jane (Parker), 2:525
Mary, 2:525
Patience, 2:525
Sarah, 2:525
Thankful, 2:525
Ives
----, 1:34, 2:525
---- (----), 1:136
Abigail, 4:685
Deborah, 3:638
Elizabeth, 3:638
Grace, 2:396, 2:525
Hannah, 2:484, 2:525
Hannah (Merriman), 4:685,
4:690
Martha (----), 2:525
Martha (Wyeth), 3:638,
4:663
Mary, 2:525, 4:685
Mary (Cook), 1:450
Mary (Yale), 4:667, 4:685
Phebe, 2:525
Sarah, 1:34, 2:525
Susanna, 2:525
Ivey
Mercy (Bartlett), 1:132,
2:526
Ivory
Ann (----), 1:475, 2:526
Dorcas, 2:470
Hannah, 2:526
Lois, 1:206, 1:309, 2:526
Mary (Davis), 2:526
Ruth, 1:94, 2:526
Sarah, 1:350, 1:475, 2:526
Tabitha, 2:526, 3:504
Jacklin/Jacklene/Jackling/etc
Hannah, 2:526
Mary, 2:526
Mehitable, 2:526
Ruth, 2:526

Susan (----), 2:526
Susanna, 2:526, 2:595
Jackman
Elizabeth, 2:526
Elizabeth (Plumer), 2:526
Esther, 2:526, 3:258
Joanna, 2:526
Joanna (----), 2:526
Mary, 2:526
Rachel (Noyes), 2:526
Sarah, 2:526, 3:341
Jackson
----, 4:336
Abigail, 2:527, 2:529-530,
3:482
Abigail (----), 2:530
Abigail (Wilson), 2:529,
4:586
Alice, 2:529
Ann, 2:529, 2:531
Bethia, 2:531
Catharine (----), 2:530
Deborah, 2:532
Deborah (----), 2:532
Deborah (Fifield), 2:158,
2:530
Deliverance, 2:529
Elinor (----), 1:143
Elizabeth, 1:209, 1:430,
2:475, 2:527-532, 3:479,
3:606
Elizabeth (----), 2:527,
2:531
Elizabeth (----) Brown,
1:274, 2:531
Elizabeth (Briscoe), 1:256,
2:527
Elizabeth (Grafton), 2:532
Elizabeth (Newgate) Oliver,
2:528, 3:273, 3:310
Elizabeth (Pilkington),
2:527
Elizabeth (Smith), 4:114
Esther, 2:531
Esther (Sealis), 2:531, 4:44
Experience, 2:529
Frances, 2:528
Frances (----), 2:528
Grace, 2:530
Grace (----), 2:529
Hannah, 2:515, 2:527-531,
3:11, 3:91, 4:333,
4:408-409, 4:586

Jackson (continued)
Hannah (Johnson), 2:532
Hannah (Trowbridge),
4:334
Jane (Thomas), 2:530,
4:280
Joanna (----), 2:530
Joanna (Pepperell), 3:392
Lydia, 2:217, 2:527-528,
2:531, 3:69-70
Margaret, 2:527-530,
4:332
Margaret (----), 2:529-531
Margery, 2:530
Martha, 1:429, 2:527
Martha (----), 2:527
Mary, 2:188, 2:527, 2:529,
2:531-532, 3:491, 4:335
Mary (----), 2:527,
2:529-530
Mary (Abbot), 1:2
Mary (Bettis), 2:530
Mary (Cole), 1:430
Mary (Cole) Gawdren,
2:527
Mary (Curtis), 2:530
Mary (Hull), 3:637, 3:639
Mary (Salter), 2:531
Mary (Whitmarsh), 4:526
Mehitable, 2:530
Patience, 2:531
Patience (Hyde), 2:531
Priscilla (Grafton), 2:289,
2:532
Rebecca, 2:528, 2:531,
3:479
Rebecca (----), 2:531
Remember (Morton),
2:527, 3:244
Ruth, 2:528
Sally, 2:531
Sarah, 1:482, 2:435,
2:527-531, 4:701
Sarah (----), 2:530
Sarah (----) Smith, 4:701
Sarah (Baker), 1:99, 2:531
Susanna, 2:527
Susanna (Jones), 2:530,
3:640
Susanna (Jones) Goose,
2:587
Theodosia, 2:529-530,
3:276, 4:616

Xene, 2:530
Jacob/Jacobs
----, 4:274
Abigail, 2:533-534
Ann, 2:533
Deborah, 1:491, 2:532-534,
4:281
Dorothy (Symonds), 4:246
Elizabeth, 1:489,
2:533-534, 3:39, 3:639,
4:345
Elizabeth (----), 2:534
Hannah, 2:532-534,
3:118-119
Hannah (----), 2:533
Hannah (Allen), 2:534
Jael, 1:491, 2:533-534
Joanna (----) Hale, 2:330,
2:534
Judith, 2:534
Lydia, 2:532-534, 3:639
Margaret, 2:532-533
Margery (Eames), 2:89,
2:533
Martha, 2:534, 4:555
Martha (Appleton), 1:61,
2:534
Mary, 1:92, 2:532-534,
3:323
Mary (----), 1:145,
2:533-534
Mary (Russell), 2:533
Mercy, 3:637, 3:639
Mercy (Barnes), 3:639,
4:674
Rebecca (Frost), 2:533
Sarah, 1:365, 1:490, 2:380,
2:532-534
Sarah (Cushing), 1:490,
2:532
Susanna (Symonds), 2:533,
4:247
Jaffrey
Ann, 3:639
Ann (----), 2:597
Elizabeth, 3:639
Elizabeth (Walker), 2:534
Hannah (----), 2:534, 4:319
Rebecca, 3:639
Sarah, 2:534, 3:639
Sarah (Jeffries), 2:597,
3:639
Sarah (Wentworth)

McPhedris, 3:639
Jagger/Jaggers
Elizabeth, 2:534-535
Elizabeth (----), 2:534,
4:363
Hannah, 2:535
Hannah (Cross), 1:516
Mary, 2:534-535, 3:405
Sarah, 2:534-535
James
Abigail, 2:537
Ann, 2:476, 4:346
Ann (----), 2:535
Ann (Collins), 2:535,
3:611
Elizabeth (----), 2:535-536,
3:639, 4:87
Jane, 1:12, 2:535
Jane (----), 2:535, 3:590
Lydia (Turner), 1:124,
2:535, 4:346
Margaret (----), 2:537
Mary, 2:536, 3:23
Mary (----), 2:536
Mary (Fuller), 2:536-537
Mehitable (----), 2:537
Rachel (Hobby), 2:437
Reana (----), 2:535
Ruth, 2:537
Ruth (Jones), 2:562
Sarah, 2:535, 3:356, 3:639
Jameson/Jamison
Esther (Martin), 3:162
Hannah, 2:264
Margaret, 2:597
Mary, 2:538
Mary (----), 2:538
Sarah (----), 2:537-538
Janes/Jeanes
Bathsheba, 2:538
Elizabeth, 2:538
Hannah, 2:538
Hannah (Bascom)
Broughton, 1:134, 1:263,
2:538
Hepzibah, 2:538
Mary, 2:538
Mary (----), 2:538
Mary (Judd), 2:538
Rachel, 2:538
Ruth, 2:538
Sarah, 2:538
Sarah (Hinsdale), 2:427,

Janes/Jeanes (continued)
Sarah (Hinsdale)
(continued)
2:538
Jaques
Abigail, 2:538, 3:35
Ann, 2:539
Ann (Knight), 2:538
Deborah (Plummer), 2:539
Elizabeth, 2:538, 3:39,
3:396
Hannah, 2:538, 3:446
Mary, 1:275, 2:538-539
Ruth, 2:119, 2:538
Ruth (Plummer), 2:539
Sarah, 2:538-539
Susanna (----), 2:538
Jaquith
Ann (Jordan), 2:539, 2:569
Annis, 1:260
Elizabeth, 2:539
Lydia, 2:195
Mary, 2:539
Mary (Adverd/Adford),
1:19, 2:539
Sarah, 2:539
Jarrad/Garrard
Mary, 3:146
Jarratt
Elizabeth, 2:539
Susanna (----), 2:539
Jarvis
---- (Porter), 3:462
Abigail, 2:539
Mary, 2:539
Rebecca (Parkman), 2:539,
3:359
Jay
Mary (Hunting), 2:503,
2:539
Jeffrey/Jeffries/Jeffrys/etc
Ann, 3:639
Ann (Clark), 2:540, 3:639
Audrey (----), 2:540
Betty (Usher), 3:509
Catharine (----), 3:298
Catharine (Eyre), 2:597,
3:639
Elizabeth, 2:539-540,
2:597
Elizabeth (Usher), 2:539,
4:363
Frances, 2:539

Hannah, 2:540
Jane, 2:539
Mary, 2:304, 2:540, 3:132
Mary (----), 2:540
Mary (Gould), 2:540
Mary (Harvey), 2:370
Priscilla, 2:540
Rebecca, 2:539, 2:597
Sarah, 1:502, 2:539-540,
2:597, 3:639
Susanna, 2:540
Jefts/Jeffs
Ann (Stowers), 2:540
Elizabeth, 3:431
Hannah, 2:540
Hannah
(Births/Booth/Borth),
2:540
Joanna, 2:540
Mary, 2:541
Sarah (----), 2:541
Jeggles
Abigail, 2:179, 2:541,
3:639
Abigail (Sharp), 2:541,
4:61
Elizabeth, 2:541
Elizabeth (----), 2:541
Mary, 2:541
Mary (----), 2:541
Mary (Weston), 2:541
Sarah, 2:541
Jellicoe
Mary (----), 2:541
Jempson
Esther (Martin), 2:541
Sarah (----), 2:541
Jenkins/Jenkin
----, 2:126
Abigail, 2:542
Ann, 2:542
Ann (----), 2:542
Bathshua, 2:542
Bethia, 4:685
Elizabeth, 2:542
Elizabeth (Oakes), 2:542,
3:302
Experience, 2:542
Experience (Hamblen),
2:542
Experience (Otis) Heard,
2:397
Hope, 2:542

Lydia, 2:542, 3:372
Lydia (Howland), 2:542
Mary, 1:74, 2:303, 2:542,
4:685
Mary (----) Fawer, 2:542
Mary (----) Ripley, 4:685
Mary (Ewer), 2:542
Mary (Farnsworth) Ripley,
3:543
Mary (Gardner), 4:682,
4:685
Mary (Lewis), 2:542
Mary (Preston) Fawer,
2:149
Mehitable, 2:342, 2:542
Mercy, 2:542
Mercy (Tufts) Wait, 4:342,
4:384
Philadelphia, 2:542
Reliance, 2:542
Ruth, 2:542
Sarah, 2:542, 3:85, 3:197,
4:685
Sarah (Gilbert), 4:685
Thankful, 2:542
Jenkinson
Mary (Savage), 4:24
Jenks
Abigail, 2:542-543
Catharine, 2:543
Catharine (Balcom), 2:542
Deborah, 2:543
Elizabeth, 2:543
Elizabeth (----), 2:543
Elizabeth (----) Floyd,
2:176, 2:543
Elizabeth (Darling), 2:543
Elizabeth (Grover), 2:320
Esther, 2:543-544
Esther (Ballard), 2:543
Hannah, 2:542-543
Joanna, 2:543
Lydia, 2:543
Margaret, 2:544
Martha, 2:542-543
Martha (Brown), 2:543
Mary, 2:542-543
Mary (Butterworth), 2:542
Mary (Jenks), 2:542-543
Mercy, 2:543-544
Patience, 2:544
Patience (Sprague), 2:544
Phebe, 2:542

Jenks (continued)
Rachel, 2:543
Ruth, 2:542
Sarah, 1:379, 2:542-543
Sarah (Meriam), 2:543,
3:87
Susanna, 2:542, 2:544
Jenner/Jenners
Alice (Pigg), 2:544, 3:435
Eleanor, 2:544, 4:714
Elizabeth, 2:544
Esther (——), 2:544
Mabel, 2:544
Mabel (Russell), 2:544
Mary (Harvey), 2:370
Rebecca, 2:544
Rebecca (Trerice), 2:544,
4:322
Sarah, 2:544
Jenness
—— (Coxe), 1:467, 2:544
Elizabeth, 2:544
Hannah, 2:544, 3:102
Mehitable, 2:544
Jennings
—— (Turney), 4:349
Captivity, 2:545
Elinor, 2:545
Elizabeth (Reynolds),
2:545
Hannah (Dickinson) Gillett,
2:48, 2:256, 2:545
Mary (Williams), 2:545
Sarah, 2:545
Susanna, 2:545
Jennison
Elizabeth, 2:545-546,
3:515
Elizabeth (——), 2:545
Grace, 2:444, 2:546
Grace (——), 2:545
Judith, 1:118, 1:163, 2:546
Judith (Macomber),
2:545-546
Lydia, 2:546
Mary, 2:546
Mercy, 2:546
Michal, 1:203, 2:545,
4:424
Rachel, 1:127, 2:546
Jenny/Jenney
Abigail, 2:546, 4:625
Ann (Lettice), 3:81

Sarah, 2:546, 3:459
Sarah (Carey), 2:546
Susanna, 2:546
Jepson/Jephson
Ann, 2:547
Apphia (Rolfe), 2:547
Emma, 2:547
Emma (——) Coddington,
1:415, 2:546
Hannah, 2:547
Hannah (——), 2:547
Martha, 2:547
Martha (——), 1:44, 2:547
Martha (——) Morris, 3:235
Ruth, 2:547
Ruth (Gardner), 1:415,
2:230, 2:546
Jess/Jesse/Jose/Joyce
Abigail, 2:547, 4:656-657
Elizabeth, 2:547
Mary, 1:547, 4:587
Mary (Wilson), 2:547,
4:587
Susanna, 2:547
Jessop/Jessup
—— (——), 4:526
Elizabeth, 2:597
Elizabeth (——), 2:597
Hannah, 2:597
Jewell
Grissel (——), 2:315
Grizel (——), 2:548
Grizell, 2:548
Hannah, 2:548
Martha, 2:547
Martha (——), 2:547
Mary, 2:548, 3:345
Mary (Smedley) Shepard,
2:548, 4:71
Mercy, 2:548
Susanna (Guilford), 2:548
Jewett
—— (Wood), 4:629
Abigail, 2:548
Ann, 1:502, 2:549,
2:597-598
Ann (——), 2:598
Ann (——) Allen, 1:29,
2:598
Ann (Allen), 1:498, 2:597
Dorcas, 2:548
Elinor (——) Boynton,
2:549

Elizabeth, 2:395, 2:549,
2:597-598
Elizabeth (——) Chadwell,
1:350, 2:548
Elizabeth (Cummings),
1:483, 2:548
Elizabeth (Kimball), 2:548
Ellen (——), 4:418
Exercise (Pierce), 2:549
Faith, 2:69, 2:549, 2:598,
3:438
Faith (Parrott), 2:597,
3:361
Faith (Parrott) Smith,
2:548, 4:121
Hannah, 1:511, 2:548,
2:598
Joanna, 2:549, 2:598
Mary, 1:549, 2:58,
2:548-549, 2:598
Mary (Griswold) Tracy,
2:590
Mary (Malinson), 2:598
Mehitable, 2:598
Mercy, 2:549
Patience, 2:548, 2:598,
4:397
Priscilla, 2:598
Rebecca, 2:548, 2:598
Rebecca (Law), 2:598
Ruth, 2:598
Ruth (——), 2:549
Ruth (Wood), 2:598, 3:131
Sarah, 2:548, 2:581,
2:597-598, 3:267
Sarah (——), 2:548
Sarah (Dickinson), 2:597
Johnson
—, 2:302, 2:551
—— (Beers), 1:155
Abigail, 2:142, 2:179,
2:549-551, 2:553-554,
2:556-558, 4:686
Abigail (May), 2:552
Abigail (Oliver), 2:554,
3:311
Abigail/Abiah (Leavitt)
Lazell, 3:65
Adeline (——), 2:419, 4:41,
4:686
Ann, 2:194, 2:557-558,
3:144, 3:457, 4:686,
4:701

Johnson (continued)
Ann (Cotton) Carr, 1:464
Ann (Stamford) Meadows,
4:685
Arbella (Clinton), 2:552
Bathsheba, 1:481, 2:554
Bethia, 2:550, 2:555,
2:559
Bethia (Read), 2:555
Catharine, 2:550-551
Catharine (----) Maverick,
2:599
Catharine (Baker), 2:551
Catharine (Skipper)
Maverick, 3:180
Christian, 4:401
Deborah, 2:551, 2:555
Deborah (Ward), 2:555
Dorcas, 2:550, 3:379
Eleanor (Ballard), 2:555
Eleanor (Brackett), 2:555
Elinor (----), 2:557
Elizabeth, 1:222, 1:512,
2:338, 2:549-551,
2:553-559, 2:599, 3:43,
3:391, 3:444, 3:620,
3:640, 4:310, 4:662,
4:686
Elizabeth (----), 2:185,
2:556, 2:558-559, 4:237
Elizabeth (Austin), 1:499
Elizabeth (Bushnell),
1:317, 2:558
Elizabeth (Dane), 2:557
Elizabeth (Disbrow), 2:554
Elizabeth (Disbrow) Ralph,
3:523
Elizabeth (Disbrow) Rolfe,
3:571
Elizabeth (Maverick),
2:555, 3:180
Elizabeth (Partridge)
Hamlin, 3:366
Elizabeth (Peters), 2:554,
3:401
Elizabeth (Porter), 2:553
Elizabeth
(Wooster/Worster), 2:550
Ellen (Cheney), 2:551
Esther, 2:550-551,
2:558-559, 2:599, 4:665
Esther (----), 2:559
Esther (Beers), 3:640

Esther (Gardner), 2:230,
2:551
Esther (Mason)
Cooledge/Coolidge, 1:452
Esther (Taylor), 2:599
Esther (Wheaden), 2:551,
4:496
Esther (Wiswall), 2:558,
4:617
Eunice, 2:550
Experience, 2:551
Frances (Hitchcock), 4:686
Grace (----) Fawer, 2:554
Grace (Negoose) Fawer,
2:148
Hannah, 1:123, 2:90,
2:212, 2:508, 2:532,
2:550, 2:553-558, 3:360,
4:414, 4:685-686, 4:701
Hannah (----), 2:557, 2:599,
4:686
Hannah (----) Bullock,
1:297
Hannah (----) Hanbury,
2:551
Hannah (Craft), 2:557
Hannah (Crosby), 1:476,
2:554
Hannah (Dorman), 2:61
Hannah (Hanbury), 2:348
Hannah (Hoadley), 2:430
Hannah (Palfrey), 2:556,
3:339
Hannah (Parmelee), 3:359
Hope, 4:686
Isabel (----) Newgate,
3:273
Joan (----), 2:551
Joanna, 2:329, 2:559
Joanna (----), 2:587
Joanna (Long), 2:599
Judith (----), 2:599
Lydia, 4:686
Mabel (Grannis), 2:290,
4:686, 4:701
Margaret, 2:552, 3:70
Margaret (----), 2:554,
2:558, 4:338, 4:629
Margaret (Morris), 3:235
Margery (----), 2:554
Martha, 1:50, 2:90, 2:551,
2:558, 3:241
Martha (Parker), 2:549

Mary, 1:130, 1:266, 2:16,
2:553, 2:554-559, 3:176,
3:232, 3:599, 4:210,
4:686
Mary (----), 1:431, 2:442,
2:550, 2:554-555, 2:557
Mary (----) Hodgkin, 3:633,
3:639
Mary (Bishop) Hodgkin,
1:185
Mary (Collins), 2:557
Mary (Cook), 2:558
Mary (Harris), 2:360,
2:553
Mary (Holt), 2:455, 2:558
Mary (Johnson), 2:556
Mary (King), 2:555
Mary (Mousall), 2:599
Mary (Newton), 3:277
Mary (Plimpton), 2:556,
3:448
Mary (Rose), 2:556, 3:576
Mary (Sage), 2:557, 4:4
Mary (Sally), 2:599
Mary (Smith), 2:556
Mary (Stone), 2:598, 4:207
Mary (Washburn), 4:429
Mehitable, 2:427, 2:551,
4:686, 4:701
Mehitable (Farnham),
2:556
Mercy, 2:557-558
Miriam (----), 2:551
Miriam (Holbrook), 2:594,
2:598
Naomi, 2:551
Penelope, 2:558
Rachel, 2:555
Rebecca, 2:550, 2:555-556,
4:665
Rebecca (Aslett), 1:69,
2:558
Rebecca (Pierson), 3:434
Rebecca (Wiswall), 2:556,
4:616
Rosamond, 2:555
Ruhamah, 2:383, 2:558,
2:599, 3:36
Ruth, 2:64, 2:551,
2:554-557, 3:180, 3:516,
4:686
Sarah, 1:337, 2:549-551,
2:554, 2:556, 2:558-559,

Johnson (continued)
Sarah (continued)
4:622, 4:686, 4:701
Sarah (----), 2:559
Sarah (Burrage), 1:510,
2:599
Sarah (Hall), 2:334, 2:559
Sarah (Hawkes), 2:551
Sarah (Lovejoy), 2:559,
3:122
Sarah (Miller), 3:211
Sarah (Neighbors), 2:555,
3:267
Sarah (Walker), 2:551
Sarah (Winn), 2:550
Susan, 2:560
Susan (----), 2:550,
2:554-555
Susanna, 2:550-551,
2:558-559, 3:478, 4:660
Susanna (----), 2:555
Susanna (Drowne), 2:74
Susanna (Sigourney), 4:94
Temperance (Ratchell),
2:558, 3:508
Zeruiah, 2:556
Johonnot
Elizabeth, 2:559
Margaret, 2:559
Marian, 2:560
Martha, 2:559
Mary, 2:559
Mary (Oliver), 2:559
Susan, 2:560
Susan (----) Johnson, 2:555
Susan (Johnson), 2:560
Susanna, 2:559
Susanna (----), 2:555
Susanna (Sigourney)
Johnson, 4:94
Jones
---, 2:569, 3:640
---- (----) Carter, 2:566
---- (----) Elithrop, 2:112
---- (Cromwell) Whetstone,
2:567
---- (Kinsley), 3:29
---- (Ruggles), 3:587
---- (Walford), 2:560,
4:392
Abigail, 1:499, 2:563-564,
2:567, 3:640
Abigail (----), 1:499, 1:512,

2:566, 2:599
Abigail (----) Elithrop,
2:566
Abigail (Atwater), 1:75,
2:564
Abigail (Heard), 2:397,
2:562
Abigail (Morse), 2:568
Abigail (Rowland), 3:581
Alice (----), 2:564
Ann, 2:563, 3:198, 3:224,
3:328
Ann (----), 2:563-564,
2:566, 4:513, 4:633,
4:686
Ann (Bibble), 1:174, 2:565,
3:301
Ann (Bullard), 2:561
Ann (Griggs), 2:315, 2:561,
3:59
Ann (Stone), 4:209
Barbara, 2:561
Barbara (----), 2:561
Bathshua (----), 3:640
Bethia, 2:564
Catharine, 2:563-564,
2:567
Catharine (----), 2:567
Catharine (Gammon),
2:567
Deborah, 2:561, 2:564,
3:640
Deborah (Clark), 2:561
Deodat, 2:567
Dorcas, 2:562
Dorcas (----), 1:319, 2:562
Dorothy, 2:367
Elizabeth, 1:212, 1:319,
1:433, 2:235, 2:560-562,
2:564-568, 3:640, 4:271
Elizabeth (----), 2:563,
2:565, 2:567
Elizabeth (----) Heath,
2:561
Elizabeth (Berry), 1:171,
2:563
Elizabeth (Field), 2:156,
2:565
Elizabeth (Folland) Hall,
2:562
Elizabeth (Pitts), 2:566,
3:442
Elizabeth (Pollard) Hall,

2:334
Elizabeth (Potter), 2:565
Elizabeth
(Voden/Voeden/etc),
4:375
Elizabeth (Wills), 3:640
Ellen (----), 2:565-566
Esther, 2:565, 4:440
Esther (Hall), 2:569
Esther (Ingersoll) Gurley,
2:325, 2:521, 2:560
Experience, 2:491, 2:561,
2:564
Hannah, 2:278, 2:561-564,
2:566-568, 3:217, 3:508,
3:640
Hannah (----), 2:563
Hannah (Brown), 2:560
Hannah (Cudworth), 1:482
Hannah (Davis), 2:561
Hannah (Eaton), 2:97,
2:567
Hannah (Heath), 2:561
Hannah (Spencer), 3:640
Hannah (Tompkins),
3:640, 4:311
Hepzibah, 1:328, 2:561
Jane, 2:565
Joan (----), 1:80, 3:640
Joan (Osgood), 2:565,
3:322
Lydia, 1:452, 2:563-564,
2:566, 3:640, 4:530
Lydia (----), 2:561
Lydia (Saunderson), 2:566,
4:22
Lydia (Treadway), 2:563,
4:325
Margaret, 2:564
Margaret (----), 2:568
Martha, 2:565, 3:640
Mary, 3:601, 1:122,
2:561-565, 2:567, 2:599,
3:492, 3:640, 4:304,
4:336, 4:483, 4:633
Mary (----), 2:561, 2:566
Mary (Bushnell), 2:565
Mary (Foster), 3:640
Mary (Fuller), 2:217,
2:564
Mary (Howard) Bass,
1:135, 2:472, 2:561
Mary (Loring), 2:566,

Jones (continued)
  Mary (Loring) (continued)
    3:118
  Mary (North), 2:566,
    3:289
  Mary (Rediat), 3:521
  Mary (Woolson), 2:215
  Mehitable, 3:272
  Mercy, 2:561, 2:564
  Mercy (Goodspeed), 2:564
  Mindwell, 2:563
  Mindwell (----), 2:563
  Patience, 2:564
  Patience (----), 2:433
  Patience (Little), 2:563,
    3:99
  Phebe, 2:563
  Rachel, 3:640
  Rachel (Clark), 1:395
  Rebecca, 2:301, 2:561-564,
    2:566-567, 3:217, 3:640
  Rebecca (----), 2:563
  Rebecca (Sally), 2:563, 4:6
  Remember, 2:327, 2:566,
    3:640
  Ruth, 2:473, 2:562-563,
    2:566, 3:587, 3:640,
    4:45
  Ruth (Wheeler), 2:561,
    4:500
  Sarah, 1:208, 1:273, 1:292,
    2:301, 2:492, 2:562-568,
    2:599, 3:473, 3:479,
    3:587, 3:640, 4:581-582,
    4:692
  Sarah (----), 2:560, 2:562,
    2:565, 2:599, 3:322
  Sarah (Farwell), 2:563
  Sarah (Topliff), 2:560,
    4:312
  Sarah (Whitman), 4:523
  Susanna, 2:530, 2:565-568,
    2:587, 3:640, 4:587
  Susanna (----), 2:562
  Susanna (Beal), 1:146,
    2:560
  Thankful, 2:564
Jordan
  ----, 2:569, 2:572
  ---- (Winter), 4:606
  Ann, 2:539, 2:569
  Deborah, 2:569
  Elizabeth, 2:483, 3:75,

  4:34
  Elizabeth (Stileman), 2:569,
    4:192
  Esther (Hall), 2:333, 2:569
  Hannah, 2:569, 4:387
  Hannah (Tristram), 2:569,
    4:331
  Jane (Wilson), 2:569
  Joanna, 1:381
  Lydia, 2:569
  Margaret (Martin), 3:136
  Mary, 2:275, 2:569, 3:561
  Mary (Whiton) Wilder,
    4:549
  Sarah, 2:569
  Sarah (Winter), 2:569
  Susanna, 3:199
  Susanna (----), 2:569
Jose
  Esther (Waldron) Elkins
    Lea, 2:112
  Esther (Waldron) Elkins
    Lee, 2:570, 3:71, 4:390
  Hannah (Martin), 2:570
  Jane, 2:570
  Jane (----), 2:569
  Joanna, 2:569-570
  Margaret, 2:569
  Mary, 2:569-570, 3:444
  Sarah, 2:570
Josselyn
  Abigail, 2:571
  Abigail (Stockbridge),
    2:571, 4:197
  Ann, 2:571
  Ann (----), 2:570
  Beatrice, 2:570-571
  Beatrice (----), 1:216,
    2:570
  Bridget (----), 2:571
  Bridget (Day), 3:640
  Dorothy, 2:571-572
  Elizabeth, 2:571-572, 3:20,
    4:668
  Esther, 2:571
  Esther (Morse), 2:571
  Hannah, 2:571
  Hannah (----), 2:572
  Hannah (Farrow), 2:147,
    2:571
  Jemima, 2:571
  Keziah, 2:571
  Margaret, 3:640

  Margaret (----) Cammock,
    1:331, 2:570
  Martha, 2:571
  Mary, 2:147, 2:570-572,
    3:640, 4:231
  Mary (Lambert), 3:640
  Mercy, 3:640
  Patience, 2:571
  Rebecca, 1:216, 1:474,
    2:364, 2:570-572, 3:282,
    4:185
  Rebecca (----), 2:572, 3:14
  Sarah, 2:571
  Sarah (Ford), 2:182, 2:571
  Sarah (King), 2:571
  Susanna, 2:571
Joston
  Rebecca, 3:282
Jourdaine/Jordan
  Jehosabeth, 2:569, 3:545
Joy
  ---- (Spencer), 4:149
  Ann, 3:641
  Ann (Pitts), 2:92, 2:572
  Deborah, 2:572
  Elizabeth, 2:573, 4:482
  Elizabeth (Spencer)
    Wellman, 2:572, 4:150,
    4:481
  Joan (Gallop), 2:222,
    2:572
  Lydia, 2:572
  Margaret, 2:572
  Mary, 2:572
  Mary (Prince), 2:572
  Ruth, 2:572-573, 3:125
  Sarah, 2:82, 2:572-573,
    3:641
  Sarah (Gaskin), 3:623,
    3:640
  Susanna (----), 2:572
  Tabitha, 2:572
Joyce
  ----, 1:136, 2:573
  Abigail, 2:573
  Dorcas, 2:573
  Dorothy, 2:573
  Dorothy (----), 2:573
  Elizabeth (Chipman),
    1:380, 2:573
  Lydia, 2:573
  Martha, 2:573
  Martha (----), 2:573

Joyce (continued)
Mary, 2:573
Mehitable, 2:573
Sarah, 2:433
Susanna, 2:481
Joyliffe
Ann (----) Cromwell
  Knight, 1:476, 2:573
Hannah, 2:573
Judd
----, 2:574
Clemence, 2:574
Clemence (----) Mason,
  2:574, 3:170
Elizabeth, 2:573-575,
  3:113, 3:641, 4:142
Elizabeth (----), 2:574
Esther, 2:574
Eunice, 2:574
Experience, 2:574
Hannah, 2:573-574
Hannah (Loomis), 2:574
Margaret, 2:574
Maria (Strong), 2:574
Mary, 2:538, 2:574-575,
  3:114
Mary (Hawkins), 2:382,
  2:574
Mary (Lewis), 2:573, 3:89
Mary (Steele), 2:575,
  4:180
Rachel, 2:574-575
Ruth, 2:574, 3:610, 4:181
Sarah, 2:573, 2:575
Sarah (Freeman), 2:204,
  3:641
Sarah (Steele), 2:574-575,
  4:180
Susanna (Woodford),
  4:638
Judkin/Judkins
Ann (----) Howard, 2:575
Elizabeth (Leavitt), 2:575,
  3:70
Hannah, 4:447
Mary (Bean), 2:575
Sarah, 2:575
Sarah (----), 2:575
Judson
Abigail, 2:576
Ann, 2:576
Ann (----), 2:505, 2:576
Ann (Welles) Steele, 2:575,

4:180, 4:477
Bridget (----), 2:576
Catharine (----) Fairchild,
  2:576
Elizabeth, 2:575, 3:641,
  4:310
Elizabeth (----) Heaton
  Wilmot, 4:580
Elizabeth (----) Wilmot,
  2:577
Elizabeth (Chapman),
  1:361, 2:576
Esther, 2:392, 2:576
Esther (Thompson), 2:576
Grace, 2:576, 3:492
Grace (----), 2:577
Hannah, 2:575-576, 4:381
Hannah (----), 2:576
Martha, 2:576
Mary, 1:377, 2:575-576
Mary (----), 2:575
Mary (----) Aldridge, 1:25,
  2:392, 2:576
Mary (Orton), 2:576
Mary (Tudor), 4:341
Mercy, 2:575, 3:608,
  3:641, 4:79
Phebe, 2:575-576
Rebecca, 2:575
Rebecca (Welles), 2:575,
  4:479
Ruth, 2:576
Sarah, 2:392, 2:477,
  2:575-576
Sarah (Foote), 2:180,
  2:575
Sarah (Porter), 2:576,
  3:461
Jupe
Grace (Keayne), 2:577
Mary, 2:577, 3:238
Jupp
Ann (Hickens), 2:411,
  2:577
Karkeet/Carkeet
Lydia (----), 3:31
Kaye
Gracy, 4:8
Keais
Mary (----) Hoddy, 3:1
Mary (Roddam) Hoddy,
  2:438

Keayne
Agnes (----), 3:2
Ann, 2:78, 3:1, 3:51, 3:332
Ann (----), 1:429, 3:2
Ann (Mansfield), 3:148
Grace, 2:577
Sarah (Dudley), 2:78,
  2:367, 3:1, 3:327
Kedall/Kedell/Keedell
Bethia, 3:2, 3:415
Mary, 3:2, 4:532
Keeler
----, 3:2
Elizabeth, 3:2
Grace (Lindall), 3:648
Mehitable (Rockwell), 3:2
Rebecca, 3:2, 3:424
Sarah, 3:2
Sarah (----) Whelpley, 3:2,
  4:504
Sarah (Sension), 3:2
Keen/Kean
Elizabeth, 3:3
Hannah, 3:3
Hannah (Dingley), 2:52,
  3:3
Jane (----), 3:2
Martha, 3:3
Martha (----), 3:3
Mary, 3:307
Sarah, 3:3
Keeny/Keny/Keeney
Agnes, 1:153
Agnes (----), 3:3
Alice (----), 3:3
Hannah, 3:3
Lydia, 3:3
Mary, 3:3
Sarah, 3:3
Sarah (Douglas), 2:63, 3:3
Susanna, 3:3, 3:355, 4:345
Keep
Elizabeth, 3:3
Hannah, 3:3
Sarah, 3:3, 3:361
Sarah (Colton), 3:3
Sarah (Leonard), 3:3, 3:79
Keese
Alice, 3:3
Ann, 3:3
Ann (Manton), 3:3, 3:150
Patience, 3:3

Keet
Hannah (French), 2:206,
3:3
Keetch
Hannah (----), 3:3
Mary, 3:3
Keith
----, 1:326
Abiah, 3:4
Abigail, 3:4
Ann, 3:4
Bethia, 3:4
Bethia (Fobes), 3:4
Constant, 3:4
Elizabeth, 3:4
Elizabeth (Fobes), 3:4
Esther, 3:4
Faithful, 3:4
Hannah, 3:4
Hannah (Fobes), 3:4
Hannah (Washburn), 3:4
Jane, 3:4
Jemima, 3:4
Kezia, 3:4
Margaret, 3:4
Martha, 3:4
Mary, 2:471, 3:4
Mary (----), 3:4
Mary (----) Williams, 3:4,
4:571
Mary (Hodges), 2:439
Mary (Lothrop), 3:4
Phebe, 3:4
Sarah, 3:4
Silence, 3:4
Susanna, 3:4
Susanna (Edson), 2:102,
3:4
Zephaniah, 3:4
Kellen/Killin/Kelling
Hannah (Trarice), 3:4
Margaret, 3:4
Kellogg
---- (Devotion), 2:43
Abigail, 3:5-6, 3:642,
4:124
Abigail (Terry), 3:5, 4:269
Ann, 3:5
Ann (Hinsdale), 3:5
Bridget (Bouton), 1:220,
3:4
Elizabeth, 3:4-5, 3:261,
3:642

Elizabeth (----), 3:642
Experience, 3:642
Hannah, 3:5
Joanna, 3:5, 4:123
Joanna (----), 3:5
Lydia, 3:4, 3:6
Lydia (----), 3:6
Margaret, 3:6
Mary, 3:4, 3:6, 3:444,
3:642
Mary (----) Lyon, 3:5
Mercy, 3:6
Prudence, 3:5
Rachel, 3:4-5, 3:278
Rebecca, 3:5
Sarah, 3:4-6, 3:279, 3:642,
3:656
Sarah (Boltwood), 1:209,
3:6
Sarah (Day) Gunn, 2:27,
2:323, 3:6
Sarah (Dickinson) Lane,
2:48, 3:5, 3:53
Sarah (Merrill), 3:199,
4:687
Sarah (Moody), 3:653
Sarah (Platt), 3:6
Sarah (Plum), 3:5
Sarah (Root), 3:6, 3:574
Kellond
Abigail (Hawkins) Moore,
2:383, 3:6, 3:230
Elizabeth, 3:6
Elizabeth (----), 3:6
Mary, 3:6
Susanna, 3:6
Kelly
---- (Wakeman), 4:388
Abiel, 3:7
Elizabeth (----), 3:6, 4:131
Elizabeth (Emery), 3:7
Hannah, 3:7, 3:477
Mary, 2:24, 3:7
Mary (Holdridge), 2:446,
3:7
Rebecca, 3:7
Sarah, 1:157, 3:7
Sarah (Knight), 3:7
Kelsey
----, 3:7
Abigail, 3:7, 4:687
Abigail (----), 4:687
Abigail (Atwood), 3:7

Hannah, 3:7
Hannah (----), 3:7
Hannah (Ingersoll), 2:520,
3:7
Lydia, 3:645
Mary, 2:256
Phebe (Disbrow), 2:52, 3:7
Priscilla, 2:586
Rebecca, 3:7, 3:202
Rebecca (Hoskins), 3:7
Ruth, 4:687
Kemp/Kempe
Bethia, 3:8
Elizabeth (----), 3:8
Esther, 3:7-8
Esther (----), 3:8
Mehitable, 3:8
Patience, 4:43
Patience (Thacher), 3:8,
3:366, 4:274
Sarah (----), 3:8
Kempster
Abigail (----), 3:8
Kempthorne
Mary (Long), 3:8, 3:109
Sarah, 3:8
Kempton
Joan (Rawlins), 3:510
Joanna, 3:8, 3:244
Joanna (Rawlins), 3:8
Julian (Bradford) Morton,
3:8
Julian (Carpenter) Morton,
3:244
Mary (----), 3:643
Mary (Reeves), 3:644,
3:661, 4:702
Patience, 3:8
Patience (Faunce), 2:148,
3:643
Kendall
---- (Tead/Teed/Ted),
4:265
Abigail, 3:9-10, 3:520
Abigail (Broughton), 3:10
Alice, 3:9
Alice (Temple), 3:9
Elizabeth, 3:9, 3:429,
4:140, 4:597
Elizabeth (Comey), 3:9
Esther, 3:9
Eunice (Brooks) Carter,
1:341, 3:9

Kendall (continued)
Hannah, 3:9-10, 3:352
Hannah (Bartlett), 1:133,
3:9
Jane, 3:10
Lydia:9
Mary, 1:282-283, 3:9-10,
4:527
Mary (Locke), 3:9, 3:103
Mary (Tidd), 3:9
Persis, 3:9
Persis (Hayward), 3:9
Phebe, 3:9
Rebecca, 1:219, 2:96,
3:9-10
Rebecca (----), 3:10
Rebecca (Mixer), 3:9,
3:223
Ruth, 3:9-10
Ruth (----), 3:10
Sarah, 3:9
Susanna, 3:9-10
Tabitha, 3:9-10, 3:378,
3:643
Kennard
Elizabeth, 3:10
Rebecca (Spencer), 3:10,
4:147
Kennedy
Annable, 3:10
Elizabeth, 3:10
Elizabeth (----), 3:10
Hannah, 3:10
Joanna, 3:10
Sarah, 3:10
Kennet
Susanna (----), 3:10
Kennicut
Joanna, 3:10
Joanna (Shepardson), 4:77
Joanna (Sheperson), 3:10
Lydia, 3:10
Kenniston/Kiniston
Dorothy (----), 3:10
Mary (Mushamore), 3:10,
3:258
Kenny/Kenney
Ann (----), 3:643
Deborah (Stokes), 4:203
Dinah, 3:10
Elizabeth, 3:643, 3:648
Elizabeth (----), 3:10
Elizabeth (Knight), 3:643

Elizabeth (Look), 3:643,
3:648
Hannah, 3:10, 3:643
Jemima, 3:10
Joanna, 3:199
Lydia, 3:643
Martha, 3:263, 4:430
Mary, 3:10, 3:437, 4:354
Mary (----), 3:643
Priscilla, 3:10
Priscilla (Lewis), 3:10
Sarah, 3:10, 3:643
Sarah (----), 3:10
Kenrick/Kenerick/Kendrick
Abigail, 3:11
Ann, 3:11
Ann (Smith), 3:11, 4:131
Deborah, 3:11
Elizabeth, 3:11
Esther, 3:11, 4:410
Esther (----), 3:11
Grace, 3:11
Hannah, 3:11, 3:202,
3:656
Hannah (Jackson), 2:515,
2:530, 3:11
Jane (----), 3:11
Judith (----), 3:11
Lydia (Cheny), 3:11
Margaret, 3:11
Maria, 3:11
Mary, 3:11
Mary (Perry), 3:11
Mercy, 3:11
Sarah, 3:11
Kent
----, 2:182
---- (Jones), 3:640
Abigail, 3:12, 3:559
Abigail (Dudley), 2:78,
3:12
Abigail (Wenchell), 3:12
Ann (----), 3:13
Deborah, 3:12
Dorothy (----), 3:12
Dorothy (Brown), 1:268
Eleanor (----) Scadlock,
3:13
Elizabeth, 3:13
Elizabeth (Winthrop),
4:607
Emma, 3:12
Emma (----), 3:12

Esther (----) Phelps, 3:13
Experience, 3:12
Frances (----), 3:12
Frances (Woodall), 3:643
Hannah, 3:11-13, 4:254
Hannah (Grissell), 3:11
Jane, 3:643
Jane (----), 3:12
Joan, 3:13
Joan (Penny), 3:13
Joanna, 3:493
Joanna (----) Davison, 3:12
Judith, 3:643
Lydia, 3:11-12
Margery (----), 3:13
Martha, 3:13
Martha (----), 3:13
Martha (Allen), 1:30
Mary, 3:11-13, 3:643
Mary (----), 3:12
Mary (----) Mears, 3:13
Mary (Hobbs), 3:12
Mercy, 3:13
Priscilla, 3:13
Priscilla (Hunter), 2:502,
3:13
Rebecca, 1:184, 2:143,
3:12-13, 4:43
Sarah, 2:308, 3:12-13,
3:643
Sarah (Woodman), 3:12
Kerley/Carsley/etc
Elizabeth, 2:474
Elizabeth (How), 3:14
Elizabeth (White), 3:13
Hannah, 2:105, 3:14
Jane (----), 3:14
Mary, 3:14
Rebecca (----) Josselyn,
2:572, 3:14
Sarah, 1:34, 3:14
Keskeys
Ruth (----), 3:14
Ruth (Graves), 2:296
Ketcham/Ketchum
Esther, 3:14
Hannah, 3:14
Martha (Betts), 1:173
Mary, 3:14
Mary (Harcutt), 2:353,
3:14
Mercy (Lindall), 3:14, 3:95
Rebecca, 3:14, 4:264

Ketcham/Ketchum
(continued)
Sarah, 3:14
Ketchell
Margaret (----), 3:32
Kettle/Kettell
Abigail, 3:15
Abigail (Austin), 1:81,
3:14
Abigail (Convers), 1:444,
3:15
Ann, 3:15
Dorothy (----) Hett, 2:407,
3:15
Elizabeth, 3:14-15, 3:643
Elizabeth (----), 3:643
Elizabeth (Allen), 3:14
Elizabeth (Ward), 3:15
Esther, 3:15
Esther (Ward), 3:15
Hannah, 1:329, 3:15
Hannah (----), 3:15
Hannah (Frothingham),
2:213, 3:15
Hannah (Kidder), 3:15
Mary, 3:14-16
Mary (Drowne), 2:74
Mary (Hett) Frothingham,
3:16
Mercy, 3:16
Mercy (Hayden), 2:386,
3:16
Rachel, 3:15
Rebecca, 2:362, 3:15
Sarah, 3:15
Sarah (Goodenow), 2:271,
3:14
Union, 3:15
Key
Dorothy, 1:500
Keyes
Elizabeth (----), 3:16
Frances (Grant), 3:16
Hannah, 3:16
Jane, 1:407, 3:16
Joanna (Cleaveland),
1:407
Judith, 3:16
Mary, 1:327, 3:16
Rebecca, 3:16
Sarah, 1:319, 3:16
Sarah (----), 2:220, 3:16
Sarah (Blandford), 1:197,

3:16
Keyser/Keasur/Keyzer/etc
Elizabeth (Holyoke), 2:456,
3:16
Hannah (Flint) Ward,
4:410
Mary, 3:179
Mary (----), 3:16
Mary (Collins), 3:643
Rebecca, 3:16
Sarah, 2:257, 3:643
Kezan
Hannah (Davis), 2:18,
3:16
Kibby/Kibbe/Kibbee
Abigail, 3:17
Abigail (Agar), 1:79
Abigail (Ager), 3:17
Abigail (Anger), 3:17
Ann, 3:17
Elizabeth, 3:17, 3:370,
3:505, 3:643
Grizzle (----), 3:17
Hannah, 3:17
Hannah (----), 3:17
Jerusha, 3:17
Mary, 3:17, 3:653
Mary (----), 3:17
Mary (Comy), 1:439, 3:17
Rachel, 3:17
Rachel (Cook), 3:17
Rebecca, 3:17
Sarah, 3:17
Sarah (Stephenson)
Lowden, 3:17
Kidder
Abigail, 3:18
Alice, 3:18
Ann, 3:18
Ann (Moore), 3:18, 3:227
Dorothy, 2:515, 3:18
Elizabeth, 3:18
Elizabeth (Bunn), 3:18
Hannah, 3:15, 3:18
Lydia (Parker), 3:18
Mary, 3:18
Mary (----), 3:18
Rachel, 3:18
Rachel (Crosby), 3:18
Sarah, 1:508, 3:18
Sarah (Griggs), 2:315, 3:18
Kilbourn/Kilborne/Kilburn
Abigail, 3:19

Abigail (Atwood), 3:19
Ann, 3:19
Dorothy, 3:20
Dorothy (Butler), 3:20
Elizabeth, 3:19-20
Elizabeth (----), 3:19-20
Elizabeth (Mitchell), 3:19
Esther, 3:20
Esther (Gibbs), 3:20
Frances, 3:20, 3:306
Frances (----), 3:20
Frances (Trumbull), 3:19
Grace, 3:19
Grace (Bulkley), 3:19
Hannah, 3:20
Hannah (Hills), 2:420,
3:20
Lydia, 2:393, 3:20, 3:306
Margaret, 3:19-20, 3:60,
3:306
Martha, 3:19
Mary, 3:19-20, 3:306,
3:572
Mary (Cheney), 1:372,
3:19
Mary (Foster), 3:20
Mary (Swan), 4:237
Naomi, 2:331, 3:19-20
Naomi (----), 3:19
Sarah, 1:472, 3:19
Sarah (Brownson), 1:280,
3:19
Sarah (Goodrich), 3:19
Susanna, 3:19
Susanna (Hills), 2:420,
3:19
Kilby
Catharine, 3:20
Elizabeth, 3:20
Elizabeth (Josselyn)
Yeomans, 2:572, 3:20,
4:668
Mary, 3:20
Miriam, 3:20
Rebecca, 3:20
Rebecca (----), 3:20
Rebecca (Simpkins), 4:101
Sarah, 3:20
Sarah (----), 3:20
Sarah (Simpkins), 4:101
Kilcup
Abigail (----), 3:85
Abigail (Dudson), 3:21

Kilcup (continued)
Grace (----), 3:21
Sarah, 3:21
Kilham/Killam/Kellum/etc
Alice (----), 3:21
Elizabeth, 2:250
Hannah, 3:644
Hannah (Goodale), 3:643-644
Lucretia, 2:40
Martha (Solart), 4:706
Ruth, 3:644
Sarah, 3:21
Sarah (----) Fairfield, 3:619, 3:643
Kilton
Jane (Blake), 1:192
Kimball
----, 1:29, 3:22
Abigail, 3:21
Ann, 3:21
Elizabeth, 2:123, 2:548, 3:21-22, 4:220
Elizabeth (----), 3:22, 3:644
Elizabeth (Potter), 3:466
Elizabeth (Trarice), 3:22
Hannah, 1:116, 2:266, 3:22, 3:347
Hannah (----), 3:21
Hannah (Bartlett), 3:22
Joanna, 3:23
Martha, 1:364, 3:22
Mary, 1:250, 3:21-22, 4:688
Mary (----), 3:21, 3:644
Mary (Brigden), 1:250, 3:22
Mary (Clark), 1:403
Mary (Hazeltine), 2:395, 3:21
Mary (Hobbs), 3:22
Mehitable, 4:297
Priscilla, 3:23
Rebecca, 3:22
Sarah, 1:250, 3:22, 3:39, 4:92
Sarah (Fownell), 2:195, 3:22
Sarah (Spofford), 4:151
Susan, 3:21
Susanna, 3:21-22
Susanna (----), 3:21
Ursula (----), 3:22

Kimberly
Abiah, 3:23
Alice (----), 3:23
Elizabeth, 3:23, 4:687, 4:689
Hannah, 3:23, 4:687
Hannah (----), 3:23, 3:644
Mary, 2:388, 3:23, 3:604, 3:644
Mary (----), 3:23
Mary (----) Preston, 4:687, 4:696
Ruth, 3:23
Ruth (Curtis), 1:487
Sarah, 3:637, 3:644, 4:675, 4:687
Kimright/Kimwright
---- (----) Holland, 3:23
Judith (----) Holland, 2:447
Kind
Jane (----), 3:23
Mary, 3:23
Sarah, 3:23
King
---- (----), 3:26
---- (Barker), 3:25
---- (Bishop), 1:186
Abigail, 3:24-27
Abigail (----), 3:24
Abigail (Strong), 3:27
Ann (----), 3:26
Ann (Hoar), 3:644
Annis, 3:24
Beriah, 3:25
Bridget (Davis), 3:26
Catharine, 3:25
Catharine (Shaflin), 4:58
Deborah, 3:24
Deliverance, 3:27, 4:350
Dorothy (----), 1:116, 2:399
Elizabeth, 1:448, 3:24-27, 3:531
Elizabeth (----), 4:687
Elizabeth (----) Corwin, 3:24
Elizabeth (Clap), 1:391, 3:26
Elizabeth (Denslow), 2:39, 3:27
Elizabeth (Goldthwait), 2:270, 3:25
Elizabeth (Walker), 3:25,

4:395
Esther, 3:25
Esther (----), 3:25
Eunice, 3:25
Experience, 3:24-26
Experience (----), 3:26
Experience (Phillips), 3:413
Hannah, 1:197, 3:24-25
Jane (----) Hatch, 2:375, 3:26
Jemima, 3:26
Joanna (----) Alvord, 3:26
Joanna (Taylor) Alvord, 1:47
Judith (Whitman), 4:523
Mary, 2:555, 3:24-27, 3:79
Mary (----), 1:493, 3:24-26
Mary (Fowler), 2:193, 3:24
Mary (French), 3:25
Mary (James), 3:23
Mary (Sprague), 3:26, 4:156
Mary (Webster), 3:27
Mary (Wilson) Jesse, 2:547, 4:587
Mehitable, 3:25, 3:27
Mehitable (Pomeroy), 3:25
Mercy, 3:530
Mindwell, 3:25
Mindwell (Pomeroy), 3:25
Mindwell (Porter), 3:25
Patience, 3:25
Rachel (Jennison) Barron, 1:127
Rhoda, 3:26, 3:562
Ruth, 1:116
Sarah, 2:571, 3:24-26, 3:266
Sarah (----), 3:26
Sarah (Griggs), 1:303, 2:315, 3:27
Sarah (Holton), 2:456, 3:24
Sarah (Whiting) Mygatt, 3:25, 3:259, 4:522
Saray, 3:24
Susanna, 2:399, 3:26
Susanna (----), 3:23, 3:26
Susanna (Jesse), 2:547
Tabitha, 3:24
Tabitha (Walker), 3:24, 4:395

King (continued)
Thankful, 3:24-25
Winifred, 1:165, 3:27
Kingman
----, 3:27, 3:327
Bethia (Howard), 2:472
Deliverance, 3:27
Elizabeth, 3:27
Elizabeth (----), 3:27
Hannah, 3:27
Joan (----), 3:27
Mercy (Randall), 3:506
Rebecca, 3:27
Rebecca (----), 3:27
Susanna, 3:27
Kingsbury
Deborah (----) Eastman,
3:29
Elizabeth, 3:28
Elizabeth (----), 3:28
Elizabeth (Fuller), 2:219,
3:28, 3:204
Esther (Judson), 2:392
Eunice (----), 4:510
Hannah, 3:28
Hannah (----), 3:28
Huldah (Corliss), 1:458,
3:29
Love (Ayers), 3:28
Margaret (----), 3:28
Mary, 3:28
Mary (----), 3:28
Mary (Bacon), 1:90, 3:29
Milicent (----), 3:28
Sarah, 3:28
Sarah (Button), 1:511,
3:28
Sarah (Haines), 3:29
Susanna, 3:28, 3:436
Susanna (----), 3:28
Kingsley/Kinsley
----, 1:471, 2:206, 3:29-30
---- (Daniels), 2:10
Abigail, 3:29
Abigail (Leonard), 3:29
Alice (----) Jones, 2:564
Alice (Daniels), 3:29
Ann, 3:29
Ann (Dickinson) Clary,
2:48
Elinor, 2:322
Elizabeth, 3:29, 3:342
Hannah, 3:29, 3:537

Hannah (----), 3:29
Hannah (Brackett), 1:229,
3:29
Martha (Brown), 1:509
Mary, 3:29-30
Mary (----), 3:29
Mary (Maury), 3:29
Mary (Morey), 3:29
Mary (Washburn), 3:30,
4:429
Mehitable (----), 1:262
Mehitable (Morey), 3:29
Remember, 3:29
Renewal, 3:29
Sarah, 3:29, 4:385
Sarah (Haynes), 2:388,
3:29
Susanna, 3:29
Kingsnoth/Kingsworth
Mary (----), 1:435
Mary (Stevens), 3:30,
4:186
Kingston
Dorothy (----), 1:516
Kinnicutt
---- (Tillinghast), 4:303
Kinsman/Kingsman
---- (Boreman), 3:30
Bridget, 2:22
Martha, 2:188
Rebecca (Budley), 1:288
Rebecca (Burley), 3:30
Sarah, 4:671
Kirby
Abigail, 3:30, 3:644
Abigail (Rowland), 3:31
Bethia, 3:30, 3:644
Elizabeth, 3:30-31, 4:4
Elizabeth (----), 3:30-31
Esther, 3:30, 4:203
Eunice, 3:30
Hannah, 1:56, 3:30
Jane (----), 3:30
Mary, 1:283, 3:30
Patience (----), 3:31
Sarah, 2:35, 2:485,
3:30-31, 3:644
Susanna, 1:481, 3:30,
3:644
Kirk
Abigail (Rawlins), 3:31,
3:509
Elizabeth, 1:114

Kirtland/Kertland/etc
Alice (----), 3:32, 4:280
Ann, 3:32
Elizabeth, 3:31-32
Hannah, 3:32, 3:476
Lydia, 3:31
Lydia (Pratt), 3:31, 3:476
Martha, 1:191, 3:31-32
Mary, 3:32
Mary (----), 1:300
Mary (Rand), 3:32
Parnell, 3:31
Parnell (----), 3:32
Priscilla, 1:433, 3:31-32
Ruth (Pierce), 3:32
Sarah, 2:19, 3:32, 3:73
Susanna, 3:32, 4:283,
4:488
Kiskeyes/Keskeys
Ruth (Graves), 3:32
Kitchell
Abigail, 3:32
Elizabeth, 3:32
Elizabeth (Wakeman),
3:32, 4:387
Grace (Pierson), 3:434
Hannah, 3:32
Joanna, 3:381
Sarah, 3:32
Kitchen/Kitchin
Abigail, 3:627, 3:644
Bethia, 3:96
Elizabeth, 3:32
Elizabeth (----), 3:32
Hannah, 3:32
Mary, 3:32, 3:663, 4:687
Priscilla, 3:644
Kitcherell/Ketcherwell/etc
Hannah, 3:33
Martha, 3:33, 4:654
Martha (----), 2:60, 3:33
Sarah, 3:33
Kitson
Alice, 3:526
Kitteredge
Hannah (French), 3:33
Knapp
Abigail, 3:33
Abigail (Wescoat), 3:34,
4:486
Ann, 3:34, 3:408
Elinor (----), 3:34
Elizabeth, 3:33-34, 4:214

Knapp (continued)
Elizabeth (----), 3:34
Elizabeth (Warren), 3:33, 4:424
Hannah, 3:33-34
Hannah (----), 1:223, 3:33
Hannah (Close), 3:33
Judith, 1:327, 3:34
Lydia, 3:34
Margaret (----), 3:34
Mary, 3:33-34, 4:134
Mary (----), 3:34
Mary (Grout), 2:319, 3:34
Priscilla, 3:34
Priscilla (----) Akers, 1:20, 3:34
Ruth, 2:155, 3:33-34
Sarah, 2:52, 3:33-34
Sarah (Austin), 3:33
Sarah (Parke), 3:348
Sarah (Young), 3:33
Unity (----) Buxton Brown, 1:274, 1:325, 3:34
Kneeland
Hannah, 3:34
Mary, 3:34
Mary (----), 3:34
Prudence (Clark), 3:610
Ruth, 3:34
Knell/Kneale/Knill
Elizabeth, 3:35
Elizabeth (----), 1:500, 3:35
Elizabeth (----) Knowles, 3:35, 3:42
Elizabeth (Newman) Knowles, 3:274, 3:644-645
Hannah, 3:35
Phebe (Nichols), 3:279
Ruth (----), 1:498, 3:35
Ruth (----) Allen, 3:35
Knight
----, 3:37
---- (----) Hill Lovering, 3:124
Abigail, 3:35-37, 3:74
Abigail (Craggin), 3:37
Abigail (Jaques), 3:35
Agnes (Coffley), 3:38
Amaziah, 3:37
Ann, 2:538, 3:38-39, 4:147, 4:688
Ann (----) Cromwell, 1:476,

2:573, 3:39
Ann (----) Ingersoll, 2:521, 3:36
Apphia, 3:35
Bathsheba (Ingersoll), 2:521, 3:36
Deborah, 3:37-38
Deborah (Coffin), 3:38
Dinah, 3:37, 3:246
Dinah (----), 3:38
Dorothy, 3:35, 3:38
Dorothy (----), 3:38
Elinor (----), 3:36
Elizabeth, 1:241, 3:22, 3:36-39, 3:237, 3:296, 3:643-644, 4:484, 4:688
Elizabeth (----), 3:35-36
Elizabeth (Jacob), 3:39
Elizabeth (Jaques), 3:39
Emma, 3:644
Hannah, 3:36-39, 3:297, 4:524
Hannah (----), 3:37-38
Hannah (----) Allen, 1:31
Hannah (Rand), 3:36
Joanna, 3:38-39
Joanna (----), 3:38
Judith, 3:38
Leah (----) Tarr, 3:37
Love, 4:687-688
Lydia, 3:38
Margery (----), 3:38
Martha, 3:37-39, 3:644
Martha (Lilly), 3:38
Mary, 1:281, 1:514, 2:65, 3:36-39, 3:299, 3:450, 3:644, 3:663, 4:688
Mary (----), 3:37
Mary (Brewster), 3:39
Mary (Bridge), 3:37
Mary (Bruster), 3:39
Mary (Bullard), 3:38
Mary (Clements), 3:36
Mary (Eaton) Hill Lovering, 2:420, 3:35
Mary (Spaule), 3:38, 4:146
Mehitable, 3:39
Persis, 3:37
Persis (----), 3:37
Rebecca, 3:37-38, 4:139, 4:711
Rebecca (Noyes), 3:37
Ruhama, 3:36

Ruhama (Johnson), 2:599, 3:36
Ruth, 1:504, 3:37-38
Ruth (Wright), 3:37
Sarah, 1:131, 3:7, 3:36-38, 3:76, 3:644, 4:531, 4:687
Sarah (----), 3:35-38
Sarah (Burt), 3:36
Sarah (Church), 1:385, 4:687
Sarah (Howe), 3:39
Sarah (Kimball), 3:22, 3:39
Sarah (Lemon), 3:644, 3:647
Sarah (Rawlins) Holdsworth, 2:594
Knott
Martha, 2:81, 3:40, 4:309
Martha (----), 3:40
Ruth (----), 3:644
Knower
----, 1:287-287, 3:40
Elizabeth, 3:41
Elizabeth (----), 3:40-41
Mary, 3:40, 3:218
Nell (----), 3:41
Sarah, 3:40-41
Sarah (Winslow), 3:40
Knowles
---- (----) Davis, 3:41
---- (Bills) Davis, 1:179
---- (Potter), 3:41
Alice, 3:42
Alice (----), 3:42
Alice/Alce (Fish), 2:161
Ann, 3:41
Apphia (Bangs), 1:111, 3:42
Barbara, 3:42, 3:188
Deborah, 3:42
Duty, 1:435
Elizabeth, 2:183, 3:41-42
Elizabeth (----), 3:35, 3:41-42
Elizabeth (Newman), 3:274, 3:644-645
Hannah, 3:42, 3:104
Martha, 3:41-42
Mary, 3:41-42, 3:98
Mary (----), 3:41
Mary (Porter), 3:460, 3:645

Knowles (continued)
Mehitable, 3:42
Mercy, 2:55, 3:42
Mercy (Freeman), 2:204,
3:42
Rebecca, 3:42
Rose, 3:42
Ruth, 3:42
Ruth (----), 3:42
Sarah, 2:70
Knowlton
Elizabeth, 3:42
Hannah (Green), 3:43
Hannah (Mirick), 3:42
Margaret (----), 3:42
Mary, 3:42
Mary (Kimball), 4:688
Mercy, 3:42
Sarah, 3:42
Sarah (----), 3:42, 4:688
Knox
Hannah (----), 3:43
Sarah, 3:43
Kostlo
Sarah, 3:43
Sarah (----), 3:43
Labarre
Mary (Burr), 1:307
Lachman
Alice (Winter), 4:606
Lacock
Alice (----), 3:43
Ladd
---- (Corliss), 1:458, 3:43
Ann (----), 3:43
Elizabeth, 2:386, 3:43,
4:127
Elizabeth (Fifield), 3:43
Elizabeth (Gilman), 2:258,
3:43
Lydia, 3:43
Lydia (Singletary), 3:43
Mary, 3:43, 3:535
Sarah, 3:43
Lahorne
Flora (----), 3:43
Laighton/Leighton
---- (Nutter), 3:44, 3:301
Catharine (Frost), 2:212,
2:345, 3:44
Elizabeth, 1:375, 1:476,
2:591, 3:44
Elizabeth (Hazard), 2:395,

3:44
Hannah (Silsbee/Silsby),
3:44, 4:98
Honor (Langdon), 3:44
Joanna (----), 1:407, 3:44
Margaret, 3:44
Martha (Booth), 1:212,
3:44
Mary, 3:44, 3:548, 4:151
Rebecca, 2:519, 3:44
Rebecca (----), 3:44
Sarah, 2:510, 3:44
Sarah (Graves), 3:44
Sarah (Redknap), 3:44,
3:522
Lake
Abigail, 3:645
Alice (----), 3:45
Ann, 1:463, 3:45, 3:173,
3:645
Ann (----), 3:45
Ann (Stratton), 3:645
Catharine (----) Child, 3:45
Hannah, 2:223, 3:45
Lucy (----), 3:45
Margaret (----), 2:223, 3:45
Martha, 2:364, 3:45
Mary, 3:45, 3:645
Mary (Coy), 1:467, 3:45
Mary (Goodyear), 2:278,
3:45
Rebecca, 3:45
Sarah, 3:45
Lakin
Abigail, 3:46
Lydia (Brown), 1:264,
3:46
Mary, 3:46, 4:553
Mary (----), 3:45, 3:163
Sarah, 3:45-46, 4:552
Lamb
Abigail, 3:47
Decline, 3:47, 4:134
Dorothy, 3:47
Dorothy (----), 2:385
Dorothy (Harbottle), 3:47
Elizabeth, 2:426, 3:46-47
Elizabeth (----), 3:47
Emory, 3:330
Eunice, 3:47
Hannah, 3:47
Huldah, 3:47
Joanna, 3:47, 4:177

Lydia (Wright) Bliss
Norton, 1:438, 3:47,
4:659, 4:693
Margaret (----), 1:35, 3:47
Mary, 3:46-48, 4:237
Mary (Alcock), 1:22, 3:47
Mary (Wise), 3:46, 4:615
Rebecca (Tilton), 4:304
Sarah, 3:47
Lambard
Abigail, 2:368
Lambert
Abigail, 3:645
Ann, 3:48, 3:267
Deborah, 3:48
Deborah (Fowler), 2:195,
3:48
Deborah (Frink), 2:209,
3:48
Edna, 1:94
Edna (Northend), 3:48,
3:290
Elinor (----) Furnell, 2:220,
3:48
Elizabeth, 1:347, 3:48,
3:645, 4:708
Elizabeth (----), 3:48
Elizabeth (Dean), 2:29
Elizabeth (Starke), 3:48
Esther, 1:213, 3:48
Eunice, 3:645
Hannah, 3:645
Jane (----), 3:48
Jemima, 1:166
Joanna (----), 3:48
Margaret, 1:239, 3:645
Martha, 3:48
Mary, 3:48, 3:640, 3:645
Mary (----), 3:645
Mary (Gray), 3:645
Mary (Lews), 3:48
Preserved, 3:645
Preserved (----), 3:645
Rachel, 3:48
Rebecca, 3:645
Sarah, 3:48, 3:645
Lamberton
---- (----), 2:278
Desire, 1:455, 3:48-49
Elizabeth, 3:49, 4:97,
4:334
Hannah, 1:43, 3:49, 4:477,
4:688

Lamberton (continued)
Hope, 4:688
Margaret (----), 3:48
Mercy, 3:48
Obedience, 3:48-49, 4:133
Lamprey/Lamphrey/etc
Elizabeth, 3:49
Elizabeth (Mitchell), 3:49
Julian (----), 3:49
Mary, 3:49
Lamson
---- (Perkins), 3:397
Azubah/Zubah, 3:49-50, 4:579
Dorothy (Mousal), 3:49
Elizabeth, 3:49
Elizabeth (----), 3:235
Elizabeth (----) Line, 4:688
Elizabeth (Mitchell), 3:49
Hannah, 1:434, 3:49
Hannah (----) Welsh, 3:49
Martha, 3:49, 3:530
Mary, 1:449, 3:49
Sarah, 1:265, 3:49
Sarah (----), 2:592, 3:50
Lancaster
Mary, 3:50, 3:219
Mary (----), 3:50
Lancton
Mary, 3:100
Lander
Sarah (Williams), 4:561
Landfear/Lamphear
----, 3:50
Abigail, 3:50
Amie, 3:50
Ann, 3:50
Elizabeth, 3:50
Esther, 3:50
Experience, 3:50
Experience (Reed), 3:50
Jerusha, 3:50
Lucy, 3:50
Mary, 3:50
Mary (----), 3:50
Prudence, 3:50
Rachel (Covey), 3:50
Sarah, 3:50
Sarah (----), 3:50
Susanna, 3:50
Zerviah, 3:50
Lane
----, 1:98, 2:497, 3:53, 3:94

---- (Kelsey), 3:7
Abigail, 3:51-52, 4:201
Abigail (Johnson) Farmer, 2:142
Ann, 2:189, 3:51-52
Ann (Keayne), 3:1, 3:51, 3:332
Asaph, 3:52
Bethia, 3:51
Bethia (Lincoln), 3:93
Catharine, 3:345, 4:350
Catharine (----) Doxy, 2:69, 3:51
Deborah, 3:51, 3:53, 3:645, 4:156
Deborah (Gill), 2:254, 3:53
Dorcas, 3:645
Dorcas (Wallis), 3:645
Dorothy, 3:52, 4:153
Dousabel (----), 3:52
Eleanor, 3:52
Elizabeth, 1:83, 2:362, 2:585, 3:51-53, 3:540, 3:645
Elizabeth (----), 3:51
Elizabeth (Beal), 1:145, 3:51
Hannah, 3:51-53, 3:645
Hannah (----), 3:51
Hannah (Brown), 1:273, 3:52
Hannah (Parke), 3:645
Hannah (Reyner), 3:52, 3:514
Hepzibah, 3:645
Jemima, 3:52-53, 4:506-507
Lydia, 3:645
Lydia (Kelsey), 3:645
Margaret, 3:645
Martha, 3:53
Mary, 1:83, 3:51-53, 3:645-646
Mary (----), 3:53
Mary (Brewer), 1:244, 3:53
Mehitable (Hobart), 3:52
Mercy (Welman), 3:645
Patience (Strong), 3:645
Priscilla, 3:52
Rachel, 3:53
Rebecca, 3:52, 3:345, 3:646

Ruth, 3:53
Sarah, 2:169, 3:51-53, 3:86, 3:645
Sarah (----), 3:52
Sarah (Beal), 1:145, 3:53
Sarah (Dickinson), 2:48, 3:5, 3:53
Sarah (Picket), 3:424, 3:645
Sarah (Webster), 3:54
Susanna, 3:51-53, 3:546
Susanna (Huet), 3:51
Susanna (Strong), 4:228
Susanna (Whipple), 3:53, 4:506
Tabitha, 3:53
Tabitha (Stodder), 3:53
Tryphena (----), 3:50-51
Zeruiah, 3:645
Laneson
Abigail, 3:54
Susanna, 3:54
Susanna (----), 3:54
Langdon
---- (----) Gridley, 3:54
Abigail, 3:54
Elizabeth, 3:54
Elizabeth (----), 3:54-55
Elizabeth (Sherburne), 3:646, 4:78
Honor, 3:44
Joanna, 3:54
Margaret, 3:54
Martha, 3:54-55
Martha (----), 3:54
Mary, 3:54
Mary (----), 3:54
Mary (Hubbard), 3:55
Mary (Porter) Royce, 3:660
Mary (Seymour) Gridley, 2:313
Phebe (----), 3:54
Rachel, 3:580
Sarah, 3:54, 3:507
Susanna, 3:54, 3:626
Langer
Ann (----), 3:55
Dinah, 3:55
Elizabeth, 3:55
Margaret, 3:55, 3:94
Susanna, 3:55

Langhorne/Longhorn
Bethia, 3:153
Constance, 3:231
Elizabeth, 2:395, 3:55
Mary, 3:55
Mercy, 3:55
Patience, 3:55
Sarah, 3:55, 4:688
Sarah (Green), 2:300, 3:55
Langley
Sarah, 3:55, 3:184
Sarah (Gill), 2:254, 3:55
Langmead
Ellen (----), 3:55
Langstaff
Sarah, 3:56
Langton/Lanckton/Lankton
----, 3:56
---- (----) Gridley, 3:646
Deliverance, 2:352, 3:56
Elizabeth, 3:56, 3:646
Elizabeth (----) Turner,
3:56
Elizabeth (Copley), 1:25
Elizabeth (Copley) Turner,
1:456
Esther, 2:351, 3:56
Hannah, 3:485, 3:646
Hannah (----) Haynes,
2:388, 3:56
Mary, 3:646
Mary (Porter) Royce,
3:646
Mercy, 3:646
Sarah, 3:646
Susanna, 3:646
Susanna (Root), 3:572,
3:646
Langworth
Rachel (Hubbard), 2:485,
3:56
Lapham
---- (Hollis), 3:56
Elizabeth, 3:56
Lydia, 1:139, 3:56
Mary, 3:56
Mary (Mann), 3:145
Mary (Tilden), 3:56, 4:301
Mercy (Mann), 3:56
Rebecca, 3:56, 4:429
Larcum
Abigail (Solart), 4:706

Large
Phebe (Lee), 3:56, 3:73
Largin
Alice (----), 3:56
Ann (----), 3:56
Susanna, 3:56
Larkin
Elizabeth, 3:57
Elizabeth (Dowse), 2:580
Elizabeth (Dowse) Miles,
2:68, 3:57
Elizabeth (Hall), 2:591,
3:57, 3:627
Hannah, 3:57, 3:271-272
Hannah (Babcock), 3:57
Hannah (Remington), 3:57
Joan (----), 3:57
Joanna, 3:57, 3:277
Joanna (----), 3:391
Joanna (Hale), 2:330, 3:57,
3:616
Lydia, 3:57
Mary, 3:57
Mary (Cottrell), 1:461,
3:57
Mary (Macoone/Mackoon),
3:141
Mary (Walker), 3:57
Mehitable, 4:239
Penelope, 3:57
Sarah, 3:57
Tabitha, 3:57
Larrabee
Alice, 3:646
Alice (Parke), 3:58, 3:348
Deborah (Ingersoll), 2:520,
3:57
Dorothy, 3:646
Elizabeth, 3:58, 3:631,
3:646
Elizabeth (Felt), 3:58
Phebe, 3:646
Phebe (----) Lee, 3:646
Sarah, 2:196, 3:58, 3:646
Laskin
Edith, 2:405
Latham
----, 3:104
---- (Singletary), 4:102
Elizabeth, 3:58, 3:74
Elizabeth (Masters)
Lockwood, 3:58, 3:104,
3:171

Frances, 3:58
Hannah, 3:58, 4:430
Jane, 2:484, 3:58, 4:563
Lydia, 3:58, 3:328
Mary (----), 3:58
Mercy, 2:361, 3:58
Rebecca (Wells), 3:58,
3:328, 4:475
Sarah, 2:472, 3:58, 4:475
Susanna, 4:601
Susanna (Winslow), 3:58,
4:601
Latoille
Catharine (Beauchamp),
1:150
Latonice
Esther, 2:2
Lattimore/Latimer
Abigail, 3:59
Ann (----), 3:59
Ann (Griggs) Jones, 2:315,
2:561, 3:59
Bathsheba, 1:78
Elisheba, 3:59
Elizabeth, 2:449, 3:59,
3:479, 4:436
Mary (Alley), 3:646
Mary (Pitt), 3:442
Naomi, 3:59
Rebecca, 3:59, 4:325
Laughton
Mary, 2:27
Launce
Mary, 2:97, 4:80, 4:554
Laurie
----, 3:59
Lydia, 3:59
Mary, 3:655
Mary (----), 3:59
Lavenuke
Isabella, 3:59
Judith, 3:59
Mary (Dival), 3:59
Law
Abigail, 3:60, 4:51
Abigail (Lane), 4:201
Ann (Eliot/Elliot/Elliott),
2:111
Elizabeth, 4:202
Elizabeth (Stodder), 4:202
Faith (----), 3:60
Lydia (Draper), 2:72, 3:60
Margaret (Kilbourn), 3:20,

Law (continued)
  Margaret (Kilbourn)
    (continued)
    3:60, 3:306
  Mary, 1:406
  Rebecca, 2:598
  Sarah, 3:60, 4:51
  Sarah (Clark), 3:60, 3:610
Lawes
  Lydia (----), 3:60
  Mary, 3:60, 3:148, 3:264
Lawrence
  ---- (Sprague), 3:63, 4:153
  Abigail, 3:60-63
  Abigail (Bellows), 1:162,
    3:61
  Ann, 3:61
  Ann (----) Phillips, 3:60,
    3:409
  Ann (Cooledge/Coolidge),
    1:452
  Ann (Coolidge) Adams,
    3:60
  Bethia, 3:63
  Christian (----), 3:61
  Deborah, 3:62
  Deliverance, 3:62
  Elizabeth, 3:60-63, 4:109,
    4:532
  Elizabeth (----), 3:61
  Elizabeth (----) Holland,
    3:61
  Elizabeth (Atkinson), 3:62
  Elizabeth (Bates), 3:63
  Elizabeth (Bennett), 3:60
  Elizabeth (Crisp), 1:473,
    3:61
  Elizabeth (Gillingham)
    Bennett, 1:505
  Elizabeth (Morse), 3:62
  Esther, 3:63
  Grace, 2:100, 3:61
  Hannah, 1:511, 3:60-62,
    4:29
  Hannah (----), 3:62
  Hannah (Mason), 3:60
  Hannah (Smith), 4:116
  Joan (----) Tuttle, 3:62
  Judith, 3:61, 4:174
  Lydia, 3:60
  Martha, 3:61-62
  Mary, 2:91, 3:60-63, 3:179,
    3:466, 4:536

Mary (----), 3:61-62
Mary (Clough), 3:60
Mary (Phillips) Munjoy,
  1:478, 3:63, 3:255,
  3:412
Mary Ann (Beauchamp),
  1:150
Maud (Russell), 3:60-61
Patience, 3:61-62
Phebe, 3:61
Rachel, 3:61
Rebecca, 3:62
Ruth (Whitney) Shattuck,
  3:61, 4:62, 4:530
Sarah, 3:60-63, 3:443,
  3:540, 4:602
Sarah (----), 3:62, 4:474
Sarah
  (Buckminster/Buck-
  master), 1:286, 3:62
Sarah (Counts), 3:60
Sarah (Morse), 3:62
Sarah (Smith), 3:62
Susanna, 1:89, 3:61-63
Susanna (----), 3:61, 4:256
Susanna (Bachelor), 1:89,
  3:61
Lawson
  Ann, 3:64
  Deborah, 3:64
  Deborah (Allen), 3:64
  Elizabeth (----), 3:63
  Jane (----), 3:64
  Mary, 3:63, 3:337
  Sarah, 3:64
Lawton
  Ann, 3:64, 4:107
  Benedicta (----), 3:64
  Elizabeth, 3:64, 4:83
  Elizabeth (Talman), 3:64
  Joanna (----) Mullins, 3:64
  Mary, 1:86, 3:64
  Mary (Broomer), 2:202,
    3:64
  Mary (Waddell/Wodell),
    3:64
  Mercy, 3:64
  Naomi (Hunt), 3:64
  Naomi (Hunt) Lawton,
    3:64
  Ruth, 3:64, 4:377
  Sarah, 3:64, 4:102
  Susanna, 3:64

Lay
  Abigail, 1:105, 3:65
  Abigail (----), 3:65
  Catharine, 3:65
  Dorothy, 3:65
  Elizabeth, 3:65
  Elizabeth (Wright), 4:654
  Marah, 3:65
  Mary, 3:65
  Mary (----), 3:65
  Mary (Stanton), 3:65
  Phebe, 2:37, 3:65
  Rebecca, 3:65, 3:512
  Sarah, 2:44, 3:65
  Sarah (----), 3:65
  Susanna, 3:65
  Temperance, 3:65
Layton
  Alice, 2:276
  Elizabeth, 3:438
Lazell
  Abiah, 3:65-66
  Abigail/Abiah (Leavitt),
    3:65, 3:70
  Deborah (Lincoln), 3:66
  Elizabeth, 3:65-66
  Elizabeth (Gates), 2:236,
    3:65
  Hannah, 3:65-66
  Lydia, 3:66
  Martha, 3:66
  Mary, 3:65-66
  Mary (----), 3:66
  Mary (Allen), 3:66
  Phebe, 3:66
  Rachel (Lincoln), 3:65
  Sarah, 3:65-66
  Sarah (----), 3:66
Leach
  Abiel, 3:67
  Abigail, 2:26, 3:66
  Abigail (Haughton), 2:378,
    3:67
  Alice, 2:116
  Alice (----), 3:67, 3:646
  Ann, 3:66
  Ann (Fuller), 3:67
  Ann (Nokes), 3:66
  Elizabeth, 2:584, 3:66,
    3:661
  Elizabeth (----), 3:67
  Elizabeth (Flint), 3:646
  Eunice, 3:66

Leach (continued)
Experience, 3:66
Hannah, 3:66-67
Hannah (----), 3:66
Hepzibah (Washburn),
3:66
Lydia, 3:66
Margaret, 3:67
Mary, 2:524, 3:66-67,
3:619
Mary (----), 3:67
Mary (Byram), 3:67
Mary (Whitman), 3:67,
4:524
Mehitable, 3:66-67
Mercy, 3:66
Phebe, 3:66
Prudence (Stetson), 3:66
Rachel, 3:66
Remember, 3:67
Sarah, 1:25, 2:406,
3:66-67, 3:212
Susanna, 3:66
Leadbetter
Catharine, 3:67, 3:373
Deliverance, 3:67
Relief (----) Dowse Foster,
2:191
Relief (Holland) Dowse
Foster, 3:67
Sarah, 3:67, 4:618
Sarah (----), 3:67
Sarah (Tolman), 3:67,
4:310
Leader
Abigail, 3:68
Abigail (----), 3:67
Alice (----), 3:68
Rebecca, 3:67
Rebecca (----), 3:68
Susanna (----), 3:68
Leager/Legare/Leger
----, 3:218
Ann, 4:394
Ann (Blake), 1:193, 3:68
Bethia, 3:68, 4:63
Hannah, 3:68
Leaman
Elizabeth, 3:68
Joanna, 3:68
Mary (----), 3:68
Rebecca, 3:68

Lear/Leare
Elizabeth, 3:647, 4:78
Elizabeth (Sherburne),
3:68
Elizabeth (Sherburne)
Langdon, 4:78
Learned/Larned/etc
Abigail, 3:68-69
Bathsheba, 3:68
Elizabeth, 2:334, 3:68-69
Goodith (----), 3:69
Hannah, 2:147, 3:68-69
Martha, 3:69
Mary, 1:127, 3:68-69
Mary (Fanning), 2:140,
3:68
Mary (Stearns), 1:302,
3:68, 4:173
Sarah, 2:132, 3:68-69,
3:122
Sarah (----), 3:68-69
Sarah (Bigelow), 3:69
Sarah (More), 3:68
Tabitha, 3:68
Thankful, 3:68
Leavensworth/Leavenworth
Grace (----), 3:69
Mary (Dorman), 2:61
Phebe (Wooster), 4:650
Leaver
Damaris (Bayley), 1:142,
3:69
Mary, 2:72
Prudence, 2:220, 3:69,
4:192
Leavitt
---- (Gilman), 2:257
Abigail, 3:70
Abigail/Abiah, 3:65, 3:70
Alice (----), 3:70
Alice (Gilman), 2:258
Asaph, 3:70
Bathsheba (Hobart), 3:70
Dorothy (Dudley), 2:77,
3:70
Elizabeth, 2:75, 2:575,
3:70
Elizabeth (Gannett), 2:225
Hannah, 2:126, 3:70,
3:102, 3:118
Hannah (Devotion), 2:43
Heriah, 3:70
Isabel (----), 3:70

Jemima, 3:70
Lydia, 3:69-70, 4:12
Lydia (Jackson), 2:527,
3:69
Margaret, 3:70
Margaret (Johnson), 3:70
Martha (Taylor), 3:69,
4:259
Mary, 3:70, 3:601
Ruth (Sleeper), 3:69
Sarah, 1:390, 3:70
Sarah (----), 3:70
LeBlonde
Ann, 3:71
Ann (----), 3:71
Marian, 3:71
Phillippa, 3:71
LeBross
Sarah (Lawrence) Winslow,
4:602
Lee
----, 3:71
---- (Brown), 3:73
Abigail, 3:72, 3:74
Abigail (Lord), 3:647
Abigail (Stevens), 4:189
Abigail (Warner), 3:72
Ann, 1:77, 3:71-72
Bridget, 2:585
Catharine, 3:73, 3:172,
4:56
Elizabeth, 2:472, 3:72-74,
3:647
Elizabeth (Bowland),
1:224
Elizabeth (Crampton),
1:470, 3:72
Elizabeth (Graham), 3:647
Elizabeth (Hubbard), 4:688
Elizabeth (Loomis), 3:647
Elizabeth (Rowland), 3:72
Elizabeth (Royce), 3:647
Elizabeth (Smith), 3:647,
4:130
Elizabeth (Woodward),
3:73
Elizabeth (Wright), 4:654
Esther (Waldron) Elkins,
2:112, 2:570, 3:71,
4:390
Hannah, 3:72-74, 3:647
Hepzibah (----) Pomeroy,
3:74

Lee (continued)
Hepzibah (Baker) Pomeroy,
3:450
Jane, 2:516, 3:73
Joanna, 3:72
Lydia, 2:242, 3:73, 3:172,
4:688
Lydia (Strong), 3:647
Margaret, 3:72
Martha, 3:647
Mary, 1:77, 2:430, 2:480,
3:71-74, 3:647, 4:362,
4:688
Mary (----), 2:317, 3:72,
3:647, 4:225
Mary (----) Engs, 2:124,
3:72
Mary (----) Fox, 3:72
Mary (Beal/Beals), 1:146
Mary (Camp), 4:688
Mary (DeWolf), 3:73
Mary (Griffing), 3:647
Mary (Hart), 2:368, 3:71
Mary (Miles) Wigley, 3:72
Mary (Woodhouse), 3:72,
4:639
Mercy, 3:73, 4:539
Mercy (Call), 1:330, 1:498,
3:73
Phebe, 3:56, 3:73
Phebe (----), 3:646
Rebecca, 3:73, 4:4
Ruth, 3:72, 3:647
Sarah, 3:72-73, 3:647
Sarah (----), 3:72
Sarah (Kirkland), 3:73
Sarah (Pixley), 3:72, 3:443
Tabitha, 3:72
Leeds
Abigail, 3:74
Abigail (Knight), 3:74
Deborah, 3:74
Elizabeth, 3:74
Elizabeth (Latham), 3:58,
3:74
Hannah, 1:390, 3:74
Joan (----), 3:74
Joanna, 3:74
Mary (Brimsmead), 1:254,
3:74
Miriam, 3:74
Miriam (Cook), 1:445,
3:74

Rebecca, 3:74
Ruth, 1:34
Leek/Leeke
Joanna, 3:75, 4:186
Mary, 3:75
Lees
Deborah, 3:75, 4:41
Elizabeth (Wright), 3:75
Leete
---- (Jordan), 2:569
Abigail, 3:75, 4:633
Ann, 1:434, 3:75, 4:333
Ann (----), 3:75
Dorothy, 2:464, 3:75
Elizabeth (Jordan), 3:75
Graciana, 3:75
Mary, 2:458, 3:75
Mary (----), 1:234, 3:75
Mary (----) Street Newman,
3:75
Mary (Chittenden), 1:382,
3:75
Mehitable, 3:75
Mercy, 3:75
Sarah, 3:75
Sarah (----) Rotherford,
3:75, 3:579
Leeth
Hannah (----), 3:75
Martha, 3:75
Leffingwell
Abigail, 3:76, 3:609
Esther, 3:76
Hannah, 2:171, 3:76
Hannah (Duntlin), 3:76
Mary, 1:317, 3:76
Mary (Bushnell), 1:318
Rachel, 3:76, 3:348
Ruth, 3:76
Sarah, 3:76
Sarah (Knight), 3:76
Tabitha, 3:76
Legat/Leggett
Ann (----) Wilson, 3:76,
4:589
Legg/Legge
---- (Stoddard), 4:201
Elizabeth (----), 3:647
Legrove
Hannah (----), 3:647
Susanna, 3:368, 3:647
Leland
Abigail, 3:77

Abigail (Hill), 3:77
Amariah, 3:76
Deborah, 3:76
Deborah (----), 3:76
Experience, 1:423, 3:77
Margaret, 3:77
Margaret (Badcock), 3:77
Martha, 3:76
Mary (Hunt), 3:76
Patience, 3:76
Patience (Holbrook), 3:77
Patience (Rice), 3:530
Patience (Sabin), 3:76
Sarah (----), 3:76
Sibella, 3:76
Susanna, 3:76
Lellock
Joanna (----), 3:77
Lemon/Lemond/etc
Elizabeth, 3:78
Grace, 3:78
Hannah, 1:145, 3:78,
3:647
Martha, 2:221, 3:78, 3:647
Mary, 3:78, 3:110, 3:647
Mary (----), 1:476, 3:77-78
Mary (Bradley), 3:77
Mary (Longley), 3:78,
3:111
Sarah, 3:644, 3:647
Lendall/Sendall
Elizabeth (----) Warren,
4:425
Lenthall
Ann, 2:105, 4:5
Leonard
---- (----), 3:361
Abigail, 3:29, 3:78-79,
4:430
Ann (Tisdale), 3:78
Catharine (Deane), 3:80
Charity, 3:395
Charity (Hodges), 2:439
Deborah, 3:79
Deliverance, 3:79
Deliverance (----), 3:79
Elizabeth, 3:79-80
Elizabeth (----), 3:80
Elizabeth (Caswell), 1:348,
3:80
Elizabeth (Lyman), 4:688
Eunice, 3:79
Experience, 3:79-80

Leonard (continued)
Hannah, 1:472, 2:29, 2:39,
2:163, 3:78-79, 4:100
Hannah (----), 3:79
Hannah (Walley) Stone,
4:400
Jerusha, 3:78
Joanna (----), 3:80
Kezia, 3:78
Lydia, 2:79, 3:79
Lydia (----), 3:80
Lydia (Gulliver), 2:322,
3:79
Margaret, 3:78, 3:80
Margaret (----), 3:79
Martha, 3:78-79, 4:382
Mary, 1:201, 3:78-80,
3:449
Mary (----), 1:152, 3:78,
3:80
Mary (Black), 3:80
Mary (Fellows), 2:151
Mary (King), 3:25, 3:79
Mary (Remington), 3:78
Mary (Watson), 3:80,
4:437
Mehitable, 3:79-80
Mercy, 3:80
Phebe, 3:80
Prudence, 3:79
Rachel, 2:349, 3:78-80
Rebecca, 1:361, 3:79,
3:211
Rebecca (----), 3:79
Rebecca (Dumbleton),
3:80
Sarah, 3:3, 3:78-80
Sarah (----), 3:79-80, 3:574,
4:305
Sarah (Dumbleton), 2:79,
3:80
Sarah (Heald), 3:79
Sarah (Scott), 3:78, 4:37
Sarah (Thrasher), 3:78,
4:294
Silence, 3:80
Susanna, 3:79
Susanna (----), 3:79
Leroy
Esther, 1:170
Lester
---- (----) Hempstead, 2:402
Ann, 3:81, 3:212, 4:441

Ann (----), 3:81, 4:558
Ann (Stedman), 4:179
Barbara (----), 3:81
Lydia (Bayley), 1:143
Mary, 2:196, 3:81
Mary (Fox), 2:196
Lettis/Lettice
Ann, 3:81
Ann (----), 3:81
Dorothy, 2:298, 3:81
Elizabeth, 3:81, 4:92
Levens/Leavens
---- (----), 1:70
Elizabeth (----), 3:81
Elizabeth (Preston), 4:688
Hannah, 3:81
Hannah (Woods), 3:81,
4:626
Rachel, 3:81
Rachel (Wright), 3:81
Leverett
Ann, 1:17, 2:484, 3:83-84
Ann (----), 3:83
Elizabeth, 1:445, 3:83
Elizabeth (----), 3:82
Hannah, 2:22, 2:489, 3:83
Hannah (Hudson), 2:489,
3:83
Jane, 3:83-84
Margaret (Rogers) Berry,
1:171, 3:562
Mary, 2:77, 3:83-84, 4:319
Rebecca, 3:83, 3:102
Rebecca (Winsor), 4:604
Sarah, 1:325, 3:82-84,
4:541
Sarah (Crisp) Harris, 1:437,
1:473, 2:366
Sarah (Payton), 3:82,
3:374
Sarah (Sedgwick), 3:83,
4:48
Leverich
Eleanor, 3:84
Martha (----) Swain, 3:84,
4:235
Mary, 3:84
Rebecca (Wright), 3:84
Lewis
Abigail, 3:85, 3:87-89,
3:647, 3:684, 4:381
Abigail (----) Kilcup, 3:85
Abigail (Ashley), 3:88

Abigail (Dudson) Kilcup,
3:21
Alice (Mattocks) Bishop,
1:185, 3:87, 3:177
Amy (----), 3:89
Ann, 3:86, 3:88, 3:241,
3:577
Ann (----), 3:87
Bathshua, 3:86
Blanch, 1:152
Deborah (Hawke/Hawkes),
2:381
Dorcas, 3:85
Elizabeth, 1:213, 3:85-89
Elizabeth (----), 3:86, 3:88
Elizabeth (Babcock), 3:85
Elizabeth (Case), 1:345,
3:88, 4:342
Elizabeth
(Hawke/Hawkes), 2:381
Elizabeth (Huntley), 3:87
Elizabeth (Orton), 3:317
Esther, 3:89
Experience (----), 3:86
Felix, 3:89, 4:50
Felix (----), 3:89
Hannah, 1:294, 2:537,
3:85-89, 3:154, 3:654
Hannah (----), 3:89, 4:688
Hannah (Baker), 3:88
Hannah (Cobb), 1:413,
3:85
Hannah (Fuller), 2:219
Hannah (Lincoln), 3:87,
3:91
Hannah (Marshall), 3:87,
3:158
Hepzibah, 3:89
Jane, 3:86
Jane (Babcock), 3:86
Jerusha, 3:88
Joanna, 3:88
Joanna (----), 3:88
Judith, 2:245
Lydia, 2:537, 3:89
Malatiah, 3:86
Margaret (----), 3:86
Martha (Brooking), 1:259,
3:87, 3:524
Mary, 1:99, 1:283, 2:537,
2:542, 2:573, 3:85-89,
3:388, 3:648, 4:103
Mary (----), 3:85, 3:88,

Lewis (continued)
  Mary (----) (continued)
    3:362
  Mary (Breadon), 3:85
  Mary (Brown), 1:264, 3:87
  Mary (Burdick), 1:301
  Mary (Button), 3:84
  Mary (Cheever), 1:371,
    3:85, 3:89, 4:702
  Mary (Davis), 2:16, 3:86,
    3:88
  Mary (Hopkins), 2:462,
    3:89
  Mary (Lewis) Skillings,
    3:86, 4:103
  Mary (Lumbard), 3:86,
    3:106
  Melatiah, 3:86
  Meletiah, 2:298
  Mercy, 3:648
  Nodiah, 3:88
  Patience (Warren), 4:425
  Phebe, 3:648
  Priscilla, 3:10
  Rebecca (----), 3:88
  Remember (Litchfield),
    3:98
  Ruth, 3:648
  Sarah, 1:209, 1:227, 1:413,
    1:480, 3:85-87, 3:89,
    3:95, 3:118, 3:273,
    3:648, 4:145, 4:433
  Sarah (----), 3:87-88
  Sarah (Babcock), 3:86
  Sarah (Jenkins), 3:85
  Sarah (Lane), 3:52, 3:86
  Sarah (Meriam) Jenks,
    2:543, 3:87
  Sarah (Moore), 3:648,
    3:654
  Sibill, 3:88
  Susanna, 1:412, 3:86
  Thankful, 3:86
  Thankful (Lyman), 3:648
  Trial, 3:87
Lews
  Mary, 3:48
Ley
  Mary (----), 3:90
Libbey
  Mary (Hanson), 2:352,
    3:90

Lidgett
  Elizabeth, 3:90, 4:363
  Elizabeth (----), 4:4
  Elizabeth (Scammon), 3:90,
    4:34
  Jane, 3:90
Lieford
  Ann, 3:90
Liet
  Sarah, 3:156
Light
  Dorothy, 3:90
  Dorothy (----), 3:90
  Mary, 3:90
Lightfoot
  Ann (----), 3:90, 4:296
  Elizabeth (----) Swasey,
    4:708
  Elizabeth (Swasey), 3:684
  Isabel, 3:90
Lilford/Lilforth
  Elizabeth (----), 3:90
Lilly/Lillie
  Abigail, 3:91
  Dorothy (----), 3:90
  Elizabeth, 3:91
  Hannah, 3:90-91
  Hannah (----), 3:90-91
  Martha, 3:38
  Mehitable, 3:91
  Mehitable (----), 1:221
  Mehitable (Frary), 2:201
  Phebe, 3:91
  Rebecca, 3:91
  Sarah, 3:91
  Susanna, 3:91
Lincoln
  ----, 4:575
  ---- (Lane), 3:53, 3:94
  Abigail, 3:93
  Ann, 3:91
  Ann (----), 3:92
  Bethia, 3:93
  Constant, 3:94
  Deborah, 3:66, 3:92-94,
    4:275
  Deborah (Hersey), 3:93
  Deborah (Hobart), 2:434,
    3:92
  Deborah (Lincoln), 3:92
  Elizabeth, 3:91-95, 3:154
  Elizabeth (----) Streete,
    3:94, 4:222

  Elizabeth (Hawke), 2:381,
    3:93
  Elizabeth (Lincoln), 3:91,
    3:94
  Hannah, 3:87, 3:91,
    3:93-94, 3:125, 3:326
  Hannah (Jackson), 3:91
  Joan (----), 3:93
  Joanna (----), 3:92
  Leah, 3:91
  Lydia, 3:93, 3:95
  Lydia (Hobart), 2:435,
    3:95
  Margaret, 3:91-93
  Margaret (Langer), 3:55,
    3:94
  Margaret (Lincoln), 3:92
  Martha, 3:91-93
  Martha (----), 3:92
  Mary, 1:115, 1:139,
    3:92-95, 4:532
  Mary (----), 3:92-93
  Mary (Chubbuck), 1:384,
    3:95
  Mary (Otis), 3:91
  Mercy, 3:94
  Prudence, 3:373
  Prudence (Ford), 2:182,
    3:92
  Rachel, 3:65, 3:91, 3:93
  Rachel (Bates), 1:138,
    3:91
  Rebecca, 3:92-93
  Ruth, 2:254, 3:91, 3:94
  Ruth (Beal/Beals), 1:145
  Sarah, 3:91-95
  Sarah (----), 3:92
  Sarah (----)
    Besbedge/etc, 1:171
  Sarah (----) Bisbee, 3:92
  Sarah (Fearing), 2:150,
    3:91
  Sarah (Lewis), 3:86, 3:95,
    4:433
  Sarah (Nichols), 3:91
  Silence, 3:91
  Susanna, 1:128, 3:91-95,
    4:433
  Susanna (----), 3:91, 3:93
  Susanna (Smith), 3:95
  Thomasin, 3:93
Lincoln, Earl of
  ---- (Fiennes), 2:158

188

Lindall/Lyndall/Lindale
Abigail, 3:95, 3:425, 4:380
Bethia (Kitchen), 3:96
Elizabeth, 3:95
Grace, 3:95, 3:648
Hannah, 3:95
Mary, 2:481, 3:95, 3:419
Mary (----), 3:95-96
Mary (Verin), 3:95, 4:371
Mercy, 3:14, 3:95
Rachel, 3:96
Rebecca, 2:169, 3:95
Rosamund (----), 3:534, 4:688
Sarah, 3:95
Susanna (----), 3:95
Lindon/Lyndon
Elizabeth (----), 3:96
Hannah, 1:450
Jane (----), 3:96
Phebe (----) Franklin, 2:201, 3:96
Lindsay/Linsey
Abigail, 3:96
Amy (Richardson), 3:96
Margaret, 3:96
Margaret (----), 3:96
Mary, 3:96
Mary (Alley), 1:39, 3:96
Naomi, 3:179, 3:648
Sarah, 3:96
Sarah (Alley), 1:39, 3:96
Lines/Loines/Line
Abia (Bassett), 3:601, 3:648
Ann (----), 4:688
Elizabeth (----), 4:688
Joanna, 3:96
Mary (Thompson), 3:97, 4:286, 4:289
Ling
Joanna (----), 2:55, 3:97
Linnell/Lynnell
Abigail, 3:97, 3:106
Bethia, 1:73, 3:97
Elizabeth, 3:97
Elizabeth (----), 3:97
Experience, 2:17, 3:97
Hannah, 2:16, 2:18, 3:97
Hannah (Shelley), 3:97, 4:71
Mary, 1:378, 3:97
Ruth (Davis), 3:97

Thankful, 3:97
Linsley
Hannah, 4:688
Mary, 4:688
Linton
Ann, 3:97, 4:434
Margaret (----), 2:419
Lippencot/Lippincot
Abigail, 3:98
Abigail (----), 3:98
Hannah (Shattuck), 4:63
Remembrance, 3:98
Restore, 3:98
Lippet/Lippitt
Ann (----), 4:45
Ann (Grove), 3:97-98
Martha, 1:303, 3:98
Mary, 1:303, 3:98
Mary (Knowles), 3:41, 3:98
Rebecca, 1:288, 2:472, 3:97-98
Rebecca (Lippet/Lippitt), 3:98
Liscom/Lyscum
Abigail (----), 3:138
Elizabeth, 4:306
Lisle
Bridget, 2:431-432, 4:363
Tryphena, 2:432
Liston
Martha (Hull), 2:492
Litchfield
Deborah, 1:466
Dependence, 2:39, 3:98
Experience, 2:39
Hannah, 3:98
Jane (Cole), 1:429
Judith, 3:98
Judith (----), 3:377
Judith (Dennis), 2:39, 3:99
Mary, 2:460
Mary (----) Long, 3:108
Remember, 2:39, 3:98
Sarah, 3:98
Sarah (Baker), 1:98, 3:98
Little
Alice (Poor), 3:99
Ann, 3:99
Ann (Warren), 3:99, 4:427
Bethia, 3:99
Bethia (----), 3:99
Constance, 3:577

Dorothy, 3:99
Elinor (----) Barnard, 3:99
Elizabeth, 3:99, 4:689
Hannah, 3:99, 4:301, 4:689
Joan (----) Hummerston, 4:688-689
Joan (Walker) Hummerston, 4:684
Judith, 3:99
Lydia (Coffin), 3:99, 3:436
Martha, 4:689
Mary, 3:99, 3:323, 4:689
Mary (Coffin), 3:99
Mary (Mayhew), 3:99
Mary (Sturdevant), 3:99
Mercy, 3:99, 4:30
Patience, 2:563, 3:99
Ruth, 3:99
Sarah, 2:517, 3:99
Sarah (Gray), 3:99
Littlefield
Ann (----), 3:100
Elizabeth, 3:100
Elizabeth (----), 4:385
Experience, 3:100
Hannah, 3:100
Jane (----), 3:100
Jemima, 3:100
Jerusha, 3:100
Lydia, 3:100
Lydia (----), 3:100
Mary, 1:125, 2:418, 3:100
Mary (----), 3:100
Mary (Hill), 3:99
Praisever, 3:100
Rebecca, 3:100
Sarah, 3:100, 4:475
Susanna, 3:100
Sybil, 3:100
Littlehale
Mary (----), 1:249
Mary (Lancton), 3:100
Liveen
Alice (----) Hallam, 3:100
Livermore
Abigail, 3:101
Ann, 3:101
Ann (Bridge), 1:248, 3:101, 4:480
Elizabeth, 3:101
Elizabeth (Grout) Allen, 1:36, 2:319, 3:101

Livermore (continued)
Grace, 2:360, 3:101
Grace (----), 3:101
Hannah, 1:451, 3:101, 3:528
Hannah (----), 3:101
Lydia, 3:101
Martha, 3:101
Mary, 3:101
Mary (----), 3:101
Mary (Coolidge), 1:451, 4:481
Rebecca (Myrick), 3:371
Sarah, 2:215, 3:101
Sarah (Nevinson) Stearns, 3:268, 4:204
Livingston
Elizabeth (Knight), 3:39
Mary (Winthrop), 4:608
Lloyd
Elizabeth, 3:102
Griselda (Sylvester), 3:102, 4:99
Hannah, 3:101
Hannah (----), 3:101
Martha, 3:102
Rebecca (Leverett), 3:83, 3:102
Tryphena (Lisle), 2:432
Lobdell/Lobden
Ann, 3:102, 4:269, 4:689
Elizabeth, 1:314, 3:102, 3:401
Elizabeth (----), 3:102
Hannah (Leavitt), 3:70, 3:102, 3:118
Martha (Ward), 3:102
Rebecca, 3:102, 3:117
Sarah, 1:180
Lochard
Rachel (Haynes), 2:389
Locke
Abigail, 2:583, 3:103-104
Abigail (Hayward), 3:103
Alice, 3:102
Ann, 3:103
Bridget (----), 3:554
Deborah, 3:103
Deborah/Dorothy (Blake), 1:192, 3:103
Dorothy, 3:103
Elizabeth, 3:102-103, 3:152

Elizabeth (Berry), 1:171, 3:102
Elizabeth (Plimpton), 3:103, 3:448
Hannah, 3:102, 3:104
Hannah (Jenness), 2:544, 3:102
Hannah (Knowles), 3:104
Hannah (Mead), 3:102, 3:190
Hannah (Pierce), 3:103
Huldah, 3:103
Jemima, 3:104
Joanna, 3:103
Lydia, 3:103
Margaret, 3:103
Margaret (Mead), 3:103, 3:190
Mary, 3:9, 3:102-103
Mary (----), 3:103
Mary (Clark), 1:404, 3:103
Mary (Day), 3:103
Mary (Winn) Wyman, 3:103, 4:665
Patience, 3:104
Phebe, 3:102
Prudence, 3:102
Rachel, 3:103
Rebecca, 3:102
Ruhamah, 3:102
Ruth, 3:103
Ruth (----), 3:103
Salome, 3:103
Salome (----), 3:103
Sarah, 1:486, 3:102-104
Sarah (Cutter), 1:496, 3:102
Sarah (Whitmore), 3:103, 4:526
Susanna (Walker), 3:102, 4:393
Tryphena, 3:102-103
Lockwood
---- (Beacham), 3:105
---- (Latham), 3:104
Abigail, 1:117, 3:104-105
Deborah, 3:105
Elizabeth, 3:104
Elizabeth (Masters), 3:58, 3:104, 3:171
Hannah (Latham), 3:58
Mary, 1:156, 2:490, 3:104-105

Mary (----), 3:104
Mary (Ferris), 2:155
Mercy (Sension), 3:104
Sarah, 3:104-105, 3:444
Susanna, 3:105
Susanna (----), 3:105
Loft
Elizabeth (----), 3:105
Logan/Logyn
Lydia, 4:275
Susanna (----), 3:105
Susanna (Cutler) Burrage, 1:511
Logee
Abigail, 3:648
Mary, 3:648
Mary (Snasher), 3:648
Loker
Mary (Draper), 3:105
Sarah (Grout), 2:319
Sarah (Rice), 3:530
Lombard/Lumbart/etc
Abigail, 1:388, 3:106
Abigail (Linnell), 3:97, 3:106
Alice, 3:106
Bathshua, 3:105, 3:107
Bethia, 3:107
Elizabeth, 3:106-107
Elizabeth (Darby/Derby), 3:107
Elizabeth (Eddy), 3:106
Experience, 3:106
Hannah, 3:106-107
Hannah (----) Whetstone, 3:105
Hannah (Wing), 3:106
Hepzibah, 3:106
Hope, 3:105
Hopestill, 3:106
Hopestill (Bullock), 3:106
Jane (Warren), 3:105, 4:426
Jemima, 1:166, 3:106
Joan (Pritchard), 3:486
Joanna (Pritchard), 3:106
Joyce (----), 3:106
Margaret, 1:437, 3:106
Martha, 3:105-106, 3:161-162
Mary, 3:86, 3:105-107, 3:123, 3:349
Mehitable, 3:106, 3:124

Lombard/Lumbart/etc
(continued)
Mercy, 3:105-106
Patience, 3:107
Rebecca, 3:107
Sarah, 3:105, 3:107
Sarah (Derby), 3:106
Sarah (Walker), 3:105
Susanna, 3:123
Temperance, 3:105
Long
—— (Hill), 2:418
Abiel, 3:107, 3:109
Abigail, 3:107, 3:109
Abigail (Norton), 3:107,
3:290
Alice (Stevens), 3:109
Ann, 1:444, 3:108-109
Ann (——) Constable, 1:443,
3:108
Ann (French), 2:206,
3:108
Catharine, 3:107-108
Deborah, 3:108-109
Eleanor, 3:108
Elizabeth, 1:501,
3:108-109, 3:351
Elizabeth (——), 2:589,
3:107-109
Elizabeth (Checkley),
3:109
Elizabeth (Green), 2:301,
3:109
Ellen, 3:108, 3:651
Hannah, 1:451, 3:107-109
Hannah (Hill), 3:107
Hannah (Hollard)
Ballantine, 2:595
Hannah (Merrill), 3:109
Hannah (Upham), 4:360
Joan (——), 3:108
Joanna, 2:599
Margaret, 3:459
Martha, 3:109
Mary, 1:236, 1:412, 1:421,
1:514, 3:8, 3:107-109,
4:14
Mary (——), 2:143, 3:108
Mary (Burr), 1:307, 3:109
Mary (Lane), 3:53
Mary (Nowell) Winslow,
3:107, 3:295
Rebecca, 3:108-109, 3:510,

3:559
Ruth, 2:595, 3:108-109
Sarah, 1:255, 2:415,
3:107-109, 4:546
Sarah (——), 4:164
Sarah (Moore), 3:109
Sarah (Tidd), 3:109
Sarah (Wilcox), 4:547
Susanna, 1:197, 3:108-109
Longe
Ellyn, 3:648
Longfellow
Abigail, 3:110
Abigail (Tompson), 3:110
Ann, 3:110
Ann (Sewall), 3:110, 4:53,
4:89
Elizabeth, 3:110
Mary (Green), 3:110
Sarah, 3:110
Longley
Ann, 3:110, 4:256
Elizabeth, 1:204, 3:110
Hannah, 3:111
Hannah (——), 3:110
Joanna (——), 1:473, 3:110
Lydia, 3:110-111, 3:301
Lydia (——), 3:111
Margaret, 3:110
Mary, 3:78, 3:110
Priscilla (——), 3:648
Sarah, 3:110-111, 3:505
Look/Looke
Deliverance, 4:650
Elizabeth, 3:111, 3:643,
3:648
Elizabeth (Bunker), 3:111,
4:676
Experience, 3:111
Jane, 3:111
Mary, 3:111
Sarah, 3:111
Looker/Luker
Mary, 3:111, 3:481
Mary (——), 3:111
Looman/Loomer
—— (——), 3:111
Mary (——), 1:7
Loomis/Lumas/Lummis/etc
——, 3:112, 3:312
—— (Judd), 2:574
Abigail, 1:113, 3:111,
3:113

Ann, 3:112-114
Catharine, 3:113
Damaris, 3:112-113
Deborah, 3:112
Deliverance, 3:114
Elizabeth, 1:509, 2:352,
3:111-114, 3:647
Elizabeth (——) Church,
3:114
Elizabeth (Ellsworth),
2:115, 3:113
Elizabeth (Judd), 3:113
Elizabeth (Moore), 1:345,
3:113, 3:228
Elizabeth (Scott), 3:112,
4:39
Elizabeth (White), 3:114
Esther, 3:112
Esther (Colt), 3:114
Esther (Gillett), 3:112
Eunice, 3:112
Frances, 3:648, 4:86
Grace, 3:113
Hannah, 2:574, 3:111-114
Hannah (Cook) Buckland
Baker, 1:97, 1:449
Hannah (Fox), 3:114
Hannah (Hansett), 2:352,
3:114
Hannah (Porter), 3:114
Hannah (Taylor), 4:264
Hepzibah, 3:111
Jane, 3:111
Jemima, 3:111
Jemima (Whitcomb),
3:111
Joanna, 3:112-113, 4:125
Joanna (Gibbs), 3:113
Lois, 3:112, 3:114
Lydia, 3:111, 3:113
Lydia (Drake), 2:70, 3:113
Mabel, 3:112, 3:114
Martha, 3:114
Mary, 3:111-114, 3:648,
4:249, 4:340, 4:706
Mary (——), 3:112, 3:648
Mary (Chauncy), 3:112
Mary (Ellsworth), 2:115,
3:111
Mary (Gaylord), 3:113
Mary (Judd), 2:574, 3:114
Mary (Porter), 3:112
Mary (Rockwell), 3:113

Loomis/Lumas/Lummis/etc
(continued)
Mindwell, 1:272,
3:112-114
Rachel, 3:113
Rebecca, 3:112-114
Rebecca (Porter), 3:114
Ruth, 3:112-114, 4:110
Ruth (Porter), 3:113
Sarah, 3:112-114
Sarah (----) Warner, 3:112
Sarah (Boltwood) Warner,
1:208, 4:419
Sarah (Hill), 2:420, 3:112
Sarah (White), 3:114
Thankful, 3:113
Thankful (Weller), 3:113
Lord
----, 1:359, 3:116
Abigail, 2:299, 3:116-117,
3:647-649
Abigail (----), 3:117, 4:514
Abigail (Hinckley), 2:425
Abigail (Warren), 3:115,
4:427-428, 4:587, 4:634
Adrian (Bayc/Baysey),
3:115
Alice (Rand), 3:116, 3:504
Amie, 3:116, 4:689
Amy, 2:250
Ann, 3:116, 4:167, 4:689
Ann (Taylor), 4:259
Catharine (----), 3:116
Dinah, 3:649
Dorothy, 2:464, 2:520,
3:115-117, 3:264
Dorothy (----), 3:116
Elizabeth, 2:594, 3:116,
3:649, 4:587
Elizabeth (----), 3:116
Hannah, 2:321, 3:116-117,
4:166
Hannah (Thurston), 3:116
Jane, 2:331, 3:649
Jane (----), 3:649
Judith, 4:689
Margaret, 3:649
Martha, 4:689
Martha (Tozer), 4:689,
4:711
Mary, 1:359, 3:116-117,
4:689, 4:691
Mary (----), 3:116-117

Mary (Moulton), 3:649
Mary (Smith), 2:460,
3:115, 4:114
Mary (Waite), 3:116
Phebe, 4:97
Rebecca (Bushnell), 1:317,
3:115
Rebecca (Eddington),
2:100, 3:116
Rebecca (Stanley), 3:116,
3:416
Sarah, 2:390, 3:115-117,
4:585, 4:689
Sarah (----), 3:115
Sarah (Shaler), 4:685,
4:689
Susanna, 1:130
Loring
Abigail, 3:119
Deborah, 1:490, 3:119
Deborah (Cushing), 1:490,
3:119
Elizabeth, 3:118
Elizabeth (Austin), 1:81
Elizabeth (Baker), 3:117
Elizabeth (Otis) Allyn,
3:117, 3:323
Elizabeth (Prince), 3:118
Hannah, 1:489, 3:117-119
Hannah (Jacob), 2:534,
3:118-119
Hannah (Leavitt), 2:126,
3:70, 3:118
Jael, 3:119
Jane, 3:118
Jane (Baker), 3:118
Jane (Newton), 3:119
Leah (Buckland), 1:285,
3:119
Lydia, 3:117-118
Lydia (Gray), 3:117
Mary, 2:566, 3:117-118
Mary (----), 2:442
Mary (Baker), 1:98, 3:118
Mary (Hawke), 2:381,
3:117
Mary (Hayman), 3:118
Priscilla, 3:117
Priscilla (Mann), 3:117
Rachel, 3:117-118
Rachel (Wheatley)
Buckland, 1:285, 3:118,
4:495

Rebecca, 3:117
Rebecca (Lobdell), 3:117
Ruth, 3:118
Sarah, 3:117-119
Sarah (Lewis), 3:118
Sarah (Young), 3:118
Susan, 3:118
Susanna, 3:117-118
Susanna (Butler), 3:118
Susanna (Coxe), 3:117
Lothrop/Lathrop/etc
Abigail, 1:394, 3:119-121
Abigail (----), 3:121
Abigail (Button) Dudson,
2:78, 3:119
Abigail (Doane), 2:56
Abigail (Edwards), 4:215
Ann, 2:469, 3:119, 3:121
Ann (----), 3:120
Barbara, 2:117, 3:120
Bathshua, 3:119-120,
4:133
Bethia, 1:388, 2:424,
3:122
Bethia (----), 2:273
Bethia (Rea), 2:289, 3:122,
3:512
Deborah, 3:122
Elizabeth, 3:119-121,
3:327, 3:569
Elizabeth (Lothrop), 3:120
Elizabeth (Scudder), 3:121,
4:43
Ellen, 1:371, 2:289
Experience, 3:120
Experience (Gorham),
3:122
Hannah, 3:119-122, 3:395,
4:235
Hannah (----) Fuller, 2:216
Hannah (Adgate), 1:18,
3:121
Hannah (Crocker), 1:475,
3:121
Hope, 3:121
Jane, 2:218, 3:120
Martha, 2:277, 3:119-120
Martha (----), 3:119
Mary, 1:278, 2:208, 3:4,
3:119-122, 3:220, 3:223,
4:174
Mary (Ansell), 3:121
Mary (Cole), 3:120

Lothrop/Lathrop/etc
(continued)
Mary (Reynolds), 3:525
Meletiah, 3:122
Mercy, 3:119
Rebecca, 3:119
Ruth, 2:60
Ruth (Royce), 3:120,
  3:570
Sarah, 3:119, 3:121
Sarah (Farrar), 2:145,
  3:121
Sarah (Larned) Ewer,
  2:132, 3:122
Susanna, 3:119, 4:92
Susanna (Clark), 1:400,
  3:119
Tabitha, 3:121
Thankful, 2:400, 3:119
Lott
Mary, 3:247
Loud/Lowd
Deborah, 3:649
Deborah (----), 3:649
Honor (Prince), 3:649
Sarah, 3:649
Sarah (----), 3:649
Love
Hannah (Thurston), 3:122
Susanna (Bennett), 1:168
Lovejoy
Abigail, 1:4, 3:122
Ann, 1:196, 3:122
Dorothy (Hoyt), 3:122
Hannah (Prichard), 3:649
Mary, 3:122, 4:585
Mary (Farnum), 3:122
Mary (Foster), 3:122
Mary (Osgood), 3:122,
  3:320
Naomi (Hoyt), 3:649,
  4:684
Sarah, 2:559, 3:122
Sarah (Prichard), 3:122
Sarah (Russ), 3:122
Lovell
Abia, 3:124
Abigail, 3:123
Ann, 3:123
Ann (----), 3:123
Beulah, 3:124
Deborah, 3:123
Eleanor, 3:124

Elinor, 3:124
Elizabeth, 2:133,
  3:123-124, 4:589
Hannah, 3:123
Hannah (Magoon), 3:143
Jane, 3:123
Jane (----), 3:123
Jane (Hatch), 2:376, 3:123
Jerusha, 3:124
Joanna (Blott), 1:206
Lydia, 3:123
Lydia (Albee/Alby), 1:498,
  3:123
Martha, 3:123
Mary, 3:123
Mary (Lombard), 3:123
Mehitable (Lombard),
  3:124
Mercy, 3:123
Patience, 1:146
Phebe, 1:298, 3:123
Rebecca, 3:123
Sarah, 1:146, 3:123
Susanna, 3:123
Susanna (Lombard), 3:123
Thankful, 3:123
Lovenam
---- (----), 3:123
Lovering
---- (----), 1:265
---- (----) Hill, 3:124
Ann (----), 3:124, 4:283
Grace, 4:407
Mary, 4:290
Mary (Eaton) Hill, 2:420,
  3:35
Lovett
Abigail, 3:124
Bethia, 3:124, 4:164
Elizabeth (Solart), 4:706
Hannah, 3:124, 3:540
Isabel (Bland), 1:197
Joanna (Blott), 3:124
Martha, 3:124
Mary, 3:124
Mary (----), 3:124
Lovewell
Hannah, 3:124
Low/Lowe
Abigail (Lane), 3:51
Elizabeth, 3:125, 3:649
Elizabeth (----), 3:125
Elizabeth (Crooker), 3:125

Elizabeth (Howland),
  2:479, 3:125
Elizabeth (Stodder), 3:125,
  4:202
Frances (----), 3:125
Hannah, 3:125
Hannah (Lincoln), 3:125
Joan (----) Peck, 3:125
Lydia (----), 3:125
Mary (Ingersoll), 2:520
Mary (Rhoades), 3:125
Ruth (Andrews), 3:125
Ruth (Joy), 2:573, 3:125
Sarah (Symonds), 3:649,
  4:245
Sarah (Thorndike), 3:125,
  4:290
Tabitha, 3:125
Lowden
---- (Cole), 1:429
Elizabeth, 3:125
Elizabeth (----), 3:125
Martha, 1:330, 3:125-126
Mary, 1:429, 2:213, 2:586,
  3:125
Mary (----), 3:125
Sarah, 3:125
Sarah (Stephenson), 3:17,
  3:125
Lowder/Louder
Elizabeth, 3:649
Elizabeth (----), 3:649
Mary (----), 3:649
Lowell
---- (Percival), 3:126
Abigail, 3:126
Abigail (Proctor), 3:126,
  3:489
Elizabeth, 3:126, 3:267,
  4:556
Elizabeth (Goodale), 3:126
Elizabeth (Sylvester),
  3:126, 4:100
Hannah, 2:84, 3:126
Hannah (Proctor), 3:126,
  3:489
Margaret, 3:126
Margaret (----), 3:127
Mary, 3:126, 4:571
Mary (----), 3:126
Mary (Chandler), 3:126
Mehitable, 3:126
Naomi (Sylvester), 3:126,

Lowell (continued)
  Naomi (Sylvester)
    (continued)
    4:100
  Patience, 3:126
  Phebe, 3:126
  Rebecca, 2:330, 3:127
  Rebecca (----), 3:126
  Ruth, 3:126
  Ruth (Woodman), 3:126
  Sarah, 3:126
Lowgie/Lougee/Lougie
  Ellyn, 3:648
  Grace, 3:127
Lucas
  Esther (Clark), 3:127
  Mary, 3:127, 4:36
Luce/Lucy
  Elizabeth (Manter), 4:689
  Mary (Brooking), 1:259,
    3:127
  Remember (----), 4:689
  Zephaniah, 4:689
Luddam
  ---- (Randall), 3:506
Ludden
  Abia, 3:127
  Alice (----), 3:127
  Eunice, 2:442
  Eunice (Holbrook), 2:442,
    3:127
  Mary, 3:127
  Sarah, 3:127
Luddington
  ---- (----), 4:698
  Dorcas, 3:128
  Dorothy, 3:128
  Elinor, 3:128
  Elizabeth, 3:128
  Ellen (----), 3:128
  Hannah, 3:128
  Martha (Rose), 3:128
  Martha (Ross), 4:698
  Mary, 3:128
  Mercy, 3:128
  Mercy (Whitehead), 3:128
Ludkin
  Elizabeth (----), 3:129
  Esther, 3:129
  Hannah, 2:69, 3:129
  Hannah (Hepbourne),
    3:129
  Hannah (Miller) Dade

  Edmonds, 2:1, 3:129,
    3:211
Ludlow
  Sarah, 1:245, 3:129
Lufkin
  Abigail, 3:649
  Elizabeth, 3:649
  Mary (----), 3:130
Lugg
  Elizabeth, 3:130
  Jane (----), 3:130
  Mary, 1:119, 3:130
Luin
  Elizabeth, 3:130
  Sarah, 3:130
  Sarah (----), 3:130
Luke
  Hannah (----), 3:130
  Hannah (Baxter), 1:503
Lum/Lumm
  Elizabeth, 2:426
  Hannah, 3:462
Lumber
  Susan, 2:113
Lumpkin
  ----, 2:107, 3:130
  ---- (----), 3:130
  Hannah, 2:298, 3:130
  Sarah (----), 4:209
  Thomasine, 3:130, 3:188,
    4:233
  Thomasine (----), 3:130
Lund
  Elizabeth, 3:131
Lunden
  Hannah (Dupper)
    Bancroft, 1:110
Lunerus
  Margaret (----) Clemens,
    3:131
Lungman
  Mary (----), 2:225
Lunt
  ---- (Wood) Jewett, 4:629
  Ann, 3:131
  Ann (----), 2:418, 3:131
  Elizabeth, 3:131, 4:448
  Hannah, 3:131
  Hannah (Coker), 3:131
  Jane, 3:131
  Jane (----), 3:131
  Mary, 3:131, 4:596
  Mary (----) Moody, 3:131

  Mary (Skerry), 3:131
  Opportunity (Hoppin),
    2:463, 3:131
  Priscilla, 3:131, 4:705
  Ruth (Wood) Jewett,
    2:598, 3:131
  Sarah, 3:131
Lupton
  Hannah, 4:689
  Hannah (Morris), 3:131,
    3:236
Luscombe
  Elinor, 4:300
Lusher
  Lydia, 2:237
  Mary (----) Gwin, 2:590,
    3:132
Luson/Leuson
  Martha (----), 3:132
  Susan, 3:132
Luther
  Experience, 3:132
Lutman
  Jane, 2:78
Lutterell/Luttrell
  Ann, 1:393
  Mary, 4:607
Lux
  Mary, 2:540, 3:132
  Mary (----) Jeffries, 2:540,
    3:132
Luxford
  Elizabeth, 3:132
  Elizabeth (----), 3:132
  Margaret, 3:132
  Margaret (----), 3:132
Lyall/Lyell/Loyal
  Alice (----), 3:133
  Mary, 1:164, 3:133
Lybrand
  Elizabeth, 4:87
Lyde
  Deborah (Byfield), 1:325,
    3:133
  Mary (Wheelwright), 1:75,
    2:512, 3:133, 4:503
  Sarah (Fernald), 3:133
  Susanna (Curwin), 1:488,
    3:133
Lyford
  ---- (----), 2:433
  ---- (Smith), 3:133, 4:135
  Ann (----), 3:133

Lyford (continued)
Judith (Gilman), 2:258
Rebecca (Dudley), 2:77,
3:133
Ruth, 1:138, 3:133-134
Lyman
Abigail (Holton), 2:455
Ann, 3:134-135
Ann (----), 3:134
Bethia, 3:134
Dorcas (Plum), 3:134,
3:445
Dorothy, 3:134
Elizabeth, 3:134-135,
3:451, 4:688
Elizabeth (Cowles), 3:134,
4:679
Elizabeth (Reynolds),
3:525
Eunice, 3:134
Experience, 3:135
Hannah, 3:134, 3:451
Hepzibah, 2:43, 3:134-135
Hepzibah (Bascom),
3:134-135
Hepzibah (Ford), 2:183,
3:134, 3:154
Joanna, 3:134
Martha, 3:134
Mary, 3:134
Mindwell, 2:362, 3:135
Mindwell (Sheldon)
Pomeroy, 3:134, 4:69
Phillis, 2:420, 3:134
Preserved, 3:135
Ruth (Holton) Baker,
2:456, 3:135, 3:599
Sarah, 3:134-135,
3:154-155, 4:659
Sarah (----), 3:134
Susanna, 3:134
Thankful, 3:135, 3:648
Wait, 3:135
Lynde
---- (Knower), 1:287
Abigail, 3:135
Ann, 2:311, 3:135-136,
3:413
Dorothy, 3:135
Elizabeth, 3:136-137,
3:273, 3:459, 4:342
Elizabeth (----), 3:135-137
Elizabeth (Tufts), 3:136,

4:342
Emma (Anderson)
Brackenbury, 1:51, 1:228,
3:135
Hannah, 3:136, 4:322
Hannah (Newgate), 3:136,
3:273
Joanna, 3:135, 3:411
Judith (Worth) Bucknam,
1:287
Lucy (Palmes) Gray, 3:343
Margaret, 3:135
Margaret (Cory/Corey),
1:460
Margaret (Martin) Jordan,
3:136
Mary, 3:136-137
Mary (----), 3:135, 3:137
Mary (----) Winthrop,
3:135
Mary (Anderson), 1:51,
2:388, 4:76
Mary (Brown), 3:135
Mehitable, 3:135
Rebecca, 3:136
Rebecca (----), 3:136
Rebecca (----) Trerice,
3:136, 4:322
Sarah, 1:402, 3:135-136,
3:433, 3:622, 4:239
Sarah (Davison), 2:24,
3:135
Susanna, 3:136
Susanna (Willoughby),
3:136
Lynn
Elizabeth, 3:137
Ellen, 2:581
Joanna, 3:137, 4:572
Rebecca, 3:137
Sarah, 3:137
Sarah (----), 3:137
Sarah (----) Gunnison,
2:324
Lyon
---- (Bateman), 3:137
Abigail, 3:137
Abigail (Gould), 3:138
Abigail (Polley), 3:137,
3:450
Alice, 2:311
Ann, 3:137-138
Bethia, 3:137

Deborah (----), 3:138
Deliverance (----), 3:138
Esther, 3:138
Hannah, 3:137-138
Hannah (Tolman), 3:137,
3:649, 4:310, 4:675
Margaret, 3:138
Maria (----), 3:138
Martha, 3:138
Mary, 3:137, 3:649
Mary (----), 3:5
Mary (Bridge), 1:248,
3:137
Mehitable, 3:138
Rachel (Ruggles), 3:138
Sarah, 3:138
Sarah (Dunkin), 3:138
Susanna, 3:137
Lytherland/Letherland/etc
Deborah, 3:139
Margaret, 3:139
Margaret (----), 3:139
Rachel (----), 3:139
Maber
Abigail, 3:236
Dorcas, 3:649
Mary (Allen), 3:649
Mable
Ann, 2:63
Macarter
Rebecca, 3:139, 3:653
Rebecca (Meacham),
3:139, 3:190, 3:653
Maccane
Deborah, 3:139
Mary, 3:139
Ruth (----), 3:139
Sarah, 3:139
Maccarty
Christian (----), 3:139
Elizabeth, 3:139
Elizabeth (----), 3:139
Esther, 3:139, 4:77
Margaret, 3:139
Sarah (----), 3:139
MacDaniel
Alice (----), 3:140
Elizabeth, 3:140
Elizabeth (Smith), 3:140
Martha, 3:140
Mary, 3:140
Mace
Ann (Winter), 2:490

Mace (continued)
Sarah (Gorton), 2:283,
3:140
MacGinnis
Rose, 3:140
Rose (Neal), 3:140
Mack
Sarah (Bagley), 3:140
Mackay
Abigail, 3:140
Elizabeth, 3:140
Hannah, 3:140
Margaret (----), 3:140
Mary, 3:140
Sarah (----), 3:140
Mackenwithy
Mary, 2:131
Mary (Everett), 2:131
Mackintosh
Jane (----), 3:140
Rachel, 3:140
Rebecca (Metcalf), 3:140,
3:204
Macklathin/Maclothlin/etc
---- (Warner), 3:140
Joanna, 3:141, 4:133
Mackmallen/Mackmillion
Elizabeth, 3:141
Elizabeth (----), 1:503,
3:141
Mary (Gilson), 3:649
Mackman
Elizabeth (Stoughton),
3:141, 4:215
Mackworth/Macworth
----, 3:263
Jane (----) Andrews, 1:55,
2:151, 3:142
Rebecca, 3:142, 4:494
Sarah, 1:8
Macomber/Macumber
Hannah, 3:506
Judith, 2:545-546
Mary (Badcock), 3:141
Sarah, 1:252, 3:141
Sarah (Crooker), 3:141
Ursilla/Ursula, 4:513
Macoone/Mackoon/etc
Abigail, 3:141
Ann (----), 3:141
Deborah, 3:141
Deborah (Bush), 3:141
Elizabeth, 3:141

Hannah, 3:141
Jemima (----), 3:141
Lois, 3:141
Margaret, 3:141
Mary, 3:141
Patience (----), 3:141
Rachel, 3:141
Sarah, 3:141
Sarah (Wood), 3:141
Macranney
Margaret (Riley), 3:141
Macy
Bethia, 2:228, 3:142,
3:650
Deborah, 3:650
Deborah (Gardner), 2:229,
3:142
Elizabeth, 2:439, 3:142
Hannah, 1:192
Mary, 1:299, 3:142, 4:702
Rebecca, 3:142, 4:559
Sarah, 3:142, 3:650, 4:653
Sarah (Hopcot), 3:142
Sarah (Norcross), 3:142,
3:286
Maddocks/Maddox/etc
Joanna, 3:142
Mary, 3:142
Mary (Wellington), 3:142,
4:481
Rachel, 3:142
Rachel (----), 3:142
Rebecca (Munnings),
3:142, 3:255
Ruth, 3:142
Ruth (----), 1:378
Ruth (Church), 3:142
Sarah, 3:142
Madiver
---- (----) Carter, 3:143
Mercy, 3:143
Rebecca (----), 3:143
Magoon/Magoun/McGown
Hannah, 3:143
Hannah (----), 3:143
Mary, 1:398, 3:143
Rebecca (----), 3:143
Recompense, 3:143
Ruth, 3:143
Ruth (----), 3:143
Sarah, 3:143
Sarah (----), 3:143

Magvarlow/Macvarlo
Margaret, 3:143, 4:202
Patience (Russell), 3:143
Mahon/Mahone
Margaret (----), 3:257
Mary (Rockwell), 3:558
Mahoone
Dinah (----), 3:143
Honor, 3:143
Maine/Mayen/Mayne
Hannah, 2:386
Mary (Wells), 3:143, 4:479
Mainor
Hannah, 2:239
Mary, 2:239
Mary (Geer), 2:239
Major
Hannah, 2:278, 3:144
Susanna (----), 3:144
Makepeace
Ann (Johnson), 3:144
Elizabeth (----) Mellows,
3:144, 3:195
Esther, 1:270, 3:144
Hannah, 2:463, 3:144
Mary, 3:144, 4:576
Waitawhile, 1:454, 3:144
Makrest
Lydia, 3:144
Lydia (Fifield), 3:144
Mary, 3:144
Malbon
Martha, 3:144
Malins
Mary, 3:144
Patience (Easton), 2:94,
3:144, 4:689
Malinson
Mary, 2:598
Mallory
Abigail, 3:144-145
Elizabeth, 3:144-145
Elizabeth (Kimberly),
4:689
Elizabeth (Trowbridge),
3:145, 4:334
Hannah, 3:144-145
Judith, 1:332, 3:145
Mabel, 3:144
Mary, 3:145
Mary (Umberfield), 3:145,
4:358
Mercy, 3:144

Mallory (continued)
  Mercy (Pinion), 3:144
  Obedience, 3:144
  Rebecca, 3:144-145, 4:700
  Silence, 3:144
  Thankful, 3:144
  Zipporah, 3:145
Malone/Maloon
  Elizabeth, 3:145
  Hannah (Clifford), 1:410,
    3:145
  Sarah, 3:145
Maltby
  Elizabeth (----), 4:689
  Hannah (Hosmer) Willard,
    2:467
  Mary, 1:282, 2:184, 3:145
  Mary (Bryan), 3:145
Man
  Rebecca (----), 1:466
Manchester
  Elizabeth (Wodell), 3:145
Mandrake
  Abigail, 3:624
Manly
  Rebecca, 3:145
  Rebecca (----), 3:145
  Sarah, 3:145
  Sarah (----), 3:145
Mann
  Alice (Teel), 3:146
  Beriah, 3:146
  Bethia, 3:146
  Deborah (----), 3:146
  Dorothy, 2:271
  Esther, 3:146
  Esther (Ware), 3:146,
    4:417
  Hannah, 3:146
  Margaret, 3:146
  Mary, 3:145-146
  Mary (----), 3:145
  Mary (Jarrad/Garrard),
    3:146
  Mary (Wheaton), 3:146
  Mercy, 3:56
  Priscilla, 3:117
  Rachel, 3:146
  Rachel (----), 3:146
Mannering
  Elizabeth, 3:650
  Sarah, 3:650

Manning
  Abigail, 3:148
  Abigail (----), 3:147
  Ann, 2:63, 3:147-148,
    3:355
  Ann (Everill) Blanchard,
    2:131
  Ann (Parker), 2:244, 3:147,
    3:355
  Anstis, 3:147
  Anstis (----), 3:147
  Betty, 3:650, 4:689
  Catharine (Innis), 4:689
  Dinah, 4:689
  Dorcas, 4:689
  Dorothy (----), 3:148
  Elizabeth, 3:147, 3:650
  Elizabeth (----), 3:147
  Elizabeth (----) Gray, 3:625,
    3:650
  Elizabeth (Stearns), 4:173
  Eunice, 4:689
  Hannah, 3:147-148, 4:174
  Hannah (----) Blanchard,
    1:197
  Hannah (Everill)
    Blanchard, 2:131, 3:147
  Hannah (Gorham), 4:689
  Margaret, 3:147, 3:650
  Mary, 1:17, 2:433,
    3:147-148
  Mary (Harraden), 3:147
  Mary (Mixer), 3:223
  Phebe, 4:689
  Rachel (Bliss), 3:147
  Rebecca, 3:147, 4:689
  Sarah, 1:293, 3:147-148,
    3:650, 4:563
  Sarah (Hobart), 2:433,
    3:147
  Susanna (----), 3:148
Mansfield
  ---- (Needham), 3:655
  Abigail, 3:650, 4:690,
    4:699
  Abigail (Yale), 4:690
  Ann, 3:148
  Bathshua, 4:690
  Bethia, 3:148-149
  Bethia (----), 3:148
  Comfort, 4:690
  Damaris, 3:650
  Damaris (----), 3:650

  Deborah, 3:148-149, 3:655
  Elizabeth, 3:148-149,
    3:655, 4:619, 4:690
  Elizabeth (----), 3:149,
    3:650
  Elizabeth (Conant), 3:148
  Elizabeth (Farnsworth),
    2:143, 3:149
  Elizabeth (Walton), 3:148
  Elizabeth (Williams),
    3:149, 4:561
  Esther, 1:438
  Gilian (----), 3:149
  Gillian (----), 2:155
  Hannah, 4:690
  Hannah (Alling), 4:690
  Hannah (Bassett), 4:690
  Hannah (Bradlee), 4:690
  Lydia, 3:148
  Margaret (Prout), 4:690
  Martha, 3:149
  Mary, 3:148-149
  Mary (----), 4:690
  Mary (Lawes) Neal, 3:60,
    3:148, 3:264
  Mercy, 4:690
  Mercy (Glover), 3:624,
    3:650
  Rebecca, 3:650
  Ruth, 3:650
  Sarah, 3:149, 4:690
  Sarah (Barsham), 3:149
  Sarah (Neal), 3:149, 3:264
  Sarah (Phelps), 3:149,
    3:407
  Silence, 4:690
Manson
  Thomasine, 1:19, 3:149
Manter
  Elizabeth, 4:689
Manton
  ---, 3:553
  Ann, 3:3, 3:150
  Elizabeth (Thornton),
    3:149
Manwaring
  Ann, 3:150
  Bathsheba, 3:150
  Elinor (Jennings), 2:545
  Elizabeth, 2:363, 3:150
  Elizabeth (Raymond),
    3:150
  Hannah, 3:150

Manwaring (continued)
Hannah (Raymond), 3:150
Judith, 3:150
Love, 3:150, 3:533
Mercy, 3:150
Prudence, 3:150
Marble
Deborah, 3:150
Elizabeth (----), 3:150
Hannah (Barnard), 3:150
Judith (----), 3:150
Mary, 3:150, 4:30
Mary (Faulkner),
2:147-148, 3:150
Rebecca (Andrews), 3:150
Marbury
Ann, 2:513
Catharine, 4:38
March
Abigail, 3:151
Bethia, 4:98
Dorcas (Blackleach), 3:151
Dorcas (Bowman)
Blackleach, 1:189, 1:225
Elizabeth, 3:151
Hannah, 3:151
Jane, 3:151
Jemima (True), 3:151
Judith, 4:295
Judith (----), 3:151
Mary, 3:150-151, 4:254
Mary (----), 2:406, 3:151
Mary (Folsom), 2:178,
3:150
Mehitable, 3:151
Rebecca (----), 3:151
Sarah, 3:151
Sarah (----), 3:609
Sarah (Healy), 3:151
Sarah (Moody), 3:151
Tabitha, 3:151
Mare
Joanna (Brunson), 3:650
Margin
Rebecca (Holdridge),
2:446, 3:151
Marion
Ann (Harrison), 2:366,
3:152
Catharine, 3:152
Elizabeth, 2:32, 3:152
Hannah, 3:152
Hannah (----), 3:152

Joanna, 3:152
Mary, 3:152
Mary (----), 3:152
Phebe (----), 3:152
Sarah (Eddy), 2:99, 3:152
Mark/Marks
Jane, 1:507
Mary, 3:152
Sarah (----), 3:152
Markham
---- (Webster), 4:449
Abigail, 3:152
Elizabeth, 3:152
Elizabeth (Locke), 3:103,
3:152
Elizabeth (Whitmore),
3:152, 4:526
Hannah, 3:152
Lydia, 2:93, 3:152-153
Martha, 3:152
Mary, 3:152
Mercy, 3:152
Patience (Harris), 2:365,
3:152
Priscilla, 2:331, 3:152
Marlo/Morely/Marlow
Elizabeth, 3:153
Martha, 3:153
Martha (Wright), 3:153
Mary, 3:153
Thankful, 3:153
Marplehead
Mary, 1:295, 3:485
Marrett
Abigail, 2:162, 3:153,
3:241, 3:531
Abigail (Richardson),
3:153
Bethia (Longhorn), 3:153
Hannah, 3:153
Lydia, 3:153
Mary, 2:470, 3:153, 3:355
Mary (Dunster), 3:153
Ruth (----) Dunster, 3:153
Susanna, 1:128, 3:153
Susanna (----), 3:153
Marsh
Ann, 2:207, 3:154
Ann (----), 3:154
Ann (Webster), 3:154,
4:449
Bathsheba (----), 3:154
Bethia, 3:154

Comfort, 3:155
Dorcas (----) Dickinson,
2:47, 3:155
Elizabeth, 1:275,
3:154-155, 3:313, 3:650
Elizabeth (----), 3:154
Elizabeth (Lincoln), 3:93,
3:154
Elizabeth (Pitkin), 3:441
Elizabeth (Spencer), 4:149
Frances, 3:154
Grace, 1:100, 3:154
Hannah, 3:154-155, 4:682
Hannah (Cutter), 3:155
Hannah (Lewis) Crow,
3:89, 3:154
Hepzibah (Ford) Lyman,
3:134, 3:154
Judith, 3:151
Lydia, 3:154
Margaret, 3:650
Mary, 2:205, 3:154-155,
3:650
Mary (Allison), 3:155
Mary (Belcher), 1:156,
3:154
Mary (Silsbee), 3:650
Mary (Very), 4:372
Phebe, 3:154
Priscilla (Tompkins),
3:650, 4:311
Rachel, 3:154, 4:476
Ruth, 2:355, 3:154, 3:650
Sarah, 3:155, 3:650
Sarah (Beal), 1:145, 3:155,
4:68
Sarah (Lewis) Crow,
1:480, 3:89
Sarah (Lincoln), 3:94
Sarah (Lyman), 3:134,
3:154-155
Sarah (Young), 3:650,
4:669
Susanna, 3:154, 3:650
Susanna (----), 3:154
Marshall
---- (Stebbins), 4:176
Abigail, 3:155-158
Abigail (----), 3:157
Abigail (Phelps), 3:155
Alice (----), 3:158
Ann, 3:155
Bethia (Parsons), 3:158

Marshall (continued)
Catharine, 3:159
Deborah, 3:157
Dorothy, 3:156
Elizabeth, 3:156-159
Elizabeth (Holcomb) Case
Slater, 1:346
Esther (Bell), 3:157
Eunice, 3:159
Frances, 2:476, 3:158
Hannah, 1:498, 3:87,
3:155, 3:157-159
Hannah (Hardy), 2:355
Joanna, 3:158
Joanna (----), 3:159
Lydia, 2:384, 3:157-158
Lydia (----), 3:159
Martha, 3:156
Mary, 1:95, 1:348,
3:156-159, 3:594
Mary (----), 3:156
Mary (Barnes), 1:121,
3:157
Mary (Burrage), 1:510
Mary (Chantrel), 3:159
Mary (Drake), 3:158-159
Mary (Hilton), 2:424,
3:159
Mary (Newberry), 3:269
Mary (Partridge), 3:156,
3:366
Mary (Sheffield) Mills,
3:157
Mary (Wilton), 3:157,
4:590
Mercy, 3:158
Milicent (----), 3:155
Naomi, 3:155
Preserved, 3:157
Prudence, 1:382
Prudence (Woodward),
3:155
Rachel, 3:159
Rebecca, 3:158
Rebecca (----), 3:158
Rebecca (Newbury), 3:157
Ruth, 1:444, 3:155,
3:157-158
Ruth (----), 2:137,
3:156-158
Sarah, 3:155-159, 3:387,
4:198, 4:401
Sarah (----), 3:156-157

Sarah (Liet), 3:156
Susanna, 3:229
Sybil (----), 3:156
Marshcroft/Mascroft/etc
Elizabeth, 3:159
Hannah, 3:159
Mary, 3:159
Mary (Gorton), 2:282,
3:159
Mehitable, 3:159
Marshfield
Abilene, 3:160
Catharine (Chapin) Bliss
Gilbert, 1:201, 1:360,
2:252, 3:160
Esther, 3:160
Esther (Wright), 3:159-160,
4:659
Hannah, 3:160
Margaret, 3:160, 3:361
Mary (Appleton), 1:61
Mercy, 3:160
Rachel (Gilbert), 2:250,
3:159
Sarah, 2:456, 3:160, 3:211
Marston, 3:651
---- (Page), 3:331
Abigail, 3:160-161, 3:481,
3:650
Abigail (Sanborn), 3:160
Abigail (Verin), 3:650,
4:371
Alice (----), 3:651
Ann, 3:160, 3:482
Bethia, 3:160
Deliverance, 3:161, 3:612,
3:651
Dinah (Sanborn), 3:160
Elizabeth, 1:134,
3:160-161
Elizabeth (----), 3:650
Elizabeth (Brown), 1:270,
3:160
Elizabeth (Poor), 3:160,
3:456
Elizabeth (Williams),
4:561
Hannah, 1:115, 3:160-161
Jane (Brackett) Haines,
2:390
Joan (----), 3:161
Lydia, 3:651
Margaret, 3:651

Martha (----), 3:161
Martha (Lombard), 3:161
Mary, 3:160-161, 3:356,
3:480, 3:651, 4:13
Mary (----), 3:651
Mary (Chichester), 3:609,
3:651
Mary (Eastow), 2:94,
2:127, 3:161
Mary (Osgood), 3:161,
3:320
Mehitable, 3:651
Melatiah, 3:161
Mercy, 3:651
Mercy (Pierce), 3:651
Patience (Rogers), 3:562
Prudence, 3:161
Rebecca (Page), 3:161
Sabina (Page), 3:161
Sarah, 3:160-161, 3:425,
3:651
Sarah (----), 3:651
Susanna, 3:651
Susanna (Stacy), 4:160
Tryphena, 3:161
Martin/Martyn
----, 3:162-163
---- (----) Atwell, 1:77,
3:162
Abigail, 1:393, 3:162-163,
3:562
Abigail (Nichols), 3:279
Abigail (Norton), 3:163
Alice, 1:393
Alice (----) Varnum, 3:163
Alice (Ellet), 3:163
Ann (----), 1:393, 2:102
Desire, 3:162
Dorothy (----), 3:162
Elizabeth, 1:90, 3:161-162,
3:164
Elizabeth (----), 3:162-163
Elizabeth (----) Edmonds,
2:102, 3:163
Elizabeth (Fullford), 2:599
Elizabeth (Gay), 2:237,
3:162
Elizabeth (Saunders),
2:353
Esther, 2:541, 3:162
Esther (Roberts), 3:162,
3:547
Grace, 3:406

Martin/Martyn (continued)
Hannah, 2:249, 2:570, 3:162, 3:164, 4:653
Hannah (----), 3:161
Joan (----), 3:162
Joanna, 3:162
Lydia, 1:457, 3:162
Margaret, 3:136
Martha, 1:393
Martha (Lombard), 3:106, 3:162
Martha (Symonds) Denison, 2:37, 4:246
Mary, 3:161-163
Mary (----), 3:161
Mary (----) Lakin, 3:46, 3:163
Mary (----) Wentworth, 3:164
Mary (Benning) Wentworth, 4:485
Mary (Billington), 1:179
Mary (Hall), 2:337, 3:161
Mary (Pindar), 3:163, 3:438
Mary (Symonds) Denison, 3:164
Mehitable, 3:162
Mercy (Billington), 3:162
Phebe (Bisby) Bracy, 1:227, 3:163
Rachel (Farnham), 2:142, 3:163
Rebecca, 3:484
Rebecca (----), 3:162
Sarah, 2:189-190, 3:161-162
Sarah (----), 3:162
Sarah (Tilton), 4:304
Sarah (Tuttle), 3:162, 4:350
Susanna, 1:96
Susanna (----), 3:651
Susanna (Holyoke), 2:456, 3:162
Susanna (North), 3:162, 3:289

Marvin
Abigail, 1:220, 3:164-165
Ann, 3:164
Elizabeth, 3:164-165, 3:312, 3:444
Elizabeth (----), 3:164

Esther, 3:165
Hannah, 1:118, 3:164-165, 4:58
Jemima, 3:164
Lydia, 3:165
Martha, 3:165
Martha (Waterman), 3:165
Mary, 1:18, 1:164, 1:318, 3:164-165, 4:399
Mary (----), 3:165
Mary (Beers), 3:164
Mehitable, 3:164
Miriam, 3:165
Phebe, 3:165
Phebe (----), 3:165
Rachel, 3:164, 4:133
Rachel (St. John), 3:164
Rhoda (St. John), 3:165
Sarah, 2:275, 3:164-165
Sarah (Clark), 1:393, 3:165, 4:96
Sarah (Graham/Grimes), 3:164
Susanna (Graham/Grimes), 3:165

Mascall/Maskell
Abigail, 3:166
Bethia, 3:166
Bethia (Parsons), 3:158, 3:166, 3:364, 4:562
Elizabeth, 3:166
Ellen (Long), 3:651
Esther (Babbage), 3:651
Mehitable, 3:165
Sarah, 3:651

Mason
---- (----) Smith Monday, 4:114
---- (Brooks), 1:262
---- (Kinsley), 3:30
---- (Peck), 3:167
Abigail, 3:166, 3:168, 3:651
Abigail (----), 3:168
Abigail (Eaton), 2:95, 3:169
Abigail (Fitch), 3:619, 3:651
Alice, 3:166
Ann, 3:166-170, 3:606, 3:651-652
Ann (----), 3:169
Ann (Colliham), 3:168

Catharine, 4:299
Christian (----), 3:652
Clemence (----), 2:574, 3:170
Content (Wales), 3:168, 4:391
Dorothy (Hobart), 1:237, 4:684
Elizabeth, 1:299, 3:167-170, 3:293, 3:619, 3:652
Elizabeth (----), 3:166, 3:170
Elizabeth (Chandler), 1:357, 3:169
Elizabeth (Hammond), 2:345, 3:168
Elizabeth (Miller), 3:170
Elizabeth (Peck), 3:652
Elizabeth (Spring), 4:157
Emma (----), 3:166
Esther, 1:452, 3:168, 4:46
Esther (----), 3:167
Esther (Howe), 2:473, 3:167
Hannah, 1:261, 3:60, 3:166-169, 3:652
Hannah (Ramsden), 3:168
Harriet, 3:170
Isabel, 1:187, 3:167-168
Jane, 3:167
Jane (----), 3:651
Joanna, 3:166
Joanna (Parker), 3:166, 3:355
Judith (Smith), 3:170
Lois, 3:166
Lucy, 3:166
Lydia, 3:168
Margaret, 3:651
Margaret (Dennison), 3:651
Margery (Partridge), 3:170
Martha, 3:166
Martha (----), 3:169
Mary, 1:515, 2:126, 3:166-170, 3:292
Mary (Dudley), 3:169
Mary (Eaton), 2:95, 3:168
Mary (Fiske), 2:166, 3:168
Mary (Holman), 2:451, 3:169
Mary (Stoddard), 3:166

Mason (continued)
Priscilla, 2:168, 3:167-168,
  3:651
Prudence (----), 3:168
Rachel, 2:415, 3:167-168
Rebecca, 3:167, 3:651
Rebecca (----), 3:167
Rebecca (Hobart), 2:435,
  3:166
Ruth, 3:167
Sarah, 1:450, 2:226,
  3:166-170, 3:620, 3:652,
  3:662
Sarah (Fitch), 3:169
Sarah (Messenger), 3:169,
  3:202
Sarah (Pepper), 3:168,
  3:392
Sarah (Reynolds), 3:169,
  3:526
Sarah (Wells), 3:652
Susan, 3:169
Susanna, 1:151, 3:168-169,
  3:294, 3:652
Susanna (Street), 4:223
Zuriel, 3:169
Massey
Ann, 3:170
Sarah, 3:170, 4:410
Sarah (Wells), 3:170,
  4:478
Masters
----, 4:711
Dores (----), 3:652
Elizabeth, 3:58, 3:104,
  3:171, 3:652
Elizabeth (Ormes), 3:652
Jane (----), 3:170
Lydia, 3:170, 4:248
Ruth (Pickworth), 3:425,
  3:652
Sarah, 3:170
Masterson
Mary (----), 4:129
Mary (Goodall), 3:171
Sarah, 3:171
Mather
---- (Holt), 3:174
---- (Stevens), 3:175
Abigail, 3:173
Abigail (Phillips), 3:171,
  3:413
Ann (Lake) Cotton, 3:45,

3:173
Catharine, 2:410, 3:171,
  3:173-175
Catharine (----), 3:174
Catharine (Atherton), 1:73,
  3:175
Catharine (Wise), 3:175
Elizabeth, 1:326, 2:310,
  3:173, 3:175, 4:97
Elizabeth (----), 3:175
Elizabeth (Clark) Hubbard,
  1:396, 2:485, 3:172
Elizabeth (Davenport),
  2:13
Elizabeth (Weeks), 4:452
Esther (Warham), 3:172,
  4:201, 4:418
Eunice, 3:172, 4:563
Hannah, 3:173, 3:175
Hannah (Treat), 3:175,
  4:327
Jerusha, 3:171, 3:173,
  3:310, 4:132
Lydia (Lee), 3:73
Lydia (Lee) George, 2:242,
  3:172
Maria, 2:589, 3:173
Maria (Cotton), 1:462,
  3:173
Mary, 3:171
Mary (----), 3:171
Mary (Cotton), 3:173
Rebecca (Stoughton),
  3:171, 4:215
Sarah, 3:173, 4:403
Sarah (----), 2:410
Sarah (----) Cotton, 3:174
Sarah (----) Day Story
  Cotton, 4:244
Sarah (----) Story Cotton,
  1:462
Sarah (Clap), 3:174
Mathes
Phebe (Davis), 2:18
Matson
Abigail, 3:175-176
Amey/Emma, 3:175
Ann, 3:175
Ann (----), 3:175
Hannah, 3:176
Mary, 3:175
Mary (----) Read, 3:176
Mary (Adams), 4:673,

4:690
Mary (Cotton), 1:464,
  3:175
Matthews
Catharine (----), 3:177
Elizabeth, 3:176, 4:690
Elizabeth (Hotchkiss),
  4:690
Esther, 3:176, 4:552,
  4:702
Joanna, 3:176
Judith, 3:176
Lydia, 3:176
Margaret (Hunt), 3:176
Martha, 3:176
Mary, 2:478, 3:177, 4:52
Mary (----), 3:177
Mary (Emerson), 3:176
Mary (Johnson), 3:176
Mary (Neighbors), 3:176,
  3:267
Mehitable, 2:332
Pentecost (Bond), 3:176
Ruth, 3:176
Sarah, 3:176, 4:262
Sarah (----), 4:690
Sarah (Cary), 2:364
Sarah (Garfield), 3:176
Sarah (Hedge), 2:400,
  3:652
Susanna, 3:177
Thomasine (----), 3:176
Matthewson
Ruth, 3:177, 4:505
Sarah (Whitman), 3:177
**Mattocks - see also
Maddocks**
Alice, 1:185, 3:87, 3:177
Constance, 3:177
Constance (Fairbanks),
  2:137, 3:177
Elizabeth, 3:177
Grace (Todd), 3:177,
  4:309
Mary, 1:276, 3:177
Mary (----), 1:451
Mehitable, 3:177
Sarah (----), 3:177, 3:510
Mattoon
Elizabeth (Boltwood),
  1:209
Jane (Hilton), 2:423, 3:178
Margaret, 3:178

Mattoon (continued)
Mary, 3:178
Rebecca (Nims), 3:178,
3:285
Sarah, 3:178
Sarah (Hawkes), 1:157,
2:381, 3:178
Maude
Mary (----) Bonner, 3:178
Maudsley
Ann (Addington), 1:17,
3:179
Cicely (----), 3:178
Elizabeth, 3:178-179
Elizabeth (----), 3:178
Hannah, 3:178
Margaret, 3:178
Martha, 3:652
Mary, 3:178-179, 4:450
Mary (Eyre), 3:652
Mary (Lawrence), 3:63,
3:179
Mary (Newbury), 3:178,
3:269
Rebecca, 3:179
Sarah (Trescott), 4:329
Maule/Mauld
Deliverance, 3:652
Elizabeth, 3:652
Margaret, 3:652
Mary (Keyser), 3:179
Naomi (Lindsay), 3:179,
3:648
Sarah, 3:652
Sarah (----), 3:179
Susanna, 3:652
Maury
Mary, 3:29
Maverick
----, 3:372
Abigail, 1:399, 2:257,
3:179-181, 4:343
Amias (----), 3:181
Ann, 3:180
Ann (Harris), 2:360, 3:180,
4:184
Catharine, 3:180
Catharine (----), 2:599
Catharine (Skipper), 3:180
Dorothy, 3:180
Elizabeth, 2:289, 2:555,
3:180-181
Eunice (----) Roberts,

3:181, 3:548
Hannah, 3:181-182
Jane, 3:180
Jane (----), 3:180
Jemima (Smith), 3:181
Margaret, 3:180, 3:473
Margaret (Sherwood),
3:180
Martha, 3:181
Martha (----), 3:182
Martha (Bradford), 1:231,
3:181
Mary, 1:76, 1:510, 2:154,
2:457, 3:180-181, 3:339,
4:503
Rebecca, 2:381, 3:180-181
Rebecca (----), 3:180
Rebecca (Wheelwright),
1:230, 2:512, 3:181,
4:503
Remember, 3:180-181,
4:641
Remember (Allerton), 1:38,
3:181
Ruth, 3:180
Sarah, 3:180-181, 3:288
Mawney
Amey, 3:182
Elizabeth, 3:182
Lydia, 3:182
Mary, 3:182
Mary (Tillinghast), 3:182
Mercy, 3:182
Mercy (Tillinghast), 4:303
Sarah, 3:182
Mawry/Mourey/etc
Elizabeth (----), 3:182
Maxfield
Elizabeth, 3:183
Elizabeth (----), 3:182
Margery, 3:183
Mary, 3:183
Mary (Davenport), 2:14,
3:183
Mary (Denman), 2:38,
3:182
Mehitable, 3:183
Maxon/Maggson/Maxson
----, 3:652
Avis, 3:652
Bethia, 3:652
Content, 3:652
Content (Rogers), 3:652

Dorothy, 3:183, 3:652
Elizabeth, 3:652
Goodith, 3:652
Hannah, 3:183, 3:652
Judith, 3:652
Judith (Clark), 3:652
Mary, 3:183, 3:652
Mary (Mosher), 3:183
Naomi, 3:652
Ruth, 3:652
Susanna, 3:652
Tacy, 3:652
Tacy (Burdick), 1:301,
3:652
May
Abigail, 2:552, 3:184
Abigail (Stansfull), 3:184
Dorothy, 1:231
Elizabeth (Franklin), 2:200,
3:183
Experience, 3:184
Joanna, 2:147, 2:227,
3:184, 4:533
Mary, 3:183-184, 3:587
Mehitable, 3:183-184
Naomi, 3:183
Prudence, 3:184
Prudence (Bridge), 1:248,
3:183
Rebecca, 2:524
Sarah, 3:183-184, 4:570
Sarah (----), 3:183
Sarah (Brewer), 1:243,
3:183
Sarah (Langley), 3:55,
3:184
Mayer
Alice (----), 3:184
Hannah, 3:184
Hannah (----), 3:184
Patience, 3:184
Mayfield
Rebecca (Armitage), 3:182,
3:184
Sarah (----), 3:415
Mayhew
----, 2:356
Ann, 4:431
Bethia, 3:185
Elizabeth, 3:184
Grace (----) Paine, 3:185
Hannah, 3:185
Jane (----), 4:17

Mayhew (continued)
Jane (----) Paine, 3:337
Jane (Paine), 3:185, 4:690
Jerusha, 4:595
Joanna, 3:184
Joanna (Christophers),
   1:383, 3:184
Martha (Parkhurst), 3:185
Mary, 3:99, 3:184-185
Patience, 3:184
Thankful (Hinckley),
   2:425, 3:184
Wait, 3:184
Maylen
Kezia (Brackett), 1:228
Maynard
---- (Blandford), 1:197
---- (Starr), 3:186, 4:169
Abigail, 3:186
Bethia, 3:186
Edith (----) Day, 2:456,
   3:185
Editha (Stebbins) Day,
   2:27
Elizabeth, 2:295, 3:186
Elizabeth (----) Heath Pell,
   2:400
Elizabeth (----) Heaton Pell,
   3:186, 3:386
Elizabeth (Price), 3:186
Eunice, 3:186
Hannah, 3:185-186
Hannah (----), 3:185-186
Hannah (Goodrich), 2:274,
   3:186
Keziah, 3:185
Lydia, 3:186, 3:229
Lydia (Richards), 3:186,
   3:533
Lydia (Ward), 3:186
Martha, 3:185
Mary, 2:488, 3:186
Mary (Axdell/Axtel), 3:186
Mary (Gates), 2:236, 3:186
Mercy, 3:185
Persis, 3:186
Ruhamah, 3:185
Ruth, 4:192
Sarah, 2:26, 3:186
Sarah (----), 3:186
Tabitha, 3:186
Mayo
Abigail, 3:189

Alice, 3:188, 3:333
Ann, 3:188
Barbara (Knowles), 3:42,
   3:188
Bathsheba, 3:188
Bathshua, 3:188
Bethia, 3:186
Content, 3:188
Elizabeth, 2:478,
   3:187-189, 4:328
Elizabeth (----), 2:224
Elizabeth (Davis),
   3:188-189
Elizabeth (Holbrook),
   3:188
Elizabeth (Wixam), 3:188,
   4:620
Hannah, 1:91, 3:187-189,
   3:235
Hannah (Freeman), 2:204,
   3:187
Hannah (Graves), 2:295,
   3:187
Hannah (Prence), 3:188,
   3:477, 4:145
Hannah (Reycraft), 3:187
Judah, 3:188
Lydia, 3:188
Margery, 3:186
Maria, 3:188
Martha, 3:188
Mary, 1:111, 3:186-189,
   4:233
Mary (----) Young, 3:188
Mary (Brown), 3:188
Mehitable, 3:187-189
Mercy, 3:187-189, 4:233
Mercy (----) Young, 3:188,
   4:670
Phebe, 3:188
Priscilla, 3:188
Rebecca, 3:187-189
Ruth, 3:188
Sarah, 3:186-189, 4:233
Sarah (----), 3:187
Sarah (Burden), 3:187
Sarah (Short), 3:188
Thankful, 3:189
Thomasine, 3:188
Thomasine (----), 3:187
Thomasine (Lumpkin),
   3:130, 3:188, 4:233

Mazure/Mazury
Abigail, 3:653
Margaret (Row), 3:652
Mary, 3:653
Mary (Kibby), 3:653
Sarah (Pickworth), 3:425,
   3:652
McDowell
Mary, 1:374
McEwen/McCune/Mekune
Abigail (Hurd), 3:190
Ann, 3:190
Charity, 3:190
Comfort, 3:189
Elizabeth, 3:189
Elizabeth/Betty, 3:189
Eunice, 3:190
Martha (Picket), 3:189
Mary, 3:189
Mary (Birdsey), 3:189
Phebe, 3:190
Rebecca, 3:189
Rebecca (Picket), 3:189
Ruth, 3:190
Sarah, 3:189-190
Sarah (Wilcockson), 3:189
McLathin
Priscilla, 4:444
McMullen
Elizabeth, 1:507
McPhedris
Sarah (Wentworth), 3:639
Meacham
---- (Brown), 1:279
Alice (Dutch), 3:617
Bethia, 2:326, 3:190
Deborah, 3:190
Deborah (----), 3:653
Deborah (----) Perkins,
   3:190
Deborah (Brown), 1:271,
   3:190
Deborah (Browning)
   Perkins, 3:396, 3:653
Hannah, 2:255, 3:190
Mary, 3:190
Mary (Cash), 1:347, 3:190
Mary (Trask), 3:190
Rebecca, 3:139, 3:190,
   3:653
Rhoda, 3:190
Sarah, 1:225, 3:190

Mead/Meade/Meades/etc
----, 3:191, 4:166
Elizabeth, 3:191
Elizabeth (----), 3:191
Elizabeth (Gulliver), 2:340
Experience, 2:399, 3:190
Grace, 3:190
Grace (Tay/Toy), 4:259
Hannah, 3:102, 3:190
Hannah (Warren), 3:190,
    4:423
Johanna (----), 3:190
Judith (----), 3:190
Lydia, 1:302, 3:190
Margaret, 3:103, 3:190
Mary, 2:21, 3:190
Mary (----), 3:191
Mary (----) Day, 3:653
Mary (Hall), 2:339, 3:190
Patience, 2:127, 3:190
Rebecca (----), 3:191
Ruth, 3:190
Ruth (Hardy), 2:355
Sarah, 2:99, 3:190
Susanna, 3:190-191
Meader
Abigail (----), 3:191
Eleanor, 3:191
Eleanor (----), 3:191
Elizabeth, 3:191
Keziah, 3:191
Lydia, 3:191
Lydia (----), 3:191
Sarah, 3:191, 4:386
Meadows/Meddowes
Ann (Stamford), 4:685
Elizabeth (Iggleden), 2:517,
    3:191
Hannah, 3:191
Mary, 2:21
Meakins/Meekins
Catharine (----), 3:191
Elizabeth (----), 3:192
Hannah, 1:158, 3:191-192
Helen, 3:192
Mary, 1:41, 1:399,
    3:191-192
Mary (----), 2:67
Mary (Biddle), 1:174,
    3:191
Mary (Bunce), 1:298,
    3:192
Mehitable, 3:192

Rebecca, 3:191
Ruth (Belknap), 1:158
Sarah, 3:191-192
Sarah (----), 3:192
Sarah (Clark) Welles,
    4:477
Mean/Meane/Means
Ann (----), 2:373, 3:192
Mary, 2:373-374, 3:192
Sarah, 2:374, 3:192
Mears
Elizabeth, 3:192-193
Elizabeth (----), 3:192-193
Hannah, 3:192
Lydia (----), 3:192
Mary, 3:193
Mary (----), 3:13,
    3:192-193
Measure/Masuer
Alice (----) Tingley, 4:306
Alice (----) Tinker, 3:193
Mecock/Maycock/etc
Mary (----), 3:193
Medbury
Sarah (----), 3:193
Mede
Experience, 2:399
Medfield
Sarah (Hooker), 2:459
Meeker/Meaker
Sarah (----), 4:685
Sarah (Preston), 4:696
Susan (Turberfield), 3:193
Meeks - see Mix
Megdaniel
Elizabeth (----), 3:653
Meigs
Concurrence, 3:193
Elizabeth, 3:193-194
Esther, 3:194
Hannah, 3:194
Lydia (----) Cruttenden,
    3:194
Mary, 3:193, 4:190
Mindwell, 3:194
Sarah, 1:130, 3:194
Sarah (Wilcoxson), 3:194,
    4:548
Trial, 3:193, 4:407
Mellard
Martha, 4:705
Mellen/Melin/Melling
Elizabeth, 3:194

Elizabeth (Dexter), 2:45,
    3:194
Elizabeth (Fiske), 2:166
Elizabeth (Spring) Gale,
    3:194, 4:157
Mary, 3:194, 4:533-534
Mary (----), 3:194
Sarah, 3:194
Mellins
Elizabeth, 1:502
Mellows/Mellhouse
Elizabeth, 3:195, 3:202
Elizabeth (----), 3:144,
    3:195
Hannah, 3:195
Hannah (----), 2:418, 3:195
Martha, 3:195, 4:434
Martha (----), 1:462, 3:195
Mary, 3:195, 4:158
Sarah, 3:195
Sarah (----), 3:195
Melville
Abigail, 3:195
Elizabeth, 3:195
Mary, 3:195
Mary (Mills) Willard,
    4:553
Mary (Willard), 3:195
Melvin
Hannah, 3:195
Hannah (----), 3:195
Melyen/Melyne/Maline
Abigail, 3:196, 4:55, 4:641
Hannah (Hubbard), 2:483,
    3:196
Susanna, 4:614
Mepham
---- (----), 3:196
Mary (----), 1:105
Mercer
Elizabeth (----), 3:196
Lucy, 3:196
Sarah, 3:196
Merchant/Marchant
Mary, 3:197, 3:653
Mary (----), 3:197, 3:653
Mary (Taylor), 4:263
Sarah (----), 3:196
Meriam
Abigail, 3:197
Ann, 1:260
Ann (Jones), 3:198
Catharine, 3:197

Meriam (continued)
  Elizabeth, 2:102, 3:197,
    4:487
  Elizabeth (----), 3:197
  Elizabeth (Brooks), 1:261
  Elizabeth (Townsend),
    3:197
  Hannah, 2:266, 3:197
  Lydia, 3:197
  Mary, 3:197, 4:265
  Mary (----), 3:197
  Mary (Cooper), 3:197
  Rebecca, 3:197
  Sarah, 2:339, 2:543, 3:87,
    ·3:197
  Sarah (----), 3:197
  Sarah (Jenkins), 3:197
  Sarah (Stone), 3:197,
    4:204
  Susanna, 3:197, 4:36
  Susanna (----), 3:197
  Thomasine, 3:197
Meridith/Merryday
  Joanna (Treworge), 4:330
Merks
  Mary, 4:259
Merrick
  Abigail, 3:198
  Abigail (Hopkins), 2:461,
    3:198
  Deborah, 3:198, 4:662
  Elizabeth, 3:198
  Elizabeth (----), 3:198, 4:35
  Elizabeth (Howes), 3:198
  Elizabeth (Tilley), 3:198,
    4:303
  Elizabeth (Wyborne),
    3:198, 4:662
  Hannah, 3:198
  Mary, 2:181, 2:462, 3:198
  Mercy (Bangs), 1:501,
    3:198
  Miriam, 3:198
  Rebecca, 3:198
  Rebecca (----), 3:198
  Ruth, 3:198
  Sarah, 2:204, 3:198
  Sarah (Stebbins), 3:198,
    4:177
Merrill/Merrills
  ----, 1:70
  Abigail, 3:199
  Abigail (Webster), 3:199

  Elizabeth (----), 3:199
  Elizabeth (Roe), 3:559
  Esther (----), 3:199
  Hannah, 3:109, 3:199,
    4:240
  Hannah (Waters), 4:433
  Hepzibah, 2:47
  Joanna (Kenney), 3:199
  Martha, 3:199
  Mary, 3:199, 4:295
  Priscilla, 3:199
  Priscilla (Chase), 1:364,
    3:199
  Prudence, 3:199
  Ruth, 3:199
  Sarah, 3:199, 4:687
  Sarah (----), 3:199
  Sarah (Clough), 3:199
  Sarah (Watson), 3:199,
    4:437
  Susanna, 1:300, 3:199
  Susanna (Jordan), 3:199
Merriman
  Abigail, 3:199, 3:632,
    3:653
  Elizabeth, 3:199, 4:690
  Grace, 3:199
  Hannah, 3:199, 4:685,
    4:690
  Joan (----), 4:690
  Mary, 3:200, 4:690
  Sarah, 3:199
Merritt
  Catharine, 2:4
  Deborah (Buck), 1:284
  Elizabeth, 3:491
  Elizabeth (----), 3:200
  Martha, 3:200
  Mary, 3:200, 4:229
  Rebecca, 3:200
Merrow/Mero
  Jane (Wallis), 3:200
Merry
  ----, 2:421, 3:200
  Constance (----), 3:200
  Elizabeth (----), 3:200
  Elizabeth (Cunnill), 3:201
  Hannah, 4:705-706
  Leah, 3:200
  Martha (Cotterill), 3:201
  Mary (----), 4:291
  Mary (Dolens), 3:200
  Mary (Dowling), 3:200

  Rachel, 3:200
  Rachel (Ballard), 3:200
  Rebecca, 3:200
  Rebecca (----), 3:200
  Sarah, 1:230, 3:200
Merryfield
  Abigail, 3:201
  Elizabeth, 3:201
  Hannah, 3:201
  Margaret (----), 3:201
  Martha, 3:201
  Mary, 3:201
  Ruth, 3:201
  Sarah, 3:201
Merwin
  Abigail, 3:201
  Ann, 3:201
  Deborah, 3:201
  Elizabeth, 3:201
  Hannah, 3:201
  Hannah (----) Miles, 3:201
  Hannah (Wilmot) Miles,
    3:207
  Martha, 3:201
  Mary, 3:201
  Mary (----), 4:676
  Mary (Adams), 1:9
  Sarah (----) Beach, 3:201
  Sarah (----) Scofield, 4:36
  Sarah (Platt) Beach, 1:144,
    3:445
  Sarah (Wooden), 3:201,
    4:638
Messenger/Messinger
  Ann, 3:201-202
  Bethia, 3:202
  Bethia (Howard), 2:472,
    3:202
  Dorcas, 3:201, 3:214
  Elizabeth, 3:202
  Elizabeth (Mellows), 3:202
  Hannah, 3:202
  Lydia, 3:201
  Martha (----), 3:202
  Mary, 1:164, 3:202
  Mehitable (Minot), 3:202,
    3:213, 3:218
  Priscilla, 3:201
  Rebecca, 3:201-202
  Rebecca (Kelsey), 3:202
  Rose (----), 3:201
  Sarah, 3:169, 3:201-202
  Sarah (----), 3:201

Messerve
Thomasine, 2:342
Metcalf
Abigail, 3:203
Abigail (----), 3:204
Ann, 3:203
Ann (Chickering) Paine,
3:336
Ann (Paine), 3:204
Elizabeth, 1:110, 3:203,
3:204
Elizabeth (----), 1:149,
3:203
Elizabeth (Fuller)
Kingsbury, 2:219, 3:28,
3:204
Grace (Williams), 4:570
Hannah, 1:296, 3:202,
3:204, 3:533
Hannah (Kenrick), 3:11,
3:202
Jane, 3:203
Joan, 4:396
Judith, 3:204
Lydia (----) Davis, 3:204
Martha, 1:254, 3:202-203,
4:111
Martha (----) Pigg/Pidge,
3:203
Mary, 3:202-204, 4:416,
4:583
Mary (----) Pigg/Pidge,
3:435
Mary (Chickering), 1:376,
3:202
Mary (Fairbanks), 2:136,
3:204
Mehitable, 3:202
Meletiah, 3:202
Meletiah (Fisher), 3:202
Rebecca, 3:140, 3:203-204
Rebecca (----), 3:203
Sarah, 3:203-204, 3:314,
4:417, 4:521
Sarah (----), 3:203
Sarah (Avery), 3:204
Sarah (Paige), 3:204
Methup/Mettup
Abigail, 3:205
Bethia, 3:204
Bethia (Beers), 1:154,
3:204
Hannah, 3:205

Mary, 3:204
Sarah, 3:204
Mew
Ann, 3:205
Ann (Gibbons), 2:245,
3:205
Michelson
Ruth, 2:303, 3:222, 3:609
Mico
Mary (Brattle), 1:239,
3:205
Middlebrook
Mary (----) Turney, 3:205,
4:349
Phebe, 3:205, 4:588
Middlecott
Jane, 1:445, 3:205
Mary, 3:205
Sarah, 3:205
Sarah (Winslow) Standish
Paine, 3:337, 4:162, 4:601
Sarah (Winslow) Standish
Payne, 3:205
Middleton
Abigail, 3:205
Alice, 3:205
Elizabeth, 3:205
Elizabeth (----), 3:205
Faith (Gillam), 2:255
Joanna, 3:205
Mighill
Bethia (Weld), 3:206
Elizabeth, 3:206
Elizabeth (Toppan), 3:205,
4:254
Ellen (----), 3:205
Grace, 3:206
Hannah, 3:206
Mary, 1:143, 3:206, 4:189
Sarah (Phillips), 3:205,
3:414
Milborne
Susanna (----), 4:344
Milbury
---- (Dixon), 3:206
Miles
---- (Harriman), 2:358
Abigail, 3:207, 3:653
Abigail (Thompson) Alsop,
3:597
Ann, 3:207, 4:223
Catherine (----), 3:207
Elizabeth, 2:358,

3:206-207
Elizabeth (Dawes), 2:24
Elizabeth (Dowes), 2:68
Elizabeth (Dowse), 3:57,
3:207
Elizabeth (Harriman),
3:206, 3:628
Esther, 3:207
Exercise (Felton), 3:653
Experience (----), 3:207
Experience (Collicott),
1:432
Frances (----), 3:207
Hannah, 3:206-207
Hannah (----), 3:201
Hannah (Wilmot), 3:207,
4:580
Martha, 3:207-208, 3:344
Mary, 2:358, 2:518, 3:72,
3:206-207, 3:653
Mary (Alsop), 1:45, 3:206
Mary (Prescott), 3:206
Mary (Whelan), 3:653
Rebecca, 3:207, 3:215
Sarah, 3:206-207
Sarah (----), 3:206
Sarah (Foster), 3:207
Susanna, 3:653
Susanna (----) Rediat,
3:206, 3:521
Milk/Milke
Mary, 3:653, 4:691
Sarah (Weston), 3:653,
4:691
Mill
Dorothy (----), 2:356
Miller
---- (----), 3:210, 4:49
Abigail, 3:211
Ann, 1:91, 3:211
Deborah, 3:211
Deborah (Templar)
Chamberlain, 4:266
Elinor, 3:208
Elinor (----), 2:404, 3:210
Elizabeth, 2:212, 3:170,
3:208-209, 3:211, 3:346,
4:161
Elizabeth (----), 3:210
Elizabeth (Smith), 3:208
Elizabeth (Turner), 3:211
Esther, 3:211
Esther (Bowen), 3:211

Miller (continued)
Esther (Jenks), 2:543
Eunice, 3:211
Experience, 3:211
Faith, 3:209, 4:603
Grace (----), 3:211
Hannah, 1:299, 2:1, 2:101,
  2:212, 2:336, 3:129,
  3:208-211, 4:296, 4:602
Hannah (Clap), 3:208
Hannah (George), 2:242,
  3:208
Hannah (Miller), 3:208
Isabel (----), 3:211
Jane, 3:209-210
Joanna, 3:210
Joanna (----), 3:210
Lydia, 1:447, 2:161, 3:209,
  3:211
Lydia (----), 3:209, 3:211
Lydia (Reynolds), 3:525
Margaret, 3:209, 3:211
Margaret (Winslow), 3:209,
  4:602
Martha, 3:208, 3:211-212,
  4:484
Mary, 3:208-209,
  3:211-212, 3:401, 4:484,
  4:534, 4:572
Mary (----), 3:209-210
Mary (----) Cutting, 1:496,
  3:210
Mary (Bushnell), 3:212
Mary (Pope), 3:210, 3:459
Mary (Rowell), 3:211
Mehitable, 1:479, 3:209,
  3:211-212
Mercy, 2:193, 3:209,
  3:212
Patience, 3:208, 3:211-212,
  3:294
Patience (----), 3:212
Rebecca, 1:369, 1:402,
  3:209, 3:211-212
Rebecca (Belcher), 3:211
Rebecca (Leonard), 3:79,
  3:211
Ruth, 3:208
Sarah, 3:210-212, 4:308
Sarah (----), 2:364
Sarah (Allen), 3:208
Sarah (Marshfield), 3:160,
  3:211

Sarah (Nettleton), 3:211
Susanna, 3:208-209, 4:515
Thankful, 1:47, 3:212
Thankful (Howes), 3:210
Wait, 3:208
Millerd/Millard/Milward
Ann, 3:212
Ann (----), 3:212, 3:427
Elizabeth, 3:212
Rebecca, 3:212, 4:293
Millet
---- (Greenoway), 3:213
Abigail, 3:212
Abigail (Coit) Eveleth,
  3:618, 3:653
Ann (Lester), 3:81, 3:212,
  4:441
Bethia, 3:213, 3:598
Elizabeth, 3:212
Hannah, 3:212
Mary, 3:212, 3:542
Mary (----), 3:212
Mary (Eveleth), 2:129,
  3:653
Mary (Greenway), 2:310
Mehitable, 3:212, 3:618
Sarah, 3:212, 4:127
Sarah (----), 3:653, 4:127
Sarah (Leach), 3:212
Millikin
Elizabeth (Alger), 1:28
Milling/Millings
Mary, 3:213, 4:294
Mary (Threeneedles),
  4:294
Millington
Sarah (Smith), 3:213
Mills
----, 1:412
Abigail, 3:215
Ann, 3:214
Dorcas (Messinger), 3:201,
  3:214
Dorothy, 3:213
Dorothy (----), 3:214
Elizabeth, 3:214-215
Elizabeth (Shove), 3:214
Frances (----), 3:215
Hannah, 2:580, 3:215
Jane (Fannin), 3:214
Jane (Warren), 3:214
Joan (----), 3:215
Joan (Porter), 3:214

Joanna, 3:214
Joanna (----), 3:214
Joanna (Alger) Oakman,
  1:27, 3:304
Joy, 3:213
Martha, 3:213
Martha (Alley), 1:39,
  3:213
Mary, 3:213-215, 3:631,
  4:553
Mary (Buell), 1:289, 3:215
Mary (Pitcher), 3:440
Mary (Sheffield), 3:157
Mehitable (Minot)
  Messinger, 3:202, 3:213,
  3:218
Prudence, 3:215
Rebecca, 3:215
Recompense, 3:213
Sarah, 1:514, 3:213-215
Sarah (----), 3:214
Susanna, 3:213-214, 3:614
Susanna (----), 3:213
Mingay
Ann (----), 2:507, 3:215
Mingo
Elizabeth (----), 3:215
Minor/Miner
Abigail, 3:216
Ann, 3:215-216
Bridget, 4:691
Bridget (----) Thompson,
  4:691
Deborah, 4:691
Elizabeth, 1:272,
  3:215-216, 4:691
Elizabeth (Booth), 1:212,
  3:216
Eunice/Hannah, 4:691
Frances (----) Willey, 3:215
Frances (Burcham) Willey,
  4:558
Grace, 3:216, 4:691
Grace (Palmer), 3:216
Hannah, 3:215-216, 4:691
Hannah (Avery), 4:691
Joanna, 3:216, 4:691
Joanna (----), 3:215
Lydia (Moore), 4:691
Martha (Wellman), 3:215,
  4:481-482
Mary, 1:373, 3:215-216,
  4:691

Minor/Miner (continued)
Mary (----), 3:216
Mary (Avery), 4:691
Mary (Lord), 4:691
Phebe, 3:215
Prudence, 4:691
Prudence (Richardson)
Hallam, 2:339, 3:535
Rebecca, 4:691
Sarah, 3:216, 4:691
Sarah (----), 3:412
Minord
Mary (----), 3:216
Minot
Elizabeth, 2:7, 3:217-218
Elizabeth (----), 3:217
Elizabeth (Breck), 1:240,
3:217
Hannah, 3:216
Hannah (Howard), 2:472,
3:217
Hannah (Jones), 3:217
Hannah (Stoughton),
3:216, 4:213, 4:216
Hepzibah (Corlet), 1:356,
1:458, 3:217
Jerusha, 3:217
Lucy, 3:217
Lydia, 3:217-218
Lydia (Butler), 1:321,
3:217
Martha, 3:217
Martha (----), 3:216
Mary, 3:217
Mary (Clark), 3:218
Mary (Dassett) Biggs,
1:177, 2:11, 3:217
Mary/Mercy (Clark), 1:392
Mehitable, 1:455, 3:202,
3:213, 3:217-218, 4:18,
4:201
Mercy, 3:217
Rebecca, 3:217-218
Rebecca (Jones), 2:563,
3:217
Rebecca (Wheeler), 3:217,
4:501
Truecross (----), 3:202
Truecross (Davenport),
2:14, 3:217
Minter
---- (----), 3:218
Hannah (----), 1:97-98

Rebecca (Bemis), 1:163,
2:50
Mirable
Elizabeth (----), 3:218
Mary (----) Whittemore,
4:535
Mary (Knower), 3:40,
3:218
Miriam
----, 2:484
Mirick/Myrick
Abigail, 3:218-219
Amity, 1:165
Ann, 3:218, 4:394
Deborah, 3:219
Elizabeth, 3:219
Elizabeth (Trowbridge),
3:218, 4:332
Hannah, 3:42, 3:218
Hannah (----), 3:218
Hopestill, 3:218
Hopestill (----), 3:218
Judith (----), 3:218
Lydia, 3:218-219
Margaret, 3:219
Mary (Lancaster), 3:219
Mercy, 3:218
Rebecca, 3:218, 3:371-372
Sarah, 1:74, 1:513, 2:428,
3:218-219
Sarah (----), 3:218
Susanna, 3:218
Thankful, 3:218
Mitchell
Abigail, 3:219
Abigail (----), 3:219
Alice, 3:219
Alice (Bradford), 3:219
Ann (----), 3:221
Constance (Moores), 3:220
Constant, 2:176
Elizabeth, 1:22, 3:19, 3:49,
3:219-221, 4:429, 4:528,
4:673, 4:691
Elizabeth (----), 3:220-221,
4:528
Esther, 3:220
Hannah, 2:393, 3:220-221,
4:84
Hannah (Spofford), 3:220
Jane (Cook), 1:446, 3:219
Joanna (Burrage), 1:510
Mabel, 3:220, 4:88

Margaret, 3:220, 4:56
Margaret (----) Shepard,
3:220
Margaret (Boradale)
Shepard, 4:76
Martha, 3:220
Mary, 3:219-221, 4:64
Mary (----), 3:220, 4:28
Mary (----) Abbe, 1:6
Mary (Bonney), 1:211,
3:220
Mary (Hayward), 2:394,
3:219
Mary (Lothrop), 3:220
Mary (Moulton), 3:221,
3:249
Mary (Prior), 3:220
Mary (Sawyer), 3:221
Mary (Thompson), 3:221,
4:285
Miriam, 3:220
Sarah, 2:392, 3:219-220
Sarah (Cotton), 1:462
Susanna, 4:84
Susanna (Pope), 3:220,
3:459
Mitchelson
Abigail, 3:222
Alice, 3:222
Bethia, 3:222, 4:456
Elizabeth, 1:75, 2:41,
3:222
Mary, 3:222
Mary (Bradshaw), 3:222
Ruth, 3:222
Ruth (Bushell), 1:317,
3:222
Mitton/Mitten
Ann, 1:228, 3:222
Elizabeth, 1:400, 3:222
Elizabeth (Cleves), 1:409,
3:222
Martha, 2:295, 2:321,
3:222
Mary, 1:229, 3:222
Sarah, 1:53, 3:222
Mix/Meeks
Abigail, 3:222-223
Ann, 3:223
Christian, 3:222
Deborah, 3:223
Dorothy, 3:223
Elizabeth, 3:222-223

Mix/Meeks (continued)
Elizabeth (Wilmot), 3:222, 4:580
Esther, 3:222
Hannah, 3:222-223, 3:312
Hannah (Chedsey), 1:370
Hannah (Fitch), 2:168, 3:223
Mary, 3:222-223
Mary (Stoddard), 3:222
Mercy, 3:222
Rebecca, 3:222
Rebecca (Turner), 3:222, 4:347
Ruth (Rockwell), 3:222, 3:557
Sarah, 3:222-223
Mixer
Abigail, 3:223-224
Abigail (Fiske), 3:224
Ann, 3:224
Ann (Jones), 3:224
Dorothy, 3:223
Elizabeth, 3:223-224
Elizabeth (Pierce), 3:224
Joanna, 2:359, 3:223, 4:412
Judith (----), 3:223
Lydia, 3:224
Mary, 1:451, 3:223-224
Mary (Coolidge), 1:451, 3:223
Mary (Lothrop) Stearns French, 3:122, 3:223, 4:174
Mehitable, 3:223
Rebecca, 3:9, 3:223-224
Rebecca (Garfield), 2:232, 3:223
Rebecca (Newton), 3:223
Sarah, 1:451, 2:328, 3:223-224, 4:174
Sarah (----), 3:223
Mokum
Hannah (----), 3:224
Monday
---- (----) Smith, 4:114
Monk
Elizabeth (----) Woodmansey, 3:224
Elizabeth (Clark) Woodmansey, 4:642
Lucy (Gardner), 2:231

Lucy (Gardner) Turner, 3:224, 4:347
Mary, 3:224
Mary (----), 3:224
Susanna, 3:224
Montague
Abigail, 3:225, 4:421
Abigail (Downing), 3:225
Hannah, 3:224
Hannah (Smith), 3:224
Margaret (----), 3:224
Martha, 2:366, 3:225
Mary, 3:225, 4:428
Mary (----) Smith, 3:225
Mary (Crow) Coleman, 1:479
Mary (Crow) Goldman, 3:225
Mary (Smith), 3:225
Sarah, 3:225
Sarah (Eastman), 2:93
Moody/Moodey
Abigail, 3:225
Deborah (----), 3:225
Elizabeth, 3:225-226, 4:44
Elizabeth (----), 3:225
Esther (Green), 3:226
Hannah, 3:225-226
Hannah (----), 3:226
Hannah (Dole), 2:59
Hannah (Sewall), 4:54
Judith, 3:225
Judith (Bradbury), 1:230, 3:225
Lydia, 3:226
Martha, 3:226, 3:592
Martha (Collins), 1:434, 3:226
Mary, 2:118, 3:225-226
Mary (----), 3:131
Mary (Cutting), 1:496, 3:226
Mehitable (Sewall), 4:53-54
Mercy (Cutting), 3:226
Sarah, 3:151, 3:225-226, 3:436, 3:447, 3:653
Sarah (----), 3:226
Sarah (Deming), 2:35, 3:226
Sarah (Pierce), 3:225
Mooers
Elizabeth, 1:365

Moone
Dorothy (----), 3:227
Moorcock/Morecock
---- (Burnham), 3:227
Mary, 3:227
Moore/More
---- (Eaton), 2:98
Abby (Eaton), 3:227
Abigail, 1:187, 3:227-228, 3:230-231
Abigail (Hawkins), 2:383, 3:6, 3:230
Alice (----), 3:230
Ann, 1:510, 3:18, 3:227
Ann (----), 3:229-230
Ann (Smith), 3:229, 4:120
Bridget (----), 3:228, 3:230
Catharine, 3:229, 3:633
Catharine (----), 3:227
Deborah, 3:227-228, 4:176
Dorothy, 3:227
Dorothy (Smith), 3:228
Dorothy (Smith) Blakeman Hall Sension, 1:195, 2:333, 4:52, 4:115
Elizabeth, 1:345, 2:247, 3:113, 3:228-231, 3:242, 3:529
Elizabeth (----), 3:228
Elizabeth (----) Periman, 3:227
Elizabeth (Wildes), 3:230
Elizabeth (Woodbury), 3:227
Ellen, 4:599
Experience, 3:231
Grace (Rice), 3:531
Hannah, 2:70, 2:373, 3:227-230
Hannah (----), 3:228
Hannah (Goffe), 2:267, 3:229
Hannah (Hempstead), 2:402
Jerusha, 3:228
Joan (----) Champney, 1:356, 3:227
Lydia, 1:493, 3:227, 3:229, 4:659, 4:691
Lydia (----), 3:229
Lydia (Maynard), 3:186, 3:229
Lydia (Post), 3:465

Moore/More (continued)
Martha, 3:229-231
Martha (----), 3:230
Martha (Flamsworth),
  3:229
Mary, 1:226, 1:461, 2:247,
  3:228-230, 3:653-654,
  4:412
Mary (----), 3:229
Mary (----) Allen, 3:231
Mary (Barlow), 1:502
Mary (Booth/Both), 3:228
Mary (Veazie), 3:231
Mary (Wellman) Howard,
  2:473, 3:231, 4:481
Mindwell, 1:187, 3:228
Miriam, 3:229, 4:558
Naomi (----), 3:230
Phebe, 3:228
Priscilla (Poor), 3:227,
  3:456
Rachel, 3:227, 3:229-230
Rebecca, 3:227, 3:230
Rebecca (----), 3:227
Remember, 3:230
Ruth, 3:227-228, 3:654,
  3:656, 4:68
Ruth (Pinion), 3:228,
  3:438
Ruth (Stanley), 3:228,
  4:164
Ruth (Starr), 3:229
Sarah, 2:253, 3:68, 3:109,
  3:227-230, 3:648,
  3:653-654
Sarah (Hodges), 3:230
Sarah (Phelps), 3:227
Susanna, 3:227, 3:229-230
Susanna (Marshall), 3:229
Tamison (Simmons),
  3:231
Moores
Ann (----), 3:231
Constance, 3:220
Constance (Longhorne),
  3:231
Dorothy, 3:231
Hannah (Plummer), 3:231
Martha, 2:276, 3:231
Mary, 3:231
Mary (Ilsley), 2:518, 3:231
Sarah, 3:231
Sarah (Cooper), 3:231

Sarah (Savory), 3:231
Morehouse/Moorhouse
---- (Keeler), 3:2
Martha (Hobby), 2:437
Mary (Wilson), 3:231,
  4:582
Morey
Abigail, 2:364, 3:232,
  3:654
Bethia, 3:232, 3:340
Elizabeth, 3:232
Hannah, 3:232, 3:654
Hannah (----), 3:654
Hannah (Lewis), 3:654
Joanna, 3:232
Joanna (Inman), 2:524,
  3:232
Martha, 3:654
Mary, 3:29, 3:232, 3:654
Mary (----), 2:398, 3:232
Mary (Bartlett) Foster,
  1:132, 2:190, 3:232
Mary (Johnson), 3:232
Mehitable, 3:29, 3:232
Sarah, 3:654
Susanna, 3:232
Susanna (Newell), 3:232,
  3:271
Morgan
Abigail, 3:232
Ann (Dart), 2:578
Bethia, 3:233
Deborah (Hart), 3:233
Dorothy (Parke), 3:348
Elizabeth, 3:233
Elizabeth (----), 3:233
Elizabeth (Bliss), 1:202,
  3:233
Elizabeth (Dixy), 3:616,
  3:654
Elizabeth (Jones), 2:568
Hannah, 3:232-233, 3:570,
  4:269
Joan (----) Bryan, 3:233
Joanna (Bryan), 1:282
Lydia, 3:233, 3:429
Margaret (----), 3:233
Margery (Hill), 3:232
Martha, 3:396
Mary, 3:232-233, 3:488
Mercy, 3:233
Prudence (----), 3:233
Rachel (Deming), 2:35,

3:233
Morley
---- (Saltonstall), 4:8
Ann, 3:233
Catherine (----), 3:233
Constant (Starr), 3:233
Martha (Wright), 4:654
Mary (Sacket), 4:2
Morrall
Mary (Butler), 3:654
Morray
Constant (Bracy), 1:227
Morrell/Morrill
Catharine, 3:234, 4:119
Elizabeth, 3:234, 3:608
Hannah, 1:243, 3:234-235,
  4:199
Hepzibah, 3:234
Jemima, 3:234
Lydia, 2:320, 3:234-235,
  4:52
Mary, 2:177, 3:234-235
Mary (----), 2:440, 3:234
Phebe (----), 3:234
Rachel, 3:234
Rebecca (Barnes), 1:123,
  3:235
Ruth, 3:235
Sarah, 1:436, 2:22,
  3:234-235, 3:252, 4:679
Sarah (----), 3:234-235
Sarah (Bradbury), 3:234
Sarah (Clement), 1:408,
  3:234
Susanna, 3:235
Susanna (----), 3:234
Morrice
Ann (----), 1:437
Sarah, 1:437
Morris
Ann, 3:235
Ann (----), 3:235
Ann (Osborn), 4:691
Desire, 3:236
Dorcas (----), 3:236
Dorothy, 3:236
Elinor (----), 3:235
Elizabeth, 1:343, 1:378,
  2:284, 3:235-236
Elizabeth (----), 3:236
Elizabeth (----) Lamson,
  3:235
Elizabeth (----) Line

Morris (continued)
Elizabeth (----) Line
Lamsom (continued)
Lamsom, 4:688
Elizabeth (Brown), 3:235
Esther, 3:236
Esther (----), 3:236
Esther (Winston), 3:236,
4:605
Grace, 1:377, 3:235
Grace (Burr/Bett), 3:235
Hannah, 3:131, 3:236
Hannah (Bishop), 3:236,
3:603
Hannah (Mayo), 3:187,
3:235
Honor, 3:235
Lenora (----), 3:236
Margaret, 3:235
Martha, 3:235
Martha (----), 3:235
Mary, 3:235, 4:304
Mary (----), 3:236
Mary (----) Pierpont, 3:235
Mary (Howard)
Coddington, 1:416
Mary (Ruggles) Pierpont,
3:432
Mehitable, 3:236
Mehitable (----), 3:236
Prudence, 3:236
Rebecca, 3:235-236
Sarah, 3:236
Morrison
Ann, 4:692
Hannah, 3:237
Hannah (----), 3:237
Margaret, 4:692
Mary, 3:237
Sarah, 4:692
Sarah (Hubbard), 2:483
Sarah (Jones), 2:568,
4:692
Silence (Hall), 2:335
Morse
---- (Clark), 1:394, 3:242
Abigail, 2:403, 2:568,
3:238-239, 3:242
Abigail (Shattuck), 3:239,
3:354, 4:63
Abigail (Stearns), 3:239,
4:173
Abigail (Woodward),

3:238, 4:645
Amity (Harris), 2:363
Ann, 3:237, 3:242, 4:295
Ann (----), 3:237-238,
3:241
Ann (Lewis), 3:241
Ann (Phillips), 3:240
Ann (Smith), 3:239
Annis (----), 3:238
Bathsheba, 2:164
Bathshua, 3:237
Bethia, 2:87, 3:237-239,
3:242, 3:400
Deborah, 3:240, 3:242
Deborah (----), 3:242
Dinah (----), 3:239
Dorcas, 3:240
Dorothy, 3:241
Dorothy (----), 3:239
Elizabeth, 2:571, 3:62,
3:237-242, 4:16-17
Elizabeth (----), 1:334,
3:237-238, 3:241-242,
3:300
Elizabeth (Barber), 3:238
Elizabeth (Bosworth),
1:216, 3:239
Elizabeth
(Goding/Godding),
2:266-267
Elizabeth (Hammant),
2:344
Elizabeth (Knight), 3:237
Elizabeth (Moore), 3:242
Esther, 1:295, 2:453,
2:571, 3:237-238, 3:240
Esther (Pierce), 3:240,
3:428
Grace (Warren), 4:423
Hannah, 3:237-242
Hannah (----), 1:225
Hannah (----) Dyer, 3:240
Hannah (Badcock), 3:240
Hannah (Phillips), 3:240
Hepzibah (Stone), 4:206
Huldah, 3:238
Joanna (----), 3:241
Joanna (Hoar), 3:238
Keziah, 3:240
Lydia, 3:237, 3:239, 3:241,
4:542
Lydia (Fisher), 2:162,
3:237

Margaret, 3:237-238
Maria, 3:240
Martha, 3:242
Martha (Johnson), 3:241
Mary, 1:119, 1:296,
3:237-241, 3:448
Mary (----), 2:93, 3:237,
3:240-241
Mary (Barber), 3:239
Mary (Barnard), 3:237
Mary (Bullen), 3:241
Mary (Clark), 1:400, 3:239
Mary (Jupe), 3:238
Mehitable, 3:240, 3:242
Mehitable (Wood), 3:240,
4:628
Miriam, 3:242
Priscilla, 3:240
Priscilla (Colburn), 3:240
Prudence, 3:237
Prudence (----), 3:237
Rachel, 3:238, 3:241
Ruth, 3:237-239,
3:241-242
Ruth (Sawyer), 3:237
Sarah, 1:455, 3:62,
3:237-242, 4:191
Sarah (----), 3:238-239
Sarah (Thurston), 3:242
Susanna, 3:240
Susanna (Shattuck), 2:149,
3:240, 4:62
Tabitha, 3:242
Morss
Mary, 2:93
Mortimer/Mortimore/etc
Ann (----), 3:242
Dorcas, 3:242
Elizabeth, 3:242, 4:557
Elizabeth (----), 3:242
Hepzibah (Munjoy), 3:255
Jane, 3:242
Jane (----), 3:242
Mary, 3:242
Morton
Ann, 2:97
Ann (----), 3:243
Ann (----) Templar, 3:244
Ann (Cooper), 3:243
Deborah, 3:244
Elizabeth, 1:216,
3:244-245, 3:506
Elizabeth (Worthington),

Morton (continued)
Elizabeth (Worthington)
(continued)
4:653
Esther, 3:244
Hannah, 1:216, 3:244,
4:423
Hannah (Phinney), 3:417
Hannah (Pritchard)
Templar, 4:266
Joanna, 3:244, 3:487
Joanna (Kempton), 3:244
Julian (Bradford), 3:8
Julian (Carpenter), 3:244
Lettice (----), 3:244, 3:542
Lydia, 2:114, 3:244
Lydia (Cooper), 3:244
Martha, 3:244
Martha (----), 3:244
Mary, 1:381, 3:244
Mary (----), 1:427, 2:591
Mary (Shelly) Harlow,
3:243, 3:628, 4:71
Mehitable (Graves), 2:294,
3:245, 4:653
Mercy, 2:81, 3:244
Patience, 2:148, 3:243-244
Phebe (----), 3:244
Phebe (Shaw), 4:65
Rebecca, 3:243
Remember, 2:527, 3:244
Ruth, 1:117, 3:244
Ruth (----), 3:245
Sarah, 1:210, 3:244
Moseley/Mosely
Ann (Addington), 3:83,
3:430
Margaret, 4:264
Mary, 1:416, 4:450
Mary (Eyre), 2:134
Sarah (Trescott), 4:329
Moses
Elizabeth, 3:245
Hannah, 3:245
Hannah (Ward) Pitman
Collins, 4:410
Margaret, 3:246
Martha, 1:516, 3:246
Mary, 2:144, 3:245-246,
4:342
Mary (Brown), 3:245
Mindwell, 3:246
Remember, 3:245

Remember (Gyles), 2:253,
3:245
Sarah, 3:245
Sarah (Tuller), 4:342
Moshier/Mosier/Mosher
Isabel, 3:492
Lydia, 3:246
Mary, 3:183
Rebecca (----), 3:246
Rebecca (Harndale), 2:357
Rebecca (Harndel), 3:246
Mosman
Ann (----), 3:246
Elizabeth, 3:246
Moss
Abiel, 3:246
Abigail, 3:246, 4:681,
4:692
Dinah (Knight), 3:246
Elizabeth, 2:429, 3:246
Elizabeth (----), 3:247
Esther, 3:246
Mary, 3:246, 3:381
Mary (----), 3:247
Mary (Alling), 3:246
Mary (Jupe), 2:577
Sarah (----), 3:246
Sarah (----) Gilbert, 3:624
Mott
Abigail, 3:247
Bethia, 3:247
Elizabeth, 2:588, 3:247,
3:538, 4:296
Hannah, 3:247
Hannah (Shooter), 3:247
Joanna (----), 3:247
Margaret, 3:247
Mary, 3:247
Mary (Lott), 3:247
Mercy, 3:247
Phebe, 3:247
Rebecca (Manning), 4:689
Sarah, 3:247
Sarah (----), 3:247
Mould
Jane, 4:198
Martha (Coit), 1:422,
3:247, 4:512
Mary, 3:247, 4:512
Mary (----), 3:247
Susanna, 3:247, 4:508
Moulder
Christian (----), 3:247

Moulthrop/Moultrop
Abigail, 3:247
Abigail (Bradley), 3:247
Elizabeth, 3:248, 3:626
Hannah, 3:248, 3:592
Hannah (Thompson),
3:248
Jane (----), 3:248
Keziah, 3:248
Lydia, 3:248
Mary, 3:248
Sarah, 3:248
Moulton
---- (Corey), 3:248
Abigail, 3:249
Abigail (----), 3:654
Abigail (Webster), 3:249
Ann, 3:248
Ann (----), 3:248
Bridget, 3:248
Dorothy, 3:249
Elizabeth, 3:249
Elizabeth (Vaughan),
4:369
Hannah, 1:16, 3:249,
3:620, 4:12
Jane, 3:248
Jane (----), 3:249
Lydia (Taylor), 3:248,
4:259
Margaret, 3:249
Margaret (Page), 3:249,
3:331, 4:11
Marian, 3:248
Martha, 3:249
Martha (----), 3:249
Mary, 2:248-249, 2:389,
3:221, 3:282, 3:649,
4:13
Mary (----), 3:160, 3:248
Mary (Cook), 3:249
Mary (Hilton), 2:422,
3:248
Miriam, 1:500, 3:249
Ruhamah (Hayden), 2:386
Ruth, 3:248-249, 4:12
Sarah, 2:389, 3:249, 4:598
Mountain
Abigail (----), 3:249
Mountfort/Munford/etc
Ann, 2:109
Elizabeth, 3:250
Elizabeth (----), 3:250

Mountfort/Munford/etc
(continued)
Hannah, 3:250
Hannah (Nichols), 3:250,
3:281, 4:93
Joanna, 3:250
Lydia, 3:250
Mary, 3:250
Mary (Cock), 3:654
Naomi, 3:250
Ruth, 3:250
Ruth (----), 3:250
Ruth (Wiswall), 3:250,
4:616
Sarah, 3:250
Susanna, 3:250
Mountjoy
Elizabeth (----) Owen,
3:250
Mousall
Alice, 2:264
Alice (----), 3:250
Ann (----), 3:251
Dorothy, 3:49
Elizabeth, 3:250-251,
3:518, 3:654, 4:360
Elizabeth (----), 3:250
Eunice, 1:260, 3:250
Joanna, 4:534
Joanna (----), 3:250
Mary, 2:599, 3:251
Mary (Richardson), 3:251,
3:537
Mercy, 3:251
Ruth, 3:250-251
Sarah (Brooks), 1:260,
3:250
Moussett
Catharine (----), 3:251
Mower
Christian, 3:251, 3:611,
3:654
Mary, 3:251
Susanna, 3:251
Moxon
Ann (----), 3:251
Martha, 3:251
Rebecca, 3:251
Moyse
Hannah (----), 3:252
Mudge
---- (----) Elsen, 2:115,
3:252

Elizabeth, 3:252
Martha, 3:252, 3:617,
4:541
Mary, 3:252
Mary (Alexander), 1:26,
3:252
Ruth (----), 3:252
Sarah, 3:252
Susanna, 3:252
Thankful, 3:252
Mudget
Ann (----), 3:252
Mary, 3:252
Sarah (Morrell), 3:252
Temperance, 3:252
Mulford
Ann, 3:252
Dorcas, 3:252
Elizabeth, 1:383, 3:252
Fredeswith (----) Osborn,
3:319
Hannah, 3:252
Hannah (----), 3:252
Jemima, 3:252
Jemima (Higgins), 3:252
Mary, 3:252
Mary (Bassett), 3:252
Patience, 3:252
Mullery
Abigail, 3:253
Abigail (----), 3:253
Ann, 3:253
Elizabeth, 3:253
Sarah, 3:253
Susanna, 3:253
Mulligan/Mullegin/Mullekin
Elinor (----), 3:252
Mary, 3:253
Rebecca, 3:252-253
Mulliner
Elizabeth, 3:253
Martha, 3:253
Martha (----), 3:253
Mullins
Ann (----) Bell, 3:253
Deborah (----) Bell, 1:160
Joanna (----), 3:64
Priscilla, 1:23, 3:253
Mumford
Abigail, 2:161, 3:253
Abigail (----), 3:253
Ann, 2:109
Content, 3:253

Elizabeth, 3:253
Elizabeth (----) Carwithy,
3:253
Elizabeth (Farnum)
Carwithy, 1:512
Esther, 3:254
Esther (Tefft), 3:254
Hannah, 3:253
Mary, 3:253-254
Mary (Bull), 3:253
Mary (Coggeshall), 3:253
Mary (Robinson), 3:553
Sarah, 1:64, 3:253-254
Tabitha, 3:254
Mun/Munn
Abigail, 1:313, 3:254,
4:178
Abigail (----), 3:533
Abigail (Burt) Ball, 1:106,
1:313, 3:254, 4:177
Abigail (Parsons), 3:254,
3:361, 3:654
Amy, 3:254
Jane, 3:254
Mary, 3:254
Munden
Ann (Munson), 3:254
Mary, 3:254, 3:448, 3:654
Munford
Elizabeth, 1:278
Munger
Abigail, 3:254
Ann, 3:254
Deliverance, 3:254
Frances, 2:269
Jane, 3:254
Mary, 3:254
Mary (Everts), 3:254
Rachel, 3:254
Sarah, 3:254
Sarah (----), 1:470, 3:254,
4:703
Sarah (Hull), 3:254, 4:692
Munjoy/Mungy
Hepzibah, 3:255
Huldah, 3:255
Martha (Walton), 4:405
Mary, 3:255, 3:341, 4:21
Mary (----), 3:255
Mary (Phillips), 1:478,
3:63, 3:255, 3:412
Munke
Ann, 4:176

Munnings/Mullings
—— (——), 4:575
Abigail, 3:255, 4:29
Ann, 3:255
Elizabeth, 3:255-256
Elizabeth (——), 3:255
Hannah, 3:256, 4:575
Hannah (——), 3:255
Hannah (Wiswall), 3:256,
3:325, 4:616
Johanna (——) Boyer, 3:255
Mary, 3:255-256
Mary (——), 3:255
Mary (Mixer), 3:223
Mehitable, 3:654
Rebecca, 3:142, 3:255
Sarah, 3:256
Takeheed, 3:255
Munroe/Monroe
Abigail, 3:256-257
Abigail (——), 3:256
Ann, 3:256
Constance, 3:256
Dorothy, 3:256
Dorothy (——), 3:256
Eleanor, 3:256-257
Elizabeth, 3:256-257
Elizabeth (——), 3:256
Eunice, 3:256
Hannah, 3:256-257
Hannah (——), 3:256
Joanna, 3:257
Joanna (Russell), 3:257
Kezia, 3:256
Lucy, 3:256
Lydia, 3:256
Martha, 3:256-257
Martha (——), 3:256
Mary, 3:256-257
Mary (——), 3:256-257
Prudence (——) Estabrook,
3:256
Rebecca, 3:256
Ruth, 3:257
Sarah, 3:256-257
Sarah (——), 3:256
Susanna, 3:256
Munson/Monson
—— (Bradley), 1:234
Ann, 3:254
Elizabeth, 2:411, 3:257
Hannah, 1:234, 3:257,
4:351

Martha, 3:257, 3:605,
4:681
Martha (Bradley), 3:257
Susan (——), 3:257
Munt/Mount
Dorothy (——), 3:257
Elinor (——), 2:420, 3:257
Faith, 3:257, 4:88
Murcock
Mary, 1:278
Murdock
Abigail (——), 3:257
Hannah, 3:257
Hannah (Stedman), 3:257
Phebe, 1:222, 4:426
Murphy
Margaret (——) Mahone,
3:257
Muscate
Dorothy (Clark), 1:402
Musgrove
Mary, 3:258
Mushamore
Mary, 3:10, 3:258
Musket
Bridget, 2:167, 4:682
Musse/Must
Esther, 3:589
Mussey/Muzzey
Alice (Dexter), 2:45, 3:258
Bethia, 3:258
Esther, 3:258
Esther (——), 3:258
Esther (Jackman), 3:258
Mary, 2:63, 3:258, 4:52
Sarah, 3:258, 4:383
Sarah (——), 3:258
Mussiloway
Ann (——) Chase, 3:258
Ann (Wheeler) Chase,
1:364
Mary (——), 3:258
Mycall
Mary, 3:284
Mary (Farr), 2:144, 3:259
Rebecca, 3:259, 4:277
Mygate/Mygatt/etc
Ann (——), 3:259
Dorothy, 3:259
Mary, 2:35, 3:259
Sarah, 2:588, 3:259
Sarah (——), 4:433
Sarah (Webster), 3:259

Sarah (Whiting), 3:25,
3:259, 4:522
Susanna, 3:259
Mylam/Milom
Abigail, 3:259
Christian (——), 3:259
Constance, 1:22, 3:259
Hannah, 3:259
Mary, 3:259
Mary (——), 3:259
Mary (Gore), 2:280, 3:259
Ruth, 3:259
Sarah, 3:259
Myles
——, 2:103
Ann (Humfrey) Palmes,
2:496, 3:344
Ann (Humphrey), 2:103,
3:259
Catharine, 1:467, 4:358
Susanna, 3:259
Mynard
Lydia (Richards), 3:533
Priscilla (Strickland), 4:224
Nabor
Elizabeth, 4:706
Naney/Nanny
Catharine (Wheelwright),
3:260, 3:263, 4:503
Elizabeth, 3:260
Mary, 3:260
Narramore
Hannah, 3:260
Hannah (——), 3:260
Sarah, 3:260
Nash
——, 3:262, 4:9
—— (Macworth), 3:263
Abigail, 3:261
Abigail (——), 3:261
Alice, 3:261
Elizabeth, 1:442, 1:445,
2:181, 3:261-262, 4:348
Elizabeth (——) Howd,
2:473
Elizabeth (——) Howe,
3:261
Elizabeth (Hitchcock)
Howd, 3:633
Elizabeth (Holbrook),
2:442, 3:262
Elizabeth (Kellogg), 3:261
Elizabeth (Porter), 3:262,

Nash (continued)
  Elizabeth (Porter)
    (continued)
    3:460
  Elizabeth (Tapp), 3:261,
    4:253
  Experience, 3:260
  Experience (Clark), 3:260
  Hannah, 1:106, 3:261-262,
    4:333
  Hannah (Coleman), 3:262
  Hannah (Curtis), 3:262
  Hannah (Porter), 3:261,
    3:463
  Hope, 3:262-263
  Joanna, 3:260, 3:263
  Joanna (Smith), 3:260
  Margaret (----), 3:262
  Margary (Baker), 3:262
  Martha, 1:405, 3:262
  Mary, 1:41, 2:331,
    3:260-263, 3:334
  Mary (----), 3:263
  Mary (Coltman), 1:438
  Mary (Combs), 3:261
  Mary (Foster), 2:188
  Mary (Scott), 3:260, 4:37
  Mercy, 3:262
  Miriam, 3:260
  Phebe (----), 3:261, 3:429
  Rebecca, 3:260-262, 4:692
  Rebecca (Smith), 3:261
  Rebecca (Stone), 3:262,
    4:208
  Sarah, 1:449, 3:261-262,
    4:252, 4:667
  Sarah (----), 3:262
  Zeruiah, 3:260
Nason
  ---- (----), 2:63
  ---- (----) Follett, 3:263
  Hannah (----) Follet, 2:178
  Hannah (Heard), 2:397,
    3:263
  Martha (Kenny), 3:263
Nayler/Naylor
  Catharine (Wheelwright),
    2:512
  Catharine (Wheelwright)
    Nanny, 3:260, 3:263,
    4:503
  Lydia, 3:263
  Tabitha, 3:263

Naziter
  Jane, 3:263, 3:377
Neal
  ---- (Laurie), 3:59
  Abigail, 3:263-264, 3:655,
    4:193
  Abigail (Penniman), 3:265,
    3:389
  Ann, 3:655
  Ann (----), 4:173
  Ann (Nichols), 3:264
  Deborah, 3:263-264, 3:333
  Dorothy, 3:655
  Dorothy (Lord), 3:264
  Elizabeth, 3:263-264,
    3:655
  Esther, 3:263
  Hannah, 2:387, 3:263-264
  Hannah (Pray), 3:264
  Jerusha, 3:263
  Joan, 3:654
  Joanna, 3:264
  Judith, 3:264
  Judith (Croade), 1:474,
    3:264
  Lydia, 3:263-264, 3:629,
    3:655
  Lydia (Paine), 3:263,
    3:335
  Margaret
    (Higason/Higginson),
    3:654
  Martha, 3:263-264
  Martha (----), 3:264
  Martha (Hart), 2:367,
    3:263
  Mary, 3:263-264, 3:655,
    4:276
  Mary (----), 3:264-265
  Mary (Buffum), 1:289,
    3:264
  Mary (Laurie/Lawes),
    3:655
  Mary (Lawes), 3:60, 3:148,
    3:264
  Milicent (----), 3:263
  Provided, 3:655
  Rachel, 3:264, 3:655
  Rebecca, 3:264
  Rose, 3:140
  Ruth, 3:264, 4:276
  Sarah, 3:149, 3:263-264,
    3:654

  Sarah (Hart), 3:264
Neave
  Margaret (----), 3:265
Needham
  ----, 3:655
  Abigail, 3:265, 3:655
  Ann, 2:407, 3:655
  Ann (Potter), 3:265, 3:466
  Deborah, 3:655
  Dorothy, 3:655
  Elizabeth, 3:265-266,
    3:655
  Elizabeth (Hicks), 2:411,
    3:266
  Hannah, 1:63, 3:265,
    3:655
  Hannah (----), 2:145
  Joan (----), 3:266
  Judith, 3:265
  Keziah (----), 3:266
  Margaret, 3:266
  Mary, 3:265, 3:629, 3:655
  Mehitable, 3:266
  Provided, 3:655
  Rachel, 3:265, 3:655
  Rebecca, 3:265, 3:609,
    3:655
  Ruth, 3:265-266
  Ruth (Chadwell), 3:265
  Sarah, 3:266
  Sarah (King), 3:24, 3:266
Neff
  Mary (Corliss), 1:457,
    3:266
Negus/Negos/Negoos
  Elizabeth, 1:120, 3:266
  Elizabeth (----), 3:266
  Grace, 2:148, 3:267
  Hannah, 3:266
  Hannah (Andrews), 3:266
  Hannah (Phillips), 3:411
  Jane (----), 3:266
  Mary, 3:266
Neighbors
  Elizabeth, 3:267
  Lettice (----), 3:267
  Martha, 2:500, 3:267
  Mary, 3:176, 3:267
  Rachel, 1:417, 3:267
  Rebecca, 3:267
  Sarah, 2:555, 3:267
Nelson
  Ann (Lambert), 3:267

Nelson (continued)
Elizabeth (----), 3:267,
4:216
Elizabeth (Lowell), 3:126,
3:267
Hannah, 2:585, 4:309
Jane, 2:148, 3:268
Jane (----), 3:267
Joanna (----), 3:267
Joanna (Dummer), 2:80
Lydia (Bartlett) Barnaby,
1:117, 1:132, 3:267
Martha, 1:413
Martha (----), 3:268
Martha (Ford), 3:268
Mary (----) Hobson, 2:438,
3:267
Mary (Hunt), 3:268
Mary (Ray), 3:267
Mercy, 3:267, 4:211
Sarah (Jewett), 2:598,
3:267
Sarah (Wood), 3:267,
4:626
Nest
Sarah (----), 3:268
Susanna, 3:268, 4:440
Nethercoot
Christian, 2:353
Nettleton
Hannah, 3:268, 4:135
Isabel, 1:366
Martha, 3:268, 3:305
Martha (Baldwin), 1:104
Sarah, 3:211
Nevers
Martha, 3:268
Martha (----), 3:268
Mary, 3:268
Nevinson
Ann, 3:268
Elizabeth, 2:374, 3:268
Elizabeth (----), 1:210,
3:268
Mary, 2:373, 3:268
Sarah, 3:268, 4:204
Newberry/Newbury
Abigail, 2:391, 3:268-269
Abigail (----) Warham,
3:268
Ann (Collins), 3:270
Ann (Ford), 2:183, 3:269
Dorcas, 3:269

Elizabeth, 3:270
Hannah, 2:350, 3:268-269
Hannah (Dewey), 3:269
Jane (----), 3:269
Marah, 3:269
Margaret, 3:268-269,
4:227
Martha, 3:269-270
Mary, 1:43, 1:392, 3:178,
3:268-270
Mary (Allyn), 1:43, 3:268
Mehitable, 3:270
Priscilla (----), 3:270
Rebecca, 3:157, 3:268-269,
3:591
Sankey, 3:270
Sarah, 1:390, 3:268-270,
4:621
Sarah (----), 3:269
Sarah (Robinson), 3:555
Newby
Elizabeth (----), 3:270
Mary (----), 3:270
Newcomb/Newcome
Abigail, 3:270
Elizabeth, 3:270
Eunice (Manning), 4:689
Grace, 3:270
Grace (----) Rix, 3:270,
3:545
Hannah, 3:270
Judith, 3:270
Leah, 3:270
Mary, 2:33, 3:270
Rachel, 3:270
Rachel (----), 3:270
Sarah, 3:270
Susanna (Cutting), 1:496,
3:270
Newell
Abigail, 3:271-272
Abigail (Rhoades), 3:271
Ann, 3:272
Ann (----), 2:592
Elizabeth, 3:271-272,
4:264
Elizabeth (----), 3:272
Elizabeth (Curtis), 1:487,
3:271
Elizabeth (Wrotham),
3:272, 4:661
Esther, 3:272, 3:655,
4:164

Eunice, 3:272
Experience, 3:271
Faith, 3:270-271
Frances (----), 3:270
Grace, 3:270-271, 4:258,
4:491
Hannah, 2:452, 3:271-272,
3:656
Hannah (----), 3:272
Hannah (Larkin), 3:57,
3:271-272
Joyce (Gleason), 3:271
Margaret (----), 3:272
Martha, 3:271-272
Martha (Gibson), 2:248,
3:271
Mary, 1:135, 3:271-272,
3:655
Mary (----), 3:271-272
Mary (Hart), 3:655
Mehitable, 3:271
Mehitable (Jones), 3:272
Mercy, 3:271-272
Rebecca, 1:373, 3:271-272,
4:638
Rebecca (Olmstead), 3:272
Ruth, 3:270-271
Sarah, 3:271-272, 3:655
Sarah (----), 3:271
Sarah (Tuttle), 3:272,
4:350
Susanna, 3:232, 3:271-272
Susanna (Rand), 3:271,
3:504
Thankful, 3:271
Newgate
Ann (----), 3:272
Elizabeth, 2:528, 3:273,
3:309
Elizabeth (----), 3:273
Hannah, 3:136, 3:272-273
Isabel (----), 3:273
Sarah, 3:273, 3:310
Sarah (Lynde), 3:136
Newhall
Elizabeth, 3:274
Elizabeth (Normanton),
3:273
Elizabeth (Payton), 3:273
Elizabeth (Potter), 3:274,
3:661
Esther (Bartram), 1:134,
3:273

Newhall (continued)
Hannah, 3:273
Jemima, 3:273, 4:372
Lydia, 3:274
Mary, 3:273-274, 3:607
Priscilla, 3:273
Rebecca, 3:273-274
Rebecca (----), 3:274
Sarah, 1:241, 3:273
Sarah (Lewis), 3:273
Susanna, 3:274, 3:631
Newland
Elizabeth, 4:492
Esther (Austin), 3:274
Mary, 3:274
Mercy, 3:274
Rose (Holloway), 3:274
Newman
---- (----), 3:274, 4:222
Ann, 3:656
Bathsheba, 3:655
Bathsheba (----), 3:656
Bethia, 3:275
Bethia (Chickering), 1:376,
3:276
Dorothy (Eames), 2:90
Elinor, 2:492
Elizabeth, 3:644-645
Elizabeth (----), 3:275
Elizabeth (Bowstreete),
1:225
Elizabeth (Rose), 4:693,
4:702
Elizabeth (Winthrop),
2:123, 3:274, 4:612
Grace, 3:275
Hannah, 3:656
Hannah (Barber), 1:501
Hannah (Bunker), 1:299,
3:276
Hannah (Kenrick), 3:656
Hope, 3:276
Hopestill, 3:275-276,
3:655-656, 4:89
Joanna (Anderson), 1:51
Joanna (Flint), 2:174,
3:275
Margaret, 3:656
Mary, 3:655-656
Mary (----), 3:75
Mercy, 3:275
Patience, 3:276, 4:144
Ruth (Emerson), 3:275

Sarah, 3:275, 4:693, 4:702,
4:711
Sybel, 3:274-275
Sybel (----), 3:276
Theodosia (Jackson)
Wiswall, 2:530, 3:276
Waitstill, 3:274
Newmarch
Dorothy (Pepperell)
Watkins, 3:392
Martha, 3:276
Martha (Gould), 2:287,
3:276
Phebe, 3:276
Sarah, 3:276
Newport
Ruth, 3:276
Ruth (----), 3:276
Newton
Abigail (----), 3:278
Alice, 3:277
Ann/Hannah (----), 3:277
Catharine (----), 3:277
Elizabeth, 3:277
Elizabeth (----), 3:277
Ellen/Elinor, 1:11, 4:603
Hannah, 3:277, 3:406
Jane, 3:119
Joan, 1:46, 3:406
Joanna (Larkin), 3:277
Lydia, 3:276
Lydia (----), 3:277
Martha, 3:278
Martha (Fenn), 2:152,
3:278
Mary, 3:276-277
Mary (Hooker), 2:459,
3:277
Mehitable (----), 3:277
Mercy, 3:276-277
Prudence, 3:277
Rebecca, 3:223
Rebecca (Newton) Mixer,
3:223
Sarah, 3:277, 3:585, 4:585
Silence, 3:277
Susanna, 3:276-277, 4:206
Nichols
----, 3:279
---- (Pierce/etc), 3:431
Abigail, 2:451, 3:279-281
Abigail (----), 3:280-281
Abigail (Bearse), 1:149,

3:279
Alice, 3:280
Alice (Hallett), 1:400,
2:340, 3:281
Ann, 3:264, 3:279-281
Ann (----), 3:279, 3:282
Ann (----) Isbell, 3:282
Ann (Wakeman), 3:278
Ann (Ward), 4:406
Bathsheba, 3:282
Ebenezer, 3:282, 4:338
Elizabeth, 2:305,
3:279-282, 4:93, 4:337
Elizabeth (----), 3:281
Elizabeth (Sargent), 1:177,
4:19
Esther, 3:278-281
Esther (----) Hawley, 3:279
Esther (Clark), 3:280
Eunice, 3:370
Experience, 3:279
Grace, 3:280
Grace (----), 3:280, 3:400
Hannah, 1:499, 3:250,
3:278-283, 4:93, 4:551,
4:622
Hannah (----), 4:413
Hannah (Hawley), 2:384,
3:281
Hannah (Whittemore),
3:280
Helen (Talcott), 3:279
Helena (Talcott), 4:251
Jemima, 3:280
Joanna (Shute), 1:286,
3:281, 4:93
Lydia, 3:278, 3:281
Lydia (----), 3:281
Margaret, 3:281
Margaret (----), 3:280
Margery, 3:280
Martha, 3:282
Mary, 1:368, 2:494,
3:279-283, 3:609, 3:656,
4:167, 4:242
Mary (----), 3:280, 3:283
Mary (Bowers), 1:223
Mary (Felt), 3:280
Mary (Moulton), 3:282
Mary (Southwick) Trask,
4:322
Mary (Spencer), 3:279,
4:149

Nichols (continued)
  Mary (Sumner), 3:280,
    4:231
  Patience, 1:54, 3:280,
    3:282
  Phebe, 3:279
  Priscilla, 3:279
  Priscilla (Shattuck), 3:280,
    4:62
  Rachel, 1:400, 3:281
  Rachel (Kellogg), 3:4,
    3:278
  Rebecca, 2:470, 3:282
  Rebecca (Josselyn), 2:572,
    3:282
  Sarah, 1:254, 1:309-310,
    2:345, 3:91, 3:278-282,
    4:59, 4:499
  Sarah (----), 3:281
  Sarah (----) Goss, 2:284,
    3:282
  Sarah (Kellogg), 3:656
  Sarah (Lincoln), 3:91
  Sarah (Whiston), 3:282
  Susanna, 3:282
  Susanna (----), 3:282
  Temperance, 3:280
Nicholson
  Dinah, 3:283
  Elizabeth, 1:55, 3:283
  Elizabeth (----), 3:283
  Hannah (Redknap), 3:283
  Jane (----), 3:283
  Mercy (----), 3:283
  Rachel, 3:283
  Rebecca, 1:339, 3:283
  Sarah, 3:283
Nick/Neck
  Bathsheba, 3:283
  Elizabeth, 4:302
  Mary (Richards), 3:283
Nickerson
  Ann, 2:400, 3:284
  Ann (Busby), 1:316, 3:284
  Elizabeth, 2:108, 3:284
  Mary, 1:477
  Mary (Bell), 1:159
  Mary (Snow), 3:284
  Mercy, 3:284
Nightingale
  Hannah (----), 3:284
  Mary (Billings) Belcher,
    3:285

Niles
  Elizabeth (Adams) Whiting,
    4:521
  Hannah, 3:284-285
  Hannah (----), 3:284
  Jane (----), 3:284
  Mary, 3:284
  Mary (----) Belcher, 3:284
  Mary (Mycall), 3:284
  Mary (Purchas), 3:284
  Sarah, 3:285
  Sarah (Sands), 3:284, 4:13
Nims
  Abigail, 3:285
  Margaret (----) Williams,
    3:285
  Mary, 3:285
  Mary (Miller) Williams,
    4:572
  Mehitable, 3:285
  Mehitable (Smead) Hull,
    2:493, 3:285
  Mercy, 3:285
  Rebecca, 3:178, 3:285
  Thankful, 3:285
Nisbett
  Elizabeth (Chauncy),
    1:368
  Sarah (Bryan) Fitch, 1:282
Nixon
  Elizabeth
    (Harwood/Harward),
    2:592
Noakes/Noake/Nokes
  Ann, 3:66
  Mary, 3:285
  Mary (Wright), 3:285
Noble
  Abigail, 3:285
  Abigail (Sacket), 3:285,
    4:2
  Ann, 3:286
  Elizabeth, 3:286
  Elizabeth (Dewey), 3:286
  Esther, 3:286
  Hannah, 3:285-286
  Hannah (----), 3:452
  Hannah (Dewey), 3:285
  Hannah (Warriner), 3:286,
    4:429
  Lois, 3:286
  Mabel, 3:285
  Mary, 3:286

  Rebecca, 3:286
  Rhoda, 3:286
  Sarah, 3:285
  Thankful, 3:286
Nock
  Elizabeth, 3:286
  Elizabeth (Emery), 3:286
  Rebecca, 3:286
  Rebecca (----), 1:166
  Rebecca (Tibbets), 3:286,
    4:299
  Sarah, 3:286
  Sarah (Adams), 3:286
Noiles
  Constance (Worcester)
    Tuckerman, 4:340, 4:651
Norcross
  Abigail, 3:287
  Adrean (----) Smith, 3:286,
    4:121
  Hannah, 3:287
  Hannah (Sanders), 3:287
  Mary, 2:249, 3:286-287,
    4:174
  Mary (----), 3:287
  Mary (Brooks), 3:287
  Mary (Gilbert), 2:249
  Mehitable, 3:287
  Mehitable (Hagar), 2:328,
    3:287
  Rose, 3:287
  Rose (Woodward), 3:287,
    4:645
  Ruth, 3:287
  Sarah, 1:378, 3:142,
    3:286-287
  Susanna, 3:287
  Susanna (----) Shattuck,
    3:287, 4:62
  Susanna (Shattuck), 3:287
Norcutt
  Sarah (Chapman), 1:362,
    3:287
Norden
  Elizabeth, 3:288
  Elizabeth (Pormort), 3:288,
    3:465
  Joanna (----), 3:287
  Mary, 3:288
  Susanna, 3:288
Norman
  — (----) Casley, 3:288
  Abigail, 3:656

Norman (continued)
Abigail (Ropes), 3:288
Ann/Hannah, 3:288
Arabella, 1:103, 3:288
Arabella (----), 3:288
Elizabeth, 1:397, 3:288
Elizabeth (Bullock), 3:607, 3:656
Lydia, 3:288
Martha, 3:288
Mary, 2:460, 3:656
Mary (----), 3:288
Mary (Ropes), 3:575, 3:656
Mary (White), 3:288
Sarah (Maverick), 3:181, 3:288
Normanton
Elizabeth, 3:273
Norris
Dorothy (----), 3:288
Elinor (----), 3:288
Elizabeth, 3:288
Mary, 3:288, 3:656
Mary (Symonds), 3:288, 4:245
North
Bathshua, 3:289
Hannah, 2:104, 3:289, 3:656, 3:660
Hannah (Newell), 3:272, 3:656
Hannah (Norton), 3:656
Hannah (Woodford), 4:638
Jane, 4:77
Lydia, 3:289, 3:656
Martha, 3:660
Martha (----), 3:660
Martha (Porter), 3:656, 3:660
Mary, 2:566, 3:289, 3:656, 4:45
Mary (Price) Petersfield, 2:81, 3:289
Mary (Warner), 4:421
Rachel, 3:660
Rebecca, 3:656
Sarah, 3:289, 3:656, 4:643
Sarah (Smith), 3:656
Susanna, 3:162, 3:289
Susanna (Francis), 3:656
Ursula (----), 3:289

Northam
Elizabeth, 3:289
Isabel (----) Catlin, 1:103, 1:349, 3:289
Mary, 3:289
Mary (Dickinson), 2:48, 3:289
Northend
Dorothy (Sewall), 3:290, 4:54
Edna, 3:290, 3:48, 3:290
Edna (----) Bailey, 3:289
Edna (Lambert) Bailey, 1:94
Elizabeth, 2:221, 2:438, 3:289
Sarah, 2:331
Northey
Sarah (Ewell), 2:132, 3:290
Northrop
Mary (Norton), 4:693
Norton
---- (Spencer), 3:290, 4:148
Abigail, 3:107, 3:163, 3:290-293, 4:330
Alice, 3:291
Ann, 3:290, 3:293, 4:420
Ann (----), 4:338
Deborah, 2:314, 2:421, 2:593, 3:290
Dorcas, 3:293
Dorothy, 3:292
Dorothy (----), 3:293
Eleanor (----), 2:458
Elizabeth, 1:249, 1:498, 1:512, 3:290-294, 3:445, 4:23, 4:242, 4:382, 4:711
Elizabeth (----), 3:293, 4:693
Elizabeth (Hubbard), 2:483, 3:292
Elizabeth (Mason), 3:168, 3:293
Flower, 3:293
Freegrace, 3:290-291
Grace, 3:293, 4:57
Grace (----), 3:293
Hannah, 3:291-293, 3:656
Hannah (----), 2:194
Hannah (Clark), 3:292
Hannah (Stone), 3:292,

4:210
Hannah (Younglove), 4:671
Joanna, 3:291
Lucy, 3:290, 3:294
Lucy (Downing), 3:293
Lydia (Wright) Bliss, 1:201, 1:438, 3:47, 3:292, 4:659, 4:693
Mary, 3:290-297, 3:558, 4:693
Mary (----), 2:194, 3:290-292, 4:184
Mary (Barber) Gillett, 2:256
Mary (Foxwell), 2:198, 3:291
Mary (Goodhue), 3:290
Mary (Mason), 3:166, 3:292
Mary (Sharp), 3:292
Mary/Mercy (Barber) Gillett, 4:693
Mehitable, 3:291
Phebe (Templar), 3:656
Priscilla, 3:293
Ruth, 1:407
Ruth (Moore/More), 3:654, 3:656
Sarah, 3:290-291, 3:293, 3:363
Sarah (----), 3:291
Susanna (Getchell), 2:235, 3:293
Susanna (Mason), 3:169, 3:294
Norwood
Abigail, 3:294, 3:618, 3:656
Alice (Donnell), 3:294
Deborah, 3:294, 3:628
Elizabeth, 3:294
Elizabeth (Andrews), 3:294, 3:598
Elizabeth (Coldam), 1:425, 3:294
Elizabeth (Ingleby), 3:294
Hannah, 3:294
Mary, 3:294, 4:18
Mary (Brown), 1:277, 3:294
Mary (Stevens), 3:294, 4:186

Nott
Ann, 3:294
Ann (----), 3:294
Elizabeth, 3:294, 3:523
Hannah, 3:294
Patience (Miller), 3:294
Thankful, 3:294
Nowell
Abigail, 3:295
Ann, 3:656
Elizabeth (----), 3:295
Lydia (----), 3:656
Lydia (Willis), 4:576
Martha, 4:610
Mary, 3:107, 3:295, 4:600
Mary (Alford) Butler
Usher, 1:27, 1:321, 3:295, 4:363
Mary (Tatchell), 3:295
Mehitable, 1:493, 2:423, 3:295
Parnell (Gray), 1:467-468, 3:295
Noyes
---- (Parker), 3:296
Abigail, 3:297-299, 3:448
Ann, 3:297-298
Ann (Belcher), 1:156, 3:298
Bethia, 3:299
Catharine (----) Jeffries, 3:298
Catharine (Eyre) Jeffries, 2:597
Dorothy, 2:389, 3:296, 3:298-299, 4:328
Dorothy (Stanton), 3:296, 4:167
Elizabeth, 2:347, 2:390, 3:296-299
Elizabeth (Darvell), 2:11, 3:298
Elizabeth (Greenleaf), 2:309, 3:299
Elizabeth (Knight), 3:36, 3:296
Hannah, 1:372, 3:297-298
Hannah (Knight), 3:36, 3:297
Judith, 3:299
Lydia, 3:297
Martha, 3:297, 3:299
Martha (Pierce), 3:299

Mary, 1:91, 2:206, 3:296-297, 3:299
Mary (----) Willard, 3:297
Mary (Cutting), 3:297
Mary (Darvell), 2:11, 3:297
Mary (Dunster) Willard, 2:82
Mary (Haynes), 2:391, 3:299
Mary (Knight), 3:36, 3:299
Mary (Norton), 3:290, 3:297
Mary (Poor), 3:297
Rachel, 2:526, 3:297, 3:299
Rebecca, 3:37, 3:296-297, 3:299
Ruth (Haynes), 2:389
Ruth (Picket), 3:297, 3:424
Sarah, 2:329, 2:389, 3:296, 3:297-299, 3:403
Sarah (----), 3:299
Sarah (Brown), 3:296
Sarah (Cogswell), 3:299
Sarah (Oliver), 3:297, 3:310
Susanna, 3:299
Nudd
---- (----), 3:299
Margaret (----), 2:63
Sarah (Dearborn), 2:32, 3:299
Nurse
----, 3:300
Abigail, 3:300
Deborah, 3:300
Elizabeth, 3:300, 3:656
Elizabeth (----) Morse, 3:300
Elizabeth (Smith), 3:300
Elizabeth (Very), 3:300, 4:372
Hannah, 3:300
Margaret, 3:300
Mary, 3:300, 4:709
Mary (Smith), 3:300
Rebecca, 2:167, 3:300, 3:483, 4:215
Rebecca (Towne), 3:300, 4:317
Sarah, 3:300

Sarah (----), 3:300
Thomasine, 3:300
Thomasine (----), 3:300
Nute
Elizabeth (Heard), 2:397, 3:301
Joanna (----), 3:300
Mary (----), 3:301
Nutt
Sarah, 2:219, 3:301, 4:664
Sibell/Sybel (----) Bibble, 1:174, 2:60, 3:301
Nutter
----, 3:44, 3:301
Abigail, 3:546
Mary, 3:301, 4:595
Mehitable
(Edenden/Eddington), 2:100
Sarah (Langstaff), 3:56
Nutting
Elizabeth, 3:301
Joanna, 3:301
Lydia, 3:301
Lydia (Longley), 3:111, 3:301
Mary, 3:301
Mary (----), 3:301
Ruth, 3:301
Sarah, 3:301
Sarah (Eggleton), 2:517, 3:301
Nye
Abigail, 3:302
Bethia, 3:302
Esther (----), 3:302
Experience, 3:302, 4:241
Hannah, 3:302
Mary, 1:302, 3:301
Remembrance, 3:302
Sarah (Gibbes), 3:302
Oakes
Abigail, 3:303
Elizabeth, 2:542, 3:302-303
Elizabeth (----), 2:393, 3:302, 4:239
Hannah, 1:58, 3:302-303, 4:384
Jane (----), 3:302
Jennet (----), 3:302
Lydia, 3:303
Martha (----), 3:302-303

Oakes (continued)
Mary, 2:174, 3:302-303,
3:657
Mehitable (Rediat), 3:302,
3:521
Ruth (Ames), 3:303
Sarah, 3:302-303
Sarah (Tufts), 3:303, 4:342
Oakman
Elizabeth (Dotey), 2:62
Joanna (Alger), 1:27,
3:304
Obbinson
Mary (----), 3:304
Ober
Abigail (Woodbury), 3:304,
4:636
Ann, 3:304, 4:636
Judith, 3:304
Mary (----), 3:304
Ockington/Okington
Mary, 2:359, 3:304
Mary (----), 3:304
Odding
Sarah, 4:83
Odell
Priscilla (----), 3:304
Rebecca, 3:304
Odlin/Odlyn
Abigail, 3:305
Abigail (Bright), 1:253,
3:305
Elizabeth (Arnold), 1:66
Elizabeth (Leavitt) Dudley
Briscoe, 2:75
Hannah, 1:394, 3:305
Margaret, 1:267, 3:305
Margaret (----), 3:305
Offitt/Uffoot/Offord
----, 3:305, 4:268
Elizabeth, 3:305
Elizabeth (----) Thele,
3:305-306, 4:279
Frances (Kilborne), 3:20,
3:306
Hannah (Hawley), 1:148,
3:305
Isabel (----), 3:305
Lydia, 3:305
Martha, 3:305
Martha (Nettleton), 3:268,
3:305
Mary, 3:305, 3:423-424

Ofield
Maudline (----), 3:306
Ogden
Elizabeth (Swain) Ward,
4:235
Okey
Mary, 3:306
Mary (----), 3:306
Tacey, 3:306
Okley/Oakley
Elizabeth, 1:265, 3:304
Sarah (----), 3:304
Olcott
Abigail, 3:306-307
Abigail (----), 3:307
Elizabeth, 2:516, 3:307
Elizabeth (----), 3:307
Hannah, 3:307
Margaret, 3:307
Mary, 1:176, 1:345,
3:306-307
Mary (----), 3:307
Mary (----) Field, 3:307
Mary (Blackleach) Welles,
1:189, 3:306, 4:380,
4:480
Rachel, 3:306
Sarah, 3:307
Sarah (Foote), 3:307
Sarah (Stocking), 3:307,
4:198
Old
Dorothy (Granger), 3:307
Mindwell, 3:307
Susanna, 3:307
Susanna
(Hanford/Hosford), 3:307
Oldage
Ann, 3:307, 3:318
Olden
Elizabeth (----), 3:307
Oldham
----, 4:693
Abigail, 3:308
Abigail (Wood), 3:308
Ann, 1:138, 3:308
Desire, 3:308
Elizabeth, 3:308
Elizabeth (Hall), 2:335
Frances (----), 1:344
Grace, 3:308
Hannah, 3:308
Hannah (----), 3:308

Hannah (Dana), 2:5
Hannah (Keen), 3:3
Lydia, 3:308
Martha (----), 1:276
Martha (Eaton), 2:98,
3:308
Mary, 3:308
Mary (Keen), 3:307
Mary (Wetherell), 3:308
Mercy, 3:308
Mercy (Sproat), 3:308,
4:158
Mindwell, 2:583
Ruth, 3:308
Sarah, 3:308
Sarah (North), 3:289
Oldstead
Sarah (Gilbert), 2:251
Oliver
----, 3:311, 4:624
Abigail, 2:554, 3:311
Ann (----), 3:311
Bridget, 1:506, 3:311
Bridget (----), 3:657
Bridget (----) Wasselbe,
3:657
Christian, 3:657
Deborah, 3:311
Elizabeth, 3:309-311,
4:615
Elizabeth (Belcher), 1:156,
3:309
Elizabeth (Brattle), 1:239,
3:310
Elizabeth (Newgate),
2:528, 3:273, 3:309
Grace, 3:311
Grace (Prentice), 3:311,
3:479
Hannah, 3:309, 3:311
Hannah (Mather), 3:173
Hopestill (Wensley), 3:310
Jerusha, 3:173, 3:310
Jerusha (Mather), 3:173,
3:310
Joanna (----), 2:244
Joanna (Goodale), 2:271,
3:309
Lydia (----), 2:163,
3:310-311
Mary, 1:61, 2:421, 2:559,
3:309-311, 4:91
Mary (----), 3:311

Oliver (continued)
  Mary (Wilson), 3:311,
    4:586
  Mercy, 3:309
  Mercy (Bradstreet), 1:236,
    3:309
  Patience, 3:310
  Sarah, 3:297, 3:309-311,
    4:332
  Sarah (Newgate), 3:273,
    3:310
  Susanna (Sweet), 3:310
Ollard
  Sarah, 4:638
Olmstead
  ---- (Loomis), 3:112, 3:312
  Damaris, 4:693
  Elizabeth, 4:693
  Elizabeth (----), 2:251,
    3:312, 4:49
  Elizabeth (Butler), 1:321
  Elizabeth (Marvin), 3:164,
    3:312
  Elizabeth (Pardee) Gregory,
    3:345
  Elizabeth (Pitkin), 3:440
  Hannah, 4:693
  Hannah (Mix), 3:312
  Hannah (Pitkin), 3:440
  Jerusha, 4:693
  Mabel, 3:312, 4:249
  Martha (----), 4:693
  Mary, 3:312, 4:693
  Mary (----) Lord, 3:116
  Mary (Benedict), 1:164,
    3:312
  Rebecca, 3:272, 3:312,
    4:693
  Sarah, 1:3, 2:235, 2:251,
    3:312, 4:693
  Sarah (Keeler), 3:2
Olney
  Amy, 3:313
  Ann, 3:313-314
  Catharine, 3:314
  Catharine (Sayles), 3:314
  Deborah, 3:314
  Elizabeth, 3:313-314
  Elizabeth (Marsh), 3:313
  Esther, 3:314
  Freelove, 3:313
  Hallelujah (Brown), 3:313
  Lydia, 3:313-314, 4:432,

4:564
  Lydia (----), 3:314
  Martha, 3:313
  Mary, 3:313-314, 4:506
  Mary (----), 3:313
  Mary (Whipple), 3:313,
    4:506
  Mercy (Williams), 3:313
  Patience (----), 3:314
  Phebe, 3:313-314
  Rachel (Coggeshall), 3:313
  Sarah, 3:313-314
Onge
  Frances (----), 3:314
  Mary, 3:314
  Mary (Underwood), 3:314,
    4:359
Onion
  Ann (Aldis), 1:24
  Deborah (Woodcock),
    3:314
  Grace, 3:314
  Grace (----), 3:314
  Hannah, 3:314
  Mary, 1:140, 3:314
  Mary (----), 3:314
  Sarah (Metcalf), 3:203,
    3:314
  Susanna, 3:314
Orchard
  Mary, 3:314
  Sarah (----), 3:314
Orcutt
  Deborah, 3:315
  Deliverance, 3:315
  Elizabeth, 3:315
  Elizabeth (Randall), 3:506
  Hannah, 3:314
  Jane, 3:315
  Jane (Washburn), 3:315,
    4:429
  Martha, 3:314-315
  Mary, 3:314-315
  Mary (Lane), 3:51
  Susanna, 3:315
Ordway
  Abigail, 3:315
  Abigail (----), 3:315
  Ann, 3:315
  Ann (Emery), 3:315
  Elizabeth, 3:315
  Esther, 3:315
  Hannah, 3:315

  Jane, 3:315
  Joanna, 3:315
  Lydia, 3:315
  Mary, 3:315
  Mary (Godfrey), 3:315
  Mary (Wood), 3:315
  Rachel, 3:315
  Rebecca, 3:315
  Sarah, 2:170, 3:315
  Sarah (----) Dennis, 2:38,
    3:315
  Sarah (Brown), 1:276
  Sarah (Clark), 3:315
  Tirzah (----) Bartlett, 3:315
  Tirzah (Titcomb) Bartlett,
    1:133
Ormes
  Ann (----), 3:315
  Edonia, 3:315
  Elizabeth, 3:315, 3:652
  Mary, 3:315, 4:376
  Mary (----), 3:315
  Rebecca (----), 3:315
Ormsbee/Ormsby
  Ann (----), 3:315
  Bethia, 3:316
  Elizabeth, 3:316
  Hannah, 3:316
  Martha, 3:316
  Mary, 2:517, 3:316
  Sarah (----), 3:316
Orne - see also Horne
  Sarah (Stevens), 4:708
Orris/Oris/Orrice
  Deborah, 4:693
  Elizabeth, 3:316
  Elizabeth (----), 3:316
  Hannah, 3:316
  Hannah (----), 3:316
  Jane, 4:693
  Martha, 3:316
  Mary, 3:316
  Mary (----), 4:229, 4:693
  Sarah, 3:316
  Sarah (----), 3:316
  Susanna, 4:693
Orton
  Abigail, 3:317
  Amie, 3:317
  Elizabeth, 3:317
  Hannah, 3:317
  Hannah (----), 3:316
  Margaret, 3:316

Orton (continued)
Margaret (Pall/Paul), 3:316
Mary, 2:576, 3:316-317
Mary (----), 3:317
Mary (Eddy), 2:99
Mary (Tudor), 3:316
Sarah, 3:317
Orvis
---- (----) Carpenter, 1:336
Abiah, 3:657
Ann, 3:317
Bethia, 3:657
Deborah, 3:317, 3:600
Deborah (----), 3:317
Elizabeth, 3:657
Elizabeth (----) Carpenter, 1:280, 3:317
Hannah, 3:317
Margaret, 3:317
Martha, 3:317
Mary, 3:317, 3:657, 4:39
Miriam (Hannison), 4:702
Sarah, 3:317
Osborn/Osbourn
Abigail, 3:318
Abigail (----), 3:319
Abigail (Eggleston), 2:106, 3:318
Abigail (Pinckney), 3:317
Ann, 3:318, 3:489, 4:691, 4:694
Ann (Oldage), 3:307, 3:318
Elizabeth, 3:317-319, 3:657, 4:152
Elizabeth (----), 3:318
Elizabeth (Ruck), 3:657
Esther, 3:318
Frezwith/Freesweed/etc (----), 3:319
Hannah, 1:68, 1:103, 2:106, 3:318-319, 3:657, 4:58
Hannah (----), 3:319
Hannah (Burton), 3:657
Joanna, 3:318
Joyce (----), 2:246
Joyce (Smith), 3:317
Martha, 3:318-319
Mary, 3:317-319, 3:326, 3:577
Mary (----), 3:317-319
Mary (----) Jones, 2:563

Mary (Merchant), 3:653
Mercy, 2:563
Mindwell, 3:318
Patience, 1:25
Priscilla, 3:319
Rebecca, 3:317, 3:319, 4:694
Recompense, 3:319
Sarah, 3:317-319, 4:657, 4:694
Sarah (----), 1:258, 3:319, 3:657
Sarah (----) Gibbard, 4:694
Sarah (Bennett), 3:318
Osgood
Abigail, 1:335, 3:320, 3:322, 4:589
Abigail (Ambrose), 1:48, 3:322
Ann, 3:320
Deborah, 3:320, 3:322, 3:577, 3:589, 3:657
Deborah (Poor), 3:322, 3:456
Dorothy, 3:320
Elizabeth, 1:271, 3:320, 3:322
Esther, 3:320
Hannah, 1:63, 1:335, 1:499, 3:320-322
Hannah (Ayers), 3:321
Hannah (Barker), 1:116, 3:320
Hannah (Belknap), 1:158, 3:320
Hannah (Blanchard), 1:196
Hannah (Dane), 3:321
Joan, 2:565, 3:322
Judith, 3:322
Lydia, 2:214, 3:320-321
Margery (----), 3:581
Margery (Fowler), 3:320, 3:657
Margery/Margaret (Fowler), 1:431, 2:194
Martha, 3:320
Martha (Ayers), 3:321
Mary, 1:69, 2:148, 2:519, 3:122, 3:161, 3:320-322, 4:536
Mary (----), 3:320
Mary (Clements), 1:408,

3:320
Mary (Hooker), 3:321
Mary (Poole), 3:322
Mary (Stephens), 3:321
Mehitable, 3:320-321
Priscilla (----), 3:320
Rebecca, 3:320
Sarah, 1:408, 3:320-322
Sarah (----), 3:320, 3:322
Sarah (----) Jones, 3:322
Susanna, 3:322
Susanna (----), 3:322
Osland
Elizabeth, 3:322-323, 4:586-587
Elizabeth (Hyde), 2:516, 3:322
Esther, 3:323
Hannah, 3:322-323, 3:479
Lydia, 3:323
Mary, 3:323
Sarah, 3:322-323, 3:478
Sarah (Hyde), 2:515, 3:323
Thankful, 3:323
Otis
Alice, 3:323
Ann, 3:323-324
Bethia, 3:324
Christina, 1:100
Deborah, 3:324
Delight, 3:324
Dorothy, 3:324
Dorothy (Joyce), 2:573
Dorothy (Thomas), 3:324, 4:281
Elizabeth, 3:117, 3:323-324
Elizabeth (----) Stream, 2:441, 3:323, 4:222
Experience, 2:397, 3:324-325
Grizzle (Warren), 3:324
Hannah, 2:254, 3:323-325
Hannah (Ensign), 3:325
Judith, 3:324-325
Margaret, 1:315, 3:323
Margaret (----), 3:323
Mary, 2:282, 3:91, 3:323-325, 4:366
Mary (Allyne), 2:62
Mary (Jacob), 2:534, 3:323
Mary (Little), 3:323
Mary (Pitman), 3:325,

Otis (continued)
Mary (Pitman) (continued)
3:441
Mercy, 3:324
Mercy (Bacon), 1:91,
3:323
Rachel, 3:324
Rebecca, 3:325
Rose, 3:324-325, 3:438
Rose (Stoughton), 3:324
Shuah (----) Heard, 2:397,
3:324
Susanna, 4:366
Susanna (----), 3:325
Otley
---- (Humfrey), 3:325
Overman
---- (----) Munnings, 4:575
Dorothy (Porter), 3:660
Hannah (Wiswall)
Munnings, 3:256, 3:325,
4:616
Oviat/Oviett
Abigail, 4:694
Amy, 4:694
Dorothy, 4:694
Frances, 4:694
Frances (----), 4:694
Hester, 4:694
Owen
---- (Grice), 2:312, 3:326
Abigail, 3:326
Ann, 3:326
Ann (----) Pettee, 3:326
Ann (Canning) Pettee,
3:404
Christian, 3:326
Deliverance, 2:99, 3:326
Elizabeth, 1:346, 3:326
Elizabeth (----), 3:250
Elizabeth (Dickinson),
3:616, 3:657
Eunice, 3:326
Hannah (Lincoln), 3:95,
3:326
Jemima, 3:326
Mary, 3:326, 4:565
Mary (Osborn), 3:318,
3:326
Rebecca, 2:586, 3:326
Rebecca (Wade), 3:326
Sarah, 3:326
Sarah (Holcomb), 3:326

Sarah (Palmer), 3:326
Tabitha, 3:326
Owens
Martha (Merritt), 3:200
Oxenbridge
Bathshua, 3:327
Frances (Woodward),
3:327
Jane (Butler), 3:327
Susanna (----), 3:327
Theodora, 3:327, 4:272
Oxston
Susanna, 2:448
Pacey/Pacy
Catharine (----), 3:327
Sarah (Dudley) Keayne,
2:78, 3:1-2, 3:327
Packard
---- (Kingman), 3:327
Abiel, 3:327
Deborah, 3:327, 4:430
Deliverance, 3:327, 4:430
Elizabeth, 1:28, 1:79,
3:327
Elizabeth (----), 3:327
Elizabeth (Lothrop), 3:121,
3:327
Faithful, 3:327
Hannah, 3:327
Jael, 3:327, 4:121
Joanna (Tuttle), 4:352
Lydia, 3:327
Margaret, 3:327
Mary, 3:327, 3:414
Sarah, 3:327
Sarah (Howard), 2:472,
3:327
Susanna, 3:327
Packer
---- (Christophers), 1:383
Elizabeth, 2:41
Elizabeth (----), 3:328
Hepzibah (----), 3:328
Jael, 4:121
Lydia (Latham), 3:58,
3:328
Mary (Williams), 3:328,
4:572
Rebecca, 3:327-328
Rebecca (Wells) Latham,
3:58, 3:328
Thomasine, 1:259

Packhurst
Pheza (----) Veazey, 4:369
Paddleford
Hannah (----), 3:328
Mary, 3:328
Mary (----), 2:91
Mary (Blanford), 3:328
Paddock
---- (Palmer), 3:343
Alice, 2:99, 3:328
Ann (Jones), 3:328
Deborah (Sears), 3:328,
4:46
Elizabeth, 2:478, 4:694
Mary, 3:328, 3:548
Sarah (Rickard), 3:540,
3:657
Susanna, 2:99, 3:328
Paddy
Alice (Freeman), 2:203,
3:329
Deborah (Waite), 3:328
Elizabeth, 3:329, 4:483
Hannah, 3:329
Margaret, 1:141
Mary, 3:329
Mary (Greenough) Payton,
3:329, 3:374
Mercy, 2:64, 3:329
Rebecca, 3:329
Padner
Ruth, 3:330
Ruth (----), 3:330
Page
---, 3:331
---- (----) Dow, 3:616
Abigail, 3:331, 4:137
Ann (----), 3:331
Ann/Hannah (----), 4:596
Bethia, 4:240
Catharine, 3:331
Damaris (Shattuck), 3:330
Elizabeth, 3:330-331,
3:338
Elizabeth (----), 3:331
Elizabeth (Beamsley),
1:148, 3:330
Emory (Lamb), 3:330
Experience, 3:331
Faith, 3:331
Faith (Dunster), 2:83,
3:330
Hannah, 2:63, 3:331,

Page (continued)
Hannah (continued)
  4:694
Hannah (—), 3:331
Humility, 3:330
Judith, 3:331
Lucy (—), 3:331
Margaret, 3:249, 3:331,
  4:11
Margery, 1:432
Martha (—), 2:300, 3:331
Martha (—) Heath, 2:399,
  3:331
Mary, 3:330-331, 3:338
Mary (—), 3:330-331
Mary (Edgecomb), 1:69,
  2:100, 3:330
Mary (Hawkesworth),
  2:382, 3:331
Mary (Marsh), 3:154
Mary (Whittier), 3:330,
  4:536
Mehitable (Green) Dow,
  3:331
Mercy, 1:411, 3:331
Meribah (—), 3:657
Mildred, 3:331
Penuel, 3:330
Phebe, 1:493, 3:330, 3:338,
  4:339
Phebe (Paine), 3:330
Rebecca, 3:161, 3:331
Sabina, 3:161
Sarah, 3:330-331, 4:22,
  4:694
Sarah (—), 4:694
Sarah (Davis), 2:17, 3:330
Sarah (Rowell), 3:331
Sarah (Smith), 3:331
Susanna, 3:331
Paige
Ann (Keayne) Lane, 3:1,
  3:51, 3:332
Elizabeth, 3:332
Joanna (—), 3:332
Sarah, 3:204, 3:332
Paine/Payne
—, 3:338
— (Bennett), 3:333
Abigail, 3:332-334, 3:337,
  3:657, 4:702
Abigail (Brockett), 1:258,
  3:657

Abigail (Frissell), 3:335
Alice, 3:333
Alice (—), 3:334
Alice (—) Parker, 3:335,
  3:357
Alice (Mayo), 3:333
Amy, 3:332
Amy (—), 3:332
Ann, 3:204, 3:333, 3:335,
  3:337, 3:623
Ann (—), 3:337
Ann (Chickering), 1:376,
  3:336
Ann (Whiting), 3:334
Bethia, 3:332
Bethia (Thacher), 3:332
Catharine, 3:337
Catharine (—), 3:336
Deborah, 3:333
Deborah (Neal), 3:333
Dorcas, 3:332, 3:337
Dorcas (—), 3:335
Dorothy, 3:334, 3:336
Dorothy (—), 3:334,
  3:658
Elizabeth, 1:10, 2:347,
  2:503, 3:330, 3:333-337,
  3:345, 3:391, 4:16,
  4:347, 4:506, 4:694,
  4:702
Elizabeth (—), 3:334-338
Elizabeth (Belcher), 4:694
Elizabeth (Colburn), 1:424
Ellen, 3:336
Ellen (Veazie), 3:336,
  4:369
Experience, 3:332
Grace (—), 3:185
Hannah, 1:61, 1:180,
  3:333-335, 3:337
Hannah (—), 3:334, 3:337
Hannah (Bass), 1:135,
  3:335
Hannah (Bray), 1:239,
  3:337
Hannah (Devotion)
  Ruggles, 2:42, 3:587
Hannah (Shaw), 3:337,
  4:65
Jane, 3:185, 3:337, 4:690
Jane (—), 3:337
Jemima (—), 4:702
Jemima (Alsop), 3:597

Judith, 3:335
Judith (—) Quincy, 2:495,
  3:334, 3:500
Lois, 3:334
Lydia, 3:263, 3:334-335,
  3:337
Margaret, 3:334, 3:337
Margaret (—), 3:337
Martha, 3:334, 4:694
Mary, 2:49, 2:500,
  3:332-337, 3:560, 3:658,
  4:54, 4:702
Mary (—), 3:334, 3:338
Mary (—) Brown, 4:676,
  4:694
Mary (Brintnall), 3:336
Mary (Craford), 1:469
Mary (Day), 2:26, 3:333
Mary (Lawson), 3:337
Mary (Nash), 3:261, 3:334
Mary (Penniman), 3:335,
  3:389
Mehitable, 3:335
Mercy, 3:333, 3:335,
  3:622, 4:694
Mercy (Carr), 1:338
Patience, 3:333
Patience (Freeman), 3:335
Patience (Sparrow), 3:333
Phebe, 3:330, 3:337
Priscilla, 3:334
Rachel, 3:334
Rebecca, 2:501, 3:333,
  3:335-336, 3:369, 3:384
Rebecca (—), 3:336
Rebecca (Doane), 3:332
Rebecca (Peck), 3:337
Rose (—), 3:332, 3:335
Rose (—) Weeden, 4:331
Sarah, 1:24, 1:178,
  3:333-336, 3:338, 3:587,
  3:658
Sarah (Clark), 3:610
Sarah (Parker), 3:333,
  3:355
Sarah (Winslow) Standish,
  3:205, 3:337, 4:162,
  4:601
Susan, 3:337
Susanna, 3:333
Thankful, 3:334
Painter
Catharine (—), 3:338

Painter (continued)
Elizabeth, 3:338
Elizabeth (----), 3:339
Palfrey
----, 3:339
---- (----), 3:339
Alice (----), 3:339
Edith (----), 3:339
Elizabeth, 3:339
Elizabeth (----) Fairfield, 2:137, 3:339
Hannah, 2:556, 3:339
Jane (----), 4:574
Lydia, 3:425
Martha, 3:339
Mary, 3:339
Rebecca, 3:339, 4:236
Rebecca (Bordman), 3:339
Remember, 1:70, 3:339
Ruth, 3:339
Palgrave/Palsgrave
Ann, 4:636
Ann (----), 3:339
Bethia, 3:339
Lydia, 3:339-340
Mary, 3:339-340, 4:481
Mary (Maverick), 2:457, 3:181, 3:339
Rebecca, 3:339
Sarah, 1:21, 3:339-340
Pall
Margaret, 3:317
Palmer
----, 3:343
---- (Fenner), 2:153
---- (Gilbert), 2:586
---- (Hilton), 2:422, 3:340
---- (Paddock), 3:343
Abigail (Allen), 1:29-30, 3:341
Abigail (Dearborn), 2:32
Alice, 1:466
Ann (----), 3:446
Ann (Denison), 2:36, 3:340
Bethia (Morey), 3:340
Bridget, 3:343
Catharine (----), 3:340
Deborah, 3:340
Dorcas, 3:341
Dorothy (----), 3:341
Dorothy (Gilbert), 2:250
Elizabeth, 1:84, 3:340-342,

3:592, 4:401
Elizabeth (----), 1:377, 3:342
Elizabeth (Alger), 1:27, 3:341
Elizabeth (Bond), 1:378
Elizabeth (Cheever), 1:371, 3:342
Elizabeth (Hodgkins), 2:439, 3:343, 4:575
Elizabeth (Kingsley), 3:342
Elizabeth (Peck) Mason, 3:652
Elizabeth (Tyler), 4:356
Esther, 2:225, 3:342
Experience, 1:486, 3:341
Frances (----), 3:342
Frances (Prentice), 3:479
Grace, 3:216, 3:342
Grace (----), 3:340
Grace (----) Rogers, 3:343, 3:569
Hannah, 2:292, 2:491, 3:341-342
Hannah (Buell), 1:289, 3:342
Hannah (Stanton), 3:341, 4:167
Joan (----) Purchase, 3:342, 3:494
Martha, 3:342-343, 4:82, 4:650
Mary, 2:206, 3:340-342, 4:192
Mary (Clark), 3:340
Mary (Gilbert), 3:342, 3:624
Mary (Munjoy), 3:255, 3:341
Mary (Pearson), 3:378, 3:658
Mary (Tyler), 4:356
Mary (Voden/Voeden/etc), 4:376
Mehitable, 2:3, 3:340
Mercy, 1:241, 3:340
Rebecca, 1:373, 3:340, 3:342-343
Rebecca (Short), 3:342
Rhoda (Hudson), 2:488
Ruth, 3:341
Sarah, 3:326, 3:341-342
Sarah (Jackman), 3:341

Palmes
Ann (Humfrey), 2:496, 3:344
Lucy, 2:299, 3:343
Lucy (Winthrop), 3:343, 4:613
Sarah, 3:343
Sarah (----) Davis, 2:23, 3:343
Pantry/Pantree
Abigail, 3:344
Ann (Tuttle), 4:352
Hannah, 3:344
Hannah (Tuttle), 3:344, 4:479
Mary, 3:344
Rebecca, 3:344
Papillans/Papillon
Catharine, 3:344
Catharine (----), 3:344
Joan (----), 3:344
Martha, 3:344
Mary, 3:344
Mercy, 3:344
Pard
Mary (----), 3:344
Pardee/Pardie
Catharine (Lane), 3:345
Elizabeth, 2:312, 3:345
Elizabeth (Paine), 3:345
Elizabeth (Yale), 3:345, 4:667
Hannah, 3:345
Martha, 3:345
Martha (Miles), 3:207, 3:344
Mary, 2:467, 3:344-345, 4:656
Mary (Denison), 3:345
Mercy, 3:345
Mercy (Ball), 1:106, 3:345
Rebecca, 3:345
Rebecca (Lane), 3:345
Sarah, 3:345
Paris
Dorothy, 3:345
Dorothy (----), 1:267, 3:345
Elizabeth, 3:345-346
Elizabeth (----), 3:346
Mary, 3:345-346
Mary (----), 3:346
Mary (Jewell), 3:345

Paris (continued)
Susanna, 3:346
Parish
Ann, 3:346
Elizabeth, 3:346
Lydia, 3:346
Mary, 3:346
Mary (----), 3:346
Mary (Blanchard), 3:346
Park/Parke/Parks
----, 3:349
Abigail, 2:166, 3:346-348
Abigail (Dix), 2:53, 3:348
Alice, 3:58, 3:348
Alice (Tompson), 3:348
Ann, 3:346-347, 3:372
Ann (Spring), 3:347, 4:157
Deborah, 3:348
Dorothy, 3:347-348
Dorothy (----), 3:348
Elizabeth, 1:168, 2:447,
3:346-348
Elizabeth (----), 3:347
Elizabeth (Billings), 3:347
Elizabeth (Miller), 3:346
Eunice, 3:347
Hannah, 3:347-348, 3:645
Hannah (Kimball), 3:347
Isabel, 3:347, 4:526
Lydia, 3:347
Margaret, 3:347
Margery, 3:347
Martha, 3:346, 3:348,
4:497, 4:560
Martha (Fiske), 3:346
Martha (Holgrave), 2:446,
3:348
Mary, 1:200, 3:347-348,
4:694
Mary (----), 3:347
Mary (Allyn), 3:348
Mindwell, 3:347
Phebe, 3:347
Rachel (Leffingwell),
3:348
Rebecca, 3:347-348, 4:16
Sarah, 3:347-348
Sarah (----), 3:347
Sarah (----) Brewster,
3:347
Sarah (Collier) Brewster,
1:245
Sarah (Cutter), 3:347

Sarah (Geer), 2:239
Theoda, 3:348-349, 4:569
Theoda (Williams) Park,
4:569
Parker
----, 3:296, 3:357
---- (Dennis), 2:39
Abiah, 3:352
Abiel, 3:354-355
Abigail, 3:349, 3:352,
3:354-355, 3:357
Abigail (Hildreth), 2:415,
3:354
Abigail (Shattuck) Morse,
3:354, 4:63
Alice, 3:354, 3:356
Alice (----), 3:335, 3:352,
3:357
Amy, 3:355
Amy (----), 3:357
Ann, 2:244, 3:147, 3:349,
3:351, 3:353-356
Ann (----), 3:349, 3:355
Beatrice (Thompson),
4:288
Bethia, 3:355
Bethia (----), 3:355
Deborah, 3:349, 3:352-353,
3:357, 4:266, 4:663
Deborah (----), 3:658
Deliverance (----), 3:353
Elizabeth, 2:240,
3:349-352, 3:354, 3:357
Elizabeth (----), 2:512,
3:354, 3:357
Elizabeth (----) Bridges,
1:249, 3:354
Elizabeth (----) Potter,
3:350
Elizabeth (Brown), 1:272,
3:350
Elizabeth (Hinckley),
2:425, 3:350
Elizabeth (Howe), 3:349
Elizabeth (Long), 3:109,
3:351
Elizabeth (Saxton), 3:354
Esther, 3:349
Eunice (----), 3:351
Experience, 3:349-350
Frances, 2:332, 3:350
Hannah, 1:204, 2:344,
3:349, 3:352, 3:354-356,

3:364, 4:355
Hannah (----), 3:354, 3:358
Hannah (Bassett), 1:136,
3:352
Hannah (Brown), 3:353
Hannah (Gilbert), 2:251,
3:354
Hannah (Kendall), 3:352
Hope, 1:450, 3:350
Jane, 2:525, 3:356
Jane (----), 3:351, 3:355,
4:256
Joanna, 3:166, 3:352,
3:355
Joanna (----), 3:350, 3:352,
4:174
Johanna, 3:355
Judith, 3:354
Judith (----) Bugby, 1:290,
3:355
Lydia, 3:18, 3:349-350,
3:352, 3:357, 4:280,
4:492
Margaret, 3:351, 3:354,
3:356, 3:658
Margaret (----), 3:353,
3:357, 4:221
Margaret (Wiswall), 3:355
Margery, 3:354
Margery (----), 3:357
Martha, 2:465, 2:549,
3:350, 3:352, 3:357
Martha (Livermore), 3:101
Mary, 1:354, 1:441, 2:23,
2:37, 2:57, 2:213, 2:335,
2:351, 3:349-357, 3:537,
3:658, 4:68, 4:447,
4:479, 4:492
Mary (----), 3:351,
3:353-354
Mary (Barsham) Bright,
1:128, 1:253, 3:350
Mary (Brown), 1:266,
3:354
Mary (Buckingham),
3:352, 4:676
Mary (Clark), 3:357
Mary (Cory), 3:612, 3:658
Mary (Fairfield), 2:137,
3:352
Mary (Fessenden), 2:583
Mary (Jones), 2:565
Mary (Lombard), 3:349

Parker (continued)
Mary (Marrett) Hovey,
3:153, 3:355
Mary (Marston), 3:160,
3:356
Mary (Parker), 3:350
Mary (Rawlins), 3:510
Mary (Rawlyns), 3:357
Mary (Turner), 3:357,
4:345
Mehitable, 3:355, 3:387
Mehitable (Barron), 1:126
Mercy (Whetstone), 4:505
Patience, 3:349, 3:357
Patience (Cobb), 1:413,
3:356
Rachel, 3:350, 3:355
Rebecca, 1:396, 2:7,
3:349-350, 3:352,
3:354-355, 3:478
Rebecca (Read), 3:353
Rose (Whitlock), 3:349
Ruhamah, 3:357
Ruth, 3:353, 3:357, 3:528
Sarah, 1:293, 2:190, 2:472,
3:333, 3:350-357, 4:1,
4:139, 4:384
Sarah (----), 3:350-351,
3:353
Sarah (Hartwell), 3:349
Sarah (Holman), 2:451,
3:356
Sarah (James), 3:356
Sarah (Short), 3:354
Susan (Short), 3:354
Susanna, 2:190, 3:355-356
Susanna (Devereux), 2:42,
3:356
Susanna (Keeny), 3:3,
3:355
Tabitha, 3:350
Thankful, 3:350
Thankful (----), 3:352
Thankful (Hemmenway),
2:401, 3:350
Parkhurst
Abigail, 3:358
Abigail (Garfield), 2:231,
3:358
Abigail (Morse), 3:239
Elizabeth, 3:358
Elizabeth (----), 3:358
Hannah, 3:358

Martha, 3:185
Mary, 3:358
Mary (Pheese), 3:358
Mary (Veazie), 3:358
Phebe, 1:66, 3:358
Rachel, 3:358
Rebecca, 3:358
Rebecca (----), 3:358
Sarah, 2:232, 3:358
Sarah (Brown), 1:264,
3:358
Susanna (----) Simpson,
3:358, 4:101
Parkman
Abigail, 4:322
Bridget (----), 2:129, 3:359
Deliverance, 3:358-359
Elizabeth, 3:359
Elizabeth (Adams), 4:673,
4:694
Hannah, 3:359
Hannah (----), 3:359
Margaret, 3:358-359
Margaret (Gardner), 2:230,
3:358
Martha (Clough), 1:411
Mary, 3:359, 4:694
Mehitable, 3:358
Mehitable (Waite), 3:358
Rebecca, 2:539, 3:359
Sarah, 3:358-359
Sarah (----), 3:359
Sarah (Trask), 3:658,
4:323
Sarah (Verin), 3:358,
4:711
Susanna (----) Gedney,
3:359
Susanna (Clark) Gedney,
2:241
Parmalee/Parmelee
---- (Kelsey), 3:7
Elizabeth (----), 2:128,
3:359
Hannah, 3:359, 4:694
Mary, 1:470
Priscilla, 4:694
Sarah, 2:386-387
Parmenter
Abigail, 3:360
Amy (----), 3:360
Ann/Annis (----) Chandler
Dane, 3:360

Bridget (----), 3:360
Elizabeth, 3:360, 3:390
Elizabeth (----), 3:360
Elizabeth (Cutler), 1:493
Hannah, 3:360
Hannah (Johnson), 3:360
Hannah (Savage) Butler,
4:24
Hannah (Williams), 3:360,
4:565
Hannah/Annis (----)
Chandler Dane, 2:6
Judith, 1:489, 3:360
Judith (----), 3:360
Leah (----), 3:360
Leah (Saunders), 4:21
Lydia, 3:359-360
Mary, 1:350, 1:445,
3:359-360
Mary (----), 3:359
Mercy, 3:359
Sarah, 3:360
Sarah (Sheffield), 3:360
Thankful, 3:360
Thomas (Rice) -
[Thomasine], 3:359
Thomasine (Rice), 3:529
Parnell
Mary, 3:658
Mary (Stacy), 3:360,
3:658, 4:159
Parris
Elizabeth, 4:365
Parrott/Parote/Parrett
---- (Pedrick), 3:385
Abigail (Clark), 3:610
Elizabeth, 4:650
Elizabeth (----), 3:361
Faith, 2:548, 2:597, 3:361,
4:121
Mary, 2:224
Parsons, 3:362
---- (----) Leonard, 3:361
Abigail, 3:254, 3:361-364,
3:654
Abigail (Haskell), 3:364
Abigail (Younglove),
3:362
Bethia, 3:158, 3:166,
3:363-364, 4:562
Bethia (Brattle), 1:239,
3:363
Catharine, 3:361

Parsons (continued)
Christian, 3:362
Elizabeth, 2:426,
3:361-364
Elizabeth (Cook), 1:445,
3:364
Elizabeth (Hardy/Hardie),
2:355
Elizabeth (Strong), 3:363,
4:227
Elizabeth (Wheelwright),
3:361, 4:503
Esther, 3:363, 4:126
Experience, 3:363
Hannah, 3:361-364
Hannah (Clap) Miller,
3:208
Hannah (Cooley), 3:362
Hannah (Parker), 3:364
Hannah (Younglove),
3:362
Isabella (Haynes), 3:363
Jemima, 3:364
Lydia, 3:363
Lydia (----), 3:451
Lydia (Brown), 3:364
Lydia (Haskell), 3:361
Margaret, 3:361
Margaret (Marshfield),
3:160, 3:361
Mary, 1:68, 3:361-364,
3:662, 4:578
Mary (----), 1:133, 2:373,
3:251
Mary (----) Lewis, 3:362
Mary (Bliss), 1:202, 3:363
Mary (Clark), 3:363
Mercy, 3:362
Priscilla (----), 3:364
Rachel, 3:362
Rhoda, 3:364
Rhoda (Tayler), 3:364
Ruth, 1:203, 3:361, 3:364,
4:20
Ruth (----), 3:362, 3:364
Ruth (Wilson), 3:361
Sarah, 2:61, 3:361-364
Sarah (----) Leonard, 4:305
Sarah (Clark), 1:404,
3:363
Sarah (Dare), 3:364
Sarah (Heald) Leonard,
3:79

Sarah (Keep), 3:361
Sarah (Norton), 3:363
Sarah (Varney), 4:366
Sarah (Vinson), 3:362,
4:375
Sarah (Vore), 3:361, 4:376
Susanna, 3:361
Partridge
---- (Cotton) Atwater,
3:366
Abiel, 3:365
Abigail, 3:365-366
Ann, 3:365
Ann (----), 3:365-366,
4:168
Deborah, 3:365
Elizabeth, 3:365-367, 4:65,
4:273
Elizabeth (----), 3:365,
3:367
Elizabeth (Rockett), 3:365,
3:557
Elizabeth (Rockwood),
3:365
Ellen (----), 3:365
Experience, 3:365
Hannah, 3:365-367
Hannah (----), 3:366-367
Hannah (Seabury), 3:365
Lydia, 1:246, 3:365
Magdalen, 3:367
Magdelen (Bullard), 3:365
Margery, 3:170
Mary, 2:86, 3:156,
3:365-367, 4:122
Mary (----), 3:365
Mary (----) Brewster, 3:365
Mary (Brown), 3:367
Mary (Cotton) Atwater,
1:76, 1:464
Mary (Fernald), 3:365
Mary (Smith), 3:367,
4:111, 4:136
Mehitable, 2:86, 3:366
Mehitable (Crow), 1:479,
3:366
Mercy, 3:365
Patience, 3:365
Patience (----), 3:366
Priscilla, 3:367
Rachel, 1:365, 3:365-367
Rebecca, 4:682
Ruth, 3:365, 4:272

Sarah, 1:35, 2:398,
3:365-367
Sarah (----), 3:365-366
Sarah (Colburn), 3:367
Sarah (Pierce), 3:367
Sarah (Tracy), 3:365,
4:321
Silence, 3:366
Thankful, 3:366
Tryphosa, 3:365
Parum
Frances (----), 3:367
Ruth, 3:658
Pasco
Dorothy, 3:367
Elizabeth (----), 3:367
Margaret, 3:658
Margery, 3:658
Mary, 3:658
Mary (Pease), 3:658
Rachel (----), 3:367
Rebecca (Terry), 3:367
Sarah, 2:327, 3:658
Sarah (----), 3:658
Pasmore/Pasmer/Pasmere
Abigail, 3:367
Alice (----), 3:367
Hannah, 3:367
Rebecca, 3:367
Rebecca (----), 3:367
Pasque
Sarah, 2:327
Passam/Passant/Passon
Ruth (----), 3:368
Patch
---- (Lee), 3:71
Bethia, 3:368
Eleanor, 3:368
Elizabeth, 3:368, 3:608
Elizabeth (----), 3:368
Elizabeth (Brackenbury),
3:368, 3:605
Ellen, 3:368
Eunice (Fraile), 2:199,
3:368
Freeborn, 3:368
Hannah, 3:368
Hannah (----), 3:368
Hannah (Eaton), 3:368
Marah, 3:369
Mary, 3:368, 4:290
Mary (----) Thompson,
3:368

Patch (continued)
Mary (Goldsmith), 3:368
Mary (Scott), 3:368
Priscilla, 3:368
Priscilla (----), 3:368
Sarah, 3:368-369
Susanna, 3:368
Susanna (Legrove), 3:368,
3:647
Patching/Patcham
Elizabeth (----) Iggleden,
2:517, 3:369
Patefield/Peatfield
Amy (----), 3:369
Mary, 3:369
Rebecca, 3:369
Patten
Abigail, 2:583
Justine (----), 3:369
Mary, 2:315, 3:369
Mary (----), 3:369
Rebecca, 3:336, 3:369
Rebecca (Adams), 1:11,
3:369
Rebecca (Paine), 3:336,
3:369
Sarah, 3:369, 4:65
Sarah (Cooper), 3:369
Patterson/Pattison
Abigail, 3:372
Ann, 3:372
Ann (----), 3:372
Ashbel, 3:371
Beulah, 3:372
Elizabeth, 3:370-371,
4:135
Elizabeth (Belknap), 1:158
Elizabeth (Kibbee), 3:370
Elizabeth (Peat), 3:370,
3:380
Elizabeth (Rithway), 3:372
Eunice, 3:371-372
Eunice (Nichols), 3:370
Faith, 3:370
Hannah, 3:370-371
Hepzibah, 3:371
Joanna (Hall), 3:371
Keziah, 3:371
Lydia, 3:371
Mary, 3:370-371, 3:490
Mary (----), 3:371-372
Mary (Hawks), 3:371
Mercy, 3:371

Mercy (Goodenow), 2:272,
3:371
Parthenia, 3:371
Rebecca, 3:371
Rebecca (Myrick)
Livermore, 3:371
Rebecca (Stevenson),
3:371
Sarah, 3:370
Sybil, 3:371
Patteshall/Paddeshall/etc
Abigail (----), 3:369
Ann, 3:369
Frances, 3:369
Martha, 3:369
Martha (----), 3:369
Mary, 2:240
Paul
---- (Maverick), 3:372
Abiel, 3:658
Abigail, 3:372
Dorothy, 3:372
Dorothy (Walker), 3:372
Elizabeth, 3:372
Esther (Bobbit), 3:372
Hannah, 3:372
Hannah (Woodie), 3:372
Lydia, 3:372
Lydia (Jenkins), 2:542,
3:372
Margaret, 3:317
Margaret (----), 4:618
Margery (Tarne), 3:658
Mary, 3:372
Mary (Breck), 1:240,
3:372, 4:310
Mary (Richmond), 3:539
Priscilla, 3:372
Sarah, 3:372
Susanna, 3:372
Payne - see Paine
Payson
Ann, 3:373-374
Ann (Parke), 3:348, 3:372
Bathsheba (Tileston),
3:373, 4:302
Catharine (Leadbetter),
3:67, 3:373
Dorcas, 3:374
Elizabeth, 2:188,
3:373-374
Elizabeth (Dowell), 3:373
Elizabeth (Partridge)

Hamlin Johnson, 3:366
Elizabeth (Phillips), 3:373,
3:414
Elizabeth (Whittingham)
Appleton, 1:62, 3:373
Hannah (----), 3:373
Joanna, 3:373
Judith (Clap), 1:388, 3:373
Mary, 1:334, 3:372-374
Mary (Eliot), 2:111, 3:372
Mary (Wiswall), 3:373,
4:617
Prudence (Lincoln), 3:373
Ruth, 3:373
Sarah, 2:187, 3:373-374,
4:615
Susanna, 1:334, 3:373
Payton
Elizabeth, 3:273
Mary, 3:374, 4:88
Mary (Greenough), 3:329,
3:374
Sarah, 3:82, 3:374
Peabody
Abiel, 3:376
Abigail (Towne), 3:375,
4:316
Alice, 3:375
Ann, 3:375
Annis, 3:375, 3:579
Bethia, 3:375
Bethia (Bridges), 1:249,
3:375
Damaris, 3:374
Elizabeth, 3:375, 3:563
Elizabeth (Alden), 1:23,
3:375
Hannah, 3:374-376
Hannah (Andrews), 1:499,
3:375
Hannah (Hale), 2:331,
3:376
Hepzibah, 3:374-375,
3:661
Isabel (----), 3:375
Jane, 4:124
Judith (----), 3:375
Keziah, 3:375
Lydia, 3:374-375
Martha, 3:375, 4:44
Mary, 2:33, 3:374-376,
4:143
Mary (Browne), 3:376

Peabody (continued)
Mary (Foster), 2:190,
3:374
Mary (Foster) Wood, 2:189
Mercy, 3:375
Philadelphia, 3:375
Priscilla, 3:375, 4:615
Rachel (Nicholson), 3:283
Ruth, 3:374-375
Ruth (----), 3:375
Sarah, 1:417, 3:374-375
Sarah (----), 3:375
Peache/Peachy
Mary (----), 3:376
Peacock
Deborah, 3:376, 3:610
Elizabeth, 3:377
Hannah, 3:376
Jane, 3:376
Jane (----), 3:376
Joyce (----), 3:376
Margery (----) Shove,
3:376, 4:705
Mary, 3:376-377, 3:601
Mary (----), 3:376
Mary (Willis), 3:377
Phebe, 3:376, 3:607
Sarah, 3:377
Sarah (Edsall), 3:377
Peak/Peake/Peaks
Abigail (Comstock), 1:440,
3:377
Dorcas, 3:377
Dorcas (French), 3:377
Elizabeth, 3:377
Elizabeth (----), 3:377
Hannah, 3:377
Judith (----) Litchfield,
3:377
Judith (Dennis) Litchfield,
3:99
Mary, 3:377
Phebe (Butler), 1:321
Ruth, 3:377
Sarah, 2:28, 3:377
Sarah (French), 3:377
Peaken
Elizabeth (----), 4:695
Pearce/Pearse - see Pierce
Peard
Jane (Naziter), 3:263,
3:377

Pearson - see also Pierson
Abigail, 3:378-379
Bethia, 3:378
Dorcas, 2:438, 3:378
Dorcas (----), 3:378
Dorcas (Johnson), 3:379
Elizabeth, 3:378-379,
3:635
Elizabeth (Hardy/Hardie),
2:355
Elizabeth (Wheelwright),
4:503
Hannah, 3:378
Hannah (Thurston), 3:378
Hepzibah, 3:378-379
Jane, 3:378
Martha, 3:379
Martha (----), 3:379
Martha (Lathrop) Goodwin,
2:277
Mary, 1:304, 3:378-379,
3:607, 3:658
Mary (French), 3:379
Mary (Pickard), 3:378,
3:422
Mary (Poor), 3:379, 3:456
Maudlin (----), 3:378
Mehitable, 3:378
Miriam, 3:378
Patience, 3:379
Phebe, 2:364, 3:378
Priscilla, 3:378
Priscilla (Hazen), 3:378
Rebecca, 3:378
Ruth, 3:378
Sarah, 3:378-379, 3:446,
4:318
Susanna, 3:378
Tabitha, 3:378
Tabitha (Kendall), 3:378,
3:643
Pease
---- (----), 3:379
Abigail, 3:379
Abigail (Randall), 3:659
Ann (Cummings),
1:483-484, 3:379
Bethia, 3:659
Bridget (----), 3:379
Deborah (Gardner) Macy,
2:229, 3:142
Deliverance, 3:659
Hannah (Walford), 4:392

Lucy (----), 3:379
Margaret (----), 3:379
Margaret (Adams), 3:658
Martha, 1:403
Mary, 3:379-380,
3:658-659
Mary (----), 3:379, 4:535
Mary (Hobbs), 3:658
Sarah, 3:380
Sarah (----), 3:380, 3:659
Susan, 3:379
Susan (----), 3:379
Peaslee/Peasley
Elizabeth, 3:380
Jane, 2:18, 3:380
Mary, 3:380, 4:536
Mary (----), 3:380
Ruth, 3:380
Ruth (Barnard), 3:380
Sarah, 3:380, 3:600, 3:659
Peat/Peate
---- (Charles), 4:677
Abigail (Harvey), 2:370
Elizabeth, 3:370, 3:380
Jane, 3:380
Sarah, 3:380
Sarah (----), 3:380
Peck
----, 3:167, 3:383
---- (Hunting), 2:503
---- (Smith), 3:381
Abigail, 3:381-382
Alice (----) Burwell, 1:316,
3:382
Ann, 3:381, 4:165
Bethia, 3:381
Bethia (----), 3:381
Deborah, 3:382
Deliverance (----), 3:382
Desire, 4:695
Elizabeth, 1:55, 3:380-384,
3:635, 3:652, 3:659
Elizabeth (----), 3:384,
4:695
Elizabeth (Baysey), 1:144,
3:383
Elizabeth (Beers), 1:155
Elizabeth (Lee), 3:647
Esther, 2:503, 3:380-381,
4:580
Hannah, 3:382-383, 3:515,
4:75
Hannah (Farnsworth),

Peck (continued)
  Hannah (Farnsworth)
  (continued)
    2:143, 3:384
  Hannah (Kitchell), 3:32
  Isabel, 4:695
  Jael, 3:384
  Joan (----), 3:125, 3:380
  Joanna, 3:381
  Joanna (Kitchell), 3:381
  Judith, 3:384
  Lydia, 3:381, 4:695
  Margery (----), 3:383
  Martha, 1:459, 3:381-383
  Martha (----), 3:382
  Mary, 2:60, 3:380-382
  Mary (Bunnell), 4:695
  Mary (Moss), 3:246, 3:381
  Mary (Richards), 3:534
  Mary (Sperry), 3:380,
    4:150
  Mehitable, 4:695
  Phebe, 3:381
  Prudence (Clap), 1:389,
    3:384
  Rachel, 3:381, 3:384
  Rachel (----), 2:442
  Rachel (Richards), 3:381
  Rebecca, 2:143, 3:337,
    3:381, 3:384
  Rebecca (Paine) Hunt,
    2:501, 3:336, 3:384
  Ruth, 1:76, 3:381-383
  Ruth (----), 3:382, 3:635
  Ruth (Ferris), 3:383
  Sarah, 3:381-384
  Sarah (----), 2:105, 3:382,
    3:384
  Sarah (----) Holt, 3:384,
    3:634
  Sarah (Alling), 3:382
  Susanna, 3:381
Pecker
  Elizabeth (Friend), 3:384
Pedrick
  ----, 3:385
  Agnes, 3:385
  Ann, 3:385
  Elizabeth, 3:385
  Joanna, 3:385
  Mary, 3:385
  Meriam, 3:385
  Meriam (----), 3:385

  Phillis (----), 3:659
  Sarah, 3:385
Peek
  Hannah (----), 3:659
Pelham
  ---- (----) Brewster, 3:386
  ---- (Waldegrave), 3:385
  Deborah, 3:386
  Elizabeth, 3:385
  Elizabeth (Bosseville) Har-
    lakenden, 2:356, 3:385
  Frances, 3:385
  Freelove, 3:385
  Freelove (Arnold), 1:64,
    3:385
  Godsgift (Arnold), 1:64,
    3:385
  Hannah, 3:386
  Mary, 3:385
  Penelope, 1:161, 3:282,
    3:385-386, 4:603
Pell
  ---- (----) Brewster, 3:386
  Ann, 4:296
  Deborah, 3:386
  Elizabeth (----) Heath,
    2:400
  Elizabeth (----) Heaton,
    3:186, 3:386
  Hannah, 3:386
  Helen, 1:227
  Lucy (----) Brewster, 1:244
  Mary, 2:242-243, 3:386
Pellet/Pellate
  ---- (----), 4:360
  Mary (Dane/Dean), 3:386
Pelton
  Mary, 3:387
  Susanna (----), 3:386
Pember
  Agnes (----), 3:387
  Ann, 3:387
  Elizabeth, 3:387
  Mercy, 3:387
Pemberton
  Alice (----), 3:387
  Elinor, 3:387
  Elizabeth, 3:387
  Elizabeth (----), 3:387
  Hannah (----), 3:387
  Jane, 3:387
  Margaret (----), 3:387
  Mary, 1:117, 3:387

  Mary (----), 3:387
  Mary (Clark), 1:396
  Mehitable, 3:387
  Sarah, 2:248, 3:387
  Sarah (----), 3:387
  Sarah (Marshall), 3:387
Pendall
  Mehitable (Parker), 3:355,
    3:387
Pendleton
  Ann, 3:388
  Eleanor (----), 3:388
  Elizabeth
    (Landfear/etc), 3:50
  Hannah (Goodenow),
    2:271, 3:388
  Mary, 2:173, 3:388, 3:590
  Mary (----), 3:388
Penewell/Pennywell
  Mary (Booth), 1:212,
    3:391
  Phebe (Newmarch), 3:276
Penfield
  Mary, 3:388
  Mary (Lewis), 3:87, 3:388
  Sarah, 3:388
Penhallow
  Ann (Wendell), 3:388
  Elizabeth, 3:389
  Mary (Cutt), 1:495, 3:388
  Susanna, 3:389
Penington
  Mary, 3:389, 4:695
  Mary (Brockett), 1:258,
    3:389-390
Penley
  Dorcas, 3:389
  Jane, 3:389
  Mary, 3:389
  Rachel (----), 3:389
Penn
  Catharine (----), 3:389
  Christian, 2:95, 3:389
  Elizabeth (Hammond),
    2:345
  Hannah, 3:389, 4:319
  Mary, 3:389
Pennell
  Mary, 2:409
  Mary (Booth), 3:389
Penniman
  Abigail, 3:265, 3:389
  Deborah, 3:390

Penniman (continued)
Elizabeth, 3:390
Elizabeth (Parmenter),
3:390
Hannah, 2:335, 3:389-390
Hannah (Billings), 1:178,
3:390
Lydia, 3:389
Lydia (----), 3:389
Lydia (Eliot), 4:543
Mary, 3:335, 3:389-390
Mary (Cross), 3:389
Sarah, 3:389
Sarah (Bass) Stone, 1:135,
3:390
Sarah (Marshall), 3:158
Waiting (Robinson), 3:390,
3:555
Penny
Agnes, 3:627
Agnes (----) Clark, 3:609
Agnes (Clark), 3:390
Ann (----), 3:390
Joan, 3:13
Joan (----) Brabrook, 3:390
Sarah (Greenwich), 3:659
Penoyer/Pennyer
---- (----) Scofield, 3:390,
4:36
Rose (----), 2:41
Pentecost/Penticus
Joan (----) Larkin, 3:57
Joanna (----) Larkin, 3:391
Pepper
Ann, 3:391
Apphia, 3:391
Apphia (Freeman), 2:204,
3:391
Bethia, 3:391-392
Bethia (Fisher), 3:391
Elizabeth, 2:130,
3:391-392
Elizabeth (Johnson), 3:391
Elizabeth (Paine), 3:336,
3:391
Mary, 2:131, 3:391-392
Mary (----), 3:391, 4:46
Rebecca, 3:391
Sarah, 3:168, 3:392
Pepperell
Dorothy, 3:392
Elizabeth, 3:392-393,
4:144

Jane, 3:392
Jane (Eliot), 2:111, 2:210,
3:392
Joanna, 3:392
Margery, 3:392-393, 4:535
Margery (----) Bray, 1:239
Margery (Bray), 3:392
Mary, 1:437, 2:211, 3:392
Mary (Hirst), 2:428, 3:393
Meriam, 3:392
Sarah, 3:392
Percival/Passevil/etc
----, 3:126
Abigail (----), 3:393
Elizabeth, 3:393
Mary (Rainsford), 3:502
Percy
Jane (Stanwood), 3:393
Mary (----), 3:393
Perham/Perrum/Peram
Rebecca, 3:393
Sarah, 3:393
Perigo
Mary (Webb), 3:394
Periman
Elizabeth (----), 3:227
Perkins
----, 3:397, 4:19
---- (Hudson), 2:488
---- (Sleeper), 2:38
Abigail, 2:178, 3:394-396
Alice, 3:395
Ann, 3:394, 3:396
Ann (Hutchinson), 3:396
Bethia (Philbrick), 3:394,
3:408
Catharine, 1:97, 3:397
Catharine (Towne), 3:394
Charity (Leonard), 3:395
Deborah, 3:396
Deborah (----), 3:190
Deborah (Browning),
1:279, 3:396, 3:653
Dorothy, 3:398
Edna (Hazen), 2:395,
3:397
Elizabeth, 3:394-398,
3:503, 4:19
Elizabeth (----), 3:395
Elizabeth (----) Clark,
1:392
Elizabeth (Brenton), 1:242
Elizabeth (Butcher), 3:394

Elizabeth (Clark), 3:398
Elizabeth (Jaques), 2:538,
3:396
Elizabeth (Lovell), 3:123
Elizabeth (Sleeper), 3:394,
4:107
Elizabeth (Sparks), 3:395,
4:145
Elizabeth (Wootton), 3:397
Esther, 3:394
Esther (Frothingham),
3:394
Eunice, 3:395
Hannah, 3:394-397, 3:408
Hannah (----), 3:395-396
Hannah (Beamsley)
Bushnell, 1:148, 3:394
Hannah (Lothrop), 3:395
Hannah (West), 3:397
Hepzibah, 3:397
Jane, 3:394
Jemima, 3:397
Jerusha, 3:396
Judith, 1:273, 3:395, 3:397
Judith (----), 3:396-397
Leah (Cox), 1:467, 3:395
Lucy, 3:395
Lydia, 3:395-396, 4:415
Martha, 3:395-397
Martha (----), 3:395-396
Martha (Morgan), 3:396
Mary, 1:230, 1:365, 2:158,
3:394-398, 3:494
Mary (----), 3:394-396
Mary (Farris), 3:394
Mary (Philbrook), 3:395
Mehitable, 3:394
Mercy, 1:358, 3:394
Mercy (----), 3:394
Phebe, 3:397, 4:317
Phebe (Gould), 2:287,
3:397
Phillis, 2:118, 3:395
Priscilla, 2:285, 3:397
Rebecca, 2:167, 2:507,
3:395, 3:397-398
Rebecca (Thompson)
Thomas, 4:279
Remember, 3:396
Remember (Hewes), 3:396
Rhoda, 3:394
Sarah, 1:235, 1:382, 3:395,
3:397

Perkins (continued)
Sarah (----), 3:396, 4:12
Sarah (Denison), 3:397
Sarah (Wainwright), 3:395, 4:382
Sarah (Wallis), 3:397
Susanna, 1:319, 2:220, 3:394-395
Susanna (----), 3:395
Susanna (Hudson) Howlett, 3:394, 3:636-637
Perley
Abigail (Towne) Peabody, 3:375, 4:316
Dorothy (----), 3:398
Hannah, 3:398
Hepzibah, 3:398
Jane (----), 3:398
Lydia (Peabody), 3:375
Martha, 1:423, 3:398
Patience, 3:398
Ruth, 3:398
Ruth (Trumbull), 3:398
Sarah, 3:398, 4:438
Susanna (----), 3:398
Perriman
Frances, 1:50, 3:398
Rebecca, 2:144, 3:399
Perrin
Abigail (Carpenter), 1:338
Ann, 3:399, 3:518
Elizabeth, 3:399
Mary, 3:399
Mary (Gridley), 2:313
Mehitable, 3:399
Sarah (Walker), 3:399, 4:395
Susanna, 1:358
Susanna (----) Roberts, 3:399, 3:547
Perry
Abiah, 1:294, 3:401
Ann, 3:401
Ann (----), 3:401
Ann (Judson), 2:576
Bethia, 3:400
Bethia (Morse), 3:400
Damaris (----), 3:400
Deborah, 3:399
Elizabeth, 1:305, 2:351, 3:399-401
Elizabeth (----), 2:255, 3:399

Elizabeth (Burge), 1:302, 3:399
Elizabeth (Lobdell), 3:401
Esther, 3:400, 4:318
Esther (Hassell), 2:372, 3:400
Grace, 3:400
Grace (----) Nichols, 3:281, 3:400
Jaciel, 3:401
Jane (----), 3:399
Joanna, 3:400
Joanna (Mason), 3:166
Mary, 3:11, 3:400, 4:222
Mary (Bailey), 1:94
Mary (Freeman), 2:203, 3:399
Mary (Miller), 3:401
Mary (Tucker), 3:401, 4:338
Mehitable, 3:399, 3:401
Remembrance, 3:399
Sarah, 3:399-401
Sarah (Carpenter), 3:400
Sarah (Clary), 1:405, 3:400
Sarah (Stedman), 3:400-401, 4:178
Susanna (Whiston), 3:401
Person
Abigail, 3:401
Elizabeth (Wheelwright), 2:512, 4:503
Mary, 3:401
Rebecca, 3:401
Sarah, 3:401
Susanna, 3:401
Tabitha, 3:401
Tabitha (----), 3:401
Pester
Dorothy (----), 3:401
Peters
Ann, 3:402
Bethia (----), 3:659
Deliverance (Sheffield), 3:402
Elizabeth, 2:554, 3:401-402
Elizabeth (Farnham), 3:401
Elizabeth (Hilliard), 3:632, 3:659
Mary, 1:358, 3:401

Mercy, 3:401
Mercy (Beamsley) Wilborne, 1:148, 3:401, 4:546
Phebe (Frye), 3:402
Petersfield
Mary (Price), 2:81, 3:289
Peterson
Marah (----), 3:403
Mary (Soule), 3:403, 4:140
Sarah, 3:403
Pettee/Petty
Ann, 3:404
Ann (----), 3:326
Ann (Canning), 3:404
Hannah, 3:404
Mary, 3:404, 4:265
Pettes/Petit
Sarah (Scofield), 3:404, 4:36
Pettibone
Sarah, 3:403
Sarah (Egglestone), 3:403
Pettingell/Pettengell
Abigail, 3:403
Jemima (Cheney) French, 1:372, 3:403
Joanna, 3:403-404
Joanna (Ingersoll), 2:521, 3:403
Mary, 1:8, 3:403-404
Mary (----), 3:403
Sarah, 3:403-404
Sarah (Noyes), 3:298, 3:403
Sarah (Poor), 3:404
Peverly
---- (Walford), 3:404
Jane (Walford), 4:392
Pheese
Mary, 3:358
Phelps
---- (Tresler), 3:405, 4:329
Abigail, 1:47, 3:155, 3:405-408
Abigail (----), 3:405
Abigail (Stebbins), 3:408, 4:176
Ann, 3:407
Ann (Gaylord), 2:239, 3:405
Annis, 3:407
Bathsheba, 3:404

Phelps (continued)
Catharine, 3:405
Catharine (----), 3:405
Damaris, 3:406, 3:659
Deborah, 3:407-408
Dorothy, 3:405
Dorothy (Ingersoll), 2:520,
 3:405
Elinor, 1:359
Elizabeth, 1:108,
 3:404-408, 3:659, 4:702
Elizabeth (----), 3:407
Elizabeth (----) Copley,
 1:456, 3:406
Elizabeth (Adams), 1:15,
 3:404
Elizabeth (Putnam), 3:406
Elizabeth (Sharp), 3:404
Elizabeth (Taylor), 4:264
Esther, 3:406, 4:702
Esther (----), 3:13
Eunice, 3:407
Eunice (----), 3:407
Frances, 3:406
Frances (----) Clark Dewey,
 2:43, 3:405
Grace, 3:406-407
Grace (Martin), 3:406
Hannah, 3:405-407, 4:702
Hannah (----), 3:405
Hannah (Bassett), 3:405
Hannah (Newton), 3:406
Isabel, 3:296
Isabel (Wilson), 3:407,
 4:588
Jane (----) Butterfield,
 3:408
Jerusha, 3:659
Lois, 3:407, 3:659
Lydia, 3:406
Mabel, 4:702
Martha, 3:407
Mary, 1:114, 1:408,
 3:406-408, 3:659, 4:702
Mary (----) Salmon, 3:406,
 4:6
Mary (Case), 3:659
Mary (Collier), 1:433,
 3:406
Mary (Dover), 4:695
Mary (Griswold), 2:316,
 3:407
Mary (Jaggers), 3:405

Mary (Pinney), 3:404,
 3:439
Mary (Porter), 3:406
Mercy, 3:406, 3:408
Mindwell, 3:406
Phillury (Randall), 3:506,
 3:659
Ruth (Andrews), 3:404
Sarah, 3:149, 3:227,
 3:405-407, 3:659, 4:379
Sarah (Buckland), 1:285,
 3:406
Sarah (Case), 1:345, 3:406
Sarah (Chandler), 1:358,
 3:407
Sarah (Gaylord), 3:407
Sarah (Griswold), 2:316,
 3:407, 3:439
Sarah (Pinney), 3:407-408,
 3:439
Sarah (Pratt), 3:407, 3:471
Sarah (Winchell), 3:406
Philbird
Mary, 2:403
Philbrick/Philbrook
---- (French) White, 2:205
Ann (----), 3:408
Ann (Knapp), 3:34, 3:408
Ann (Roberts), 3:408,
 3:547
Bethia, 3:394, 3:408
Elizabeth, 1:365, 2:232,
 3:408-409, 3:548
Elizabeth (Barron), 1:126
Hannah, 3:408-409, 4:12,
 4:47, 4:394
Hannah (French) White,
 3:409, 4:511
Hannah (Perkins), 3:408
Martha, 1:347, 3:408-409
Mary, 3:395, 3:408-409
Mary (----), 3:409
Mehitable (---), 3:409
Sarah, 3:408
Phillips
---- (----) Cobb, 3:414
Abiah, 3:409
Abiel, 3:410
Abigail, 1:118, 2:92, 3:171,
 3:409-413, 4:403, 4:635
Abigail (Bromfield), 1:258
Alice, 3:413, 4:196
Ann, 3:240, 3:409,

3:414-415
Ann (----), 3:60, 3:409,
 3:416
Ann (----) White, 3:417,
 4:510
Ann (Foster), 2:584, 3:409
Ann (Hunt), 2:501, 3:415
Ann (Hunting), 3:410
Ann (Lynde) Greenwood,
 3:413
Ann (Torry), 3:413
Bethia, 3:415
Bethia (Bedell), 3:415
Bethia (Keedell), 3:2,
 3:415
Bridget, 3:415
Bridget (----), 3:413, 3:416
Bridget (----) Sanford, 4:14
Catharine, 3:412
Catharine (Anderson), 1:51,
 3:412
Christian (Barker), 1:502
Deborah, 4:130
Deborah (----), 3:417
Dorcas, 3:414
Elizabeth, 1:23, 1:184,
 2:131, 3:373, 3:409-411,
 3:413-417, 4:393
Elizabeth (----), 3:409-410,
 3:416-417
Elizabeth (----) Bill, 3:409
Elizabeth (----) Welden,
 3:410, 4:474
Elizabeth (Ames), 3:411
Elizabeth (Brock), 3:410
Elizabeth (Edson), 2:102,
 3:414
Experience, 3:413
Faith, 3:414
Faith (----), 3:412
Faith (----) Dotey, 3:412
Faith (Clark) Dotey, 1:403,
 2:62
Grace, 3:412
Grace (----) Holloway,
 3:412
Hannah, 3:240, 3:410-415,
 3:417, 4:509
Hannah (----), 3:413, 3:415
Hannah (Gillam), 2:255,
 3:414
Hannah (Salter), 3:413, 4:7
Joan (----), 3:417

Phillips (continued)
Joanna, 3:409
Joanna (----), 3:412
Joanna (Lynd) Everton, 3:411
Lydia, 3:415
Martha, 3:412, 3:417
Martha (Franklin), 3:417
Mary, 1:478, 2:223, 3:63, 3:255, 3:409-412, 3:414-416, 3:420
Mary (----), 3:411-412, 3:414, 3:416
Mary (Bennett), 3:415
Mary (Crandall), 1:471
Mary (Dwight), 2:85, 3:410
Mary (Emerson), 3:415
Mary (Faneuil), 3:414
Mary (Foster) Smith, 2:584
Mary (Grosse), 2:319
Mary (Hayman), 2:388, 3:413
Mary (Packard), 3:327, 3:414
Mary (Smith), 3:415
Mehitable, 3:411-412, 3:414
Patience, 3:415
Phebe, 2:252, 2:255, 3:416
Philippa (----), 3:414
Rachel (----), 3:414
Ruth, 3:413
Ruth (Burdick), 1:301
Sarah, 3:205, 3:411-417
Sarah (----), 3:329, 3:412, 3:415
Sarah (----) Mayfield, 3:415
Sarah (----) Minor, 3:412
Sarah (Appleton), 1:61, 3:414
Sarah (Cutler), 3:409
Sarah (Hallet), 3:410
Sarah (Holland), 1:163, 2:447, 3:413
Sarah (Smith), 3:409
Sarah (Stedman) Brackett Alcock Graves, 1:22, 1:229, 2:297, 3:413, 4:179
Sarah (Stiles) Bancroft, 4:195
Sarah (Thomas), 3:409

Susanna, 3:414
Susanna (----), 1:71
Susanna (----) Stanley, 3:116, 3:416, 4:164, 4:297
Philpot
Ann (----) Hunn, 2:499, 3:417
Phinney/Finney
Abigail (----) Coggin, 1:420, 3:417
Christian (----), 3:417
Elizabeth, 3:417
Elizabeth (Bayley), 3:417
Elizabeth (Warren), 3:417, 4:425
Hannah, 3:417
Mary, 3:417
Mary (Rogers), 3:417
Melatiah, 3:417
Mercy, 3:417
Phebe (Ripley), 3:418
Reliance, 3:417
Phippen/Phippenney/etc
Abigail, 3:418
Ann, 3:418-419, 4:502
Ann (Cromwell) Auger, 1:78, 1:476, 3:418
Damaris (----) Searle, 3:419
Dorcas, 3:419
Dorcas (Wood), 3:419
Elinor (----), 3:418
Elizabeth, 3:418-419
Elizabeth (----), 3:418
Hannah, 2:248, 3:418
Jane, 3:418
Joanna, 3:419
Judith, 2:392, 3:418-419
Mary, 3:418-419, 4:83
Mary (Lindall), 3:419
Mary (Standford), 3:419
Mehitable, 2:183, 3:418
Naomi, 2:492
Rachel, 3:419
Rachel (Guppy), 3:419
Rebecca, 3:418, 4:78, 4:373
Sarah, 2:378, 2:439, 3:418-419, 4:110, 4:668
Sarah (----), 2:492, 3:418
Sarah (Purchase), 3:418
Seaborn/Sibborn (Good-

win, etc), 3:419
Wilmot (----), 3:418
Phips/Phipps
---- (Hayes), 2:387
Ann, 3:420
Catharine (----), 3:420
Elizabeth, 3:420, 3:583
Elizabeth (----), 3:420
Elizabeth (Hutchinson), 2:510
Emma, 4:342
Margaret, 3:420
Mary, 3:420
Mary (Danforth), 1:277, 2:9, 3:420
Mary (Phillips), 3:420
Mary (Spencer) Hall, 4:18
Mary (Spencer) Hull, 2:493, 3:421, 4:148
Mehitable, 3:420
Pickard
Elizabeth (Bradstreet), 3:422
Elizabeth (Hale), 3:422
Jane (Crosby), 3:422
Mary, 3:378, 3:422
Sarah, 2:347
Picke
Abigail, 3:422
Mary (----), 3:422
Pickels/Pickles
Abigail, 3:422
Alice, 3:424
Alice (Hatch), 2:375, 3:424, 3:576
Lydia, 3:424
Mary, 1:490, 3:424
Mary (----), 3:422
Mercy, 1:490
Miriam (Turner), 3:424, 4:346
Pickeram
Esther (----), 3:422
Joan, 3:422
Pickering
Alice (Flint), 2:175, 3:423
Ann, 3:423
Elizabeth, 3:422-423
Elizabeth (----), 2:28, 3:422
Hannah, 3:423
Jane, 3:423
Jane (Cromwell), 1:476, 3:423

Pickering (continued)
Lydia, 3:423
Mary, 3:423, 3:444
Mary (----), 3:423
Mary (Stanyan), 3:423,
4:168
Mercy, 3:423
Sarah, 3:423
Sarah (----), 3:423
Picket
Abigail, 3:424
Abigail (Seymour), 3:424,
4:58
Comfort, 3:424
Elizabeth (----), 3:424
Elizabeth (Mulford)
Christophers, 1:383
Elizabeth (Stow), 3:423
Hannah, 3:424
Hannah (Wetherell), 3:423,
4:491
Margaret, 3:424
Margaret (----), 3:424
Martha, 3:189
Mary, 3:424, 4:59
Mary (Cross), 1:516, 3:424
Mary (Offitt), 3:305,
3:423-424
Mercy, 2:185, 3:424
Rebecca, 3:189, 3:424,
4:51
Rebecca (Keeler), 3:424
Ruth, 3:297, 3:424
Ruth (----), 2:415
Ruth (Brewster), 1:245,
2:415, 3:424
Sarah, 3:424, 3:645
Pickman - see also Pitman
---- (Hasket), 3:425
---- (Palfrey), 3:339
Abigail, 3:425
Abigail (Lindall), 3:425
Bethia, 3:425
Elizabeth, 3:425
Elizabeth (Eastwick),
3:425
Elizabeth (Hardy), 2:355,
3:424
Hannah, 4:703
Hannah (Weeks), 3:659,
4:453
Lydia, 3:425
Lydia (Palfrey), 3:425

Martha, 1:141, 3:424-425
Mary, 3:425, 3:633
Nicholas, 3:424-425
Rachel, 3:425
Sarah, 3:425
Susanna, 3:424-425
Tabitha, 2:155, 3:425
Tabitha (----), 3:425
Pickton
Ann (----), 3:425
Pickworth
Abigail, 3:425
Ann (----), 3:425
Elizabeth (----), 3:425
Hannah, 3:425-426
Mary, 3:426
Rachel, 3:425, 4:93
Ruth, 3:425, 3:652
Sarah, 3:425-426, 3:652
Sarah (Marston), 3:425
Pidcock/Pidcoke
Sarah (Richards), 3:426
Pidge - see Pigg
Pierce/Pearse/Pears/Peirse
----, 3:429, 4:252
---- (Cole), 1:429
---- (Howe), 2:473
---- (Stevens), 3:430
Abia, 3:430
Abia/Abigail, 3:659
Abigail, 2:442, 3:427,
3:430-431, 3:515
Abigail (Somers), 3:432
Abigail (Symonds), 3:430,
4:246
Abigail (Warren), 3:432
Alice, 3:426
Alice (Hart), 3:427
Ann, 3:427, 3:430
Ann (----), 3:426, 3:430,
3:432
Ann (----) Millerd, 3:427
Ann (Addington)
Maudsley, 3:179
Ann (Addington) Mosely,
3:430
Ann (Greenway), 2:310,
3:430
Ann (Huthwit), 2:513
Barbara, 3:429, 3:659
Catharine, 3:427
Deborah, 3:426, 3:429-430
Deborah (Converse), 1:444,

3:429
Dorothy (Pike), 3:429,
3:437
Elinor (----), 3:428
Elizabeth, 1:106, 2:599,
3:224, 3:427-432, 3:659,
4:535, 4:588
Elizabeth (----), 3:427-429,
3:431, 3:659
Elizabeth (----) Foster,
3:430
Elizabeth (----) Tufts,
3:431
Elizabeth (----) Whittemore
Foster, 2:584
Elizabeth (Kendall), 3:9
Elizabeth (Kendall)
Winship, 3:429, 4:597
Esther, 3:240, 3:426,
3:428
Esther (----), 3:432
Esther (Spencer), 3:432
Exercise, 2:549, 3:428
Grace, 3:426
Grace (Tucker), 3:427,
4:339
Hannah, 3:103, 3:426-429,
3:431
Hannah (----), 3:426
Hannah (Baker), 1:95
Hannah (Brooks), 1:261,
3:426
Hannah (Convers), 1:515,
3:430
Hannah (Holbrook), 2:442,
3:427
Hannah (Johnson), 2:555
Hannah (Munroe), 3:257
Hannah (Wilson), 3:429
Isabel (----), 3:429
Jael, 3:429
Jane (----) Stanwood,
4:168
Jane (Stanwood), 3:428
Jerusha, 3:426
Joanna, 3:427
Joanna (----), 3:427
Judith, 3:426, 3:429, 3:431,
3:659, 4:29, 4:664
Lydia, 3:426, 3:429, 3:431
Lydia (Bacon), 3:431
Lydia (Morgan), 3:233,
3:429

Pierce/Pearse/Pears/Peirse
(continued)
Martha, 3:299, 3:426-427,
3:429, 3:432
Martha (----), 3:429
Martha (Adams), 1:11,
3:426
Martha (Brayton), 1:240
Mary, 2:406, 3:426-432,
3:517, 4:144, 4:324,
4:341, 4:394
Mary (----), 2:487, 3:426,
3:430-431, 3:659
Mary (Budlong), 1:288
Mary (Giddings), 2:249
Mary (Knight), 3:37
Mary (Proctor), 3:431-432
Mary (Ratchell), 3:429, ⸱
3:508
Mary (Richardson), 3:429
Mary (Warren), 4:424
Mary (Woodhouse), 3:427,
4:640
Mehitable, 3:428, 3:561
Mercy, 3:428, 3:651,
4:324
Parnell (----), 3:428
Patience (Dodson), 2:58,
3:429
Persis, 2:234, 3:426,
3:430-431, 4:75, 4:675,
4:686, 4:695
Phebe (----) Nash, 3:261,
3:429
Rachel, 3:659
Rebecca, 3:426, 3:428
Rebecca (----), 3:426
Rebecca (----) Wheeler,
3:428, 4:500
Rebecca (Budlong), 1:288
Ruth, 3:32, 3:428-430
Ruth (Bishop), 1:185,
3:428-429
Ruth (Holland), 2:447
Sarah, 2:444, 3:225, 3:367,
3:426-427, 3:431-432
Sarah (----), 3:426-427
Sarah (Colbron), 3:432
Sarah (Colburn), 1:424
Sarah (Cotton), 1:464,
3:430
Sarah (Eyre), 3:431
Sarah (Keen/Kean), 3:3

Susanna, 1:279, 3:427,
3:430
Tabitha, 3:426, 3:431
Tabitha (----), 3:431
Pierpont
Abigail, 3:432
Abigail (Davenport), 2:13,
3:432
Elizabeth, 1:91, 3:433
Elizabeth (Angier), 1:58,
3:433
Experience, 3:433
Margaret, 3:433
Margaret (----), 3:432
Mary, 3:432-433, 4:695
Mary (----), 3:235
Mary (Hooker), 2:459,
3:432
Mary (Ruggles), 3:432
Sarah, 3:433, 4:695
Sarah (Haynes), 2:390,
3:432
Sarah (Lynde), 3:136,
3:433
Thankful, 3:432-433
Thankful (Stow), 3:432,
4:217
Pierson - see also Pearson
Abigail, 2:13, 3:433-434
Abigail (Clark), 3:609
Alice (----), 3:434
Elizabeth, 3:434
Grace, 3:433-434
Hannah, 3:434
Martha, 3:434
Mary, 3:434-435, 3:536
Mary (Harrison), 3:434
Mary (Taintor/Tainter),
4:248
Mary (Tomlinson), 4:310
Rebecca, 3:433-434
Ruth, 3:434
Sarah, 3:434
Susanna, 1:159, 3:433-434
Ursula (----), 3:434
Pigg/Pidge
Alice, 2:544, 3:435
Hannah, 3:435
Margaret (----), 3:435,
4:274
Martha, 1:294, 3:435
Martha (----), 3:203
Mary, 3:435

Mary (----), 3:435
Sarah, 3:435
Pike
Abigail, 3:436
Ann, 3:436
Dorothy, 2:403, 3:429,
3:435-437
Elizabeth, 1:339,
3:436-437
Hannah, 3:436, 3:599
Israel, 3:436, 4:334
Jessie, 3:436
Joanna, 3:436
Judith, 3:436
Lydia, 3:436
Lydia (Coffin) Little, 3:436
Margaret, 3:436
Martha (Goldwyer), 2:270,
3:437
Mary, 3:436, 4:653
Mary (----), 3:436
Naomi, 3:435
Naomi (----), 3:435
Nicholas (Pickman), 3:425
Prudence (Edmaster),
2:581
Rachel, 3:435
Ruth, 3:436, 4:254
Sarah, 1:230, 3:436-437,
4:199
Sarah (----), 3:435
Sarah (Brown), 3:435
Sarah (Moody), 3:226,
3:436
Sarah (Sanders), 3:436
Sarah (Saunders), 4:20
Susanna, 3:436
Susanna (----), 3:436
Susanna (Kingsbury), 3:28,
3:436
Pilgrim
---- (Gardner), 2:227
Pilkington
Elizabeth, 2:527
Pilsbury
Apphia, 3:437
Catharine (Gavett), 3:437
Deborah, 3:437
Dorothy, 3:437
Dorothy (Crosby), 3:437
Elizabeth, 3:437
Experience, 3:437
Hannah, 3:437

Pilsbury (continued)
  Judith, 3:437
  Lydia, 3:437
  Mary (----), 3:437
  Mary (Kenny), 3:437
  Susanna, 3:437
  Susanna (Whipple) Worth,
    3:437, 4:653
  Thankful, 3:437
Pinckney/Pinkney
  Abigail, 3:317
  Jane, 2:492
  Susanna (Welch)
    Edes/Eads/etc, 3:617
Pindar/Pinder/etc
  ---- (Wilson), 3:438, 4:589
  Ann, 3:438
  Catharine, 3:438
  Joanna, 3:438, 3:581
  Mary, 3:163, 3:438
  Mary (----), 3:438
Pingree/Pingrew/etc
  Abigail (Clement), 1:408,
    3:438
  Faith (Jewett), 2:598,
    3:438
  Lydia, 1:305
Pinion
  Abigail, 3:438
  Christiana, 3:438
  Elizabeth (----), 3:438
  Experience, 4:695
  Hannah, 3:438
  Mary, 3:438, 4:695
  Mary (Coffin), 4:696
  Mercy, 3:144
  Mercy (----), 4:695
  Ruth, 3:228, 3:438
Pinkham
  Deborah, 3:438
  Elizabeth, 3:438
  Elizabeth (Layton), 3:438
  Mary (Coffin), 2:228
  Rose, 3:438
  Rose (Otis), 3:325, 3:438
  Sarah, 3:438
Pinney
  Abigail, 1:12, 3:439
  Elizabeth, 3:439
  Elizabeth (Rand), 3:439,
    3:505, 4:704
  Hannah, 3:439
  Joice (Bissell), 1:187

Joice/Joyce (Bissell), 3:439
Mary, 1:9, 3:404, 3:439
Mary (Griswold) Phelps,
  2:590
Mary (Hull), 2:492, 3:439
Sarah, 3:407-408, 3:439
Sarah (Clark), 1:392,
  3:439
Sarah (Griswold) Phelps,
  3:407, 3:439
Pinson/Pinchin/Pincin
  Ann, 3:439
  Ann (Cooper), 1:454,
    3:439
  Elizabeth (White), 3:439,
    4:509
  Hannah, 3:439, 4:669
  Jane (Standlake), 3:439
  Sarah (Dexter), 2:579,
    3:439
  Sarah (Turner), 3:439
  Waitstill, 3:439
Piper
  Alice, 3:440
  Alice (Darby), 3:440
  Margaret, 2:309, 3:440
  Mary, 3:440
  Sarah, 3:440
  Sarah (----), 3:439-440
Pirne/Perne
  Rachel, 3:511
Pitcher
  Experience, 1:289, 3:440
  Frances, 1:490
  Margaret (----), 3:440
  Mary, 3:440
  Mary (Blake), 1:192
  Mary (Clap), 3:440
  Nazareth, 1:490
  Ruth, 3:440
Pitkin
  Abigail, 3:440
  Ann, 3:440
  Deborah, 3:440
  Dorothy, 3:440
  Elizabeth, 3:440-441,
    4:696
  Elizabeth (Green), 3:440
  Elizabeth (Stanley), 3:441,
    4:163
  Elizabeth (Whiting), 3:440
  Esther, 3:440
  Esther (Cadwell), 3:440

Esther (Hosmer), 3:440
Hannah, 3:440-441
Hannah (Goodwin), 2:278,
  3:441
Hannah (Stanley), 3:440,
  4:164
Jerusha, 3:441
Mabel, 3:440-441
Martha, 1:392, 3:440-441,
  4:623
Mary, 3:440, 4:587, 4:634
Rachel, 3:440
Ruth, 3:440
Sarah, 3:441
Pitman - see also Pickman
  Abigail, 4:558
  Barbara (Evans), 3:441
  Bethia, 4:98
  Elizabeth, 1:513
  Elizabeth (----), 1:316
  Hannah (Ward), 4:410
  Mary, 3:325, 3:441
  Tabitha (----) Dix, 2:53
  Temperance (Welles),
    3:441
Pitney
  Abigail, 3:442
  Margaret, 3:442
  Sarah, 3:442, 4:280
  Sarah (----), 3:442
Pittee/Pitty/Pittey
  Mary, 1:10, 3:442
  Mary (----), 3:442
  Sarah, 3:442
  Sarah (----), 3:442
Pitts/Pitt
  Ann, 2:92, 2:572
  Deborah, 2:471, 3:442
  Elizabeth, 1:81, 2:566,
    3:442
  Elizabeth (Bowdoin),
    1:221
  Mary, 1:293, 3:442
  Mary (Andrews)
    Hodges/Hedges, 3:443
  Sarah, 2:450
  Sarah (Bobbit), 1:207,
    3:443
  Susanna (----) Alley, 1:39,
    3:443, 3:646
Pittums/Pittoms
  Elizabeth, 3:443
  Mary, 3:443

Pittums/Pittoms (continued)
Mary (----), 3:443
Pixley
Abigail, 3:443
Abigail (Clark), 1:395,
3:443
Lydia (Dibble), 2:46, 3:443
Mary, 3:443
Mary (Strong), 3:443
Sarah, 3:72, 3:443
Sarah (Lawrence), 3:443
Place/Plaise
Alice (----), 3:443
Dinah, 3:443
Elizabeth, 3:443
Hannah, 3:443
Margaret (Stafford), 4:160
Sarah, 3:443
Sarah (----), 3:443
Plaisted/Playstead
Hannah (----), 3:444
Mary, 3:444
Mary (Jose), 2:570, 3:444
Mary (Pickering), 3:423,
3:444
Olive (----), 3:444
Platt
Abigail, 3:444
Elizabeth, 3:444
Elizabeth (Johnson), 3:444
Elizabeth (Marvin), 3:165,
3:444
Hannah, 1:439, 3:444-445
Hannah (Clark), 3:444,
3:609
Hannah (Hanford), 2:350,
3:444
Hannah (Marvin), 3:165
Lydia (Bayley), 1:142
Mary, 1:74, 3:445, 4:528
Mary (----), 3:445
Mary (Kellogg), 3:4, 3:444
Rebecca, 3:445
Rebecca (Benedict), 3:445
Sarah, 1:144, 3:6,
3:444-445
Sarah (----), 3:444
Sarah (Campfield), 4:677
Sarah (Lockwood), 3:104,
3:444
Platts
Elizabeth, 1:258
Mary, 3:480

Sarah, 1:378
Plum/Plumb/Plumbe
Dorcas, 3:134, 3:445
Dorothy, 3:446
Elizabeth, 3:445-446
Elizabeth (Norton), 3:445
Mary, 3:445-446, 4:643
Mary (----), 2:92
Mary (Baldwin), 1:105,
3:446
Mercy, 3:445
Ruth (Clark), 3:609
Sarah, 3:5, 3:445
Plumer
Elizabeth, 2:526
Plumly
Esther (----), 3:446
Plummer
Abigail, 2:517, 3:447
Ann, 4:10
Ann (----) Palmer, 3:446
Bathshua, 3:447
Beatrice (----) Canterbury,
1:333
Beatrice (----) Cantlebury,
3:446
Deborah, 2:539, 3:447
Eleanor, 3:447
Elizabeth, 3:446-447
Elizabeth (Dole), 3:447
Emma, 3:446
Hannah, 3:231, 3:446-447
Hannah (Jaques), 2:538,
3:446
Hannah (Swett), 3:447
Joanna (Woodbury), 3:447,
4:636
Lydia, 3:447
Mary, 1:121, 1:372,
3:446-447, 4:240
Mary (----), 3:447
Mary (Bidfield/Bedfield),
1:175
Mary (Elithorp), 3:446
Mary (Wood), 3:446
Miriam, 3:447
Ruth, 2:539, 3:446-447
Ruth (----), 3:446
Sarah, 3:446-447
Sarah (Cheney), 3:446
Sarah (Moody), 3:447
Sarah (Pearson), 3:446

Plympton/Plimpton
Abigail, 3:448
Abigail (Noyes), 3:298,
3:448
Abigail (Thompson), 3:448
Dorothy, 3:448
Elizabeth, 3:103, 3:298,
3:448
Elizabeth (----) Rutter,
3:595
Elizabeth (Fisher), 3:448,
3:619
Hannah, 3:447-448, 4:708
Jane, 3:447-448
Jane (----), 3:638
Jane (Dummer),
3:447-448
Mary, 2:556, 3:447-448,
3:632
Mary (Morse), 3:448
Mary (Munden), 3:448,
3:654
Mehitable, 3:447-448
Rhoda, 3:447
Sarah, 3:448
Sarah (Turner), 3:448
Pole - see Pool
Pollard
Ann, 3:449, 3:549, 4:195
Ann (----), 3:449
Barbara, 3:449
Deliverance (----), 3:448
Elizabeth, 2:333-334,
3:449
Hannah, 3:448-449
Margaret (----), 3:450
Mary, 3:449
Mary (----), 3:449
Mary (Leonard), 3:80,
3:449
Mary (Taintor), 4:249
Mary (Winslow), 3:449
Sarah, 3:449
Sarah (Farmer), 2:141,
3:449
Sarah (Jones), 2:566
Pollen/Poland
Bethia (----), 3:660
Polley/Polly
Abigail, 3:137, 3:450
Abigail (----) Sharswood,
4:61
Bethia, 3:450

Polley/Polly (continued)
Elizabeth, 1:272, 3:450
Elizabeth (Winn), 3:450,
4:596
Hannah, 1:97, 1:485,
3:450
Hannah (----), 3:450
Jane (Walter), 3:450
Joanna, 3:450
Mary, 3:450
Mary (----), 3:450
Mary (Knight), 3:450
Mercy, 3:450
Miriam, 3:450
Priscilla, 3:450
Priscilla (----), 3:450
Rebecca, 3:450
Sarah, 3:450
Susanna, 3:450, 4:458
Susanna (----), 3:450
Susanna (Ives), 2:525
Pomeroy/Pomroy/Pummery
Abigail, 3:450-451
Abigail (----), 2:480
Abigail (Cook), 1:449,
3:451
Abigail (Strong) Chauncy,
1:369, 3:452, 4:227
Elizabeth, 3:451, 3:660
Elizabeth (French), 2:206
Elizabeth (Lyman), 3:134,
3:451
Esther (----), 3:451
Experience (Woodward),
3:451, 4:644
Hannah, 1:500, 3:450-451
Hannah (----) Noble, 3:452
Hannah (Lyman), 3:134,
3:451
Hannah (Warriner) Noble,
3:286
Hepzibah, 3:450
Hepzibah (----), 3:74
Hepzibah (Baker), 3:450
Lydia, 3:451
Lydia (----) Parsons, 3:451
Lydia (Brown) Parsons),
3:364
Mary, 3:450-451, 3:660
Mary (----), 3:450
Mary (Cowes), 3:660
Mehitable, 3:25, 3:451
Mercy, 3:450

Mindwell, 3:25, 3:451
Mindwell (Sheldon), 3:134,
4:69
Rachel, 3:660
Rebecca (Brooking), 1:259,
3:452
Repent (----), 3:451
Sarah, 3:450-451
Sarah (King), 3:25
Susanna, 3:660
Susanna (Cunliff), 1:484,
3:451
Thankful, 3:451
Pomfret
----, 3:452, 4:517
Martha, 2:4, 3:452
Pond
---- (----), 3:453
Abigail, 1:389, 2:26, 3:452
Abigail (Shepard), 3:452,
4:71
Ann, 3:453
Ann (----), 3:452
Deborah, 3:452
Deborah (Hawes), 3:452
Elizabeth, 3:453
Hannah, 3:452
Hannah (----), 3:452
Hannah (Griffin), 2:313,
3:452
Joanna (----), 3:453
Judith, 3:453
Martha, 3:453
Mary, 1:125, 1:190, 3:453
Mary (----), 2:404, 4:71
Mary (Ball), 1:34, 3:453
Mary (Dyer), 2:88, 3:453
Mindwell, 3:453
Miriam (Blatchley), 1:198,
3:453
Rachel, 3:452
Rachel (----), 3:452
Rebecca, 3:453
Sarah, 1:388, 2:481,
3:452-453
Sarah (----), 3:453
Thankful, 3:453, 4:619
Ponder
Elizabeth, 3:453
Lydia (Pomeroy), 3:451
Martha, 3:453
Mary, 3:453
Sarah, 3:453

Susanna, 3:453
Temperance (Buckland),
1:285, 3:453
Pontus
Hannah, 1:386, 3:454,
3:540
Mary, 2:34, 2:259, 3:454
Pool/Poole/Pole
----, 3:454
---- (----) Champney, 1:126
Abigail, 3:455
Abigail (Ballard), 3:455
Ann, 3:455
Bethesda, 2:158,
3:455-456
Deborah (Dodge), 3:455
Elishama (----), 3:454
Elizabeth, 1:282,
3:454-455, 4:144
Elizabeth (----), 3:455,
4:291
Elizabeth (Brenton), 1:242,
3:454
Elizabeth (Holmes), 3:455
Hannah, 3:455
Jane, 1:282, 3:454
Joanna, 3:455
Joanna (----), 3:455
Judah, 3:455
Margaret, 3:454-455
Margaret (----), 3:454
Mary, 2:103, 2:402, 3:322,
3:454-455
Mary (----), 3:455
Mary (Richmond), 3:455
Mercy (----), 3:455
Miriam, 3:455
Return, 3:455
Sarah, 1:111, 1:356,
3:454-455
Sarah (----) Woodbury,
3:455
Sarah (Solart), 4:706
Silence (Saxton), 3:455,
4:32
Susanna, 3:455
Poor/Poore
Abigail, 3:456-457
Abigail (Hale), 3:456
Alce, 3:456-457
Alice, 3:99, 3:456
Ann, 3:456
Ann (Johnson), 3:457

Poor/Poore (continued)
Bethia, 3:457
Catharine, 3:457
Deborah, 3:322, 3:456-457
Eleanor, 3:457
Elizabeth, 3:160,
3:456-457
Elizabeth (----), 3:456
Elizabeth (Burrage) Dean,
1:308, 2:31, 3:457
Esther, 4:528
Hannah, 2:6, 2:517,
3:456-457
Judith, 3:457
Lucy, 3:456
Lydia, 3:456-457, 4:307
Martha, 2:290, 2:329,
3:456
Mary, 1:397, 3:297, 3:379,
3:456-457, 4:192, 4:488,
4:528
Mary (----) Hardy, 3:456
Mary (Farnum), 2:143,
3:456
Mary (Titcomb), 3:457
Mary (Wellington), 3:457
Mehitable, 3:456
Mehitable (----), 3:456
Priscilla, 3:227, 3:456
Rachel (Bailey), 3:457
Rebecca, 3:457
Ruth, 3:456
Sarah, 3:404, 3:456-457,
4:30
Sarah (Brown), 1:270,
3:457
Silence, 3:457
Pope
Alice, 3:459
Alice (----), 3:457
Ann (Fallowell), 3:459
Bathshua, 3:458
Bathshua (Folger), 2:177,
3:458
Beatrice (----), 3:458
Damaris, 1:289, 3:458
Damaris (Shattuck), 3:457,
4:62
Elizabeth, 3:457, 3:459
Eunice, 3:459
Exercise (Smith), 3:458
Gertrude, 3:458
Gertrude (----), 3:458

Hannah, 1:289, 3:458-459
Jane, 3:458
Jane (----), 3:457-458
Jerusha, 3:458
Margaret, 3:458
Margaret (----), 3:458-459
Margaret (Long), 3:459
Mary, 3:210, 3:458
Mindwell, 3:459
Patience, 1:192, 3:458
Ruth, 3:459
Sarah, 2:425, 3:458
Sarah (Jenny), 2:546,
3:459
Susanna, 2:546, 3:220,
3:459
Pore
Elizabeth (Lane), 3:52
Portage/Pordage
Elizabeth, 3:459
Elizabeth (Lynde), 3:136,
3:459
Hannah, 1:221, 3:459
Judith, 3:459
Porter
----, 1:376, 2:358, 3:462
---- (----), 4:696, 4:703
Abigail, 3:462, 3:464
Abigail (----), 2:442
Abigail (Cowles), 3:464
Abigail (Williams), 3:460
Ann, 1:272, 2:239, 2:239,
3:459-462, 3:660, 4:696
Ann (----) Simmons, 3:459,
4:100
Ann (Hathorne), 2:377,
3:462
Bathshua (Reed), 3:520
Deborah, 3:460
Deborah (----), 3:460
Deliverance (----), 3:461
Dorothy, 3:464, 3:660
Elizabeth, 1:56, 2:553,
3:262, 3:460, 3:462-464,
3:496, 3:660
Elizabeth (----), 3:460
Elizabeth (Baldwin), 1:102
Elizabeth (Groves), 2:321,
3:462
Elizabeth (Hathorne),
2:377, 3:460
Elizabeth (Pitkin), 4:696
Elizabeth (Rising), 3:463

Esther, 3:461, 3:660
Esther (Dickinson) Smith,
4:127
Eunice (----), 3:462, 4:114
Gingen, 3:460
Grace (----) Rogers, 3:463
Grace (----) Rogers Palmer,
3:343
Hannah, 2:51, 2:321,
3:114, 3:261, 3:460-463,
3:660, 4:545, 4:679
Hannah (----) Freeman,
2:204, 3:462
Hannah (Buel), 3:462
Hannah (Dodge), 2:57,
3:463, 4:636
Hannah (Groves), 3:462
Hannah (Lum), 3:462
Hannah (Stanley), 3:463,
4:165
Hepzibah, 3:462
Joan, 3:214, 3:463
Joanna, 3:461-462, 3:464,
3:660, 4:264
Joanna (Cook), 3:463
Joanna (Gaylord), 2:238,
3:461
Lois, 3:460, 3:464, 3:660
Lois (Stanley), 3:464,
4:165
Lydia, 3:462, 3:660
Lydia (----), 3:660
Margaret (----), 3:461
Martha, 3:463, 3:656,
3:660
Martha (----) North, 3:660
Martha (Freeman), 3:660
Martha (Porter) North,
3:656, 3:660
Mary, 1:168, 2:231, 2:292,
3:112, 3:406, 3:459-464,
3:645-646, 3:660-661,
4:681
Mary (----), 3:459, 3:461
Mary (Bissell), 3:460
Mary (Scott), 3:462, 4:39
Mary (Stanley), 3:461,
4:165
Mehitable, 2:277,
3:462-463, 3:660
Mindwell, 3:25
Rachel, 3:660
Rebecca, 3:114, 3:460-461,

Porter (continued)
  Rebecca (continued)
    3:660
  Rebecca (----), 3:661
  Rebecca (Woodford),
    3:461, 4:638
  Rose, 3:460, 3:463
  Rose (----), 3:460
  Ruth, 2:321, 3:113,
    3:461-464, 3:573, 3:660,
    4:133
  Ruth (----), 3:462
  Sally, 3:660
  Sarah, 1:52, 2:69, 2:321,
    2:576, 3:460-464, 4:591
  Sarah (Burt), 1:313, 3:463
  Sarah (Hart), 2:368, 3:464
  Sarah (Tudor), 3:460,
    4:341
  Susan, 3:463
  Susanna, 3:461
  Susanna (Sewall), 4:56
  Thankful (----), 3:661
Portis
  Hannah, 4:457
Portland
  Dorothy, 3:582
Portman
  Mehitable (Waite), 4:383
Portmort/Pormort/Purmont
  Ann, 3:464
  Elizabeth, 1:14, 3:288,
    3:465
  Elizabeth (----), 3:465
  Martha, 3:465
  Pedaiah, 3:464
  Susan (----), 3:464
Post
  Abigail, 3:465
  Ann, 3:465
  Catharine, 1:352, 3:465
  Elinor, 3:465
  Elizabeth, 3:465
  Esther, 3:465
  Esther (Hyde), 2:516,
    3:465
  Hannah, 3:465
  Hannah (Hosmer), 2:467
  Joanna, 3:465
  Lydia, 3:465
  Margaret, 1:6, 3:465
  Mary, 3:465, 3:585
  Mary (----), 1:249

  Mary (Andrews), 3:465
  Mary (Tyler), 3:465
  Rebecca (Bruen), 1:281,
    3:465
  Sarah, 2:468, 3:465
  Sarah (Reynolds), 3:465,
    3:525
  Susanna (Sutton), 3:465
Potter
  ----, 3:41
  Abigail, 3:466
  Alice (----), 3:467
  Ann, 1:500, 3:265, 3:466
  Ann (Collins), 1:434
  Bethia, 3:466-467
  Content, 3:466
  Deliverance, 2:301, 3:467
  Dorothy, 3:466
  Dorothy (----), 1:20, 3:467
  Elizabeth, 2:353, 2:565,
    3:274, 3:466-467, 3:661
  Elizabeth (----), 3:350,
    3:466
  Elizabeth (Hawes), 4:696
  Elizabeth (Rose), 3:466
  Elizabeth (Stone), 4:204
  Elizabeth (Whipple), 3:466,
    4:505
  Eunice, 2:214, 3:466
  Frances, 3:466
  Frances (----), 3:468
  Grace (Brooks), 1:261
  Hannah, 1:189, 3:466-467,
    3:661-662, 4:15, 4:675,
    4:696
  Hannah (----), 1:153, 3:468
  Hannah (Cooper), 1:454,
    3:466
  Hannah (Russell), 3:595,
    4:696
  Hope, 3:468, 4:696, 4:698
  Isabel, 1:316, 3:466
  Isabel (----), 3:467
  Judith, 1:500
  Judith (----), 2:160
  Judith (----) Graves, 3:468
  Judith (Alward) Graves,
    2:295
  Lydia, 3:466-467, 3:496
  Margaret, 3:466
  Martha, 3:468
  Martha (Hall), 3:468
  Martha (Hazard), 2:395,

    3:466
  Mary, 1:223, 3:466-468,
    3:556
  Mary (----), 3:466
  Mary (----) Russell, 3:466
  Mary (Edmands), 2:102,
    3:466
  Mary (Gedney), 3:467
  Mary (Hitchcock) Russell,
    4:699
  Mary (Lawrence), 3:61,
    3:466
  Mercy (Robinson), 3:553
  Phebe (----), 4:696, 4:698
  Rachel (Warner), 3:466,
    4:420
  Rebecca, 1:16, 1:92, 3:466,
    3:468, 4:696
  Ruth, 3:466-467
  Ruth (Driver), 3:467
  Ruth (Fisher), 2:163,
    3:466
  Sarah, 3:467-468, 4:30
  Sarah (----), 3:467, 4:14
  Sarah (Wilson), 4:588
  Susanna, 3:468
  Susanna (Tripp), 3:468,
    4:331
Potts
  Joanna (----), 3:468
  Mary, 3:468
Poulter
  Elizabeth, 2:7, 3:469
  Hannah, 2:75, 3:469
  Hannah (Hammond),
    2:345, 3:469
  Mary, 3:469, 4:598
  Rachel (Eliot), 2:109,
    3:468, 3:527
Powell
  Abigail (----), 3:469
  Alce (Traharen), 3:470
  Ann, 3:470
  Ann (Dummer), 2:79
  Dorothy, 3:469
  Eliz, 1:282
  Elizabeth, 1:282, 2:448,
    3:469-470
  Elizabeth (----), 3:469-470
  Esther, 3:469
  Hannah, 3:469-470, 4:352
  Isabel (----), 3:469
  Margaret, 3:469

Powell (continued)
  Martha, 3:469-470
  Martha (Clement), 3:469
  Martha (Deane) Clement,
    1:175, 1:407
  Mary, 3:469-470, 4:14,
    4:655, 4:696
  Mary (Bromfield), 1:259
  Priscilla, 3:469, 4:286
  Priscilla (----), 3:470
  Sarah, 2:86, 3:469
  Sarah (----), 1:197, 3:469
  Sarah (Bromfield), 1:259
Power
  Hope, 1:394, 3:470
  Jane (----), 3:470
  Mary, 3:471
  Mercy (Tillinghast), 4:303
  Rebecca (Rhodes), 3:470,
    3:527, 4:559
  Sarah, 3:471
  Sarah (----), 3:470
  Trial (Shepard), 3:470,
    4:75
Powers
  Mary (Poulter) Winship,
    4:598
Powning/Pounding
  Hannah, 3:471
  Sarah, 3:471
Powsland/Powsley/etc
  Mary (----) Barnes, 3:471
Pratt
  ----, 3:473
  ---- (Cuthbertson), 1:492,
    3:475
  ---- (Sumner), 4:232
  Abial, 1:175, 3:475
  Abigail, 3:471, 3:473
  Abigail (Wood), 3:473
  Ann, 3:474
  Ann (----), 3:473
  Ann (Williams) Barker,
    4:561
  Bathsheba, 3:473
  Bathsheba (----), 2:2, 3:474
  Bethia, 3:473-474
  Deborah, 3:474, 3:476
  Deborah (Cooper), 3:476
  Deliverance, 3:473
  Dorcas, 3:474
  Dorcas (Folger), 2:177,
    3:474

Elizabeth, 1:89, 1:178,
    1:364, 2:43, 2:277,
    2:380, 3:471-472,
    3:474-476
  Elizabeth (----), 3:471-472,
    4:70
  Elizabeth (Baker), 1:98,
    3:476
  Elizabeth (Clark), 1:394,
    3:476
  Elizabeth (Griswold)
    Rogers, 1:152, 2:317,
    3:474, 3:563
  Esther, 3:471
  Experience, 3:474-475
  Experience (----), 3:476
  Grace (Shippey), 3:476,
    4:705
  Hannah, 1:392, 2:470,
    3:471-476, 4:147, 4:152,
    4:707
  Hannah (Boosy), 1:211,
    3:472
  Hannah (Kirtland), 3:32,
    3:476
  Hannah (Rogers), 3:475,
    3:561
  Hepzibah (----), 3:473, 4:3
  Joanna, 3:476
  Joanna (----), 3:471
  Judah, 3:475
  Judith, 3:475
  Lydia, 3:31, 3:473-474,
    3:476
  Lydia (Parmenter), 3:360
  Margaret, 3:474
  Margaret (Maverick),
    3:473
  Martha, 3:473, 3:475
  Martha (----), 3:473
  Martha (Pratt), 3:473,
    3:475
  Mary, 3:471, 3:473-476,
    4:105, 4:126, 4:236,
    4:515, 4:523, 4:537,
    4:653
  Mary (----), 3:472-473,
    3:475-476
  Mary (Andrews), 3:473
  Mary (Flagg), 2:171
  Mary (Pitkin), 3:440
  Mary (Whitman),
    3:472-473, 4:523

Mehitable, 3:473, 4:65
  Meleltiah, 3:473
  Mercy, 3:473, 3:475
  Mercy (----), 3:473
  Patience (----), 3:475
  Persis (Dunham), 2:81,
    3:471, 4:65
  Phebe (----), 3:471
  Priscilla, 3:473
  Prudence, 3:476
  Rachel, 3:471
  Rebecca, 3:476
  Rebecca (----), 3:473
  Ruth, 3:472
  Ruth (Huntington), 2:503
  Ruth (Warner), 4:418
  Sarah, 3:407, 3:471-476,
    4:431, 4:661
  Sarah (----), 3:473-475
  Sarah (Beament), 3:474
  Sarah (Chapman), 1:362,
    3:474
  Sarah (Jones), 2:566,
    3:473
  Susanna, 3:473-474
  Susanna (----), 3:475
  Temperance, 3:474
  Thankful, 3:476
Pray
  ---- (----) Herendean, 3:476
  Dorothy, 3:476, 4:277
  Elizabeth, 3:476
  Elizabeth (Hayden), 2:386,
    3:476
  Hannah, 3:264, 3:476
  Joanna (Dowman), 3:476
  Mary, 3:476
  Ruth, 3:476
  Sarah, 3:476
Preble
  Hannah (----), 3:477
  Hannah (Kelly), 3:477
  Judith (Tilden), 3:477,
    4:301
  Mary, 3:477
Prence
  Elizabeth, 3:477
  Hannah, 3:188, 3:477,
    4:145
  Jane, 3:477, 4:138
  Judith, 1:115, 3:477
  Mary, 3:477, 4:320
  Mary (----) Freeman, 3:477

Prence (continued)
Mary (Collier), 1:433,
3:477
Mary (Collier) Freeman,
2:204
Mercy, 2:204, 3:477
Patience (Brewster), 1:246,
3:477
Rebecca, 2:203, 3:477
Sarah, 3:477
Susanna, 3:477
Susanna (----), 3:477
Prentall
---- (Pedrick), 3:385
Prentice
----, 3:480, 4:166
---- (Nichols), 3:279
Abiah, 3:478
Abigail, 3:480
Abigail (Walker), 3:480
Alice, 3:480
Alice (----), 3:480, 4:437
Ann, 3:479
Bethia, 3:479
Bethia (----), 3:479
Elizabeth, 1:25, 3:478-479
Elizabeth (----), 3:478-480
Elizabeth (Bartlett), 1:131,
3:478
Elizabeth (Jackson), 1:209,
2:528, 3:479
Elizabeth (Latimer), 3:59,
3:479
Esther, 2:222, 3:478,
3:480
Esther (----), 3:478
Esther (Hammond), 3:479
Experience, 3:479
Frances, 3:479
Grace, 3:311, 3:479-480
Grace (----), 3:479
Hannah, 2:550, 3:478-479
Hannah (Chesebrough),
1:373
Hannah (Osland), 3:323,
3:479
Hepzibah (----), 3:479
Irene, 3:479
Joanna (----), 2:248, 3:478
Lydia (----), 3:478
Mary, 2:349, 3:478-479
Mercy, 3:478
Patience, 3:479-480

Praise, 3:479
Rebecca, 3:479-480
Rebecca (Jackson), 2:528,
3:479
Rebecca (Parker), 3:355,
3:478
Rose, 3:478
Sarah, 3:478-479, 4:123
Sarah (Jones), 2:564,
3:479
Sarah (Osland), 3:323,
3:478
Sarah (Stanton), 2:38,
3:480, 4:167
Susanna, 2:550, 3:478
Susanna (Johnson), 2:550,
3:478
Presbury
Catharine (----), 1:351
Mary, 2:385
Prescott
Abigail, 3:480-481
Abigail (----) Sanborn,
3:480
Abigail (Marston), 3:160,
3:481
Ann (Marston), 3:160,
3:482
Dorothy, 3:481
Dorothy (----), 3:481
Elizabeth, 3:481
Elizabeth (----), 3:481
Elizabeth (Hoar), 3:481
Elizabeth (Redington),
3:482
Lucy, 3:480
Lydia, 2:136, 3:481
Martha, 3:481, 3:585
Mary, 3:206, 3:480-482,
4:31
Mary (Boulter), 3:480
Mary (Haynes) Howe,
2:476
Mary (Looker), 3:111,
3:481
Mary (Marston), 3:161,
3:480
Mary (Pepperell) Frost
Colman, 1:437, 2:211,
3:392
Mary (Platts), 3:480
Rebecca, 3:480-481, 4:12
Rebecca (----) Bulkely,

3:481
Rebecca (Bulkley), 1:292,
3:481
Rebecca (Wheeler) Bulkley,
1:292
Ruth (Brown), 3:481
Sarah, 3:480-481, 4:499
Sarah (----), 3:481
Temperance, 3:480
Thankful (Wheeler), 3:481
Pressie
Mary, 3:482
Mary (Gage), 3:482
Presson
Elizabeth
(Voden/Voeden/etc),
4:376
Preston
---- (----), 2:455, 3:483
---- (Seabrook), 3:483, 4:43
Abigail, 3:482
Abigail (Jackson), 2:530,
3:482
Deliverance, 1:337, 3:482
Elizabeth, 1:45, 1:180,
3:482-483, 3:631, 4:688
Elizabeth (Beach), 1:504,
3:482
Elizabeth
(Voden/Voeden/etc),
4:376
Emma, 3:482
Emma (Fairchild), 2:137,
3:482
Hannah, 3:482
Lydia, 3:482
Margaret (----), 3:482
Martha, 3:483
Martha (Bradley) Munson,
3:257
Mary, 1:337, 2:149,
3:482-483, 3:638
Mary (----), 3:482-483,
4:685, 4:687, 4:696
Mary (Haynes), 2:390
Rebecca, 3:483
Rebecca (Nurse), 3:300,
3:483
Relief, 3:482
Remember, 3:482
Sarah, 3:482-483, 4:696
Sarah (----), 3:483
Sarah (Bridges), 3:483

Preston (continued)
Sarah (Gardner), 3:483
Susanna (----) Read, 3:482,
3:518
Susanna (Gutterson),
3:483
Pretious/Pretiose
Mary, 3:484
Rebecca (Martin), 3:484
Price
Abigail, 3:484
Ann, 2:517, 3:484-485
Ann (Wood), 1:235, 3:484
Elizabeth, 1:120, 1:473,
3:186, 3:484-485, 3:584,
4:54
Elizabeth (----), 3:484-485
Elizabeth (Cromwell),
1:476, 3:484
Elizabeth (Hirst), 2:428
Grace, 3:485
Grace (Waite), 3:484
Hannah, 3:484-485, 4:371
Hannah (Baxter) Luke,
1:503
Joyliffe, 3:484
Margaret, 3:484
Margaret (Child), 3:484
Mary, 2:81, 3:289,
3:484-485
Mary (Marplehead), 3:485
Mary (Rouse), 3:579
Mehitable, 3:484
Mindwell, 3:484
Sarah, 3:484-485
Sarah (----), 3:484
Sarah (Wolcott), 3:484,
4:621
Susanna, 2:314
Prichard/Pritchard
Abigail, 3:485
Alice, 1:234, 3:486
Ann (----), 3:485
Elinor (----), 3:485
Elizabeth, 1:33, 3:486
Elizabeth (----), 3:486
Elizabeth (Prudden)
Slough, 3:486, 4:108
Frances (----), 3:486
Hannah, 3:649, 4:266,
4:474
Hannah (----) Davis, 3:485
Hannah (Langton), 3:485

Joan, 3:486
Joanna, 3:106
Margery (----), 3:485
Phebe, 3:485
Rebecca (----), 3:486
Sarah, 3:122
Templer, 3:485
Pride
Elizabeth, 4:253
Prideaux
Bridget (Wilson), 4:584
Priest
---- Allerton, 1:498
Deliverance, 4:278
Elizabeth, 3:486, 3:585
Elizabeth (----), 3:486
Elizabeth (Gray), 3:486
Hannah, 3:486
Hannah (Hagar), 2:328
Leah (----), 3:486
Lydia, 3:486
Sarah (----), 1:492
Sarah (Allerton) Vincent,
3:486
Prime
Ann (----), 3:487
Rebecca, 3:487, 4:136
Sarah, 3:487
Sarah (----), 3:487
Prince
Ann, 2:517
Ann (----) Barstow, 1:129,
3:487
Deborah, 3:487
Elizabeth, 2:479, 3:118,
3:487, 3:496
Elizabeth (Harraden),
3:488
Honor, 3:649
Joanna (Morton), 3:244,
3:487
Margaret (----), 3:487-488
Martha, 3:487
Martha (Barstow), 1:129,
3:487-488
Martha (Merwin), 3:201
Mary, 2:572, 2:577,
3:487-488, 3:580
Mary (----), 3:487
Mary (Hinckley), 3:488
Mary (Turner), 3:487,
4:346
Mercy (Hinckley), 2:425

Rebecca, 3:496
Rebecca (----) Baldwin,
1:104
Rebecca (Phippen), 3:418
Ruth (Turner), 3:488
Sarah, 2:478, 3:487
Sarah (Rix), 3:487
Sarah (Warren), 3:487
Prindle
Elizabeth (Hobby), 2:437
Hannah, 2:494
Pringle
Hannah, 4:696
Joanna, 4:696
Mary, 3:488
Mary (Desbrough), 3:488
Phebe, 3:488
Sarah, 4:696
Pringrydays
Mary (Morgan), 3:488
Prior
Ann, 3:489
Ann (Osborn), 3:318,
3:489
Eleanor (Childs), 3:489
Elizabeth, 3:489
Mary, 3:220, 3:489
Mary (----), 3:488
Sarah, 1:403, 2:588,
3:488-489
Sarah (Eggleston), 3:488
Sarah (Prime), 3:487
Pritchet
---- (Langton), 3:56
Esther, 2:351
Hannah (Langton), 3:646
Proctor
Abigail, 3:126, 3:489
Edith (----), 3:489
Elizabeth, 3:490, 4:373
Elizabeth (Bassett), 3:489
Elizabeth (Thorndike),
3:489, 4:290
Hannah, 3:126, 3:489
Hannah (----), 3:490
Hannah (Felton) Endicott,
2:152
Jane (Hildreth), 3:490
Lydia, 3:490
Martha, 3:489
Martha (----), 3:489
Martha (Wainwright),
3:490, 4:382

Proctor (continued)
  Mary, 3:431-432,
    3:489-490
  Mary (----), 3:490
  Mary (Patterson), 3:371,
    3:490
  Sarah, 1:354, 2:56,
    3:489-490
Prouse
  Abigail, 3:490
  Hannah (----), 3:490
  Hannah (Barnes), 3:490
Prout
  Deborah (----), 3:491
  Deborah (Symmes), 4:244
  Elizabeth (----), 3:491
  Elizabeth (Upshall)
    Greenough, 2:310, 4:362
  Elizabeth (Wheeler), 3:490,
    4:501
  Eunice, 3:490
  Grace (----), 3:490
  Love (----), 3:491
  Margaret, 3:490-491,
    4:690
  Margaret (----), 3:491
  Mary, 2:55, 3:490
  Mary (Jackson), 3:491
  Mary (Rutherford) Hall,
    3:490, 3:627, 4:699
  Sarah, 3:490
  Susanna, 3:491, 4:697
Prouty
  Elizabeth (Howe), 3:491
  Elizabeth (Merritt), 3:491
  Margaret, 3:491
Prudden
  Abigail, 3:492, 4:394
  Ann, 1:431, 3:491
  Elizabeth, 3:486,
    3:491-492, 4:107
  Grace (Judson), 2:576,
    3:492
  Joanna, 3:492
  Joanna (----), 4:557
  Joanna (Boyse), 3:492
  Joanna (Willet), 1:185
  Mary, 3:492
  Mildred, 1:105, 3:492
  Sarah, 3:492
Pudeater
  Ann (----), 3:492, 3:603
  Isabel (Mosier), 3:492

  Jane, 3:613
Pudney
  Abigail, 3:492
  Hannah, 3:492
  Joanna, 3:492
  Judith, 3:492
  Judith (Cooke), 3:492
  Mary, 3:492
  Mary (Jones), 3:492
Puffer/Poffer
  Abigail (Everett), 2:131,
    3:493
  Esther, 3:493
  Martha, 3:492
  Mary (----), 3:492-493
  Ruth (----), 3:493
  Ruth (Farnsworth), 3:493
Pullen
  Joan, 2:234
  Susanna, 2:254
Pulling
  Elinor (Brackett), 1:228
Pulsifer
  Elizabeth, 3:493
  Joanna, 3:493
  Joanna (Kent), 3:493
  Margaret, 3:493
  Mary, 3:493
  Sarah (Loud/Lowd), 3:649
  Susanna, 3:493
  Susanna (Waters), 3:493,
    4:435
Punchard
  Abigail, 3:493
  Abigail (Waters), 3:493,
    4:435
  Hannah (Brown), 4:v,
    4:697
  Margaret (Hooper), 3:493
  Mary, 3:493
  Sarah, 3:493
Punderson
  Abigail, 3:493
  Damaris, 3:493
  Damaris (Atwater), 1:75,
    3:493
  Hannah, 2:246, 3:493
  Margaret (----), 3:493
  Mary, 3:493
Purchase/Purchas/Purkas
  ----, 1:333
  Elizabeth, 1:346, 3:494
  Elizabeth (----), 1:197,

    3:494
  Elizabeth (Williams),
    3:494
  Hannah, 1:204
  Jane, 3:494
  Joan (----), 3:342, 3:494
  Mary, 3:284, 3:494, 4:151
  Mary (----), 3:494
  Mary (Perkins), 3:397,
    3:494
  Priscilla, 3:494, 4:590
  Ruth, 3:494
  Ruth (Williams), 3:494,
    4:561
  Sarah, 3:418, 3:494
  Sarah (----), 3:494
Purdy
  Frances, 3:495
  Mary, 3:495
Purple
  Hannah (Ackley), 3:495
Purrington
  Sarah, 3:495
  Sarah (----), 3:495
Purryer
  Alice (----), 3:495
  Catharine, 3:495
  Mary, 3:495
  Sarah, 3:495
Putnam/Putman
  ---- (Gedney), 3:496
  ---- (Hutchinson), 2:512
  Abigail, 3:496-497
  Ann, 3:496-497, 3:661,
    4:323
  Ann (Carr), 3:497, 4:677
  Ann (Holyoke), 2:456,
    3:497
  Ann (Trask), 3:661
  Apphia, 3:495
  Deliverance, 3:497, 4:388
  Elizabeth, 2:174, 3:406,
    3:495-497
  Elizabeth (----), 1:433,
    3:495, 3:497
  Elizabeth (Porter), 3:496
  Elizabeth (Prince), 3:496
  Esther, 3:496
  Eunice, 3:496
  Hannah, 1:267, 3:495-496
  Hannah (----), 3:496
  Hannah (Boardman),
    3:495

Putnam/Putman (continued)
Hannah (Cutler), 3:496
Huldah, 3:496
Joanna, 3:496
Lydia, 3:496
Lydia (Potter), 3:466,
3:496
Mary, 3:495-497, 4:341
Mary (----) Veren, 3:497
Mary (Holton), 3:495
Mehitable, 3:496
Miriam, 3:496
Priscilla, 3:496
Priscilla (----), 3:496
Prudence, 3:495, 3:497,
4:666
Rachel, 3:496
Rebecca, 3:496, 3:622,
4:700, 4:704
Rebecca (Prince), 3:496
Ruth, 3:496
Sarah, 2:511, 3:495-497
Sarah (----), 3:495
Sarah (Holton), 3:495
Sarah (Hutchinson) Root,
2:596
Sarah (Miles), 3:206
Susanna, 3:496-497
Pygan
Jane, 2:304, 3:497
Judith (Redfield), 3:497,
3:521
Lydia, 3:497
Lydia (----) Boyes, 3:497
Lydia (Beamond) Boyes,
1:147, 1:226
Sarah, 2:339, 3:497
Pynchon
---- (----) Smith Sanford,
4:114
Amy (Wyllys), 3:497,
4:574
Ann, 3:498, 4:114
Bathsheba (Taylor), 4:259
Frances (----) (Smith)
Sanford, 3:498
Joanna (Edgecomb), 2:100
Margaret, 2:23, 3:498
Margaret (Hubbard), 2:487,
3:498
Mary, 2:456, 3:497-498,
4:519
Mehitable, 3:497

Quarles
Joanna, 3:499, 4:130
Mary (----), 3:499
Quelch
Elizabeth (----), 3:499
Quick
Ann (----), 3:499
Elizabeth (Cooke), 1:446
Quiddington
Ann, 3:499
Elizabeth, 3:499
Sarah (----), 3:499
Quilter
Frances (Swan), 3:499,
4:237
Mary, 3:499
Rebecca, 3:499
Sarah, 3:499
Quimby/Quinby
Ann, 4:229
Elizabeth (Osgood), 3:322
Lydia, 3:500, 3:634
Quincy
Ann, 3:500
Ann (Shepard), 1:239,
2:166, 3:500
Dorothy, 3:501
Dorothy (Flynt), 3:501
Elizabeth, 2:279,
3:500-501
Elizabeth (Gookin) Eliot,
2:110, 2:279, 3:500
Experience, 3:500-501,
4:28
Hannah (Shepard), 4:76
Joanna, 2:433, 3:500-501
Joanna (Hoar), 2:431,
3:500
Judith, 2:493, 3:500-501,
3:514
Judith (----), 2:495, 3:334,
3:500
Mary, 3:500-501, 4:23
Ruth, 2:500, 3:500-501
Quinny
Mary (Topping), 4:255
Rabey/Rabbe
Catharine (----), 3:501
Rachell
Judith (Hart), 2:367
Ragland
Mary (----), 3:501

Rainsborough/Rainsborow
---, 3:502
Judith, 4:613
Martha, 1:467-468
Rainsford/Ransford
Ann, 2:468, 3:502
Dorothy, 3:502
Elizabeth, 2:310, 3:502,
4:370
Elizabeth (----), 3:502
Hannah, 3:502-503, 4:370
Hannah (Griggs), 2:315
Mary, 3:502, 3:563, 4:370
Mary (Allen), 1:32
Mary (Sunderland), 3:502,
4:233
Ranis, 1:157, 3:502
Susanna, 3:502, 4:370
Susanna (Vergoose), 3:502,
4:370
Raisin
Elizabeth (Dyer), 2:88
Ramsdell/Ramsden
Dorcas, 3:503
Eleanor, 3:503
Eleanor (Vinton), 3:503,
4:375
Elizabeth, 3:503, 4:64
Elizabeth (Perkins), 3:397,
3:503
Hannah, 3:168, 3:503
Mary (Savory), 3:503
Priscilla (----), 3:503
Rachel (Eaton), 2:95,
3:503
Sarah, 3:503
Ramsey
Martha, 1:417
Rand
Abigail, 3:504
Abigail (----), 3:504
Alice, 3:116, 3:504, 4:155
Alice (Sharp), 3:504
Deborah, 3:505
Elizabeth, 1:244, 2:336,
3:439, 3:504-505, 4:704
Elizabeth (----), 3:504
Hannah, 3:36, 3:504-505
Isabel, 3:504
Margery, 2:68, 3:504
Mary, 3:32, 3:504-505
Mary (Carter), 1:341,
3:504

Rand (continued)
Mary (Crane), 3:504
Mary (Randall), 3:504
Mary (Rogers), 3:561
Mary (Walton), 3:505
Mehitable, 3:504
Mehitable (Call), 3:504
Persis (----), 3:505
Rebecca, 3:504
Remembrance (Alt), 1:42, 3:504
Sarah, 2:333, 3:504-505
Sarah (Edenden), 2:100, 3:505
Sarah (Longley), 3:111, 3:505
Susanna, 3:271, 3:504
Tabitha (Ivory), 2:526, 3:504
Randall
----, 3:506
Abigail, 3:505, 3:507, 3:659
Deborah, 3:505, 3:507
Deborah (Buck), 3:505
Dorcas, 4:585
Elizabeth, 1:514, 2:18, 3:506-507
Elizabeth (----), 3:507
Elizabeth (Gleason), 3:506
Elizabeth (Ines/Innes/etc), 2:518
Elizabeth (Kibby), 3:505
Elizabeth (Morton), 3:506
Elizabeth (Tozer), 4:697, 4:711
Grace, 3:505
Hannah, 3:506-507, 4:344, 4:417
Hannah (----), 3:507
Hannah (Macomber), 3:506
Hannah (Packard), 3:327
Hannah (Warfield), 3:506
Judith, 3:506
Lydia, 3:505
Margaret, 3:506
Mary, 3:504-507, 4:168, 4:248-249
Mary (----), 3:505-507
Mary (French), 2:207
Mercy, 3:506
Mercy (----), 3:506

Patience, 3:506
Patience (Parker), 3:357
Phillury, 3:405, 3:506, 3:659
Rachel, 3:505
Rachel (Waite), 3:506
Rebecca (----), 3:507
Ruth, 3:505
Sarah, 3:505-507
Sarah (----), 3:506
Sarah (Brown), 1:509
Sarah (Langdon), 3:54, 3:507
Susanna, 3:505-506, 4:29, 4:63
Susanna (----), 3:505
Susanna (Barron), 1:126, 3:506
Susanna (Barstow), 3:505
Susanna (Kimball), 3:21
Ranger
Mary (----), 3:507
Prudence, 3:507
Sarah, 3:507
Sarah (----), 3:507
Rankin
Martha (----), 3:507
Ranney
Elizabeth, 3:508
Esther, 3:508, 4:25
Hannah (Turner), 3:507
Mary, 3:508, 4:25
Mary (Hubbard), 2:483, 3:507
Mary (Starr), 3:507
Rebecca (----), 4:510
Rebecca (Willet), 3:508
Sarah (Warner), 3:507
Ransom
Hannah (Jones), 3:508
Raper
Martha, 3:508
Martha (----), 3:508
Mercy, 3:508
Rasor
Exercise (Blackleach), 1:189, 3:508
Ratchell/Rachell
Ann, 2:332, 3:508
Judith, 3:520
Judith (----), 3:520
Judith (Hart), 1:296, 2:367, 3:508

Mary, 3:429, 3:508
Temperance, 2:558, 3:508
Ratcliff/Ratliffe
Alice (----), 3:508
Elizabeth, 3:508
Elizabeth (Thele), 3:509, 4:279
Rauchon/Ronshon
Mary, 1:150, 4:95
Mary (Beauchamp), 1:150
Ravenscroft
Dionysia, 3:509
Dionysia (Savage), 3:509, 4:25, 4:27
Sarah, 3:509
Rawlins/Rawlings/Rollins
Abigail, 3:31, 3:509
Abigail (----), 3:509
Ann, 3:509
Elizabeth, 3:509-510, 4:313
Elizabeth (Wilmot), 3:509, 4:581
Emma (----), 3:510
Eunice, 4:313
Hannah (----), 3:510
Hannah (----) Griggs, 3:509
Joan, 3:510
Joan (----), 3:509
Joanna, 3:8
Judah (----), 3:509
Lydia (Sylvester), 3:509, 4:100, 4:655-656
Martha, 3:510
Mary, 3:357, 3:509-510
Mary (----), 3:510
Patience, 3:510
Rebecca, 3:510
Rebecca (Long), 3:510
Ruth, 3:510
Sarah, 2:446, 2:594
Sarah (----), 3:510
Sarah (----) Mattocks, 3:177, 3:510
Rawson
Ann, 3:511
Ann (Glover), 2:262, 3:511
Dorothy, 3:511
Elizabeth, 3:511
Grindall, 3:511-512
Margaret, 3:511

Rawson (continued)
  Mary, 3:511-512, 4:314
  Pirne/Parnell, 3:511
  Rachel, 1:78, 3:511
  Rachel (Pirne/Perne),
    3:511
  Rebecca, 3:511, 3:588,
    3:588
  Sarah, 1:264, 3:511
  Susanna, 3:511
  Susanna (Wilson), 3:511,
    4:585
  Thankful, 3:511
Ray - see Rea
Raymond/Rayment
  ---- (Scruggs), 4:42
  Abigail, 3:661
  Ann, 3:513
  Bathsheba, 3:513
  Bathshua, 1:453
  Bethia, 3:661
  Elizabeth, 3:150,
    3:512-513, 3:532, 3:661
  Elizabeth (----), 2:38
  Elizabeth (Harris), 3:512
  Elizabeth (Smith), 3:513,
    4:127
  Experience, 3:513
  Hannah, 3:150, 3:513
  Hannah (Bishop), 1:506,
    3:513
  Judith (----), 3:513
  Mary, 1:357, 3:513
  Mary (Betts), 1:173, 3:513
  Mary (Smith), 3:513,
    4:127
  Mehitable, 3:513
  Mercy (Sands), 4:13
  Rachel, 3:661
  Rachel (----), 3:661
  Rebecca (Lay), 3:512
  Ruth (Hall), 3:513
  Sarah, 3:512
Rayner/Reyner
  ---- (Boyes), 3:514
  Abigail, 1:263, 3:514
  Abigail (Hathorne), 3:514
  Ann, 2:438, 3:513
  Catharine (----), 3:514
  Dorothy, 3:514
  Elizabeth, 3:514, 4:143
  Elizabeth (----), 3:514
  Elizabeth (----) Gilbert,

2:249, 3:515
Elizabeth (Denison), 3:513
Esther, 4:540
Frances (Clark), 3:514
Hannah, 2:476, 3:514,
  4:597
Hannah/Ann, 3:52
Joanna (----) Edwards,
  3:513
Judith, 2:196, 3:514, 4:357
Judith (Quincy), 3:501,
  3:514
Lydia, 3:514
Martha, 3:513, 4:506
Martha (----), 3:515
Mary, 3:513
Mary (----), 3:514
Sarah, 3:514
Raynes/Raines
  ----, 3:502, 4:641
Raynsford - see Rainsford
Razor
  Exercise, 2:439
Rea/Ray
  ---- (----) Hewett, 3:512
  Bethia, 2:289, 3:122,
    3:512
  Bethia (----), 3:512
  Dorothy, 3:512
  Elizabeth, 3:512, 3:661
  Elizabeth (----), 3:512
  Elizabeth (Leach), 3:661
  Elizabeth (Phips), 3:420
  Hannah, 3:512
  Hepzibah (Peabody), 3:375,
    3:661
  Jemima, 3:661
  Mary, 2:33, 3:267, 3:512
  Mary (----), 3:512
  Mary (Thomas), 3:512,
    4:281
  Rebecca, 3:512, 4:188,
    4:708
  Sarah, 2:391, 3:512, 3:661
  Sarah (Waters), 3:512,
    4:435
  Sibel, 3:512
Read/Reed
  ---- (Randall), 3:506
  Abigail, 3:515-516,
    3:518-519, 4:664
  Abigail (----), 3:517
  Abigail (Baldwin), 3:516

Abigail (Kendall), 3:9,
  3:520
Abigail (Pierce), 3:515
Agnes, 2:89
Alice (----), 3:515
Amy, 1:346
Ann, 3:516-517
Ann (----) Derby), 2:40
Ann (Perrin), 3:399, 3:518
Ann (Swift), 3:517, 4:241
Bathshua, 3:520
Bethia, 2:555, 3:515
Bethia (Frye), 2:213, 3:516
Deborah, 2:200, 3:517
Elizabeth, 1:336, 2:165,
  3:515-520, 4:612
Elizabeth (----), 3:517,
  3:520
Elizabeth (Clark), 3:518
Elizabeth (Green), 3:516
Elizabeth (Holden), 2:446,
  3:516
Elizabeth (Jennison),
  2:545, 3:515
Elizabeth (Mousall), 3:518,
  3:654
Elsy (----), 3:518
Esther, 1:332, 3:519-520
Esther (Thompson), 3:520
Experience, 3:50, 3:517
Grace (Holloway), 3:517
Hannah, 3:515-519, 4:141,
  4:704
Hannah (----), 3:517, 3:520
Hannah (Peck), 3:515
Hopestill (Holbrook),
  3:518
Jemima, 3:516
Joan (Stone), 3:661
Joanna, 3:518
Joanna (----), 3:517
Lydia, 4:394
Mabel (----), 3:519
Margaret, 3:519, 4:228
Margaret (----), 2:478
Martha, 3:516, 3:519,
  4:246
Martha (Boyden), 3:519
Mary, 1:90, 2:87,
  3:515-520, 4:374, 4:710
Mary (----), 3:176, 3:515,
  3:517-518
Mary (Goodrich), 2:274,

Read/Reed (continued)
Mary (Goodrich)
   (continued)
   3:519
Mary (Kendall), 3:9
Mary (Oldham), 3:308
Mary (Pierce), 3:426,
   3:517
Mary (Winter), 3:516,
   4:605
Mehitable, 3:516
Mercy, 3:520, 3:518
Patience, 3:516
Persis, 3:519
Persis (----), 3:519
Prudence, 3:517
Rachel, 4:230, 4:581
Rebecca, 3:353, 3:517
Rebecca (Fitch), 3:517
Rebecca (Ruggles), 3:516
Remember, 3:518
Ruth, 3:516, 3:519, 4:523
Ruth (Crook), 3:519
Ruth (Johnson), 3:516
Ruth (Talcott), 4:251
Sarah, 1:502, 3:515-520,
   4:198, 4:316, 4:396
Sarah (----), 3:516, 3:519
Sarah (Sawyer), 3:519
Susanna, 3:516-519, 4:132
Susanna (----), 3:482,
   3:518-519
Susanna (Richmond),
   3:516, 3:539
Sybel (----) Rice, 3:515
Reape
Joanna (----) Rhoades,
   3:520
Joanna (Arnold) Rhoades,
   3:527
Judith (----) Ratchell, 3:520
Judith (Hart) Ratchell,
   3:508
Sarah, 3:520
Sarah (----), 3:520
Rease
Judith (Hart) Ratchell,
   2:367
Record
Hannah (Hobart), 2:436,
   3:520
Redding/Reading/Riddan
----, 2:59

Abigail, 3:520
Elizabeth (----), 3:520
Elizabeth (King), 3:24
Hannah, 3:520
Mary (Bassett), 3:520
Sarah, 3:520
Reddock
----, 2:382, 3:521
Redfield
Deborah (Sturges), 3:521,
   4:708
Elizabeth, 3:521
Elizabeth (Howe), 3:521,
   3:636
Judith, 3:497, 3:521
Lydia, 1:143, 3:521, 4:291
Margaret, 3:521
Rebecca, 3:521, 3:545
Rebecca (----), 3:521
Sarah, 3:521
Redfyn
Lydia, 1:143
Rediat/Ridiat/Radyate
Ann (----), 3:521
Deborah, 3:521, 4:190
Dorothy, 2:144, 3:521
Elizabeth, 3:521
Mary, 2:515, 3:521
Mehitable, 3:302, 3:521
Susanna, 3:521
Susanna (----), 3:206,
   3:521
Redington
Elizabeth, 3:482
Mary, 2:406
Mary (Gould), 2:287,
   3:521
Sarah, 3:580
Redknap
Hannah, 3:283, 3:521
Rebecca, 3:521
Sarah, 3:44, 3:521-522
Redman
Luce (----), 3:522
Martha (Cass), 1:347,
   3:522
Mercy, 3:522
Ruth, 3:522
Redway/Readaway/etc
Lydia, 4:308
Sarah, 1:337, 3:522
Reeve/Reeves
----, 3:523

Ann, 3:523
Dorothy (Howell), 2:478
Elizabeth, 3:523, 3:661
Elizabeth (----), 3:523
Elizabeth (Collins), 3:523
Elizabeth (Nott), 3:294,
   3:523
Freeborn, 3:523
Hannah, 3:523
Hannah (----), 2:133
Hannah (Rowe), 3:523
Jane (----), 3:522
Mary, 3:523, 3:644, 3:661,
   4:450, 4:702
Mehitable, 3:523
Sarah, 3:523
Reick
Elizabeth, 1:114
Reith
Elizabeth (George), 3:523
Relph/Ralph/Relf
Alice, 3:523
Deliverance, 3:523
Elizabeth (Disbrow), 2:554,
   3:523
Mary (----) Cooke, 1:447,
   3:523
Sarah, 3:523
Remington
Abigail (----), 3:524
Ann, 2:113, 3:524
Elizabeth, 2:248, 4:179
Elizabeth (----), 3:524
Hannah, 3:57, 3:524
Martha, 3:524
Martha (Belcher), 1:155,
   3:524
Mary, 3:78
Mehitable (----), 3:524
Remember (Stowell),
   3:524, 4:219
Rhoda (----) Gore, 2:280,
   3:524
Sarah, 3:524, 3:559
Sarah (Rose), 3:524
Rendall
Martha (Brooking) Lewis,
   1:259, 3:87, 3:524
Rew
Sarah (Richmond), 3:525,
   3:539, 4:394
Rex
Grace (----), 3:525

Rex (continued)
  Mary, 3:525
Reycraft
  Hannah, 3:187
Reynolds/Renold/Renolds
  Alice (Kitson), 3:526
  Ann, 3:525-526
  Ann (----), 3:525
  Ann (Holbrook), 2:443
  Elizabeth, 2:194, 2:545,
    3:525-526
  Elizabeth (----), 2:449,
    3:526
  Elizabeth (Green), 2:301,
    3:525
  Eunice/Catharine, 4:171
  Hannah, 4:476
  Judith, 1:173
  Kezia, 3:525
  Lydia, 3:525
  Mary, 3:525-526, 4:16
  Mary (----), 3:526
  Mary (Green), 2:301,
    3:525
  Priscilla (----), 3:526
  Rebecca, 3:525
  Rebina, 3:525
  Ruth, 3:526, 4:529
  Sarah, 1:507, 3:169, 3:465,
    3:525-526
  Sarah (----), 3:525
  Sarah (Clark), 3:526
  Sarah (Dwight), 2:85,
    3:526
  Sarah (Green), 2:301,
    3:525
  Susanna, 3:525
  Tabitha, 1:6, 3:526
Rhodes/Roads/Rhoads
  Abigail, 3:271
  Abigail (Coates), 1:412,
    3:527
  Ann (Graves), 3:527
  Elizabeth, 3:526-527
  Elizabeth (Coates), 3:527
  Hannah, 3:527
  Jane, 3:527
  Jane (Coates), 3:527
  Joanna (----), 3:520
  Joanna (Arnold), 1:67,
    3:527
  Mary, 3:125, 3:527
  Mary (Carder), 1:335,

    3:527
  Mercy (Williams)
    Waterman Winsor, 3:526,
    4:432, 4:569, 4:605
  Phebe, 3:526
  Rebecca, 3:470, 3:527,
    4:559
  Sarah, 3:527
  Susanna, 3:527
  Waite, 3:526
  Waite (----), 3:526
Rice
  Abiel, 3:531
  Abigail, 3:528-531
  Abigail (Marrett), 3:153,
    3:531
  Agnes (Bent), 1:169,
    3:528
  Ann, 3:528-529, 3:531
  Ann (----), 3:528, 3:531
  Ann (Bent), 1:169
  Ann (Churchill), 1:387
  Ann (Derby), 3:530
  Barbara, 3:529
  Bathshua (----), 3:530
  Beriah, 3:531
  Berzela, 3:529
  Bethia, 3:527
  Bethia (Ward), 3:527
  Bethia (Williams), 4:570
  Damaris, 3:527
  Deborah, 3:527, 3:530,
    4:29
  Deborah (Caulkins), 1:349,
    3:529
  Deliverance, 3:529
  Dinah, 3:528-529
  Dorcas, 3:528, 4:389
  Dorothy, 3:530
  Elizabeth, 1:244, 2:390,
    3:527-531
  Elizabeth (----), 3:530-531,
    4:257
  Elizabeth (Holden), 2:445,
    3:529
  Elizabeth (King), 3:531
  Elizabeth (Moore), 3:529
  Elizabeth (Wheeler), 3:529
  Elizabeth (Willard), 3:531
  Elnathan, 3:529
  Elnathan (Whipple), 3:529
  Esther, 2:483, 3:531
  Frances, 3:529-531

  Grace, 3:528-529, 3:531
  Hannah, 3:528-529, 3:531,
    4:407
  Hannah (----), 3:528
  Hannah (Livermore),
    3:528
  Hannah (Walker), 3:528
  Hepzibah, 3:527
  Huldah, 3:528
  Jaazaniah, 3:529
  Joyce, 3:528
  Joyce (Russell), 3:528,
    3:595
  Kezia, 3:527
  Lydia, 3:527-529
  Lydia (Fairbanks), 3:528
  Martha, 1:169, 1:451,
    3:527, 3:529-530
  Martha (----), 3:529-530
  Martha (Lamson), 3:530
  Mary, 1:304, 3:527,
    3:529-531, 4:204
  Mary (----), 3:529-531
  Mary (----) Brown, 3:531
  Mary (Beers), 1:155, 3:530
  Mary (Brown), 1:172,
    1:277, 3:527
  Mary (Dix) Brown, 1:264
  Mary (Graves), 3:527
  Mary (Spinning), 4:150
  Mary (Ward), 3:527
  Mercy, 3:529
  Mercy (----) Brigham,
    3:528
  Mercy (Hurd) Brigham,
    1:252, 2:502
  Mercy (King), 3:530
  Patience, 3:530-531
  Patience (----) Stone, 3:530
  Priscilla, 3:527
  Prudence, 3:529
  Rachel, 2:75, 3:527, 3:529
  Rebecca, 3:527, 3:530
  Rebecca (----), 3:530
  Rebecca (Howe), 2:474
  Rebecca (Watson), 3:529
  Ruth, 2:373, 3:528-530,
    4:477
  Ruth (Parker), 3:528
  Sarah, 3:527, 3:529-531
  Sarah (----), 3:529-530
  Sarah (----) Hoyt, 2:481
  Sarah (Prescott) Wheeler,

Rice (continued)
Sarah (Prescott) Wheeler
(continued)
4:499
Sybel (----), 3:515
Sybilla, 3:529
Sybilla (----), 3:529
Tabitha, 3:529
Tabitha (Stone), 3:529,
4:205
Tamar, 3:529
Thankful, 3:528
Thomasine, 3:529
Thomasine (----), 3:528
Vashti, 3:531
Zephaniah, 3:530
Zipporah, 3:530
Rich
Ann (----), 3:532
Bethia, 3:661
Bethia (Williams), 3:661
Eunice, 3:547
Huldah, 3:532
Lydia, 3:547
Margaret, 3:661
Mary, 3:661
Priscilla, 3:532
Rebecca, 3:532
Sarah, 3:532
Sarah (Roberts), 3:532,
3:547
Richard
Hannah (Pontus) Churchill,
1:387
Jane (Tilson), 4:304
Richards
----, 3:532
---- (Stocking), 4:198
Abigail, 3:532-533
Abigail (----) Mun, 3:533
Abigail (Parsons) Mun,
3:361, 3:654
Alice, 1:232, 3:534
Ann, 3:532-534
Ann (Winthrop), 3:533,
4:613
Bathsheba, 1:254
Bathshua, 3:533
Deborah, 3:533, 4:523
Dorcas, 3:532
Elizabeth, 2:15, 2:414,
3:532-534, 3:661
Elizabeth (Hawkins)

Winthrop, 2:383, 3:533,
4:607
Elizabeth (Raymond),
3:532
Elizabeth (Reeves), 3:661
Esther, 3:534
Grace, 3:533
Grace (----), 3:535
Hannah, 2:166, 3:533-534,
4:40
Hannah (Andrews), 1:54,
3:534
Hannah (Hudson), 1:473,
2:489, 3:532
Hannah (Metcalf), 3:533
Jerusha, 2:15, 3:532
Joanna, 3:534, 3:661,
4:157
Joanna (Dodd), 3:534,
4:680
Love (Manwaring), 3:150,
3:533
Lydia, 3:186, 3:533
Lydia (Stocking), 3:533
Mary, 1:26, 1:295, 2:425,
3:283, 3:382, 3:532-534,
3:661, 4:37, 4:524
Mary (----), 3:533
Mary (Aldis), 1:24, 3:534
Mary (Brewer), 3:533
Mary (Graves), 3:534
Mary (Parsons), 3:361,
3:662
Mehitable (Ruggles),
3:588
Penelope, 3:533
Rachel, 3:381, 3:534
Rosamund (----) Lindall,
3:534, 4:688
Ruth (----), 3:533
Sarah, 2:15, 3:426,
3:532-534
Sarah (----), 2:14, 3:533
Sarah (Gibbons), 2:245,
3:532, 4:357
Susanna (----), 3:533
Susanna (Hunting), 3:532
Welthian (----), 3:534
Richardson
----, 1:63, 3:537
Abigail, 1:137, 3:153,
3:537-538
Abigail (Wyman), 3:538,

4:664
Amy, 3:96
Amy (Graves), 3:537
Amy/Ann (Graves), 3:662
Ann, 3:662
Ann (Bartlett), 3:535
Bridget, 3:538
Bridget (Henchman),
1:359, 2:403, 3:536
Catharine, 1:499,
3:535-536, 4:101
Deborah, 3:536
Deborah (Fuller), 3:536
Deliverance (Scott), 3:538,
4:38
Elizabeth, 1:28, 1:408,
3:536-537, 4:92, 4:664
Elizabeth (Arnold), 3:662
Elizabeth (Bacon), 3:536
Elizabeth (Borden), 3:538
Elizabeth (Mott), 3:538
Elizabeth (Swan), 4:236
Elizabeth (Tryer), 3:536
Elizabeth (Wiseman),
3:538
Esther, 3:537-538
Hannah, 1:102, 3:536-538
Hannah (Green), 3:536,
4:683
Hannah (Kingsley), 3:537
Jane (----), 3:537
Joanna, 3:537-538
Joanna (----), 3:537
Judith, 3:537
Lydia, 2:142
Lydia (Coleman), 3:537
Lydia (Gilbert), 2:250
Margaret, 3:535
Margaret (Godfrey), 2:266,
3:536
Margaret (Warner), 3:662
Margaret (Willing), 3:536
Martha, 3:537
Martha (----), 3:537
Mary, 1:103, 1:261, 2:141,
2:236, 2:343, 3:251,
3:429, 3:535-538, 3:541,
3:662, 4:339, 4:586,
4:665
Mary (----), 3:535-538
Mary (Champney), 1:356,
3:538
Mary (French), 2:205

Richardson (continued)
Mary (Ladd), 3:535
Mary (Parker), 3:537
Mary (Pierson), 3:536
Mercy, 3:536
Phebe, 1:102, 3:536-538
Phebe (Baldwin), 3:537
Prudence, 2:339, 3:535,
   3:538
Rebecca, 3:538
Rebecca (----), 4:87
Rebecca (Clark), 1:398
Remembrance, 3:537
Remembrance
   (Underwood), 3:537
Rhoda, 1:359
Ruth, 3:535-536, 3:538
Ruth (Wheeler), 3:662
Sarah, 1:91, 3:535-538,
   4:561
Sarah (----) Hayward,
   3:537
Susanna (----), 3:535
Richmond
Abigail, 3:539
Abigail (----), 3:539
Abigail (Rogers), 3:563
Ann, 2:385
Ann (Sproat), 4:158
Mary, 2:266, 3:455, 3:539
Mary (Andrews), 3:539
Mehitable (Andrews),
   3:539
Sarah, 3:525, 3:539, 4:394
Susanna, 3:516, 3:539
Rickard/Ricker/Ricket
Eleanor, 3:539
Eleanor (----), 3:539
Elizabeth, 3:539
Esther (Barnes), 3:540
Hannah, 3:539
Hannah (Dunham), 3:540
Hannah (Pontus) Churchill,
   3:454, 3:540
Joan (Tilson), 3:540
Judith, 2:148, 3:539
Judith (----), 3:540
Lydia, 3:540
Mary, 3:539-540
Mercy, 3:540
Rebecca, 1:491
Sarah, 3:540, 3:657
Sarah (----), 3:540

Ricketson
Elizabeth, 3:540
Elizabeth (----), 3:540
Rebecca, 3:540
Ricroft
Frances (Pitcher), 1:490
Riddan/Riddaine
Abigail, 3:540
Elizabeth (----), 3:540
Hannah, 3:540, 3:662
Sarah, 3:662
Rider
Ann (----), 4:697
Elizabeth, 1:207, 1:428,
   3:540, 4:697
Elizabeth (Lane), 3:53,
   3:540
Esther, 4:697
Hannah, 3:540-541, 4:697
Hannah (----), 3:540
Hannah (Lovett), 3:540
Lydia, 4:697
Lydia (Tilden), 3:540
Mary, 4:697
Mary (----), 3:540, 4:697
Mary (Gray), 4:697
Rebecca, 4:697
Sarah, 3:540, 4:697
Sarah (----) Matthews,
   4:690
Sarah (Bartlett), 1:132,
   3:540
Sarah (Lawrence), 3:61,
   3:540
Sarah/Mary (Bartlett),
   4:697
Thankful, 4:697
Ridgdale/Rigdale
Alice (----), 3:541
Ridge
Martha (----), 3:541
Ridgeway/Ridgway
Mary (----), 3:541
Mary (Brackenbury),
   1:228
Ridland
Patience (Davis), 2:578
Rigby
Abigail, 2:451, 3:541
Elizabeth, 1:73, 3:541
Isabel (----), 1:240
Mehitable, 3:541, 4:348
Silence, 3:541

Riggs
Abigail, 3:542
Ann, 3:542, 4:712
Ann (Wheeler), 3:542
Elizabeth, 3:541-542
Elizabeth (----), 3:541
Elizabeth (Frese), 3:542
Elizabeth (Rooke), 3:541
Hannah, 3:541
Lydia, 3:541
Mary, 2:371, 3:541-542
Mary (Millet), 3:542
Mary (Richardson), 3:541
Ruth (Wheeler), 3:541
Sarah, 3:542, 4:339
Sarah (Baldwin), 1:104,
   3:541
Right
Hannah, 3:542
Riker
Joanna, 1:173
Riland
Joanna, 1:408, 4:6
Riley
Grace, 2:275, 3:542
Grace (----), 3:542
Margaret, 3:141, 3:542
Margaret (----), 3:542
Mary, 3:542
Mary (Frost), 2:212
Sarah, 3:542
Rindge
Elizabeth (Dutch), 2:84,
   3:542
Sarah (Shatswell), 4:61
Ring
Deborah, 3:542
Deborah (Hopkins), 2:462,
   3:542
Elizabeth, 2:30, 2:314,
   3:542-543
Elizabeth (----), 3:543
Hannah, 3:543
Hannah (Fowler), 3:543
Lettice (----) Morton,
   3:244, 3:542
Martha, 3:543
Mary, 3:542, 4:415-416
Mary (----), 1:400, 4:536
Mary (Bray), 3:543, 3:605
Mary (Shaw), 4:65
Priscilla (----), 3:543
Susanna, 1:400, 3:542

Ripley
----, 3:543
---- (Gager), 2:221
Elizabeth (----) Thaxter,
  2:85, 3:543, 4:275
Elizabeth (Hobart), 2:435,
  3:543
Hannah (Bradford), 1:232,
  3:543
Joanna (----), 3:543
Mary, 3:543
Mary (----), 4:685
Mary (Farnsworth), 2:143,
  3:543
Phebe, 3:418
Sarah, 1:145, 3:543
Sarah (Lazell), 3:66
Risden
Beatrice (----), 3:543
Sarah, 3:543
Rishworth
----, 2:80
---- (Wheelwright), 2:512,
  3:543-544, 4:503
Mary, 3:544, 4:503
Susanna (Wheelwright)
  Hutchinson, 2:513
Rising
Elizabeth, 3:463
Elizabeth (Hinsdale), 2:427,
  3:544
Hannah, 3:662
Rebecca (Adams), 4:697
Risley/Risley
Sarah, 3:544
Rist
Sarah (----), 3:544
Rithway
Elizabeth, 3:372
Rix
Abigail, 3:545
Abigail (Ingersoll), 2:520,
  3:545, 4:579
Bridget (----) Fiske, 3:662
Bridget (Musket) Fiske,
  4:682
Charity, 3:544
Charity (----), 3:544
Elizabeth, 3:544
Esther, 3:545
Grace (----), 3:270, 3:545
Margaret (----), 3:662
Mary, 3:544-545

Remember, 3:545
Sarah, 3:487, 3:545
Sarah (----), 2:270, 3:545
Roach
Elizabeth, 3:662
Hannah, 3:662
Hannah (Potter),
  3:661-662
Mary, 3:662
Rebecca (Redfield), 3:521,
  3:545
Roanes/Roane
Wilmott (----) Start, 3:545,
  4:173
Roath
Elizabeth, 3:545
Hannah, 3:545
Mary, 3:545
Sarah, 3:545
Sarah (Saxton), 3:545,
  4:32
Robbins
---- (----), 3:546, 4:148
Ann (----), 3:546
Comfort, 3:545
Elizabeth (----), 3:545
Elizabeth (Bowdoin),
  1:222
Esther (----), 3:546
Hannah, 3:545-546
Hannah (Chandler), 1:359
Isabel (----), 3:662
Jehosabeth (Jordan), 2:569
Jehosabeth (Jourdaine),
  3:545
Mary, 3:545-546, 4:326
Mary (----), 3:545-546
Mary (----) Abbot, 1:4,
  3:545
Mary (----) Bishop, 3:662
Rebecca, 3:546, 4:645
Rebecca (----), 3:546
Sarah (----), 4:710
Sarah (Brooks), 3:545,
  3:606, 4:697
Susanna (Lane), 3:546
Roberts
---- (Harris), 3:548
Abigail, 2:335, 2:591,
  3:546-548
Abigail (Nutter), 3:546
Alce, 3:546
Alice, 3:548

Ann, 3:408, 3:547-548
Catharine, 4:528
Christian (Baker), 1:95,
  3:547
Deborah, 3:546
Elizabeth, 1:467, 2:397,
  3:546-547, 4:91, 4:347
Elizabeth (----), 3:547, 4:91
Elizabeth (Stone)
  Sedgwick, 3:547, 4:49,
  4:208
Elizabeth (Tower), 3:548
Esther, 3:162, 3:547
Eunice, 3:546
Eunice (----), 3:181,
  3:547-548
Experience (----), 3:547
Hannah (Bray), 1:240,
  3:547
Jane, 3:546
Joanna, 3:546
Joanna (----), 3:548
Joanna (Brooks), 3:546
Lydia, 1:134, 3:546-548
Margery, 3:546
Mary, 3:546-547
Mary (Caulkins), 1:349,
  3:546
Mary (Leighton), 3:44,
  3:548
Mary (Paddock), 3:328,
  3:548
Mehitable, 3:546
Patience, 3:547
Ruth, 3:546
Sarah, 3:532, 3:546-547
Susanna (----), 3:399,
  3:547
Susanna (Lane), 3:52
Robie/Roby
Abigail (Curtis), 3:548
Ann, 3:549
Ann (Pollard), 3:549
Dorothy, 3:549
Elizabeth, 3:548
Elizabeth (Greenough),
  2:310, 3:549
Elizabeth (Philbrick) Chase
  Garland, 1:365, 2:232,
  3:409, 3:548
Hannah, 3:548
Judith, 3:548
Lois (----), 3:549

Robie/Roby (continued)
Mary, 2:32, 2:178,
3:548-549
Mehitable, 3:549
Mehitable (Sewall), 3:549,
4:56
Mercy, 3:549
Priscilla (----), 3:548
Ruth, 3:548
Sarah, 3:549
Sarah (----), 3:548
Robineau
Mary, 1:85
Robinson
---- (Baker), 1:98, 3:554
---- (Manton), 3:553
Abigail, 3:549, 3:552,
3:555-556
Abigail (Gardiner) Hazard,
3:556
Alithea, 3:552
Ann, 2:76, 3:549, 3:555
Ann (----), 3:551-552
Beriah, 3:550
Catherine, 3:553
Damaris, 3:553
Damaris (----), 3:553
Deborah, 3:549
Dorcas, 3:549
Dorothy, 2:147, 3:553
Elizabeth, 3:549,
3:551-553, 3:555-556,
4:566
Elizabeth (----), 2:308,
3:550, 3:553, 3:555-556
Elizabeth (----) Sherman,
3:554
Elizabeth (Bushnell),
1:317
Elizabeth (Gaille), 3:550
Elizabeth (Weeks), 3:552
Esther, 3:555
Experience (----), 3:551
Faith, 3:552
Fear, 1:99, 3:550, 3:552
Frances, 2:287
Hannah, 3:549, 3:551-553,
3:555-556
Hannah (Wiswall), 3:552
Hope (Potter), 4:696,
4:698
Isabella, 3:552
Isabella (----), 3:555

Jane, 3:549, 3:554
Kate, 2:182
Lucretia (Foxwell), 2:198,
3:552
Margaret, 3:556
Margaret (----), 3:554
Margaret (Hanford), 2:350,
3:550
Martha, 3:550, 3:556,
3:663
Martha (Buck), 3:551
Martha (Hawkins), 3:663
Mary, 2:126, 2:589, 3:549,
3:551-556, 3:625, 3:663,
4:128, 4:581, 4:698
Mary (----), 1:277, 3:549,
3:555-556, 3:628, 4:393
Mary (Alcock), 1:22, 3:551
Mary (Allen), 3:553
Mary (Beamsley), 1:148,
2:39, 3:554
Mary (Bushnell),
1:317-318, 3:550
Mary (Coggan) Woody,
1:420, 3:554, 4:637
Mary (Harraden), 3:549
Mary (Hazard), 3:552
Mary (Kitchen), 3:663,
4:687
Mary (Potter), 3:556
Mary (Silver), 3:553, 4:98
Mary (Wells), 4:475
Mercy, 3:550, 3:552-554,
4:454
Phebe (Dane), 2:6, 3:553
Prudence, 1:248, 3:555
Rebecca (----), 3:553
Ruth, 3:552
Sarah, 3:549, 3:551-555,
3:608, 3:662
Sarah (----), 3:550, 3:554
Sarah (Behoney), 1:155,
3:550
Sarah (Denison), 3:615
Sarah (Hitchcock), 3:551
Sarah (Mason), 3:166,
3:662
Sarah (Sanborn), 3:550
Sarah (Smith), 4:127
Silence (----), 3:554
Susanna, 3:550
Susanna (----), 3:552
Thankful, 3:556

Ursula (----), 1:469
Ursula (----) Hosier Streeter,
2:466, 3:555
Waiting, 3:390, 3:555
Robison - see Robinson
Robitail
Grizzle (Warren) Otis
Baker, 3:324
Rock
Elizabeth, 3:556
Elizabeth (----), 3:551
Elizabeth (Coggan), 1:420,
3:556
Hannah, 1:232, 1:241,
3:551, 3:556
Lydia, 3:556
Mary, 1:408
Mary (----), 3:556
Rebecca, 3:556
Sarah, 3:556
Rocke
Mary (Wilson) Danforth,
2:8
Rockett
Agnes (Bicknell), 3:557
Bethia, 3:556-557
Deliverance, 3:556
Elizabeth, 3:365, 3:557
Hannah, 3:557
Hannah (Ellis), 2:113
Jane (----), 3:557
Joanna, 3:557
Judith, 3:556
Judith (----), 3:556
Margaret (Holbrook),
2:441, 3:557
Mary, 3:556-557
Mary (Twitchell), 3:557
Mary (Wilmouth), 3:557
Mehitable, 3:557
Patience, 3:556
Sarah (Wheelock), 3:557
Silence (----), 3:557
Trial, 3:556
Rockwell
----, 3:557, 4:16
Abigail, 3:558
Ann (Bliss), 3:558
Deliverance (----), 4:422
Deliverance (Haynes),
3:557
Elizabeth, 3:557-558
Elizabeth (Foster), 3:557

Rockwell (continued)
Hannah, 3:557-558
Jerusha, 3:558
Joan, 1:96, 2:523, 3:558
Lydia, 3:557, 3:598
Mary, 3:113, 3:557-558,
4:438
Mary (----), 3:557
Mary (Norton), 3:293,
3:558
Mehitable, 3:2
Ruth, 2:503, 3:222,
3:557-558
Sarah, 1:470, 2:238,
3:557-558
Sarah (Ensign), 2:125,
3:557
Susanna (----), 2:292
Susanna (Chapin), 3:558
Rockwood
Abigail, 3:558
Deliverance, 3:558
Elizabeth, 3:365
Hannah, 3:558
Hannah (Ellis), 2:113,
3:558
Margaret (Holbrook),
2:441
Patience, 3:558
Phebe, 4:261
Sarah (----), 3:558
Susanna, 3:558
Roddam
Mary, 2:438
Rodman
Ann, 4:698
Charity, 4:698
Elizabeth, 4:698
Hannah, 4:698
Hannah (Clark), 3:559,
4:678
Mary, 4:698
Mary (----), 4:698
Mary (Willet), 4:698
Patience, 4:698
Patience (Easton) Malins ,
4:689, 4:698
Roe - see also Rowe
Abigail, 3:559, 4:265
Abigail (----), 3:559
Bridget (----), 1:432
Elizabeth, 3:559
Esther, 3:559

Martha (George), 2:242
Mary, 2:78, 3:559, 3:617
Rebecca (Long), 3:559
Ruth, 3:559
Ruth (----), 3:559
Sarah (Remington), 3:559
Rogers
----, 3:561, 3:590
---- (Wilson), 3:560
Abiel, 4:428
Abigail, 1:37, 3:560-563,
3:568, 4:423, 4:668,
4:698
Abigail (Barker), 1:116
Abigail (Brown), 1:276
Abigail (Martin), 3:562
Alice, 1:480
Ann, 2:488, 3:561, 3:568,
4:492
Ann (Churchman), 1:387,
3:561
Ann (Fisen), 3:564
Bathsheba, 3:560, 4:130
Bathshua, 2:196
Content, 3:652
Dorothy, 3:560
Elizabeth, 1:61, 2:259,
2:411-412, 2:474,
3:559-564, 3:568-569,
4:111, 4:118, 4:193,
4:564
Elizabeth (----), 3:563-564
Elizabeth (Baxter), 3:663
Elizabeth (Denison), 2:36,
3:562
Elizabeth (Griswold),
1:152, 2:317, 3:474,
3:563
Elizabeth (Knowles) Ford,
2:183
Elizabeth (Peabody), 3:375,
3:563
Elizabeth (Pemberton),
3:387
Elizabeth (Rowland),
3:560, 3:581
Elizabeth (Snow), 3:569
Elizabeth (Taintor), 3:568,
4:249
Elizabeth (Twining), 3:563,
4:353
Ester (Foxwell), 2:198
Eunice (Stetson), 4:183

Experience, 3:563, 3:569
Frances (----), 3:561
Grace (----), 3:343, 3:463,
3:569
Hannah, 1:232, 3:475,
3:561-564, 3:569, 4:307
Jane, 3:560
Joanna, 4:328
Judah, 3:563
Judith (----), 3:561
Judith (Appleton), 1:61,
3:568
Lois (Ivory) Bly, 2:526
Lydia, 3:561, 3:563, 3:569,
4:512
Margaret, 1:171, 2:486,
3:559-562, 3:564, 3:568
Margaret (----), 3:569,
4:137
Margaret (Crane), 3:564
Margaret (Hubbard) Scott,
2:486, 3:560, 4:39
Martha, 3:560, 3:563,
3:568, 4:633, 4:698
Martha (Barnard), 4:674,
4:698
Martha (Whittingham),
3:563
Mary, 1:427, 2:2, 2:251,
3:417, 3:559-564,
3:568-569, 4:352, 4:698
Mary (----), 2:474, 3:569
Mary (----) Barker, 1:116,
3:560
Mary (Bates), 3:563
Mary (Exell), 2:133, 3:560
Mary (Jordan), 3:561
Mary (Paine), 3:337, 3:560
Mary (Ransford), 3:563
Mary (Stanton), 3:568,
4:167
Mehitable, 3:561, 3:563
Mehitable (Pierce), 3:428,
3:561
Mercy (----), 3:560
Naomi (Burdick), 1:301,
3:563
Orange, 4:677, 4:698
Patience, 3:559, 3:562
Priscilla, 1:452, 3:559,
3:561-562
Priscilla (Dawes), 3:561
Rhoda (King), 3:26, 3:562

Rogers (continued)
Ruth, 3:559, 3:563, 3:569
Ruth (Brown), 3:569
Sarah, 3:559, 3:561,
3:563-564, 3:568
Sarah (—), 3:568, 4:639
Sarah (Appleton), 1:61,
3:559
Sarah (Everard), 3:559
Sarah (Wade), 3:568,
4:378
Susanna, 3:564, 3:568-569
Susanna (----), 3:568-569,
4:282
Susanna (Dean), 2:30,
3:564, 4:139
Roise - see Royce
Rokeby
Elizabeth, 4:373
Rolestone
Mary, 3:570
Mary (----), 3:570
Rolfe
— (Collins), 3:570
Abigail, 3:570-571
Abigail (Bond), 1:209,
3:571
Ann (----), 3:571
Apphia, 2:547, 3:570
Apphia (----), 3:570
Dorothy (----), 3:571
Elizabeth, 1:370, 3:570
Elizabeth (Disbrow), 3:571
Esther, 3:571, 4:20
Esther (----), 3:571
Hannah, 2:58, 3:571
Hannah (Bradstreet),
1:235, 2:455, 3:570
Honour (----), 3:571
Martha, 3:571
Mary, 3:570-571
Mary (Scallard), 3:12
Mary (Scullard), 3:571,
4:43
Rebecca, 1:496, 3:571
Sarah, 3:571
Rollo
Hannah (Kirby) Andrews,
1:56
Rood
Mary, 3:572
Rachel, 3:572
Sarah, 3:572

Rook/Rooke
Elizabeth, 3:541
Sarah (Hall), 2:591
Rookman
Elizabeth (----), 3:572
Roome/Rome
Ann (—), 3:572
Root
— (Frary), 2:201
Abigail, 3:573-574
Abigail (Alvord), 1:46,
3:574
Ann, 3:573
Ann (—), 3:573
Ann (Gull), 2:322, 3:573
Bethia, 3:573
Bethiah, 3:573
Dorcas (----), 3:573
Dorothy, 1:360
Dorothy (Abbot), 1:2
Dorothy (Ingersoll) Phelps,
2:520, 3:405
Elizabeth, 3:572-574
Elizabeth (Gale), 2:221,
3:574
Elizabeth (Salmon), 3:572,
4:6
Elizabeth (Warner), 3:573
Esther, 3:573
Hannah, 3:573-574
Hannah (Haynes), 2:388,
3:573
Joanna, 3:572
Margaret, 3:572
Margaret (----), 3:573,
3:663, 4:337
Mary, 3:572-574
Mary (----), 3:573, 4:421
Mary (----) Burt, 3:573
Mary (----) Ruggles, 3:588
Mary (Ashley), 1:69, 3:572
Mary (Frary), 3:572
Mary (Gridley), 2:313,
3:574
Mary (Holton) Burt, 1:313
Mary (Kilbourn), 3:20,
3:306, 3:572
Mary (Orton), 3:317
Mary (Spencer), 3:574
Mary (Woodruff), 4:642
Mary/Mercy (Frary), 3:572
Mehitable, 3:572
Mehitable (----) Hinsdale,

3:573
Mehitable (Frary), 1:47,
2:201, 3:572
Mehitable (Johnson)
Hinsdale, 2:427
Mercy, 3:572-573
Ruth, 3:572
Ruth (Porter) Smith, 3:464,
3:573, 4:133
Sarah, 1:109, 3:6,
3:572-574, 4:656
Sarah (----) Leonard, 3:574
Sarah (Clark), 1:395
Sarah (Dumbleton)
Leonard, 3:80
Sarah (Hutchinson), 2:596
Sarah (Wadsworth), 3:573,
4:380
Susanna, 3:572-573, 3:646
Thankful, 3:573-574,
4:480
Rooten/Rowton
Ann (----), 3:574
Roper
Alice, 1:16, 3:575
Alice (----), 2:48, 3:575
Elizabeth, 2:84, 3:574-575
Hannah, 1:501, 3:575
Hannah (—) Goble, 3:574
Mary, 2:84, 3:574-575
Mary (Caldwell), 1:329
Rachel, 3:575
Ruth, 3:574
Sarah, 3:575
Susan (----), 3:575
Ropes
Abigail, 3:288, 3:575
Elizabeth, 3:575
Lydia, 3:575
Lydia (Wells), 3:575
Mary, 3:575, 3:656
Mary (----), 3:575
Ruth, 3:575
Ruth (Ingersoll), 3:575
Sarah, 3:575, 4:410
Sarah (----), 3:575
Sarah (Ingersoll), 2:520,
3:575
Rose
— (—) Potter, 4:696
— (Charles), 4:677, 4:698
Abigail, 3:575
Abigail (Barker) Foot,

Rose (continued)
Abigail (Barker) Foot
(continued)
2:181
Abigail (Grant), 2:291,
3:576
Abigail (Hale), 3:576
Alice (Hatch) Pickels,
3:576
Constance (----), 3:576
Dorcas, 3:576, 4:234
Dorothy, 3:575
Elizabeth, 3:466,
3:575-576, 4:693, 4:698,
4:702
Elizabeth (----) Potter,
3:466
Elizabeth (Bumpus), 3:576
Elizabeth (Collamore),
3:576
Elizabeth (Goodrich),
2:274, 3:575
Ellen (----) Luddington,
3:128
Hannah, 3:575-576, 4:698
Hannah (Allyn), 1:44,
3:576
Lydia, 3:575
Margery (----), 3:576
Martha, 3:128
Mary, 2:556, 3:575-576,
4:698
Mary (Fleming), 2:172
Mary (Foote), 3:576
Phebe (----) Potter, 4:698
Phebe (Bassett), 3:601
Rebecca (----), 4:698
Sarah, 2:180, 3:524,
3:575-576
Sarah (Remington), 3:524
Rosewell
Sarah, 4:645
Ross
---- (----) Luddington,
4:698
Ann (Lewis), 3:86, 3:577
Constance (Little), 3:577
Deborah (Osgood), 3:577,
3:657
Dorothy, 3:577, 4:529
Elizabeth, 4:698
Hannah, 1:289, 4:698
Margaret, 3:577

Martha, 4:698
Mary, 2:260, 2:295, 3:577,
4:698
Mary (----), 3:577
Mary (Knight), 3:663,
4:688
Mary (Osborn), 3:318,
3:577
Sarah, 3:577
Seeth (Holman), 2:451,
3:577
Rosseter/Rossiter/Rocester
Elizabeth, 3:578
Elizabeth (----), 3:577
Jane, 2:251, 3:578
Joanna, 1:462, 3:577-578
Mary, 3:578
Mary (Gilbert), 2:250,
2:455, 3:578
Patience, 3:578
Sarah, 3:577-578
Sarah (Sherman), 3:578
Susanna, 3:577-578
Roswell/Rosewell
Catharine, 3:578
Catharine (Russell), 3:578,
3:594
Dorcas, 3:578
Elizabeth, 3:578-579
Lydia, 3:578
Lydia (Trowbridge), 3:578,
4:333
Maud, 3:579
Sarah, 3:578
Rotherford/Rutherford
Elizabeth, 4:699
Lydia, 4:699
Mary, 2:332, 3:490, 3:579,
3:627, 4:699
Sarah, 3:579, 4:333
Sarah (----), 3:75, 3:579
Roundy/Roundee/Rounday
Ann (Bush), 3:579
Mary, 3:579
Rous/Rouse/Rowse
---- (Brooking/Brucken),
1:259
Ann, 3:579
Annis (Peabody), 3:375,
3:579
Elizabeth, 1:219, 1:452,
3:579
Elizabeth (Dotey), 3:579

Judith, 3:579
Judith (----), 3:579
Mary, 3:579
Mercy, 3:579
Sarah, 3:579
Sarah (----), 3:579
Suretrust (----), 3:579
Suretrust (Starr),
3:233-234
Thankful, 1:297
Rowden
---- (----) Hammond, 3:580
Elizabeth (----) Hammond,
2:346
Rowe/Row
Abigail, 3:580
Abigail (Alsop), 1:45,
3:580
Ann, 2:452
Bridget (----), 3:580, 3:611
Elizabeth, 3:580
Elizabeth (----), 3:580
Hannah, 3:523, 3:580
Jane, 2:3, 3:580
Margaret, 3:580, 3:652
Martha (George), 2:242
Mary, 3:580, 3:614
Mary (----), 3:618
Mary (Dickinson), 3:580
Mary (Prince), 3:580
Rachel, 3:580, 3:615
Rachel (Langdon), 3:580
Rebecca, 3:580
Rebecca (Long), 3:109
Ruth, 3:580, 3:615
Sarah, 3:580
Sarah (Abbot), 1:4
Sarah (Redington), 3:580
Rowell
Joanna (Pindar), 3:438,
3:581
Margery (----) Osgood,
3:581
Margery (Fowler) Osgood,
1:431, 3:657
Mary, 3:211, 3:581
Sarah, 3:331, 3:581
Sarah (Barnes), 1:123
Rowland
Abigail, 3:31, 3:581
Elizabeth, 3:72, 3:560,
3:581
Mary, 3:581

Rowland (continued)
Mary (Smith), 3:581
Rebecca, 3:581, 4:112
Rowlandson
— (----), 2:252
Ann, 3:582
Dorothy (Portland), 3:582
Elizabeth, 3:582
Hannah (Wilson), 3:582,
4:587
Martha, 3:582
Mary, 1:203, 3:581-582
Mary (White), 3:13, 3:581,
4:511
Sarah, 1:209, 3:581-582
Rowley
Abigail, 3:582
Ann, 3:582
Ann (----) Blossom, 1:205,
3:582
Catharine (Crippin), 1:515,
3:582
Elizabeth (Fuller), 2:217,
3:582
Grace, 3:582
Hannah, 3:582
Martha, 3:582
Mary, 3:582, 4:541
Mary (Denslow), 2:39,
3:582
Mehitable, 3:582
Sarah, 3:582, 3:630
Violet (Stedman), 3:582
Rowton
Ann (----), 3:583
Roy
Elizabeth, 3:583
Elizabeth (Phipps), 3:583
Mary, 3:583
Royal/Ryall
----, 3:583
Elizabeth (Dodd), 3:583
Jemima, 3:583
Jerusha, 3:583
Mary, 3:583
Mary (----), 3:583
Phebe, 3:583
Phebe (Green), 1:430,
3:583
Ruth, 3:583
Ruth (Tolman), 3:583,
4:310
Sarah, 3:583, 4:356

Sarah (----), 3:583
Royce/Roise
— (----), 4:287
Abigail, 3:570
Abigail (----) Hoyt, 3:570
Abigail (Cook) Pomeroy
Hoyt, 1:449
Deborah, 3:570
Deborah (Caulkins), 1:349,
3:569
Elizabeth, 3:569, 3:647
Elizabeth (----), 3:570
Elizabeth (Lothrop), 3:121,
3:569
Hannah, 3:570
Hannah (Churchwood),
1:387, 3:570
Hannah (Morgan), 3:570
Hannah (Wilcoxson)
Farnham, 2:143
Mary (----), 3:570
Mary (Porter), 3:646,
3:660
Patience, 3:570
Ruth, 3:120, 3:570
Sarah, 1:349, 3:569-570
Ruck
----, 1:311
Abigail, 3:584, 3:663
Bethia, 3:663
Elizabeth, 3:584, 3:657,
4:152
Elizabeth (----), 3:584
Elizabeth (Price) Croade,
1:473, 3:485, 3:584
Hannah, 1:241, 2:243,
3:584, 4:152
Hannah (Spooner), 3:584,
4:152
Joan, 2:341
Joane, 3:584
Margaret, 3:584
Margaret (Clark), 3:584
Mary, 3:584
Mary (Clark), 3:610
Mary (Wilson) Danforth,
2:8
Rebecca, 1:61, 3:584
Ruth, 3:663
Sarah, 3:584, 4:152
Sarah (Flint), 3:663
Rudd
Abigail, 3:585

Lydia, 3:585
Mary, 1:180, 3:585
Mary (Post), 3:585
Mercy, 3:585
Mercy (----), 3:585
Patience, 1:318, 3:584
Ruel
Emma (Seeley), 3:585,
4:50
Rugg
Abigail, 3:585
Bathsheba, 3:585
Elizabeth, 3:585
Elizabeth (----), 3:585
Elizabeth (Munroe), 3:257
Elizabeth (Priest), 3:585
Hannah, 3:585
Hannah (----), 3:585
Hannah (Singletary), 3:585
Hepzibah, 3:585
Martha, 3:585
Martha (Prescott), 3:481,
3:585
Mary, 3:585
Mehitable, 3:585
Mercy, 3:585
Milicent, 3:585
Rebecca, 3:585
Ruth, 3:585
Sarah, 3:585
Sarah (Newton), 3:585
Tabitha, 3:585
Ruggles
----, 3:587
---- (Day), 2:26
Abigail, 3:587
Abigail (Crafts), 1:469,
3:586
Ann, 3:587
Ann (----), 3:587
Ann (Bright), 1:253, 3:587
Ann (Fowle), 3:621
Barbara (----), 3:586
Dorothy, 3:587
Elizabeth, 1:278,
3:586-587
Elizabeth (----), 3:580,
3:586
Elizabeth (Phillips), 3:411
Frances (----), 3:586
Hannah, 3:587-588
Hannah (Devotion), 2:42,
3:587

Ruggles (continued)
Hannah (Fowle), 3:587
Huldah, 3:587
Lucy, 3:588
Margaret (----), 3:586
Martha, 3:587-588
Martha (Devotion), 2:42, 3:587
Martha (Maudsley), 3:652
Martha (Woodbridge), 3:588
Mary, 3:432, 3:586-588
Mary (----), 3:588
Mary (Gibson), 2:248, 3:586
Mary (May), 3:183, 3:587
Mehitable, 3:586, 3:588
Mercy (Veazie), 4:369
Patience, 3:588
Rachel, 3:138, 3:586, 4:158
Rebecca, 3:516, 3:586-587
Rebecca (----), 3:587
Ruth (----), 3:586
Sarah, 3:586-588, 4:580
Sarah (----), 3:588
Sarah (Dyer), 3:586
Sarah (Fielder), 2:157
Sarah (Paine), 3:587
Rule
Margaret, 4:292
Rumball
Bethia, 3:588, 4:191
Rumery
Sarah, 4:516
Rumney
Rebecca (Willet), 4:556
Rumrill/Rumerell/etc
Sarah, 3:588
Sarah (Fairman), 3:588
Rumsey/Rumsie
Rachel (Frost), 2:211
Rebecca (Rawson), 3:511, 3:588
Rundell
Abigail (Tyler), 4:356
Rusco
Esther (----), 3:258
Esther (Musse/Must), 3:589
Joanna (Corlet), 3:589
Mary, 3:589, 4:474
Rebecca (----), 3:589

Rebecca (Beebe), 3:589
Sarah, 1:426, 3:589
Rush
Elizabeth, 3:589
Elizabeth (----), 3:589
Judith (----), 3:589
Thankful, 3:589
Russ
Deborah (Osgood), 3:320, 3:589
Margaret (----), 3:589
Mary, 2:186, 3:589
Sarah, 3:122, 3:589
Russell
---- (----), 1:251
---- (----) James, 2:536
---- (----) Smith, 4:132
---- (Rogers), 3:561, 3:590
Abigail, 1:248, 3:592, 3:594
Abigail (Curwin) Hathorne, 1:488, 2:377, 3:590
Abigail (Whiting), 3:594, 4:518
Abigail (Winship), 3:595
Alice (----) Sparrow, 3:595
Ann, 2:507
Catharine, 3:578, 3:594
Catharine (Thornton) Cannon Edwards, 4:293
Dorothy (----), 3:592
Dorothy (----) Smith, 3:591, 4:115
Elizabeth, 2:295, 2:404, 3:590-595, 3:663, 4:589
Elizabeth (----), 3:591-592
Elizabeth (Baker), 3:591
Elizabeth (Fiske), 2:165
Elizabeth (Gibbs), 2:247
Elizabeth (Nurse), 3:300
Elizabeth (Palmer), 3:592
Elizabeth (Russell), 3:663
Elizabeth (Terry), 3:593, 4:269
Esther, 3:593-594
Esther (Tuttle), 3:594
Hannah, 2:290, 3:592-593, 3:595, 4:696, 4:699
Hannah (----), 2:25, 3:592
Hannah (Moulthrop), 3:248, 3:592
Jane (----), 3:590
Jane (----) James, 3:590

Jane (Blackman), 3:593
Joanna, 3:257, 3:593, 4:115
Joanna (Cutler), 1:493
Joanna (Smith), 3:593, 4:115
Joyce, 3:528, 3:589, 3:595
Lydia, 3:592
Mabel, 2:544, 3:590, 3:592
Mabel (Haynes), 2:389, 3:590
Martha, 3:590, 3:592, 3:594
Martha (----), 1:234, 2:338, 3:594
Martha (Moody), 3:226, 3:592
Mary, 1:262, 2:455, 2:533, 3:590-594, 3:663
Mary (----), 3:466, 3:590
Mary (----) Chester, 1:438, 3:594
Mary (Belcher), 3:592, 3:602
Mary (Bridge), 1:248
Mary (Church), 1:385, 3:593
Mary (Hamlin), 2:344, 3:593
Mary (Hitchcock), 3:593, 3:632, 4:699
Mary (Hubbard), 3:590
Mary (Marshall), 3:159, 3:594
Mary (Pendleton), 3:590
Mary (Talcott), 3:591, 4:250
Mary (Wade) Sharpe Chester, 1:375
Mary (Wolcott), 3:590, 4:621
Maud, 3:60-61, 3:590
Maud (----), 3:593
Mehitable, 1:357, 3:589, 3:593
Mehitable (Wyllis), 2:188, 3:589, 4:577, 4:633
Patience, 3:143
Phebe, 3:594
Phebe (Gregson) Whiting, 2:316, 4:518
Prudence, 3:592, 3:594

Russell (continued)
Prudence (Chester), 1:375, 3:594
Rachel, 3:592
Rebecca, 1:422, 3:589-590, 3:592
Rebecca (----), 3:589
Rebecca (Newberry), 3:269, 3:591
Ruth, 3:592
Sarah, 2:519, 3:589, 3:591-592
Sarah (Brooks), 1:259
Sarah (Champney), 3:591
Sarah (Davis), 2:23, 3:595
Rust
Elizabeth (Rogers), 3:569
Experience, 2:324, 3:595
Mary, 1:131
Mary (Morgan) Pringrydays, 3:488
Rebecca, 3:595
Rebecca (Clark), 1:404, 3:595
Sarah, 1:35, 3:595
Rutherford - see Rotherford
Rutter
Elizabeth, 3:595
Elizabeth (----), 3:595
Elizabeth (Plympton), 3:448
Jane, 1:50
Mary, 2:444
Rutty
Abigail, 3:596
Cary, 3:596
Mercy, 3:596
Phebe, 3:596
Rebecca, 3:596
Rebecca (Stevens), 3:596, 4:188
Ryder
Mary (Gray), 2:298
Sabin
Abigail, 1:296, 4:1
Experience, 4:1
Hannah, 1:34
Margaret, 1:336, 4:2
Mary, 4:1-2
Mehitable, 4:1
Mercy, 4:2, 4:454
Patience, 3:76, 4:1
Sarah, 4:1

Sarah (Parker), 4:1
Sacket/Sackett
Abigail, 3:285, 4:2
Abigail (Hannum), 2:351
Agnes (Tinkham), 4:2
Ann (----), 4:2
Deborah, 4:2
Deborah (----), 4:2
Elizabeth, 4:2
Elizabeth (Betts), 1:173, 4:2
Hannah, 4:2
Isabel (----), 4:2
Martha, 4:2, 4:638
Mary, 3:605, 4:2
Mary (Wooden), 4:638
Mercy (Whitehead) Betts, 1:173, 4:2
Rebecca, 4:2
Sarah, 4:2
Sarah (Blomfield), 1:204, 4:2
Sarah (Cram), 4:2
Sarah (Denison), 2:37
Sarah (Stiles) Stewart, 4:2, 4:191, 4:194
Sadd
Hannah, 4:3
Hepzibah, 4:3
Hepzibah (----) Pratt, 3:473, 4:3
Sadler
Abiel, 4:3
Ann, 1:36, 2:369
Ann (Coke), 4:567
Deborah (----), 4:3
Martha (Cheney), 1:316, 1:372, 4:3
Rebecca (----), 4:3
Saffin/Saffyn
Elizabeth (----) Lidget, 4:4
Elizabeth (Scammon) Lidgett, 3:90
Martha (Willet), 1:270, 4:3, 4:557
Rebecca (Lee), 3:73, 4:4
Sage
Elizabeth, 4:4
Elizabeth (Kirby), 3:30, 4:4
Mary, 2:557, 4:4
Mercy, 4:4
Mercy (----), 4:4
Susanna, 1:25

Sale/Seale/Saile
Abigail, 4:5
Alice (----), 4:5
Hepzibah, 4:5
Margaret (----), 4:5
Mary, 4:5
Mary (----), 4:413
Mary (Foster), 2:187, 4:5
Sarah, 4:5
Sarah (----), 4:5
Sarah (James), 2:535
Thankful, 4:5
Salisbury
Annabel (----), 4:5
Bridget (----), 4:5
Elizabeth (----), 4:5
Susanna (----), 4:5
Salisbury, Earl of
Catharine, 2:66
Sallows
----, 4:5, 4:582
Freeborn (----), 4:703
Hannah, 4:5, 4:703
Martha, 4:5
Mary, 3:647, 4:5, 4:703
Sarah, 4:5
Salls
Ann (Lenthall), 4:5
Sally/Sallee
Mary, 2:599
Mary (----), 4:6
Rebecca, 2:563, 4:6
Sarah (----), 4:6
Salmon/Sammon/etc
Ann, 4:703
Ann (Thompson), 4:703
Elizabeth, 3:572, 4:6, 4:703
Joanna (Riland), 4:6
Margery, 4:198
Martha, 4:703
Mary, 4:6, 4:703
Mary (----), 3:406, 4:6, 4:703
Remember (Felton), 4:703
Ruth, 4:6
Sarah, 2:73, 4:703
Susanna, 4:703
Salter
----, 4:7
Abigail, 1:106
Ann (Condy), 3:612, 4:703
Elizabeth, 4:6

Salter (continued)
Elizabeth (----), 4:6
Hannah, 3:413, 4:7
Hannah (----), 4:6
Joan (----), 4:6
Lydia, 4:7
Mary, 2:531, 4:6-7
Mary (----), 4:6-7
Mehitable, 4:7
Sarah, 4:6
Saltonstall
----, 4:8
Abigail, 4:8
Elizabeth, 1:463, 2:37, 4:7,
4:9, 4:678
Elizabeth (Roswell), 3:579
Elizabeth (Ward), 4:7,
4:408
Grace, 4:8-9
Gracy (Kaye), 4:8
Jerusha (Richards), 2:15,
3:532
Martha, 1:395
Martha (Wilford), 4:8
Meriel (Gurdon), 4:8
Rosamond, 4:8-9
Sampson
----, 2:357, 4:10
---- (----) Stodder, 4:10,
4:202
---- (Haynes), 2:390, 4:10
---- (Nash), 3:262, 4:9
Abigail, 4:9-10
Ann (Plummer), 4:10
Bridget (Clopton), 4:10
Dorcas, 1:211, 4:10
Elizabeth, 4:10, 4:158
Elizabeth (----), 4:9
Grace, 4:9
Hannah, 2:453, 4:10
Judith, 4:10
Lora, 4:9
Lydia, 4:10, 4:509
Lydia (Standish), 4:10
Martha, 4:10
Mary, 4:10, 4:230
Mary (Standish), 4:9
Priscilla, 4:10
Rachel, 4:9
Rebecca, 4:9
Ruth, 4:10
Sarah, 4:9
Sarah (Standish), 4:9

Sams/Sammes
Elizabeth (----), 4:10
Mary, 2:103, 4:11
Mercy, 4:11
Samuel
Lucy (----) Wight, 4:11
Samways/Samois/Samwise
Esther, 2:465
Esther (----), 4:11
Sanborn
---- (Bachiler), 1:89, 4:11
Abigail, 2:31, 3:160,
4:11-13
Abigail (----), 3:480
Abigail (Gove) Dalton,
4:11
Amy, 4:13
Ann, 4:11-12
Deborah, 4:12
Dinah, 3:160
Dorothy, 4:11-12
Elizabeth, 4:12
Elizabeth (Dearborn), 2:32
Elizabeth (Sherburne),
4:12
Hannah, 2:388, 4:12
Hannah (Moulton), 4:12
Hannah (Philbrick), 4:12
Huldah, 4:12
Jemima, 4:11
Joanna, 4:11
Judith, 2:287, 4:11-12
Judith (Coffin), 4:12
Keziah, 4:12
Love, 4:12
Lydia, 4:12
Lydia (Leavitt), 4:12
Margaret, 4:12
Margaret (----) Webster
Godfrey, 2:266
Margaret (Page) Moulton,
4:11
Mary, 1:347, 4:11-13
Mary (----) Boulter, 4:12
Mary (Gove), 2:288, 4:12
Mary (Marston), 3:161,
4:13
Mary (Moulton), 3:248,
4:13
Mary (Tuck), 4:11, 4:337
Meribah (----) Tilton, 4:11
Phebe, 4:13
Rachel, 4:12

Rebecca (Prescott), 3:480,
4:12
Ruth, 4:12
Ruth (Moulton), 4:12
Sarah, 3:550, 4:11-13
Sarah (----), 4:11-12
Sarah (----) Perkins, 4:12
Susanna, 4:11
Theodate, 4:11
Sanders
Ann, 2:45
Hannah, 3:287
Sarah, 3:436
Sanderson
---- (----) Cross, 3:390
Abigail (Fiske), 2:166
Hannah (Price), 3:485
Sands/Sandes
Ann (Manning), 3:355
Mercy, 4:13
Sarah, 3:284, 4:13
Sarah (----), 4:13
Sandy/Sandie
Ann (Holmes), 4:13
Elizabeth, 4:13
Mary, 4:13
Sandys
Ann (Manning), 3:147
Deliverance, 4:13
Mary, 4:13
Sybil (----), 4:13
Sanford/Sandford/etc
---- (----) Smith, 4:114
---- (Rockwell), 3:557,
4:16
Abigail, 4:13, 4:15-16
Ann, 4:14-16
Ann (Adams), 1:11, 4:15
Bathsheba, 1:181
Bathshua, 4:15
Bridget, 4:15
Bridget (----), 4:14
Deborah, 4:16
Elizabeth, 1:43, 1:433,
4:13-16, 4:685
Elizabeth (----), 4:15
Elizabeth (Paine), 4:16,
4:694
Elizabeth (Smith), 4:14,
4:113
Elizabeth (Spatchurst),
4:14
Elizabeth (Webb), 4:444

Sanford/Sandford/etc
(continued)
Esther, 4:14
Frances (----) Smith, 3:498
Hannah, 1:352, 4:13,
4:15-16
Hannah (----), 4:15
Jane, 4:15
Margery (----), 4:15
Martha, 4:13-14
Mary, 1:331, 4:13-15,
4:345, 4:587
Mary (Botsford), 1:217,
4:14
Mary (Brenton), 1:242,
4:15
Mary (Gorton) Greene,
2:283, 2:305, 4:14
Mary (Long), 3:108, 4:14
Mary (Powell), 4:14, 4:696
Mary (Pratt), 3:471
Rebecca, 4:14, 4:16
Rebecca (----), 4:14
Ruth, 1:318, 4:16
Sarah, 4:14-16, 4:93
Sarah (----), 4:15
Sarah (----) Potter, 3:467,
4:14
Sarah (Arnold), 1:66
Sarah (Waddell), 4:15,
4:377
Sarah (Willet), 4:16, 4:556
Susanna, 4:14
Susanna (----), 1:323, 4:15
Sanger
Abigail, 4:17
Deborah, 4:17
Elizabeth, 4:16-17
Elizabeth (Morse), 4:16-17
Esther, 4:17
Hannah, 4:17
Jane, 4:16
Mary, 2:362, 4:16-17
Mary (Cutter), 1:496, 4:16
Mary (Reynolds), 3:526,
4:16
Mehitable, 4:16
Rebecca, 4:16
Rebecca (Park), 3:348,
4:16
Ruth (----), 4:16
Sarah, 4:16-17
Sarah (----), 4:16

Sape
Mary, 3:311
Sargent/Sargeant/etc
----, 4:18
Abigail, 4:17, 4:19, 4:190
Abigail (Clark), 1:393,
4:19
Ann, 3:618, 4:19
Catharine (----) Brown,
4:17
Deborah, 4:17
Deborah (Hillier), 4:17
Dorothy (----), 4:18
Elizabeth, 1:177, 1:424,
2:172, 4:17-19, 4:341
Elizabeth (----), 4:17
Elizabeth (Perkins), 3:396,
4:19
Esther, 4:17
Esther (Mccarty), 4:17
Hannah, 3:619, 4:17-19
Hannah (Haraden), 4:18
Hannah (Howard), 4:18
Hannah (Short), 4:20
Hope, 4:17
Lydia, 4:17
Lydia (Chipman), 1:380,
4:17
Margaret, 4:18
Martha (Baker), 4:18
Mary, 1:352, 4:17-19
Mary (Bense), 4:17
Mary (Colby), 1:424, 4:19
Mary (Duncan), 3:617,
4:19
Mary (Norwood), 4:18
Mary (Spencer) Hall Phips,
4:18
Mary (Spencer) Hull Phips,
2:493, 3:422, 4:148
Mary (Stevens), 4:18
Mehitable, 4:17
Mehitable (Minot) Cooper,
1:455, 3:217, 4:18,
4:201
Naomi (Stanwood), 4:20
Rachel, 4:17
Rachel (Barnes), 1:123,
4:18
Ruth, 1:218, 4:17, 4:19,
4:601
Sarah, 1:93, 4:17, 4:19,
4:257

Sarah (----), 4:19
Sarah (----) Bradstreet,
1:235
Sarah (Harvey), 4:18
Sarson
Ann, 4:652
Jane (----) Mayhew, 4:17
Jane (Paine) Mayhew,
3:185, 4:690
Mehitable, 4:703
Satterly/Shatterly/Saterlee
Rebecca, 4:20
Rebecca (Bemis) Minter
Dymond, 1:163
Sarah, 4:20
Saunders
----, 4:21
---- (Grafton), 4:21
---- (Hardier), 2:353
Abiah, 4:20
Abigail, 4:21
Abigail (Bissell), 4:20
Ann (----), 4:21
Elizabeth, 1:139, 2:353,
4:20-22, 4:369, 4:620,
4:703
Elizabeth (----) Bancroft,
1:110, 1:248, 4:21
Esther, 4:20
Esther (----), 2:261
Esther (Rolfe), 3:571, 4:20
Hannah, 4:20, 4:703
Hannah (Pickman), 4:703
Judith, 4:21
Leah, 4:21
Lydia, 4:22
Lydia (Hardier), 4:21
Mary, 2:108, 4:20-21
Mary (Clark), 4:22
Mary (Munjoy), 4:21
Mary (Saxton), 4:20, 4:32
Rachel, 4:21
Rachel (----), 4:21
Return (Shattuck), 4:21,
4:62
Ruth, 4:21
Sarah, 4:20-21
Sarah (----), 4:21
Susanna, 4:20
Saunderson
Abia, 4:22
Abial/Abia (Bartlett), 1:133,
4:22

264

Saunderson (continued)
Abigail (Traine), 4:23
Ann (Shattuck), 4:23
Elizabeth (—), 4:23
Esther, 4:22
Hannah, 4:22-23
Lydia, 2:566, 4:22-23
Lydia (—), 4:22
Mary, 4:22-23
Mary (—), 4:22
Mary (—) Cross, 1:477,
4:22
Mary (Eggleston), 4:22
Sarah, 4:22-23
Sarah (—), 4:23
Sarah (Crow), 4:23
Sarah (Page), 4:22
Susanna, 4:22
Savage
Abigail, 4:24-25, 4:71
Christian (—), 4:27
Dionysia, 3:509, 4:25-27
Elizabeth, 1:162, 4:23-27,
4:513
Elizabeth (Brown) Butler,
1:321, 4:23
Elizabeth (Dubbin), 4:24
Elizabeth (Norton)
Symmes, 4:23, 4:242
Elizabeth (Scottow), 4:27,
4:40
Elizabeth (Walford), 4:24,
4:392
Esther, 4:25
Esther (Ranney), 3:508,
4:25
Faith, 4:27
Faith (Hutchinson),
2:512-513, 4:26
Faith (Phillips), 3:414
Hannah, 2:255, 2:279,
4:23-27, 4:99, 4:357
Hannah (Phillips)
Anderson, 3:414
Hannah (Tyng), 2:279,
4:24, 4:357
Lydia, 4:27
Margaret, 1:27
Martha (Allen), 1:29, 4:23
Mary, 4:23-27, 4:274,
4:357, 4:473, 4:527
Mary (Quincy), 3:500,
4:23

Mary (Ranney), 3:508,
4:25
Mary (Symmes), 4:26,
4:200, 4:244
Mercy, 4:25
Rachel, 4:24-25
Sarah, 2:414, 4:23-27,
4:546
Sarah (—), 1:263
Sarah (Bowen), 4:24
Sarah (Hough), 2:468,
4:23
Susanna, 4:24-25
Savil
— (Tidd), 4:265
Abigail, 4:27
Bethia, 4:27
Deborah, 4:27-28
Deborah (Faxon), 2:149,
4:28
Experience (Quincy),
3:501, 4:28
Hannah, 4:27
Hannah (—), 4:27
Hannah (Adams), 1:13,
4:27
Judith, 4:28
Lydia (—), 4:27
Mary, 4:27
Mehitable, 4:27
Mehitable (—), 4:27
Sarah, 4:27
Sarah (—), 2:149
Sarah (Gamitt/Jarmill),
4:27
Savory/Savorie/Savary
Catharine (Busby), 1:316
Mary, 3:503, 4:28
Mary (—) Mitchell, 4:28
Mary (Sawyer) Mitchell,
3:221
Sarah, 3:231, 4:28
Susanna, 4:28
Sawdy
Ann (—), 4:29
Elizabeth, 4:29
Mary, 4:29
Sawin
Abigail, 4:29
Abigail (—), 4:29
Abigail (Munning), 4:29
Deborah, 4:29
Deborah (Rice), 3:530,

4:29
Elizabeth, 4:29
Judith (Pierce), 3:426, 4:29
Mary, 4:29
Mercy, 4:29
Ruth, 4:29
Sarah, 4:29
Sarah (Stone), 4:29, 4:206
Sawtell/Sartell/Sautell/etc
Abigail, 4:29
Ann, 4:30
Bethia, 4:29-30
Elizabeth, 4:29-30
Elizabeth (—), 4:30
Elizabeth (Harris), 4:30
Hannah, 4:29-30, 4:597
Hannah (Lawrence), 3:61,
4:29
Margaret, 4:649
Mary, 4:29-30
Mary (—), 4:29-30
Ruth, 2:407, 4:29-30
Sarah, 4:29
Susanna, 4:29
Susanna (Randall), 3:505,
4:29
Sawyer
Abigail, 4:30
Ann, 4:30
Ann (—), 4:30
Elizabeth, 4:30-31
Hannah, 4:30-31, 4:703
Hannah (Very) Foster,
3:621
Martha, 4:30
Mary, 1:478, 2:119, 2:136,
3:221, 4:30-31, 4:641
Mary (—), 4:30
Mary (Emery), 2:119, 4:31
Mary (Marble), 4:30
Mary (Prescott), 3:481,
4:31
Mercy, 2:90
Mercy (Little), 3:99, 4:30
Rebecca (—) Snow, 4:30
Rebecca (Baker) Snow,
4:138
Ruth, 3:237, 4:30-31,
4:703
Ruth (—), 4:31
Sarah, 1:273, 3:519,
4:30-31
Sarah (—), 4:703

Sawyer (continued)
Sarah (——) Wells, 4:31
Sarah (Bray), 3:605, 4:30
Sarah (Littlefield) Wells,
  4:475
Sarah (Poor), 4:30
Sarah (Potter), 4:30
Saxton/Sexton
Ann (Copp) Atwood, 1:77,
  4:32
Catharine (——), 4:31
Elizabeth, 3:354, 4:31-32
Hannah, 4:31-32
Hannah (——), 4:31
Hannah (Denison), 2:36,
  4:32
Hannah (Denison)
  Chesebrough, 1:373
Hannah (Fowler), 2:193,
  4:32
Hannah (Wright), 4:32,
  4:654
Jerusha, 4:32
Lucy (——), 4:32
Mary, 4:20, 4:31-32
Mary (——), 4:32
Mary (Hill), 2:418, 4:32
Mary (Woodward), 1:107
Mercy, 4:32
Mindwell, 4:32
Patience, 4:32
Phebe, 4:31
Sarah, 3:545, 4:31-32
Sarah (Bancroft), 4:31
Sarah (Cook), 4:32
Sarah (Knight), 4:687
Silence, 3:455, 4:32
Sayer/Sayre/Sayers
Mary (Hubbard), 4:32
Sarah, 2:477
Sarah (——), 4:33
Sayle/Sayles
——, 2:301, 2:305
Catharine, 3:314
Elizabeth (Comstock),
  4:33
Mary, 4:33
Mary (——), 4:33
Sayward/Sayword
Mary (——), 4:33
Mary (Webb), 4:447
Saywell
Abigail (Buttolph), 1:180,

1:323, 4:33
Elizabeth, 2:19, 4:33
Susan (——), 4:33
Scadlock
Eleanor (——), 3:13
Elinor (——), 4:33
Rebecca, 4:33
Sarah, 4:33
Susanna, 4:33
Scammon/Scammond/etc
Ann, 4:390
Elizabeth, 3:90, 4:34
Elizabeth (Jordan), 4:34
Elizabeth (Wakeley), 4:387
Jane, 2:31, 4:34
Mary, 4:34
Prudence, 4:34
Prudence (Waldron), 4:34,
  4:391
Rebecca, 4:34
Scamp
Joan (Collins), 1:435, 4:34
Mary, 4:34
Scant
Joanna, 4:428, 4:428
Sarah, 4:34
Sarah (Brown), 4:34
Susanna, 4:34, 4:277
Scarborough
Bethia (——), 4:34
Deborah, 4:34
Hannah, 4:34
Mary (——), 4:313
Mary (Smith), 4:34, 4:131
Scarlet
——, 4:35
Elizabeth, 4:35
Jane, 4:35
Margaret, 4:35
Mary, 4:35
Mary (——), 4:35
Rebecca, 4:69-70
Thomasine, 4:35
Thomasine (——), 4:35
Scate
Sarah (——), 4:35
Scathe
Ann, 4:35
Schrick
Mary (Varleet) Ambeck,
  1:48, 4:35, 4:366
Scofield/Scovil/Scovel/etc
—— (——), 3:390, 4:36

Abigail (Merwin), 3:201
Amie, 4:35
Ann (——), 4:35
Elizabeth, 4:35-36
Elizabeth (——), 4:35
Hannah (Benton), 1:170,
  4:36
Hannah (Richards), 4:40
Joanna, 4:36
Mary, 4:36
Mary (Lucas), 4:36
Mary/Mercy, 4:36
Rachel (——), 4:35
Sarah, 3:404, 4:35-36
Sarah (——), 4:36
Sarah (Barnes), 3:600,
  4:36
Scolley
Hannah, 4:36
Hannah (Barrett), 1:125,
  4:36
Mary, 4:36
Sarah, 4:36
Scoon/Scone
Elizabeth, 4:36
Sarah, 4:36
Sarah (Hart), 4:36
Score
Sarah (Hart), 2:367
Scotchford
Susanna (Meriam), 4:36
Scott
—— (——) Porter, 4:696,
  4:703
Abigail, 4:39
Abigail (——), 4:38
Abigail (Neal), 3:264
Ann, 4:37
Ann (——), 2:183, 4:39
Bathshua (Oxenbridge),
  3:327
Bridget, 4:37
Catharine, 4:37
Catharine (Marbury), 4:38
Deborah, 4:37
Deliverance, 3:538, 4:38
Elizabeth, 3:112, 4:37,
  4:36-39, 4:653
Elizabeth (——), 4:38-39
Elizabeth (——) Upson,
  4:36
Elizabeth (Fuller) Upson,
  4:362

Scott (continued)
  Elizabeth (Webster), 4:37
  Hannah, 1:403, 2:194,
    4:36-39, 4:443
  Hannah (Allis), 1:42, 4:39
  Hannah (Duncan/Dunkin),
    4:38
  Hannah (Hawks), 2:381,
    4:38
  Joanna (Jenks), 2:543
  Margaret, 4:37-38
  Margaret (----), 4:36
  Margaret (Hubbard), 2:486,
    3:560, 4:39
  Martha, 4:38-39
  Martha (----), 4:39
  Mary, 2:119, 2:446, 3:260,
    3:368, 3:462, 4:37-39
  Mary (Orvis), 3:657, 4:39
  Mary (Richards), 4:37
  Mehitable, 4:39
  Patience, 1:154, 4:38
  Rebecca, 4:506, 4:551
  Rebecca (----), 4:37
  Redemption, 4:38
  Sarah, 3:78, 4:37-39,
    4:164, 4:269
  Sarah (----), 4:38
  Sarah (Bliss), 1:202, 4:37
  Susanna, 4:77
  Susanna (Searle), 4:36
Scottow/Scottaway
  Elizabeth, 4:27, 4:39-40
  Joan (----), 4:40
  Lydia, 1:369, 2:245,
    4:39-40
  Lydia (----), 4:39-40
  Mary, 1:369, 4:39-40
  Mehitable, 4:40
  Rebecca, 1:194, 4:39-40
  Rebecca (----), 4:39
  Sarah, 4:40, 4:396
  Sarah (----), 4:40
  Sarah (Symmes), 4:40
  Thomasine, 4:40
  Thomasine (----), 4:39
Scranton
  Adeline (----) Johnson Hill,
    3:632, 4:41, 4:686
  Ann, 4:41
  Deborah, 4:41
  Deborah (----) Thompson,
    4:41

Deborah (Dudley)
    Thompson, 2:78
  Elizabeth, 4:41
  Elizabeth (Bishop) Clark,
    1:185
  Elizabeth (Clark), 4:41
  Elizabeth (Goodrich), 4:41
  Hannah, 4:41
  Hannah (----), 1:41
  Joanna (----), 4:41
  Mary, 4:41
  Mary (Seward), 4:41, 4:57
  Mehitable, 4:41
  Mercy, 2:558, 4:41
  Sarah, 1:317, 4:41
  Sarah (----) Munger, 4:703
  Sarah (Hull) Munger,
    4:692
  Sarah (Stafford), 4:160
Scribner/Scrivener
  Deborah (Lees), 3:75, 4:41
  Hannah (Crampton), 1:470,
    4:41
  Mary, 4:41
  Rebecca, 4:41
Scripture
  Abigail, 4:41
  Elizabeth (----), 4:41
  Jemima, 4:41
  Lydia, 4:41
  Mary, 4:41
  Mary (----), 4:41
  Ruth, 4:41
  Sarah, 4:41
Scriven/Screven/Scrieven
  Alice (Knowles), 3:42
  Bridget (----), 4:41
  Bridget (Cutts), 1:495
  Elizabeth, 2:93, 4:41
  Mary (----), 4:41
Scruggs
  ----, 4:42
  Margery (----), 4:42
Scudder
  Deborah, 4:43
  Elizabeth, 3:121, 4:43
  Elizabeth (----), 4:43
  Elizabeth (Hamblen),
    2:343
  Elizabeth (Hamlin), 4:43
  Experience, 4:43
  Hannah, 1:112, 2:375,
    4:43

Joanna (Betts), 1:173, 4:43
  Mary, 4:43
  Phebe (Titus), 4:43
  Rachel (----), 4:43
  Reliance, 4:43
  Sarah, 4:43
Scullard
  Martha, 4:43
  Mary, 3:12, 3:571, 4:43
  Rebecca, 4:43
  Rebecca (Kent), 1:184,
    3:12, 4:43
  Sarah, 4:43
Seabrook
  ----, 2:137, 3:483, 4:43
Seabury
  Elizabeth, 4:43
  Grace, 4:44
  Grace (----), 4:43
  Hannah, 3:365, 4:44
  Martha, 4:44
  Martha (Peabody), 3:375,
    4:44
  Patience, 4:44
  Patience (Kemp), 4:43
  Sarah, 4:44
Seager/Seeger/Seger
  Abigail, 4:44
  Elizabeth, 4:44
  Elizabeth (----), 4:44
  Elizabeth (Moody), 3:226,
    4:44
  Margaret, 4:44
  Mary, 4:44
  Mercy, 4:44
  Sarah, 4:44
  Sarah (Bishop), 4:44
  Sarah (Wheeler), 4:44
  Thankful, 4:44
Seale
  Rebecca, 2:523
Sealey - see also Seeley
  Elizabeth (Washburn)
    Howard, 4:429
Sealis
  ---- (Hatherly) Hanford,
    2:186
  Eglin (Hatherly) Hanford,
    2:349, 4:44
  Esther, 2:531, 4:44
  Hannah, 4:44, 4:592
Search
  Ann (----), 4:45

Search (continued)
Catharine (----), 4:45
Searle
Abigail, 4:703
Ann (----) Lippit, 4:45
Ann (Grove) Lippit,
3:97-98
Catharine (----) Warner,
4:45
Damaris (----), 3:419,
4:704
Deborah, 4:45
Deborah (----), 4:45
Deliverance (Tyng), 4:45,
4:357
Joan (Calverly) White,
4:45
Joanna, 4:428
Lydia, 4:45
Mary, 4:45, 4:703-704
Mary (----), 4:703
Mary (North), 3:289, 4:45
Mary (Ruggles), 3:586
Miriam, 1:338
Rebecca, 2:523
Ruth, 4:45
Ruth (Janes/Jeanes), 2:538
Ruth (Jones), 4:45
Sarah, 4:45
Sarah (----), 2:103
Sarah (Baldwin), 4:45
Susanna, 4:36
Sears
Ann (----) Farrar, 4:46
Deborah, 3:328, 4:46
Deborah (Willard), 4:46,
4:553
Dorothy, 4:704
Dorothy (----), 4:46
Dorothy (Thacher), 4:704
Elizabeth, 4:704
Elizabeth (Dimmock), 4:46
Esther (Mason), 4:46
Hannah, 4:46
Mary, 1:339, 4:46, 4:356
Mary (----), 2:507, 4:46
Mary (Downer), 4:46
Mary (Hilton), 4:46
Mercy (Mayo), 4:233
Rebecca, 2:232, 4:46
Sarah (Graham/Grimes)
Marvin, 3:164
Susanna (----), 4:46

Seaver
Abigail, 4:47
Abigail (Twelves), 4:353
Elizabeth, 1:470, 2:441,
4:46
Elizabeth (Allard), 1:28,
4:46
Elizabeth (Ballard/Bullard),
4:46
Hannah, 4:46-47
Hannah (Wilson), 4:47,
4:586
Lucy, 2:264
Mary, 4:46
Mary (----), 4:46
Mary (----) Pepper, 3:391,
4:46
Rebecca (Wilson), 4:586
Sarah, 4:46
Sarah (Inglesby/Ingoldsby),
4:46
Thankful, 4:47
Seaverns/Seavern/Seborn
Abigail, 4:47
Deborah, 4:47
Elizabeth, 4:47
Mary, 4:47
Mary (----), 4:47
Rebecca, 4:47
Rebecca (Stratton), 4:47
Sarah, 4:47
Sarah (Grant), 2:291, 4:47
Seavey/Seavy
Elizabeth (----), 4:47
Hannah (Philbrick) Walker,
3:409, 4:394
Hannah (Philbrook)
Walker, 4:47
Sebborn/Sibborne/Seaborn
Deborah, 4:47
Elizabeth, 2:143, 4:47
Esther, 2:503
Mary, 4:47
Mary (----), 4:47
Seccomb
Ann, 4:48
Ann (----), 4:48
Dorothy, 4:48
Hannah (Willis), 4:47
Rebecca (Willis), 4:48
Susanna, 4:47
Sedgwick
Abigail, 4:49

Elizabeth, 4:49
Elizabeth (----), 4:48
Elizabeth (Stone), 3:547,
4:49, 4:208
Hannah, 4:48
Joanna (----), 1:36, 4:48
Mary, 4:49
Mary (Hopkins), 2:462,
4:48-49
Mercy, 4:49
Sarah, 3:83, 4:48
Sarah (----), 4:48
Thankful, 4:49
Seeley/Seely
---- (----) Miller, 3:210,
4:49
Dorcas, 2:245, 4:50
Elizabeth (----) Olmstead
Gilbert, 4:49
Emma, 3:585, 4:50
Mary, 4:49
Mary (----), 4:50
Mary (Turney), 4:49,
4:349
Phebe, 4:49
Rebecca, 4:49
Rebecca (Sanford), 4:14
Sarah, 4:49
Sarah (Squire), 4:49, 4:158
Selden/Seldon
Esther, 4:50
Esther (----), 4:50, 4:418
Felix (Lewis), 3:89, 4:50
Hannah, 4:50
Mary, 4:50, 4:261
Mercy, 4:50
Rebecca, 4:50, 4:475
Rebecca (Church), 1:385,
4:50
Sarah, 4:50
Sellick/Silleck/Selleck
Abigail (Gold), 2:286
Abigail (Law), 3:60, 4:51
Elizabeth, 4:50
Joanna, 4:50-51
Martha (Gold), 2:13, 2:286,
4:51
Sarah, 4:51
Sarah (Law), 3:60, 4:51
Susanna, 4:50-51
Susanna (----), 4:50
Semond
Ann (Barrell), 1:124, 4:51

Semond (continued)
Hannah, 4:51
Sendall
Elizabeth (----) Warren,
2:392, 4:51, 4:587
Joanna, 2:498, 4:51
Joanna (----), 4:51
Mary, 4:51
Sension/Sention/Senchion
Dorothy (Smith) Blakeman
Hall, 1:195, 2:333, 4:52,
4:115
Elizabeth, 4:51-52
Elizabeth (Haite), 4:52
Elizabeth (Stanley), 4:51,
4:165
Mary, 2:514
Mercy, 3:104
Rebecca (Picket), 3:424,
4:51
Sarah, 3:2, 4:51-52
Senter
Hannah (Read), 3:518,
4:704
Mary (Matthews), 3:177,
4:52
Mary (Muzzey), 4:52
Sarah (----), 1:430
Sessions
Elizabeth, 1:339
Elizabeth (Spofford), 4:52,
4:151
Severance/Severence/Severns
---- (----) Ambrose, 1:48,
3:322
---- (Kimball), 3:22
Abigail, 1:385, 4:52-53
Abigail (----), 4:52
Dinah, 4:52
Elizabeth, 2:93, 4:52
Lydia, 4:52
Lydia (Morrill), 3:234,
4:52
Mary, 1:418, 4:52-53
Mary (----), 4:52
Sarah, 4:52
Susanna (----) Ambrose,
4:52
Sewall/Sewell/Seawall
---- (Batchelder) Titcomb,
4:56
Abigail, 4:56
Abigail (Melyen)

Woodmansey Tilley, 4:55,
4:641
Ann, 3:110, 4:53, 4:89
Ann/Ellen (Hunt), 4:53
Catharine, 4:54
Catharine (Lee) Howell,
3:73, 4:56
Dorothy, 3:290, 4:53-54
Elizabeth, 2:428, 4:54-55,
4:704
Elizabeth (Alford), 4:54
Elizabeth (Price), 4:54
Elizabeth (Titcomb), 4:54
Elizabeth (Walley), 4:54,
4:400
Esther (Wigglesworth),
4:54, 4:542
Hannah, 4:53-56, 4:254
Hannah (----), 4:254
Hannah (Fessenden),
2:583, 4:54
Hannah (Hull), 2:493, 4:55
Jane, 2:243, 4:53-54, 4:56
Jane (Dummer), 2:80, 4:53
Judith, 4:55
Lydia, 4:56
Lydia (Storer), 4:56
Margaret, 4:54, 4:56
Margaret (Mitchell), 3:220,
4:56
Mary, 4:54-56
Mary (Cabot), 4:54
Mary (Payne), 4:54
Mary (Shrimpton) Gibbs,
4:55
Mehitable, 3:549, 4:53-54,
4:56
Mehitable (Storer), 4:54
Rebecca, 4:56
Rebecca (Dudley), 2:76,
4:56
Sarah, 4:54-56
Sarah (Hale), 4:704
Susanna, 4:56
Seward
Abigail, 4:57
Abigail (Bushnell), 1:318,
4:57
Deborah, 4:57
Grace (Norton), 3:293,
4:57
Hannah, 2:349, 4:57
Judith, 4:57

Judith (Bushnell), 1:318,
4:57
Lydia, 4:57
Lydia (Bushnell), 1:318,
4:57
Mary, 4:41, 4:57
Temperance, 4:57
Seymour
Abigail, 3:424, 4:58
Elizabeth, 4:58
Hannah, 4:58
Hannah (Hawkins), 2:382,
4:58
Hannah (Marvin), 3:164,
4:58
Hannah (Woodruff), 4:643
Margaret, 4:58
Mary, 2:313, 4:58
Mary (Waters), 4:433
Mary (Watson), 4:58,
4:437
Mercy, 4:58
Mercy (----), 4:58, 4:707
Rebecca, 4:58
Ruth, 4:58
Sarah, 4:58
Shaddock/Chaddock
Hannah, 4:58, 4:487
Shaflin
Alice (----), 4:58
Catharine, 4:58
Elizabeth (----), 4:58
Sarah, 4:58
Shaler
Alice (Spencer) Brooks,
1:262, 4:59, 4:147
Ann, 4:59
Sarah, 4:685, 4:689
Shannon
Abigail (Vaughan), 4:59,
4:369
Shapleigh/Shapley
Abigail (Gould/Gold),
2:286
Alice (----), 4:60
Ann, 1:83, 2:185, 4:59
Ann (----), 4:59
Catharine, 2:422, 4:59,
4:330
Jane, 4:59
Mary, 4:59, 4:336
Mary (Picket), 3:424, 4:59
Ruth, 4:59

Shapleigh/Shapley
(continued)
Sarah, 1:177
Share
Sarah (Gibbs), 2:246
Sharp/Sharpe
— (----), 2:224
Abigail, 2:541, 4:60-61
Abigail (----), 1:390, 4:60
Alice, 1:70, 3:504
Alice (----), 4:61
Elizabeth, 3:404
Elizabeth (----), 4:60
Elizabeth (Stedman)
Upham Thompson, 4:178
Experience, 4:61
Hannah, 4:61
Hannah (Frost), 2:211
Hannah (Gillam), 2:255
Martha, 1:286
Martha (----), 4:60
Mary, 3:292, 3:504,
4:60-61, 4:555
Mary (Wade), 1:375
Sarah, 4:570
Sarah (Williams), 4:570
Sharswood
Abigail, 4:61
Abigail (----), 4:61
Catharine, 4:61
Mary, 4:61
Shatswell/Satchells/etc
Ann, 4:61
Elinor (Cheney), 4:61
Hannah, 4:61
Joanna, 2:302, 4:61
Joanna (----), 2:302, 4:61
Mary, 4:61
Rebecca (----), 4:61
Sarah, 4:61
Sarah (Younglove), 4:61,
4:671
Susanna (----), 4:61
Shattuck
Abigail, 3:239, 3:354,
4:62-63
Abigail (----), 4:62
Ann, 4:23, 4:62
Damaris, 3:330, 3:457,
4:62
Damaris (----), 4:62, 4:700
Deborah, 4:62
Deborah (Barstow), 1:129,

4:62
Elizabeth, 2:265, 4:63
Exercise, 4:63
Grace (----), 4:704
Hannah, 4:62-63, 4:140,
4:487
Hannah (----), 4:63
Hannah (Osborn), 2:106,
3:318, 4:58
Hepzibah (Hammond),
2:345
Joanna, 4:62-63
Margaret, 4:62
Martha, 4:62
Mary, 1:272, 2:108,
4:62-63, 4:322
Mary (Morse), 3:239
Patience, 4:62, 4:123
Priscilla, 3:280, 4:62
Rebecca, 1:386, 4:62
Rebecca (Boltwood),
1:209
Rebecca (Chamberlain),
4:62
Retire, 4:62
Return, 4:21, 4:62
Ruth, 4:62
Ruth (Whitney), 3:61, 4:61,
4:530
Sarah, 2:229, 4:62
Sarah (Bucknam), 1:287,
4:62
Susanna, 2:149, 2:446,
3:240, 3:287, 4:62
Susanna (----), 3:287, 4:62
Susanna (Randall), 3:506,
4:63
Shaw
—, 1:326
Abiah, 4:449
Abial, 1:277, 4:65
Abigail, 1:283, 4:63-65
Alice, 4:64-65
Alice (----), 4:64
Alice (Phillips), 3:413
Alice (Stonard), 4:63
Ann, 4:64
Ann (----), 4:65
Bethia (Leager), 3:68, 4:63
Constance (Doane),
4:63-64
Deborah (----), 4:65
Deliverance, 4:304

Elizabeth, 4:63-66, 4:207,
4:706
Elizabeth (----), 4:64
Elizabeth (Booth), 4:699,
4:704
Elizabeth (Fraile), 2:199,
4:66
Elizabeth (Partridge),
3:366, 4:65
Elizabeth (Phillips), 3:413
Elizabeth (Ramsdell),
3:503, 4:64
Esther, 4:65
Hannah, 3:337, 4:63-65
Hannah (----), 4:63-64
Jane (----), 4:63
Judith, 4:64-65
Judith (----), 4:64-65
Judith (Whitmarsh), 4:525
Lydia, 4:63, 4:65
Lydia (Waterman), 4:63
Margaret, 4:63, 4:66
Martha, 4:63-64
Martha (----), 4:64
Mary, 4:63-65
Mary (----), 1:192, 2:199,
4:66
Mary (Darling), 4:65
Mary (Mitchell), 3:220,
4:64
Mary (Souther), 4:65,
4:141
Mary/Martha, 4:63
Mehitable, 4:65
Mehitable (Pratt), 4:65
Persis, 4:65
Persis (Dunham) Pratt,
4:65
Phebe, 4:63, 4:65
Phebe (Watson), 4:65,
4:437
Priscilla, 4:64-65
Rebecca, 4:63-65
Rebecca (Beebe), 1:153
Sarah (Patten), 4:65
Sarah (Waters), 4:64
Susanna, 4:63, 4:704
Susanna (----) Tilton, 4:65,
4:305
Shea
Hannah (Shearman), 4:704
Sheaffe
—, 4:66

Sheaffe (continued)
Elizabeth, 1:488, 2:247,
4:66, 4:444
Elizabeth (Cotton), 4:66
Elizabeth (Rand) Pinney,
4:704
Joan, 1:382
Joanna (----), 4:66
Margaret (Webb), 4:66,
4:273, 4:444
Mary, 2:35, 4:67
Mary (----), 4:67
Mehitable, 4:66-67
Mehitable (Sheaffe),
4:66-67
Rebecca, 4:66
Ruth (Wood), 4:67
Sarah, 4:66
Shearer
Hannah (Bumstead), 1:298,
4:67
Shearman - see also Sherman
Abigail, 4:704
Elizabeth (Lawton), 3:64
Hannah, 4:704
Isbell (Tripp), 4:331
Martha (Tripp), 4:331
Martha (Wilbor), 4:545
Sarah (Spooner), 4:704
Sarah (Wilbor), 4:545
Shears/Sheares/Sheeres
Ann (----) Grosse, 4:67
Elizabeth (Heath), 2:398,
4:67
Grace, 4:67
Judith, 4:67
Mary, 4:67
Mary (----), 4:67
Mehitable, 4:67
Susanna (----) Green,
2:304, 4:67
Sheather
Deborah, 4:67
Elizabeth, 4:67
Elizabeth (Wellman), 4:67
Hannah, 2:338, 4:67
Mary, 4:67
Mary (----), 1:362
Rachel, 4:67
Susanna, 4:67
Susanna (----), 2:269
Shed
Agnes, 4:68

Ann (----), 4:68
Elizabeth, 4:67
Elizabeth (----), 4:68
Eunice, 4:67
Hannah, 4:67-68
Mary, 4:67
Mary (----), 4:67
Rachel, 2:142
Ruth (Moore), 3:227, 4:68
Sarah, 4:67
Sarah (Chamberlain), 4:68
Susanna, 4:67
Sheffield
Ann, 4:68
Catharine, 4:68
Deborah, 4:68
Deliverance, 3:402
Elizabeth, 4:68-69
Hannah, 4:68-69
Hannah (Bullard), 4:69
Martha, 4:69
Mary, 3:157, 4:68-69
Mary (----), 4:68
Mary (Parker), 3:350, 4:68
Mary (Shrieve), 4:68
Mary (Woody), 4:68
Rachel, 4:68-69
Sarah, 3:360, 4:68-69
Sarah (Beal) Marsh, 1:145,
3:155, 4:68
Susanna, 4:69
Tamosin, 4:69
Sheldon/Shelden
Abigail, 4:70
Abigail (Tillinghast), 4:70,
4:303
Alice (----), 4:69
Ary, 4:70
Catharine, 4:69
Elizabeth (----) Pratt, 4:70
Elizabeth (Foote/Foot),
2:180
Esther, 4:69
Eunicee, 4:70
Hannah, 1:360, 4:69-70
Hannah (Stebbins), 4:70,
4:176
Jemima, 4:69-70
Joanna (Vincent), 4:70,
4:374
Martha, 4:70
Mary, 1:250, 4:69-70
Mary (----), 4:70

Mary (Converse)
Thompson, 1:444
Mary (Hinsdale), 4:70
Mary (Hunt), 4:69
Mary (Southwell), 4:70
Mary (Thompson), 4:70
Mary (Whiting), 4:70
Mary (Woodford), 4:69,
4:639
Mehitable, 4:70
Mehitable (Gunn) Ensign,
2:124, 2:324, 4:69
Mercy, 4:69-70
Mindwell, 3:134, 4:69-70
Miriam, 4:69
Rachel, 4:70
Rebecca, 4:70
Rebecca (Scarlet), 4:69-70
Remembrance, 4:70
Ruth, 4:69, 4:228, 4:657
Sarah, 4:69
Sarah (Warner), 4:69
Silence, 4:70
Susanna, 4:704
Thankful, 2:103, 4:69-70
Shelley/Shelly
Ann, 2:198
Hannah, 3:97, 4:71
Judith (Garnett), 2:233,
4:71
Mary, 2:357, 3:243, 3:628,
4:71
Susanna, 2:230
Shelstone
Ann, 4:71
Ann (----), 4:71
Elizabeth, 4:71
Mary, 4:71
Prudence, 4:71
Susanna, 4:71
Shelton
Elizabeth, 4:71
Elizabeth (Welles), 4:71,
4:477
Sarah, 4:71
Shepard/Shepherd/etc
---- (----) Pond, 3:453
Abigail, 3:452, 4:71,
4:74-76
Abigail (Savage), 4:24,
4:71
Alice (Mason), 3:166
Ann, 1:239, 2:166, 3:500,

Shepard/Shepherd/etc
(continued)
  Ann (continued)
    4:71
  Ann (Tyng), 4:358
  Bethia, 4:76
  Deborah, 2:136, 4:71,
    4:74-75, 4:77, 4:509
  Dorothy (Flint), 2:174,
    4:75
  Elizabeth, 1:264, 4:71,
    4:74-75, 4:77
  Elizabeth (Fuller), 4:72
  Hannah, 1:196, 2:594,
    4:71-72, 4:74-76
  Hannah (----), 4:75
  Hannah (Blanchard),
    1:195, 4:76
  Hannah (Ensign), 2:125,
    4:76, 4:361
  Hannah (Peck), 3:383,
    4:75
  Hannah (Tyng), 4:76
  Hepzibah, 4:71
  Jane, 4:75, 4:77
  Jane (North), 4:77
  Joanna (----), 4:76
  Joanna (Hooker), 2:459,
    4:76
  Judith, 4:71
  Judith (Sill), 4:71
  Margaret, 4:72, 4:76
  Margaret (----), 3:220, 4:73
  Margaret (Boradale), 4:76
  Margaret (Touteville), 4:76
  Martha, 2:373, 4:71
  Martha (----) Henbury,
    2:402, 4:74-75
  Mary, 2:364, 4:71-72, 4:76
  Mary (----), 4:75
  Mary (----) Bigelow, 4:75
  Mary (----) Pond, 4:71
  Mary (Anderson) Lynde,
    1:51, 2:388, 4:76
  Mary (Benton) Bigelow,
    1:176
  Mary (Smedley), 2:548,
    4:71, 4:109
  Mary (Wainwright), 4:72,
    4:382
  Mehitable, 4:72
  Mercy (Chickering), 1:377,
    4:72

  Persis, 4:75
  Persis (Pierce), 4:75
  Rebecca, 1:176, 4:74-75,
    4:77
  Rebecca (Greenhill), 2:308,
    4:74
  Rebecca (Putnam) Fuller,
    4:700, 4:704
  Ruth, 4:76
  Sarah, 4:71, 4:74-77,
    4:288
  Sarah (Eastman) French,
    2:93, 2:207, 4:76
  Susanna, 4:77
  Susanna (----) Goodwin,
    2:278
  Susanna (Scott), 4:77
  Thanks, 4:71, 4:75
  Thanks (----), 4:75
  Trial, 3:470, 4:75
  Violet, 4:74-75, 4:77
  Violet (----), 4:71
Shepardson
  Elizabeth (Call) Tingley,
    1:511, 4:77, 4:305
  Joanna, 4:77
  Joanna (----), 1:330, 4:77
  Lydia, 1:330, 4:77
Sheperson
  Joanna, 3:10
Shepley/Shipley
  Ann (----), 4:77
  Lydia, 4:77
Shepreve
  Elizabeth (Jeffrey/Jeffries),
    2:597
Shepway
  Ann (----), 4:77
Sherand
  Sarah (Winsor), 4:604
Sherburne/Sherborne
  Elizabeth, 3:68, 3:646,
    4:12, 4:77-78
  Elizabeth (Tuck), 4:78
  Frances, 2:58
  Love (Hutchins), 2:508,
    4:78
  Martha, 4:78
  Mary, 4:77-78, 4:107
  Mary (Jackson), 2:532
  Rachel, 4:78
  Rebecca, 4:78
  Rebecca (Gibbons), 2:245,

    4:77
  Ruth, 4:78
  Sarah, 4:78
  Sarah (----) Abbot, 1:5,
    4:78
  Sarah (Wiggin), 4:540
Sheritt/Sherritt
  Elizabeth (----) Griffin,
    2:313, 4:86
Sherman
  Abiah, 4:81
  Abiah (Street), 4:223
  Abiah/Abigail (Streete),
    4:78-79
  Abiel, 4:84
  Abigail, 4:79, 4:81-83,
    4:554
  Abigail (Thompson) Curtis
    Hurst, 3:637
  Abigail (Thompson) Curtis
    Huse, 4:85, 4:710
  Alice, 4:84
  Ann, 4:83
  Desire (Dotey), 2:62,
    2:452, 4:85, 4:161-162
  Eleanor, 4:85
  Elizabeth, 2:234, 4:79,
    4:81-83, 4:85
  Elizabeth (----), 3:554,
    4:82-83
  Elizabeth (Lawton), 4:83
  Elizabeth (Winship), 4:83
  Esther, 4:81
  Eunice, 4:79
  Experience, 4:85
  Grace, 4:81-82, 4:85
  Grace (----), 4:83-84
  Hannah, 4:82-83, 4:85
  Hannah (----), 4:83
  Isabel, 4:83
  Isbel (Tripp), 4:84
  Jane (Hatch), 4:82
  Joanna, 4:81
  Martha, 1:224, 3:463,
    4:82-84
  Martha (----), 3:463
  Martha (Knowles), 3:42
  Martha (Palmer), 3:343,
    4:82
  Martha (Tripp), 4:85
  Martha (Wilbor), 4:85
  Mary, 1:29, 1:127, 2:383,
    3:463, 4:79-85

Sherman (continued)
Mary (----), 4:80, 4:83
Mary (Launce), 4:80, 4:554
Mary (Phippeny), 4:83
Mary (Titterton), 4:85
Mary (Walker), 4:79
Mehitable, 4:85
Mehitable (Wellington), 4:83, 4:480
Mercy, 1:120, 4:81-82
Mercy (Judson), 4:79
Mercy (White), 4:85, 4:513
Naomi (----), 4:85
Patience, 4:85, 4:486
Priscilla, 4:83
Prudence (Hill), 4:85
Rebecca (Phippeny), 4:78
Sarah, 3:463, 3:578, 4:79, 4:82-85
Sarah (----), 4:85
Sarah (Odding), 4:83
Susanna, 4:82, 4:85
Susanna (----), 4:79
Susanna (Hardy), 2:355
Ursula, 4:610
Sherwin
Abigail, 4:86
Alice, 4:86
Elinor, 4:86
Frances, 4:86
Frances (Loomis), 3:648, 4:86
Mary, 3:621, 4:86
Mary (Chandler), 1:359, 4:86
Sarah, 4:86
Sherwood
Alice (----), 4:86
Ann, 4:86
Elizabeth, 4:195
Hannah (Bumstead), 1:298
Jane (Burr), 1:306
Margaret, 3:180
Mary, 4:298, 4:705
Rebecca, 4:86
Rebecca (Burr), 1:307
Rebecca (Turney), 4:86, 4:349
Rose, 4:86
Ruth, 2:444
Sarah, 4:498

Sarah (----), 4:705
Sarah (Wheeler), 4:501
Shether/Sheather/Shedar
Elizabeth, 4:86
Elizabeth (Wellman), 4:86, 4:482
Hannah, 4:86
Rachel, 4:86
Susanna, 4:86
Susanna (----), 4:86
Shipman
Abigail, 4:87
Alice (Hand), 4:87
Elizabeth, 2:463, 4:87
Elizabeth (Comstock), 4:87
Hannah, 4:87
Mary (Andrews), 4:87
Shippen
Abigail (Grosse), 2:319, 4:87
Ann, 4:87
Elizabeth, 4:87
Elizabeth (----) James, 4:87
Elizabeth (Lybrand), 4:87
Mary, 4:87
Rebecca (----) Richardson, 4:87
Shippey/Sheppy/Shippie
Elizabeth (----), 4:88
Grace, 3:476, 4:87-88, 4:705
Grace (----), 4:87
Mabel, 4:88
Mabel (----), 2:595
Mabel (Mitchell), 4:88
Margaret, 4:88
Mary, 4:87-88
Sarah, 4:87
Thanklord (----), 4:88
Shooter
Hannah, 3:247, 4:88
Hannah (----), 4:88
Shore
Abigail, 2:489, 4:88
Abigail (----), 4:88
Ann, 4:88
Elizabeth, 4:88
Mary (Paddy), 3:329
Mary (Payton), 3:374, 4:88
Phebe, 4:88
Priscilla (Hathorne), 4:88
Susanna, 4:88

Shoreborne
Abigail (----), 4:88
Short
Ann (----), 4:88
Ann (Sewall) Longfellow, 3:110, 4:53, 4:89
Elizabeth (----), 4:88
Faith (Munt), 3:257, 4:88
Hannah, 4:20, 4:89
Jane, 4:89
Lydia, 4:89
Mary, 4:89
Mehitable, 4:89
Rebecca, 3:342
Sarah, 3:188, 3:354, 4:88-89
Sarah (----), 1:15
Sarah (Glover), 4:88
Sarah (Whipple), 4:89
Susan, 3:354
Shorthose
Catharine (----), 4:89
Elizabeth, 4:89
Shortridge
Ann, 2:32, 4:89, 4:402
Esther (Dearborn), 2:32, 4:89
Shotten/Shatton
Alice (----), 1:466, 4:89
Rachel, 2:440, 4:89
Shove
Elizabeth, 3:214, 4:89
Hannah, 4:89
Hannah (Bacon) Walley, 4:674, 4:705, 4:712
Hope (Newman), 3:276
Hopestill (Newman), 3:275-276, 4:89
Joanna, 4:90
Lydia, 4:89
Lydia (----), 4:89
Margery (----), 3:376, 4:89, 4:705
Mary, 4:89-90
Ruth, 4:89
Sarah, 2:310, 4:90
Sarah (----) Farwell, 2:147, 4:90
Yetmercy, 4:90
Shreve/Sherive/Shrieve
Elizabeth, 4:90
Jane (Havens), 2:378, 4:90
Martha, 4:90

Shreve/Sherive/Shrieve
(continued)
Martha (----), 4:90
Mary, 4:68, 4:90
Shrimpton
Abigail, 4:90-91
Bethia, 4:90-91
Elinor (----), 4:90-91
Elizabeth, 4:90-92
Elizabeth (----), 4:90, 4:201
Elizabeth (Richardson),
    4:92
Elizabeth (Roberts), 4:91
Lydia, 4:90
Martha, 4:91
Mary, 2:247, 4:55, 4:90-91
Mary (----) Hawkins Fenn,
    2:152, 2:383, 4:90
Mary (Oliver), 3:310, 4:91
Mehitable, 4:90
Rebecca (----), 4:90
Sarah, 1:397, 2:510,
    4:90-91
Shurtleff/Shirtley/Shetle
Abiel, 4:92
Abigail, 4:92
Elizabeth, 4:92
Elizabeth (----), 1:446
Elizabeth (Lettice), 3:81,
    4:92
Hannah, 4:92
Lydia, 4:92
Lydia (Barnes), 4:92
Mary, 4:92
Sarah, 4:92
Sarah (Kimball), 4:92
Susanna, 4:92
Susanna (Lothrop), 4:92
Shute
Catharine (----), 4:92
Elizabeth, 4:93
Elizabeth (----), 4:92
Hopestill (Viall), 4:93,
    4:377
Joanna, 1:286, 3:281, 4:93
Lydia, 4:93
Lydia (----), 4:93
Mary, 4:93
Mary (Rainsford), 3:502,
    4:370
Sarah, 4:93
Sarah (Sanford), 4:16, 4:93

Sibley/Sibly/Sebley/Sybley
Abigail, 4:93
Damaris, 4:94, 4:653
Elizabeth, 4:93-94
Hannah, 4:93-94
Hannah (----), 4:94
Lydia, 4:94
Mary, 4:93-94, 4:388
Mary (----), 4:94
Rachel, 4:93-94
Rachel (Pickworth), 3:425,
    4:93
Rebecca, 4:94
Ruth, 4:94
Ruth (----) Small, 4:94
Sarah, 2:86, 4:93-94
Sarah (----), 1:376, 4:93
Sarah (How), 1:224
Sarah (Wells), 4:94
Susanna (Follet), 4:93
Sigourney
Elizabeth, 4:95
Elizabeth (Breed), 4:95
Hannah, 4:95
Jane, 4:95
Joanna, 4:95
Joanna (Tileston), 4:95
Mary, 4:94
Mary (Germaine), 4:94
Mary (Ronshon), 1:150,
    4:95
Mary (Varney), 4:95
Mary (Waters), 4:95
Rachel, 4:95
Rebecca (Tileston), 4:95
Susanna, 4:94-95
Sigsworth
Esther (----), 4:95
Isabel, 4:95
Sikes/Syckes/Sykes
Abigail, 4:95
Abigail (Fowler), 2:193,
    4:95
Elizabeth (Burt), 1:314,
    4:96
Elizabeth (Granger), 2:290,
    4:96
Experience, 4:96
Hannah, 4:96
Hannah (Bagg), 1:93, 4:96
Mary (----) Trumbull, 4:96,
    4:337
Phebe, 4:95

Phebe (----), 4:96
Rebecca, 1:314, 4:95
Sill/Syll/Scill
Elizabeth, 2:306, 2:410,
    4:96-97
Elizabeth (Mather), 4:97
Jemima, 2:335, 4:96-97
Jemima (Belcher), 1:155,
    4:96
Joanna, 4:97
Joanna (----), 4:96
Judith, 4:71
Lucy, 4:97
Phebe, 4:97
Phebe (Lord), 4:97
Sarah, 4:97
Sarah (Clark) Marvin,
    1:393, 3:165, 4:96
Sillevant/Sillivant
Abigail (Cole), 1:427,
    4:97-98
Elizabeth (Lamberton),
    3:49, 4:97, 4:334
Silliman
Abigail, 4:97
Abigail (----), 4:97
Hannah (----) Hendrickson,
    4:97
Jemima, 4:97
Martha, 4:97
Mary, 4:97
Peaceable, 4:97
Peaceable (----) Egleton,
    2:106, 4:97
Rebecca, 4:97
Sarah, 4:97
Sarah (Hull), 2:492, 4:97
Silsbee/Silsby
Bethia, 4:98
Bethia (----), 1:425
Bethia (March), 4:98
Bethia (Pickman), 3:425
Bethia (Pitman), 4:98
Deborah (Tompkins), 4:98,
    4:710
Dorothy (----), 4:98
Elizabeth, 4:98
Grace (----) Eaton, 4:98
Hannah, 3:44, 4:98
Margaret, 4:98
Mary, 3:650, 4:98
Mary (Biscoe), 4:98
Rachel (----), 4:98

Silsbee/Silsby (continued)
  Sarah, 4:98
Silver
  Catharine (----), 4:98
  Elizabeth, 4:98
  Hannah, 1:7, 4:98
  Martha, 4:98, 4:556
  Mary, 3:553, 4:98
  Mary (----), 4:98, 4:382
  Mary (Williams), 4:98
  Sarah, 1:43, 4:98
Silvester - see Sylvester
Simmons/Symons/Simones
  Ann (----), 3:459, 4:100
  Elizabeth, 2:85, 4:100
  Hannah, 4:100
  Hannah (Wells), 4:705
  Martha (----), 4:100
  Mary, 1:24, 1:166, 4:100
  Mary (Woodworth), 4:648
  Patience (----), 1:99
  Patience (Barstow), 1:129
  Sarah, 4:100
  Sarah (----), 4:100
  Tamison, 3:231
  Welthea (----) Goddard,
    2:264
Simonds - see Symonds
Simpkins
  ---- (Ackerly), 4:101
  Catharine (Richardson),
    4:101
  Deborah, 1:309, 4:101
  Elizabeth (Paige), 3:332
  Isabel (----), 4:101
  Margaret (Barton), 1:134
  Miriam, 4:101, 4:356
  Miriam (----), 4:101
  Rebecca, 4:101, 4:307
  Sarah, 4:101
Simson/Simpson/Symson
  Abigail, 4:101
  Abigail (----), 4:101
  Deborah, 4:101
  Elizabeth, 4:101
  Hannah, 4:101
  Mary, 1:157, 2:569, 4:101
  Mary (Coley), 1:432,
    4:222
  Sarah, 4:101
  Susanna, 4:101
  Susanna (----), 3:358,
    4:101

Tabitha (Benton), 3:603
  Wait, 4:101
  Wait (Clap), 1:390, 4:101
Sinclair/St.Clair
  Mary (----), 4:102
Singletary/Singletery
  ----, 4:102
  Eunice/Unice, 2:98, 4:102
  Hannah, 3:585, 4:102
  Lydia, 3:43, 4:102
  Mary, 4:102
  Mary (----), 4:102
  Mary (Stockbridge), 4:102
  Sarah, 2:212, 4:102
  Sarah (Belknap), 4:102
  Susanna, 4:102
  Susanna (----), 4:102
  Susanna (Cooke), 4:102
  Waitstill, 4:102
Singleton
  Mary, 1:492
Sinnet/Sennot/Sennitt
  Elizabeth, 4:102
  Mary, 4:102, 4:145
  Mary (----), 4:102
  Sarah, 4:102
Sisson
  Abigail, 4:102
  Ann, 4:102
  Elizabeth, 1:29, 4:102-103
  Hope, 4:102
  Mary, 4:102
  Rachel (Burdick), 1:301
  Ruth, 4:102
  Sarah (Lawton), 3:64,
    4:102
Skate
  Sarah (----), 4:705
Skeath
  Joanna, 4:103
  Mary, 4:103
  Rebecca, 4:103
  Sarah, 4:103
  Sarah (----), 4:103
Skeel
  Abigail, 4:103
  Elizabeth, 4:103
  Hannah, 2:409, 4:103
  Hannah (Terrill), 4:103
Skelling/Skilling/Skillings
  Abigail, 1:458, 1:484,
    4:105
  Deborah, 4:103

Deborah (----), 4:103
  Mary (Lewis), 3:86, 4:103
Skerry
  Ann, 4:705
  Bridget (----), 4:104
  Elizabeth, 4:104
  Elizabeth (----), 4:104,
    4:705
  Hannah, 4:705
  Martha, 4:705
  Martha (Mellard), 4:705
  Mary, 3:131, 4:104
  Priscilla, 4:705
  Priscilla (Lunt), 4:705
Skidmore
  Dorothy, 3:626, 4:105
  Ellen (----), 4:104
  Joanna (----) Westcoat
    Baldwin, 1:104, 4:705
Skiff
  Bathshua, 1:219, 4:105
  Beulah, 4:706
  Elizabeth, 4:105, 4:706
  Elizabeth (Nabor), 4:706
  Hannah, 4:706
  Hannah (Merry),
    4:705-706
  Hepzibah (Codman), 4:706
  Mary, 4:105, 4:706
  Mary (Chipman), 4:706
  Patience, 1:218, 4:105,
    4:706
  Sarah, 4:706
  Sarah (Barnard), 4:674,
    4:706
Skilling
  Abigail, 1:458
Skinner
  Abigail, 4:106
  Elizabeth, 4:105
  Elizabeth (Maverick),
    3:181
  Elizabeth (Maverick)
    Grafton, 2:289
  Hannah (----), 4:105
  Mary, 4:105
  Mary (----), 4:105
  Mary (Filley), 2:159, 4:105
  Mary (Gould), 2:286,
    4:105-106
  Mary (Loomis), 3:112,
    4:340, 4:706
  Mary (Pratt), 3:475, 4:105

Skinner (continued)
  Rachel (Pratt), 3:471
  Sarah, 4:105
Skipper
  Catharine, 3:180, 4:706
  Jane, 1:264, 4:106
Slack
  Mary (----), 4:106
Slater
  Elizabeth (----), 4:106
  Elizabeth (Holcomb) Case,
    1:346
Slaughter
  Abiah (----) Bartlett, 4:106
Slawson
  ----, 2:285, 4:106
  Betty (Benedict), 1:164
  Elizabeth (Benedict),
    4:106
  Mary, 4:106
  Mary (Williamson), 4:106
  Sarah, 4:106
  Sarah (Tuttle), 4:106,
    4:352
Sleeper
  ----, 2:38
  Abigail, 4:706
  Elizabeth, 3:394, 4:107,
    4:706
  Elizabeth (----), 4:107
  Elizabeth (Shaw), 4:706
  Joanna (----), 4:107
  Mary, 4:706
  Mehitable, 4:706
  Naomi, 4:706
  Ruth, 3:69
  Sarah (----), 4:706
Sley/Slye
  Elizabeth (----), 4:107
Slocum/Slocome
  ----, 2:300, 2:305
  Ann (Lawton), 3:64, 4:107
  Elizabeth, 4:107
  Joan (----), 4:107
  Joanna, 4:107
  Mary, 4:107
  Mary (Holder), 2:446
  Sarah, 4:107
Sloman/Sluman/Slowman
  Abigail, 4:107
  Elizabeth, 4:107
  Hannah (----), 4:107
  Mary, 4:107

Rebecca, 4:107
Sarah, 1:349, 4:107
Sarah (Bliss), 4:107
Sloper
  Bridget, 4:107
  Elizabeth, 4:107
  Martha, 4:107
  Mary, 4:107
  Mary (Sherburne), 4:78,
    4:107
  Rebecca, 4:107
  Sarah, 4:107
  Susanna, 4:107
  Tabitha, 4:107
Slough
  Elizabeth (Prudden), 3:486,
    3:491, 4:107
  Hasadiah, 4:107
Small
  Ann, 4:108
  Hannah, 4:108
  Hannah (Sibley), 4:93
  Lydia, 2:511, 4:108, 4:709
  Mary, 1:325, 4:138
  Ruth (----), 4:94, 4:108
Smalley
  Hannah, 1:111, 4:108
  Mary, 4:108
Smallidge
  Abigail, 4:108
  Johanna, 4:108
  Mary (----), 4:108
Smead
  ---- (Stoughton), 2:38
  Elizabeth, 2:21, 4:109
  Elizabeth (Lawrence), 3:63,
    4:109
  Judith, 2:380, 4:109
  Judith (Stoughton), 4:109
  Mehitable, 2:493, 3:285,
    4:109
  Thankful, 4:109
  Waitstill, 4:109
Smedley
  Mary, 2:548, 4:71, 4:109
  Sarah (Wheeler), 4:109
Smith, 3:287
  ----, 3:133, 3:381, 4:135,
    4:360
  ---- (----), 1:69, 1:289,
    1:455, 4:114, 4:126
  ---- (Comstock), 4:120
  ---- (Davis), 2:17

---- (Eliot), 2:111, 4:122
---- (Hudson), 2:488
---- (Palfrey), 3:339
---- (Parke), 3:349
---- (Pratt), 3:473
Abiel, 4:116
Abigail, 1:15, 4:110-112,
  4:114, 4:118, 4:122,
  4:124, 4:127, 4:133,
  4:135-137, 4:342
Abigail (----), 4:123
Abigail (Carter), 1:342,
  4:123
Abigail (Fowle), 2:192,
  4:137
Abigail (Kellogg), 4:124
Abigail (Page), 4:137
Abigail (Rice), 3:529
Adrean (----), 3:286, 4:121
Alice, 4:120, 4:506
Alice (----), 4:111, 4:120
Amphyllis (Angell), 4:112
Andrean (----), 4:121
Ann, 1:43, 3:11, 3:60,
  3:229, 3:239, 4:114-115,
  4:120-121, 4:126-127,
  4:131, 4:135-136
Ann (----), 4:121, 4:127,
  4:136
Ann (Bourne), 1:219,
  4:127
Ann (Fuller), 4:125-126
Ann (Pynchon), 3:498,
  4:114
Bathsheba, 4:111, 4:130
Bathsheba (Rogers), 4:130
Bathshua (Lothrop), 4:133
Bathshua (Rogers), 2:196,
  3:560
Beriah, 2:196, 4:122,
  4:130
Bethia, 4:122, 4:130,
  4:200
Bethia (Snow), 4:123
Bridget, 4:116
Canada (Waite), 4:383
Catharine, 4:117
Catharine (----), 4:120
Catharine (Morrill), 3:234,
  4:119
Cathrine, 2:580
Clemence (----) Hunt,
  4:120

Smith (continued)
Clemence (Hosmer) Hunt, 2:501
Content, 4:112
Damaris, 4:113
Deborah, 1:88, 4:120, 4:123-124, 4:129, 4:134
Deborah (—), 1:388
Deborah (Howland), 2:478, 4:121
Decline (Lamb), 3:47, 4:134
Dinah, 4:124
Dorcas, 4:119, 4:652
Dorothy, 1:195, 2:333, 3:228, 4:52, 4:115, 4:122, 4:132, 4:136, 4:250
Dorothy (—), 3:591, 4:115-116
Dorothy (Cotton), 1:464, 4:125
Eleanor, 4:128
Elian, 4:114
Elizabeth, 1:331, 1:389, 2:180, 2:223, 2:251, 2:322, 2:335, 2:591, 3:140, 3:208, 3:300, 3:513, 3:647, 4:14, 4:110-111, 4:113-117, 4:119-127, 4:130-137, 4:288, 4:440, 4:530, 1:505
Elizabeth (—), 2:442, 3:603, 4:111-113, 4:116, 4:125, 4:131, 4:133, 4:135
Elizabeth (—) Kelly, 3:6, 4:131
Elizabeth (—) Walker, 4:396
Elizabeth (Ames), 1:49
Elizabeth (Bliss), 4:112
Elizabeth (Cook), 4:116
Elizabeth (Farrand), 2:144, 4:136
Elizabeth (Frost), 2:212
Elizabeth (Golding), 2:269
Elizabeth (Ladd), 3:43, 4:127
Elizabeth (Patterson), 3:370, 4:135
Elizabeth (Rogers), 4:111,

4:118
Elizabeth (Standley), 4:136
Elizabeth (Wicks) Townsend, 4:319, 4:539
Esther, 4:111, 4:123, 4:125, 4:130, 4:132, 4:224
Esther (Chickering), 1:376, 4:111
Esther (Dickinson), 4:127
Esther (Goodyear), 3:625, 4:127
Esther (Parsons), 3:363, 4:126
Eunice (—) Porter, 3:462, 4:114
Exercise, 3:458
Experience, 1:7, 4:116, 4:123, 4:125, 4:127
Experience (—), 4:127
Faith (Parrott), 2:548, 4:121
Frances (—), 3:498
Grace, 4:111, 4:132
Grace (—), 4:120, 4:706
Grace (Winston), 4:605
Hannah, 1:234, 1:485, 2:167, 2:396, 2:418, 3:224, 4:110-111, 4:113, 4:116-118, 4:122-123, 4:125-128, 4:132, 4:134-135, 4:137, 4:511
Hannah (—), 4:111
Hannah (Astwood), 4:118
Hannah (Bliss) Haley, 2:332, 4:134
Hannah (Coolidge), 1:452
Hannah (Goodenow), 2:272, 4:117
Hannah (Graves), 4:137
Hannah (Hitchcock), 2:428, 4:111
Hannah (Nettleton), 3:268, 4:135
Hannah (Tidd), 4:125
Hannah (Williams), 4:122
Hepzibah, 4:136
Hope (Stow), 4:110, 4:218
Huldah, 2:33
Huldah (—), 4:122
Huldah (Hussey), 2:507
Isabel (—), 4:118
Jael (Packard), 3:327,

4:121
Jael (Packer), 4:121
Jane, 2:286
Jane (—), 4:126
Jane (Barnard), 1:119
Jane (Harris), 2:286, 2:364
Jane (Kent), 3:643
Jane (Peabody), 4:124
Jane (Tudor), 4:341
Jehoidan (—), 4:110
Jemima, 3:181, 4:126, 4:134
Jerusha, 4:123, 4:127
Jerusha (Mather), 4:132
Joan (Clark), 1:402
Joanna, 3:260, 3:593, 4:114-115, 4:123, 4:125, 4:131, 4:135, 4:668
Joanna (—), 4:121, 4:134
Joanna (Barber), 4:136
Joanna (Erickson) Bigelow, 1:175
Joanna (Kellogg), 3:5, 4:123
Joanna (Loomis), 4:125
Joanna (Macklathlin), 3:141, 4:133
Joanna (Quarles), 3:499, 4:130
Joyce, 3:317
Judith, 3:170, 4:111, 4:116, 4:320
Judith (—), 4:111, 4:116
Lucy, 2:231, 4:130
Lydia, 3:621, 4:110, 4:112, 4:116, 4:123-125, 4:127, 4:134-135, 4:148, 4:638
Lydia (—), 2:365, 4:121, 4:125
Lydia (Bristol), 4:125
Lydia (Buck), 4:116
Lydia (Carpenter), 1:338, 4:110, 4:125
Lydia (Huet), 2:490, 4:124
Lydia (Winchester), 4:127
Lydia (Wright), 4:124, 4:660
Margaret, 4:114, 4:123, 4:128, 4:134-135, 4:616, 4:706
Margaret (—), 2:368, 4:110, 4:120-121
Margaret (Buffum), 4:706

Smith (continued)
Margaret (Swilloway), 4:131, 4:242
Martha, 4:113-114, 4:124-128, 4:133-134
Martha (----), 4:109
Martha (Bushnell), 1:317, 4:124
Martha (Golding), 2:269
Martha (Metcalf) Brignall, 1:254, 3:203, 4:111
Martha (Varney), 4:366
Mary, 1:77, 1:249, 1:453, 2:81, 2:262, 2:323, 2:425, 2:460, 2:462, 2:556, 3:115, 3:203, 3:225, 3:234, 3:300, 3:367, 3:415, 3:513, 3:581, 4:34, 4:109-122, 4:124-134, 4:136-137, 4:221, 4:326, 4:654
Mary (----), 2:114, 3:225, 4:116-117, 4:121, 4:126, 4:131, 4:133, 4:135
Mary (----) Masterson, 4:129
Mary (Baldwin), 1:105, 4:110
Mary (Barber), 1:65
Mary (Barker), 1:502, 4:112
Mary (Beers), 1:154, 4:122
Mary (Bird), 4:124
Mary (Bliss), 4:128
Mary (Burritt), 1:310
Mary (Chamberlain), 1:354
Mary (Church), 4:133
Mary (Cutler), 1:493, 4:126
Mary (Dickinson), 4:127
Mary (Eldridge), 2:108, 4:122
Mary (Ensign), 2:125, 4:132
Mary (Fairbanks), 2:136, 3:203, 4:111
Mary (Fones), 2:179
Mary (Foster), 2:584
Mary (Goodall) Masterson, 3:171
Mary (Grant), 2:291, 4:111
Mary (Hall), 2:337, 4:112

Mary (Hopkins), 4:132
Mary (Horn), 2:464
Mary (Hosmer), 2:467, 4:135
Mary (Knapp), 3:34, 4:134
Mary (Maverick), 1:76
Mary (Partridge), 3:367, 4:122
Mary (Pratt), 4:126
Mary (Robinson), 4:128
Mary (Smith), 4:133
Mary (Swift), 4:133
Mary (Young), 4:112, 4:670
Mary (Younglove), 4:136, 4:671
Mary/Mercy (Tibbals), 4:128
May, 4:112
May/Mary, 4:117
Mehitable, 1:331, 4:120, 4:122, 4:124, 4:133, 4:136
Mehitable (Holdridge), 2:446
Mercy, 1:165, 4:113, 4:118, 4:120, 4:122, 4:124-125, 4:127, 4:133
Mercy (Golding), 2:269
Mercy (Tibbals), 4:298
Mercy/Mary (----), 4:119
Mindwell, 4:123
Miriam, 4:116, 4:121, 4:123
Miriam (----), 4:121, 4:625
Obedience (Lamberton), 3:49, 4:133
Patience (Shattuck), 4:62, 4:123
Penninah, 4:111
Phebe, 4:110, 4:112, 4:317
Phebe (----), 4:110
Phebe (Campfield), 4:123, 4:677
Preserved, 4:132
Prudence, 4:123-124
Rachel, 2:371, 4:110, 4:112, 4:119, 4:123, 4:646
Rachel (Cole), 1:428, 4:112
Rachel (Marvin), 3:164-165, 4:133

Rachel (Steele), 4:124
Rebecca, 1:225, 1:361, 2:583, 3:261, 3:613, 4:111, 4:114-116, 4:120, 4:122-125, 4:127-128, 4:132-136, 4:196, 4:240, 4:551
Rebecca (----), 4:122, 4:134
Rebecca (Dickinson), 2:48, 4:125
Rebecca (Foote), 1:445, 2:180, 4:128
Rebecca (Glover), 2:261, 4:135
Rebecca (Page), 3:331
Rebecca (Prime), 3:487, 4:136
Rebecca (Rowland), 3:581, 4:112
Rebecca (Smith), 1:225, 4:115, 4:132
Ruhamah, 4:128
Ruth, 4:110-111, 4:125, 4:133, 4:136
Ruth (----), 4:126
Ruth (Loomis), 3:114, 4:110
Ruth (Maverick), 3:180
Ruth (Porter), 3:464, 3:573, 4:133
Ruth (Wickenden), 4:135, 4:538
Sarah, 1:66, 1:277, 1:396, 1:444, 2:164, 3:62, 3:213, 3:331, 3:409, 3:631, 3:656, 4:110-114, 4:117, 4:119-125, 4:127-128, 4:132-135, 4:137, 4:287, 4:637, 4:678
Sarah (----), 4:110-111, 4:113, 4:119-120, 4:123-124, 4:127-128, 4:131, 4:701
Sarah (----) Millet, 4:127
Sarah (----) Wilmot, 4:123
Sarah (Adams), 1:15
Sarah (Allen), 1:30
Sarah (Boylston), 1:226, 4:135
Sarah (Chandler), 4:130
Sarah (Coker), 1:423,

Smith (continued)
  Sarah (Coker) (continued)
    4:117
  Sarah (Davis), 2:18, 4:117
  Sarah (Fowler), 2:195,
    4:120
  Sarah (Frost), 2:211, 4:133
  Sarah (Hammond), 2:347
  Sarah (Jones), 2:599
  Sarah (Millet), 4:127
  Sarah (Newell), 3:272
  Sarah (Phippen) Haughton,
    2:378, 3:418, 4:110
  Sarah (Prentice), 4:123
  Sarah (Ruggles) Wilmot,
    4:580
  Sarah (Stafford), 4:160
  Sarah (Tully), 4:343
  Sarah (Whipple), 4:506
  Sarah (Woodward), 4:121
  Susanna, 3:95, 4:111-112,
    4:124-127, 4:132-133,
    4:136, 4:552
  Susanna (----), 4:123
  Susanna (Hinckley), 4:119
  Susanna (Read), 3:519,
    4:132
  Tabitha, 4:117
  Tamosin, 4:706
  Temperance (Howard),
    2:472
  Thankful, 4:123, 4:125
  Thankful (Gibson), 2:248
  Zephaniah, 4:125
Smyth
  Ann (----) Collins, 1:434,
    4:118
  Hannah (----), 4:120
Snasher
  Mary, 3:648
Snell
  Hannah (Alcock), 1:21
  Martha (Harris), 2:360
  Martha (Matthews), 3:176
Snelling
  ---, 3:560
  Ann, 2:12, 4:137
  Jane (Adams), 1:8
  Margaret (----) Rogers,
    3:569, 4:137
  Margaret (Rogers), 3:560
  Margery (Stagg), 4:137
  Mary, 4:137

  Mary (Hibbert), 2:408,
    4:137
Snooke
  Margaret (----), 4:137
Snow
  Abiah, 4:138
  Abigail, 2:183, 4:138-139
  Abigail (Warren), 4:138,
    4:427
  Alice, 4:138
  Ann, 1:77, 4:138
  Ann (Cook), 1:448, 4:138
  Bathshua, 4:139
  Bethia, 4:123, 4:139
  Constance (Hopkins),
    2:462, 4:138
  Deborah, 4:138-139
  Elizabeth, 3:569, 4:138
  Elizabeth (----), 4:138
  Grace, 4:138
  Hannah, 1:430, 4:138-139
  Jane, 4:138
  Jane (Prence), 3:477,
    4:138
  Joanna, 4:139
  Lydia, 4:138-139
  Lydia (Shaw), 4:65
  Mary, 3:284, 4:138-139
  Mary (Small), 4:138
  Mary (Smalley), 4:108
  Mehitable, 4:139
  Meletiah, 4:139, 4:682
  Melita, 4:139
  Mercy, 4:138
  Milcah (----), 4:139
  Milcha, 2:164
  Naomi (Whitman), 4:139,
    4:524
  Phebe, 4:138
  Rebecca, 4:138-139
  Rebecca (----), 4:30
  Rebecca (Baker), 4:138
  Rebecca (Barker), 1:116,
    4:139
  Ruth, 1:428, 4:138
  Sarah, 4:138-139, 4:397,
    4:432
  Sarah (----), 4:139
  Sarah (Parker), 3:352,
    4:139
  Susanna, 4:138
  Susanna (Dean) Rogers,
    2:30, 3:564, 4:139

  Zerubabel, 4:138
Soane
  Elizabeth (----), 4:197
Solart
  Abigail, 4:706
  Bethia, 4:706
  Elizabeth, 4:706
  Hannah, 4:706, 4:711
  Martha, 4:706
  Mary, 4:706
  Sarah, 4:706
  Sarah (----), 4:139, 4:706
Soley/Solly
  Abigail, 4:139
  Abigail (----), 4:139
  Dorcas (Coffin), 4:706
  Mary, 4:139
  Rebecca, 4:139
  Sarah, 4:139
  Sarah (----), 4:139
Sollenden/Salindine
  Alice, 4:139
  Elizabeth (Usher), 4:139
  Sarah, 4:139
Somerby
  Abiel, 4:140
  Abigail, 2:308, 4:140
  Abigail (----), 4:140
  Elizabeth, 1:399, 2:329,
    4:140
  Judith (Greenleaf), 1:420,
    2:308, 4:140
  Rebecca, 4:140
  Rebecca (Knight), 4:139
  Sarah, 2:330, 4:140
Somers
  Abigail, 3:432
  Elizabeth, 4:140
  Elizabeth (----), 4:140
  Mary, 4:140
Somes
  Alice, 4:140
  Elizabeth (Kendall), 3:9,
    4:140
  Hannah, 4:140
  Hannah (Shattuck), 4:62,
    4:140
  Jane, 4:140
  Jane (Stanwood), 4:140
  Lydia, 4:140
  Margery (----), 4:140
  Mary, 2:345, 4:140
  Sarah, 4:140, 4:517, 4:713

Soper
 Elizabeth (Alcock), 1:22,
  4:140
 Sarah, 4:650
Soule/Sole/Soul
 ----, 4:489
 Elizabeth, 4:140, 4:392
 Esther (----), 4:141
 Margaret (----), 4:141
 Mary, 3:403, 4:140
 Mary (Becket), 4:140
 Patience, 4:140
Southack
 Elizabeth (Foy), 3:622
Souther/Souter/Sowther
 Alice (----), 4:141
 Dinah, 4:141
 Elizabeth (Fairfield), 2:137,
  4:141
 Hannah, 2:348, 4:141
 Hannah (Read), 4:141
 Mary, 4:65, 4:141
 Sarah (----) Hill, 4:141
 Sarah (Burrill), 1:309
Southmayd/Southmead
 Ann, 4:142
 Esther, 4:142
 Esther (Hamlin), 2:344,
  4:142
 Margaret, 4:142
 Margaret (Allyn), 1:43,
  4:142
 Milicent, 4:142
 Milicent (Addis), 1:18,
  1:67, 1:153, 4:141
Southwell
 Abigail, 4:142
 Elizabeth, 4:142
 Elizabeth (Judd), 4:142
 Hannah, 4:142
 Mary, 4:70, 4:142
 Sarah, 4:142
 Sarah (Stebbins), 4:142,
  4:176
Southwick
 Cassandra, 4:707
 Cassandra (----), 4:142
 Clarissa, 4:142
 Deborah, 4:142-143
 Elinor, 4:707
 Elizabeth, 4:707
 Esther, 4:707
 Esther (Boyce), 4:707

 Hannah, 4:707
 Mary, 1:314, 4:142, 4:322,
  4:707
 Mary (----), 4:707
 Provided, 3:623
 Ruth, 4:707
 Sarah, 1:227, 1:289, 4:707
 Sarah (----), 3:612
 Sarah (----) Tidd, 4:707,
  4:710
Southworth
 Alice, 1:384, 4:143
 Alice (Carpenter), 1:231,
  4:143
 Desire (Gray), 2:298,
  4:143
 Elizabeth, 2:177, 2:480,
  4:143
 Elizabeth (Collier), 1:433,
  4:143
 Elizabeth (Reyner), 4:143
 Esther (Hodges), 2:439
 Mary, 1:23, 4:143
 Mary (Peabody), 4:143
 Mercy, 2:204, 4:143
 Priscilla, 4:143
 Rebecca (----), 4:143
Sowell
 Elizabeth (----), 4:144
 Hannah, 4:144
Sowers
 Elizabeth, 4:387
Spalding/Spaulding/etc
 Deborah, 4:146
 Dinah, 4:145
 Dorothy, 4:146
 Eunice, 4:146
 Grace, 4:145
 Hannah (Hale), 4:146
 Margaret (----), 4:145
 Mary (Stow), 4:218
 Olive (Farwell), 2:147,
  4:145
 Priscilla (Underwood),
  4:146
 Rachel (----), 4:145
Sparhawk
 Abigail, 4:144-145
 Abigail (Gates), 4:144
 Ann, 1:454, 4:144
 Catharine (----), 4:144
 Elizabeth, 4:144
 Elizabeth (Pepperell),

 3:392, 4:144
 Elizabeth (Poole), 4:144
 Esther, 1:15, 4:144
 Mary, 1:126, 4:144
 Mary (----), 4:144
 Patience (Newman), 3:276,
  4:144
 Ruth, 4:144
 Sarah (Whiting), 4:145
 Sybil/Sybell, 1:82, 4:144,
  4:541
Spark/Sparks/Sparke
 Elizabeth, 3:395, 3:575,
  4:145
 Margaret, 3:575
 Mary (Sinnet), 4:102,
  4:145
 Rose, 3:575
 Sarah, 3:575
 Susan, 3:575
Sparr
 Mary, 1:472
Sparrow
 Alice (----), 3:595
 Apphia, 4:145
 Apphia (Freeman), 4:145
 Elizabeth, 4:145
 Hannah (Prence) Mayo,
  3:188, 3:477, 4:145
 Mary, 4:145
 Pandora (----), 4:145
 Patience, 3:333
 Priscilla, 4:145
 Rebecca, 2:204-205, 4:145
 Rebecca (Bangs), 1:111,
  4:145
 Sarah (Lewis) Cobb, 1:413,
  3:86, 4:145
Spatchurst
 Elizabeth, 4:14
Spaule/Spowell/Spaul
 Alice (----), 4:146
 Elizabeth, 3:554, 4:146,
  4:153
 Elizabeth (----), 4:146
 Elizabeth (Buckminster),
  1:286
 Mary, 3:38, 4:146
 Mary (----), 4:146
 Mary (----) Guttridge,
  4:146
 Mary (Guttridge), 4:146
 Mehitable, 4:146

Spawle/Sprawle
Elizabeth, 4:84
Mary, 4:84
Spear
Abigail, 4:146
Deborah, 4:147
Dorothy, 4:147
Elizabeth, 4:147
Hannah, 4:146-147
Hannah (Holman), 4:147
Lydia, 4:147
Margaret, 4:147
Mary, 2:399, 4:146-147
Mary (----), 4:146
Mary (Deering), 4:147-148
Mehitable, 4:147
Rachel, 4:146
Rachel (Deering), 4:146
Rebecca, 4:147
Sarah, 4:146
Speck
Mary (Purchase), 3:494,
4:151
Speed
Mary, 1:237
Spencer
----, 3:290, 4:148-149,
4:330
---- (----) Hungeford, 4:149
---- (----) Robbins, 3:546,
4:148
---- (Greene), 4:148
Abigail, 4:149, 4:245
Abigail (Atkinson), 1:75,
4:147
Agnes, 2:497, 4:149
Agnes (----), 2:104, 4:150
Alice, 1:262, 4:59, 4:147
Ann, 4:149
Audry/Susanna, 4:707
Deborah, 4:150
Dorothy, 4:148
Elizabeth, 2:572,
4:147-150, 4:262, 4:481
Elizabeth (Marshcroft/etc),
3:159
Elizabeth (Phippen), 3:418
Esther, 3:432, 4:149
Esther (Andrews), 4:149
Grace, 4:148
Hannah, 1:237, 3:640,
4:147, 4:149-150
Hannah (----), 4:147

Hannah (Pratt), 4:147
Hannah (Willey)
Blatchford, 1:198, 4:149,
4:558
Hannah (Willey)
Hungerford Blatchford,
2:498
Hepzibah, 4:149
Hepzibah (Church), 1:385,
4:149
Joanna, 4:148
Lydia, 4:148
Lydia (Smith), 4:135,
4:148
Margaret, 4:150
Martha, 4:149
Mary, 2:493, 3:279, 3:421,
3:574, 4:18, 4:147-149
Mary (Disbrow), 2:52,
4:148
Mehitable, 1:442, 4:147
Mercy (Selden), 4:50
Patience (Chadbourne),
4:149
Rachel, 4:149
Rebecca, 1:167, 1:497,
3:10, 4:147-148, 4:707
Rebecca (Ackley), 1:497
Rebecca (Hayward), 2:393
Rebecca (Howard), 4:148
Rebecca (Parker) Clark,
1:396
Rebecca (Sweetman),
4:148, 4:239
Ruth, 1:399, 4:147, 4:150
Sarah, 1:345, 2:514, 4:147,
4:149-150
Sarah (----), 4:149
Sarah (Ackley), 1:497,
4:150
Sarah (Barding), 1:114,
4:149
Sarah (Meakins), 3:191
Sarah (Smith), 4:125
Susanna, 1:90, 4:148
Susanna (Green), 2:303,
4:148
Theodosia (Waite), 4:148
Sperry
Abigail (Dickerman), 2:47
Elizabeth, 4:700
Elizabeth (----), 4:150,
4:700

Elizabeth (----) Bunnell,
4:707
Elizabeth (Fernes), 3:619,
4:151
Esther, 3:635, 4:150,
4:675
Mary, 3:380, 4:150
Sarah (Dickerman), 2:47
Spicer
Abigail, 4:151
Hannah, 4:151
Jane, 4:151
Margaret (Parke), 3:347
Mary (Bassaker/Bussicot),
1:136
Mary (Busicot), 4:151
Ruth, 4:151
Spink
Margaret, 4:151, 4:368
Spinning
Abigail (Hubbard), 2:483,
4:150
Deborah (Bartlett), 1:131
Mary, 4:150
Spofford/Spafford
Abigail, 4:151
Abigail (Haggett), 2:329,
4:151
Elizabeth, 4:52, 4:151
Elizabeth (----), 4:151
Hannah, 3:220, 4:151
Lydia, 4:151
Martha, 4:151
Mary, 4:151
Mary (Leighton), 3:44,
4:151
Mehitable, 4:151
Ruth, 4:151
Sarah, 4:151
Sarah (Birkbee), 4:151
Sarah (Wheeler), 4:151,
4:496
Spooner
Abigail, 4:153
Ann, 4:152
Ann (----), 4:152
Bethia, 4:152
Beulah, 4:152
Deborah, 4:152
Eleanor, 4:152
Elizabeth, 4:152
Elizabeth (----), 4:152,
4:702

Spooner (continued)
Experience, 4:152
Experience (----), 4:152
Hannah, 3:584, 4:152
Hannah (Pratt), 4:152,
4:707
Martha, 1:452, 4:152
Mary, 4:152
Mercy, 4:152
Mercy (Branch), 3:605,
4:152
Phebe, 4:152
Rebecca, 4:152
Sarah, 4:153, 4:704
Susanna, 4:152
Sprague
----, 2:91, 3:63, 4:153
Abiah, 4:154, 4:156
Abigail, 4:154
Alice (Rand), 4:155
Ann, 4:153
Catharine (Anderson),
4:156
Deborah, 4:153, 4:156
Deborah (Lane), 3:51,
4:156
Desire, 4:153
Dorcas, 4:153
Dorothy, 4:153
Dorothy (Lane), 3:52,
4:153
Elizabeth, 4:153-154,
4:156
Elizabeth (----), 1:271,
4:154
Elizabeth (Bartlett), 1:132,
4:153
Elizabeth (Holbrook),
4:153
Eunice (Chester), 1:375,
4:155
Hannah, 4:154, 4:156
Hannah (Harris) Cook,
2:360
Joan (----), 4:154
Joan (Corbin), 4:155
Joanna, 1:385, 4:154,
4:156
Joanna (----), 1:444
Lydia, 2:267, 4:153
Lydia (Goffe), 2:267,
4:153
Mary, 2:101, 3:26,

4:153-156
Mary (----), 4:154-155
Mary (Carrington), 1:340,
4:154
Mary (Sharp), 3:504
Mercy, 4:153, 4:337
Milicent, 4:154
Milicent (Eames), 4:156
Patience, 2:544
Persis, 2:2, 4:154, 4:156
Rebecca, 1:80, 4:156
Rebecca (Crawford), 4:156
Ruth, 4:153
Ruth (Bassett), 4:153,
4:675, 4:680
Sarah, 4:153-154, 4:156
Sarah (Chillingworth),
1:379, 4:156
Sarah (Hasey), 4:154
Tabitha, 4:154
Spring
Abiah, 4:157
Abigail, 4:157, 4:415
Ann, 3:347, 4:157
Deborah, 4:157
Elinor (----), 4:157
Elizabeth, 2:222, 3:194,
4:156-157
Elizabeth (Traine), 4:157
Hannah, 4:157
Hannah (Barsham), 1:128,
4:157
Joanna (Richards), 4:157
Lydia, 4:157
Lydia (Cutting), 1:497,
4:157
Mary, 2:18, 4:157, 4:409
Mehitable, 2:265, 4:157
Mehitable (Bartlett), 1:133,
4:156
Rebecca, 4:157
Sarah, 4:157
Susanna, 4:157
Susanna (----) Cook, 4:157
Susanna (----) Goodwin
Cook, 1:446
Springfield
Mary (Mellows), 3:195,
4:158
Sproat
Ann, 4:158
Elizabeth, 4:158
Elizabeth (Sampson), 4:10,

4:158
Hannah, 4:158
Mary, 4:158
Mercy, 3:308, 4:158
Spurr/Spoure/etc
Elizabeth, 4:158, 4:662
Elizabeth (----), 4:158
Elizabeth (Tilestone),
4:158
Martha, 4:158
Mary, 4:158
Patience, 4:158
Waitstill, 4:158
Spurwell
Jane (----), 1:411
Squire
Bridget (----), 4:158
Elizabeth, 4:159, 4:386
Hannah, 4:159
Martha, 4:159
Mary, 4:158
Mary (----), 4:158
Rachel (Ruggles), 3:586,
4:158
Sarah, 4:49, 4:158-159
St. John
----, 4:520
Rachel, 3:164
Rhoda, 3:165
Stackhouse
Abigail, 4:159
Hannah, 4:159
Mary, 4:159
Ruth, 4:159
Susanna (----), 4:159
Stacy/Stacey/Stacie
---- (Pedrick), 3:385
Deborah, 4:159
Elinor (----), 4:159
Elizabeth, 4:159-160
Hannah, 4:159
Hannah (Ingalls), 2:519,
4:159
Mary, 1:118, 3:360, 3:658,
4:159
Priscilla, 4:v
Priscilla (Bulkley), 4:v
Rebecca, 1:288, 4:159
Sarah, 4:v, 4:159
Susanna, 4:159-160
Susanna (Worcester),
4:159

Stafford
Deborah, 4:160, 4:486
Elizabeth, 4:160
Elizabeth (----), 4:160
Frances, 4:160
Freelove, 4:160
Hannah, 1:259, 4:160
Jane (Dodge), 4:160
Margaret, 4:160
Mary, 4:160
Mary (Burlingame), 1:303
Mercy, 4:160
Mercy (Westcott), 4:160, 4:487
Patience, 4:160
Sarah, 4:160, 4:486
Sarah (Holden), 2:445, 4:160
Stagg
Margery, 4:137
Staines
Ann, 4:160
Joice (----), 4:160
Rebecca, 4:160
Sarah, 4:160
Stallion
Christian (----) Chappell, 4:161
Deborah, 1:82, 4:161
Elizabeth (Miller), 4:161
Margaret, 2:181, 4:161
Margaret (----), 4:161
Sarah, 2:100, 4:161
Stamford
Ann, 4:685
Stanbury/Stanborough/etc
Alse (----) Wheeler, 4:161, 4:501
Martha, 4:161
Martha (----), 4:161
Sarah, 4:161
Stancliffe
Abigail, 4:161
Abigail (Bevans), 4:161
Esther, 4:161
Esther (Adams), 4:161
Jerusha, 4:161
Martha, 4:161
Mary, 4:161
Olive, 4:161
Olive (----) Wright, 4:161
Sarah, 4:161
Sibbil, 4:161

Standish
Barbara (----), 4:162
Desire, 4:162
Desire (Dotey) Sherman Holmes, 2:62, 2:452, 4:85, 4:161
Elizabeth, 2:34, 4:161
Eunice, 4:163, 4:200
Lois, 4:162
Lora, 4:161-162
Lydia, 4:10, 4:161
Martha, 4:162
Mary, 4:9, 4:162
Mary (Church), 1:385
Mary (Dingley), 2:52, 4:162
Mehitable, 4:162
Mercy, 4:161-162
Rose (----), 4:162
Sarah, 4:9, 4:161, 4:661
Sarah (----), 2:596, 4:162
Sarah (Alden), 1:23, 4:161
Sarah (Allen), 1:35, 4:162
Sarah (Winslow), 3:205, 3:337, 4:162, 4:601
Susanna (----), 4:163
Standlake
Jane, 3:439
Lydia, 4:98
Lydia (----) Barstow, 1:128, 4:163
Stanford/Standford
Mary, 3:419
Mary (----) Williamson, 4:163
Mary (Howland) Williamson, 4:573
Stanhope/Stanape/Stanup
Hannah, 4:163
Hannah (Bradish), 4:163
Jemima, 4:163
Mary, 4:163
Rebecca, 4:163
Sarah, 4:163
Sarah (Griffin), 4:163
Susanna, 4:163
Susanna (Ayer), 4:163
Staniford/Staniforth
Elizabeth, 4:163
Margaret (Harris), 2:364, 4:163
Martha, 4:163
Mary, 4:590

Rebecca, 4:163
Sarah (----), 4:163
Sarah (----) Jones, 2:599
Stanley/Standley
Abigail, 1:430, 2:458, 4:164-165
Ann, 4:164-165
Ann (Peck), 3:381, 4:165
Bennet (----), 4:165, 4:590
Bethia (Lovett), 4:164
Elizabeth, 1:71, 3:416, 3:441, 4:51, 4:136, 4:163-165, 4:380
Elizabeth (----), 1:89-90, 4:165
Esther, 4:164
Esther (Newell), 3:272, 4:164
Hannah, 3:440, 3:463, 4:163-165
Hannah (Cowles), 4:163, 4:679
Hannah (Spencer), 4:149
Lois, 3:464, 4:165
Lydia (Wilson), 4:164
Martha, 3:416, 4:297
Mary, 2:156, 2:458, 3:416, 3:461, 4:164-165
Mary (Strong), 4:165, 4:227
Mary/Martha, 3:416
Rebecca, 3:116, 3:416
Ruth, 3:228, 4:164
Sarah, 2:238, 2:458, 4:164-165, 4:379
Sarah (----) Long, 4:164
Sarah (Boosey), 1:211, 4:165
Sarah (Fletcher), 2:173, 4:164
Sarah (Moore) Long, 3:109
Sarah (Scott), 4:39, 4:164
Susanna, 4:165
Susanna (----), 3:116, 3:416, 4:164, 4:297
Stansfull
Abigail, 3:184
Stanton
---- (Mead), 3:191, 4:166
---- (Prentice), 4:166
Ann, 4:166-167
Ann (Lord), 3:116, 4:167

Stanton (continued)
Avis (----), 4:166
Borrodell (Denison), 2:36,
4:167
Content, 4:166
Dorothy, 3:296, 4:166-167
Elizabeth, 4:166
Elizabeth (----), 4:166
Elizabeth (Brown), 1:267
Hannah, 2:357, 3:341,
4:166-167
Hannah (----), 4:166
Hannah (Lord), 4:166
Joanna, 4:167
Joanna (Gardner), 2:231,
4:167
Lucy, 4:167
Margaret (Chesebrough),
1:373
Martha, 4:166
Mary, 2:357, 3:65, 3:568,
4:166-167
Mary (Clark) Cranston,
1:394, 1:472
Mary (Harndel), 2:357,
2:464, 4:166
Patience, 4:166
Prudence, 4:166
Ruth, 4:166
Sarah, 1:373, 2:37-38,
3:480, 4:166-167
Sarah (Denison), 2:36,
4:167
Stanwood/Stainwood
Esther (Bray), 3:605,
4:168
Hannah, 4:168
Hannah (Babson), 4:168
Jane, 3:393, 3:428, 4:140,
4:168
Jane (----), 4:168
Lydia (Butler), 4:167
Mary (Blackwell), 4:168
Mary (Nichols), 4:167
Naomi, 4:20, 4:168
Ruth, 3:627, 4:168
Stanyan/Stanian/Stanion
Ann (----) Partridge, 3:366,
4:168
Mary, 3:423, 4:168
Mary (----), 4:168
Mary (Bradbury), 1:230,
4:168

Staples/Staple
----, 1:144, 2:370, 4:169
Abigail (Campfield), 4:677
Amy/Ann, 4:169
Hannah, 4:168-169
Hannah (----), 4:168
Margery (----), 4:168
Martha, 4:168
Mary, 4:168-169
Mary (----), 4:168-169
Mary (Coles), 4:169
Mary (Randall), 3:506,
4:168
Mehitable, 4:168-169
Mehitable (----), 4:168
Rachel, 4:169
Rebecca, 4:168
Sarah, 4:169, 4:231
Sarah (----), 4:169
Stapleton
Ann, 4:169
Elizabeth, 4:169
Mary, 4:169
Mary (White), 4:169
Starboard/Starbird
Abigail, 4:171
Abigail (Dam), 4:171
Agnes, 4:171
Elizabeth, 4:171
Starbuck
Abigail, 1:419, 4:171-172
Ann, 4:707
Dorcas, 2:237, 4:171
Dorcas (Gayer), 2:238,
4:172
Elizabeth, 1:419, 4:172
Esther, 4:171-172
Eunice, 2:227, 4:172
Eunice/Catharine
(Reynolds), 4:171
Hepzibah, 4:172
Mary, 2:227, 4:172
Mary (Coffin), 1:420,
4:172
Priscilla, 4:707
Sarah, 1:81, 4:171-172,
4:213, 4:366
Starke/Start
----, 4:172
Deborah (Loud/Lowd),
3:649
Elizabeth, 3:48
Wilmott (----), 3:545,

4:173
Starkey
Mary, 1:512
Starkweather
Ann (----), 4:172
Deborah, 4:173
Elizabeth, 4:173
Jennet (----), 4:173
Lydia, 4:173
Starr
----, 3:186, 4:169
---- (Hollingworth), 2:595,
4:170
---- (Stowers/Stower),
4:219
Abigail, 4:170
Constant, 3:233, 4:171
Elizabeth, 2:154,
4:169-171
Elizabeth (----), 4:169
Elizabeth (Allerton), 1:39,
2:134, 4:169
Elizabeth (Hopson), 2:464
Hannah, 1:494, 4:169-170,
4:707
Hannah (Brewster), 3:606,
4:170
Lydia, 2:134, 4:170
Marah (Weld), 4:458
Martha (----), 4:170
Mary, 3:507, 4:170, 4:707
Mary (Conklin), 4:707
Mary (Stone), 4:170, 4:209
Mary (Weld), 4:170
Rachel, 4:170
Rachel (----), 4:171
Rachel (Harris), 4:170
Ruth, 3:229
Sarah, 4:707
Suretrust, 3:233-234
Susan (----), 4:171
Susanna, 4:707
Susanna (Hollingsworth),
4:707
Staunton
Ann (Thompson), 4:289
Hannah (Thompson),
4:283
Stearns
Abigail, 3:239, 4:173-174
Ann, 4:173
Elizabeth, 4:173-174
Elizabeth (Stone), 4:209

Stearns (continued)
Hannah, 1:256, 4:174-175
Hannah (—), 4:173-174
Hannah (Manning), 4:174
Joanna (—) Parker, 3:350, 4:174
Judith, 4:174
Judith (Lawrence), 3:61, 4:174
Martha, 4:173
Mary, 1:302, 1:494, 3:68, 4:173-175, 4:543
Mary (—), 4:173
Mary (Lothrop), 2:208, 3:122, 3:223, 4:174
Mary (Norcross), 3:287, 4:174
Mehitable (—), 4:174
Rebecca, 4:173-174, 4:321
Rebecca (Gibson), 2:248, 4:173
Rebecca (Stearns), 4:173
Sarah, 4:173-174, 4:208
Sarah (Beers), 1:155, 4:174
Sarah (Mixer), 3:223, 4:174
Sarah (Nevinson), 3:268, 4:204
Stebbins
—, 4:175-176
Abigail, 3:408, 4:175-178
Abigail (Bartlett), 1:132, 4:176, 4:225
Abigail (Brooks), 4:177
Abigail (Burt) Ball Mun, 1:106, 1:313, 3:254, 4:177
Abigail (Denton), 2:40, 4:175
Abigail (Mun), 1:313, 3:254, 4:178
Ann, 4:176
Ann (—) —, 4:176
Ann (Munke), 4:176
Bethia (Comstock), 1:439, 4:175
Deborah, 1:46, 1:313, 4:176
Deborah (Moore), 4:176
Dorothy (Alexander), 1:26, 4:176
Editha, 2:26-27

Elizabeth, 1:328, 1:396, 4:175, 4:177-178, 4:588, 4:659
Elizabeth (Wright), 4:178, 4:659
Esther, 4:175
Experience, 4:178
Frances (—), 4:175
Hannah, 4:70, 4:176-178, 4:578
Hannah (—) Edwards, 4:175
Hannah (Wright), 4:177
Jane (Green), 2:307, 4:177
Joanna, 4:177
Joanna (Lamb), 3:47, 4:177
Lydia, 4:175
Margaret (—), 4:176
Martha, 4:177
Mary, 2:238, 4:175-178
Mary (—), 4:428
Mary (—) Ball, 1:107, 4:175
Mary (—) Bennet, 4:175
Mary (—) Colton, 4:175
Mary (—) Ely, 4:178
Mary (Ashley), 4:175
Mary (Broughton) Bennett, 1:167
Mary (Day) Ely, 1:431, 2:27, 2:117
Mary (French), 2:206, 4:177
Mary/Margaret (—), 4:175
Mehitable, 4:177
Mercy, 4:175, 4:177
Mindwell, 4:175
Miriam, 4:578
Rebecca, 4:176
Rebecca (—) Hawkins, 4:176
Sarah, 3:198, 4:142, 4:175-178, 4:578
Sarah (—), 4:177
Sarah (Dorchester), 2:60, 4:176-177
Sarah (Graves), 4:175
Sarah (Williams), 4:177
Thankful, 4:175-176, 4:225

Stedman
Abigail (Andrews), 1:55
Alice (—), 4:178
Ann, 4:179
Ann (—), 4:179
Elizabeth, 2:81, 2:346-347, 4:178-179, 4:285, 4:361
Elizabeth (—), 4:178
Elizabeth (Remington), 2:248, 4:179
Hannah, 1:501, 2:516, 3:257, 4:178
Hannah (Coburn), 4:178
Hannah (Isbell), 2:196, 4:179
Martha, 1:448, 4:178-179
Mary, 4:178-179, 4:438
Mary (Trowbridge), 4:332
Mary (Watson), 4:179, 4:437
Pilgrim (Eddy) Baker, 1:100, 2:99
Sarah, 1:22, 1:228, 2:297, 2:346, 3:400-401, 3:413, 4:178-179
Sarah (Hammond), 2:346, 4:179
Violet, 3:582
Violet (Shepard), 4:75
Steele
Abiel, 4:181
Ann, 4:180
Ann (Bishop), 4:180
Ann (Welles), 2:575, 4:180, 4:477
Bethia (Bishop), 1:185
Bethia (Hopkins) Stocking, 2:461, 4:180, 4:199
Elizabeth, 4:180-181, 4:439
Hannah, 4:180-181
Jerusha, 4:181
Lydia, 1:182, 4:180
Mary, 2:575, 4:179-181, 4:286, 4:707
Mary (—) Seymour, 4:180
Mary (Boosy), 1:211, 4:181
Mary (Warner), 2:420, 4:181, 4:418
Mary/Mercy (—) Seymour, 4:707
Mary/Mercy (Bradford),

Steele (continued)
Mary/Mercy (Bradford)
(continued)
4:181
Meletiah (Bradford), 1:232
Mercy (----) Seymour, 4:58
Mercy (Bradford), 1:232
Prudence, 4:180
Rachel, 4:124, 4:180-181,
4:673
Rachel (----), 4:180
Ruth, 4:181
Ruth (Judd), 2:574, 4:181
Sarah, 1:214, 2:574-575,
4:179-181
Sarah (Barnard), 1:118,
4:180
Sarah (Hart), 4:179
Steere
Elizabeth (----) Wheeler,
4:181, 4:498
Hannah (Wickenden),
4:181, 4:538
Stent/Stint
---- (----), 1:150, 4:181
Dorothy, 4:181-182
Elizabeth, 1:150, 2:366,
4:181-182
Elizabeth (----), 4:182
Elizabeth (Burwell), 4:676
Hannah, 4:182
Margaret, 3:629
Mary, 4:181
Mehitable, 4:181-182
Sarah (Butler), 4:181
Stephens - see Stevens
Stephenson
Abigail, 4:182, 4:516
Ann, 1:374
Deborah, 4:182, 4:588
Elizabeth, 4:182
Hannah, 4:182
Jane (----), 4:182
Lydia, 4:182
Margaret, 4:182, 4:572
Margaret (----), 4:182
Mary, 2:508, 4:182
Mary (Clark), 4:182
Naomi, 4:398
Naomi (----), 4:190
Rebecca, 3:371, 4:182
Sarah, 3:17, 3:125, 4:182
Sarah (----), 1:199, 4:182

Sterling
Ann (----) Neal, 4:173
Ann (Nichols) Neal, 3:264
Mary (Sawtell), 4:30
Sterry
Hannah (----) Huet, 4:183
Hannah (Palmer) Huet,
2:491
Stertt/Steritt
Jane (----), 4:183
Sarah, 4:183
Stetson/Stedson/Studson/etc
----, 1:117, 4:184
---- (Barlow), 4:184
Abigail, 4:183
Abigail (----), 4:183
Abigail (Hudson), 2:489
Ann, 4:183
Ann (Harris) Maverick,
3:180
Bethia, 4:183
Bethia (----), 4:183
Bethia (Hawke), 2:381
Deborah, 4:183-184
Deborah (Brooks), 1:263,
4:183
Desire, 4:183
Elizabeth, 4:184
Elizabeth (----) Harris,
2:360, 4:184
Eunice, 4:183
Hannah, 4:183-184
Honour, 4:183
Joanna (Brooks), 4:183
Lois, 4:183
Lydia, 4:184
Margaret, 4:183-184
Mary, 4:183-184
Mary (----) Bryant, 4:183
Mary (----) Norton, 4:184
Mary (Collamore), 1:432
Mary/Mercy (----), 4:184
Patience, 4:184
Prudence, 3:66, 4:183
Prudence (----), 4:183
Rachel, 4:184
Ruth, 1:381, 4:184
Sarah, 4:183-184
Sarah (Dodson), 2:58,
4:184
Stevens
----, 3:175, 3:430
---- (Hall), 2:591

---- (Royal), 3:583
Abigail, 4:189
Abigail (Cole), 1:426
Abigail (Green), 4:190
Abigail (Sargent), 4:19,
4:190
Abzubah, 4:187
Alice, 3:109
Alice (----), 4:185
Alice (Cook) Whiting,
1:448, 4:189, 4:519
Ann, 4:188
Ann (----), 4:190
Catharine, 2:31, 4:184
Catharine (----), 4:186
Deborah, 4:185
Dionis, 1:419
Dorothy, 4:184, 4:187
Elizabeth, 4:184-187,
4:189, 4:339, 4:641
Elizabeth (----), 4:185-186,
4:308
Elizabeth (Abbot), 1:2
Elizabeth (Aspinwall), 1:70
Elizabeth (Bidfield), 1:175,
4:190
Elizabeth (Clark), 1:401
Elizabeth (Gallop), 2:223,
4:186
Esther (Barker), 1:116,
4:187
Eunice, 4:189
Eunice (Chester), 4:189
Grace (Barron), 1:126
Hannah, 4:184-186, 4:189
Hannah (----), 4:187
Hannah (Barnard), 1:120,
4:184, 4:187
Hannah (Evarts), 2:128
Jane, 1:18
Joanna, 4:185
Joanna (Leek), 3:75
Joanna (Leeke), 4:186
Joanna (Thorn), 4:187
Judith, 4:187, 4:190
Love (Holyroad), 4:707
Lucy, 4:187
Margery/Mary, 2:457
Maria, 4:189
Martha, 2:482, 4:189
Martha (Bartlett), 4:189
Mary, 1:116, 1:359, 1:422,
2:56, 2:457, 3:30, 3:294,

Stevens (continued)
  Mary (continued)
    3:321, 3:611, 4:18,,
    4:184-190, 4:660, 4:707
  Mary (----), 4:185, 4:188
  Mary (Blaisdale), 4:187
  Mary (Buckminster),
    1:286
  Mary (Calef), 1:329
  Mary (Chase), 1:364,
    4:187
  Mary (Coit), 1:422, 4:187
  Mary (Fletcher), 2:173
  Mary (Ingalls), 2:519,
    4:187
  Mary (Meigs), 3:193,
    4:190
  Mary (Mighill), 4:189
  Mary (Wakeley), 4:386
  Mary (Willard), 4:184,
    4:555
  Mehitable, 4:185
  Mehitable (Colcord), 1:424,
    4:188
  Mindwell, 4:187
  Naomi, 2:592
  Patience, 4:185
  Phebe, 4:189
  Philippa (----), 4:189
  Prudence (----), 4:187
  Rebecca, 3:596, 4:188
  Rebecca (----), 3:635,
    4:188
  Rebecca (Josselyn), 1:216
  Rebecca (Josselyn)
    Croakham Harris, 2:570,
    4:185
  Rebecca (Rea), 3:512,
    4:188, 4:708
  Ruth, 2:263, 4:189
  Ruth (Poor), 3:456
  Sarah, 1:70, 2:56, 4:185,
    4:187-189, 4:708
  Sarah (----), 4:186-188
  Sarah (Abbot), 1:2, 4:185
  Sarah (Davis), 4:189
  Sarah (Hough) Carpenter,
    1:336
  Susanna (Eveleth), 3:618,
    4:186
  Susanna (Welch)
    Edes/Eads/etc Pinckney,
    3:617

  Thomasin, 4:188
  Trial, 4:187
Stevenson - see Stephenson
Stewart/Steward/Stuart
  Abigail, 4:191
  Ann, 4:191
  Ann (----), 4:191
  Bethia (Rumball), 3:588,
    4:191
  Deborah, 4:191
  Deborah (Rediat) Farrabas,
    4:190
  Dorothy (Rediat) Farrabas,
    2:144
  Elizabeth, 4:191, 4:485
  Elizabeth (----), 4:191
  Hannah, 4:190
  Hannah (----), 4:190
  Hannah (Templar), 3:485
  Margaret, 4:190
  Martha, 2:202, 4:190
  Mary, 3:621
  Mary (----), 4:191
  Phebe, 4:191
  Sarah, 1:5, 2:356, 3:621
  Sarah (----), 4:191
  Sarah (Stiles), 4:2, 4:191,
    4:194
  Susanna, 4:191
Stickney
  Dorothy, 4:192
  Elizabeth, 4:192, 4:267
  Elizabeth (----), 4:192
  Elizabeth (Chute), 4:192
  Faith, 2:220, 4:192
  Hannah, 4:191
  Hannah (Brocklebank),
    1:258, 4:192
  Julian (Swan), 4:237
  Julian/Susan (Swan),
    4:192
  Mary, 4:192
  Mary (----), 4:192
  Mary (Palmer), 4:192
  Mary (Poor), 4:192
  Mercy, 4:192
  Prudence, 4:192
  Prudence (Leaver) Gage,
    2:220, 3:69, 4:192
  Rebecca, 4:191
  Rebecca (----), 4:191
  Sarah, 4:191-192
  Sarah (----), 1:7

  Sarah (Morse), 3:237,
    4:191
Stileman
  Elizabeth, 2:569,
    4:192-193
  Hannah (----), 4:193
  Judith (----), 4:192
  Mary, 4:193
  Mary (----), 4:193
  Ruth, 1:319, 4:192
  Ruth (Maynard), 4:192
  Sarah, 4:193
Stiles
  Abigail, 4:193
  Abigail (Neal), 3:263,
    4:193
  Abigail (Rogers), 4:698
  Bathsheba (Tomlinson),
    4:193
  Bathshua (Tomlinson),
    4:310
  Bethia (Hanmer), 4:196
  Deborah, 4:194
  Dorcas (Burt), 1:313,
    4:195
  Elizabeth, 4:193-195
  Elizabeth (Frye), 2:214,
    4:195
  Elizabeth (Rogers), 4:193
  Elizabeth (Sherwood),
    4:195
  Elizabeth (Wilcockson),
    4:194, 4:548
  Hannah, 1:201, 2:426,
    4:193-195
  Hannah (Rose), 3:576
  Jane (----), 4:194
  Keziah (Taylor), 4:195,
    4:259
  Lydia, 4:194
  Margaret, 4:194-195
  Mary, 4:194-195, 4:429
  Mary (----), 4:195
  Mindwell, 4:194
  Phebe, 4:193
  Rachel, 4:193
  Rachel (----), 4:193
  Ruth, 4:193, 4:195
  Ruth (----) Wheeler, 4:193,
    4:499
  Ruth (Bancroft), 4:195
  Sarah, 1:110, 4:2, 4:191,
    4:193-195

Stiles (continued)
Sarah (----), 1:400, 4:194
Still
Ann, 1:367
Stillman
Ann, 4:196
Ann (Southmayd), 4:142
Elizabeth, 4:196
Hannah, 4:196
Lydia, 4:196
Martha, 4:196
Mary, 4:196
Rebecca, 4:196
Rebecca (Smith), 4:128,
4:196
Sarah, 4:196
Stillwell
Elizabeth, 2:295, 4:196
Elizabeth (----), 4:196
Stilson
----, 4:196
Agnes, 4:196
Mary (----), 4:196
Stimpson/Stimson
Abigail, 4:196-197
Abigail (----), 4:196-197
Alice, 4:196
Alice (Phillips), 4:196
Bethia, 4:196
Deborah, 4:196
Elizabeth, 4:196-197
Elizabeth (Stubbs), 4:196,
4:228
Jane (----), 4:196
Lydia, 4:196
Mary, 4:196-197
Mehitable (Spring), 4:157
Mercy, 4:196
Rebecca, 4:196-197
Sarah, 4:196
Susanna, 4:196
Wait (----), 4:197
Stitson
Mary (----) Norton, 3:290
Stockbridge
Abigail, 2:571, 4:197
Abigail (----), 4:197
Ann, 4:198
Ann (----), 4:197
Barshua, 4:198
Deborah, 4:198
Elizabeth, 2:516, 4:197,
4:344

Elizabeth (----) Soane,
4:197
Esther, 4:197
Experience, 4:197
Grace, 4:198
Hannah, 4:197, 4:300
Judith, 4:197
Lydia (Barrell), 4:198
Margaret, 4:198
Margaret (Turner), 4:198
Mary, 3:633, 4:102,
4:197-198
Mary (----), 2:403, 4:197
Mary (Tilden), 4:197
Rachel, 4:197
Ruth, 4:197
Sarah, 4:197-198, 4:345,
4:647
Sarah (Reed), 4:198
Susanna, 4:198
Stocker
Elizabeth, 4:198
Margery (Salmon), 4:198
Martha (----), 4:198
Mary, 1:351, 2:340
Mary (Witt), 4:198, 4:713
Sarah, 4:198
Sarah (Marshall), 3:158,
4:198
Stocking/Stockin/Stocken
----, 4:198
Bethia, 4:198, 4:219
Bethia (Hopkins), 2:461,
4:180, 4:198
Elizabeth, 4:198
Elizabeth (----), 4:198
Hannah, 4:198
Jane, 4:198
Jane (Mould), 4:198
Lydia, 3:533, 4:198
Sarah, 3:307, 4:198
Stockman
Dorothy, 4:199
Hannah (Morrell), 4:199
Sarah (Pike) Bradbury,
1:230, 3:437, 4:199
Stockton
Prudence, 2:456
Stockwell
Abigail (----), 4:199
Elizabeth (Shaw), 4:66
Stoddard
----, 4:201

Barbara (----) Weld, 4:199,
4:458
Bethia (Smith), 4:130,
4:200
Christian, 4:199-200
Christian (----), 4:199
Deborah, 4:200
Dorothy, 4:200
Elizabeth, 4:200-201
Elizabeth (----) Shrimpton,
4:201
Elizabeth (Curtis), 1:487,
4:200
Esther, 2:104, 4:201
Esther (Warham) Mather,
3:172, 4:201, 4:418
Eunice (Standish), 4:163,
4:200
Grace, 4:200
Hannah, 4:201
Jane, 4:200
Lydia, 4:199, 4:344
Martha, 4:200-201
Martha (Belcher), 1:156
Mary, 3:166, 3:222,
4:200-201
Mary (----), 4:200-201
Mary (Downing), 2:66,
4:199
Mary (Foote), 2:180, 2:274,
4:200
Mary (Mortimer), 3:242
Mary (Symmes) Savage,
4:26, 4:200, 4:244
Mehitable (Minot) Cooper
Sargent, 1:455, 3:217,
4:18, 4:201
Mercy, 4:200
Rebecca, 2:384, 4:201
Sarah, 4:199, 4:201
Susanna (----), 4:200
Stodder
--- (----), 4:10
Abigail, 4:201-202
Abigail (Lane) Law, 4:201
Abigail (Lane) Low, 3:51
Ann (----), 4:202
Bathsheba, 4:202
Deborah, 4:201
Elizabeth, 3:125, 4:202
Elizabeth (Gill), 2:254,
4:202
Eunice, 4:202

Stodder (continued)
Hannah, 4:202, 4:502
Hannah (----), 4:202
Hannah (Bryant), 1:283,
4:202
Jael, 4:201
Lois, 4:202
Lois (Sylvester), 4:202
Lydia, 4:202
Margaret (Magvarlow/etc),
3:143, 4:202
Martha, 4:202
Martha (Beal) Chubbuck,
1:146, 4:203
Mary, 4:201-203
Mary (----), 4:202
Mary (Sylvester), 4:201
Mercy (----), 4:202
Rachel, 4:203
Ruth, 4:202
Sarah, 4:201-202
Sarah (Howard), 4:202
Tabitha, 3:53, 4:202-203
Stokes
Deborah, 4:203
Grace, 4:203
Stonard
Alice, 4:63
Stone
---- (----) Cooper, 2:164
---- (----) Lumpkin, 3:130
Abigail, 4:203-205,
4:207-210
Abigail (----), 4:204, 4:206
Abigail (Bassaker/Busicot),
1:136, 4:205
Abigail (Wheeler), 4:203
Abigail (Wilson), 4:204
Ann, 4:203, 4:206-207,
4:209
Ann (----), 4:206
Ann (Howe), 2:474, 4:205
Bathshua, 4:209
Catharine, 4:708
Deborah, 2:558, 4:206,
4:209
Dorcas, 4:203-204
Dorcas (----), 4:203
Dorcas (Jones), 2:562
Dorothy, 4:210
Elizabeth, 1:119, 3:547,
4:49, 4:203-210, 4:381,
4:708

Elizabeth (----), 2:227,
4:203
Elizabeth (Allen), 1:36,
4:208
Elizabeth (Herrick), 4:209
Elizabeth (Shaw), 4:207
Esther, 4:203
Esther (Kirby), 3:30, 4:203
Experience, 4:204
Frances, 2:300, 4:209
Hannah, 1:169, 3:292,
4:204-207, 4:210
Hannah (----), 4:207, 4:210
Hannah (Eager), 4:708
Hannah (Foster), 4:204
Hannah (Jamison), 2:264
Hannah (Walley), 4:400
Hannah (Wolfe), 4:210
Hepzibah, 4:206
Hepzibah (Coolidge),
4:206
Hopestill, 4:207
Joan, 3:661
Joan (----), 4:206
Joan/Jane (Clark), 4:209
Joanna, 4:206, 4:249,
4:587
Joanna (----), 4:203
Joanna (Parker), 3:352
Lydia, 4:208-210
Lydia (----) Cooper, 1:454,
4:204
Margaret, 1:278, 2:286,
4:204-205
Margaret (Trowbridge),
4:204, 4:332
Mary, 1:459, 2:169, 2:195,
2:424, 2:500, 2:598,
4:170, 4:203-210, 4:708
Mary (----), 4:203,
4:205-207, 4:210, 4:499
Mary (----) Hughes, 2:491,
4:210
Mary (----) Ward, 4:203
Mary (Barsham), 4:206
Mary (Bartlett), 1:131,
4:207
Mary (Greenough), 2:310
Mary (Johnson), 2:558,
4:210
Mary (Moore) Ward, 4:412
Mary (Plympton), 3:448
Mary (Rice), 4:204

Mary (Whipple), 4:209,
4:505
Mehitable, 4:203
Mercy, 4:204
Mindwell, 4:204
Patience (----), 3:530
Priscilla, 4:207
Rachel, 4:206
Rebecca, 3:262, 4:204,
4:206, 4:208
Reliance, 4:207
Reliance (Hinckley),
2:425-426, 4:207
Ruth (Eddy), 4:206
Ruth (Haynes), 4:203
Sarah, 1:321, 1:409, 1:444,
2:416, 2:471, 3:197,
4:29, 4:203-209, 4:446,
4:708
Sarah (----), 4:206-207,
4:210
Sarah (----) Lumpkin,
4:209
Sarah (Bass), 1:135, 3:390
Sarah (Hildreth), 4:204
Sarah (Nevinson) Stearns
Livermore, 4:204
Sarah (Shaflin), 4:58
Sarah (Shepard), 4:75
Sarah (Stearns), 4:173,
4:208
Sarah (Tainter), 4:209,
4:249
Sarah (Wait), 4:207
Susanna, 2:264, 4:204,
4:209-210
Susanna (----), 4:204
Susanna (Newton), 3:277,
4:206
Tabitha, 2:388, 3:529,
4:203, 4:205
Thankful, 4:207
Storer
Abigail, 4:210
Elizabeth (----), 2:495,
4:210
Hannah, 4:210
Hannah (Hill), 4:210
Jemima, 4:210
Keziah, 4:210
Lydia, 4:56, 4:210
Mary, 4:210
Mehitable, 4:54, 4:210

Storer (continued)
Sarah, 4:210
Stores/Storrs
Ann, 4:211
Catharine (----) Bicknell,
4:211
Elizabeth, 4:211
Esther, 4:211
Esther (Egard), 4:211
Hannah, 4:211
Hannah (Wood), 4:211
Lydia, 4:211
Martha, 4:211
Martha (----), 4:211
Mary, 4:211
Mary (Huckins), 2:487,
4:211
Mehitable, 4:211
Mehitable (----), 4:211
Rebecca, 4:211
Sarah, 4:211
Zeruiah, 4:211
Storke
Mercy (Nelson), 4:211
Story
Abigail, 4:212
Ann, 4:212
Ann (Belcher), 4:212
Bethia, 4:212
Bethia (----), 4:212
Damaris, 4:212
Elinor, 2:595
Elizabeth, 3:610, 4:213
Elizabeth (----), 4:212
Hannah, 4:212
Margaret (----), 2:3
Martha, 4:212
Mary (Williams), 4:570
Rebecca, 4:212
Sarah, 4:396
Sarah (----), 1:462, 4:212
Sarah (----) Day, 4:244
Sarah (Foster), 2:189-190
Sarah (Starbuck), 1:81,
4:172, 4:213, 4:366
Susanna (----), 1:397
Susanna (Fuller), 4:213
Stoughton
----, 2:38, 3:613
---- (Clark), 1:402
Abigail, 4:215
Abigail (Edwards) Lothrop,
4:215

Catharine, 4:546
Dorothy (Talcott), 4:215,
4:251
Elizabeth, 3:141,
4:213-215
Elizabeth (----), 4:213
Elizabeth (Bissell), 1:187,
4:213
Elizabeth (Knapp), 3:33,
4:214
Hannah, 3:216, 4:214-215
Judith, 4:109
Mabel, 4:215
Margaret (----) Huntington,
2:503, 4:214
Mary, 2:144, 4:214-215
Mary (Wadsworth), 4:214,
4:381
Rebecca, 3:171, 4:215
Rose, 3:324
Sarah (Fitch), 4:214
Sarah (Hoar), 2:594, 4:214
Stover
Sarah (Very) Cook/Cooke,
3:612
Stow
----, 4:218
---- (Bigg), 4:217
Abigail, 4:216
Bethia, 4:219
Bethia (Stocking), 4:198,
4:219
Dorothy, 2:250, 4:218
Elizabeth, 1:62, 1:121,
1:175, 3:423, 4:216-218
Elizabeth (----), 4:216-217
Elizabeth (Stone), 4:205
Esther (Cornwell) Wilcox,
1:459, 4:217
Experience, 4:217
Hannah, 4:217, 4:219
Hannah (Wetmore), 4:217
Hope, 4:110, 4:216-218
Hope (Fletcher), 4:218
Hopestill (Foster), 4:217
Margaret, 4:218, 4:526
Mary, 2:78, 3:617,
4:217-219
Mary (Atwater), 1:76,
4:216
Mary (Gragg/Griggs),
4:218
Mary (Wetmore), 4:217

Rachel, 4:218, 4:526
Rachel (Pond), 3:452
Sarah, 1:393, 4:217
Sarah (Woodward) Gates,
4:644
Thankful, 3:432,
4:216-218, 4:334
Stowell
Elizabeth (Eells/Ells/etc),
2:105
Mary, 2:228, 4:219
Mary (----), 1:146, 2:435
Mary (Beal), 1:146, 4:219
Mary (Farrow), 2:146,
4:219
Rachel (Gill), 2:254, 4:219
Remember, 3:524, 4:219
Stowers/Stower
----, 4:219
Abigail, 4:219
Abigail (Knight), 3:36
Amy (----), 4:219
Ann, 2:540
Elizabeth, 4:219
Hannah, 2:415, 4:220
Hannah (----), 4:220
Jane, 4:219
Jane (----), 4:219
Joanna (----), 4:220
Mary, 1:348, 4:219-220
Mary (Blaisdell), 1:191,
4:219
Phebe (----), 4:219
Sarah, 1:512, 4:219-220
Susanna, 4:497
Straight/Straite
Elizabeth, 4:220, 4:480
Elizabeth (Kimball), 3:21,
4:220
Mary (----), 4:220
Mary (Long), 3:108
Susanna, 4:220, 4:480
Strange
Alice, 4:220
Comfort, 4:220
Grizigon, 2:161
Mary (----), 4:220
Sarah, 4:220
Sarah (----), 1:486, 4:220
Stratford
Elizabeth, 4:445
Stratton
Abigail, 4:221

Stratton (continued)
Abigail (——), 4:221
Ann, 3:645
Ann/Hannah, 4:221
Bethshua (Applin), 1:62
Elizabeth, 4:221-222,
4:566
Elizabeth (Train), 4:221,
4:321
Hannah (Wheat), 4:221
Judy, 4:221
Margaret (——) Parker,
4:221
Mary, 2:430, 4:221
Mary (Butters), 4:221
Mary (Frye), 4:221
Mary (Perry), 4:222
Mary (Smith), 4:221
Mercy, 4:221
Rebecca, 4:47, 4:221
Sarah, 4:221-222
Sarah (Howe), 2:474,
4:221
Susan (——), 2:2
Susanna (——), 4:221
Stream/Streame
Abigail, 4:222, 4:298
Elizabeth, 3:323
Elizabeth (——), 2:441,
3:323, 4:222
Martha, 1:432, 4:222
Martha (Beard), 3:602,
4:222
Mary, 1:102, 4:222
Mary (Coley) Simpson,
1:432, 4:222
Sarah, 4:222
Street/Streete
—— (——) Newman, 3:274,
4:222
Abiah, 4:222-223
Abiah/Abigail, 4:78-79
Alice (——), 4:222
Ann, 4:223
Ann (Miles), 3:207, 4:223
Eleanor, 4:223
Elizabeth (——), 3:94, 4:222
Hannah, 4:222-223
Hannah (Glover), 4:223
Mary, 4:222-223
Mary (——) Newman, 3:75
Maudlin (Daniels), 4:223
Sarah, 2:399, 4:222-223

Susanna, 4:222-223
Streeter
Deborah, 4:223
Deborah (——), 4:223
Hannah, 4:223
Mary, 3:555
Mary (——), 4:223
Rebecca, 4:223
Rebecca (——), 4:223
Sarah, 4:223
Ursula (——), 2:466, 3:555,
4:223
Stretton
Elizabeth (——), 4:223
Strickland/Stickland
Ann, 4:224
Elizabeth, 1:55, 2:578,
4:224
Elizabeth (——), 2:52, 4:224
Esther (Smith), 4:130,
4:224
Mary, 4:224
Priscilla, 4:224
Rebecca, 4:224
Sarah, 4:224
Striker
Abigail, 4:224
Deborah, 4:224
Dorcas, 4:224
Hannah, 4:224
Hannah (Waters), 4:224,
4:435
Strong
—— (Holton), 2:456
Abiah (Ingersoll), 2:521
Abigail, 1:369, 3:27, 3:452,
4:225-228
Abigail (Bartlett) Stebbins,
4:176, 4:225
Abigail (Bissell), 4:225
Abigail (Ford), 2:183,
4:226-227
Abigail (Ingersoll), 2:521
Bela, 4:225
Christian, 4:228
Damaris, 4:227
Eleanor/Elinor, 2:31, 4:226
Elizabeth, 1:214, 2:417,
3:363, 4:225-227, 4:655
Elizabeth (Warriner),
4:227, 4:429
Esther, 1:187, 4:226-228
Esther (Clap), 1:389,

4:228
Eunice, 4:225
Experience, 2:158,
4:225-227
Freedom (Woodward),
4:225, 4:644
Hannah, 1:335-336, 1:405,
1:509, 4:225-227
Hannah (Clap), 1:390,
4:225
Hannah (Trumbull), 4:227,
4:336
Joanna, 4:227
Joanna (Gillet), 4:227
Lydia, 3:647, 4:225
Margaret, 4:227
Margaret (Newberry),
3:269, 4:227
Maria, 2:574, 4:228
Martha, 4:566
Mary, 1:396-397, 3:443,
4:165, 4:225-228
Mary (——) Lee, 4:225
Mary (Clark), 1:398,
4:226-227
Mary (Hart) Lee, 3:72
Mary (Hewett), 4:228
Mary (Huet), 2:490
Mary (Stebbins), 4:176
Patience, 3:645
Rachel, 4:228
Rachel (——), 1:234
Rachel (Holton), 2:456,
4:228
Rebecca (Stebbins), 4:176
Ruth, 4:228
Ruth (Sheldon) Wright,
4:69, 4:228, 4:657
Sarah, 1:119, 4:225-227,
4:476
Sarah (Warham), 4:227,
4:418
Selah, 4:228
Submit, 4:228
Susanna, 4:228
Tabitha (Lee), 3:72
Thankful, 4:225-227
Thankful (Stebbins), 4:176,
4:225
Waitstill, 4:228
Stroud
Mary, 4:708
Mary (——), 4:708

Stuard - see Stewart
Stubbs
Abigail (Benjamin), 1:166,
4:228, 4:645
Dinah (Manning), 4:689
Elizabeth, 4:196, 4:228
Margaret (Reed), 3:519,
4:228
Mary, 4:228, 4:321
Stuckey
Ann (Quimby), 4:229
Elizabeth, 4:229
Elizabeth (----), 4:229
Studley
Deborah, 4:229
Elizabeth, 4:229
Elizabeth (----), 4:229
Mary, 4:229
Mary (Merritt), 4:229
Sarah (Brooks), 1:263
Sturgis/Sturges
Abigail, 4:229
Abigail (----), 4:229
Deborah, 3:521, 4:708
Deborah (Barlow), 1:117
Elizabeth, 4:229
Fear, 2:453
Hannah, 4:229
Mary, 4:229
Mary (----) Orris, 4:229,
4:693
Mary (----) Rider, 4:697
Mary (Hedge), 2:400,
4:229
Susanna (Banks), 1:112
Thankful, 4:229
Sturtevant/Sturdevant
Ann, 4:229-230,
4:431-432
Hannah, 4:230
Hannah (Winslow) Crow,
4:229, 4:602
Lydia, 4:230
Mary, 3:99, 4:230
Sarah, 4:230
Stutch
Sarah, 4:230
Sarah (----), 4:230
Sullivan
Margaret, 2:67
Summers
Mary (Sampson), 4:10,
4:230

Rachel (Reed), 4:230
Sumner
---, 4:232
Abigail, 4:230-232
Ann, 4:231-232
Ann (Tucker), 4:231
Deliverance, 4:232, 4:452
Elizabeth, 2:404,
4:230-232
Elizabeth (Badcock), 4:230
Elizabeth (Clap),
4:230-231
Elizabeth (Clement), 1:514,
4:232
Esther (Puffer), 3:493
Experience, 4:232
Hannah, 2:268, 4:231-232
Hannah (----), 4:232
Jaazaniah, 4:230
Joan, 4:232, 4:439
Margaret, 4:230
Margaret (Harris), 4:230
Mary, 2:282, 2:476, 3:280,
4:231-232
Mary (----), 4:232
Mary (Baker), 1:95, 4:231
Mary (Josselyn), 2:572,
4:231
Mehitable, 4:230-232
Mercy, 2:287, 4:232
Rachel (Avery), 1:83
Rebecca, 4:230-232, 4:582
Rebecca (----), 4:232
Sarah, 4:231-232
Sarah (----), 4:231
Sarah (Staples), 4:231
Silence, 4:230
Silence (----), 4:230
Susanna, 4:231
Thankful, 4:230-232
Waitstill, 4:231, 4:339
Sunderland/Synderland
Dorothy, 4:233
Dorothy (----), 4:233
Hannah, 4:233
Mary, 3:502, 4:233
Mary (Vial), 4:233, 4:377
Thomasine (Lumpkin)
Mayo, 3:130, 4:233
Surney/Turney
Ruth, 1:298
Sussell
Abigail (Davis), 4:233

Sutliffe
Hannah (Plympton), 3:448,
4:708
Sarah (----), 4:233
Sutton
Alice, 4:234
Catharine, 4:233
Damaris (Bishop), 4:234
Eliphael (----), 4:233
Elizabeth, 4:233-234
Elizabeth (House), 4:233
Esther, 4:234
Hannah, 4:233-234
Hannah (----), 4:233
Lydia, 4:233
Martha (----), 4:233
Mary, 4:234
Mary (Gassell/Gaffell),
4:234
Rachel (----), 4:234
Sarah, 4:233-234
Sarah (----), 4:234
Sarah (Tilden), 4:233,
4:301
Susanna, 3:465
Swain
Abigail, 4:235
Bethia, 4:236
Christian, 4:235
Deborah, 4:234, 4:356
Dorcas, 1:435, 4:234,
4:248
Dorcas (Rose), 4:234
Dorothy, 1:361, 4:235
Elizabeth, 4:235, 4:441
Elizabeth (----), 4:235
Eunice, 4:235
Experience (Folger), 2:177
Hannah, 4:234-236, 4:252
Hannah (Lothrop), 3:120,
4:235
Jane (----) Bunker, 4:235
Jane (Godfrey) Bunker,
1:299
Martha (----), 3:84, 4:234
Mary, 4:235-236, 4:708
Mary (Wyer), 4:235, 4:663
Mary/Mercy (----), 4:235
Patience, 4:708
Phebe, 4:235
Prudence, 4:236
Prudence (----), 4:236
Rachel, 4:234

Swain (continued)
Sarah, 4:235
Swan
----, 2:463, 4:237
Abigail, 4:236-237
Ann, 4:237, 4:336
Ann (----), 4:237
Dorothy, 4:237
Elizabeth, 4:236
Elizabeth (----), 4:236-237
Frances, 3:499, 4:237
Hannah, 4:236
Joan (----), 4:236
Julian, 4:237
Julian/Susan, 4:192, 4:237
Lydia, 4:236
Mary, 4:236-237
Mary (Lamb), 3:48, 4:237
Mary (Pratt), 4:236
Mercy, 4:422
Prudence (Wade), 4:237
Rebecca, 4:236
Rebecca (Palfrey), 4:236
Ruth, 4:236
Sarah, 1:227, 4:236-237
Sarah (Holden), 2:446, 4:236
Swasey/Swazey/Swasy
Abigail, 4:708
Elizabeth, 3:648, 4:237, 4:708
Elizabeth (----), 4:708
Elizabeth (Lambert), 4:708
Mary, 4:708
Mary (----), 4:708
Mary (Betts), 1:173
Rebecca (Satterly/Shatterly), 4:20
Swayne
Rebecca, 4:709
Sweat
Mercy (Rouse), 3:579
Sweet/Swaite/Sweete
Abigail, 4:238
Deborah, 4:238
Elizabeth, 4:238
Elizabeth (----), 4:238, 4:708
Elizabeth (Walker), 4:238, 4:395
Margaret, 4:238
Mary, 4:238
Mary (----), 2:448, 4:238

Mary (Green), 2:302, 4:238
Mehitable, 4:238
Mehitable (Larkin), 4:239
Meribah, 2:243, 4:238
Priscilla (Carpenter), 1:338, 4:239
Rachel (----), 4:238
Renewed, 4:238
Sarah, 4:238
Susanna, 3:310, 4:238
Susanna (----), 4:238
Temperance, 4:238
Temperance (----), 4:238
Sweetman/Swetman
Bethia, 2:407, 4:239
Elizabeth, 4:239, 4:480
Hepzibah, 4:239
Isabel (----), 4:239
Mehitable, 4:239
Rebecca, 4:148, 4:239
Ruhamah, 4:239
Sarah, 4:239, 4:324
Sweetser/Switzer
Bethia (----), 4:239
Elizabeth, 4:239
Elizabeth (----), 2:472, 4:239
Elizabeth (----) Oakes, 2:394, 3:302, 4:239
Hannah, 4:239
Mary, 1:196, 4:239
Sarah, 4:239
Sarah (Lynde) Clark, 1:402, 4:239
Swetland/Sweetland
Agnes (----), 4:708-709
Grace, 4:709
Swett
Bethia (Page), 4:240
Deliverance, 4:240
Elizabeth, 4:239-240
Elizabeth (----), 4:240
Esther, 4:239-240
Esther (----), 2:309
Esther (Weare), 4:239
Hannah, 1:93, 3:447, 4:239-240
Hannah (Merrill), 3:199, 4:240
Huldah, 4:240
Mary, 4:239-240
Mary (Baxter) Buttolph,

1:323
Mary (Hussey), 4:240
Mary (Plummer), 4:240
Mercy, 3:234
Phebe (----), 4:240
Rebecca, 2:222, 4:240
Rebecca (Smith), 4:134, 4:240
Sarah, 2:436, 4:239-240
Sarah (----), 4:240
Swift
Abigail, 4:241
Abigail (----), 4:241
Abigail (Blake), 1:192
Abigail (Gibbs), 4:241
Ann, 3:517, 4:241
Dinah, 4:242
Elizabeth, 4:241, 4:445
Elizabeth (----), 4:242
Elizabeth (Capen), 4:241
Elizabeth (Vose), 4:241, 4:376
Esther, 4:242
Experience, 1:32
Experience (Nye), 4:241
Hannah, 4:241-242, 4:593
Hopestill, 4:241
Jirah, 4:242
Joan, 1:96, 4:241
Joan (----), 4:241
Joanna, 4:241
Mary, 4:133, 4:241-242
Mary (----), 4:241
Mary (Bodfish), 4:241
Remember, 4:241
Rest, 4:241
Rest (Atherton), 1:73, 4:241
Ruth, 2:310, 4:241
Ruth (----), 4:242
Sarah, 4:241
Sarah (----), 4:241
Susanna, 1:389, 4:241
Temperance, 4:242
Swilloway
Hannah, 4:242
Margaret, 4:131, 4:242
Swinerton/Swannerton
---- (Gardner), 2:227
Elizabeth, 4:709
Elizabeth (----), 4:242
Esther (Baker), 4:709
Hannah (----), 4:242

Swinerton/Swannerton
(continued)
Hannah (----) Brown,
4:709
Joanna, 4:709
Mary, 4:709
Mary (----), 4:709
Mary (Sumner), 4:231
Ruth, 4:242, 4:709
Ruth (Symonds), 4:242,
4:245
Sarah, 4:709
Sylvester/Silvester
Ann, 4:99
Barshua, 4:99
Deborah, 4:99
Dinah, 4:100
Elizabeth, 3:126, 4:100
Esther, 4:100
Griselda, 3:102, 4:99
Grizel (Brinley), 1:255,
4:99
Grizzle, 4:99
Hannah (----), 4:364
Hannah (Leonard), 4:100
Hannah (Savage), 4:25
Hannah (Savage) Gillam,
2:255, 4:27, 4:99
Lois, 4:99, 4:202
Lydia, 3:509, 4:99-100,
4:655-656
Lydia (Standlake), 4:98
Martha, 4:99
Mary, 1:484, 2:100, 4:99,
4:201
Mary (----), 4:99
Mary (Brinley), 1:255
Naomi, 3:126, 4:99-100
Naomi (Torrey), 4:100
Sarah, 4:99
Sarah (Grant), 4:100
Silence, 4:99
Symmes
---- (----), 4:243
Catharine, 4:244
Deborah, 4:243-244
Elizabeth, 2:7, 4:242-244,
4:363
Elizabeth (Collamore)
Rose, 3:576
Elizabeth (Norton), 3:290,
4:23, 4:242
Hannah, 4:243-244

Huldah, 2:23, 4:243-244
Mary, 4:26, 4:200,
4:243-244
Mary (----), 4:314
Mary (Nichols), 4:242
Mehitable (----) Dalton,
4:244
Mehitable (Palmer) Dalton,
2:3
Rebecca, 1:212, 4:243-244
Ruth, 4:243-244, 4:573
Ruth (Convers), 4:243
Sarah, 1:257, 2:166, 2:468,
4:40, 4:243-244
Sarah (----), 4:243-244
Susanna, 1:513, 1:513
Susanna (Graves), 2:297,
4:244
Symonds
Abigail, 3:430, 4:245-247
Abigail (Spencer), 4:149,
4:245
Ann, 4:245
Bethia, 4:247
Betty (Day), 4:244
Catharine, 4:245, 4:316
Dorothy, 2:366, 4:246-247
Dorothy (----), 4:246
Dorothy (Harlakenden),
4:709
Elizabeth, 2:125,
4:245-247
Elizabeth (----), 4:244-245,
4:247
Elizabeth (Andrews),
1:499, 4:247
Elizabeth (Browning),
1:279, 4:245
Elizabeth (Day), 4:244
Huldah, 4:244, 4:247
Joan, 4:247
Joanna (----), 4:246
Judith, 4:244, 4:247
Judith (----) Hayward,
4:247
Judith (Phippen) Hayward,
2:392
Martha, 2:37, 4:246-247
Martha (----) Epes, 1:387,
2:125, 4:246
Martha (Reed) Epes, 4:246
Mary, 1:358-361, 3:164,
3:288, 4:245-247, 4:372

Mary (Epes), 2:80
Mary (Wade), 4:247,
4:378
Priscilla, 1:99, 4:246-247,
4:420
Rebecca, 4:244
Rebecca (----), 4:244,
4:246
Rebecca (----) Byley Hall
Worcester, 1:326, 4:246
Rebecca (Swayne), 4:709
Richgrace, 4:245
Ruth, 2:108, 2:117, 4:242,
4:245-247
Sarah, 2:330, 2:408, 3:649,
4:244-245, 4:247, 4:709
Sarah (----), 4:247
Sarah (Bacon), 4:244
Sarah (Waters), 4:709
Susan (----), 4:245
Susanna, 2:533, 3:598,
4:245-247
Susanna (----), 4:393
Susanna (Blodget), 4:245
Tabitha, 4:247
Tabor/Taber
---- (Cooke), 3:612, 4:248
Abigail, 4:248
Bethia, 4:248
Elizabeth (Tillinghast),
4:303
Esther, 4:248
Lydia, 4:248, 4:303
Lydia (Masters), 3:170,
4:248
Mary, 4:248
Mary (----), 4:248
Sarah, 4:248
Tainer
Ann, 4:248
Elizabeth, 4:248
Elizabeth (Condy), 4:248
Joanna, 4:248
Rebecca (Dike), 3:616,
4:248
Taintor/Tainter/Taynter
----, 1:112
---- (Guy), 2:325
Ann, 4:249
Catharine (----), 4:249
Dorcas (Swain), 1:435,
4:234, 4:248
Dorothy, 2:325, 4:249

294

Taintor/Tainter/Taynter
(continued)
Elizabeth, 3:568,
4:248-249
Elizabeth (----), 4:249
Elizabeth (Warren), 4:248,
4:423
Hannah, 2:325
Joanna, 2:256, 4:249
Joanna (Stone), 4:206,
4:249
Mabel (----) Butler, 1:320
Mabel (Olmstead) Butler,
4:249
Mary, 2:325, 4:248-249
Mary (----), 4:248
Mary (Guy), 4:249
Mary (Loomis), 3:114,
4:249
Mary (Randall), 4:248
Rebecca, 2:325, 4:249
Sarah, 1:154, 2:325, 4:209,
4:249
Susanna, 4:248
Talbot
Cicely (----), 4:250
Judith, 4:250
Martha (Barstow), 4:249
Mary, 4:249-250
Rebecca (Hathaway),
4:249
Sarah (Andrews), 4:249
Talby/Tolby
Difficulty, 4:250
Dorothy (----), 4:250
Hannah (----), 4:250
Talcott
Abigail, 4:251
Abigail (Clarke), 4:251
Dorothy, 4:215, 4:250-251
Dorothy (Smith), 4:250
Elizabeth, 4:250-251,
4:380
Ellen (Wakeman), 4:387
Eunice, 4:251
Hannah, 2:286, 4:250-251
Hannah (Holyoke), 2:456,
4:251
Helen, 3:279
Helena, 4:250-251
Helena/Ellen (Wakeman),
4:250
Jerusha, 4:251

Mary, 2:103, 3:591,
4:250-251
Mary (----), 4:251
Mary (Cook), 4:250
Rachel, 4:250-251
Ruth, 4:250-251
Sarah, 4:250
Talley/Tally
Abigail, 4:252
Elizabeth (Grosse), 4:252
Hannah, 4:252
Jane, 4:252
Mary, 4:252
Mary (----), 4:252
Sarah, 4:252
Sarah (----), 4:252
Sarah (Blake), 1:192,
4:252
Talmadge/Talmage
---- (Alsop/Alsup), 1:45
---- (Peirce), 3:429, 4:252
Abigail, 4:252
Abigail (Bishop), 3:603,
4:709
Elizabeth, 4:252
Elizabeth (Alsop), 3:597
Hannah (Yale), 4:252,
4:667, 4:709
Mary, 4:252
Sarah, 2:439, 2:467, 4:252
Sarah (Nash), 3:262, 4:252
Talman/Tallman
Ann (----), 4:253
Ann (----) Walstone, 4:253
Ann (Wright) Walstone,
4:402
Elizabeth, 3:64, 4:252-253
Hannah, 4:253
Hannah (Swain), 4:252
Jemima, 4:252
Mary, 4:252
Mary (Devoll), 2:42, 4:252
Tankersly
Tabitha (----), 4:253
Tanner/Tanners
Joanna (Lewis), 3:88
Mary (Babcock), 1:86
Rebecca (Spencer)
Kennard, 3:10, 4:147
Tapley
Elizabeth, 4:253
Elizabeth (Cash), 1:347,
4:253

Elizabeth (Pride), 4:253
Hannah, 4:253
Lydia, 4:709
Lydia (Small), 4:709
Mary, 1:267, 4:253, 4:709
Thomasine (----), 4:253
Tapp
----, 2:195, 4:253
Ann, 1:57, 2:244, 4:253
Elizabeth, 3:261, 4:253
Jane, 4:253, 4:327
Tappan/Topping/etc
---- (----) Mepham Baldwin,
3:196
---- (Hill), 2:417
Abigail (Wigglesworth),
4:255, 4:542
Alice (----), 4:255
Ann, 4:254
Ann (----), 4:254
Elizabeth, 1:399, 3:205,
4:253-255
Emma (----), 4:255
Esther (Wigglesworth)
Sewall, 4:54, 4:542
Hannah, 4:254, 4:414
Hannah (----) Sewall,
4:254
Hannah (Fessenden)
Sewall, 4:54
Hannah (Kent), 3:13,
4:254
Hannah (Sewall), 4:53,
4:254
Jane, 4:254-255
Jane (Batt), 1:140, 4:255
Judith (----), 4:255
Lydia (----) Wilford, 4:255,
4:550
Marian (----), 4:255
Martha, 4:255
Martha (----), 4:254
Mary, 4:254
Mary (----) Baldwin, 4:255
Mary (----) Mepham
Baldwin, 1:105
Mary (March), 4:254
Mary (Woodmansey),
4:254
Ruth (Pike), 4:254
Sarah (Angier), 1:58,
4:254
Sarah (Greenleaf), 4:255

Tappan/Topping/etc
(continued)
Sarah (Kent), 3:643
Susanna, 4:253
Susanna (Goodale), 2:271,
4:253
Tapper
Hannah (----), 4:255
Lydia, 4:255
Tarbell/Tarball/Tarbole
Abigail, 4:255, 4:531
Ann, 4:256
Ann (Longley), 4:256
Elizabeth, 1:505, 4:256,
4:709
Elizabeth (Blood), 1:205
Hannah (Longley), 3:111
Mary, 4:256, 4:709
Mary (Nurse), 3:300,
4:709
Sarah, 4:709
Susanna (----) Lawrence,
3:62, 4:256
Tarbox
Experience, 4:256
Hannah, 4:256
Joanna, 4:256
Mary, 4:256
Mary (Haven), 2:379,
4:256
Rebecca, 4:256
Rebecca (Armitage), 1:63,
4:256
Sarah, 4:256
Susanna, 4:256
Tare
Jane (----) Parker, 3:351,
4:256
Tarleton/Tarlton
Deborah (Cushing), 1:489,
4:256
Mary (----), 4:256
Ruth, 4:257
Ruth (----), 4:256
Tarne/Terney/Tarney
Deliverance, 4:257
Elizabeth (----) Rice, 3:531,
4:257
Hannah, 4:257
Margery, 3:658
Sarah, 1:207, 4:257
Sarah (----), 4:257

Tarr
Abigail, 4:257
Elizabeth, 4:257
Elizabeth (Felt), 4:257
Elizabeth (Williams),
4:257
Grace (Hodgkins), 4:257
Hazelelponi, 4:257
Honour, 4:257
Leah (----), 3:37
Martha, 4:257
Martha (----), 4:257
Mary, 4:257
Rebecca (----) Card, 4:257
Sarah, 4:257
Sarah (Sargent), 4:257
Tart
Elizabeth, 4:257
Eunice, 4:258
Tatchell
Mary, 3:295
Tatenham
Mary (----), 4:258
Tatman/Totman
Deborah (Turner), 4:258,
4:346
Elizabeth, 4:258
Sarah, 4:258
Taunton
Elizabeth, 4:258
Susanna (----), 4:258
Tawley
Hannah, 4:258
Jane, 4:258
Mary (----), 4:258
Tay/Toy
Abiel, 4:258
Bathsheba (Wyman),
4:258, 4:664
Elizabeth, 4:258
Grace (Newell), 3:270,
4:258
Mercy, 4:258
Mercy (----), 4:258
Tayler
Ann, 2:19
Rhoda, 3:364
Taylor
---- (Burgess), 4:263
Abigail, 4:259, 4:261,
4:264-265
Abigail (Bissell), 4:262
Abigail (Roe), 3:559,

4:265
Achsa (----), 4:260
Alice, 4:263
Ann, 1:408, 4:259-264
Ann (----), 4:263
Bathsheba, 4:259
Catharine, 4:262
Catharine (----), 4:261-262
Deborah, 4:264
Deborah (----), 4:261
Deborah (Godfrey), 2:266
Dorothy, 4:265
Dorothy (Rogers), 3:560
Dorothy (Taintor), 4:249
Elinor, 4:261
Elizabeth, 1:413-414,
4:259-265, 4:419
Elizabeth (----), 4:261,
4:263-264
Elizabeth (Fitch), 2:168,
4:259
Elizabeth (Newell), 4:264
Elizabeth (Richards) Davie,
2:15, 3:533
Elizabeth (Spencer), 4:262
Elizabeth(----)Bancroft
Saunders Bridge, 1:110,
1:248, 4:21
Esther, 2:599, 4:262,
4:419
Experience, 4:259, 4:261
Experience (Williamson),
4:262
Frances, 4:263
Hannah, 1:474, 4:260-261,
4:263-265
Hannah (----), 4:259, 4:264
Hannah (----) Axtell, 1:84
Hannah (Cole), 1:426
Hannah (Fitzrandle), 2:170,
4:261
Hannah (Granger), 4:265
Hannah (Rice) Ward,
3:529, 4:407
Hope, 4:261
Isabel/Elizabeth
(Tompkins), 4:260
Jerusha, 4:265
Joan, 4:263
Joanna, 1:47, 4:261, 4:264
Joanna (Cole), 1:426
Joanna (Porter), 3:464,
3:660, 4:264

Taylor (continued)
Judith, 4:259
Keziah, 4:195, 4:259,
4:263, 4:265
Lydia, 3:248, 4:259,
4:260-261, 4:265
Lydia (Hatch), 2:376,
4:260
Mabel, 4:264-265
Margaret, 4:263-265
Margaret (Mosely), 4:264
Martha, 1:149, 3:69, 4:259,
4:263-264
Martha (Way), 4:440
Mary, 2:89, 4:259-265
Mary (----), 2:477, 4:260,
4:262-263, 4:265
Mary (Banks), 1:112
Mary (Harrington), 2:592,
4:264
Mary (Hodges), 4:263
Mary (Meriam), 4:265
Mary (Merks), 4:259
Mary (Petty), 4:265
Mary (Selden), 4:50, 4:261
Mary (Taylor), 4:260,
4:262
Mehitable, 4:259-260,
4:263
Mercy, 4:261-262, 4:264
Mindwell, 2:290, 4:261,
4:264
Naomi, 4:259
Phebe (Rockwood), 4:261
Rachel, 4:260
Rebecca, 2:325, 4:260-262,
4:264
Rebecca (----), 4:261,
4:265
Rebecca (Ketcham), 3:14,
4:264
Rhoda, 4:260-261
Rhoda (----), 4:261
Rhoda (Dewey), 4:260
Ruth, 4:259, 4:263-264
Ruth (Burgess), 4:263
Ruth (Cogan), 4:264
Ruth (Wyllys), 4:259,
4:577
Sarah, 4:259, 4:261-264
Sarah (----), 4:260,
4:263-264
Sarah (Barron), 1:126

Sarah (Brooks), 4:262
Sarah (Hosford),
4:264-265
Sarah (Matthews), 4:262
Sarah (Newton), 3:277
Sarah (White), 2:427,
4:264, 4:510
Sarah (Younglove), 4:262,
4:671
Susanna (Drake) Brackett,
2:69
Thankful, 4:260-262,
4:264, 4:654
Thankful (Day), 4:260
Thankful (Woodward),
4:261, 4:644
Thomasin (----), 4:262
Thomasine (Scarlet), 4:35
Tead/Teed/Ted - see also
Tidd
----, 4:265
Alice (----), 4:265
Elizabeth, 4:265
Hannah, 4:265
Margaret (----), 4:265
Mary, 4:265
Sarah (----), 4:265
Teal/Teel
Abigail (Coggan), 1:514
Alice, 3:146
Tefft
Elizabeth (Jenks), 2:543
Esther, 3:254
Tell
Abigail, 4:266
Elizabeth, 4:266
Mary (----), 4:266
Rachel, 4:266
Templar/Templer/Temple
----, 1:221
Abigail, 1:227, 4:266
Alice, 3:9
Ann (----), 3:244
Deborah, 1:512, 3:485,
4:266
Deborah (Hadlock), 4:266
Deborah (Parker), 4:266
Elizabeth, 4:266
Elizabeth (Bowdoin),
1:221
Esther, 4:266
Hannah, 3:485, 4:266
Hannah (Pritchard), 4:266

Joanna (----), 4:266
Margaret, 2:249
Mary, 4:266
Phebe, 3:656, 4:266
Ruth, 4:266
Sarah (----), 4:266
Tenney/Tenny
---- (Warwick), 4:268,
4:429
Abigail, 4:268
Abigail (Bailey), 4:268
Ann (----), 4:268
Catharine (----), 4:710
Elizabeth, 4:710
Elizabeth (Hagborn), 4:267
Elizabeth (Stickney), 4:192,
4:267
Hannah, 4:709
Martha (----), 4:268
Mary, 4:709-710
Mary (----), 4:267
Mercy, 2:355
Ruhamah, 4:268
Ruth, 2:355
Sarah, 1:78, 4:710
Sarah (Boynton), 4:268
Terhan/Turhan
Abigail, 4:268
Mary (----) Wise, 4:268
Terrill/Tirrell/Turrall
---- (Offitt), 3:305
---- (Ufford), 4:268
Abigail, 4:268, 4:356
Hannah, 4:103
Martha, 4:268
Rebecca (Simpkins), 4:101
Sarah, 1:77, 4:268
Sarah (----), 4:268
Sarah (Willey), 4:268,
4:558
Terry
Abigail, 3:5, 4:269
Ann, 4:269
Ann (Lobdell), 3:102,
4:269
Elizabeth, 3:593,
4:268-269
Elizabeth (Wadsworth),
4:268, 4:381
Hannah, 4:269
Hannah (Eggleston), 4:268
Hannah (Morgan), 4:269
Martha, 4:269

Terry (continued)
Martha (Credan) Crane,
4:269
Mary, 2:274, 4:268-269
Mary (Cooley), 4:270
Rebecca, 3:367, 4:268-269,
4:654
Sarah, 4:268
Sarah (Bliss) Scott, 4:37
Sarah (Scott), 4:269
Tew
Elnathan, 4:270
Mary, 2:360, 4:270
Mary (Clark), 4:270
Seaborn, 1:178, 4:270
Tewksbury
Elizabeth, 4:270
Hannah, 4:270
Martha (----) Harvey,
2:370, 4:270
Naomi, 4:270
Ruth, 4:270
Thacher/Thatcher
Abigail, 4:273
Ann, 4:271-272
Bathsheba, 4:272
Bethia, 2:479, 3:332,
4:271
Desire, 4:271
Dorothy, 4:704
Edith, 4:270
Elizabeth, 2:13, 2:21,
3:623, 4:271-274
Elizabeth (Jones), 4:271
Elizabeth (Partridge),
3:366, 4:273
Elizabeth (Thacher) Gee,
3:623
Elizabeth (Thornton) Gee,
2:241, 4:292
Hannah, 2:452, 4:271-273
Hannah (----), 4:272
Hannah (Curwin), 4:274
Lydia, 4:271-272
Lydia (Gorham), 2:281,
4:271
Margaret (Webb) Sheaffe,
4:66, 4:273, 4:444
Mary, 3:616, 4:270-274
Mary (----), 4:271
Mary (Farnsworth), 2:143,
4:273
Mary (Savage), 4:25, 4:27,

4:274
Mary (Thornton), 4:272,
4:292
Mercy, 4:271, 4:273
Patience, 3:8, 3:366,
4:273-274
Rebecca, 4:271
Rebecca (Winslow), 4:271,
4:602
Ruth, 4:272
Ruth (Partridge), 3:365,
4:272
Sarah, 4:273
Susanna (----) Bailey, 1:94,
4:272
Theodora, 4:272
Theodora (Oxenbridge),
3:327, 4:272
Tharpe
Elizabeth, 4:274
Margaret (----) Pigg, 3:435,
4:274
Sarah (----) Robbins, 4:710
Sarah (Brooks) Robbins,
4:697
Thaxter
---- (Jacob), 4:274
Abigail, 4:275
Abigail (Church), 1:386,
4:275
Deborah, 1:491, 4:274-275
Deborah (Lincoln), 3:94,
4:275
Elizabeth, 1:489,
4:274-275
Elizabeth (----), 2:85, 3:543,
4:275
Elizabeth (Jacob), 1:489,
2:534
Hannah (Gridley), 4:275
Lydia (Logan), 4:275
Mary, 1:491, 4:274-275
Mary (----), 4:275
Mary (Buttolph), 2:276
Sarah, 4:274-275, 4:297
Thayer
Abigail, 4:275-278
Abigail (Hayden), 2:386,
4:275
Abigail (Veazie), 4:278,
4:369
Ann, 4:277
Ann (----), 4:278

Bathsheba, 4:276
Bethia, 4:278
Comfort, 4:276
Deborah, 2:149, 4:276-278
Deborah (----), 4:277
Deliverance (Priest), 4:278
Dorothy, 4:277
Dorothy (Pray), 4:277
Elizabeth, 4:276-278
Elizabeth (----), 4:276
Esther, 4:276
Experience, 2:206, 4:278
Freelove, 4:278
Grace, 4:275-276
Hannah, 2:387, 4:276-278
Hannah (----) Hayward,
4:278
Hannah (Hayden), 2:386,
4:277
Hannah (Hayward), 4:275
Hulda, 4:276
Hulda (Hayward), 4:276
Huldah, 4:276-277
Jael, 2:353, 4:277
Jemima, 4:278
Joanna, 1:478, 4:277
Lydia, 4:275, 4:277
Margaret, 4:275, 4:278
Margery (----), 4:278
Martha (----), 4:276
Mary, 1:93, 4:276-278
Mary (----), 4:276-278
Mary (Barrett), 4:278
Mary (Neal), 3:264, 4:276
Mercy, 4:276
Mercy (----), 4:276
Miriam, 4:276
Naomi, 4:276
Naphtali, 4:276
Priscilla, 4:276
Rachel, 4:278
Rebecca, 4:276-277
Rebecca (Mycall), 3:259,
4:277
Ruth, 4:275-277
Ruth (Neal), 3:264, 4:276
Sarah, 2:21, 2:392-393,
4:275-277
Sarah (----), 4:276
Sarah (Bass), 4:276
Sarah (Hayward), 4:275
Susanna, 4:276-277
Susanna (Scant), 4:277

Thayer (continued)
Temperance, 4:278
Trial, 4:278
Theale/Thele/Theele/Thale
Elizabeth, 3:509, 4:279
Elizabeth (——), 3:306,
4:279
Thing
Abigail (Gilman), 2:258,
4:279
Elizabeth, 4:279
Mary, 2:77
Mary (Gilman), 2:258,
4:279
Mary (Vaughan), 4:368
Thistle/Thissell
Elizabeth (Patch), 3:368
Jane, 4:279
Mary, 4:279
Thomas
——, 4:282
—— (Goddard), 2:264
—— (Winthrop), 4:611
Abigail, 4:280-281
Alice (——) Kirtland, 1:349,
3:32, 4:280
Ann, 4:279
Ann (——) Lovering, 4:283
Ann (Belding), 4:279
Bethia, 4:280
Clement (——), 4:280
Deborah, 1:473-474,
4:281-282
Deborah (Jacobs), 2:534,
4:281
Dinah, 4:279
Dorcas, 4:280
Dorothy, 3:324, 4:279,
4:281, 4:316
Elizabeth, 1:375, 1:476,
2:454, 4:280-281, 4:710
Elizabeth (——), 4:283
Elizabeth (——) Condy,
1:441, 4:281
Elizabeth (Burrows), 1:311,
4:282
Elizabeth (Dolberry),
4:281
Hannah, 4:281, 4:710
Jane, 2:530, 4:279-280
Jane (——), 4:279
Joanna, 4:283
Lydia, 4:280

Lydia (Parker), 3:350,
4:280
Mary, 2:6, 3:512,
4:279-282, 4:710
Mary (——), 4:281
Mary (Appleton), 1:61
Mary (Graves), 4:710
Mary (Roby), 3:549
Mary (Walford), 4:392
Mercy, 4:281-282
Mercy (Ford), 2:184, 4:282
Priscilla, 4:280
Rebecca, 4:281
Rebecca (——), 4:280
Rebecca (Iyans), 2:518,
4:280
Rebecca (Maverick), 3:180
Rebecca (Thompson),
4:279
Recompense, 4:279
Ruth, 4:710
Sarah, 3:409, 4:279-281,
4:581
Sarah (Chapin), 1:360,
4:282
Sarah (Pitney), 3:442,
4:280
Susanna (——) Rogers,
3:568, 4:282
Tabitha, 3:634, 4:280
Tabitha (——), 4:280
Thankful, 4:280
Thompson
—— (——), 2:366
—— (——) Royce, 4:287
—— (Brewer), 4:287
—— (Hopkins), 4:287
Abigail, 1:45, 1:486, 3:110,
3:448, 3:597, 3:613,
3:637, 4:85, 4:283-288,
4:710
Abigail (——), 4:285,
4:288-289
Abigail (Gardner), 2:585
Alice, 3:348
Ann, 1:233, 1:370,
4:283-286, 4:288-289,
4:703
Ann (——) Crosby, 1:477,
4:289
Ann (Vicaris), 4:710
Ann (Wells), 2:382, 4:288,
4:478

Ann/Hannah, 4:286
Beatrice, 4:288
Bridget, 1:223, 4:283,
4:289
Bridget (——), 4:290, 4:691
Bridget (Chesebrough),
1:373
Catharine (——), 1:331,
4:283
Catharine (Treat), 4:289,
4:326
Deborah, 4:288
Deborah (——), 4:41
Deborah (Dudley), 2:78,
4:284
Elinor, 2:206, 4:283, 4:289,
4:369
Elizabeth, 1:233, 4:283,
4:285-286, 4:288-289
Elizabeth (——), 2:159,
4:285
Elizabeth (Billings), 4:288
Elizabeth (Lothrop) Royce,
3:569
Elizabeth (Smith), 4:110,
4:288
Elizabeth (Stedman)
Upham, 4:178, 4:285,
4:361
Ellen (Harrison), 4:285
Esther, 2:224, 2:576,
3:520, 3:626, 4:284-288
Frances (Whitmore), 4:526
Hannah, 3:248, 4:283-285,
4:288
Hannah (Walker), 4:285
Joanna, 4:290
Judith, 4:290
Lydia, 1:481, 4:283,
4:285-286, 4:289
Margaret, 4:288
Margaret (——), 4:285
Martha, 2:586, 4:284
Martha (Fiske), 4:284
Mary, 1:454, 2:7, 3:97,
3:221, 4:70, 4:283-289,
4:614
Mary (——), 3:368
Mary (Brackett), 1:229,
4:287
Mary (Converse), 1:444,
4:288
Mary (Holmes), 2:453

Thompson (continued)
Mary (Lovering), 4:290
Mary (Steele), 4:286,
4:707
Mercy, 4:288, 4:626
Mirable (----), 4:285
Olive, 1:493
Philadelphia, 4:290
Philadelphia (Tileston),
4:290
Priscilla, 1:370, 4:286
Priscilla (Powell), 3:470,
4:286
Rachel, 4:290
Rachel (Glover), 4:288
Rebecca, 4:279, 4:285,
4:288
Rebecca (Bishop), 3:603,
4:288
Rebecca (Daniel), 2:10
Sarah, 1:106, 2:170, 2:403,
2:505, 3:601, 3:637,
4:283-288
Sarah (----), 4:283-284
Sarah (Coggan), 4:290
Sarah (Gold), 2:286
Sarah (Shepard), 4:288
Sarah (Smith), 4:287
Susanna, 4:283, 4:287
Susanna (----) Blodget,
1:203, 4:285
Susanna (Blodget), 1:203,
4:287
Susanna (Kirtland), 4:283
Thomson
Bridget, 2:36
Mary (Cooke), 1:446
Thorndike
Alice, 4:290, 4:710
Ann, 4:290
Elizabeth, 3:489, 4:290
Elizabeth (----), 4:290
Hannah, 4:290
Martha, 4:290, 4:710
Mary, 4:290
Mary (Patch), 3:368, 4:290
Sarah, 3:125, 4:290
Thorne/Thorn
Desiretruth, 1:8, 4:291
Hannah, 4:291
Joanna, 4:187
Lydia (Redfield) Bayley,
1:143, 4:291

Thornton
Ann, 2:336, 4:292
Catharine, 4:292-293
Elizabeth, 2:241, 3:149,
4:291-293
Elizabeth (Danforth),
4:293
Elizabeth (Gilbert), 4:291
Experience, 4:291-293
Experience (Brooking),
4:292
Hannah, 4:293
Hannah (Farrand), 2:144,
4:292
Joanna, 4:293
Lydia, 4:291
Mary, 4:272, 4:292-293
Mary (----), 4:291
Mary (----) Merry, 4:291
Mary (Boylston) Coussens,
4:291
Mary (Dolens) Merry,
3:200
Mary (Dowling) Merry,
3:200
Priscilla, 4:292
Sarah (----), 4:292
Thomas [?Thomasine],
4:292
Thorpe/Thorp
----, 1:294, 4:293
Alice, 2:23
Alice (----), 4:293
Elizabeth, 2:60, 4:293
Hannah, 1:295, 4:293
Margaret (----) Pigg, 3:435
Martha (Pierce/etc), 3:427
Mary, 1:377
Mary (Benton), 3:603
Mary (Ford), 2:183
Rebecca (Milward), 3:212,
4:293
Thrall/Trall
Abigail, 4:293, 4:323
Deborah, 4:293, 4:323
Deborah (Gunn), 2:324,
4:293, 4:323
Elizabeth, 4:293, 4:323
Elizabeth (Owen), 1:346
Martha, 4:293, 4:323
Mehitable, 1:400, 4:293,
4:323
Philippa, 2:465, 4:293

Phillis, 4:323
Thrasher/Thresher
Bethia (Brooks), 4:294
Dorothy, 4:294
Hannah, 1:348, 4:294
Hannah (Thrasher), 4:294
Mary, 4:294
Mary (Caswell), 1:348,
4:294
Mary (Goodrich), 4:294
Sarah, 3:78, 4:294
Threeneedles
Damaris, 4:294
Damaris (Hawkins), 2:382,
4:294
Elizabeth, 4:294
Mary, 4:294
Ruth, 4:294
Sarah, 4:294
Susanna, 4:294
Throgmorton
Patience, 1:421, 4:294
Thurber/Thurbar
Abigail, 4:295
Bethia, 4:295
Elizabeth, 4:295
Mary, 1:297, 4:295
Mary (----), 4:295
Mercy, 4:160
Priscilla, 4:295
Rachel, 4:295
Rachel (Wheeler), 4:295
Ruth, 4:295
Ruth (----), 4:295
Welthean (----) Tourtelott,
4:295
Thurlo/Thurla/Thurrell/etc
Abigail, 4:295
Ann, 4:295
Ann (Morse), 3:242, 4:295
Bethia, 4:295
Elizabeth, 4:295
Hannah, 4:295
Jane (----), 4:295
Judith, 4:295-296
Judith (March), 4:295
Lydia, 4:295, 4:710
Martha, 2:72
Mary, 4:295, 4:622
Mary (----), 4:295
Mary (Merrill), 4:295
Prudence, 4:295
Sarah, 2:9, 4:295

Thurlo/Thurla/Thurrell/etc
(continued)
Sarah (Howe), 4:295
Tamosin, 3:598
Thurston
Abigail, 4:296
Ann, 4:296
Ann (----) Lightfoot, 4:296
Ann (Pell), 4:296
Catharine, 2:507
Content, 4:296
Dorcas, 4:296
Elinor, 2:378, 4:296
Elizabeth (Mott), 4:296
Elizabeth (Walker), 4:296,
    4:396
Ellen, 4:296
Esther (----), 4:297
Hannah, 3:116, 3:122,
    3:378, 4:296
Hannah (Miller), 4:296
Judith, 4:297, 4:324
Margaret (----), 4:297
Martha, 4:296
Martha (Stanley), 4:297
Mary, 4:296-297
Mary (----), 4:296
Mary (Stedman), 4:179
Mary (Wood), 4:297,
    4:628
Mary/Martha (Stanley),
    3:416
Mehitable, 4:297
Mehitable (----), 4:297
Mehitable (Kimball), 4:297
Mehitable (Mayo), 3:187
Phebe, 4:296
Rebecca, 1:404, 4:296
Sarah, 3:242, 4:296
Sarah (Thaxter), 4:275,
    4:297
Thwing
Abigail (----), 4:298
Deborah, 4:298
Deborah (----), 4:298
Elizabeth, 4:298
Elizabeth (----), 4:298
Hannah, 4:298
Lydia, 4:298
Mary, 4:298
Mary (----), 4:298
Rachel, 4:298
Sarah, 4:298

Tibbal/Tibbals
Abigail (Streame), 4:222,
    4:298
Ann (Arnold), 1:66
Hannah, 1:453, 4:298
Mary, 4:298
Mary (----), 4:298
Mary (Sherwood), 4:298
Mary/Mercy, 4:128
Mercy, 4:298
Sarah, 1:434, 4:298
Tibbets/Tybbot/Tebbets
----, 1:393
---- (----), 3:628
Abigail, 4:299
Agnes, 4:299
Ann, 4:299
Bridget, 4:299
Catharine, 4:299
Catharine (Mason), 4:299
Dorothy (Tuttle), 4:299,
    4:350
Elizabeth, 1:151, 4:299
Elizabeth (----), 4:299
Hannah, 4:299
Joyce (----), 4:299
Judith, 4:299
Judith (Dam), 2:3, 4:299
Lydia, 4:299
Margery, 4:299
Martha, 4:299
Mary, 2:372, 4:299
Mary (----), 4:299
Mary (Canney), 1:332,
    4:299
Rebecca, 3:286, 4:299
Remembrance, 4:299
Rose, 4:299
Rose (Austin), 4:299
Susanna, 4:299
Tichenor
Abigail, 4:710
Hannah, 4:710
Mary (Charles), 4:677,
    4:710
Ticknor/Tickner
Deborah (Hyland), 2:516,
    4:300
Hannah (Stockbridge),
    4:197, 4:300
Lydia, 4:300
Lydia (Tilden), 4:300

Tidd
Elizabeth, 2:219, 4:300,
    4:710
Elizabeth (----), 4:300
Hannah, 4:125, 4:300
Mary, 3:9, 4:300
Rebecca, 1:203, 4:300
Rebecca (Wood), 4:300
Sarah, 3:109
Sarah (----), 4:707, 4:710
Tidmarsh
Mary (Felmingham), 4:710
Tiff/Tift/Teffe
Ann (----), 4:300
Lydia, 2:46, 4:300
Tabitha, 4:301, 4:588
Tiffany
Elizabeth (----), 4:300
Sarah, 4:300
Tilden
Abigail, 4:301
Alice/Elizabeth (Twisden),
    4:301, 4:354
Elizabeth, 4:301
Elizabeth (----), 4:302
Hannah, 4:301
Hannah (Little), 3:99,
    4:301
Judith, 3:477, 4:301
Lydia, 1:219, 2:233, 3:540,
    4:300-301
Lydia (----), 2:377, 4:301
Lydia (Bourne), 1:219,
    4:301
Mary, 3:56, 4:197, 4:301
Mary (Holmes), 4:302
Mercy, 4:301
Rebecca, 1:251, 4:301
Ruth, 4:301
Sarah, 4:233, 4:301
Susanna, 4:302
Tileston/Tilestone/Tillston
Ann, 4:302
Bathsheba, 3:373, 4:302
Elizabeth, 4:158, 4:302
Elizabeth (----), 4:302
Joanna, 4:95
Naomi, 4:302
Philadelphia, 4:290
Rebecca, 4:95
Ruth, 2:40, 2:191, 4:302
Sarah, 4:302
Sarah (Bridgeman/Bridgman)

Tileston/Tilestone/Tillston
(continued)
Sarah
(Bridgeman/Bridgman)
(continued)
(Bridgeman/Bridgman),
1:250, 4:302
Till/Tylls
Elizabeth (Nick), 4:302
Tilley
---- (----), 4:302
Abigail (Melyen), 3:196
Abigail (Melyen)
Woodmansey, 4:55, 4:641
Alice (----), 4:303
Elizabeth, 1:343, 2:479,
3:198, 4:303
Tillinghast
----, 4:303
Abigail, 4:70, 4:303
Ann, 4:304
Elizabeth, 4:303
Freelove (Stafford), 4:160
Hannah, 4:303
Lydia, 4:304
Lydia (----), 4:303
Lydia (Tabor), 4:248,
4:303
Martha, 4:304
Martha (Holmes), 4:303
Mary, 3:182, 4:303-304,
4:412
Mercy, 4:303
Paris, 4:303
Sarah, 4:304
Tillotson
Dorcas (Coleman), 4:304
Jane (Evans), 4:304
Martha, 4:304
Mary, 4:304
Mary (Jones), 4:304
Mary (Morris), 3:235,
4:304
Philadelphia, 4:304
Tilson
Elizabeth, 2:80, 4:304
Elizabeth (Haskins), 2:466
Elizabeth (Hoskins), 4:304
Jane, 4:304
Joan, 3:540
Mary, 1:427, 2:81, 4:304
Tilton
---- (----) Leonard Parsons,

3:361
Abigail, 4:304
Deliverance (Shaw), 4:304
Elizabeth, 4:305
Elizabeth (----), 4:305
Mary, 2:92, 2:322,
4:304-305
Mary (----), 4:305
Mehitable (Weare), 4:305
Meribah (----), 4:11
Rebecca, 4:304
Sarah, 4:304
Sarah (----) Leonard
Parsons, 4:305
Sarah (Heald) Leonard
Parsons, 3:79
Susanna (----), 4:65, 4:305
Timberlake
Elizabeth, 1:421, 4:305
Tindal
Margaret, 4:610
Tingley/Tingle
Alice (----), 4:306
Elizabeth (Call), 1:511,
4:77, 4:305
Mary, 4:306
Rhoda, 4:306
Sarah, 4:306
Tinker
Alice (----), 3:193
Tinkham
---- (Brown), 4:710
Agnes, 4:2
Elizabeth (Liscom), 4:306
Esther (----), 4:306
Mary, 4:306
Tirrell/Turrell/Terrall/etc
Abigail, 4:307
Abigail (----), 4:307
Hannah (----), 4:306
Martha, 4:307
Mary, 4:306-307
Miriam, 4:306
Rebecca, 4:307
Rebecca (Simpkins), 4:101,
4:307
Sarah, 4:307
Sarah (Willey), 4:306
Tisdale
Abigail, 4:307
Ann, 3:78, 4:307
Hannah (Rogers), 3:563,
4:307

Mary, 2:207
Mary (Avery), 1:83, 4:307
Mindwell, 3:620
Remember, 4:307
Sarah (----), 4:307
Sarah (Walker), 4:398
Titcomb/Titcome
---- (Batchelder), 4:56
Ann, 4:307-308
Ann (Cottle), 4:308
Elizabeth, 1:132, 4:54,
4:307-308
Elizabeth (----) Stevens,
4:308
Hannah, 4:307
Joanna, 4:308
Joanna (Bartlett), 4:307
Judith, 4:307
Lydia, 1:398, 4:308
Lydia (Poor), 4:307
Mary, 3:457, 4:307-308
Mary (Dam), 4:307
Millicent, 4:308
Rebecca, 4:308, 4:325
Sarah, 4:307-308, 4:325
Sarah (Brown), 4:307
Tirzah, 1:133, 4:308
Titerton/Titterton
---- (Wilcockson), 4:308
Elizabeth, 4:308
Jane (----), 4:308
Mary, 4:85, 4:308
Titus
---- (Carpenter), 4:308
Abigail, 2:216
Content, 4:308
Hannah, 4:308
Hannah (----), 4:308
Lydia, 4:308
Lydia (Redway), 4:308
Mary, 1:222-223, 4:309
Phebe, 4:43
Sarah (Battelle), 1:140
Sarah (Miller), 4:308
Tobey
Hannah (Nelson), 4:309
Martha (Knott), 3:40,
4:309
Todd
Catharine, 4:309
Elizabeth (Brocklebank),
4:309
Grace, 3:177, 4:309

Todd (continued)
Grace (----), 4:309
Hannah, 4:309
Margaret (----) Barton, 1:134, 4:309
Mary, 4:309, 4:345
Mary (Bradley), 1:234, 4:309
Mehitable, 4:710
Mercy, 1:136, 4:309
Priscilla (----), 4:309
Rachel (----), 2:273
Sarah, 4:309
Sarah (Blackman), 4:309
Sarah (Gilbert), 3:624, 4:309
Susanna (----), 4:309
Toll - see Towle
Tolman
Ann, 1:240, 4:310
Elizabeth, 4:310
Elizabeth (Collins), 4:310
Elizabeth (Johnson), 3:640, 4:310
Hannah, 3:649, 4:310, 4:675
Hannah/Ann, 3:137
Mary, 4:310
Mary (Breck) Paul, 3:372, 4:310
Rebecca, 4:310, 4:338
Rebecca (Burrows), 1:311
Ruth, 3:583, 4:310
Sarah, 3:67, 4:310
Sarah (----), 4:310
Tomlin/Tomline/Tomlins
Sarah, 4:594
Sarah (Barnes), 1:121, 4:311
Sarah (Wing), 4:594
Tomlinson
Alice (----), 1:301, 3:603, 4:310
Bathsheba, 4:193
Bathshua, 4:310
Elizabeth (Judson), 3:641, 4:310
Hannah (----), 4:310
Margaret, 2:356, 4:310
Mary, 4:310
Phebe, 4:310
Sarah (Welles) Hawley, 4:477

Tabitha, 4:310, 4:649
Tompkins
Abigail, 4:311
Deborah, 4:98, 4:311, 4:710-711
Elizabeth, 1:184, 4:311, 4:711
Elizabeth (----), 4:311
Hannah, 3:640, 4:311
Isabel/Elizabeth, 4:260
Lettice (Foster), 4:311
Margaret, 4:711
Margaret (----), 4:311
Mary, 4:311, 4:700, 4:711
Mary (----), 4:311
Mary (Penington), 4:695
Mary (Read), 4:710
Priscilla, 3:650, 4:311
Rebecca, 4:311, 4:711
Rebecca (Knight), 4:711
Ruth, 4:311
Sarah, 4:311, 4:434
Tompson - see Thompson
Tomson
Sarah (Shepard), 4:71
Tongue
Deborah, 4:312
Elizabeth, 4:312, 4:608
Hannah, 4:312
Joanna, 4:312
Margery (----), 4:312
Mary, 4:312, 4:539
Mary (----), 4:312
Sarah, 4:312
Toogood/Towgood/Twogood
Elizabeth, 4:312
Elizabeth (----), 4:312
Toolly/Tolly/Tooley
Agnes, 4:312
Elizabeth, 4:312
Elizabeth (----), 4:312
Esther, 4:312
Joanna, 4:312
Judith, 4:312
Mary, 4:312
Toothaker
---- (Hill), 2:418
Margaret, 2:418
Margaret (----), 4:312
Martha, 2:418
Topliff
Mehitable, 4:313
Obedience, 1:456,

4:312-313
Patience, 2:453, 4:312-313
Patience (----), 4:313
Sarah, 2:560, 4:312-313
Sarah (----), 4:312
Thankful, 4:313
Waitstill, 4:313
Torrey/Torry/Torie
---- (----) Symmes, 4:243
---- (Green), 2:303, 4:313
Angel, 4:314
Ann, 3:413, 4:313
Ann (Hatch), 2:376, 4:313
Bethia, 4:313
Damaris, 4:313
Deborah (----), 4:314
Elizabeth (Rawlins), 3:510, 4:313
Eunice (----) Dean, 2:30
Eunice (Rawlins), 4:313
Joanna, 4:313
Lydia (Wills), 4:313, 4:578
Mary, 4:313-314
Mary (----) Scarborough, 4:313
Mary (----) Symmes, 4:314
Mary (Rawson), 3:511, 4:314
Mary (Smith) Scarborough, 4:34, 4:131
Naomi, 4:100, 4:314
Ruth, 4:313
Ruth (Frye), 2:213, 4:313
Sarah, 4:313
Susanna, 4:313
Susanna (----), 4:313
Totenham
Alice, 4:315
Alice (----), 4:315
Ann, 4:315
Ann (----), 4:315
Arminell, 4:315
Elizabeth, 4:315
Mary, 4:315
Mary (----), 4:314
Rebecca, 4:315
Rebecca (----), 4:315
Sarah, 4:315
Totman
---- (Parker), 3:357
Deborah, 4:566
Judith, 3:357
Lydia, 3:357

Toung/Tong
Elizabeth (Hagborn), 4:315
Tourtellet/Tourtellott
Esther, 4:315
Mary (----), 4:315
Mary (Bernon), 1:170,
4:315
Welthean (----), 4:295
Tousey/Tousley
Dorothy (----) Finch
Edwards, 2:103, 2:159,
4:315
Elizabeth, 4:315
Margaret, 4:76
Touzell
Susanna (English), 2:582
Tower
Elizabeth, 3:548
Elizabeth (Goodale), 4:316
Hannah, 4:316, 4:505
Judith, 2:231
Margaret (Ibrook), 2:516,
4:316
Towle/Toll/Toule/etc
Catharine (----), 4:316
Dorothy (Thomas), 4:279,
4:316
Mary, 4:316
Mary (----), 4:316
Rebecca, 2:319-320
Sarah (----), 4:316
Sarah (Reed), 4:316
Towne
Abigail, 3:375, 4:316-317
Ann (----), 4:316
Catharine, 3:394, 4:316
Catharine (Symonds),
4:245, 4:316
Deliverance, 4:317
Ednah, 4:317
Elizabeth, 4:316
Emma, 4:317
Emma (----), 4:317
Esther, 4:317
Experience, 4:317
Hannah (----), 4:317
Joanna, 4:317
Joanna (----), 4:317
Joanna (Blessing), 4:317
Martha, 4:317
Martha (----), 4:318
Mary, 2:94, 4:316-318
Mary (----), 4:317

Mary (Browning), 1:279,
4:316
Mercy, 4:317
Phebe, 4:317
Phebe (----), 4:317
Phebe (Perkins), 3:397,
4:317
Phebe (Smith), 4:317
Rebecca, 3:300, 4:316-317
Ruth, 4:317
Sarah, 1:249, 3:300,
4:316-317
Sarah (French), 4:317
Susanna, 4:317
Zerviah, 4:317
Townsend
Abigail, 4:318
Abigail (----), 4:319
Abigail (Collins), 3:611,
4:318
Abigail (Train), 4:318,
4:321
Ann, 4:318-319
Ann (----), 4:319
Ann (Cole), 1:429, 4:318
Deliverance (Cole), 4:319
Dinah, 4:319
Dorothy (----), 4:318
Elizabeth, 3:197, 4:318
Elizabeth (----), 4:318
Elizabeth (Cole), 1:429,
4:318
Elizabeth (Wicks), 4:319,
4:539
Esther (Perry), 4:318
Hannah, 2:495, 4:318-320,
4:440-441
Hannah (----) Jaffrey,
2:534, 4:319
Hannah (Penn), 4:319
Leah, 4:319
Lydia, 1:455, 4:319
Lydia (----), 4:319
Margaret, 4:319
Margaret (----), 4:319
Mary, 4:318, 4:320
Mary (----), 4:318-319
Mary (Leverett) Dudley,
2:77, 3:83, 4:319
Mary (Welcome), 4:456
Meribah (Harcutt), 2:353,
4:318
Patience, 4:319

Rebecca, 4:319
Rebecca (Maudsley),
3:179
Rose, 4:318, 4:539
Sarah, 4:318-319
Sarah (Addington), 1:17,
3:83, 4:318
Sarah (Livermore), 3:101
Sarah (Pearson), 3:378,
4:318
Susanna, 4:319
Towsly
Mary, 4:320
Mary (Hussey), 4:320
Toy - see Tay
Tozer/Tosier/Tozier
---- (Blott), 1:206, 4:320
Abigail, 4:320
Elizabeth, 4:697, 4:711
Elizabeth (Wentworth),
4:320, 4:486
Judith, 4:320
Judith (Smith), 4:320
Martha, 4:320, 4:688,
4:711
Mary, 4:320
Mary (----), 4:320
Mary (Beebe), 1:153
Sarah, 4:320
Susanna, 4:320
Tracy
Abigail (Adgate), 1:18,
4:320
Elizabeth, 4:320
Martha (Bourne) Bradford,
1:219, 1:230
Mary, 4:321
Mary (Foote) Stoddard
Goodrich, 2:180, 2:274
Mary (Griswold), 2:317,
2:590
Mary (Prence), 3:477,
4:320
Mary (Winslow), 4:320,
4:602
Miriam, 4:321, 4:433
Rebecca, 4:321
Ruth, 4:321
Sarah, 3:365, 4:320-321
Tryphosa (----), 4:320
Traharen
Alce, 3:470

Train/Traine
Abigail, 4:23, 4:318, 4:321
Abigail (Bent), 4:321
Deborah, 4:321
Elizabeth, 4:157, 4:221,
4:321
Hannah, 1:378, 4:321
Margaret, 4:321
Margaret (----), 4:321
Mary, 4:321
Mary (Stubbs), 4:228,
4:321
Rebecca, 1:129, 4:321
Rebecca (Stearns), 4:321
Sarah, 1:427, 4:321
Trarice/Trerice/etc
Elizabeth, 3:22
Hannah, 1:81, 3:4, 4:322
Hannah (Lynde), 3:136,
4:322
Rebecca, 2:544, 3:136,
4:322
Rebecca (----), 4:322
Sarah, 2:587
Trask
Abigail, 4:322
Abigail (Parkman), 4:322
Ann, 3:661, 4:322-323
Ann (----), 4:323
Ann (Putnam), 3:661,
4:323
Ann (White), 4:512
Christian, 4:322
Christian (Woodbury),
4:322, 4:634
Elizabeth, 4:322-323
Elizabeth (Gally), 2:223,
2:253, 4:322
Hannah (Solart), 4:706,
4:711
Mary, 3:190, 4:322-323
Mary (----), 4:322
Mary (Shattuck), 4:62,
4:322
Mary (Southwick), 4:142,
4:322
Rebecca, 4:322
Sarah, 3:658, 4:322-323
Sarah (----), 4:323
Susanna, 2:581, 4:323
Travers/Travis
---- (----), 1:170
Bridget (----), 4:324, 4:593

Elizabeth, 1:170, 4:324
Esther (----), 4:323
Grace (Clements), 4:324
Mercy, 4:528
Mercy (Pierce), 4:324
Sarah, 4:324, 4:401
Treadway/Treadaway/etc
Abigail, 4:324
Bethia, 4:324
Catharine, 4:324
Deborah, 2:265, 4:324-325
Dorothy (Bell) Cutler,
1:516, 4:324
Elizabeth, 2:352, 4:324
Hannah, 4:324
Huldah, 4:324
Judith (Thurston), 4:324
Lydia, 2:563, 4:324-325
Mary, 2:163, 2:383, 4:324
Sarah, 4:324
Sarah (Sweetman), 4:239,
4:324
Sufferance (Haynes),
2:391, 3:299, 4:324
Sufferance (Howe), 2:474,
4:324
Susanna, 4:324
Tabitha, 4:324
Treadwell
Abigail, 4:325
Abigail (Wells), 4:325,
4:478
Ann, 4:325
Elizabeth, 2:393, 4:325
Esther, 2:470, 4:325
Hannah, 4:325
Martha, 1:478, 4:325
Mary, 4:325
Mary (----), 4:325
Rebecca, 4:325
Rebecca (Titcomb), 4:308,
4:325
Sarah, 4:325
Sarah (Titcomb), 4:308,
4:325
Treat
Abigail, 1:52, 2:449,
4:326-328
Abigail (Willard) Estabrook,
4:328
Alice (----), 4:326
Ann, 4:327-328
Catharine, 4:289,

4:326-327
Catharine (Bulkley), 1:290,
4:327
Dorcas, 4:326
Dorotheus, 4:328
Dorothy, 4:328
Dorothy (Bulkley), 1:290,
4:328
Dorothy (Noyes), 4:328
Eliz (Powell) Hollingworth
Bryan Durand, 1:282
Elizabeth, 4:326, 4:328
Elizabeth (----) Bryan,
4:327
Elizabeth (Mayo), 3:188,
4:328
Eunice, 4:326, 4:328
Frances (Bryan), 1:282
Hannah, 3:175, 4:327
Hannah (Wright)
Boardman, 4:326
Honour, 2:35, 4:326
Jane, 4:327-328
Jane (Tapp), 4:253, 4:327
Jemima, 4:325
Jerusha, 2:274, 4:325-326,
4:328, 4:480
Joanna, 2:449, 4:326
Joanna (----), 4:326
Mabel, 4:325
Mary, 4:327-328, 4:622
Mary (Robbins), 4:326
Mary (Smith), 4:129,
4:326, 4:654
Prudence, 4:326, 4:328
Prudence (Chester), 4:326
Rebecca, 4:325-326, 4:328
Rebecca (Latimer), 4:325
Sarah, 1:332, 2:182, 2:274,
4:325-328
Sarah (Andrews), 1:53,
2:182, 4:325
Sarah (Coleman), 1:431,
4:326
Susanna, 4:326, 4:449
Treby/Trebie
Mary (----), 4:328
Tree
Joanna (Rogers), 4:328
Trescott
Abigail, 4:329, 4:452
Ann (—), 4:329
Elizabeth, 4:329

Trescott (continued)
Elizabeth (Dyer), 2:88, 4:329
Martha, 2:408, 4:329
Mary, 2:401, 4:329
Mary (Savage) Jenkinson, 4:24
Patience, 4:329
Rebecca (----), 4:329
Sarah, 4:329
Thankful, 4:329
Tresler/Trusler
---, 3:405, 4:329
Elinor (----), 4:329
Elizabeth, 4:329
Treswell
Martha (----), 4:329
Sarah, 4:329
Trew
Mary (Sumner) Howe, 4:232
Treworgy/Treworthy/etc
---- (Spencer), 4:330
Catharine (Shapleigh), 2:422, 4:59, 4:330
Elizabeth, 2:257, 4:330
Joanna, 1:48, 4:330
Lucy, 1:350, 4:330, 4:579
Mary (----), 4:330
Trians
Abigail (Norton), 3:293, 4:330
Trickey/Trickett
Rebecca (----), 4:330
Trill
Ann (----), 4:330
Salome, 4:300
Trimmings
Susanna (----), 4:330
Tripp/Trippe
---, 4:377
Abiel, 4:330
Alice, 2:339, 4:331
Deliverance (Hall), 4:330
Isbel/Isbell, 4:84, 4:331
Martha, 4:85, 4:331
Mary, 4:331
Mary (----), 2:519, 4:331
Mehitable (Fish), 2:161
Mercy (Lawton), 3:64
Rose, 2:347
Susanna, 3:468, 4:331
Susanna (Anthony), 1:59,

4:331
Tristram
Freegrace, 4:331
Hannah, 2:569, 4:331
Rachel, 4:331
Ruth, 4:331
Troop
Mary, 4:331
Mary (Chapman), 1:362, 4:331
Trotman
Catharine (----), 4:331
Trott
Abigail, 4:331, 4:711
Ann, 4:711
Ann (----), 4:711
Deliverance (----)
Withington, 4:331, 4:619
Dinah, 4:711
Elizabeth, 4:677, 4:711
Elizabeth (Norton), 4:711
Mary, 2:318, 4:331, 4:711
Preserved, 1:97, 4:331-332
Priscilla, 4:331, 4:711
Rachel, 4:331, 4:711
Sarah, 1:333, 4:331-332
Sarah (----), 4:332
Tabitha, 4:331, 4:711
Thankful, 2:424, 4:331-332
Trotter
Abigail, 4:332
Cutbury (Gibbs), 4:332
Mary, 4:332
Rebecca, 4:332
Sarah, 4:332
Trowbridge
Abigail, 4:332-334
Abigail (Beardsley), 4:333
Ann, 4:333
Ann (Leete), 1:434, 3:75, 4:333
Bethia, 4:334
Deliverance, 4:332, 4:407
Elizabeth, 2:440, 3:145, 3:218, 4:332-334
Elizabeth (Lamberton) Sillevant, 4:97, 4:334
Esther (Howe), 3:636, 4:332
Experience, 4:332, 4:334, 4:589
Hannah, 2:311, 4:332-334,

4:519
Hannah (Bacon), 4:333
Hannah (Jackson), 4:333
Hannah (Nash) Ball, 1:106, 3:261, 4:333
Hannah (Walter), 4:332, 4:403
Huldah, 4:334
Jemima, 4:333
Lydia, 2:5, 3:578, 4:333-334
Lydia (Alsop), 1:45, 4:332
Margaret, 4:204, 4:332-334
Margaret (Atherton), 1:73, 4:332
Margaret (Jackson), 2:530, 4:332
Maria, 4:332
Mary, 2:252, 4:332-334
Mary (----), 4:332
Mary (Goffe), 2:268, 4:333
Mary (Winston), 4:333, 4:605
Mindwell, 2:217, 4:332
Sarah, 4:332-334
Sarah (----), 4:333
Sarah (Fullam), 4:334
Sarah (Oliver), 4:332
Sarah (Rutherford), 3:579, 4:333
Sarah (Ward), 4:334, 4:409
Sarah (Wilson), 4:333
Susanna (----), 4:334
Thankful, 4:332, 4:334, 4:412
Thankful (Stow), 4:218, 4:334
Truant
Hannah, 2:90, 4:334
Mary, 1:378
Mehitable, 2:2, 4:334
True
Israel, 4:335
Israel (Pike), 3:436, 4:334
Jane, 4:335
Jane (Bradbury), 1:230, 4:334
Jemima, 3:151, 4:334-335
Lydia, 4:334
Mary, 2:95, 4:334

True (continued)
Ruth, 4:335
Ruth (Whittier), 4:335,
4:536
Truesdale/Trusdell/Truesdall
Elizabeth (Hammond)
Woodward, 4:335, 4:644
Experience, 4:335
Mary, 4:335
Mary (----), 4:335
Mary (Hood), 2:457
Mary (Jackson), 2:530,
4:335
Mindwell, 4:335
Rebecca, 4:335
Trull
Sarah, 4:335
Sarah (French), 2:208,
4:335
Truman
Ann, 4:336
Elizabeth, 4:336
Mary, 4:336
Mary (Shapley), 4:336
Trumbull/Trumble/etc
---- (Blackman), 1:190
---- (Jackson), 4:336
Abigail, 4:711
Ammi, 4:336
Ann (Swan), 4:237, 4:336
Elizabeth, 4:336
Elizabeth (----), 4:336
Ellen (----), 4:711
Faith (Robinson), 3:552
Frances, 3:19
Hannah, 1:141, 4:227,
4:336, 4:711
Hannah (Higley), 2:414,
4:336
Mary, 1:506, 2:115,
4:336-337
Mary (----), 4:96, 4:337
Mary (Jones), 2:599, 4:336
Ruth, 3:398, 4:711
Trusdale
Mary (Hood), 2:457
Try/Tray
Margaret (----) Root, 3:663,
4:337
Sarah, 2:321, 4:337
Tryer
Elizabeth, 3:536

Tubbs
Bethia, 4:337
Dorcas, 4:337
Mary, 4:337
Mary (Willey), 4:337,
4:558
Mercy (Sprague), 4:153,
4:337
Tuck/Tucke/Tewk
Bethia (----), 4:337
Bethia (Hobbs), 2:437
Catharine, 4:337
Elizabeth, 4:78
Elizabeth (Nichols), 3:282,
4:337
Joanna (----), 4:337
Mary, 4:11, 4:337-338
Mary (Philbrick), 3:409
Tucker
---- (----), 2:510
Abigail, 4:339
Amy (----), 4:338
Ann, 4:231
Ann (----), 4:338
Ann (----) Norton, 4:338
Ebenezer, 4:338
Ebenezer (Nichols), 3:282,
4:338
Elizabeth, 4:338-339
Elizabeth (----), 4:339-340
Elizabeth (Coe), 1:418
Elizabeth (Hobart), 2:433,
4:339
Elizabeth (Stevens), 4:186,
4:339
Elizabeth (Williams),
4:570
Grace, 3:427, 4:339
Hannah, 4:338
Hannah (Gulliver), 2:322
Margaret (----), 4:339
Martha, 4:338
Martha (----), 4:338
Mary, 1:385, 1:454, 2:46,
2:558, 3:401, 4:338-339
Mary (Brimblecombe),
3:606
Mary (Randall) Taintor,
4:249
Mary (Richardson), 4:339
Phebe (Page), 4:339
Rebecca (Tolman), 4:310,
4:338

Sarah, 4:338-340, 4:426
Sarah (----), 4:338
Sarah (Riggs), 3:542,
4:339
Waitstill (Sumner), 4:231,
4:339
Tuckerman
Christian, 4:340
Constance (Worcester),
4:340, 4:651
Elizabeth, 4:340
Emma (----), 4:340
Martha, 4:340
Martha (----), 4:340
Priscilla, 4:340
Sarah, 4:340
Sarah (----), 4:340
Susanna (Chamberlain),
1:353, 4:340
Tudman
Rebecca (Fitch), 3:620
Sarah, 3:601
Tudor
Abigail, 4:341
Abigail (Bissell), 4:341
Elizabeth, 4:341
Elizabeth (----), 4:340
Jane, 4:340-341
Joanna (Porter) Taylor,
3:660
Margaret, 4:341
Mary, 3:316, 4:340-341
Mary (----) Skinner, 4:105
Mary (Loomis) Skinner,
3:112, 4:340
Sarah, 3:460, 4:340-341
Tuf
Martha, 4:572
Tufton
Jane (Mason), 3:167
Tufts
Abigail, 4:341-342
Abigail (Smith), 4:342
Ann, 4:342
Catharine, 4:342
Dorothy, 4:342
Elizabeth, 3:136,
4:341-342
Elizabeth (----), 3:431
Elizabeth (Lynde), 3:137,
4:342
Elizabeth (Sargent), 4:341
Emma (Phips), 4:342

Tufts (continued)
Lydia, 4:342
Mary, 2:100, 4:341-342
Mary (Cotton), 4:342
Mary (Pierce), 3:431,
  4:341
Mary (Putnam), 3:496-497,
  4:341
Mercy, 4:341-342, 4:384
Mercy (Cotton), 1:464
Persis, 4:341
Prudence (----), 4:342
Rebecca, 4:341
Rebecca (Waite), 4:341,
  4:383
Sarah, 3:303, 4:341-342
Sarah (Bradstreet), 4:341
Tuller
Damaris (Cornish), 4:342
Elizabeth (Case) Lewis,
  1:345, 3:88, 4:342
Mabel, 4:342
Mary, 4:342
Mary (Moses), 4:342
Sarah, 4:342
Tully
Abigail, 4:343
Abigail (Maverick), 4:343
Deborah, 4:343
Hepzibah, 4:343
Lucy, 4:343
Lydia, 4:343
Margaret, 4:343
Mary, 4:343
Mary (Beamond/Beaman),
  1:147, 4:342
Sarah, 4:342-343
Turand
Mary (Colburn) Barrell,
  1:424
Turbat/Turbutt
Elizabeth, 4:343
Sarah (----), 4:343
Turbefield/Turberfield
Ann, 4:343
Susan, 3:193
Turell
---- (Colman), 4:344
Ann, 4:343-344
Ann (----), 4:344
Christian, 4:344
Elizabeth, 4:344
Lydia, 4:343-344

Lydia (----), 4:344
Lydia (Blott), 4:343
Lydia (Stoddard), 4:344
Mary, 4:344
Mary (Colbron) Barrell,
  1:124, 1:424, 4:343
Rebecca, 4:344
Rebecca (----), 4:344
Sarah, 4:344
Sarah (----), 4:344
Sarah (Sumner), 4:232
Turfry/Turfree
Mary (----), 4:344
Turin
---- (Blott), 1:206
Mary (Colburn) Barrell,
  1:424
Turner
----, 2:266
---- (----), 4:347, 4:365
---- (----) Winter, 4:606
---- (Gardner), 2:227
Abiah, 4:347
Abigail, 2:440, 4:345-347
Abigail (----) Stockbridge,
  4:197
Ann, 2:304, 4:346
Ann (Heath), 2:398
Ann (James), 4:346
Bathsheba (Hobart), 2:435,
  4:347
Bathsheba (Hobart) Leavitt,
  3:70
Deborah, 4:258, 4:346
Deborah (----), 4:346
Elizabeth, 2:240, 3:211,
  3:624, 4:345-348
Elizabeth (----), 3:56,
  4:346-348
Elizabeth (Copley), 1:456
Elizabeth (Jacob), 4:345
Elizabeth (Marsh), 3:154
Elizabeth (Nash), 4:348
Elizabeth (Roberts), 4:347
Elizabeth (Stockbridge),
  4:197, 4:344
Eunice, 4:347
Frances, 4:349
Freestone, 4:347
Grace, 1:383
Hannah, 1:225, 2:451,
  2:462, 3:507, 4:345-348
Hannah (Hudson), 2:488,

4:346
Hannah (Lazell), 3:66
Hannah (Randall), 4:344
Isabel (Gill), 4:346
Jane, 4:345
Jane (Vining), 4:345,
  4:374
Joanna (Bowman), 1:225
Lucy (Gardner), 3:224,
  4:346
Lydia, 1:124, 2:62, 2:535,
  4:345-346
Lydia (----), 4:345
Margaret, 4:198
Martha (Besbedge), 1:171,
  4:347
Mary, 1:64, 1:220, 1:352,
  3:357, 3:487, 4:345-347,
  4:667, 4:711
Mary (----), 4:345
Mary (----) Alsop, 1:45,
  4:349
Mary (----) Pratt, 3:472
Mary (Brewster), 1:245,
  4:346
Mary (Gardner), 2:227,
  4:711
Mary (Nichols), 3:279
Mary (Sanford), 4:15,
  4:345
Mary (Todd), 4:309, 4:345
Mehitable (Hett), 2:407,
  4:345
Mehitable (Rigby), 4:348
Mercy, 2:227, 4:345
Miriam, 3:424, 4:346
Osiah (Wing), 4:594
Penelope, 4:347
Penelope (----), 4:347-348
Prudence, 4:349
Rebecca, 3:222, 4:347
Ruth, 3:488, 4:346
Sarah, 2:138, 2:441, 3:439,
  3:448, 4:346-348
Sarah (----), 4:347
Sarah (Adams), 1:9
Sarah (Hyland), 2:516,
  4:348
Sarah (Stockbridge), 4:197,
  4:345
Susanna (Keeny), 4:345
Susanna (Merrill), 3:199

Turney
---, 4:349
Ann, 4:349
Elizabeth, 4:349
Elizabeth (---), 4:349
Jemima, 4:349
Judith, 4:349
Martha, 4:349
Mary, 4:49, 4:349
Mary (---), 3:205, 4:349
Rebecca, 4:86, 4:349
Rebecca (---), 4:349
Ruth, 1:298, 4:349
Sarah, 4:349
Turvill
Judith (---), 4:349
Tuttle/Tuttel/Tuthill
---, 4:351-352
--- (Lee), 3:71
Abigail, 4:350-352, 4:422
Ann, 4:351-352
Ann (---), 4:352
Catharine (Lane), 4:350
Deliverance, 4:351
Deliverance (King), 4:350
Dorothy, 4:299, 4:350-351
Dorothy (---), 4:350
Elizabeth, 2:103,
4:350-352
Elizabeth (---), 4:352
Esther, 3:594, 4:352
Hannah, 3:344, 4:350-352,
4:479, 4:678, 4:711
Hannah (Munson), 1:234,
3:257, 4:351
Hannah (Powell), 3:470,
4:352
Isabel (---), 4:352
Jane, 2:249, 4:350
Joan (---), 3:62, 4:350
Joanna, 4:351-352
Judith (Otis), 3:325
Margaret, 4:352
Martha, 4:351-352
Martha (Ward), 4:351
Mary, 1:304, 1:340, 2:387,
4:350-352, 4:401
Mary (---), 4:351
Mary (Holyoke), 2:456,
4:350
Mary (Rogers), 4:352
Mercy, 1:275, 4:352
Phebe, 4:351

Rebecca, 4:350-352
Rebecca (Bell), 1:159,
4:351
Ruth, 4:352
Sarah, 2:25, 3:162, 3:272,
4:106, 4:350, 4:352,
4:684, 4:711
Sarah (---), 4:351
Sarah (Cogswell), 1:422,
4:352
Sarah (Howe), 3:636,
4:351
Sarah (Newman), 4:711
Sarah (Young), 4:351
Susanna, 4:351-352
Temperance, 4:351
Twelves
Abigail, 4:353
Hannah, 4:353
Martha, 4:353
Martha (Brackett), 1:229,
4:353
Mary, 4:353
Rachel, 2:209, 4:353
Sarah, 4:353
Twining
Abigail (Young), 4:353,
4:670
Ann, 1:179, 4:353
Ann (---), 4:353
Elizabeth, 3:563, 4:353
Elizabeth (Dean), 2:30,
4:353
Hannah, 4:353
Isabel, 1:95
Joanna, 1:179, 4:353
Mercy, 4:353
Ruth, 4:353
Ruth (Cole), 4:353
Susanna, 4:353
Thankful, 4:353
Twisden
Alice/Elizabeth, 4:301,
4:353-354
Mary (Alcock), 1:21
Twitchell
Abiel, 4:354
Abigail, 4:354
Bethia, 4:354
Hannah, 4:354
Hannah (Hinman), 2:426
Mary, 3:557, 4:354
Mary (---), 4:354

Mary (Riggs), 3:541
Mary (White), 4:354
Patience, 2:90
Twombly/Twambly
Elizabeth, 4:354
Elizabeth (---), 4:354
Esther, 4:354
Hannah, 4:354
Hope, 4:354
Mary, 4:354
Mary (Kenney), 4:354
Rachel, 4:354
Rachel (---), 4:354
Sarah, 4:354
Tyler
Abigail, 4:354-356
Abigail (Terrill), 4:268,
4:356
Ann, 4:354
Ann (Geer), 2:239
Catharine, 4:355
Deborah, 4:354, 4:356
Deborah (Swain), 4:234,
4:356
Dorcas, 4:356
Elizabeth, 4:354, 4:356
Elizabeth (Stent/Stint),
4:182
Hannah, 1:319, 4:354,
4:356
Hannah (---), 4:354, 4:356
Hannah (Freeman), 4:354
Hannah (Parker), 4:355
Hannah (Stent), 4:182
Hannah (Whitehead),
4:356
Hope, 4:355
Jane (---), 4:355
Jane (Pepperell) Clark,
3:392
Joan (---), 2:47, 4:355
Joanna, 4:355
Martha, 2:240, 4:355
Mary, 2:143, 3:465,
4:355-356
Mary (---), 4:354-355
Meriam (Pepperell), 3:392
Miriam, 4:356
Miriam (Simpkins), 4:101,
4:356
Patience, 4:356
Phebe (Chandler), 1:359
Prudence (Blake), 1:192,

Tyler (continued)
  Prudence (Blake)
    (continued)
    4:355
  Ruth, 4:356
  Sarah, 4:355-356
  Sarah (----), 4:355
  Sarah (Havens), 2:379,
    4:355
  Sarah (Royal), 3:583,
    4:356
  Tamar, 1:450, 4:355
  Tirzah, 4:356
Tyng
  Ann, 4:358
  Ann (Brown), 4:358
  Barsheba, 4:357
  Bethia, 4:358, 4:494
  Deliverance, 4:45, 4:357
  Elizabeth, 1:238,
    4:357-358
  Elizabeth (Clark), 1:400,
    4:357
  Elizabeth (Coytemore),
    1:467-468, 4:358
  Eunice, 4:357, 4:554
  Hannah, 2:279, 4:24, 4:76,
    4:357
  Jane (----) Hunt, 4:358
  Judith (Reyner) Fox, 2:196,
    4:357
  Mary, 4:357
  Mary (----), 4:357
  Mary (Sears), 4:356
  Mary (Twelves), 4:353
  Mercy, 1:236, 4:358
  Rebecca, 2:76, 4:357
  Sarah (----) Richards Davie,
    2:15
  Sarah (Gibbons) Richards
    Davie, 3:532, 4:357
  Sarah (Usher), 4:357,
    4:363
Uffoot/Ufford - see Offitt
Umberfield/Umprevile/etc
  ----, 4:358
  Ann, 4:358
  Elizabeth, 4:358
  Esther, 4:358
  Mary, 2:65, 3:145, 4:358
  Sarah, 4:358
Underhill
  Elizabeth, 4:359

Elizabeth (----), 4:359
Elizabeth (Field), 2:156
Helena (----), 4:359
Underwood
  ---- (----) Pellet, 4:360
  Deborah, 4:360
  Elizabeth, 4:359
  Elizabeth (----), 1:294,
    4:359
  Hannah, 2:248, 4:359
  Jane, 4:359
  Jane (----), 4:359
  Magdalen (----), 4:360
  Marable, 1:344
  Martha, 4:359
  Martha (Fiske), 4:359
  Mary, 3:314, 4:359
  Mary (----), 4:359
  Mary (How), 4:359
  Priscilla, 4:146, 4:360
  Remembrance, 3:537,
    4:360
  Sarah, 4:359-360
Unthank
  Mary, 1:45, 4:360
  Susanna (----), 4:360
Updike
  ---- (Smith), 4:360
Upham
  ----, 4:535
  Abigail (Hayward), 2:394,
    4:361
  Catharine (----) Hollard,
    2:447, 4:360
  Dorothy (Wigglesworth),
    4:542
  Elizabeth, 4:360-361,
    4:455
  Elizabeth (----), 4:360
  Elizabeth (Mousal), 4:360
  Elizabeth (Stedman), 4:178,
    4:285, 4:361
  Hannah, 4:360
  Mary, 4:360, 4:534
  Priscilla, 1:479, 4:360
  Ruth, 4:361
  Ruth (Wood), 4:361
Upshall/Upsall
  Ann, 4:361
  Dorothy (----), 2:351
  Dorothy (Capen), 4:361
  Elizabeth, 2:309,
    4:361-362

Susanna, 1:467, 4:361,
    4:679
Upshur
  Susanna, 1:428
Upson
  Elizabeth, 4:362
  Elizabeth (----), 2:313, 4:36
  Elizabeth (Fuller), 4:362
  Hannah, 2:313, 4:362
  Mary, 4:362
  Mary (Lee), 3:72, 4:362
  Tabitha, 4:362
  Thankful, 4:362
Upton
  Ann, 4:362
  Elinor, 4:711
  Elinor (----), 4:711
  Isabel, 4:711
  Mary, 4:711
Urann/Urin
  Rebecca (Cate), 4:362
Usher
  Betty, 3:509
  Bridget (Lisle) Hoar, 2:432,
    4:363
  Elizabeth, 2:539, 4:139,
    4:362-363
  Elizabeth (----) Jagger,
    2:534, 4:363
  Elizabeth (Allen), 1:36,
    4:363
  Elizabeth (Lidgett), 3:90,
    4:363
  Elizabeth (Symmes), 4:244,
    4:363
  Frances, 4:363
  Frances (----), 4:362
  Hannah, 4:363
  Mary (Alford) Butler, 1:27,
    1:321, 3:295, 4:363
  Rebecca, 1:264, 4:362-363
  Sarah, 4:357, 4:363
Utley/Uttley
  Hannah (Hatch), 2:376,
    4:364
  Lydia, 2:491, 4:364
Utting
  Ann (----), 4:364
Vale/Vail/Vayle
  Abigail, 4:364
  Ann (----), 4:364
  Sarah, 4:364

Vales/Fales
Abigail (Hawes), 2:138
Van der Donck
---- (Doughty), 2:62
Van Zandt
Margaret, 1:418
Vane
---- (Fitzroy), 4:365
Vangoodenhausen
---- (----) Turner, 4:347,
    4:365
Elizabeth, 4:365
Elizabeth (Parris), 4:365
Varleet
Jane, 4:366
Judith, 4:366
Judith (----), 4:366
Mary, 1:47, 4:35, 4:366
Varney
Abigail, 4:366
Abigail (----), 4:366
Abigail (Proctor), 3:489
Ann, 4:366
Bridget, 4:366
Bridget (----), 4:366
Elizabeth, 4:366
Elizabeth (----), 4:366
Esther (Starbuck), 4:172
Hannah, 4:366
Judith, 4:366
Lydia, 4:366
Martha, 4:366
Mary, 1:383, 4:95, 4:366
Mary (----), 4:366
Mary (Otis), 4:366
Mercy, 4:366
Rachel, 4:366, 4:374
Sarah, 4:366
Sarah (Starbuck) Story
    Austin, 1:81, 4:172, 4:213,
    4:366
Susanna (----) Otis, 3:325
Susanna (Otis), 4:366
Varnum
Alice (----), 3:163
Hannah, 4:367
Hannah (----), 4:367
Vassall
----, 4:367
Ann, 4:367
Ann (----), 4:367
Frances, 1:11, 4:367
Judith, 4:367, 4:514

Margaret, 4:367
Mary, 4:367
Vaughan/Vahan/Vahen
Abigail, 4:59, 4:368-369
Ann, 4:368
Bridget, 4:368-369
Eleanor, 4:368, 4:390
Elizabeth, 2:479,
    4:368-369
Elizabeth (Eliot), 2:111,
    4:368
Elizabeth (Henchman),
    2:402, 4:368
Frances (----) Clarke, 4:368
Gillian (----), 4:368
Jane, 4:368
Joanna, 4:368
Margaret, 4:368-369
Margaret (Cutt), 1:495,
    4:368
Margaret (Spink), 4:151,
    4:368
Mary, 4:368, 4:430
Mary (Belcher), 1:156,
    4:368
Sarah, 4:368
Susanna (Grimes), 2:316,
    4:368
Veazey/Veazie/Veesie/Vesey
Abigail, 4:278, 4:369
Elinor (Thompson), 2:206,
    4:289, 4:369
Elizabeth, 4:369
Elizabeth (Saunders), 4:22,
    4:369
Ellen, 3:336, 4:369
Hannah, 2:308, 4:369
Mary, 3:231, 3:358, 4:369
Mehitable, 2:164, 4:369
Mercy, 4:369
Pheza (----), 4:369
Venner
Ann, 4:369
Ventris
Elizabeth, 2:294
Elizabeth (----), 4:370
Grace, 4:370, 4:675
Mary, 4:370
Mary (Graves), 4:370
Sarah, 4:370, 4:676
Susanna, 4:370, 4:675
Verden
---- (Masters), 4:711

Elizabeth, 4:711
Mary, 4:711
Vere
Mary, 4:517
Veren/Verin/Vering
Abigail, 3:650, 4:371
Bethia, 4:371
Deliverance, 4:370-371
Dorcas, 3:632, 4:371
Dorcas (----), 4:371
Hannah, 1:441, 4:371
Hannah (Price), 3:485,
    4:371
Jane (----), 4:371
Joanna (----), 4:371
Mary, 3:95, 4:370-371,
    4:569
Mary (----), 1:441, 3:497,
    4:371
Mary (Conant), 4:370
Mary (Wiseman), 4:371,
    4:615
Mehitable, 4:371
Mercy, 4:371
Penelope (----), 4:371
Sarah, 3:358, 4:371, 4:711
Vergoose
Ann, 4:370
Elizabeth, 4:370
Elizabeth (Foster), 4:370
Hannah, 4:370
Lydia, 4:370
Mary, 4:370
Mary (Balstone), 1:109,
    4:370
Prudence, 4:370
Susanna, 3:502, 4:370
Susanna (----), 3:502,
    4:370
Vermaes/Vermayes
Abigail, 1:324, 2:509,
    4:372
Alice (----), 4:371-372
Mercy (Bradford), 1:231,
    4:371
Vernon
Ann (Hutchinson) Dyer,
    2:509, 4:372
Very
Abigail, 1:55, 4:372-373
Abigail (Woodin), 4:372
Alice, 4:373
Alice (Woodhouse), 4:372,

Very (continued)
Alice (Woodhouse)
(continued)
4:639
Bethia, 4:372
Bridget, 4:372
Bridget (----), 2:253, 4:372
Desire, 4:372
Elizabeth, 3:300,
4:372-373, 4:639
Elizabeth (Proctor), 4:373
Hannah, 2:186, 3:621,
4:372
Hannah (----), 4:372
Hannah (Giles/Gyles),
2:325, 4:372
Jemima, 4:372
Jemima (Newhall), 3:273,
4:372
Keziah, 4:372
Martha, 4:372
Mary, 1:494, 4:372
Mary (----), 4:372
Mary (Symonds), 4:372
Ruth, 4:372
Sarah, 3:612, 4:372, 4:639
Vial/Viall/Viol/Vyall
Abigail, 4:376
Elizabeth, 4:377
Elizabeth (----), 4:377
Hopestill, 4:93, 4:376-377
Mary, 4:233, 4:376-377
Mary (----), 4:376
Mary (Williams), 4:377,
4:564
Sarah, 4:376
Susanna (Pickman), 3:425
Vicaris
Ann, 4:710
Vicars/Vickers/Vickery/etc
Dorcas (Paine), 3:337
Elizabeth (Binney), 1:180
Hannah (----), 4:373
Hannah (Pardee), 3:345
Rebecca, 1:180
Rebecca (Hull), 2:492
Rebecca (Phippeny), 3:418,
4:373
Vicory
Elizabeth (Hudson), 2:489
Vinal
Ann (----), 4:373
Elizabeth (Baker), 1:98,

4:373
Mary, 1:381, 4:373
Mary (Baker), 1:98, 4:373
Vincent
---- (Carpenter), 1:337
Abigail, 2:116
Elizabeth, 2:227
Elizabeth (Rokeby), 4:373
Hannah, 1:265, 2:112,
4:373
Jane, 4:373
Joanna, 4:70, 4:374
Mary, 3:627
Priscilla (Carpenter), 1:338,
4:374
Rachel (Varney), 4:366,
4:374
Rebecca (----), 4:373
Sarah, 2:45
Sarah (Allerton), 3:486
Vine
Elizabeth, 4:374
Elizabeth (Harrington),
2:592, 4:374
Vining
Jane, 4:345, 4:374
Margaret, 4:374
Mary, 4:374
Mary (Read), 3:517, 3:519,
4:374
Naomi (----), 4:374
Sarah, 4:524
Vinson
Abigail, 4:375
Elizabeth, 2:227, 4:375
Hannah, 4:375
Rachel (----) Cooke, 3:612
Rachel (Cooke), 4:375
Sarah, 3:362, 4:375
Sarah (----), 4:374-375
Vinting
Sarah, 2:361
Vinton
Abiathar, 4:375
Ann, 2:396, 4:375
Ann (----), 4:375
Eleanor, 3:503, 4:375
Elizabeth, 4:375
Hannah, 2:418, 4:375
Hannah (Green), 4:375
Hannah (Hills), 4:375
Lydia (Hayden), 2:386,
4:375

Mary, 4:375
Rebecca, 4:375
Sarah, 2:361, 4:375
Vixen
Elizabeth, 4:375
Jemineth, 4:375
Voaker
Mary, 3:610
Voden/Voeden/Vouden/etc
---- (Waters), 4:375
Elizabeth, 4:375-376
Mary, 4:375-376
Mary (Ormes), 4:376
Vore/Voar
Abigail, 1:285, 4:376
Lydia, 1:448, 4:376
Mary, 1:46, 4:376
Sarah, 3:361, 4:376
Vose
Abigail, 4:376
Abigail (----), 4:376
Elizabeth, 4:241, 4:376
Martha, 4:376
Waitstill (Wyatt), 4:376,
4:661
Wacombe/Wackham
Mary (----), 4:377
Wadd
Ann, 3:331
Waddams - see Wadom
Waddell/Wodel
---- (Tripp), 4:377
Alice, 1:59, 4:377
Elizabeth, 3:145
Frances, 1:60, 4:377
Innocent, 4:377
Mary, 3:64, 4:377
Mary (----), 2:235, 4:377
Ruth (Lawton), 3:64,
4:377
Sarah, 4:15, 4:377
Wade
Ann, 4:378
Catharine, 4:378
Deborah, 2:82, 4:378
Deborah (Dudley), 2:78,
4:378
Dorothy, 4:378
Elizabeth, 4:378, 4:415
Elizabeth (----), 4:378
Elizabeth (Cogswell),
4:379
Elizabeth (Ensign), 2:125,

Wade (continued)
Elizabeth (Ensign)
(continued)
4:378
Elizabeth (Thornton),
4:293
Mary, 1:375, 4:247,
4:377-378
Mercy, 4:378
Mercy (Bradstreet), 1:236,
4:378
Prudence, 1:464, 1:477,
4:237, 4:378
Rebecca, 3:326
Ruth (Garrett), 2:233
Sarah, 3:568, 4:377-378
Sarah (Phelps), 3:407,
4:379
Susanna, 4:378
Susanna (----), 4:377-378
Wadland/Wadlen
Agnes, 2:586
Elizabeth (----), 4:379
Wadleigh
Elizabeth (Gilman) Ladd,
2:258
Wadley
Mary (----), 3:641
Wadom/Wadams/Wadoms
Hannah (----), 4:379
Hannah (Biddle), 1:174
Susanna, 4:379
Susanna (----), 4:379
Wadsworth
Abigail, 4:381
Abigail (Andrews), 1:54
Abigail (Lewis), 3:648,
4:381
Abigail (Lindall), 3:95,
4:380
Dorothy (Ball), 4:380
Elizabeth, 4:268,
4:380-381
Elizabeth (----), 4:381
Elizabeth (Barnard), 1:118,
4:380
Elizabeth (Stanley), 4:164,
4:380
Elizabeth (Stone), 4:381
Elizabeth (Talcott), 4:251,
4:380
Esther, 4:380
Eunice, 4:380

Grace (----), 4:379
Hannah, 4:380-381
Hannah (Judson), 4:381
Lydia, 4:380
Mary, 4:214, 4:379-381
Mary (----), 4:379
Mary (----) Gridley, 4:380
Mary (Blackleach) Welles
Olcott, 1:189, 3:307, 4:380,
4:480
Mary (Humphrey) Gridley,
3:626
Mary (Wiswall), 4:616
Mercy, 4:380
Rebecca, 4:381
Ruth, 4:380
Ruth (Bordman), 3:604
Sarah, 1:68, 3:573,
4:379-381, 4:546
Sarah (Bunce), 4:381
Sarah (Stanley), 4:165,
4:379
Susanna, 4:381
Susanna (----), 4:381
Wager
Sarah (Edes), 3:617
Waight - see Wait
Wainwright
Ann, 4:382
Elizabeth, 1:422, 4:382
Elizabeth (----), 1:18
Elizabeth (Norton), 1:498,
3:294, 4:382
Hannah (----), 2:125, 4:382
Lucy, 2:76, 4:382
Martha, 3:490, 4:382
Mary, 1:235, 4:72, 4:382
Mary (----) Silver, 4:382
Mary (Dudley), 2:76
Mary (Williams) Silver,
4:98
Mehitable, 1:76, 4:382
Philippa (----), 4:382
Sarah, 2:210, 3:395, 4:382
Sarah (Gilbert), 4:382
Sarah (Whipple), 4:382
Wait/Waite
---- (Hills), 4:383
Abigail, 4:384-385
Alice (----), 4:385
Ann, 4:385
Ann (Webb), 4:385
Canada, 4:382-383

Catharine (Carroll), 1:340
Deborah, 3:328, 4:383
Eleanor, 4:384
Elizabeth (----), 4:384
Eunice, 4:384
Experience, 4:385
Grace, 3:484, 4:383
Grace (----), 4:383
Hannah, 1:287, 4:383-384
Hannah (Billings), 4:384
Hannah (Oakes), 3:302,
4:384
Jemima, 4:385
Lucy, 4:384
Lydia, 4:384
Martha, 4:382-385
Martha (Leonard), 3:79,
4:382
Mary, 1:60, 1:131, 3:116,
4:382-385, 4:474
Mary (----), 4:383, 4:385
Mary (Belding), 4:384
Mary (Graves), 4:383
Mary (Warner), 4:384
Mary (Woodward), 4:383,
4:643-644
Mehitable, 3:358, 4:383
Mehitable (Bucknam),
1:287, 4:385
Mercy (Tufts), 4:342,
4:384
Miriam, 4:383
Phebe, 4:385
Rachel, 3:506, 4:383
Rebecca, 4:341, 4:383
Rebecca (----), 4:384
Rhoda, 4:384
Ruhamah, 4:384
Ruhamah (Hagar), 2:328,
4:384
Sarah, 4:207, 4:382-385
Sarah (----), 4:383, 4:385
Sarah (Cutler), 1:493
Sarah (Kingsley), 4:385
Sarah (Mussey), 3:258,
4:383
Sarah (Parker), 4:384
Thankful, 4:385
Theodosia, 4:148
Wake
Catharine, 4:385
Wakefield
Ann, 4:386

Wakefield (continued)
Ann (----), 4:385, 4:700
Deborah, 4:386
Deliverance, 4:386
Deliverance (----), 4:386
Dorcas, 4:386
Elizabeth, 2:211-212,
  4:386
Elizabeth (----), 4:386
Elizabeth (----) Littlefield,
  4:385
Elizabeth (Littlefield),
  3:100
Experience (Thornton),
  4:293
Hannah, 2:290, 4:385-386
Martha, 1:285, 4:386
Mary, 2:46, 4:386
Susanna (----), 4:386
Wakeham
Sarah (Meader), 3:191,
  4:386
Wakeley/Wakely/Wakelin
Abigail, 4:386
Alice (----) Boosy, 1:211,
  4:387
Elizabeth, 1:418,
  4:387-388
Elizabeth (Dubbin), 4:24
Elizabeth (Sowers), 4:387
Hannah, 4:387
Mary, 4:386
Patience, 4:386
Sarah (----), 4:386
Sarah (Burt) Gregory,
  1:313, 2:312
Wakeman/Wakman
----, 1:412, 4:388
Abigail, 4:387
Ann, 3:278
Elizabeth, 3:32
Elizabeth (----), 4:387-388,
  4:556
Ellen, 4:387
Hannah, 3:278
Hannah (----), 1:137
Hannah (Goodyear), 2:278,
  4:388
Hannah (Jordan), 4:387
Helena/Ellen, 4:250
Joanna, 2:327, 4:388
Martha, 2:22-23
Mary (Burr), 1:307

Sarah, 3:278
Walcot/Walcott/Walcut
Abigail (Briggs), 4:388
Alice (Ingersoll), 2:521
Ann, 4:388
Deliverance (Putnam),
  4:388
Elizabeth, 4:388
Hannah, 4:388
Jerusha, 4:388
Mary, 4:388, 4:622
Mary (----), 4:388
Mary (Freake), 2:202
Mary (Freke), 4:388
Mary (Sibley), 4:93, 4:388
Penelope (----), 4:388
Ruth (Hooper), 4:388
Waldegrave
----, 3:385
Walden
Elizabeth, 4:388
Elizabeth (----), 2:288
Hannah, 2:144, 4:388
Mary, 4:388
Naomi, 4:388
Ruth, 4:388
Thomasin, 4:388
Waldo
---- (Cogswell), 1:422,
  4:389
Elizabeth, 1:80, 1:229,
  4:389
Rebecca, 1:16
Rebecca (Adams), 1:16,
  4:389
Susanna, 1:16
Waldron/Walderne/etc
Abigail, 4:390
Ann, 2:243, 4:390
Ann (Scammon), 4:390
Constant (----), 4:389
Dorcas (Rice), 4:389
Dorothy (----), 4:389
Eleanor, 4:390
Eleanor (Vaughan), 4:368,
  4:390
Elizabeth, 2:243, 4:390
Elizabeth (----) Horn,
  2:464, 4:389
Esther, 2:112, 2:570, 3:71,
  4:390
Hannah (Cutt), 1:495,
  4:390

Margaret, 4:390
Mary, 4:389-390
Naomi, 4:389
Priscilla, 4:389
Priscilla (----), 4:389
Prudence, 4:34, 4:391
Rachel (----), 4:389
Sarah, 4:389
Tabitha, 4:389
Tamisin, 4:389
Wales
Content, 3:168, 4:391
Deborah, 4:391
Elizabeth, 1:49, 4:391
Elizabeth (----), 4:391
Hannah, 1:177
Hannah (----), 4:391
Isabel (----), 4:391
Joanna, 4:391
Joanna (Faxon), 2:149,
  4:391
Mary, 4:391
Rachel, 4:391
Sarah, 4:391
Susan (----), 4:391
Susanna (Blake), 1:192
Walford
----, 2:426, 2:452, 2:560,
  3:404, 4:392
Elizabeth, 4:24, 4:392
Hannah, 4:392
Jane, 4:392
Jane (----), 4:392
Martha, 4:392
Mary, 1:259, 4:392
Mary (----), 4:392
Walker
---- (Leager), 3:218
Abigail, 3:480, 4:392-395,
  4:397-398
Abigail (----), 4:660
Abigail (Prudden), 3:492,
  4:394
Abigail/Elizabeth, 3:630
Agnes (----) Alger, 1:27
Ann, 4:392, 4:394-395,
  4:397
Ann (----), 4:397
Ann (----) Houlton, 2:455,
  4:395
Ann (Leager), 4:394
Ann (Mirick), 3:218, 4:394
Barsheba (----), 4:394

Walker (continued)
Bathsheba, 4:394
Bathsheba (Brooks), 4:394
Catharine, 4:395
Deborah, 2:587
Dorcas, 4:398
Dorothy, 3:372, 4:392
Dorothy (----), 4:392
Dorothy (Abell), 4:392
Elishua, 4:396
Elizabeth, 2:534, 3:25,
  4:238, 4:296, 4:393-395,
  4:397-398
Elizabeth (----), 4:393,
  4:396
Elizabeth (----) Blakeman,
  4:393
Elizabeth (Fowle), 3:627
Elizabeth (Phillips), 3:416,
  4:393
Elizabeth (Soule), 4:141,
  4:392
Elizabeth (Wheeler)
  Blakeman, 1:195
Elizabeth (Woodbury),
  4:394, 4:634
Esther, 1:77, 4:393-395,
  4:627
Eunice, 4:394, 4:634
Experience, 4:393, 4:395
Grace (----), 4:394, 4:436
Hannah, 2:338, 3:528,
  4:285, 4:392-397
Hannah (----), 4:392-393
Hannah (Hutchinson),
  2:509-510, 4:395
Hannah (Leffingwell)
  Flagg, 2:171
Hannah (Philbrick), 3:409,
  4:394
Hannah (Philbrook), 4:47
Jane (Butterworth), 4:395
Jane (Metcalf), 3:203
Joan, 2:496, 4:684
Joan (Metcalf), 4:396
Judith (----) Alger, 4:396
Leah, 4:393
Lydia, 4:394
Lydia (Read), 4:394
Martha, 4:394-397, 4:530
Martha (How), 4:397
Martha (Ide), 2:517, 4:396
Mary, 1:270, 3:57, 4:79,

4:392-397, 4:649, 4:678
Mary (----), 4:397
Mary (----) Robinson
  Brown, 3:549, 3:607,
  4:393
Mary (Bowen), 4:395
Mary (Gardner), 4:392
Mary (Pierce), 4:394
Mary (Prudden), 3:492
Mary (Walford) Brooking,
  1:259, 4:392
Mehitable, 4:394
Mercy, 4:393-394
Patience, 4:393, 4:396
Patience (----), 2:59
Patience (Jewett), 2:598,
  4:397
Persis (----), 4:395
Phebe, 4:393
Rebecca, 4:394
Rejoice, 4:393
Sarah, 1:270, 2:551, 3:105,
  3:399, 4:393-398, 4:426,
  4:634
Sarah (----), 4:395-396
Sarah (Goodnow), 4:397
Sarah (Read), 4:396
Sarah (Richmond) Rew,
  3:525, 3:539, 4:394
Sarah (Scottow), 4:40,
  4:396
Sarah (Snow), 4:397
Sarah (Story), 4:396
Sarah (Wyman), 4:395,
  4:664
Susan (----) Symonds,
  4:245
Susanna, 3:102, 4:392-393
Susanna (----), 4:393,
  4:398
Susanna (----) Symonds,
  4:393
Susanna (Collins), 1:435,
  4:397
Susanna (Rossiter), 3:577
Tabitha, 3:24, 4:395
Walkup
Naomi, 4:398
Naomi (Stephenson),
  4:398
Rachel, 4:398
Thankful, 4:398

Wall
Elizabeth, 2:370, 4:398
Joan, 4:398
Sarah, 2:64, 4:398
Wallen/Walling/Walline
Jane, 2:334, 3:627
Joyce (----), 4:398
Margaret (----) Caldwell,
  4:399
Mary (----), 4:399
Waller
Jane, 4:399
Joan (----), 1:474, 4:399
Lydia, 4:399
Lydia (----), 4:399
Margaret (----), 4:399
Martha (----), 4:399
Mary (----), 4:399
Mary (Durin), 4:399
Mary (Marvin), 3:165,
  4:399
Mehitable, 4:399
Rebecca, 4:399
Sarah, 4:399
Sarah (----), 4:399
Walley
Abiel, 4:400
Christian (Johnson), 4:401
Elizabeth, 4:54, 4:399-400
Elizabeth (----), 4:399,
  4:555
Elizabeth (Alden), 1:23,
  4:400
Elizabeth (Wing), 4:399,
  4:595
Hannah, 1:44, 4:399-400
Hannah (----), 4:401
Hannah (Bacon), 4:674,
  4:705, 4:712
Lydia, 4:400
Mary, 1:474, 4:401
Ruth, 2:132, 2:582
Sarah, 1:368, 4:399-400
Sarah (----), 4:399
Sarah (Marshal), 4:401
Sarah (Walter), 4:403
Wallingford/Wallinsford
Elizabeth (Palmer), 4:401
Mary (Tuttle), 4:351,
  4:401
Sarah, 2:463
Sarah (----), 4:401
Sarah (Travers), 4:324

Wallington
Hannah, 4:401
Mary, 4:401
Sarah, 4:401
Sarah (Travers), 4:324, 4:401
Wallis/Wallace
---- (Bradstreet), 1:235, 4:402
Ann (Shortridge), 4:89, 4:402
Dorcas, 3:645
Jane, 3:200
Jane (Drake), 2:70
Margaret (----), 4:402
Sarah, 3:397
Walsby/Wallsbee
Hannah (----), 4:402
Ruth (Ball), 4:402
Walston/Walstone
Ann, 4:253
Ann (Wright), 4:402, 4:654
Jane, 4:403
Walter/Walters
Abigail, 4:403
Abigail (Phillips) Woodbury East, 2:92, 4:403, 4:635
Hannah, 4:332, 4:403
Hannah (----), 4:403
Jane, 3:450
Maria, 4:403
Mary (Roundy/Roundee/etc), 3:579
Rebecca, 4:403
Rebecca (Abbot), 4:403
Rebecca (Belcher), 4:403
Sarah, 4:403
Sarah (----), 4:403
Sarah (Mather), 3:173, 4:403
Waltham
Ann, 4:404
Phyllis, 4:404
Walton
Abigail, 4:404
Alice (----), 4:404
Dorcas, 4:404
Elizabeth, 3:148, 4:404-405
Elizabeth (----), 4:405

Martha, 4:405
Mary, 1:132, 3:505, 4:404-405
Mary (----), 4:404
Sarah, 4:404
Sarah (Maverick), 3:180
Walworth
Abigail (----), 4:405
Joanna, 4:405
Martha, 4:405
Mary, 4:405
Wandell
---- (----) Herrick, 4:405
Wanton
---- (Freeborn), 4:406
Elizabeth, 4:406
Hannah, 4:406
Margaret, 4:406
Mary, 4:406
Ruth, 4:406
Ruth (Bryant), 4:406
Sarah, 4:406
Sarah (Freeborn), 4:406
Susanna, 4:406
Waples/Whapples/Whaples
Hannah, 4:406
Jane, 4:406
Rebecca, 4:406
Ward
---- (Tuttle), 4:352
Abigail, 3:181, 4:406-407, 4:409-410
Abigail (Collins), 1:436
Abigail (Hall), 4:409
Abigail (Spring), 4:157, 4:415
Alice, 4:411
Alice (----), 1:500
Alice (Edmunds), 4:408
Amy, 4:412
Amy/Ammi (----), 4:414
Ann, 4:406-407, 4:414, 4:420
Ann (Tappin), 4:254
Bathsheba, 4:415
Beriah, 4:412
Bethia, 3:527, 4:411, 4:413-415
Christian (Swain), 4:235
Deborah, 2:555, 4:409, 4:414, 4:663
Deborah (Joy), 2:572
Deliverance (Trowbridge),

4:332, 4:407
Dinah, 4:415
Dorcas, 4:410
Dorinada/Dorinda, 4:412
Dorothy, 4:414
Elizabeth, 2:217, 2:227, 2:352, 2:572, 3:15, 4:7, 4:407-414
Elizabeth (----), 4:412-414
Elizabeth (Beers), 1:155
Elizabeth (Flood), 4:412
Elizabeth (Rockwell), 3:557
Elizabeth (Swain), 4:235
Esther, 3:15, 4:407, 4:409-410
Esther (----), 2:384, 4:406, 4:414
Esther (Kenrick), 4:410
Frances, 2:146
Frances (----), 4:413
Grace (Lovering), 4:407
Hannah, 2:311, 2:473, 4:407, 4:409-414
Hannah (----) Nichols, 4:413
Hannah (Flint), 3:621, 4:410
Hannah (Jackson), 2:528, 4:408-409, 4:586
Hannah (Johnson) Eames, 2:90, 2:557, 4:414
Hannah (Rice), 3:529, 4:407
Hannah (Tappan), 4:414
Hopestill, 4:414
Isabel, 4:412
Jane, 4:411
Jane (----) Hopkins, 2:461, 4:411
Jemima, 4:415
Joanna, 4:413-414, 4:558
Joanna (Mixer) Harrington, 2:359, 3:223, 4:412
Joyce (----), 4:407, 4:409, 4:412, 4:414
Judith, 4:415
Judith (----), 4:415
Keziah, 4:415
Lydia, 2:259, 3:186, 4:410, 4:412
Margaret, 2:414, 4:410, 4:412, 4:414, 4:454

316

Ward (continued)
Margaret (----), 4:410
Margaret (Winthrop),
4:613
Martha, 2:181, 3:102,
3:181, 4:351, 4:410
Mary, 1:66, 1:306, 2:32,
2:173, 2:222, 2:251,
3:181, 3:527, 4:406-414,
4:422, 4:631
Mary (----), 4:203, 4:407,
4:411, 4:413
Mary (---) Sale, 4:413
Mary (Carter), 4:413
Mary (Foster) Sale, 4:5
Mary (Harris), 2:250,
2:365, 4:409
Mary (Joy), 2:572
Mary (Moore), 3:229,
4:412
Mary (Spring), 4:157,
4:409
Mary (Tillinghast), 4:303,
4:412
Mercy, 4:409, 4:412
Phebe, 4:409, 4:414
Phebe (----), 4:414
Prudence, 4:411
Rebecca, 4:407, 4:409
Record, 4:407
Record (----), 4:407
Remember, 4:410
Remember (Farrow),
2:146, 4:407
Ruth, 4:407
Sarah, 1:307, 1:500, 2:291,
3:628, 4:334, 4:406-407,
4:409-411, 4:413-414
Sarah (----), 4:409, 4:412,
4:414
Sarah (Bradstreet)
Hubbard, 1:236, 2:485,
4:413
Sarah (Hills), 2:420
Sarah (Howe), 2:475,
4:413
Sarah (Massey), 3:170,
4:410
Sarah (Nicholson), 3:283
Sarah (Ropes), 4:410
Silence, 4:412
Susan, 2:160, 4:411
Susanna, 2:152, 4:414

Tabitha, 4:407
Tamar, 4:413
Thankful, 4:409, 4:412
Thankful (Trowbridge),
4:332, 4:412
Trial (Meigs), 3:193, 4:407
Ursula, 4:413
Wardell/Wardwell/etc
Abigail, 4:416
Alice, 4:416
Alice (----), 4:416
Catharine (Chickering,
1:513
Elizabeth, 4:415
Elizabeth (----), 4:415
Elizabeth (----) Gillet,
4:416
Elizabeth (----) Perry Gillett,
2:256
Elizabeth (Jellett), 2:541
Elizabeth (Wade), 4:415
Hannah, 4:416
Leah, 4:416
Lydia (Perkins), 4:415
Martha, 4:415
Mary, 4:416
Mary (Ring), 4:415-416
Mercy, 4:415
Meribah, 4:416
Prudence, 4:415
Sarah (Hawkes), 4:415
Susanna, 4:415
Warden
Mehitable (Hinckley),
2:425
Ware
---- (Vassall), 4:367
Dorothy (Rice), 3:530
Elizabeth, 2:254, 4:417
Elizabeth (----), 4:417
Esther, 3:146, 4:416-417
Hannah, 4:416
Hannah (----), 4:416
Joanna (----), 4:416
Margaret, 4:417
Margaret (Hunting), 2:503,
4:416
Mary, 4:416
Mary (Metcalf), 3:204,
4:416
Sarah, 4:417
Sarah (Metcalf), 3:204,
4:417

Warfield
Hannah (Randall), 3:506,
4:417
Warham
Abigail, 1:44, 4:417
Abigail (----), 3:268
Abigail (----) Branker,
1:238, 3:201, 4:417
Esther, 3:172, 4:201,
4:418
Hannah (Adams), 1:15,
4:418
Hepzibah, 4:418
Jane (----), 4:418
Sarah, 4:227, 4:418
Warner
----, 3:140, 4:422
Abigail, 3:72, 4:418-419,
4:421-422, 4:527
Abigail (Abby/Abbey), 1:6
Abigail (Montague), 3:225,
4:421
Abigail (Tuttle), 4:352,
4:422
Ann, 2:484, 4:419, 4:421
Ann (Gorton), 2:283,
4:421
Ann (Norton), 3:293,
4:420
Ann (Ward), 4:420
Bethia, 4:422
Catharine (----), 4:45
Deborah (----) Crow, 1:480
Deliverance (----) Rockwell,
4:422
Dorcas, 4:419
Dorcas (----), 4:419
Dorothy, 4:422
Elizabeth, 2:397, 3:573,
4:418-419, 4:421-422
Elizabeth (----), 4:418,
4:422
Elizabeth (Coggeshall),
1:421
Elizabeth (Goodman),
4:419
Elizabeth (Grant), 4:422
Elizabeth (Ranney), 3:508
Elizabeth (Taylor), 4:419
Ellen (----) Jewett, 4:418
Esther, 4:419
Esther (----), 4:427
Esther (----) Selden, 4:50,

Warner (continued)
Esther (----) Selden
(continued)
4:418
Esther (Taylor), 4:419
Faith (Brown), 4:418
Hannah, 4:418-419,
4:421-422
Hannah (----), 4:422
Hannah (Batchellor),
1:87-88, 4:421
Hannah (Boynton), 4:421
Hope (Nash), 3:263
Joanna, 4:419
Joanna (Gardner), 4:421
Lydia, 1:280, 4:419-421
Lydia (Boltwood), 1:208,
4:421
Margaret, 3:662, 4:422
Margaret (----), 4:420
Martha, 4:419, 4:422
Martha (Boltwood), 1:208,
4:419
Mary, 1:130, 1:480, 2:71,
2:420, 4:181, 4:384,
4:418-422
Mary (----), 4:419
Mary (----) Root, 4:421
Mary (Ward), 4:422
Mehitable, 4:419-420,
4:422
Mercy, 4:419
Mercy (Swan), 4:422
Priscilla, 1:483, 4:421-422
Priscilla (Holliman), 2:448,
4:420
Priscilla (Symonds), 4:246,
4:420
Rachel, 3:466, 4:420
Rebecca, 4:418-419
Rebecca (----), 4:419
Rebecca (----) Cooley,
4:421
Rebecca (Fletcher), 1:11,
2:173, 4:418
Ruth, 4:418-419, 4:422
Sarah, 2:414, 3:507, 3:618,
4:69, 4:418-422
Sarah (----), 3:112
Sarah (Boltwood), 1:208,
4:419
Sarah (Dane), 2:6, 4:419
Sarah (Ferry), 4:421

Sarah (Golding), 2:269
Sarah (Warner), 4:421
Susan, 4:420
Susanna, 4:418, 4:421
Thankful, 4:419
Warren
Abiel (Rogers), 4:428
Abigail, 3:115, 3:432, 4:51,
4:138, 4:423, 4:425-428,
4:587, 4:634, 4:657
Abigail (Hastings), 4:425
Abigail (Rogers), 3:561,
4:423
Alice, 2:247, 4:424, 4:426
Ann, 2:167, 3:99, 4:427
Deborah, 4:426
Deborah (Williams), 4:425
Deborah (Wilson), 4:424
Deliverance, 4:423
Elizabeth, 1:372, 1:386,
2:433, 3:33, 3:417,
4:248, 4:423-427
Elizabeth (----), 2:392, 4:51,
4:423, 4:425, 4:427,
4:587
Elizabeth (----) Barlow
Coombs, 1:117, 1:439,
4:424
Elizabeth (Crow), 1:479,
4:427
Elizabeth (Seaverns), 4:47
Elizabeth (Whitney), 4:423,
4:530
Esther (----) Cushman,
4:423
Esther (----) Woodward,
4:427
Esther (Cushman), 4:423
Esther (Woodward), 4:427
Grace, 4:423-424
Grizzel, 4:424
Grizzle, 3:324
Hannah, 2:34, 3:190,
4:423, 4:426-427
Hannah (----), 4:426
Hannah (Morton), 4:423
Hope, 4:424, 4:426
Jane, 3:105, 3:214, 4:426
Lucy, 4:425
Lydia, 4:426-427
Lydia (Cutting), 4:427
Lydia (Fiske), 4:425
Margaret, 4:424

Margaret (----), 4:424
Mary, 1:132, 1:175, 1:307,
1:378, 2:167, 3:626,
4:423-424, 4:426-428,
4:448, 4:587
Mary (----), 4:424
Mary (Barron), 1:126,
4:423
Mary (Brown), 4:425
Mehitable (Clark), 1:401,
4:402
Mehitable (Wilder), 4:425
Mercy, 1:232, 2:34,
4:424-426
Michal (Jennison) Blois,
1:203, 2:545, 4:424
Patience, 4:424-425
Phebe (Murdock), 4:426
Priscilla, 4:423, 4:425
Priscilla (Faunce), 2:148,
4:425
Prudence, 4:426
Rebecca, 4:426
Rebecca (Church), 4:426
Ruth, 4:423
Sarah, 1:447, 2:233, 3:487,
4:423-427
Sarah (Dotey), 2:62, 4:424
Sarah (Fitch), 4:427
Sarah (Tucker), 4:340,
4:426
Sarah (Walker), 4:426
Susanna, 4:423, 4:426
Warriner/Warrener
---- (Thomas), 4:282
Abigail, 4:428
Dorcas, 4:428
Elizabeth, 4:227,
4:428-429
Elizabeth (----), 1:103
Elizabeth (----) Hitchcock,
4:428
Elizabeth (Baldwin), 1:103,
4:428
Hannah, 3:286, 4:428-429
Joanna, 4:428
Joanna (Scant), 4:428
Joanna (Searl), 4:428
Lydia (----) Hitchcock,
4:428
Mary, 1:213, 4:428
Mary (----) Ball Stebbins,
4:175

318

Warriner/Warrener
(continued)
Mary (----) Stebbins, 4:428
Mary (Montague), 3:225,
4:428
Sarah, 4:428
Sarah (----), 1:6
Sarah (----) Collins, 4:428
Sarah (Alvord), 1:46,
4:428
Sarah (Scant), 4:428
Sarah (Tibbals) Collins,
1:434, 4:298
Warwick
----, 4:268, 4:429
Joan, 2:401, 4:429
Wase
Ann, 1:255
Washburn/Washborne
Abigail, 4:430
Abigail (Leonard), 4:430
Ann, 4:429
Deborah (Packard), 3:327,
4:430
Deliverance, 4:430
Deliverance (Packard),
3:327, 4:430
Elizabeth, 2:471,
4:429-430
Elizabeth (Mitchell),
3:219-220, 4:429
Hannah, 3:4, 4:430
Hannah (Latham), 3:58,
4:430
Hannah (Wooster), 4:429
Hepzibah, 3:66, 4:430
Jane, 3:315, 4:429
Joanna, 4:430
Margaret (----), 4:429
Martha, 4:429-430
Mary, 3:30, 4:429
Mary (----), 2:410
Mary (Bowden), 4:429
Mary (Butler), 1:321,
4:429
Mary (Stiles), 4:194, 4:429
Mary (Vaughan), 4:368,
4:430
Patience, 4:430
Rebecca, 4:430
Rebecca (Lapham), 4:429
Sarah, 4:429

Wass/Wasse
Catharine (----), 4:430
Wasselbe
Bridget (----), 3:657
Wasson
Martha (Kenney), 4:430
Waterbury
Alice (----), 4:431
Mary, 4:430
Mary (----), 4:430
Rachel, 4:430
Rose (----), 2:233, 4:430
Sarah, 2:47, 4:430, 4:449
Waterhouse
Ann, 4:431
Ann (Douglas), 4:431
Ann (Mayhew), 4:431
Elizabeth, 4:431
Hannah (----), 4:431
Rebecca, 4:431, 4:537
Rebecca (Clarke), 4:431
Ruth, 4:431
Sarah, 4:431
Sarah (----), 4:431
Sarah (Pratt), 3:476, 4:431
Waterman
Abigail, 4:432
Ann, 4:432-433
Ann (Olney), 3:313
Ann (Sturdevant), 4:230,
4:431-432
Bethia, 2:445, 4:432
Elizabeth, 3:620,
4:432-433
Elizabeth (Bourne), 1:219,
4:433
Hannah, 4:433
Hannah (----), 4:433
Lydia, 4:63, 4:432-433
Lydia (Olney), 4:432
Martha, 3:165, 4:433
Mary/Mercy, 4:432
Mehitable, 4:432
Mercy (Williams), 3:526,
4:432, 4:569, 4:605
Miriam, 4:433
Miriam (Tracy), 4:321,
4:433
Sarah, 4:432
Sarah (Lewis) Lincoln,
3:86, 3:95, 4:433
Sarah (Snow), 4:432
Susanna, 4:433

Susanna (Carder), 4:432
Susanna (Lincoln), 3:91,
4:433
Waiting, 4:432
Waters
----, 4:375
Abigail, 3:493, 4:434-435
Ann (Linton), 3:97, 4:434
Dorothy, 4:435
Elizabeth, 4:434-435
Elizabeth (Lattimore),
4:436
Frances (----), 4:434
Hannah, 4:224, 4:433-435
Hannah (----), 4:434
Joanna, 4:435
Joyce, 4:434
Joyce (----), 4:434-435
Martha, 4:434-435
Martha (Mellows), 3:195,
4:434
Mary, 2:123, 4:95,
4:433-435
Mary (----), 4:435
Mehitable, 4:435
Phebe, 4:435, 4:488
Rachel, 4:434
Rebecca, 4:434-435
Rebecca (----), 4:435
Sarah, 1:170, 3:512, 4:64,
4:433-435, 4:709
Sarah (----), 4:434-435
Sarah (----) Mygott, 4:433
Sarah (Fenn), 4:435
Sarah (Tompkins), 4:311,
4:434
Sarah (Webster) Mygate,
3:259
Susanna, 3:493, 4:434-435
Watkins
Bridget, 2:13
Dorothy (Pepperell), 3:392
Elizabeth, 4:436
Elizabeth (----), 4:436
Hannah, 4:436
Mehitable, 4:436
Sarah, 4:436
Sarah (----), 4:436
Watson
---- (Prentice), 3:480
Abigail (Dudley), 2:77
Alice (----) Prentice, 4:437
Ann, 4:437-438

Watson (continued)
Ann (----), 4:437
Ann (Bridge), 1:248
Dorcas, 2:86, 4:436-437
Dorothy (Bissell), 4:438
Elizabeth, 1:248,
4:437-438, 4:563
Elizabeth (Frost), 2:298
Elizabeth (Hudson), 4:438
Eunice (Barker), 1:115,
4:437
Grace, 4:436
Grace (----) Walker, 4:394,
4:436
Hannah, 1:183, 4:438
Joan (----), 4:438
Margaret (----), 4:437
Margery, 2:273
Martha, 1:248
Mary, 2:330, 3:80, 4:58,
4:179, 4:437-438
Mary (----), 4:437, 4:527
Mary (Butterfield), 4:436
Mary (Clark) Gaylord,
1:392
Mary (Hyde), 2:514, 4:436
Mary (Rockwell), 3:557,
4:438
Mercy, 4:437
Mercy (----), 4:437
Phebe, 4:65, 4:437
Phebe (Hicks), 2:410,
4:437
Rebecca, 3:529, 4:437
Rebecca (Errington), 4:437
Rebecca (Wells) Latham
Packer, 3:328
Ruth (Griffin), 4:438
Sarah, 3:199, 4:437-438
Sarah (Perley), 4:438
Susanna (----), 4:344
Watts
Eleanor, 1:273, 4:439
Elizabeth, 2:483, 4:439
Elizabeth (----), 4:439
Elizabeth (Steele), 4:180,
4:439
Waugh
Dorothy, 4:439
Way
Agnes, 2:363
Ann (Lester), 4:441
Bethia (----), 4:440

Elizabeth, 2:566, 4:440,
4:476
Elizabeth (----), 4:440
Elizabeth (Jones), 2:566
Elizabeth (Smith), 4:122,
4:440
Esther (Jones), 4:440
Hannah, 4:440
Hannah (Townsend) Hull,
2:495, 4:320, 4:440-441
Irene (----), 4:439
Joan (Sumner), 4:439
Lydia, 4:440
Martha, 1:30, 4:440
Mary (----), 4:440
Mary (Maverick), 3:180
Sarah, 4:440, 4:475
Susanna, 4:439
Susanna (Nest), 3:268,
4:440
Wayne
Mary, 3:251
Weare
---- (Gooch), 2:270
Elizabeth (Swain), 4:235,
4:441
Esther, 4:239
Hannah, 2:270
Mary, 2:270
Mehitable, 4:305
Phebe, 2:270
Ruth, 2:270
Sarah, 2:291
Weatherhead
Mary, 4:442
Weaver
Elizabeth (----), 4:442
Margaret (----), 4:442
Mary (Freeborn), 4:442
Sarah, 4:442
Webb
Abigail, 4:443
Abigail (Austin), 1:499
Ann, 4:385, 4:445-446
Ann (----), 4:445
Bethia (Adams), 1:13,
4:445
Bridget, 4:445
Bridget (Whitford), 4:445
Dosabell (----), 4:444
Elizabeth, 2:306,
4:443-444
Elizabeth (----), 2:10, 4:446

Elizabeth (Nichols), 3:280
Elizabeth (Stratford), 4:445
Elizabeth (Swift), 4:445
Esther, 4:444
Experience, 4:444
Frances (Bromfield), 1:258
Grace (----), 4:445
Hannah, 1:12, 4:443,
4:445
Hannah (Scott), 4:36,
4:443
Jane (Woolford), 4:444
Joanna, 4:444
Lydia, 4:445
Margaret, 4:66, 4:273,
4:443-444
Margery, 4:445
Mary, 1:14, 2:91, 3:394,
4:443, 4:445
Mary (----), 4:445-446
Mary (----) Fayerweather,
2:273
Mary (Adams), 1:13, 4:446
Mary (Bass), 1:456
Mary (Becket), 1:151,
4:443
Mary (Fosdick), 2:185
Mary (Wilson) Hannah,
2:350, 4:588
Mercy (Bucknam), 1:287,
4:443
Mindwell, 4:445
Patience, 4:446
Patience (----), 4:446
Priscilla, 4:444
Priscilla (McLathin), 4:444
Rebecca (----), 1:63, 4:446
Sarah, 1:63, 1:181, 1:287,
2:157, 4:444-446
Sarah (----), 4:444
Susanna (Cunliffe) Cole,
1:484, 4:445
Thankful, 4:445-446
Webber
Bathsheba, 4:447
Deborah, 4:447
Deborah (----), 4:447
Dorcas, 4:447
Elizabeth, 4:446
Elizabeth (----), 4:446
Martha, 4:446
Mary, 4:446
Mary (----), 4:447

320

Webber (continued)
Mary (Parker), 3:351,
4:447
Mehitable, 4:447
Sarah, 4:447
Sarah (----), 4:447
Waitstill, 4:447
Webster
----, 4:449
---- (Godfrey), 4:450
Abiah, 4:449
Abiah (Shaw), 4:449
Abigail, 3:199, 3:249,
4:448-450
Abigail (Alexander), 1:26,
4:450
Agnes (----), 4:448
Alice, 4:450
Ann, 3:154, 4:447-449
Ann (Batt), 4:449
Bridget (Huggins), 4:449
Charity, 4:449
Dorcas (Hopkins), 2:462
Elizabeth, 4:37, 4:447-450,
4:652
Elizabeth (Brown), 4:448
Elizabeth (Lunt), 4:448
Esther (----), 4:447
Hannah, 4:447-450
Hannah (Ayer), 1:84,
4:450
Hannah (Beckley), 1:504
Hannah (Judkins), 4:447
Joanna, 4:450
Lucy, 4:449
Lydia, 4:448
Margaret (----), 2:266
Margery (----), 4:450
Mary, 2:404, 3:27, 4:128,
4:449-450
Mary (----), 2:119, 4:448
Mary (Hutchins), 4:447
Mary (Maudsley), 3:179,
4:450
Mary (Reeve), 3:523,
4:450
Mary (Shatswell), 4:61
Rachel, 4:447, 4:449
Sarah, 2:316, 3:54, 3:259,
4:447, 4:449-450
Sarah (----), 4:449-450
Sarah (Brewer), 1:244,
4:450

Sarah (Clark), 4:450
Sarah (Mygate), 2:588,
3:259
Sarah (Nichols), 3:279
Sarah (Waterbury) Dibble,
2:47, 4:430, 4:449
Susanna, 4:447, 4:449
Susanna (Batchelder),
4:447
Susanna (Treat), 4:326,
4:449
Susannah, 4:447
Thankful, 4:450
Wedgewood
Abigail, 4:451
Mary, 4:451
Mary (----), 4:451
Rachel (Davis) Haynes,
2:20
Weed
---- (Wensley), 4:482
Ann, 4:451
Bethia (Holley), 4:451
Deborah, 1:130, 4:451
Deborah (Wensley), 4:451
Dorcas, 4:451, 4:656
Hannah, 4:451
Joanna (Westcoat), 4:451,
4:486
Mary, 4:451
Mary (----), 4:451
Sarah, 4:451
Weeden
Dorothy, 4:452
Elizabeth, 1:429, 4:452
Elizabeth (Cole), 1:430,
4:452
Hannah, 4:452
Hannah (Proctor), 3:489
Jane (----), 4:452
Mary, 4:452
Mary (----), 4:452
Rose (----) Paine, 3:332,
4:331
Ruth (----), 4:452
Sarah, 4:452
Weeks
Abigail, 4:452-453
Abigail (Trescott), 4:329,
4:452
Bethia, 4:453
Deliverance (Sumner),
4:232, 4:452

Elizabeth, 3:552,
4:452-454
Elizabeth (----), 4:452
Elizabeth (Haynes), 2:390,
4:453
Experience, 4:453, 4:712
Hannah, 3:659, 4:452-453
Jane, 1:190, 4:452, 4:454
Jane (----), 2:497
Jane (Clap), 4:453
Jemima, 4:453
Lydia, 4:712
Margaret, 4:453
Martha, 4:453
Mary, 2:306, 4:452-454,
4:509, 4:712
Mary (----), 4:452-453
Mary (Atherton), 1:73,
4:453
Mary (Haynes/Haines),
2:390
Mehitable, 4:712
Mercy, 4:712
Mercy (Robinson), 3:550,
4:454
Rebecca, 4:453
Renew, 1:335, 4:454
Repent, 4:453
Sarah, 4:453-454, 4:712
Sarah (----), 4:453
Sarah (Hammond), 4:453
Sarah (Sumner) Turell,
4:232
Susanna, 4:453
Susanna (Barnes), 4:453
Thankful, 4:452-453
Weightman
Margaret (Ward), 4:414,
4:454
Welch
Ann, 4:676
Elizabeth, 4:454
Elizabeth (----), 4:454-455
Elizabeth (Upham), 4:455
Esther, 4:455, 4:676
Hannah (Buckingham),
4:455, 4:676
Hannah (Haggert), 4:455
Lydia, 4:455
Mary, 4:455
Mercy (Sabin), 4:454
Rachel, 4:454
Sarah, 4:455, 4:676

Welch (continued)
Susanna, 3:617, 4:454
Welcome
Mary, 4:456
Mary (----), 4:456
Weld
Abigail, 4:457
Alice (----), 4:456
Ann (----) Hyde, 2:514,
4:456
Barbara, 4:456
Barbara (----), 4:199, 4:457
Bethia, 3:206, 4:456
Bethia (Mitchelson), 3:222,
4:456
Deborah, 4:458
Dorcas, 4:456
Dorothy, 2:38, 4:457-458,
4:473, 4:570
Dorothy (Whiting), 4:473,
4:520
Elizabeth, 2:36, 2:281,
4:456-458, 4:473
Elizabeth (----), 4:457
Elizabeth (Chamberlain),
1:353
Elizabeth (Devotion), 2:42,
4:458
Elizabeth (White), 4:457
Elizabeth (Wilson), 4:473
Esther, 4:457
Hannah, 2:399, 4:457-458
Hannah (Portis), 4:457
Joanna, 4:457
Judith (----), 4:459
Marah, 4:458
Margaret, 4:457-458,
4:473
Margaret (----), 4:458-459
Margaret (Bowen), 4:457
Mary, 2:229, 2:360, 4:170,
4:456-458
Mary (Savage), 4:24,
4:473
Mehitable, 4:456
Sarah, 2:201, 4:457-458
Sarah (Faxon), 2:149,
4:458
Susanna (Polley), 3:450,
4:458
Welden/Weldon
Elizabeth (----), 3:410,
4:474

Sarah, 4:504
Weller
Ann (Wilson), 4:474
Deliverance, 4:474
Deliverance (Hanchet),
2:352, 4:474
Elizabeth, 4:474
Elizabeth (----) Curtis,
4:474
Elizabeth (Abell) Curtis,
1:485
Experience, 4:474
Hannah, 4:474
Hannah (Pritchard), 4:474
Mary, 4:474
Mary (Alvord), 1:46, 4:474
Rebecca, 4:474
Sarah, 2:351, 4:474
Thankful, 3:113, 4:474
Welles/Wells
---- (Warner), 4:422
Abigail, 4:325, 4:476-478
Abigail (Allis), 4:474
Abigail (Ingersoll) Rix,
2:520
Ann, 2:382, 2:575, 4:180,
4:288, 4:475-478
Ann (----), 4:478
Ann (Tuttle) Pantry, 4:352
Comfort, 4:476
Dorothy (Worthen), 4:653
Elizabeth, 2:362, 4:71,
4:475-478
Elizabeth (----), 4:475,
4:477, 4:479, 4:547
Elizabeth (----) Foote,
4:478
Elizabeth (Bourne), 4:475
Elizabeth (Curtis), 1:485
Elizabeth (Deming) Foote,
2:180
Elizabeth (Goodrich),
2:275, 4:477
Elizabeth (Hollister), 4:477
Elizabeth (Way), 4:440,
4:476
Esther, 4:476
Frances (----), 1:431, 4:479
Hannah, 4:476-479, 4:512,
4:705
Hannah (Buckland), 1:285
Hannah (Lamberton), 1:43,
3:49, 4:477

Hannah (Reynolds), 4:476
Hannah (Tuttle) Pantry,
3:344, 4:479
Hepzibah, 4:480
Hepzibah (Buell), 1:157,
1:289, 4:479
Hepzibah (Colton), 4:476
Hopestill, 4:474
Jerusha (Treat), 2:274,
4:325, 4:480
Lucy (Treworgy)
Chadbourne, 4:330
Lydia, 3:575, 4:476, 4:478
Lydia (----), 4:476
Margaret, 4:476
Margaret (----), 4:476
Martha, 4:474-475
Mary, 1:431, 2:250, 2:331,
2:480, 2:487, 3:143,
3:604, 4:474-479
Mary (----), 1:158, 4:477,
4:479
Mary (Blackleach), 1:189,
3:306, 4:380, 4:480
Mary (Greenleaf), 4:476
Mary (Hollister), 2:449,
4:476
Mary (Parker), 4:479
Mary (Rusco), 3:589,
4:474
Mary (Waite), 4:383,
4:474
Mary (White), 4:476,
4:508
Mercy, 4:477
Naomi (----), 4:479
Prudence, 4:477
Rachel (Marsh), 4:476
Rebecca, 2:575, 3:58,
3:328, 4:475, 4:477,
4:479
Rebecca (Selden), 4:50,
4:475
Ruth, 4:477, 4:479
Ruth (----), 4:477
Ruth (Rice), 4:477
Sarah, 1:144, 1:174, 1:375,
2:384, 2:480, 3:170,
3:652, 4:94, 4:475-480
Sarah (----), 1:158, 4:31,
4:474, 4:480
Sarah (----) Lawrence,
4:474

Welles/Wells (continued)
Sarah (Clark), 4:477
Sarah (Littlefield), 3:100,
  4:475
Sarah (Savage), 4:24
Sarah (Smith) Lawrence,
  3:62
Sarah (Strong) Barnard,
  4:226, 4:476
Sarah (Way), 4:440, 4:475
Susan, 4:475
Susanna, 4:475
Temperance, 3:441, 4:475
Thankful (Root), 4:480
Wait, 4:480
Wellington
Ann (Bridge) Livermore,
  1:248, 3:101, 4:480
Elizabeth, 4:480
Elizabeth (Straight), 4:220,
  4:480
Elizabeth (Sweetman),
  4:239, 4:480
Mary, 3:142, 3:457,
  4:480-481
Mary (Palgrave), 3:340,
  4:481
Mehitable, 4:83, 4:480
Ruhamah, 1:273, 4:480
Sarah (----), 4:480
Sarah (Bond), 1:210,
  4:481
Susanna, 4:480
Susanna (Straight), 4:220,
  4:480
Wellman
Abigail, 4:481
Elizabeth, 4:67, 4:86,
  4:481-482
Elizabeth (----), 4:481
Elizabeth (----) Griswold,
  4:482
Elizabeth (Cogswell),
  4:481
Elizabeth (Joy), 4:482
Elizabeth (Spencer), 2:572,
  4:150, 4:481
Hannah (Adams), 4:481
Martha, 3:215, 4:481-482
Mary, 2:473, 3:231,
  4:481-482
Mercy, 3:645
Rachel, 4:481

Sarah, 4:481
Welsh
Deborah, 1:328
Elizabeth (Upham), 4:360
Hannah (----), 3:49
Hannah (Haggett), 2:329
Welsteed/Welstead
---- (Hutchinson), 4:482
Catharine (Long), 3:108
Elizabeth (Dering), 2:41,
  4:482
Mehitable, 1:81, 1:499
Mehitable (Cary), 4:482
Welton
Else, 4:482
Hannah, 4:482
Mary, 4:482
Mary (----), 4:482
Wenbourne/Winborn/etc
Elizabeth (----), 4:482
Wenchell
Abigail, 3:12
Wendell
Ann, 3:388
Wensley/Winsley/Winslye
----, 4:482
Ann (----) Boade, 1:207,
  4:483
Deborah, 4:451, 4:483
Elizabeth, 4:482-483
Elizabeth (----), 4:483
Elizabeth (Paddy), 3:329,
  4:483
Hannah, 4:482
Hopestill, 3:310
Martha, 4:482
Mary, 2:205, 4:482
Mary (Greely), 4:482
Mary (Jones), 3:640, 4:483
Mercy, 1:250, 1:491,
  4:483
Sarah, 3:330, 4:483
Wentworth
Abigail, 4:484
Abra, 4:484
Catharine, 4:485
Catharine (----), 4:485
Dorothy, 4:484-485
Elizabeth, 4:320, 4:484,
  4:486
Elizabeth (----), 4:486
Elizabeth (Knight), 3:36,
  4:484

Elizabeth (Stewart), 4:485
Hannah (French), 4:484
Martha, 4:484-485
Martha (Miller), 3:208,
  4:484
Mary, 4:484-485
Mary (----), 3:164
Mary (Benning), 4:485
Mary (Miller), 3:208,
  3:211, 4:484
Mercy, 4:485
Rebecca (Jeffrey/Jeffries),
  2:597
Sarah, 3:639, 4:484-486
Sarah (Allen), 4:484
Sarah (Cromwell), 1:476,
  4:485
Sarah (Hunking), 2:498
Susanna, 4:484
Tamasin, 4:484
Tamosine, 4:484
Thomasin, 2:387
Wermall/Wormall
Esther, 4:486
Mary (Barrows), 4:486
Mehitable, 4:486
Mercy, 4:486
Miriam (----), 4:486
Patience (Sherman), 4:486
Sarah, 4:486
Wescott/Westcott/Westcoat
Abigail, 3:34, 4:486, 4:705
Catharine, 4:487
Catharine (----), 4:487
Damaris, 1:64, 4:487
Deborah (Stafford), 4:160,
  4:486
Dinah, 4:487
Elenor, 4:486
Ellen (England), 2:123,
  4:486
Joanna, 4:451, 4:486,
  4:705
Joanna (----), 1:104, 4:486,
  4:705
Mary, 4:487
Mercy, 4:160, 4:487
Sarah, 4:487
Sarah (Stafford), 4:160,
  4:486
West
----, 2:332, 4:488
Abigail, 4:487

West (continued)
Catharine (Almy), 1:45
Elizabeth, 1:361,
4:487-488
Elizabeth (----), 4:488
Elizabeth (----) Atwood,
1:78
Elizabeth (Meriam), 4:487
Hannah, 3:397, 4:487
Hannah (Haddock), 4:487
Hannah (Hadlock), 4:487
Hannah (Shaddock), 4:58,
4:487
Joan, 1:422
Mary, 4:487-488
Mary (Hilliard), 2:421,
4:488
Mary (Poor), 4:488
Mehitable (----), 4:488
Phebe (Waters), 4:435,
4:488
Rhoda (Meacham), 3:190
Sarah (----), 4:488
Susanna, 4:487
Tryphosa (Partridge),
3:365
Westall/Westell/Westoll
Susanna, 4:488
Susanna (Kirtland), 4:488
Westbrook
---- (Walford) Hinckson,
4:392
Martha (Walford), 4:392
Sarah (Woodcock), 2:392
Westcar
Hannah (Barnard), 1:118,
4:489
Westead/Wesstead
Eleanor, 4:489
Westgate
Mary, 4:489
Mary (----), 4:489
Westoe
Susanna, 2:412
Weston/Wesson
---- (----) Pease, 3:379
---- (Soule), 4:489
Elizabeth, 4:490
Mary, 2:541, 4:490, 4:691
Sarah, 3:653, 4:490, 4:691
Sarah (Fitch), 2:170
Westover
Abigail (Case), 1:345

Elizabeth, 4:491
Hannah, 4:491
Hannah (----), 4:490
Jane, 4:491, 4:571
Joanna, 4:491
Margaret, 4:490-491
Mary, 1:346, 4:491
Westwood
Bridget (----), 4:491
Sarah, 1:445, 4:491
Wetherbee/Wetherby
Elizabeth (Whitney), 4:531
Mary (----), 4:491
Mary (Howe), 2:475
Wetherell/Wetherill/etc
Ann (Rogers), 4:492
Dorothy, 4:492
Dorothy (----), 4:492
Elizabeth, 1:283, 4:492
Elizabeth (Newland),
4:492
Grace (----), 4:491
Grace (Brewster), 1:245,
4:491
Hannah, 3:423, 4:491-492
Isabel (----), 4:492
Lydia (Parker), 4:492
Lydia (Totman), 3:357
Mary, 2:364, 3:308, 4:491
Mary (----), 4:492
Mary (Parker), 3:357,
4:492
Sarah, 2:433-434, 4:492
Susanna (----), 4:491
Wetmore
Elizabeth (Hubbard), 2:484
Hannah, 4:217
Margaret (Stow), 4:218
Mary, 4:217
Mary (Platt) Atkinson,
1:74, 3:445
Rachel (Stow), 4:218
Weymouth
Elizabeth, 4:493
Esther (Hodsden), 4:493
Esther (Hodsdon), 2:440
Mary (----), 4:493
Tabitha, 4:493
Whale
---- (Harrington), 4:493
---- (Hopkins), 4:493
Ann, 4:493
Elizabeth, 4:493

Elizabeth (----), 4:493
Elizabeth (Griffin), 4:493
Joan, 4:493
Lydia, 4:493
Martha, 4:493
Sarah (Cakebread), 1:328,
4:493
Theodosia, 4:493
Whaley
Catharine (----), 4:493
Whalley
----, 2:458
---- (Goffe), 4:494
Frances, 2:268
Wharff
Ann (Riggs), 4:712
Charity, 4:712
Experience, 4:712
Hannah, 4:712
Lydia, 4:712
Mary, 4:712
Patience, 4:712
Rebecca, 4:712
Rebecca (Mackworth),
3:142, 4:494
Wharton
Ann, 4:495
Bethia, 4:494
Bethia (Tyng), 4:358,
4:494
Dorothy, 4:495
Martha, 4:495
Martha (Winthrop), 4:494,
4:613
Mary (----), 4:494
Rebecca, 4:494
Sarah, 1:461, 4:494
Sarah (Higginson), 2:414,
4:494
Wheat/Wheate
Elizabeth (----), 4:495
Elizabeth (Mansfield),
3:655
Hannah, 4:221, 4:495
Remembrance, 4:495
Sarah, 4:495
Tamsen (----), 4:495
Thomasine (----), 4:495
Wheatley
Elinor (----), 4:495
Jane, 4:495
Rachel, 1:285, 3:118,
4:495

324

Wheaton
Elizabeth (—), 4:495
Hannah, 1:323
Margaret, 2:282
Mary, 3:146
Mehitable, 4:495
Sarah, 4:495
Whedon/Wheaden/Wheedon
Abigail, 4:496
Ann (Harvey), 4:496
Esther, 2:551, 4:496
Hannah, 4:496
Hannah (—), 4:496
Jane (Ault), 2:101
Martha, 4:496
Rebecca, 4:496
Sarah, 4:496
Wheeler
— (Turney), 4:349
Abigail, 1:115, 2:406,
  2:419, 4:203, 4:496-499
Abigail (—), 4:496-497
Abigail (Allen), 1:37
Alce/Alice (—), 4:501
Alice, 4:500
Alse (—), 4:161
Ann, 1:364, 3:542,
  4:497-498, 4:500, 4:502
Ann (—), 4:496-497,
  4:501
Ann (Buss/Bussey), 1:319
Ann (French), 3:622
Ann (Phippen), 3:418,
  4:502
Catharine (—), 4:496
Deborah, 4:499
Dinah, 4:498
Dorcas (Swain) Taintor,
  4:234, 4:248
Dorothy, 4:497
Elizabeth, 1:195, 1:439,
  1:449, 2:173, 2:223,
  2:307, 3:490, 3:529,
  4:496-501, 4:620
Elizabeth (—), 4:181,
  4:498-499
Elizabeth (Harris), 4:499
Elizabeth (Rowland)
  Rogers, 3:581
Esther, 1:195
Esther (Botsford), 1:217,
  4:499-500
Experience, 4:497

Frances (—), 1:449, 2:306,
  4:497
Hannah, 1:167, 4:496,
  4:498, 4:501-502
Hannah (—), 4:500, 4:626
Hannah (Buss/Bussey),
  4:501-502
Hannah (French), 2:205,
  4:497
Hannah (Harrod), 4:501
Jane (—), 4:501
Joan (—), 4:500
Joanna, 4:499
Judith, 4:496, 4:498
Lydia, 2:90, 4:496
Martha, 4:497
Martha (Parke), 3:348,
  4:497
Martha (Wigglesworth),
  4:542
Mary, 1:19, 2:195,
  4:496-501, 4:559
Mary (—), 4:500
Mary (—) Stone, 4:206,
  4:499
Mary (Brooks), 1:262,
  4:501
Mary (Burr), 1:306
Mary (Giles), 2:253
Mary (Holbrook), 2:442,
  4:496
Mary (Wilson), 4:499
Mercy, 4:497, 4:499
Miriam, 1:195, 3:604,
  4:499
Rachel, 4:295, 4:497
Rachel (—), 1:29, 4:497
Rebecca, 1:291, 1:486,
  3:217, 4:496, 4:498-502
Rebecca (—), 3:428,
  4:499
Ruth, 2:369, 2:561, 3:541,
  3:662, 4:496-500
Ruth (—), 4:193,
  4:498-499
Ruth (Fuller), 4:501
Ruth (Wood), 4:500, 4:630
Sarah, 1:256, 1:449, 2:75,
  2:147, 2:303, 4:44,
  4:109, 4:151, 4:496-501
Sarah (—), 1:263, 4:496,
  4:498, 4:500-501
Sarah (Badger), 4:498

Sarah (Beers) Stearns,
  1:155, 4:174
Sarah (Nichols), 3:279,
  4:499
Sarah (Prescott), 3:481,
  4:499
Sarah (Sherwood), 4:498
Sarah (Stearns), 4:174
Sarah (Wise), 4:496
Susanna, 4:499
Susanna (—), 2:277
Susanna (Stowers), 4:497
Thankful, 3:481
Wheelock
Elizabeth (Bullen), 1:296
Elizabeth (French), 4:502
Elizabeth (Fuller), 4:502
Experience, 4:502
Hannah, 4:502
Hannah (Stodder), 4:202,
  4:502
Lydia (Rice), 3:529
Mercy (Standish), 4:162
Rebecca, 1:469, 4:502
Rebecca (—), 4:502
Record, 4:502
Ruth (Huntington), 4:162
Sarah, 3:557
Wheelwright
—, 2:512, 3:543, 3:544,
  4:503
— (Hutchinson), 2:512
Catharine, 2:512, 3:260,
  3:263, 4:502-503
Elizabeth, 2:512, 3:361,
  4:503
Esther (Houchin), 2:468,
  4:504
Hannah, 1:369, 2:512,
  4:503
Mary, 1:75, 2:513, 3:133,
  4:502-503
Mary (Hutchinson), 2:508,
  2:513, 4:502
Rebecca, 1:230, 2:512,
  3:181, 4:503
Sarah, 1:473, 2:512, 3:544,
  4:503, 4:503
Sarah (—), 2:508
Susanna, 2:513
Whelan
Mary, 3:653

Whelden/Wheldon
Catharine, 2:461, 4:504
Margaret (----), 4:504
Sarah, 4:504
Whelpley
Deborah (----), 4:504
Rebecca, 4:504
Rebecca (Bulkley), 1:292, 4:504
Sarah, 4:504
Sarah (----), 3:2, 4:504
Whetstone
---- (Cromwell), 2:567
Hannah (----), 3:105
Mercy, 4:505
Whidden
Elizabeth, 4:505
Jane (----), 4:505
Sarah, 4:505
Sarah (----), 4:505
Whight
Mary, 2:250
Whinyard
Hannah (Gold), 2:588
Whipple
Abigail, 2:463, 4:505-506
Abigail (Jenks), 2:543
Alice, 4:505-507
Alice (Angell), 1:57, 4:505
Alice (Smith), 4:506
Amphillis, 4:506
Ann, 4:506
Deborah, 4:505
Deliverance, 4:506
Dorothy, 4:506
Elizabeth, 3:466, 4:505-506
Elizabeth (Eddy), 2:99, 4:507
Elizabeth (Paine), 4:506
Elizabeth (Woodman), 4:506
Elnathan, 3:529, 4:506
Experience (Hinckley), 2:425, 4:505
Freelove, 4:506
Hannah, 4:505
Hannah (Tower), 4:505
Hope, 4:507
Jemima (Lane), 3:52, 4:506-507
Jennet (----), 4:505
Joanna (Appleton), 1:61

Lydia (Hoar), 2:594
Margaret, 4:505
Margery, 4:506
Margery (----), 4:506
Martha, 1:275
Martha (Denison), 2:37
Martha (Reyner), 3:513, 4:506
Mary, 1:334, 3:313, 4:209, 4:505-506
Mary (Bartholomew), 1:130, 2:589, 4:506
Mary (Olney), 3:313, 4:506
Rebecca (Scott), 4:506
Rose (----), 4:506
Ruth, 4:505
Ruth (Matthewson), 3:177, 4:505
Sarah, 2:272, 4:89, 4:382, 4:500, 4:505
Sarah (----), 4:505-506
Susanna, 3:53, 3:437, 4:505-506, 4:652-653
Whippo
Abigail (Hammond) Greenough, 2:346, 4:507
Elizabeth, 4:507
Jane, 4:507
Margaret, 4:507
Martha, 4:507
Whiston
Sarah, 3:282
Susanna, 3:401
Whitaker/Whitacre
Elizabeth, 4:507
Elizabeth (----), 4:507
Mehitable, 4:507
Whitcomb/Whetcumbe
Abigail, 4:507-508
Catharine, 2:114, 4:507
Damaris, 4:508
Elizabeth, 4:508
Elizabeth (Buck), 1:284
Frances (----), 4:507
Hannah, 4:508
Hannah (----), 4:508
Jemima, 3:111, 4:507
Joanna, 4:508
Mary, 4:507-508
Mary (----), 4:507
Mary (Cudworth), 1:482, 4:508

Rebecca, 4:508
Rebecca (----), 4:507-508
Ruth, 4:508
Sarah, 4:508
White
--- (French), 2:205
Abigail, 2:476, 4:508-510
Abigail (----) Lord, 3:117, 4:514
Abigail (Mather) Blake, 3:173
Abigail (Rogers), 3:562
Ann, 2:392, 4:508-509, 4:511-512, 4:514
Ann (----), 3:417, 4:510, 4:514
Ann (----) Jones, 4:513, 4:633, 4:686
Bridget (----), 4:513
Catharine (----), 4:509, 4:515
Charity, 4:516
Deborah, 4:509
Deborah (Shepard), 4:75, 4:509
Dorcas, 4:513, 4:515
Elizabeth, 1:51, 1:83, 1:342, 3:13, 3:114, 3:439, 4:457, 4:508-509, 4:511-515
Elizabeth (----), 4:509, 4:511-512, 4:515
Elizabeth (----) Withington, 4:510, 4:619
Elizabeth (Bowles), 1:224, 4:511
Elizabeth (Bunce), 1:298, 4:509
Elizabeth (Chamberlain), 4:515
Elizabeth (Herbert), 1:488
Elizabeth (Humphrey), 2:497
Elizabeth (Savage), 4:513
Esther, 2:115
Esther (Strong), 4:228
Eunice, 4:512
Eunice (----) Kingsbury, 4:510
Experience, 4:509-510, 4:512, 4:514
Frances (----), 2:423
Grace (Hall), 4:508

White (continued)
Hannah, 1:141, 4:508-514
Hannah (----), 4:512
Hannah (French), 3:409,
4:511
Hannah (Hunt), 4:508
Hannah (Phillips), 3:413,
4:509
Hannah (Smith), 4:511
Hannah (Wells), 4:512
Jerusha, 4:509, 4:512
Joan, 4:511
Joan (Calverly), 4:45
Joanna, 4:508
Judith (Vassall), 4:367,
4:514
Lydia, 4:509, 4:512, 4:514
Lydia (Gilman), 2:258
Lydia (Rogers), 3:561,
4:512
Lydia (Sampson), 4:509
Margery (----), 2:391
Martha, 2:477, 4:509-512,
4:515
Martha (----), 4:509
Martha (Coit) Mould,
1:422, 3:247, 4:512
Martha (Montague)
Harrison, 3:225
Martha (Proctor), 3:489
Mary, 1:459, 2:230, 2:250,
2:443, 2:460, 3:13,
3:288, 3:581, 4:169,
4:354, 4:476, 4:508-515
Mary (----), 4:510-511,
4:516
Mary (Beck), 1:150
Mary (Dyer), 4:514
Mary (Frothingham),
2:213, 4:515
Mary (Mould), 3:247,
4:512
Mary (Pratt), 4:515
Mary (Rice), 3:531
Mary (Rishworth), 3:544,
4:503
Mary (Rowlandson), 4:511
Mary (Swift), 4:241
Mary (Weeks), 4:454,
4:509
Mehitable, 4:508
Mehitable (Adams), 1:13
Mercy, 4:85, 4:513

Philippa (Wood), 4:515
Rachel, 4:509, 4:514
Rachel (----), 4:514
Rebecca, 4:509-510
Rebecca (----) Ranney,
4:510
Rebecca (Bemis), 1:163,
2:360, 4:511
Remembrance (----), 4:712
Return, 4:509
Ruth, 4:509, 4:515
Ruth (----), 4:510-511,
4:515
Ruth (Burrage), 1:510,
4:509
Ruth (Edmunds), 2:581
Sarah, 1:94, 1:436, 2:411,
2:427, 2:467, 3:114,
4:264, 4:508-515, 4:671
Sarah (----) Foster, 4:516
Sarah (Baker), 1:501,
4:510
Sarah (Bassett), 1:136,
4:513
Sarah (Bunce), 1:298,
4:511, 4:653
Sarah (Crow), 1:479,
4:508
Sarah (Rumery), 4:516
Submit, 4:509
Susanna, 4:508-509, 4:511,
4:514
Susanna (----), 2:408,
4:514-515, 4:599
Susanna (Cogswell), 4:508
Susanna (Humphrey),
2:497, 4:513
Susanna (Miller), 4:515
Susanna (Mould), 3:247,
4:508
Thankful, 4:510-511,
4:514
Ursilla/Ursula (Macomber),
4:513
Whitehead
Abigail (Stephenson),
4:182, 4:516
Damaris, 4:516
Elizabeth, 4:516
Grace, 4:516
Hannah, 4:356, 4:516
Joanna, 1:269
Martha, 4:516

Martha (Bradfield), 4:516
Mary, 4:516
Mary (----), 4:517
Mary (----) Hopkins, 2:462,
3:89, 4:516
Mary (Brown), 1:509
Mehitable (Bishop), 1:186
Mercy, 1:173, 3:128, 4:2,
4:516
Sarah, 4:516
Sarah (Gregson) Gilbert,
2:250, 2:316, 4:517
Susanna, 4:516, 4:700,
4:713
Tabitha (----), 4:517
Whitehouse
---- (Pomfret), 3:452,
4:517
Whiterig
Abigail, 1:503
Whitfield
---- (Sheaffe), 4:66
Abigail, 4:517
Sarah, 2:413, 4:517
Whitford
Bridget, 4:445
Bridget (----), 4:517
Whitham
Sarah (Somes), 4:517
Whiting
----, 2:434, 4:522
---- (Gay), 2:237
---- (St. John), 4:520
Abigail, 2:71, 3:594, 4:518,
4:520
Alice, 4:519
Alice (Cook), 1:448, 4:189,
4:519
Ann, 3:334, 3:620,
4:519-521
Ann (Allyn), 1:43, 4:519
Ann (Danforth), 2:7, 4:520
Dorcas (Chester), 1:375,
4:521
Dorothy, 4:473, 4:520-521
Elizabeth, 1:402, 3:440,
4:518-521, 4:684
Elizabeth (Adams), 4:521
Elizabeth (Barlow), 1:502
Eunice, 4:519, 4:521
Hannah, 4:519-520
Hannah (----), 4:520
Hannah (Dwight), 2:85,

327

Whiting (continued)
  Hannah (Dwight)
  (continued)
    4:519
  Hannah (Trowbridge),
    4:333, 4:519
  Jerusha, 4:587
  Margaret, 4:519
  Martha, 1:282, 4:518,
    4:521
  Mary, 1:436, 2:368, 4:70,
    4:518-522
  Mary (----), 2:169
  Mary (Allyn), 1:43, 4:522
  Mary (Billings), 4:519
  Mary (Pynchon), 3:498,
    4:519
  Phebe, 4:519
  Phebe (Gregson), 2:316,
    4:518
  Rebecca (Hackett), 2:326
  Sarah, 1:293, 3:25, 3:259,
    4:145, 4:518-520, 4:522
  Sarah (Danforth), 4:519
  Sarah (Metcalf), 3:204,
    4:521
  Sibyl/Sybil (Collins), 1:434,
    4:518
  Susanna, 4:519
  Susanna (----), 4:521
  Sybil, 1:282, 4:518, 4:521
Whitlock
  Rose, 3:349
Whitman
  Abiah, 4:523
  Abigail, 4:523-524
  Abigail (Burnham), 4:523
  Abigail (Byram), 1:326,
    4:524
  Abigail (Hollis), 4:523
  Ann, 4:523
  Christina (Farrar), 4:524
  Deborah, 4:523
  Deborah (Richards), 4:523
  Dorothy, 4:524
  Dorothy (----), 4:524
  Elinor, 4:523
  Elizabeth, 2:304,
    4:523-524
  Experience, 4:523
  Hannah, 2:207, 4:523-524
  Hannah (Knight), 4:524
  Joanna, 4:525

Judith, 4:523
Lydia, 4:523
Mary, 3:67, 3:472-473,
  4:523-525
Mary (----), 4:524
Mary (Cary), 4:524
Mary (Conant), 4:524
Mary (Ford), 4:523
Mary (Pratt), 4:523
Mary (Richards), 4:524
Naomi, 4:139, 4:524
Ruth, 4:523-524
Ruth (Reed), 4:523
Sarah, 3:177, 4:523-525
Sarah (----), 4:524-525
Sarah (Alcock), 1:22,
  4:525
Sarah (Bartlett), 4:524
Sarah (Vining), 4:524
Silence, 4:523
Susanna, 4:524, 4:573
Susanna (----), 4:524
Whitmarsh
  Alice, 4:525-526
  Bathsheba (----), 4:525
  Christian (----), 4:525
  Deborah, 4:525
  Elizabeth, 4:525
  Elizabeth (----), 4:525
  Hannah, 4:525
  Hannah (----), 4:525
  Jane, 4:525
  Judith, 4:525
  Mary, 4:525-526
  Mary (----), 4:525
  Mercy (Read/Reed), 3:520
  Ruth, 4:525-526
  Sarah, 4:525
  Sarah (----), 4:525
  Sarah (Holbrook), 2:442
  Susanna, 4:525
Whitmore/Wetmore
  ---- (----) Jessup, 4:526
  Abigail, 4:526-528, 4:547
  Abigail (Warner), 4:527
  Ann, 2:146, 4:526-527
  Beriah, 4:526, 4:528
  Bethia, 4:526-527
  Catharine (Roberts), 4:528
  Deborah, 4:527
  Dorcas (----) Allen, 4:527
  Edith, 4:526
  Elizabeth, 1:18-19, 3:152,

4:526-528
Elizabeth (Hubbard), 4:528
Esther, 4:527
Frances, 4:526
Hannah, 4:526, 4:528
Hannah (Harris), 3:629,
  4:526
Hope, 4:526
Isabel, 4:526
Isabel (Park), 4:526
Lydia, 4:527
Lydia (Bacon), 4:527
Margaret, 1:342, 4:526
Margaret (Harty), 4:526
Margaret (Stow), 4:526
Margery, 4:526
Martha, 4:526
Mary, 1:244, 4:526-528
Mary (----), 4:528
Mary (----) Watson), 4:527
Mary (Allen), 4:526
Mary (Bacon), 4:527
Mary (Butterfield) Watson,
  4:436
Mary (Kendall), 4:527
Mary (Platt) Atkinson,
  1:74, 4:528
Mary (Savage), 4:24,
  4:527
Mehitable, 4:527-528
Rachel (Eliot) Poulter,
  2:109, 3:469, 4:527
Rachel (Stow), 4:526
Rebecca, 4:527
Rebecca (Cutler), 4:527
Rebecca (Gardner), 4:527
Sarah, 3:103, 4:526-528
Sarah (Hall), 2:334, 4:528
Whitnell
  Elizabeth (----) Mitchell,
    3:221, 4:528
Whitney
  Abigail, 1:141, 4:528,
    4:530-532
  Abigail (----), 4:531
  Abigail (Bridge), 1:248
  Abigail (Hagar), 2:328,
    4:528
  Abigail (Tarbell), 4:531
  Alice, 4:531
  Ann, 4:530
  Ann/Hannah, 2:162
  Deborah, 4:531

Whitney (continued)
Dorothy, 4:529
Dorothy (Ross), 3:577, 4:529
Elinor, 4:530
Elinor (----), 4:529
Elizabeth, 4:423, 4:528-532
Elizabeth (----), 4:528, 4:531
Elizabeth (Harris), 2:363, 4:530
Elizabeth (Lawrence), 3:61, 4:532
Elizabeth (Smith), 4:530
Esther (Poor), 4:528
Grace, 4:531
Hannah, 4:529-531
Hepzibah, 4:531
Jane, 4:528
Jane (----), 4:528
Joanna, 4:531
Judith (Clement), 4:529
Lydia, 1:14, 4:530
Lydia (----), 4:531
Lydia (Jones), 2:564, 4:530
Martha, 4:530-532
Martha (Beach), 1:144, 4:530
Martha (Coldham), 4:531
Martha (Walker), 4:530
Mary, 4:529-532
Mary (----), 4:531
Mary (Bemis), 1:163, 4:532
Mary (Hapgood), 2:352, 4:530
Mary (Kedell/Keedell), 3:2, 4:532
Mary (Poor), 4:528
Mercy, 4:531
Mercy (Travis), 4:528
Rebecca, 4:531
Rebecca (Burge), 4:531
Ruhamah, 4:531
Ruth, 3:61, 4:61, 4:528-530
Ruth (Reynolds), 3:526, 4:529
Sarah, 2:359, 4:529-532
Sarah (Hagar), 2:328, 4:531

Sarah (Hapgood), 2:352, 4:530
Sarah (Haven), 2:379, 4:530
Sarah (Knight), 4:531
Sarah (Woodward), 4:529
Susanna, 4:532
Tabitha, 4:530
Winifred (----), 4:532
Whiton/Whitton/Whitten
Abigail, 4:532
Abigail (----), 4:532
Audry (----), 4:533
Bethia, 4:532
Deborah (----) Howard, 4:533
Elizabeth, 4:533
Hannah, 4:532
Jael, 4:533
Joanna, 4:533
Joanna (Garnett), 2:233
Joanna (May) Gardner, 2:147, 2:227, 4:533
Judith, 4:532
Leah, 4:533
Lydia, 4:533
Margaret, 4:532
Mary, 4:532-533, 4:549
Mary (Beal), 1:145, 4:532
Mary (Kedell/Keedell), 4:532
Mary (Lincoln), 3:93, 4:532
Rachel, 4:533
Rebecca, 4:532
Susanna, 4:533
Whitred/Whitridge/etc
Charity (----), 4:533
Elizabeth (----), 4:533
Florence (----), 4:533
Mary, 2:368
Mary (Bulkley), 4:676
Rebecca, 1:410, 4:533
Susanna (----) Colby, 1:424, 4:533
Whittemore/Whitamore
---- (Upham), 4:535
Abiel, 4:534
Abigail, 4:534-535
Ann, 4:534
Elizabeth, 4:533-535, 4:598
Elizabeth (----), 2:188,

2:584, 4:534
Elizabeth (Annable), 4:534
Elizabeth (Bucknam), 1:287, 4:533
Elizabeth (Pierce), 4:535
Esther, 4:533
Esther (Brooks), 1:261, 4:533
Experience, 4:534
Grace, 4:533
Hannah, 3:280, 4:533-535
Hannah (----), 1:322, 4:535, 4:713
Huldah, 4:534
Isabel (Parke), 3:347
Joanna, 4:534
Joanna (Mousall), 4:534
Lydia, 4:534
Lydia (Bassett), 4:534
Margery, 4:535
Margery (Pepperell), 3:392, 4:535
Martha, 4:535
Mary, 4:533-535
Mary (----), 4:535
Mary (----) Pease, 4:535
Mary (Mellen), 4:533-534
Mary (Miller), 3:209, 4:534
Mary (Upham), 4:360, 4:534
Mehitable, 4:533
Rebecca, 4:534-535
Sarah, 4:534-535
Sarah (----), 4:534-535, 4:713
Sarah (Hall), 2:337
Susanna, 4:533-535
Susanna (Frost), 4:534
Whittier
Mary, 3:330, 4:536
Mary (----) Ring, 4:536
Mary (Osgood), 4:536
Mary (Peaslee), 3:380, 4:536
Ruth, 4:335, 4:536
Ruth (----), 4:536
Whittingham
Elizabeth, 1:62, 3:373, 4:536-537
Judith, 4:536
Martha, 1:396, 3:563, 4:536-537

Whittingham (continued)
Martha (Hubbard), 2:133,
2:486, 4:536
Mary, 4:537
Mary (Lawrence), 3:62,
4:536
Whittlesey
Hannah, 4:537
Lydia (Way), 4:440
Martha (Jones), 2:565
Mary, 4:537
Mary (Pratt), 4:537
Rebecca, 4:537
Rebecca (Waterhouse),
4:537
Ruth, 4:537
Ruth (Dudley), 2:78, 4:537
Sarah, 4:537
Whitwell
Joanna (----), 4:537
Mary (----), 4:537
Wickenden
Hannah, 4:181, 4:538
Plain, 4:538, 4:552
Ruth, 4:135, 4:538
Wickham/Wickum/Wicom/etc
Ann, 4:538
Barbara (Holden), 2:445,
4:538
Mary, 4:538
Mary (----), 4:538
Sarah, 4:538
Sarah (----), 4:538
Sarah (Churchill), 1:387
Sarah (Satterly/Shatterly),
4:20
Wicks - see also Weeks
Alice (----), 4:539
Ann, 4:538-539
Ann/Hannah, 1:315
Bethia, 4:539
Elizabeth, 3:626, 4:319,
4:538-539
Hannah, 4:539
Isabel (Harcut), 2:353,
4:539
Mary, 2:259, 4:538-539
Mary (----), 4:538
Mary (Lynde), 3:136
Mercy (Call) Lee, 1:330
Mercy (Lee), 3:73, 4:539
Rose (Townsend), 4:318,
4:539

Sarah, 4:539
Wickson/Wixam
Elizabeth, 3:188, 4:620
Wickwire
Ann, 4:539
Elizabeth, 4:539
Mary (Tongue), 4:312,
4:539
Wiggin
---- (Whiting), 4:522
Abigail, 4:540
Catharine (----), 4:540
Dorothy, 4:540
Hannah, 4:539
Hannah (Bradstreet),
1:236, 4:539
Mary, 2:257, 4:539-540
Sarah, 4:539-540
Sarah (Barefoot), 4:540
Susanna, 4:540
Wigglesworth
Abigail, 4:255, 4:540-542
Catharine, 4:542
Dorothy, 4:541-542
Elizabeth, 4:542
Esther, 4:54, 4:541-542
Esther (Rayner), 4:540
Martha, 4:541-542
Martha (Brown), 1:275,
4:542
Martha (Mudge), 3:252,
4:541
Mary, 4:541-542
Mary (Brintnal), 4:542
Mary (Reyner), 3:513
Mary (Rowley), 4:541
Mercy, 4:541
Phebe, 4:542
Rebecca, 4:541
Rebecca (Coolidge), 4:541
Sarah, 4:542
Sarah (Leverett), 4:541
Sybil, 4:541
Sybil/Sybell (Sparhawk),
4:144
Sybil/Sybell (Sparhawk)
Avery, 1:82, 4:541
Wight
Abigail, 4:543
Alice (----), 4:543
Ann (----), 1:295, 4:543
Ann (Dewing), 2:44
Bethia, 4:542

Deborah, 4:542-543
Deborah (Colburn), 4:543
Elizabeth, 4:543
Elizabeth (Hawes), 4:543
Esther, 4:542
Hannah, 4:543
Hannah (Albee), 1:20,
4:543
Hannah (Dewing), 4:542
Jane, 4:543
Jane (Goodenow), 2:272,
4:543
Lucy (----), 4:11
Lydia, 4:542
Lydia (Eliot) Penniman,
4:543
Lydia (Morse), 4:542
Marah, 4:543
Mary, 2:114, 4:543
Mary (Stearns), 4:543
Mehitable, 4:543
Mehitable (----), 4:543
Miriam, 4:542-543
Ruth, 4:542
Sarah, 4:543
Sarah (Avery) Metcalf,
3:204
Wigley
Mary (Miles), 3:72
Wilbor/Wilbur/Wildbore
----, 4:545
Ann, 4:544-545
Ann (Bradford), 4:544
Elizabeth, 2:202, 4:545
Elizabeth (----), 1:184,
4:544
Elizabeth (Farwell), 2:147
Hannah, 4:545
Hannah (Porter), 3:461,
4:545
Martha, 4:85, 4:545
Mary, 2:184, 4:545
Mehitable (Deane), 4:544
Rebecca, 1:279, 2:593,
4:545
Sarah, 2:432, 4:545
Wilborne
Mercy (Beamsley), 1:148,
3:401, 4:546
Wilcocks/Wilcox
----, 4:547
Abigail, 4:547
Abigail (Whitmore), 4:526,

Wilcocks/Wilcox (continued)
Abigail (Whitmore)
(continued)
4:547
Ann, 2:591, 4:546
Catharine (Stoughton),
4:546
Christian, 4:547
Elizabeth (Cook), 1:447,
4:546, 4:681
Elizabeth (Crandall), 1:471
Esther, 4:546-547
Esther (Cornwell), 1:459,
4:217, 4:547
Hannah, 4:546
Hannah (----), 4:546
Hannah (Hazard), 2:395,
4:547
Jane, 4:546
Lydia (Alling), 1:41
Mary, 4:546-547
Mary (----), 2:109,
4:546-547
Sarah, 4:546-547
Sarah (Savage), 4:546
Sarah (Wadsworth), 4:381,
4:546
Silence (Hands), 4:546
Susan, 4:547
Thankful, 4:546
Wilcockson/Wilcoxson
----, 1:302, 4:308
---- (Kelsey), 3:7
Ann (----), 4:547
Elizabeth, 3:602, 4:194,
4:547-548
Elizabeth (----) Welles,
4:547
Elizabeth (Bourne) Welles,
4:475
Elizabeth (Curtis) Welles,
1:485
Hannah, 2:143, 2:386,
3:604, 4:547-548
Janna, 4:548
Jemima, 4:548
Joanna, 4:548
Joanna (Birdseye), 1:183,
1:302, 4:548
Lydia, 4:547
Lydia (----), 4:547
Margaret, 4:547
Margaret (----), 2:387,

4:548
Mary, 4:547
Mary (----), 4:547
Mindwell, 4:548
Patience, 1:195, 4:547
Phebe, 3:603, 4:548
Rebecca, 4:548
Sarah, 3:189, 3:194, 4:548
Silence, 4:548
Silence (----), 4:547
Thankful, 4:548
Wild/Wilde/Wildes/Wylde
Alice (----), 4:549
Elizabeth, 3:230, 4:548
Elizabeth (----), 4:549
Martha, 4:548-549
Phebe, 3:615, 4:548
Priscilla, 4:548
Priscilla (Gould), 2:287,
4:548
Sarah, 1:506, 4:548-549
Sarah (----), 4:549
Wilder
Ann, 4:549
Ann (----), 4:549
Ann (Eells/Ells/Eels/Eales),
2:105
Elizabeth, 2:125, 2:150,
4:549
Elizabeth (Eames), 4:549
Hannah, 4:549
Hannah (----), 4:549
Martha (----), 4:549-550
Mary, 4:549-550
Mary (----), 4:549
Mary (Whiton), 4:532,
4:549
Mehitable, 4:425
Sarah, 4:550
Wildish
----, 2:465
Wilford
Bridget (----), 4:550
Lydia (----), 4:255, 4:550
Martha, 4:8
Wilkey/Wilkie
Elizabeth (----), 1:489,
4:550
Mary, 4:550
Wilkins
Abigail, 3:617, 4:551
Elizabeth, 4:551
Hannah (Nichols), 3:283,

4:551
Mary, 4:551
Mary (----), 4:551
Mary (Lewis) Skilling
Lewis, 3:86, 4:103
Wilkinson/Wilkeson
Abigail, 4:551
Ann (----), 4:552
Deborah (----), 4:551
Elizabeth, 2:151, 4:551
Freelove, 4:551
Hannah, 4:551
Isabel (----), 4:552
Jane, 2:53, 4:552, 4:597
Jemima, 4:551
Joanna, 4:552
Margaret, 2:267, 4:552
Mercy, 4:551
Plain (Wickenden), 4:538,
4:552
Prudence (----), 1:287,
2:151, 4:551
Rebecca, 4:551
Rebecca (Scott), 4:551
Rebecca (Smith), 4:116,
4:551
Rebecca (Winsor) Leverett,
4:604
Ruth, 2:463, 4:551-552
Sarah, 4:551
Susanna, 2:472, 2:593,
4:552
Susanna (Smith), 4:111,
4:552
Tabitha, 1:186
Thankful, 4:551
Wilks/Wilkes
Joan (----), 4:550
Mary, 4:550, 4:635
Willard/Willerd
Abigail, 2:126, 4:328,
4:553-554
Abigail (Sherman), 4:82,
4:554
Abovehope, 4:555
Ann, 4:553
Ann (Wilder), 4:549
Deborah, 4:46, 4:553
Dorcas (----), 1:162
Dorcas (Cutler), 4:553
Dorothy, 4:552, 4:554-555
Elizabeth, 1:205, 3:531,
4:553-555

Willard/Willerd (continued)
Elizabeth (----) Walley,
4:555
Elizabeth (Alden) Walley,
1:23, 4:400
Elizabeth (Dunster), 2:82,
4:555
Elizabeth (Phelps), 3:405
Esther, 4:552
Esther (Matthews), 4:552,
4:702
Eunice, 4:554
Eunice (Tyng), 4:357,
4:554
Hannah, 1:255, 4:552-555
Hannah (Cutler), 4:552
Hannah (Hosmer), 2:467,
4:554
Hepzibah, 4:553
Margaret, 4:552, 4:554
Margery, 2:16
Martha, 4:555
Martha (Jacob), 4:555
Mary, 2:581, 3:195, 4:184,
4:553-555
Mary (----), 3:297
Mary (Brown), 1:277,
4:553
Mary (Dunster), 2:82,
4:555
Mary (Hayward), 4:553
Mary (Lakin), 3:46, 4:553
Mary (Mills), 4:553
Mary (Sharpe), 4:555
Mary (White), 4:508
Mehitable, 4:553
Mercy, 4:553
Priscilla (Buttolph), 4:555
Sarah, 2:472, 4:552-555
Sarah (Bartlett), 1:131
Sarah (Lakin), 3:46, 4:552
Susanna, 4:553
Tabitha, 4:553
Willet
Abigail, 1:185, 4:556
Abigail (Collins), 1:434,
2:346, 4:556
Ann, 4:556
Ann (Brown), 4:556
Dinah (Townsend), 4:319
Eleanor (Adams), 4:556
Elinor (Adams), 1:11
Elizabeth (----) Wakeman,

4:387, 4:556
Elizabeth (Hunt), 2:501,
4:556
Elizabeth (Lowell), 4:556
Esther, 2:174, 4:557
Hannah, 4:556
Hannah (Brown), 1:270
Joanna, 1:185, 3:617
Joanna (----) Prudden,
4:557
Joanna (Boyse) Prudden,
3:492
Judith, 4:556
Martha, 1:270, 4:3,
4:556-557
Martha (Silver), 4:98,
4:556
Mary, 2:458, 4:556-557,
4:698
Mary (Brown), 1:269-270,
4:557
Mary (Edes), 3:617
Rebecca, 3:508, 4:556-557
Ruth, 4:556, 4:558
Sarah, 2:110, 4:16,
4:556-557
Susanna (Holbrook), 2:443,
4:555
Willey
Abigail (Pitman), 4:558
Alice, 2:234
Alice (----), 4:557
Ann (----) Lester, 4:558
Elizabeth (Mortimer),
3:242, 4:557
Elizabeth (Willis), 4:558,
4:574
Frances (----), 3:215
Frances (Burcham), 1:300,
4:558
Frances (Marshall), 2:476
Hannah, 1:198, 1:507,
2:498, 4:149, 4:558
Isabel, 4:558
Jane, 4:557
Margaret (----), 4:558
Margaret (Winthrop) Ward,
4:613
Mary, 4:337, 4:558
Mary (----), 4:558
Miriam, 4:558
Miriam (Moore), 3:229,
4:558

Ruth, 4:558, 4:574
Sarah, 4:268, 4:306, 4:558
William
Joan (----) Ames, 1:49
Williams, 4:570
—, 4:571
—— (Bliss), 1:202, 4:571
---- (Hart), 4:560
Abiel, 4:561, 4:565
Abigail, 2:590, 3:460,
4:561, 4:563, 4:565,
4:569
Abigail (----), 4:570
Abigail (Allen), 4:563
Abigail (Allyn) Bissell,
1:186
Abigail (Cloyce), 1:411
Alice (----), 4:571
Ann, 1:115, 4:561-562,
4:571
Ann (----), 4:561
Ann (Alcock), 1:22, 4:562
Anstis, 4:563
Arabella, 4:562
Bathsheba, 4:565
Bathsheba (----), 4:566
Bethia, 3:661, 4:559-560,
4:570-571
Bethia (Parsons)
Mascall/Maskell, 3:166,
3:364, 4:562
Catharine, 4:570
Catharine (----) Carter,
1:238, 1:340, 4:559
Damaris, 4:571
Deborah, 3:625, 4:425,
4:569
Dorothy (Weld) Denison,
2:38, 4:473, 4:570
Elizabeth, 1:182, 1:396,
2:419, 3:149, 3:494,
4:257, 4:558-565, 4:567,
4:569-572
Elizabeth (----), 4:559,
4:561
Elizabeth (Cotton), 1:464
Elizabeth (Jackson), 2:527
Elizabeth (Rogers), 3:562,
4:564
Elizabeth (Stratton), 4:566
Elizabeth (Tart), 4:257
Elizabeth (Watson), 4:437,
4:563

Williams (continued)
Esther, 4:563
Esther (----) Bond, 4:563
Esther (----) Egglestone,
4:562
Esther (Blakely) Bond,
1:209
Eunice, 4:563
Eunice (Mather), 3:172,
4:563
Frances (----), 4:567
Frances (Dighton), 4:565
Freeborn, 1:403, 1:472,
2:368, 4:569
Grace, 4:570
Hannah, 1:110, 3:360,
4:122, 4:559-562,
4:564-565, 4:570-571
Hannah (----), 4:559
Hannah (Geer), 2:239
Hepzibah, 4:561, 4:567
Jane, 4:572
Jane (----), 4:561
Jane (Gilbert), 2:251,
4:570
Jane (Latham) Hubbard,
2:484, 4:563
Jane (Westover), 4:571
Joanna, 4:572
Joanna (----), 4:571
Joanna (Lynn), 3:137,
4:572
Joanna (Ward), 4:558
Judith (Cooper), 4:560
Keziah, 4:565
Leah (Townsend), 4:319
Lydia, 4:558, 4:561, 4:564
Lydia (----), 4:563
Lydia (Bates), 1:138,
4:567
Lydia (Olney), 3:313,
4:564
Margaret (----), 3:285
Margaret (----) Fearing,
2:150, 4:566
Margaret (Stephenson),
4:182, 4:572
Margery (----), 4:561,
4:567
Martha, 2:501, 4:559-560,
4:562, 4:565, 4:567,
4:569-570
Martha (Hall), 2:337,

4:559
Martha (Parke), 3:349,
4:560
Martha (Strong), 4:566
Martha (Tuf), 4:572
Mary, 1:233, 1:383, 2:57,
2:323, 2:515, 2:545,
3:328, 4:98, 4:377,
4:559-567, 4:569-572,
4:628
Mary (----), 1:229, 3:4,
4:371, 4:560, 4:562,
4:564, 4:568-569, 4:571
Mary
(Burkly/Brelly/Burleigh),
4:561
Mary (Fuller), 2:218,
4:564
Mary (Holden), 2:445-446,
4:571
Mary (Lowell), 4:571
Mary (Miller), 4:572
Mary (Oliver) Shrimpton,
3:310, 4:91
Mary (Owen), 3:326,
4:565
Mary (Palfrey), 3:339
Mary (Veren), 4:569
Mary (Wheeler), 4:559
Mehitable, 4:563, 4:571
Mercy, 3:313, 3:526,
4:432, 4:563, 4:569,
4:571, 4:605
Naomi, 4:565
Orpha, 4:565
Patience, 4:559
Phebe, 2:106, 4:563,
4:565-566
Priscilla (----), 4:565
Providence, 4:559, 4:569
Rachel, 4:562
Rachel (----), 4:559
Rebecca, 2:522, 4:559,
4:561, 4:563, 4:565,
4:571
Rebecca (----), 4:559,
4:571
Rebecca (Colby), 1:424,
4:562
Rebecca (Macy), 3:142,
4:559
Rebecca (Rhodes) Power,
3:470, 4:559

Ruth, 3:494, 4:561, 4:564,
4:571-572
Ruth (----), 4:559
Ruth (Bradley), 1:233
Sarah, 1:84, 2:28, 4:177,
4:264, 4:560-565,
4:569-572
Sarah (----), 4:560, 4:572
Sarah (Browning), 1:279,
4:563
Sarah (Coytemore),
1:467-468
Sarah (Geer), 4:559
Sarah (Hammond), 4:559
Sarah (Manning), 3:147,
4:563
Sarah (May), 3:183, 4:570
Sarah (Richardson), 3:538,
4:561
Sarah (Taylor), 4:264
Sarah (Wise), 4:570, 4:615
Selina, 4:559
Susanna, 4:558, 4:563,
4:571
Susanna (----), 4:564
Theoda, 4:559, 4:565,
4:569-570
Theoda (Park), 3:349,
4:569
Williamson
Abigail, 4:573
Ann, 4:573
Experience, 4:262, 4:573
Joanna, 4:573
Martha, 4:572-573
Mary, 2:226, 4:106,
4:572-573
Mary (----), 4:163, 4:573
Mary (Cobb), 4:572
Mary (Howland), 2:478,
4:573
Mercy, 4:572-573
Ruhama (Clark), 1:400
Sarah, 4:572-573
Willing
Margaret, 3:536
Willis
---- (----) Palfrey, 3:339
---- (Lincoln), 4:575
Abigail, 1:177, 4:576-577
Amy, 4:574
Amy (Glass), 2:260, 4:574
Ann (----), 4:576

Willis (continued)
Bethia, 4:576
Bridget, 2:512
Bridget (Hutchinson),
2:513
Deliverance, 4:576
Elizabeth, 4:558,
4:573-575
Elizabeth (—), 4:574,
4:576
Elizabeth (Boulton), 1:217
Elizabeth (Hobart), 4:574
Elizabeth (Hodgkins)
Palmer, 2:439, 3:343,
4:575
Esther, 2:354
Experience, 4:575
Experience (Byram), 1:326,
4:575
Experience (Newell),
3:271
Grace, 2:338
Grace (—), 4:577
Hannah, 2:393, 4:47,
4:575-577
Hannah (Eliot), 2:109,
4:577
Hannah (Else), 4:575
Hannah (Munnings),
3:256, 4:575
Hester, 4:574
Jane, 2:335-336, 4:577
Jane (—), 4:575
Jane (—) Palfrey, 4:574
Joan (—), 4:576
Joanna, 4:576
Judith, 4:574, 4:713
Lucy, 4:578
Lydia, 1:362, 1:410, 4:313,
4:576-578
Lydia (—), 4:576
Mabel, 4:574
Mary, 3:377, 4:574-577,
4:713
Mary (—), 4:574
Mary (Blake), 1:194
Mary (Makepeace), 3:144,
4:576
Mercy (—), 4:574
Mildred (—), 4:576
Patience (Bonham), 1:210,
4:577
Rebecca, 4:48, 4:577

Ruth, 4:574
Ruth (Haynes), 4:577
Ruth (Symmes), 4:244,
4:573
Sarah, 1:49, 4:575-577
Sarah (—), 4:577
Sarah (Lincoln), 3:94
Susanna, 4:573
Susanna (Whitman), 4:524,
4:573
Temperance, 4:574, 4:576
Williston/Willingstone
Beulah, 4:578
Consider, 4:578
Hannah, 4:578
Hannah (Stebbins), 4:578
Margaret, 4:578
Mary, 4:578
Mary (Parsons) Ashley,
3:363, 4:578
Mary Ann, 4:578
Miriam, 4:578
Miriam (Stebbins), 4:578
Phebe, 4:578
Sarah, 4:578
Sarah (—), 4:578
Sarah (—) Stebbins, 4:578
Willix
Mary (—) Hawksworth,
2:382, 4:578
Willoughby
—, 1:332, 4:579
— (Gardner), 2:227
Abigail, 4:579
Abigail (Bartholomew),
1:129, 4:579
Elizabeth, 4:579, 4:713
Grizzel (—), 4:579
Hannah, 4:578
Jerinnah, 4:578
Margaret (—), 2:346,
4:578
Mary, 1:134, 4:579
Mary (—), 4:578
Sarah, 4:578-579
Sarah (—), 4:578
Sarah (Walley) Chauncy,
4:400
Susanna, 3:136, 4:578-579
Wills
— (Abbot), 1:5
Abigail (Ingersoll) Rix,
3:545, 4:579

Azubah/Zubah (Lamson),
3:50, 4:579
Elizabeth, 3:640
Elizabeth (Neighbors),
3:267
Hannah, 4:579
Hannah (Buckland), 4:579
Joanna, 1:495, 4:579
Lucy (Treworgy) Chad-
bourne, 1:350, 4:579
Lydia, 1:362, 4:313
Sarah, 1:5
Susanna, 4:579
Wilmot/Wilmarth/etc
—, 4:581
— (Brown), 4:580
Abigail, 1:8, 4:580-581
Ann, 1:300, 4:580-581
Dorothy, 4:580
Elizabeth, 2:217, 3:222,
3:509, 4:580-581, 4:691
Elizabeth (—), 2:577
Elizabeth (—) Heaton,
4:580
Esther, 4:580
Esther (Peck), 3:381,
4:580
Hannah, 1:14, 3:207,
4:580-581
Mary, 3:557, 4:580-581,
4:681
Mary (—), 4:580-581
Mary (Chedsey), 1:370
Mary (Robinson), 4:581
Mary/Mercy, 4:580
Mehitable, 4:580-581
Rachel (Read), 4:581
Rebecca, 4:580
Ruth, 4:580
Sarah, 3:635, 4:580-581
Sarah (—), 4:123
Sarah (Ruggles), 3:586,
4:580
Sarah (Thomas), 4:280,
4:581
Tabitha, 4:581
Wilson
—, 3:438, 3:560, 4:589
— (Buffum), 1:289, 4:588
— (Hooker), 3:416
— (Sallows), 4:5, 4:582
Abigail, 2:415, 2:529,
4:204, 4:583, 4:585-589

Wilson (continued)
Abigail (Osgood), 3:320,
 4:589
Alice, 4:583
Ann, 1:515, 2:505, 4:474,
 4:582-583
Ann (----), 3:76, 3:621,
 4:582, 4:588-589
Ann (Lambert), 3:48
Bethia (----), 4:581
Bridget, 4:584
Catharine, 4:582
Damaris, 4:581
Deborah, 4:424, 4:581,
 4:583, 4:588-589
Deborah (----), 4:583
Deborah (Stephenson),
 4:182, 4:588
Deliverance, 4:586
Deliverance (----), 4:586
Dorcas, 1:406
Dorcas (Randall), 4:585
Elizabeth, 4:473,
 4:582-583, 4:585-586,
 4:588
Elizabeth (----), 4:583,
 4:589
Elizabeth (----) Warren
 Sendall Hayward, 2:392,
 4:51, 4:425, 4:587
Elizabeth (Crow) Warren,
 1:479
Elizabeth (Mansfield),
 3:148
Elizabeth (Osland), 3:323,
 4:586-587
Elizabeth (Pierce), 4:588
Elizabeth (Stebbins), 1:328,
 4:175, 4:588
Elizabeth/Isabel, 4:588
Esther (----), 4:582
Experience, 4:586, 4:589
Experience (Trowbridge),
 4:332, 4:589
Grace (----), 4:582
Hannah, 3:429, 3:582,
 4:47, 4:581, 4:583,
 4:585-589
Hannah (----), 4:581, 4:589
Hannah (Crafts), 1:469,
 4:586
Hannah (Jackson), 2:528,
 4:586

Isabel, 3:407, 4:588
Jane, 2:569
Jane (----), 4:588
Jezabel, 4:588
Joanna, 4:582
Judith, 4:583
Judith (Hersey), 2:407,
 4:583
Lydia, 4:164, 4:589
Lydia (Cole), 1:428, 4:585
Lydia (Stebbins), 4:175
Margaret, 4:586, 4:589
Mary, 1:239, 2:8, 2:350,
 2:547, 3:231, 3:311,
 4:499, 4:581-589
Mary (----), 4:583,
 4:586-587
Mary (Griffin), 2:313,
 4:588
Mary (Hale), 2:330, 4:582
Mary (Lovejoy), 3:122,
 4:585
Mary (Metcalf), 3:203,
 4:583
Mary (Richardson), 4:586
Mary (Sanford), 4:15,
 4:587
Mercy, 4:581
Mindwell, 4:588
Newgrace, 4:589
Patience (----), 4:589
Phebe (Middlebrook),
 3:205, 4:588
Priscilla, 4:590
Priscilla (Purchase), 3:494,
 4:590
Rachel (----) Brandish,
 4:581
Rachel (----) Brandisly,
 1:238
Rachel (----) Brundish,
 1:281
Rebecca, 4:582, 4:586-588
Rebecca (Sumner), 4:582
Relief, 4:587
Rose (Knowles), 3:42
Ruth, 3:361
Ruth (Duntlen), 4:582
Sarah, 2:480, 4:333,
 4:581-583, 4:585-586,
 4:588, 4:590
Sarah (----), 3:603, 4:582,
 4:585

Sarah (Baxter), 1:503
Sarah (Blood), 1:204
Sarah (Hooker), 2:459
Sarah (Hurst), 4:588
Sarah (Jones) Bulkley,
 1:292, 2:562, 4:581-582
Sarah (Kilcup), 3:21
Sarah (Lord), 4:585
Sarah (Newton), 3:277,
 4:585
Seaborn, 2:164, 4:263,
 4:589
Silence, 4:586
Susanna, 2:254, 3:511,
 4:583, 4:585-586
Susanna (----) Rediat Miles,
 3:206
Susanna (Andrews), 4:583
Susanna (Jones), 2:568,
 4:587
Tabitha (Tift), 4:301,
 4:588
Thankful, 2:311,
 4:586-587
Thankful (Beaman), 1:504
Wilterton
Jane (----), 4:590
Wilton
Catharine (----), 2:467,
 4:590
Mary, 3:157, 4:590
Mary (Staniford), 4:590
Winborne
Elizabeth (Hart), 2:367,
 4:590
Winch
Deborah, 4:590
Elizabeth, 4:590
Elizabeth (----), 4:590
Hannah, 4:590
Hannah (Gibbs), 2:247,
 4:590
Mary, 2:131, 4:177, 4:591
Sarah (----) Barnard, 1:118,
 4:591
Silence, 4:590
Winchcomb
Elizabeth, 4:591
Mary (----), 4:591
Mary (Harris), 2:360
Winchell/Winshall
Abigail, 4:591
Abigail (Brownson), 4:591

Winchell/Winshall
(continued)
Christian, 4:591
Elizabeth, 4:591
Elizabeth (----), 4:591
Elizabeth (Filley), 2:159,
  4:591
Martha, 4:591
Mary, 4:591
Phebe, 4:591
Sarah, 3:406, 4:591
Sarah (Porter), 3:464,
  4:591
Winchester
Elizabeth, 4:592
Hannah, 4:592
Hannah (----), 4:592
Hannah (Sealis), 4:44,
  4:592
Joanna (----), 4:592
Lydia, 4:127, 4:592
Mary, 1:24, 4:591-592
Wincol/Wincall/Winkle
Beatrice (----), 4:592
Elizabeth (----), 4:592
Window
---- (----) Travers, 1:170
Ann, 4:593, 4:635
Bridget (----) Travers,
  4:324, 4:593
Elinor (----), 4:593
Winds/Wendes/Wines
Bridget, 4:312
Bridget (----), 4:593
Wing
Abigail, 4:595
Ann (Hoxie), 2:385
Beulah, 4:594
Deborah, 4:593-595
Deborah (Bachiler), 1:89,
  4:594
Deborah (Dillingham),
  4:594
Desire, 4:594
Dorothy (----), 2:385
Elizabeth, 2:385, 4:399,
  4:594-595
Hannah, 3:106-106,
  4:593-595
Hannah (----), 4:593
Hannah (Swift), 4:241,
  4:593
Hepzibah, 4:594

Jerusha (Mayhew), 4:595
Joan (----), 4:595
Joanna, 4:594
Josebeth (Davis), 2:17
Joshabeth, 4:594
Joshabeth (Davis), 4:594
Judith (----), 4:595
Lydia, 4:593
Mercy, 4:595
Miriam (Dean), 4:594,
  4:680
Osiah, 4:594
Oziah (Dillingham), 4:595
Sarah, 4:594-595
Sarah (Briggs), 4:595
Susanna, 4:594
Wingate
Abigail, 4:595-596
Ann, 4:595-596
Ann (----), 4:595
Elizabeth, 4:596
Jane, 4:596
Joanna, 4:595
Love, 4:596
Martha, 4:596
Mary, 4:595-596
Mary (----), 2:387
Mary (Lunt), 4:596
Mary (Nutter), 3:301,
  4:595
Mehitable, 4:595
Sarah, 2:388, 4:596
Sarah (----) Canney, 1:332,
  4:595
Winn
Abigail, 4:597
Ann, 1:406, 4:596-597
Ann/Hannah (----) Page
  Wood, 4:596
Elizabeth, 3:450, 4:596
Elizabeth (----), 4:597
Hannah, 4:597
Hannah (Sawtell), 4:30,
  4:597
Joanna, 4:597
Joanna/Jane (----), 4:596
Mary, 3:103, 4:597, 4:665
Mary (Richardson)
  Wyman, 4:665
Rebecca, 4:597
Sarah, 2:550, 4:596-597
Sarah (Beal), 4:596

Winship/Windship/etc
Abigail, 3:595, 4:597-598
Elizabeth, 4:83, 4:597-598
Elizabeth (----), 4:597
Elizabeth (Kendall), 3:429,
  4:597
Hannah (Rayner), 3:514,
  4:597
Jane (----), 4:617
Jane (Fessenden), 2:583
Jane (Wilkinson), 4:552,
  4:597
Joanna, 4:597, 4:617
Margery, 2:49, 4:597-598
Mary, 1:265, 4:597-598
Mary (Poulter), 3:469,
  4:598
Mehitable, 4:597
Rebecca (Barsham), 1:128,
  4:597
Sarah, 2:484, 4:597
Sarah (----), 4:597-598
Sarah (Harrington), 2:360
Susanna, 4:597
Winslead/Wenslad/etc
Elizabeth (Whittemore),
  4:598
Mary, 4:598
Sarah, 4:598
Sarah (Moulton), 4:598
Winslow
---- (Hutchinson), 2:510
Ann, 4:600-601
Catharine, 4:600
Elinor, 1:99, 4:601, 4:603
Elizabeth, 1:260, 1:262,
  1:315, 1:516, 4:599-600,
  4:602-603
Elizabeth (----), 4:601
Elizabeth (Barker), 4:599
Elizabeth (Hutchinson),
  2:509, 4:600
Ellen, 4:603
Ellen/Elinor (Newton)
  Adams, 1:11, 4:603
Faith, 4:603
Faith (Miller), 3:209, 4:603
Hannah, 1:480, 4:229,
  4:602
Hannah (Briggs), 1:252,
  4:603
Judith (----), 4:601
Margaret, 3:209, 4:602

336

Winslow (continued)
Margaret (Bourne), 1:219,
4:602
Mary, 2:298, 3:449, 4:320,
4:600-603
Mary (Chilton), 1:379,
4:601
Mary (Jones), 3:640
Mary (Nowell), 3:107,
3:295, 4:600
Mercy (----), 4:603
Parnell, 2:190, 4:600-601
Penelope (Pelham), 3:385,
4:603
Rebecca, 4:271, 4:602
Ruth (Sargent), 1:218,
4:19, 4:601
Sarah, 3:40, 3:205, 3:337,
4:162, 4:600-601
Sarah (Hilton), 4:600
Sarah (Lawrence), 4:602
Sarah (Wensley), 3:330,
4:483
Susanna, 3:58, 4:601-602
Susanna (----) White, 4:513,
4:515, 4:599
Winsor/Windsor
Constance, 4:604
Elizabeth, 4:604
Elizabeth (Arnold), 1:66
Hannah, 1:345, 4:605
Lydia, 4:604
Martha, 4:603-604
Mary, 4:604-605
Mary (----), 4:603
Mercy (Williams)
Waterman, 3:526, 4:432,
4:569, 4:605
Rachel (----), 4:605
Rebecca, 4:604-605
Rebecca (----), 4:604
Sarah, 4:604
Sarah (----), 4:604
Susanna, 4:604
Winston/Winstone/etc
Ann, 4:605
Elizabeth, 1:41, 4:605
Elizabeth (Daniel), 2:10,
4:605
Esther, 3:236, 4:605
Grace, 4:605
Mary, 4:333, 4:605

Winsworth
Rebecca (----), 4:605
Winter
----, 4:606
---- (----), 4:606
Abigail, 4:606
Alice, 4:606
Ann, 1:139, 2:490
Catharine, 4:606
Hannah, 1:301, 2:359,
4:606
Jane (Cooper), 4:605
Martha, 2:490, 4:605
Mary, 3:516, 4:605-606
Patience, 4:606
Sarah, 2:569, 4:606
Winthrop
----, 4:611
---- (Rainsborow), 3:502
---- (Temple), 1:221
Ann, 3:533, 4:610,
4:612-613
Ann (Dudley), 2:76
Ann (Wainwright), 4:382
Catharine (Brattle) Eyre,
1:239, 2:133, 4:614
Elizabeth, 2:123, 3:274,
4:607, 4:612-613
Elizabeth (Fones), 2:150,
4:608
Elizabeth (Glover), 2:262,
4:606
Elizabeth (Hawkins),
2:383, 3:533, 4:607
Elizabeth (Read), 4:612
Elizabeth (Tongue), 4:312,
4:608
Jane (Borland), 1:215
Joanna, 4:613
Judith, 4:613
Judith (----), 1:109, 2:394,
2:406
Judith (Rainsborough),
4:613
Lucy, 2:65, 3:343,
4:612-613
Margaret, 1:488,
4:607-608, 4:612-613
Margaret (Tindal), 4:610
Martha, 4:494, 4:608,
4:612-613
Martha (----), 4:607
Martha (----) Coytemore,

1:420
Martha (Fones), 4:611
Martha (Nowell) Coyt-
more, 4:610-611
Martha (Rainsborough)
Coytemore, 1:468
Mary, 1:107, 2:77,
4:607-608, 4:610-612
Mary (----), 3:135
Mary (Brown), 1:277,
4:613
Mary (Forth), 4:610
Mary (Luttrell), 4:607
Mercy, 4:607-608
Priscilla, 4:607-608
Sarah, 4:607, 4:610
Sarah (Glover), 2:262,
4:607
Thomasine (Clopton),
4:610
Winus
Susanna, 4:614
Susanna (Melyen), 4:614
Wise
Abigail, 4:615
Abigail (Gardner), 2:229,
2:231, 4:614
Ammi Ruhami, 4:614
Ann, 4:614
Bethia, 4:614
Catharine, 3:175
Emma, 4:614
Jane (----), 4:539, 4:615
Lucy, 4:614
Mary, 3:46, 4:614-615
Mary (----), 4:268, 4:614
Mary (Thompson), 4:289,
4:614
Sarah, 4:496, 4:570,
4:614-615
Susan (----), 2:307
Susanna (----), 4:614
Wiseman
Alice, 1:476
Dorothy (----), 4:615
Elizabeth, 3:538
Mary, 4:371, 4:615
Mercy/Mary, 4:615
Sarah, 4:615
Wiswall
----, 4:616
Deborah, 4:615-616
Elizabeth, 2:311,

Wiswall (continued)
  Elizabeth (continued)
    4:615-617
  Elizabeth (----), 4:617
  Elizabeth (Oliver), 3:310,
    4:615
  Esther, 2:558, 4:615-617
  Hannah, 3:256, 3:325,
    3:552, 4:615-616
  Hannah (Baker), 1:98,
    4:616
  Isabella (----) Farmer,
    2:141
  Isabella (Barbage) Farmer,
    4:617
  Lydia, 4:616
  Margaret, 3:355, 4:616
  Margaret (Smith), 4:616
  Martha, 1:516, 4:616
  Mary, 3:373, 4:615-617
  Mercy, 4:615
  Priscilla, 4:615
  Priscilla (Peabody), 3:375,
    4:615
  Rebecca, 2:556, 4:616
  Ruth, 3:250, 4:616
  Sarah, 4:616-617
  Sarah (Baker), 4:617
  Sarah (Payson) Foster,
    2:187, 3:373, 4:615
  Susanna, 4:615
  Theodosia (Jackson),
    2:530, 3:276, 4:616
Witchfield
  ---- (----) Goffe, 4:621
  Margaret (----) Goffe,
    4:617
  Margaret (Wilkinson)
    Goffe, 2:267, 4:552
With
  Mary (----), 4:618
Witham
  Lydia (Griffin), 4:713
  Sarah (Somes), 4:140,
    4:713
Witherdin
  Mary, 1:412
Witherell
  Dorothy, 2:524
Witherton
  Mary (Brock), 2:434
Withie
  Mary, 4:618

Susan, 4:618
Withington
  ----, 2:292
  Abia, 4:619
  Abigail, 4:619
  Ann, 1:139, 4:618
  Constant, 4:619
  Deliverance (----), 4:331,
    4:619
  Elizabeth, 2:336,
    4:618-619
  Elizabeth (----), 4:510,
    4:618
  Elizabeth (Eliot), 2:111,
    4:619
  Faith, 1:98, 4:618
  Hannah, 4:619
  Margaret (----) Paul, 4:618
  Margery (Tarne) Paul,
    3:658
  Mary, 2:8, 4:618
  Mary (----), 4:618
  Sarah, 4:618-619
  Sarah (----), 4:619
  Sarah (Leadbetter), 3:67,
    4:618
  Silence, 4:618-619
  Submit, 4:619
  Susanna, 4:619
  Thankful, 4:619
  Thankful (Pond), 3:453,
    4:619
Withman
  Susanna (----), 4:619
Withridge - see Whitred
Witt
  Ann, 1:123, 4:619
  Elizabeth, 4:619
  Elizabeth (Baker), 4:619
  Elizabeth (Mansfield),
    3:148, 4:619
  Esther, 2:377, 4:619
  Martha, 4:619
  Mary, 4:198, 4:619, 4:713
  Mary (Diven), 2:53, 4:619
  Sarah, 4:619
  Sarah (----), 4:619
Witter
  ---- (Crandall), 1:471
  Annis (----), 4:620
  Elizabeth, 4:620
  Elizabeth (Wheeler), 4:620
  Hannah, 4:620

Mary, 4:620
Witteridge - see Whitred
Wittingham
  Martha (Hubbard), 2:133
Wittoms
  Elizabeth, 4:620
  Mary, 4:620
  Redigan (Clark), 4:620
Witty
  Sarah (Spear), 4:146
Wixam/Wickson
  Elizabeth, 4:620
  Lydia, 4:620
  Sarah (----), 4:620
Woad
  Susanna (----), 2:152
Wodell - see Waddell
Wolcott
  Abia, 4:624
  Abia (Hawley), 4:624
  Abiah, 4:621
  Abiah (Goffe), 2:267,
    4:621
  Abigail, 4:623
  Abigail (----), 4:622
  Abigail (Walter), 4:403
  Alice (Ingersol), 4:622
  Ann, 2:317, 4:621
  Elizabeth, 1:453, 1:458,
    1:498, 4:620-623
  Elizabeth (----), 4:620
  Elizabeth (Saunders),
    4:620
  Eunice, 4:623
  Hannah, 4:621-623
  Hannah (Newberry), 3:269
  Hannah (Nichols), 4:622
  Hepzibah, 4:623
  Jane (Allen), 4:622
  Joanna, 4:622-623
  Joanna (Cook), 4:623
  Judith (Appleton), 1:61,
    4:623
  Lucia, 4:624
  Lucy, 4:623
  Lydia, 4:622
  Martha, 1:44, 4:622-624
  Martha (Pitkin), 1:392,
    3:441, 4:623
  Mary, 2:70, 3:590,
    4:620-623
  Mary (Chester), 4:622
  Mary (Emerson), 4:622

Wolcott (continued)
Mary (Thorla), 4:622
Mary (Treat), 4:622
Mary Ann, 4:623
Mehitable, 4:623
Mercy, 4:620
Penelope (Curwin), 1:488,
  4:622
Rachel, 4:622
Rebecca (Granger), 2:290,
  4:622
Sarah, 1:351, 1:368, 1:405,
  3:484, 4:621-623
Sarah (Chester), 4:623
Sarah (Drake), 4:623
Sarah (Johnson), 4:622,
  4:686
Sarah (Newberry), 3:269,
  4:621
Ursula, 4:623
Wolfall
---- (Oliver), 3:311, 4:624
Wolfe/Woolfe
Hannah, 4:210
Martha (----), 4:624
Susanna, 4:624
Wollaston
Mary (----), 4:624
Wolterton
Bennet (----) Stanley,
  4:165, 4:590
Jane (----), 4:590
Wood/Woods
----, 4:629
---- (Dunham), 2:81, 4:629
Abiah, 4:625
Abiah (Bowen), 4:625
Abigail, 2:467, 3:308,
  3:473, 4:625-630
Abigail (----), 4:627, 4:629
Abigail (Jenny), 2:546,
  4:625
Alice, 4:629
Alice (----), 4:628-629
Alice (Whitney), 4:531
Amy (----), 4:630
Ann, 1:235, 3:484
Ann (----), 4:628-629
Ann/Hannah (----) Page,
  4:596
Bathsheba, 4:628
Bethia, 1:495, 4:628
Catharine, 4:626

Catharine (----), 4:625
Dinah, 4:626
Dorcas, 3:419
Dorothy, 4:625
Dorothy (Badcock), 1:92,
  4:625
Dorothy (Witherell) Irish,
  2:524, 4:492
Elizabeth, 4:626-630
Elizabeth (----), 4:625
Elizabeth (Foster), 4:629
Elizabeth (Hall), 2:337,
  4:627
Elizabeth (Hancock),
  2:592, 4:628
Ellen (----), 4:626
Esther, 4:629
Esther (Walker), 4:394,
  4:627
Experience (Fuller), 2:219
Frances, 2:475
Frances (----), 4:629
Hannah, 1:373, 2:354,
  3:81, 4:211, 4:625-629
Hannah (----), 4:626, 4:629
Hannah (----) Page, 3:331
Hannah (----) Wheeler,
  4:626
Hazabelponah (----), 4:628
Hopestill (----), 4:626
Jemima, 4:629
Jerusha, 4:625
Joanna, 4:626
Lydia, 4:627
Lydia (----), 4:627
Lydia (Bacon), 4:627
Margaret, 2:358,
  4:627-629
Margaret (----), 4:628,
  4:630
Margaret (----) Smith,
  4:121
Margaret (Elithorpe),
  4:629
Martha, 4:629-630
Martha (Earle), 2:134,
  4:630
Martha (Foster), 2:188,
  4:629
Mary, 1:77, 1:162, 1:232,
  1:387, 2:452, 3:315,
  3:446, 4:297, 4:626-630
Mary (----), 4:626, 4:628

Mary (Buddington), 4:627
Mary (Chappell), 1:364
Mary (Davenport), 2:13
Mary (Foster), 2:189
Mary (Grover), 4:625
Mary (Healey), 4:627
Mary (Parmenter), 3:360
Mary (Pigg/Pidge), 3:435
Mary (Williams), 4:566,
  4:628
Mehitable, 2:31, 3:240,
  4:625, 4:628
Mercy, 4:627
Mercy (Thompson), 4:288,
  4:626
Milicent, 4:626
Miriam, 4:629-630
Miriam (----), 4:629
Miriam (----) Smith, 4:625
Phebe, 4:628
Philippa, 4:515
Rachel, 4:629
Rebecca, 4:300
Rebecca (----), 4:629
Rebecca (Benedict), 1:164
Ruth, 2:598, 3:131, 4:67,
  4:361, 4:500, 4:625,
  4:627, 4:630
Ruth (----), 4:625
Ruth (Mousall), 3:251
Sarah, 1:135, 1:160-161,
  2:138, 2:546, 3:141,
  3:267, 4:625-628
Sarah (----), 4:625
Sarah (Masterson), 3:171
Silence, 4:627
Susanna, 4:628-629
Susanna (----), 2:152
Tabitha, 4:625
Tryall, 4:629
Woodall
Frances, 3:643
Woodbridge
Abigail (Leete), 3:75,
  4:633
Abigail (Warren) Lord,
  4:427, 4:587, 4:634
Ann, 4:632
Deborah (Cushing)
  Tarleton, 1:489, 4:256
Dorothy, 2:214, 4:632
Dorothy (Lamb), 3:47
Dorothy (Lamb)

Woodbridge (continued)
Dorothy (Lamb)
Woodbridge (continued)
Woodbridge, 3:47
Elizabeth, 1:397
Lucy, 1:236, 2:125, 4:632
Margaret, 4:633
Martha, 3:588, 4:632
Martha (Rogers), 4:633
Mary, 1:461, 4:633
Mary (----), 1:423
Mary (Jones), 4:633
Mary (Pitkin), 4:634
Mary (Ward), 4:408, 4:631
Mehitable (Russell)
Hubbard, 3:589
Mehitable (Wyllis) Russell
Foster, 2:188, 3:589,
4:577, 4:633
Mercy (Dudley), 2:78,
4:632
Sarah, 4:632
Susanna, 4:633
Woodbury/Woodberry
Abigail, 3:304, 4:635-636
Abigail (Phillips), 2:92,
4:403, 4:635
Agnes (----), 4:635
Ann, 4:635
Ann (Palsgrave), 4:636
Ann (Window), 4:635
Bethia, 4:635
Christian, 4:322, 4:634
Elizabeth, 3:227, 4:394,
4:634-635
Elizabeth (----), 4:634-636
Hannah, 1:95, 4:634-636
Hannah (Dodge) Porter,
2:57, 3:463, 4:636
Joanna, 3:447, 4:636
Mary, 4:550, 4:634-635
Mary (----), 2:141, 4:634,
4:636
Mary (Dixey), 4:634
Mary (Wilks), 4:550,
4:635
Priscilla, 4:634
Sarah, 4:713
Sarah (----), 3:455
Sarah (Dodge), 2:57, 4:636
Sarah (Haskell) , 4:636
Susan, 4:634
Susanna, 1:133, 4:634-635

Woodcock
Bridget, 4:637
Deborah, 3:314
Hannah (----), 4:637
Mary, 3:627
Mary (Newman), 3:656
Sarah, 1:101, 2:392, 4:637
Sarah (Judson) , 2:392
Sarah (Smith), 4:637
Wooden/Woodin/Wooding
Abigail, 3:632, 4:372,
4:638
Martha (Sacket), 4:638
Mary, 4:638
Sarah, 3:201, 4:638
Sarah (Ollard), 4:638
Susan, 4:638
Woodfield
Esther (----), 4:638
Woodford
Abigail, 4:638
Elizabeth, 4:638
Esther, 4:638
Hannah, 1:35, 4:638-639
Lydia, 4:638
Lydia (Smith), 4:638
Mary, 4:69, 4:638-639
Mary (Blott), 1:205, 4:639
Rebecca, 3:461, 4:638
Rebecca (Newell), 3:272,
4:638
Sarah, 1:34, 1:303,
4:638-639
Susanna, 4:638
Woodham
Mary, 3:598, 4:637
Mary (----), 4:637
Woodhead
Mary, 2:288
Woodhouse/Woodis/etc
Alice, 4:372, 4:639
Elinor, 4:639
Elinor (Hopkinson), 4:639
Elizabeth, 4:639
Hannah, 4:639
Mary, 3:72, 3:427,
4:639-640
Mary (----), 4:639
Melicent/Milicent, 2:126,
4:639
Sarah, 4:639
Sarah (----), 4:639
Sarah (----) Rogers, 4:639

Sarah (Wade) Rogers,
3:568
Woodland
Martha (----), 4:640
Woodley
Elizabeth (----), 4:640
Miriam, 4:640
Woodman
--- (Raynes), 3:502, 4:641
Dorothy (Chapman), 4:640
Elizabeth, 4:506, 4:640
Elizabeth (----), 4:640
Elizabeth (Stevens), 4:641
Hannah, 4:641
Hannah (----), 4:640
Hannah (Hilton), 4:641
Joanna (----), 4:640
Judith, 4:641
Margaret, 4:641
Mary, 1:271, 2:119,
4:640-641
Mary (Field), 4:641
Mary (Goodridge), 2:276,
4:640
Mary (Sawyer), 4:641
Mehitable, 4:641
Rebecca, 4:641
Remember (Maverick),
3:181, 4:641
Ruth, 3:126, 4:640-641
Sarah, 3:12, 4:640-641
Woodmansey
Abigail (Melyen), 4:55,
4:641
Ann, 1:493, 4:642
Bethia, 4:642
Elizabeth, 4:641
Elizabeth (----), 3:224
Elizabeth (Carr), 1:338,
4:641
Elizabeth (Clark), 1:398,
4:641
Margaret, 3:224, 4:641
Margaret (----), 4:641-642
Mary, 4:254, 4:641
Sarah, 4:641-642
Woodruff/Woodrow
Abigail, 4:642-643
Elizabeth, 1:263, 4:643
Elizabeth (Thompson),
4:289
Hannah, 4:642-643
Hannah (----), 4:642

Woodruff/Woodrow
(continued)
Hannah (Clark), 1:396,
4:642
Margaret, 4:642
Mary, 4:642-643, 4:714
Mary (Plum), 3:446, 4:643
Phebe, 4:642
Rachel, 4:643
Rebecca, 4:643
Rebecca (----), 4:714
Rebecca (Canterbury),
1:333, 4:642
Rebecca (Clark), 3:610,
4:643
Ruth, 4:643
Sarah, 4:643
Sarah (North), 3:289,
4:643
Woodward
Abigail, 3:238, 4:645-646
Abigail (Benjamin) Stubbs,
4:228, 4:645
Abigail (Hall) Ward, 4:410
Ann, 4:643, 4:646
Ann (----) Gates, 2:236,
4:646
Ann (Beamsley), 1:148,
4:643
Ann (Dewey), 4:645
Deliverance, 4:646
Deliverance (----) Butts,
1:322
Deliverance (Dana), 2:5
Elizabeth, 3:73, 4:643-645,
4:647
Elizabeth (----), 4:644
Elizabeth (Dana), 2:5,
4:643
Elizabeth (Hammond),
2:346, 4:335, 4:644
Esther, 4:427, 4:647
Esther (----), 4:427
Experience, 3:451, 4:644
Frances, 3:327
Freedom, 4:225, 4:644
Hannah, 4:643, 4:647
Jane, 1:413
Jane (Godfrey), 4:644
Judith, 4:646
Lydia, 4:644
Lydia (Brown), 1:264,
4:644

Margaret, 4:643
Martha, 2:118, 4:643
Mary, 1:107, 2:264, 4:383,
4:643-647
Mary (----), 4:644, 4:646
Mary (Goose), 2:280,
4:647
Mehitable, 4:646-647
Mehitable (----), 4:646
Mercy, 4:644
Prudence, 3:155, 4:643
Rachel, 4:643, 4:647
Rachel (Smith), 2:371,
4:119, 4:646
Rebecca, 2:164, 4:643-646
Rebecca (Robbins), 3:546,
4:645
Rose, 3:287, 4:645
Rose (----), 4:646
Sarah, 2:236, 4:121, 4:529,
4:643-644, 4:646
Sarah (----), 4:643
Sarah (----) Solart, 4:706,
4:714
Sarah (Blomfield) Sacket,
1:204
Sarah (Crossman), 4:645
Sarah (Dean), 2:30
Sarah (Goodnow), 4:645
Sarah (Rosewell), 4:645
Silence, 4:646
Submit, 4:646
Susanna, 4:644
Susanna (Grout), 2:319
Thankful, 4:261, 4:644,
4:646
Thankful (----), 4:646
Woodwell
Ann (----), 4:647
Dorcas, 4:647
Elizabeth, 4:160, 4:647
Elizabeth (Stacey), 4:160
Margaret, 4:647
Mary, 4:647, 4:714
Mary (----), 4:647
Thomasine (----), 4:647
Woodworth
Abigail, 4:647
Catharine, 4:648
Deborah, 4:647
Deborah (Daman), 2:4,
4:647
Elizabeth, 4:647

Eunice, 4:647
Martha, 2:4, 4:648
Mary, 4:647-648
Ruth, 4:647
Sarah, 4:647
Sarah (Stockbridge), 4:198,
4:647
Woody/Woodie/Wooddy
Ann, 4:637
Ann (----), 4:637
Dorcas (Harper), 2:358,
4:637
Elizabeth, 4:637
Frances (Dexter), 4:637
Hannah, 3:372
Martha, 4:637
Mary, 4:68, 4:637
Mary (Coggan), 1:420,
3:554, 4:637
Sarah, 4:638
Woolcot - see Wolcott
Woolderson
Frances, 1:126
Woolen
Jane, 2:334, 3:627
Woolery/Woolsworth
Abia, 4:648
Elizabeth, 4:648
Hannah, 4:648
Hannah (Huggins), 4:648
Mary, 4:648
Wooley/Woolly
Elizabeth, 4:648
Elizabeth (----), 4:648
Grace, 4:648
Mary, 4:648
Ruth, 4:648
Woolford
Jane, 4:444
Woolland
Elizabeth, 1:472
Woolridge/Woolrych
Sarah (----), 4:648
Woolson
Beulah, 4:649
Elizabeth, 4:649
Elizabeth (Chadwick),
4:649
Hannah, 4:649
Hannah (----), 4:649
Mary, 2:215, 4:649
Sarah, 1:210, 4:649
Sarah (Hyde), 4:649

Woolson (continued)
Thankful, 4:649
Woory/Woorey/Woorie
Hannah, 4:649
Margaret (----), 4:649
Wooster/Woster
Alice, 4:650
Ann, 4:650
Ann (----), 4:650
Damaris, 4:650
Elizabeth, 2:550,
   4:649-650
Hannah, 4:429, 4:649
Jerusha, 4:649
Margaret (Sawtell), 4:649
Mary, 4:649
Mary (----), 4:649
Mary (Walker), 4:649
Persis, 4:649
Phebe, 4:650
Phebe (----), 4:650
Phebe (Tomlinson), 4:310
Ruth, 1:223, 4:649-650
Sarah, 4:649
Susanna, 4:650
Susanna (----), 4:650
Tabitha, 4:649-650
Tabitha (Tomlinson),
   4:310, 4:649
Tamar, 4:649
Zervia, 4:650
Wootton
Elizabeth, 3:397
Worcester/Worster
Constance, 4:340, 4:651
Constant (----), 4:651
Deliverance (Looke),
   4:650
Dorothy, 4:650
Elizabeth, 2:550,
   4:650-651
Elizabeth (Parrott), 4:650
Hannah, 4:650
Hannah (----), 4:650
Hulda (Cheney), 1:372,
   4:651
Jane, 4:650
Jemima, 4:650
Lydia, 4:651
Martha (Cheney), 1:372
Martha (Palmer), 4:650
Mary, 4:650
Mary (Cheney), 1:372,

4:650
Rebecca, 4:651
Rebecca (----) Byley Hall,
   1:326, 2:334, 4:246,
   4:651
Sarah, 4:650-651
Sarah (----), 4:650-651
Sarah (Soper), 4:650
Susanna, 4:159, 4:650-651
Susanna (----), 1:48,
   4:650-651
Worden
Jane, 4:651
Mary, 1:302, 4:651
Mary (----), 4:651
Mehitable (Hinckley), 1:83,
   4:651
Wormall/Wormell
Esther, 2:81, 4:652
Miriam (----), 4:652, 4:714
Sarah, 4:652
Wormwood
---- (----), 1:156
Elizabeth, 4:652
Esther, 4:652
Mary, 1:156
Wornum
Christian (----), 4:652
Worth
Ann (Sarson), 4:652
Damaris (Sibley), 4:653
Dorcas, 4:652
Dorcas (Smith), 4:652
Elizabeth, 4:652
Elizabeth (Webster), 4:652
Judith, 1:287, 4:652-653
Mary, 4:652-653
Mary (Pike), 4:653
Miriam (Gardner), 2:229,
   4:652
Sarah, 2:254, 4:652-653
Sarah (Macy), 3:142,
   4:653
Susanna, 4:653
Susanna (Whipple), 3:437,
   4:505, 4:652-653
Worthen
Dorothy, 2:481, 4:653
Hannah, 2:195, 4:653
Hannah (Martin), 3:162,
   4:653
Worthington
Amy, 4:653

Elizabeth, 1:223, 4:653
Elizabeth (Scott), 4:37,
   4:653
Margaret, 4:653
Mary, 4:653
Mary (Pratt), 4:653
Mehitable, 4:653
Mehitable (Graves) Mor-
   ton, 2:294, 3:245, 4:653
Sarah, 4:653
Sarah (Bunce) White,
   1:298, 4:511, 4:653
Susanna (----), 1:106,
   4:653
Worthlike
Alice, 4:654
Hannah, 4:654
Mary, 4:654
Sarah, 4:654
Wright
--- (----) Elson, 2:115
--- (Deming), 2:35
--- (Pratt), 3:473
Abigail, 4:655, 4:657,
   4:660
Abigail (----) Walker, 4:660
Abigail (Jess), 2:547,
   4:656-657
Abigail (Warren), 4:423,
   4:657
Alice (----), 4:657
Ann, 2:221, 4:402,
   4:654-655
Clemence, 4:655
Deborah, 1:377, 4:656-657
Dorcas, 4:660
Dorcas (Weed), 4:451,
   4:656
Dorothy, 1:261, 4:655,
   4:660
Dorothy (----), 1:197,
   4:655
Eleanor, 1:283
Elizabeth, 1:137, 3:75,
   4:178, 4:654-660
Elizabeth (----), 2:48,
   4:655-656, 4:660
Elizabeth (Bateman),
   4:658
Elizabeth (Burt), 1:313,
   4:659
Elizabeth (Chittenden),
   1:382, 4:660

Wright (continued)
Elizabeth (Hassell), 2:372,
  4:658
Elizabeth (Stebbins), 4:659
Elizabeth (Stoddard),
  4:200
Elizabeth (Strong), 4:655
Esther, 3:159-160, 4:655,
  4:657-659
Esther (Cooke), 1:446
Experience, 4:655
Grace, 4:656
Hannah, 1:214, 2:274,
  2:432, 3:542, 4:32,
  4:177, 4:326, 4:654-657,
  4:659-660
Hannah (Albee), 4:659
Hannah (Axtell), 4:655
Hannah (Bliss), 4:656
Hannah (Hunt), 4:655
Helped, 4:657, 4:659
Hepzibah, 4:656
Isabel, 4:660
Jane, 2:349, 4:654
Jane (----), 4:654
Joanna/Hannah, 4:658
Keziah, 4:660
Lois, 4:656
Lydia, 1:201, 1:438, 3:47,
  3:292, 4:124, 4:657,
  4:659-660, 4:693
Lydia (Moore), 1:493,
  3:229, 4:659
Lydia (Sylvester) Rawlins,
  3:510, 4:655-656
Mabel, 4:659
Margaret, 4:659
Margaret (----), 4:659
Margaret (----) Hilliard
  Elson, 2:421, 4:660
Martha, 3:153, 4:654-656,
  4:658
Martha (Kitcherell), 3:33,
  4:654
Mary, 3:285, 4:654-660
Mary (----), 4:656-657,
  4:659
Mary (Barker), 4:655
Mary (Belden), 4:655
Mary (Butler), 1:321,
  4:659
Mary (Case), 4:660
Mary (Chapin), 4:655

Mary (Dudley), 2:76
Mary (Pardee), 4:656
Mary (Powell), 4:655
Mary (Smith) Treat, 4:326,
  4:654
Mary (Stevens), 4:185,
  4:660
Mary (Stoddard), 4:200
Mehitable, 4:656, 4:660
Mehitable (Hinsdale),
  2:427
Mercy, 4:656-658, 4:660
Mercy (----), 4:657
Mercy (Burt), 1:313, 4:658
Mercy (Stoddard), 4:200
Mercy (Wardwell), 4:415
Mindwell, 4:655,
  4:657-658
Miriam, 4:656
Olive (----), 4:161
Patience, 4:658
Preserved, 4:657
Priscilla, 2:369
Priscilla (----), 1:454, 4:657,
  4:661
Rachel, 3:81, 4:658
Rebecca, 3:84, 4:654-655
Rebecca (Barrett), 4:655
Rebecca (Crafts), 4:660
Rebecca (Goodrich), 4:655
Rebecca (Terry), 4:654
Ruth, 3:37, 4:657-658
Ruth (----) Center, 1:350,
  4:658
Ruth (Sheldon), 4:69,
  4:228, 4:657
Sarah, 1:434, 4:654-659
Sarah (----) Burk, 4:658
Sarah (Benton), 3:603,
  4:660
Sarah (Lyman), 4:659
Sarah (Osborne), 4:657
Sarah (Root), 4:656
Susanna (Johnson), 4:660
Tabitha, 4:656
Thankful, 4:654-655
Thankful (Taylor), 4:654
Wrotham
Elizabeth, 3:272, 4:661
Sarah (----), 4:661
Susanna, 2:468, 4:661
Wyard
Eunice, 4:661

Lois, 4:661
Sarah, 4:661
Sarah (Standish), 4:661
Wyatt/Wiat/Wyat
Dorcas, 4:661
Elizabeth, 2:323,
  4:661-662
Elizabeth (Spurr), 4:662
Hannah, 4:661
Hannah (Parker), 3:355
Hepzibah, 4:661
Joanna, 2:156, 4:662
Joanna/Hannah, 4:661
Mary, 4:661
Mary (----), 2:295, 4:661
Mary (Bronson), 1:42,
  1:280, 4:661
Mercy, 4:662
Rebecca, 4:662
Sarah, 1:188, 2:294, 2:397,
  4:661-662
Sarah (Pratt), 4:661
Susanna, 4:661
Waitstill, 4:376, 4:661
Wyborne/Wiborne/etc
Abigail, 4:662
Abigail (Eliot), 2:109,
  4:662
Elizabeth, 3:198, 4:662
Elizabeth (----), 4:662
Mary, 4:662
Ruth (----), 4:662
Wyer/Wier
Catharine, 4:662
Eleanor, 4:714
Eleanor (Jenner), 4:714
Elizabeth, 4:662
Elizabeth (Johnson), 2:558,
  2:599, 4:662
Hannah, 4:662
Mary, 4:235, 4:663
Mary (----), 4:663
Ruhamah, 4:663
Ruth (----), 4:714
Sarah, 4:663
Sarah (----), 4:663
Wyeth/Withe/Wieth
Deborah, 4:663
Deborah (Parker), 4:663
Deborah (Ward), 4:409,
  4:663
Elizabeth, 4:663
Lydia (Fiske), 2:164-165,

Wyeth/Withe/Wieth
(continued)
Lydia (Fiske) (continued)
4:663
Martha, 2:583, 3:638,
4:663
Mary, 4:663
Rebecca (----), 4:682
Rebecca (----) Andrews,
1:56, 4:663
Sarah, 2:165, 4:663
Wyley/Wiley
Sarah, 4:663
Susanna, 4:663
**Wyllis/Wyllys - see also
Willis**
---- (Hobart), 2:434
Amy, 3:497, 4:574
Mary, 2:111, 4:577
Mehitable, 2:188, 3:589,
4:577, 4:633
Ruth, 4:259, 4:577
Ruth (Haynes), 2:389
Wyman/Weyman
Abigail, 3:538, 4:663-665
Abigail (Fowle), 4:665
Abigail (Read), 4:664
Ann, 4:665-666
Bathsheba, 4:258, 4:664
Catharine, 4:663
Deliverance, 4:666
Elizabeth, 4:663-666
Elizabeth (Coggin), 4:664
Elizabeth (Hancock),
4:663
Elizabeth (Richardson),
4:664
Esther, 4:665-666
Esther (Johnson), 2:559,
4:665
Eunice, 4:663, 4:665
Hannah, 4:665
Hannah (----), 4:665
Hannah (Farrar), 4:665
Hannah (Fowle), 4:665
Isabel, 4:664
Isabel (Farmer), 1:204,
2:141-142, 4:664
Jerusha, 4:663
Joanna, 4:665
Judith, 4:664, 4:666
Judith (Pierce), 3:659,
4:664

Kezia, 4:665
Love, 4:665
Lucy, 4:663
Lydia, 4:665
Martha, 4:664
Mary, 4:664-665
Mary (Carter), 1:88, 1:342,
4:664
Mary (Richardson), 4:665
Mary (Winn), 3:103, 4:665
Patience, 4:664-665
Phebe, 4:665
Prudence, 4:666
Prudence (Putnam), 4:666
Rachel, 4:665
Rebecca, 4:665
Rebecca (Johnson), 2:556,
4:665
Ruth, 4:665
Sarah, 2:219, 4:395,
4:664-665
Sarah (Nutt), 2:219, 3:301,
4:664
Susanna, 4:665
Tabitha, 4:663
Yale
---- (----), 4:667
Abigail, 4:667, 4:690
Ann, 2:461, 4:666-667
Ann (Morton), 2:97
Elizabeth, 3:345,
4:666-667
Hannah, 4:252, 4:667,
4:709
Martha, 4:667
Mary, 4:667, 4:685
Mary (Turner), 4:347,
4:667
Rebecca, 4:667
Rebecca (----), 4:666
Rebecca (Gibbard), 2:244,
4:667
Ruth (Bishop), 3:603,
4:667
Sarah (Nash), 3:261, 4:667
Ursula (----), 4:666
Yates
Abigail (Rogers), 4:668
Dinah, 4:668
Dorothy, 4:668
Mary, 2:412, 4:668
Mary (----), 4:668

Yeales
Ann, 4:668
Naomi (Frye), 2:213,
4:668
Yelings
Elizabeth (----), 4:668
Yell
Elizabeth, 4:668
Joanna (Smith), 4:668
Yeo/Yow
Elizabeth, 4:668
Sarah (Hull), 2:492
Sarah (Phippen), 3:418,
4:668
Yeomans
Elizabeth (Josselyn), 2:572,
3:20, 4:668
Susanna (----), 4:668
Yescutt
Alice (----), 4:668
York/Yorke
Abigail, 1:153
Deborah (----), 2:109,
4:669
Elizabeth (----), 4:669
Hannah, 3:628
Hannah (----), 4:669
Patience, 3:629
Ruth (----), 4:669
Young
Abigail, 4:353, 4:669-670
Abigail (----), 4:670
Alice, 1:147
Ann, 4:669
Ann (Doane), 4:669
Dorcas, 4:669
Elizabeth, 4:669
Elizabeth
(Hagborne/Hackborne),
2:328
Elizabeth (Harcutt), 2:353,
4:671
Esther, 4:669
Hannah, 4:669
Hannah (Pinson), 3:439,
4:669
Jennet, 4:671
Joanna, 4:670
Joanna (Hicks), 4:670
Judith, 4:669
Lois, 4:669
Lydia, 4:670
Margaret, 2:203

Young (continued)
Margery, 4:669
Margery (----), 4:670
Margery (Batson), 1:139
Martha, 4:669
Mary, 4:112, 4:670
Mary (----), 3:188
Mercy (----), 3:188, 4:670
Naomi, 4:669
Patience, 4:669
Priscilla, 4:669
Priscilla (----), 4:669
Rebecca, 4:669
Reliance, 4:669
Ruth, 4:669
Ruth (----), 4:669
Ruth (Cole), 1:112, 1:426,
  4:670
Sarah, 3:33, 3:118, 3:650,
  4:351, 4:669, 4:671
Sarah (----), 4:669
Sarah (Davis), 2:21, 4:670
Sarah (White), 4:513,
  4:671
Susanna, 4:669
Susanna (Matthews),
  3:177
Younglove
Abigail, 3:362
Hannah, 3:362, 4:671
Lydia, 2:290, 4:671
Margaret (----), 4:671
Mary, 4:136, 4:671
Mary (----), 4:671
Mercy, 4:671
Sarah, 4:61, 4:262, 4:671
Sarah (----), 4:671
Sarah (Kinsman), 4:671
Youngman
Ann, 4:672
Ann (----) Heath,
  4:671-672
Ann (Fisher) Heath, 2:398
Elizabeth, 4:672
Leah, 4:672
Youngs
Ann, 4:672
Joan (----), 4:672
Mary, 1:277, 4:672
Rachel, 4:672

CPSIA information can be obtained
at www.ICGtesting.com
Printed in the USA
FSHW010234301018
53368FS